WORDSWORTH CLASSICS
OF WORLD LITERATURE

General Editor: Tom Griffith

LONDON LABOUR AND
THE LONDON POOR

HENRY MAYHEW

London Labour and the London Poor

*A Selection by Rosemary O'Day
and David Englander*

**WORDSWORTH CLASSICS
OF WORLD LITERATURE**

2

Customers interested in other titles from
Wordsworth Editions can visit our website at
www.wordsworth-editions.com

For our latest list and a full mail order service contact
Bibliophile Books, Unit 5 Datapoint,
South Crescent, London E16 4TL
Tel: +44 020 74 74 24 74
Fax: +44 020 74 74 85 89
orders@bibliophilebooks.com
www.bibliophilebooks.com

This edition published 2008 by Wordsworth Editions Limited
8B East Street, Ware, Hertfordshire SG12 9HJ

ISBN 978 1 84022 619 5

This edition © Wordsworth Editions Limited 2008
Introduction © Rosemary O'Day 2008

Wordsworth® is a registered trademark of
Wordsworth Editions Limited

Typeset in Great Britain by Roperford Editorial
Printed and bound by Clays Ltd, St Ives plc

CONTENTS

INTRODUCTION   xiii

MAYHEW'S PREFACE   xlix

1 STREET-FOLK   1

  Of wandering tribes in general   3

  Wandering tribes in this country   6

  Of the number of costermongers and other street-folk   7

  Of the varieties of street-folk in general, and costermongers
    in particular   11

  Habits and amusements of costermongers   13

  Gambling of costermongers   20

  The 'Vic. Gallery'   25

  The politics of costermongers – policemen   29

  Marriage and concubinage of costermongers   31

  Religion of costermongers   32

  Of the uneducated state of costermongers   34

  Language of costermongers   36

  Of the nicknames of costermongers   37

  Of the education of costermongers' children   38

  The literature of costermongers   39

  Of the costermongers' capital   40

  Of the 'slang' weights and measures   41

  Of the boys of the costermongers, and their bunts   42

  Education of the 'coster-lads'   44

  The life of a coster-lad   46

  Of the 'penny gaff'   49

  Of the coster-girls   56

  The life of a coster-girl   61

  Of the homes of the costermongers   65

  Of the dress of the costermongers   70

  Of the diet and drink of costermongers   73

  Of the earnings of costermongers   74

  Of the capital and income of the costermongers   78

  Of the providence and improvidence of costermongers   78

  Of the costermongers in bad weather and during the cholera   80

  Of the costermongers' raffles   81

  Of the tricks of costermongers   82

2 MINORITIES   85
  Of the street-Irish   87
    Of the causes which have made the Irish turn costermongers   89
    How the street-Irish displanted the Jews in the orange trade   92
    Of the religion of the street-Irish   94
    Of the education, literature, amusements and politics of the
      street-Irish   98
    The homes of the street-Irish   99
    Irish lodging-houses for immigrants   104
    Of the diet, drink and expense of living of the street-Irish   109
    Of the resources of the street-Irish as regards 'stock-money',
      sickness, burials, &c.   113
    Of the history of some Irish street-sellers   115
    Of the Irish 'refuse'-sellers   118
  The street-Jews   121
    Of the trades and localities of the street-Jews   122
    Of the Jew old-clothes men   125
    Of a Jew street-seller   131
    Of the Jew-boy street-sellers   132
    Of the pursuits, dwellings, traffic, etc., of the Jew-boy street-sellers 135
    Of the street Jewesses and street Jew-girls   136
    Of the synagogues and the religion of the street- and other Jews   139
    Of the politics, literature, and amusements of the Jews   141
    Of the charities, schools, and education of the Jews   143
  The Negro crossing-sweeper, who had lost both his legs   148
  The Negro cook   156

3 VOICES OF THE POOR: the employed and the destitute   159
  Street-sellers of 'wet' fish   161
    Street-sellers of 'wet' fish   162
    Street-sellers of sprats   164
    Street-sellers of shell-fish   167
  Street-sellers of fruit and vegetables   170
    Superior or 'aristocratic' vegetable-sellers   171
    Of the character of the street-stalls   173
    A fruit-stall keeper   174
  The London flower-girls   177
    Of two orphan flower-girls   177
    Of the life of a flower-girl [who had kept 'loose' company]   180
  The street-sellers of fried fish   182
    'Fishy' the trader in fried fish   182
  The street-sellers of baked-potatoes   186
    A baked-potato vendor   186

The cats'- and dogs'-meat dealers 188
  A cats'-meat carrier 189
Street-sellers of drinkables (coffee) 190
  A coffee-vendor in a small way of business 192
  Sellers of hot-cross buns 194
  The muffin-man 196
Street-orators 198
  Of running patterers 198
The street-buyers 199
  Mayhew's introduction to the subject 199
  Street-buyers of rags and bones 200
  The rag-and-bone man 200
Street-sellers of second-hand articles 203
  Seller of second-hand metal-wares 203
The 'pure'-finders 205
  A female 'pure'-finder 206
The mud-larks 210
  A child mud-lark 210
  The experiences of a juvenile mud-lark 212
Scavengers 216
  A 'regular' scavager 216
Omnibus drivers and conductors 220
  An omnibus driver 220
  An omnibus conductor 223
Carmen and porters 225
  Van-driver 226
Crossing-sweepers 227
  The old dame who supports a pensioner 227
  Mary, who had been a serving-maid 229
  'Gander', 'captain' of the boy crossing-sweepers 233
  The street where the boy-sweepers lodged 239
  The boy-sweepers' room 241
Flushermen 242
  The flusherman who had been a seaman 242
Cesspool-sewermen 245
  A cesspool-sewerman's statement 246
Chimney-sweeps 247
  A 'knuller' or 'querier' 248
Ballast-heavers and coal-whippers 250
  The meeting of the ballast-heavers' wives 251
Asylum for the houseless poor 257
  A homeless painter 258
  A homeless carpenter 260
  A homeless tailor 262

4 THE LONDON LABOUR MARKET AND
  THE CASUAL LABOUR PROBLEM   265
  Casual labour   267
    Of the casual labourers among the rubbish-carters   317
    The effects of casual labour in general   322
    Of the scurf trade among the rubbish-carters   325
  Skilled and unskilled   341
    'Garret-masters'   341
  Scavengers etc.   351
    Scavengers   351
    'Casual hands' among the scavengers   359
  Coal-heavers and dock-labourers   370
    Coal-heavers and -whippers   370
    Dock-labourers   382
    The London Dock   384
  The problem of low wages   401
    Review of the problem of low wages   401

5 SIGHTS OF LONDON   413
  Of the orange and nut market   415
  Of London street-markets on a Saturday night   418
  The Sunday morning markets   422
  Of Covent-garden market   423
  Of the Old Clothes Exchange   427
  The London Dock   431
  The West and East India Docks   434
  The St Katherine's Dock   436

6 CULTURE AND BELIEF   441
  Punch   443
    Punch talk   451
    Scene with two Punchmen   451
    The Punchman at the theatre   452
    The history of Punch   453
  Guy Fawkes   454
    Guy Fawkes (man)   454
  Silly Billy   463
  Of the experience of a street-bookseller   470
  Street-vocalists   472
    Street negro serenaders   472
    Statement of another Ethiopian serenader   475
  A standing patterer   481
  The wooden-legged sweeper   482
  Street-seller of saws   486

7 THE POOR AT HOME: *poverty and the domestic economy*   489
  Questionnaire of street-orderlies   491
  Mayhew's survey of the inmates of a lodging-house   502
    Cheap lodging-houses   502
  Of the life of a street-seller of dog-collars   515
  The home comforts of a cats'-meat carrier   519
  Street-seller of cutlery   520

8 PAUPERS AND CRIMINALS   525
  London vagrants   527
    Characteristics of the various classes of vagrants   534
    Statement of a returned convict   545
    Lives of the boy inmates of the casual wards of the
      London workhouses   550

9 CLASSIFICATION OF THE WORKERS AND NON-WORKERS   557
  Of the workers and non-workers   559

10 ANSWERS TO CORRESPONDENTS   573
  Money donated for the London Poor   578
  A journeyman on coconuts   581
  The library of a model dwelling-house   582
  Free-trade and the working man   584
  A draper on surveying his trade   585
  The causes of prostitution   586
  The Coal-Whippers' Journal   589
  A letter from a bricklayer's labourer   592
  A debate about labour and capital between F. B. B. and
    Henry Mayhew   593

APPENDIX 1: A MAYHEW BIBLIOGRAPHY   599

APPENDIX 2: MAYHEW'S TABLE OF CONTENTS   605

APPENDIX 3: MAYHEW'S AUTHORITIES

ILLUSTRATIONS

The London costermonger	2
The coster-girl	57
Hindoo tract-seller	86
The Jew old-clothes man	129
The street-seller of nutmeg-graters	160
The oyster-stall	169
The London coffee-stall	191
Cab-driver	221
The London scavager	266
Orange-mart, Duke's Place	414
Punch's showmen	442
Guy Fawkes	455
A street-seller of crockery-ware	490
A dinner at a cheap lodging-house	526
Gang of coal-whippers at work below bridge	558
Asylum for the Houseless Poor, Cripplegate	574

MAPS

Map showing the density of the population	568
Map showing the intensity of ignorance	569
Map showing the intensity of the criminality	570
Map showing the criminality of females	571

In memory of my beloved husband
David Englander
3 June 1949 – 7 April 1999

PREFACE

David Englander was informed that he had terminal lung cancer three weeks before he died on April 7 1999. During that last three weeks he and I spent as always much time in one another's company. We discussed the present book and worked on the shape of the introduction together. We were determined to offer the reader a useful aid to reading Mayhew, to set his four-volume *London Labour and the London Poor* in the context of his other work, to include material on how and why Mayhew worked as he did, emphasising in particular the contribution of the interviews, and to explain why we decided not to confine the selection to Mayhew's showy 'characters' but to include also materials which are frequently overlooked in collections for the general reader. David hoped that he would live on to see completion of this work but this was not to be.

I take full responsibility, of course, for the text as it stands. I have tried to do justice to both David's great scholarship and his imaginative flair, inspecting every statement and conclusion in the light of what I know he would have said and thought, listening all the time to his voice in my ear. It has been a heavy responsibility and the editor, Tom Griffith, has been extremely patient with the delays consequent upon events. The edition was ready for publication in 2000 but publication was unavoidably postponed until 2008. Minimal changes have been made since 2000. I would like to thank Dr Laurence Marlow for the benefit of his great erudition and also for his support and that of his wife Jo during these dark days. I am also exceptionally grateful to Mrs Valerie Humphrey for her help in preparing the edition for handover. I hope that this volume will be a fitting memorial to David's and my partnership.

ROSEMARY O'DAY
The Open University
December 2007

INTRODUCTION

I

'London Labour and the London Poor' in the context of Mayhew's work

London Labour and the London Poor is a masterpiece of personal inquiry and social observation. It is the classic account of life below the margins in the greatest metropolis in the world and a compelling portrait of the habits, tastes, amusements, appearance, speech, humour, earnings and opinions of the labouring poor at the time of the Great Exhibition. In scope, depth and detail it remains unrivalled. London as presented here is an ingeniously contrived machine in which social relations arising from the production of goods and services are cast as an organised parasitism. Workers in the luxury and bespoke trades who danced attendance on aristocratic and fashionable London are thus connected with the nightmen and pure-finders who subsist upon the removal of decaying organic matter. And so we descend into the abyss, into a world without fixed employment where skills were declining and insecurity mounting, a world of criminality, pauperism and vice, of unorthodox personal relations and fluid families, a world from which regularity was absent and prosperity departed.

To make sense of so strange an environment required curiosity, imagination and a novelist's eye for detail. Henry Mayhew possessed all three in good measure. His interest, once aroused, developed into an unsentimental appreciation of the vicissitudes of the poor accompanied by a growing respect for their durability. His considerable energies and literary gifts were mobilised in their defence. At its best his writing was disciplined and controlled. Mayhew's artistry, his reliance upon individual and collective biography, came from the possession of great descriptive power

and tremendous compositional skills. The construction of situations through which the humanity of the poor might be conveyed was a speciality. Ears as well as eyes played a part. Mayhew
was remarkably sensitive to the language of the poor – to the
burr of the Irish, the cries of the costermongers and the spiel
of the patterers. The decision to represent Londoners through
the demotic, with dropped aitches and displaced 'v's, but minus
the generous use of expletives, served to enliven the text, suggest
the authenticity of its narratives and accuracy of its findings,
and express forms of social criticism which might otherwise be
deemed unseemly or improper. No previous writer had succeeded in presenting the poor through their own stories and in
their own words. Even Dickens found Mayhew's work suggestive. *London Labour and the London Poor* is, in fact, closer to
literature than is sometimes imagined. To pass from one to the
other, writes one authority, is merely to cross sides of the same
street. 'Knowledge of Mayhew persuades us that Dickens the
comic–caricaturist is in essence a great *realist,* just as reading
Dickens persuades us that Mayhew was not merely a fine reporter
but a superb artist.'[1]

Of Dickens we know plenty; of Mayhew precious little. Henry
Mayhew was born on 25 November 1812, the son of Joshua
Mayhew and his wife Mary Ann Fenn. His father, a successful
London solicitor, was a stern, autocratic paterfamilias; his mother
remains a shadowy figure. Seven of the seventeen Mayhew
children were boys. All joined their father's practice and all,
with one exception, abandoned the law for journalism. From
the little we know of them the brothers Mayhew appear to
have been spirited sorts who disregarded their father's wishes –
but not his allowances – to pursue literary and theatrical interests, turning out popular farces, almanacks, comic novels, travel
accounts – anything for which there was a ready market – and
contributing to regular newspapers and journals while parti-
cipating in the founding and editing of miscellaneous money-
making ventures. Most were failures. None of the Mayhew
brothers had any business sense, two were bankrupts and all
seem to have experienced a good deal of financial insecurity. In
the case of the eldest, it led to tragedy. Thomas Mayhew, editor
of the radical *Poor Man's Guardian,* who died by his own hand

in 1834, was also unusual in his complete identification with the popular radical movement. The descent of his siblings was less steep.

Headstrong Henry, having dropped out of respectable society, fell into a middle-class bohemia where he came into contact with W. M. Thackeray, Charles Dickens and Douglas Jerrold, whose daughter, Jane, he married in 1844. It was a comfortable, convivial and creative environment peopled by dramatists, journalists, and witty, talented types meeting in pubs and clubs, scribbling satires and dreaming up all sorts of theatrical and literary projects. Some faces were familiar. The illustrated comic weekly, *Figaro in London,* which Mayhew edited between 1835 and 1839, was owned by his Westminster contemporary and one-time partner Gilbert Beckett. *Punch,* the climax of such ventures, was founded in 1841, and although Mayhew was ousted from the editorial chair in 1842, he continued his association with the journal until 1845. Twelve months later, Mayhew, like Beckett before him, was bankrupted. The next three years witnessed a desperate casting around for cash. There followed several potboilers, written in collaboration with his brother Augustus, before fortune again smiled in October 1849 with the invitation from the editors of the *Morning Chronicle* to act as the Metropolitan Correspondent for its national investigation of 'Labour and the Poor'.

With this appointment began the three serial inquiries, conducted during the next five years, which together constitute the Mayhew survey, as it will be described below. In 1849–50 Mayhew produced some eighty-two letters for the *Morning Chronicle,* about a million words in all, devoted primarily to the condition of the London manufacturing trades. In the next two years he published the equally weighty *London Labour and the London Poor,* an investigation in sixty-three weekly parts of the metropolitan street trades. Included on the wrappers was a correspondence column ('intended to be cut off in binding'),[2] which foreshadowed the attempted critique of political economy that was developed in *Low Wages,* a separate part-work, also published in 1851, which folded after four issues. The same fate befell the *Great World of London,* a projected panorama, which appeared in monthly instalments between March and November 1856. Its most substantial legacy, the partially finished survey of the prison population, was later completed with outside assistance and published in book form in 1862.[3] All three inquiries were closely connected. About a third of the material published in the *Morning Chronicle* was incorporated in *London Labour and the London Poor,* which also also supplied the key reference for the sequel, *The Criminal Prisons of London*.[4] In *London Labour and the London Poor* there was also frequent cross-referencing between volumes and also to the *Morning Chronicle* survey: 'For a more detailed account of the mode of business as conducted at the Old Clothes Exchange I refer the reader to p. 368, vol. i. Subsequent visits have shown me nothing to alter in that description, although written (in one of my letters to the *Morning Chronicle)* nearly two years ago.'[5]

Unsold numbers *of London Labour and the London Poor* were bound and published in book form as a four-parts-in-one-volume, monumental and unwieldy *Cyclopaedia of the Condition and Earnings of Those that Will Work, Those that Cannot Work, and Those that Will Not Work*, by John Howden (George Woodfall and Son of Angel Court, Skinner Street, London, being the printer) in 1851. It included, in response to popular demand, the *Answers to Correspondents*. The edition of *London Labour and the London Poor* in most frequent modern use is that which was published by Griffin Bohn and Company, London, in 1861-2.[6] This differed in several respects from the first edition; internal evidence indicates that Mayhew was adding materially to it certainly as late as 1856.[7] Whole sections on street entertainers seem to have appeared for the first time in this version. Similarly dock labourers, cabmen and porters found their way into its pages. Maps and tables relevant to the study of criminality in England and Wales, which were dispersed throughout the final section of the 1851 edition, appear in a separate appendix in the edition of 1861-2. This later edition also contained much work that was neither undertaken by nor obviously supervised by Mayhew himself and which did not appear at all in 1851. Mayhew's intellectual laziness probably accounted for his failure to organise and prune the work for this edition.

Mayhew's brief in the letters to the *Morning Chronicle* was to provide a reliable account of the earnings of labouring London. The survey population for this purpose included:

. . . all those persons whose incomings are insufficient for the satisfaction of their wants – a want being, according to *my* idea, contra-distinguished from a mere *desire* by a positive physical pain, instead of a mental uneasiness, accompanying it. The large and comparatively unknown body of people included in this definition I shall contemplate in *two* distinct classes, viz., the honest and dishonest poor, and the first of these I propose subdividing into the striving and the disabled – or in other words, I shall consider the whole of the metropolitan poor under three separate phases, according as they will work, they can't work and they won't work.[8]

The trades were largely self-selecting. The weavers of Spital-fields, dock labourers and the slop-clothing workers, universally acknowledged as paradigmatic low-wage trades, supplied an obvious starting point. Attention then shifted to those artisanal trades where, in consequence of the reorganisation of the social relations of production, the degradation of working conditions and deterioration of living standards was most pronounced. Included here were the tailors, hatters, boot and shoemakers, carpenters, joiners and cabinet-makers; excluded were the metal and engineering trades, precision manufactures and printing and paperwork. Unskilled labourers and service workers were under-represented. Domestic service, the largest single source of employment, was omitted.[9]

The want of 'trustworthy information' which supplied the rationale for the inquiry posed formidable problems.[10] The growth of the statistical movement, as Michael Cullen has shown, was an expression of middle-class anxieties provoked by the narrow informational basis of the Condition of England Question. Mayhew, though not part of any of the various social reform networks, was closer to the mainstream than is sometimes suggested. The great parliamentary inquiries of the period did not pass over him as the Angel of Death had passed the Children of Israel. Mayhew, like Engels, was an assiduous reader of official publications. The reports of police authorities, Poor Law commissioners, the registrar-general, factory inspectors and other regulatory agencies were scrutinised for evidence and argument and their strengths as well as their defects readily exposed.[11] The blue book sociology that framed the values, assumptions and concepts of contemporaries also supplied the point of departure for his particular method of social inquiry. The possibilities of a scientific representation of the social order obtained through details in direct personal testimony seized his imagination. Mayhew's solution was to combine the ethos and interrogative approach of the royal commission with the reporting skills of the journalist. The technique, perfected in *London Labour and the London Poor*, enabled him to justify the work as 'the first commission of inquiry into the state of the people undertaken by a private individual, and the first "blue book" ever published in twopenny numbers'.[12]

The sanitary science, which in London as in Paris thrived on the panic provoked by the conjunction of cholera and crime and the displaced fears of social change expressed by them, provided another point of reference. Mayhew, who had spent time in the French capital, knew of the work of the public hygienists, and wrote as though his readers might be familiar with Thenard's researches or with toxicologists like D'Arcet, whose work was published in the *Annales d'hygiene publique*.[13] Here in Paris too, perhaps, he first encountered the work of Alexander Parent-Duchatelet, a one-time editor and authority on sewerage and industrial hygiene, who was also the author of *De la prostitution dans la ville de Paris* (1836), which Mayhew cites with approval.[14] He certainly knew of his work on sewerage by the late 1840s: 'The late M. Parent du Chatelet, a high authority on this matter, stated (in 1833) that the emanations from the Voirie were insupportable . . . '.[15] Parent-Duchatelet's extraordinary study of the pathology of Paris reveals an intellectual framework of public inquiry that was well in advance of developments on this side of the Channel. Parent-Duchatelet was remarkable in his use of social statistics and in the path-breaking application of field observation and personal interview to social research. The point at which Mayhew read the Frenchman's work on crime remains to be established. What is clear, though, is that he fully shared contemporary concerns in respect of the connection between labouring and dangerous classes. His survey, defined as a fact-gathering exercise on wages and incomes, addressed a particular debate on poverty and criminality and the re-establishment of social order.

The requirements of the work led him into strange company. Labourers were summoned by cab to the newspaper offices; testimonies were taken at public meetings, in the workplace, in private interviews held in trade societies and in small gatherings in low-lodging houses. Mayhew consorted with coal-heavers and convicts, spoke with street-walkers and slop-workers, fraternised with beggars, visited the poor at home, and even received them in Mrs Mayhew's parlour! The extraordinary rapport that developed between writer and audience found expression in the letter columns of the *Morning Chronicle* and in the pathetic appeals from distressed needlewomen, the wives of impoverished railway guards and like-minded correspondents who cast him as a finder of jobs and distributor of alms.[16] These roles he was not willing to perform. Mayhew's mission, as he himself defined it, was to act as an intermediary between the classes, and to explain to one half how the other half lived. The keeping of low company was a requirement of social science, not evidence of weakened class loyalties. 'To this middle class we ourselves belong,' he wrote, 'and, if we ever wandered out of it, we did so but to regard the other forms of life with the same eyes as a comparative anatomist loves to lay bare the organism and vital machinery of a zoophyte, or an ape, in the hope of linking together the lower and the higher forms of animal existence.'[17]

Whom did Mayhew interview? In the course of writing *London Labour and the London Poor* (Volumes I to III) Henry Mayhew drew upon 436 separate interviews (including seven collective interviews) involving more than 700 individuals.[18] These were undertaken by Mayhew and assistants. Mayhew was aware of an inbuilt bias in his interview population; it was that imposed by who was willing to talk to him. When reporting the words of an oyster-seller about his diet he observed: 'I have found the Irish far more communicative than the English. Many a poor untaught Englishman will shrink from speaking of his spare diet . . . a reserve, too, much more noticeable among the men than the women.'[19] Unsurprisingly therefore he did speak to those who would speak to him, whether or not they were representative of the groups among the poor in which he was most interested. Women and children were often more loquacious than middle-aged men. A sixth of the interviewees were women and of these ten were definitely aged sixteen or below. Sixteen of the females interviewed were described as Irish and only one as English. The women were derived from just a few broad occupational categories (retail, cleansing, labouring and vagrants). The wives of the ballast-heavers excepted (31), most were either single or widowed. Young boys of sixteen years and under accounted for 46 of the 436 interviews. But it wasn't simply a matter of numbers. As indicated above, some people were more forthcoming than others and, when people were willing to talk, Mayhew was more than willing to report.

Preliminary analysis of Mayhew's interviewees where detail is specified

Breakdown by gender (where specified):

Male	Female	Total
361	73	434

Breakdown by marital status:

Married	Single	Widowed	Unstated
127	132	26	137

Breakdown of single interviewees by gender (where stated):

Single	Males	Females
132	107	25

Breakdown of young interviewees by gender:

Young	Males	Females
59	46	13

For the relationship between the reported interviews and the survey as a whole also had a bearing upon the interview population. Mayhew's survey was not questionnaire-led or even interview-led. He was not interested in offering the life histories of a representative sample. He did not discuss the concept of representative sampling or his thought processes as he decided who to interview and who to pass over. He never presented a statistical analysis of all his interviews.[20]

Breakdown of interviews by occupation

Breakdown by broad occupational category[a]

Cleansers[b]	42
Collectors	10
Entertainers	67
Labourers	58
Sewage	5
Skilled artisans	17
Street sellers	159
Thieves and vagrants	61
Transport	7
Other	12
Total	436

Breakdown of interviews within five occupational categories[c]

1. Cleansers: 42

Crossing-sweepers	24
Street-sweepers	4
Chimney-sweeps	3
Rubbish-carters	4
Vermin-destroyers	2
Labourers	5
Other	0

2. Collectors: 10

Mudlarks	4
Pure-finders (manure)	2
Bonegrubber	1
Dustman	1
Dredger-men	2

3. Entertainers: 67

Acrobat	1
Animal act (excluding exhibits)	2
Artist	1
Clown	5

a This is based upon a preliminary analysis of the Mayhew interviews. It should be noted that some of these interviews were reported in extraordinary length and detail while others were recorded briefly. There were also large numbers of so-called 'informants', who are not represented in this analysis, many of whom were perhaps also interviewees.

b Mayhew's category merges imperceptibly with those of collectors, refuse sellers and sewage workers. They are treated separately for the purposes of this table.

c Other categories are difficult to break down precisely. For example, there were two collective interviews of thieves and vagrants. At the first eleven individuals were singled out for special mention; at the second there were 50 vagrants, of whom 31 were singled out. These vagrants were described as for the most part thieves.

Conjuror	1
Dancer	1
Exhibitors of animals or birds	2
Other exhibitors	1
Fire-eater	1
Guy Fawkes-related	2
Jugglers	1
Musicians	27
Punch & Judy	1
Photographers	3
Profile-cutters	2
Showmen	5
Strolling players	1
Sword-swallowers	1
Other	0

4. Skilled artisans: 17

Tailors	4
Furniture-makers	6
Boot- and shoe-makers	2
Looking-glass maker	1
Chamber-master	1
Doll-maker	1
Other	1

5. Street-sellers: 159

Pets and their needs	7
Prepared foods	17
Fresh fruit and vegetables	32
Flowers	5
Meat	9
Fish and shellfish	8
Clothing	12
Dry goods such as stationery	13
Sewing goods	3
Metal, tools etc	4
Coke and coal	3
Skins (fur)	2
Tea leaves	3
Turf	3
Other	0

The interviews were used by Mayhew to elucidate and give credence to the points he made about each occupation and its place in the casual economy of the metropolis. He did not muse upon the dangers of assuming that individual statements had a wider applicability. There are some sections of the work which rely much more heavily upon interview materials than others. The vicious circle which seems to have existed between Mayhew's conclusions and his sources (both oral and written) meant that he would always select those interviews which expressed and supported his own views most dramatically, while these same interviews stimulated his thoughts. The original verbatim interview reports are no longer (if they ever existed) extant. The format of the extracts included in the work indicates that questioning followed reasonably uniform lines.[21] Yet the length, richness and content of the individual interviews was more important to the balance of the overall inquiry than their number; it determined what use Mayhew made of them in the completed text. Witness, for example, the apparent garrulousness of the boy crossing-sweepers, thieves and mud-larks when compared with the seemingly uncommunicative utterances of such as the steam-boat seller of periodicals or the boxmaker.[22] Was it simply that one individual spoke less than another or that Mayhew considered their speech less worthy of inclusion in his account? Were street entertainers included in such numbers because of contemporary concerns about noise and other forms of pollution or because of their colourful appeal or because they were easy to observe and willing to talk – important factors when Mayhew was seeking to enliven somewhat dry sections of his work? The weight which Mayhew accorded such considerations must, it seems, always be a matter of speculation.

The powerful and compelling quality of the Mayhew survey, though it drew something from his widening social sympathies and the use of open-ended questions, owed more to the ways in which the interviews were written up. Mayhew insisted that the experiences told to him were taken down on the spot and 'repeated to the public in the selfsame words in which they were told to me'.[23] The language of the poor it may have been; spontaneous it was not. To be sure, the actors were unscripted, but the production was carefully staged. Cues were given and the audience prepared for the lines about to be delivered. Historians have also noted the heightened effect created by the elimination of the reporter's questions and the presentation of each interview as if it were an autobiographical statement in the 'voice' of the worker.[24]

Mayhew was assisted by his brother Augustus and two former London City Missionaries – Henry Wood and Richard Knight. The latter were described 'as gentlemen who have been engaged with me from nearly the commencement of my inquiries, and to whose hearty co-operation both myself and the public are indebted for a large increase of knowledge. Mr Wood, indeed, has contributed so large a proportion of the contents of the present volume [Volume 1 of *LL&LP*] that he may fairly be considered one of its authors'.[25] This suggests that they were more than the 'stenographers' suggested in the Report of the Transportation Committee of 1856. He also had two clerks 'continually engaged' 'in collecting information and making general statistics for me'. [26] Interviews generally began with questions about wages and working conditions. No reliable wage series existed when Mayhew began his inquiry. Employers, small and large, who paid the lowest wages, were generally uncooperative. When he came to discuss dust-carting he observed: 'It is impossible to obtain any definite statistics on this part of the subject. Not one in *every* ten of the contractors keeps any account of the amount [of dust] that comes into the "yard".' [27] Workers, though helpful, were poor record-keepers, 'and it is only with considerable difficulty and cross-questioning that one is able to obtain from them an account of the expenses necessarily attendant upon their labour, and so, by deducting these from the price paid to them, to arrive at the amount of their clear earnings'.[28] Mayhew, in an attempt to construct the average rate of wages, took extraordinary pains to secure reliable information. Assuming that his informants were 'naturally disposed' to understate their earnings and that his readers expected them to do so, he explained his procedure thus:

My first inquiries are into a particular branch of the trade under investigation upon which the workman is engaged. I then request to be informed whether the individual has his or her work first or second-handed; that is to say, whether he or she obtains it direct from the employer, or through the intervention of some chamber or piece-master. If the work comes to the operative in question second-handed, I then endeavour to find out the prices paid for the work itself to the first hand, as well as the number of work people that the first hand generally employs. This done, I seek to be informed whether the work of the individual I am visiting is piece or day work. If day work, I learn the usual hours of labour per day, and the rate of wages per week. If it be piece-work, I request to be made acquainted with the prices paid for each description of work seriatim, the time that each particular article takes to make, and the number of hours that the party usually works per day. By these means I arrive at the gross daily earnings. I then ascertain the cost of trimmings, candles, and such other expenses as are necessary to the completion of each particular article; and, deducting these from the gross gains per day, I find what are the clear daily earnings of the individual in question. I then check this account by obtaining from the workman a statement as to the number of such articles that he can make in a week; and, deducting expenses, I see whether the clear weekly earnings agree with those of the clear daily ones. After this I request to know the amount of the earnings for the last week, then those for the week before; and then those for the week before that. Beyond this point I find that the memory generally fails. Out of the scores of operatives that I have now visited, I have found only one instance in which the workman keeps a regular account of his weekly gains

When I have obtained an account of the clear earnings of the workpeople during such times as they are fully employed, I seek to procure from them a statement of what they imagine to be their weekly earnings, taking one week with another, throughout the year. Having got this I then set about to discover how often in the course of the year they are 'standing still', as they term it. I inquire into the number and duration of 'the slacks'. This done, I strive to obtain from the operative an average of the weekly earnings during such times. I then make a calculation of the total of the workpeople's gains when fully employed for so many months, and when partially occupied for the remainder of the year. By this means I am enabled to arrive at an average of their weekly earnings throughout the whole year; and I then compare this with the amount I have previously received from them on the subject . . . I finally check the whole account of their earnings by a statement of their expenditure. I generally see their rent-book, and so learn the sum that they pay for rent; and I likewise get a detail of their mode and cost of living inquired into, especially with regard to the truthfulness, industry and sobriety of the individual.[29]

The personal visits and lengthy interviews with operatives required to elicit incomes data were perhaps the most time-consuming part of the whole inquiry for the Morning Chronicle. The bias towards the skilled worker, which has drawn criticism in some quarters, owed as much to Mayhew's developed record-keeping practices as to any other virtues. The comparative expenditure of time and effort in securing reliable information on earnings made him appreciative of the intelligent artisan, above all of the 'Society' man, who could more readily supply standard list prices and other essential documents. One such informant who 'placed in my hands a variety of statistical papers connected with the trade' was, he concluded, 'a person of superior understanding'. The difference between those who stored information on paper and those who relied purely upon memory was for Mayhew and his associates a personal as much as a cultural consideration. 'Indeed,' he wrote, 'the change from the squalor, foetor and wretchedness of the homes of the poor people that I had lately visited, to the comfort, cleanliness and cheerfulness of the operative tailors, has been as refreshing to my feelings as the general sagacity of the workmen has been instrumental in the lightening of my labours.' [30]

Mayhew, though, was concerned with more than the calculation of wage rates. The survey, undertaken at a key moment in the transformation of the urban economy, recorded the changes in manufacturing activity associated with the expansion of the sweated industries. Captivated by the articulate artisans with whom he consorted, Mayhew developed a quite remarkable understanding of the cultural and material changes that flowed from the increasing degradation of labour. Before Marx there were few who had a better grasp of its defining elements. Mayhew, who spent time in the workshops and petty manufactures, separates work into its constituent parts, and proceeds from an analysis of the labour process to chart the changes in the division of labour in order to show how labour power had become a commodity organised and cheapened to suit the needs of its purchasers. He describes the disruption of the labour market, the expansion of the sweated, slop or dishonourable sector and the varying forms of work process, work organisation and wage payment that were applied to increase labour productivity. [31] Small wonder that he saw the role of tables as markedly inferior to narrative and life histories in his scheme of things. [32]

Mayhew's comparative method − the cross-checking of statements and juxtaposition of empirically grounded conclusions with received truths − did not necessarily yield reliable results, but it did make the investigator increasingly critical of official sources of information and the explanatory framework into which they were organised. He was scathing in his critique of the national census, 'whose insufficiency is a national disgrace to us, for there the trading and working classes are all jumbled together in the most perplexing confusion, and the occupations classified in a manner that would shame the merest tyro in logic':[33]

> The census of 1841, as I have pointed out, mentions no dustman whatever! . . . But I have so often had instances of the defects of this national numbering of the people that I have long since ceased to place much faith in its returns connected with the humbler grades of labour. The costermongers, for example, I estimate at about 10,000, whereas the government reports, as has been before mentioned, ignore the very existence of such a class of people.[34]

In particular, he became sceptical of the representation of society as a spontaneous and self-adjusting order, and began to doubt whether prevailing economic arrangements were either natural or necessary.[35] The gloomy implications of the Malthusian theory of population and its rationalisation of the subsistence theory of wages struck him as both vicious and contentious. He took up arms against the wage-fund theory and ridiculed the view, imputed to J. S. Mill, that 'there is no hope for the working men of this country until they imitate the Catholic priests and register vows in Heaven of perpetual celibacy'.[36]

Mayhew not only documented the downward pressures on the artisan at work but also recorded the sense of loss experienced by the destruction of craftsmanship and the communities it sustained. The silk weavers of Spitalfields, 'formerly, almost the only botanists in the Metropolis', with their once-flourishing entomological, floricultural and mathematical societies, exemplify the severance of science and art, and the despair among craft workers at the loss of skill, independence and control.[37]

Mayhew was just as concerned with the social relations of production, with the values, beliefs and assumptions of his informants, with their traditions and memories, and the connection between their work and their way of life. Taking his cue from the craft trades, he recorded the enormous cultural variations between skilled and unskilled occupations and how these distinctions affected their corporate consciousness and political outlook.

He noted, with respect to the waterside trades, how regularity of habits was incompatible with irregularity of income. He noted, too, how different groups of workers responded to technical and economic change and the pressures which transformed coal-whippers into special constables and costermongers into Chartists.

Moving from the streets to the prisons and reformatories, Mayhew explored how the prison operated and how it was organised. *The Criminal Prisons of London,* a text that says as much about civil society as about the penal system, has not received the attention it merits.[38] The prison population, so often viewed as an undifferentiated mass, is here disaggregated and presented as men, women and juveniles whose condition highlights the place of punishment and prison in the social system. New punishment regimes were examined, the goals and methods of the organisation of penal life scrutinised and the prison assessed as both school and factory. Direct personal testimony taken from inmates, ticket-of-leave men and young offenders, as always makes compelling reading and reinforces the connection between prisoners and civilians.[39]

II
Mayhew and the framework for an analysis of poverty

The disjuncture between the process of production and wealth creation as represented by political economy and the exploitation revealed by his investigations into the manufacturing trades, raised questions which Mayhew felt impelled to answer. Having been led to the view that inadequate remuneration rather than inefficient expenditure was the principal cause of poverty, he switched attention from observation to analysis.

Apart from a well-thumbed copy of Mill's *Principles of Political Economy,* the key texts were those of Smith and Ricardo. Mayhew also read Charles Babbage's *Economy of Machinery and Manufacturers* (1832), Andrew Ure's *Philosophy of Manufacturers* (1835), Chalmers, McCulloch and others.[40] Of the unorthodox economists there was no mention. The writings of the Ricardian socialists, who between 1820 and 1840 advanced the claim of labour to the whole product of industry, seems to have passed him by. So he began with Mill's statement that the rate of wages was determined by the law of demand and supply and sought its refutation and reformulation from the standpoint of workers as observed in the productive process. His definition of wages as the ratio of the remuneration of the labourer to the quantity of the work performed differed markedly from the orthodox view (in which wages depended on the proportion between population and capital). It enabled him to focus attention on employer strategies for controlling the labour process to show how the supply and remuneration of labour was affected by organisational systems, wage systems and the mechanisation of production rather than by any increase in population. His conclusion, baldly summarised, was that overwork rather than overpopulation was the more influential cause of the surplus of labour.

Mayhew located the crux of the problem in a growing disequilibrium between the funds available for the maintenance of labour and the funds absorbed by capital. His conclusions, though, were almost as pessimistic as those of the classical economists. He envisaged a future of increasing competition in which the relentless downward pressure on wages and employment provoked crises of overproduction and underconsumption, distress and disturbance. No relief was possible, he argued, until wages were made to better reflect the value created by the worker. Justice, rather than the market, should rule, and the workman receive a fairer share of the 'increased value that . . . [he] by the exercise of his skill, gives to the materials on which he operates'.[41] What was required, then, was a 'new partnership' between 'the man of money and the man of muscles'.[42] The reconciliation of the classes through the development of an equitable wage system, he concluded, would best secure material and moral progress.[43]

Mayhew's claim to revise economic theory in the light of the evidence he had collected, to be, in his own words, 'the first who has sought to evolve the truths of the Labour Question by personal investigation', represents an aspiration rather than an achievement.[44] What went wrong? Scholarly approaches here are of two kinds. Some assert that Mayhew's 'unreliability and lack of tenacity' accounts for the poverty of his theory; others direct attention to certain shortcomings in his assumptions and procedures.[45]

Mayhew, in the second approach, is presented as the victim of his own sources. His economics, it has been argued, express an artisan trade consciousness which helps to account for the uneasy shifting from fact to value to reach conclusions that do not proceed from theoretical considerations.[46]

Low Wages, Mayhew's attempt to gather his thinking into a general statement, is widely perceived as an exercise that displays his limitations rather than his strengths. 'Mayhew's economic analysis,' writes Gareth Stedman Jones, 'consisted largely of antinomies – the disclosure of phenomena not easily accounted for, or indeed, even mentioned in the conventional economics of the period, accompanied by an inability or unwillingness to locate them in an alternative theoretical structure. Such an ambivalence made it unclear even to himself whether he was engaged in a critique of political economy or an extension of it.' But whereas previous commentators have fixed upon Mayhew's alleged fecklessness to account for the abandonment of serious social analysis, Stedman Jones presents him as the victim of economic and political change, beached by the onset of mid-Victorian stability, and thus deprived of the radical constituency which might have sustained his project.[47]

Plausible though it is, the interpretation rests on a counterfactual that cannot be tested. The outcome of the Mayhew survey, had it been undertaken at the beginning rather than the close of the 1840s, must remain a matter of conjecture. The extent to which Mayhew had been radicalised by his experience as Metropolitan Commissioner may also be questioned. It will be seen below that, for all his advances in respect of the labour question, he accepted far more of the assumptions of liberalism than he ever criticised. Mayhew's commitment to private property, support of emigration, qualified approval of trade unions, and liking for profit-sharing arrangements, locate him squarely within the ranks of the enlightened middle classes. Even his concern with unequal exchange was connected with a continuing preoccupation with the formation of the dangerous and criminal classes. Thus Chalmers, whose opinions Mill considered erroneous, was mustered by Mayhew in defence of the principle that wages should be sufficient to prevent pauperism. The 'immense mass of surplus labourers, who are continually vagabondising through the country', he claimed, partly reflected the want of such a wage.[48] Viewed in the round, his theoretical interventions seem much more like an attempt to modify or moralise political economy than an attempt to replace it.

Mayhew's search for an organising framework for his findings was not exhausted by his encounter with political economy. The need of an alternative anchorage became pressing after the break with the *Morning Chronicle* and the shift towards the street trades and the criminal classes. Those readily available did not at first seem promising. 'The phrenologists alone have looked into the subject, but unfortunately they are theorists with a disposition to warp rather than discover facts,' he wrote. Of ethnography he was equally critical. 'Ethnologists,' he observed, 'have done little or nothing towards increasing our knowledge of the physical conformation of the predatory and vagabond races of the world.' [49] It was the descriptive force and evolutionist assumptions of ethnography that caught his imagination. Two features were striking: the division of mankind into two anatomically and morally distinct classes, the civilised settlers and the unproductive wanderers, and the parasitism of the latter upon the former. The similarities between the social order as portrayed by contemporary anthropology and that which formed the subject of his investigation seemed to Mayhew to constitute:

. . . points of coincidence so striking that, when placed before the mind, makes us marvel that the analogy should have remained thus long unnoticed. The resemblance once discovered, however, becomes of great service in enabling us to use the moral characteristics of the nomad races of other countries, as a means of comprehending the more readily, those of the vagabonds and outcasts of our own.' [50]

How well versed Mayhew was in the anthropology and travel literature of his day is uncertain. Mayhew himself, one literary scholar has recently noted, is unspecific almost to the point of mystification about his ethnographic references. [51]

London Labour and the London Poor acknowledges, but does not engage with, the writings of Pritchard, Lewis and others. [52] There was no good reason why it should. Ethnology, as presented here, was not a set of testable propositions, but a strategy that enabled the author to develop his role as social explorer and interpreter of the poor. Mayhew's borrowings were largely for purposes of illustration; his citations were included as a reassurance for disturbed readers rather than as an invitation to further research.

The nomadic poor are likened to primeval savages, who are ruled by brute passions and animal appetites, and live without structure and restraint. They are dangerous and depraved, restless and indulgent, improvident, licentious and lewd. These people, unknown to the census enumerators, supplied the recruits to the vagabond hordes that were said to be roaming the country. Questions concerning numbers, though, were less urgent than the possibilities of redemption and rehabilitation. Here there were grounds for optimism. On closer inspection, Mayhew found regularities and system in the lives of the poor, and shows them trying to create order and meaning out of the apparently meaningless chaos of their everyday existence. The significance of this discovery, however, has been obscured by a Whiggish preoccupation with the origins of modern British sociology and the modern idea of culture. Of such things contemporaries knew little. Mayhew, who well understood the needs of his audience, showed that, notwithstanding appearance to the contrary, the outcast poor might be susceptible to rational analysis and perhaps also to rational reform.

III

Mayhew and Utilitarianism

Scientist in spirit, and with a lifelong enthusiasm for chemistry, Mayhew had set out to apply the techniques of natural science to the study of social phenomena. 'I have undertaken the subject with a rigid determination neither to be biased nor prejudiced by my own individual notions,' he wrote. 'I know that as in science the love of theorising warps the mind, and causes it to see only those natural phenomena that it wishes to see . . . '.[53] He saw himself as a recorder of facts and an inductive reasoner.

Empirical investigation, too, was influenced by the moral categories of Benthamite social analysis. His eligibility supplied a perspective on social research as well as a basis for public policy. Mayhew shared with contemporaries numerous preconceptions about poverty and the poor, and readily classified individuals as respectable and worthy or depraved and vicious. Thus the informants and respondents by whom he set such store were all located within the same evaluative framework. With the workshy, thrift-less and criminal elements he had no truck: 'Those who desire to live by the industry of others, form no portion of the honest and independent race of workmen in this country whom Mr Mayhew wishes to befriend,' he informed one correspondent. 'The deserv-ing poor are those who cannot live by their labour, whether from underpayment, want of employment, or physical or mental incap-acity, and these Mr Mayhew wishes, and will most cheerfully do all he can, at any time and in any way, to assist.' [54]

The origins of these distinctions were also accountable in Utilit-arian terms. Mayhew's analysis of the formation of labouring and dangerous classes thus combined aspects of sensationalist psych-ology with an appreciation of the special circumstances of time and place. The genesis of criminality, though rooted in an impatience of steady labour, was primarily a result of the neglect and tyranny of parents and masters, and a consequent failure to engender a love of industry.[55] Men and women, Mayhew believed, were born egoists. 'Theft,' he wrote, 'is a natural propensity of the human condition and honesty an artificial and educated sentiment. We do not come into the world with an instinctive sense of the rights of property implanted in our bosom, to teach us to respect the possessions of others, but rather with an innate desire to app-ropriate whatever we may fancy.' [56] Chadwick's formulation – 'Crime is mostly the result of a desire to obtain property with a less degree of labour than by regular industry' – was also cited with approbation.[57] Prostitution, too, he believed, arose among those 'who are born in labour for their bread, but who find the work inordinately irksome to their natures, and pleasure as inordinately agreeable to them'.[58]

Mayhew's concern with the roots of criminality also led him to an appreciation of Mandeville's sensationalist hedonism. Apart from the irreverent tone and mordant wit, and the telling use of vignettes, anecdotes and sketches – all of them no doubt congenial to the founder editor of *Punch* – it was the satirist-philosopher's assertion that pride was the key to social organisation that caught his imagination. Mayhew, though he balked at the egoistic re-duction of morality, found the idea of self-love as a socialising agent, capable of converting human animals into human beings, particularly pertinent to his inquiries. What was most suggestive about Mandeville's writing was the unfolding possibilities of moral progress through the balancing of the weaker passions against the stronger. The role of the legislator and moralist to promote such adjustments as were necessary to secure the continuing victory of reason over passion seemed equally apposite.[59] Mayhew, like the political economists who drank at the same trough, readily endorsed Mandeville's view that the desire to be admired, and the disinclination to be despised, constituted an insight of great importance in the shaping of social and market relations. The spirit of emulation, properly mobilised, Mayhew asserted, represented 'one of the great means of moral government in a State'. Its absence among the lowest social classes accounted for prostitution and crime.[60] Mayhew, though, did not believe that such people could not be reached. His proposal for the formation of self-regulating street-trading communities was a measure designed to channel restlessness into respectability.[61]

The idea of man as a creature of desires who seeks to satisfy them as abundantly as he can at the least cost to himself served to distance him from Evangelical educational initiatives and allied strategies for social reform. Apart from a misguided preoccupation with externals, Evangelical social action was, he believed, too narrow in its scope to address the labour question effectively. His attempts to demonstrate this empirically by a case study of the Ragged School Union brought down the wrath of the philanthropic establishment upon his head, and opened the rift with his employers that was to culminate in his departure from the *Morning Chronicle*. Mayhew, though 'pelted with dirt from every evangelical assembly throughout the country', declined to go down gently.[62] Charges against the 'religious gentry' were repeated and embellished in subsequent publications. He scorned educational systems in which children were 'duly taught to spell and to write, and to chatter catechisms and creeds that they cannot understand', and condemned the influence of parson and chaplain as harmful. 'No man,' he wrote, 'can have a deeper loathing and contempt for those outward shows of godliness – those continued "lip services" – the everlasting "praying in public places", which the revelation of our every-day's commercial and prison history teaches us to believe, constitute the flagrant "shams" of the age.' [63] In place of chaplain and bible worship he recommended 'really good sound wholesome labour training'.[64]

For Mayhew, it was the formation or non-formation of habits of industry that was central to his understanding of the social question. Mayhew, though he was not attached to any particular group or programme, drew selectively upon the stock of ideas that formed the basis of middle-class radicalism and shared in full its civilising mission. His belief that criminal behaviour reflected a want of self-control due in large part to an unwholesome environment, underscored the importance not only of the family but also of employment in the key initiatory stages of social development. Apart from the production of necessities, work provided the most direct evidence of the subordination of the passions. For Mayhew, as for his contemporaries, an aptitude for labour was readily perceived as a direct measure of the restraint and discipline upon which social order rested. The tripartite division of the metropolitan poor into those that will work, those that cannot work, and those that will not work, as the organising principle of the Mayhew survey, expressed middle-class fears of the growth of pauperisation and the consequent descent of the labouring classes into the dangerous classes. The utilitarian roots of his thinking were also evident in his conception of work as a necessary form of suffering in which pain might be mitigated and industry encouraged through education, example and deliberation.[65]

Mayhew's concept of education, though, was wider than that sanctioned by philosophical radicalism. Coleridge's insight into the complexities of the human intellect and feelings impressed him. He, in turn, insisted upon the separation of learning skills and knowledge and was critical of those Evangelical initiatives in which the two were confounded. 'Of course,' he wrote in respect of the rehabilitation of young offenders, 'the teaching of reading and writing is a negative good but it becomes almost an evil when people get to believe that it has any positive or moral religious effect, per se, and so to forego . . . all education of the feelings, and principles, and even the tastes, of those confined within them. The most valuable of all schooling is surely that of the heart, and the next that of the hands, especially for the poorer classes, who are mostly the inmates of our jails.' [66] Cooke Taylor's dictum that 'reading and writing are no more education than a knife and fork is a good dinner' was quoted with approval on several occasions.[67] The cultivation of the feelings and education of the moral sentiments, he argued, supplied the basis for a curriculum that directly addressed the social crisis.

Why is it, then, that Mayhew's ideas have proved difficult to place? Mayhew's want of system and failure to locate his ideas within a coherent programme of social reform, suggest one line of inquiry. It is possible, however, that the difficulty lies in ourselves, in our assumptions about the Victorian middle classes and Mayhew's place within them. To be sure, Mayhew's own humanity did get in the way of the utilitarian precepts he was trying to uphold. But was that so unusual? Is it not likely that his alleged antagonism to a unified bourgeoisie makes him seem rather more marginal than was the case? In truth, we do not know. The teleological bias of histories of social science, and the tendency of recent work to focus upon text rather than context, diverts us from the more fruitful study of how his work was received and understood in his own day rather than how it is 'read' in ours.

IV

Journalism

We cannot and should not forget that Mayhew was a journalist – an investigative journalist but a journalist none the less. Perhaps it is this fact that makes him worthy of our attention – through his popular presentation of the people and poverty he influenced as many of the population of mid-Victorian England as did any more serious author – ranking alongside Charles Dickens as a leading shaper of opinion. If 13,000 copies weekly of the numbers of *London Labour and the London Poor* were sold as against 40,000 of Dickens's *Household Words*, this makes clear Dickens's greater popularity but does not diminish Mayhew's own outreach. What is more, Mayhew deliberately encouraged dialogue with his public. While it is permissible to criticise Mayhew for his unsystematic and repetitive presentation, for his rambling prose, for his imprecise referencing and for his failure clearly to signal remedies for the social ills he identified, it is not possible to deny that it was Mayhew who was (and is) read and his London and Londoners that are remembered.

If Mayhew was a journalist, then his survey was also journalism. As indicated above, it would be inappropriate to see his investigation as systematic or bound by the application of modern, or even emerging contemporary, survey methodologies. This is not say, however, that Mayhew was not serious in his attempt to convey to his readers a real sense of the condition of the poor of the metropolis, of their relationship to the labour economy, of the problems that beset them and their possible remedies. He did (especially in the context of his collective interviews) attempt systematic and statistical analyses of small populations. But in order to realise his overall aims Mayhew combined a number of techniques, ranging from the sober and statistical to the sensationalist. In order to persuade his readers to consider serious issues it was important to make the text vivid and entertaining: the direct reporting of the speech of men, women and children who, even to the Victorian middle classes, must have seemed quaint and 'foreign'; the use of photographs (through woodcuts based on daguerreotypes) as the basis of a social record; [68] the inclusion of descriptions of occupations which were already disappearing and of those which were new and strange ('I don't think they'll ever take greatly in the streets,' declared the ice-cream seller, 'but there's no saying.');[69] the digest histories of occupations and the digressions into discussions of the derivation of words; the appeal to contemporary interests in political economy, popular science and anthropology – all played their part in encouraging readers to read on and engage with the text.

V

Social inquiry and social reform

Mayhew's work, we are told, is lively and some describe it as 'scientific'.[70] The curiosity and commitment, enthusiasm and energy, sympathy and humanity felt by its author spring out from the pages, tapping equivalent emotions in his readership, and drawing the reader in to the subject. Mayhew adopted a camera technique in the presentation of his findings. He sought to convey his impressions through a narrowing focus. Direct quotation and the reproduction of idiomatic expression or the use of dialect strategems which so easily relieved the oppressive weight of detail and humanised his findings – were applied lavishly. He operated the zoom facility on his camera with consummate skill.

Mayhew's 'twopenny numbers' typically begin with an introductory section – often historical and scientific in emphasis – on the 'occupation' he is about to address. Generalisation rendered in a passive voice gives way to contemporary profiles in specific settings, generally reported in the first person, which are full of interesting detail and display a sensitivity to the language and sentiments of those who work and those who cannot work. These reports were carefully worked up from original interviews conducted either by himself or his helpers. They illustrate and confirm the points he has been trying to make in the general introduction, seemingly effortlessly carrying his readers along with his argument. He responds to individuals in ways that reinforce our involvement with them and make his case entirely credible. There is no attempt to attain uniformity and comparability in reporting, although Mayhew's interest in certain issues (such as former occupation, education, religion, child abuse, diet, housing, earnings and language) is reflected with some regularity in the longer and in the collective interviews. Mayhew's qualities of vividness, immediacy, and preciseness convince.[71]

It would be cynical to imply that Mayhew's strategy of presentation was a conscious one. He had a genuine commitment to empirical inquiry based upon observation and classification and, on occasion, he reflected upon the superiority of his own methodology:

I was determined to avail myself of the acquaintances I made in this quarter, in order to arrive at some more definite information upon those places than has yet been made public. The only positive knowledge the public have hitherto had of the people assembling in the cheap lodging-houses of London is derived chiefly from the Report of the Constabulary Commissioners, and partly from the Report upon Vagrancy. But this information, having been procured through others, was so faulty, that having now obtained the privilege of personal inspection and communication, I was desirous of turning it to good account. Consequently I gave notice that I wished all that had dined there on last Sunday to attend me yesterday evening, so that I might obtain from then generally an account of their past and present career. [72]

He then interviewed between fifty and sixty inhabitants of the cheap lodging-house, incorporating a kind of oral questionnaire – the results of which are given in the form of collective statistics.[73] He collected much statistical data himself, for instance from the Billingsgate salesmen.[74] He would go to enormous lengths to find comparable data and be extremely critical of its quality.[75] Elsewhere he seemed uncertain of the value of quantitative data. He pondered on the relationship between the different types of evidence he was presenting to his readers in support of his arguments: the role of tables of statistics is inferior to that of narrative and life histories.[76]

Curious and ample as this Table of Refuse is – one, moreover, perfectly original – it is not sufficient, by the mere range of figures, to convey to the mind of the reader a full comprehension of the *ramified* vastness of the second-hand trade of the metropolis. Indeed tables are for reference more than for the current information to be yielded by a history or a narrative.

Mayhew's belief in the possibilities of a scientifically sound representation of the social order based upon the largest possible number of direct personal testimonies made his project unmanageable and defeated him. Time and again the project ran away from him. *London Labour and the London Poor* grew from a part work into an expanded and expansive four-volume work. What structure it had was spoiled by Mayhew's journalistic indulgence. But this same journalistic indulgence gained Mayhew a popular audience which, for example, the un-sensationalist Charles Booth never commanded.

Questions of identity and status were inseparable from survey investigation as practised by Mayhew. He was conscious of the social, material and physical distance that separated the well-fed classes from the labouring poor, and devised stratagems for their reduction. The hindrance to personal understanding made great demands on Mayhew who, with minimal preparation, found himself required to make sense of a world from which reason, it was supposed, had fled. When he visited a prison he spent time on the treadmill. When he interviewed a blind man he deliberately conversed with him in the dark. He walked the streets and visited the homes of the poor. His struggle for self-control and mastery of class prejudice constitutes one of the heroic themes of his survey. Mayhew possessed an unusual curiosity and sensitivity. The achievements of working-class culture and its possibilities for further progress impressed him; he found much that was admirable in the institutions and values of skilled workers and was repelled by the social wreckage below him.

Mayhew's position as an expert on social questions perhaps needs to be revised in the light of recent findings. In May 1852 he was called by Frederick James Furnivall to appear 'before the Committee of the House of Commons on the Ballast Heavers Bill' and pledged 'to do all I can to assist the ballast heavers'; at the same time he was engaged in a lecture tour 'expressly with a view of assisting in putting an end to the iniquities practised upon these wretched men'.[77] Mayhew's collective interview with the ballast-heavers and their wives either inspired Furnivall to request Mayhew's evidence or was in some other way allied with this request. This is an early example of an investigative journalist using his knowledge and influence to organise a campaign for reform. Mayhew was also called to give evidence before the Committee on Transportation, another cause dear to his heart. He joined the Royal Statistical Society and Benthamite reform groups. His association with the young Furnivall, who was a founder of the Working Men's College on Red Lion Street, London, and a Christian Socialist supporter of trade unionism, while on a formal footing, seems important. In 1857 another letter to an unknown correspondent reveals that Mayhew was in some demand as a lecturer as far afield as Dumfries, Aberdeen and Peterhead, as well as at the Marylebone Institute. At Birmingham he had commanded an audience of 2,500, at Brighton 1,500, and at Glasgow 2,000.[78]

His position, however, was insecure. His expertise was not revered. His methods and procedures were challenged, as was his integrity. The want of specialisation and an alleged want of character denied Mayhew standing. In part this was because

Mayhew drew no distinction between his serious investigative journalism and other writings. The serialised version of *London Labour and the London Poor* thus carried advertisements for the part issues of a novel, co-authored with William Cruikshank, on the Great Exhibition, and also informed readers of *Mr Mayhew's Spelling Book for the Working Classes,* 'explaining the sound meaning and derivation of the Greek, Latin and Saxon words of the English language', issued in eighteen one-penny parts.[79] Mayhew, as a litterateur and journalist, was, in fact, as well known for his non-sociological writings as for his survey research, and was particularly well regarded as a young people's author. 'No writer could have treated the story more successfully than he has done,' ran the review of his *Young Humphrey Davy* in 1855. In respect of this literary genre, declared another, Mayhew was the equal of Miss Edgeworth.[80] His travel writings were scarcely less popular, *The Upper Rhine and its Picturesque Scenery* being listed 'among the best gifts of the season'.[81] His works of social inquiry, by contrast, were compromised by his earlier associations and practices. Mayhew found it difficult to live down his reputation as a writer of comic stories and farces, who resorted to scissors-and-paste methods and took as much care with the truth as he did with other people's copy.[82]

Mayhew was a sceptic with regard to political economy. He felt that it was in need of revision and hoped to supply some of the necessary empirical data for that purpose. He eventually became a protectionist. He was no socialist. Rather he was convinced that theoretical and social requirements could be satisfied without the wholesale transformation of property relations. His rejection of political economy was partial. The utilitarian cast of his social analysis, above all its underlying hedonism, gave his social policies a repressive aspect. Mayhew's opinions on the poorest elements were not significantly different from Charles Booth's some fifty years later. Their terms varied but not the substance. Booth's distinction between the self-supporting or 'true' working class and the outcast poor would not have seemed odd to the author of *London Labour and the London Poor,* who never used the term 'residuum' of the poor in his writings but applied an equally vivid degenerationalist vocabulary to the depiction of its condition. Mayhew also accepted the case for special action outside the

Poor Law and found nothing objectionable in the suggestion that 'habitual vagrants' should be placed under police supervision.[83] For habitual criminals he was even more severe. 'Transportation I think very valuable to old and confirmed offenders, people who are called vagabonds, and who have certain primitive notions of society upon them,' he remarked; and added, 'I think it is for the good of society to get rid of such people, and send them into a primitive country, where vagabond habits are consistent as it were with liberty.'[84]

Mayhew was acutely aware of the problems of the labour market. Unlike Charles Booth, his successor in so many respects, he formulated no proposal for the de-casualisation of dock labour or scheme for rationalisation of the labour market and removal of the residual elements from it. Mayhew, though he had broken with general theories of over-population, found it difficult to think of social advance in other terms.[85] His analysis of the operation and overstocking of the London labour market, for all its remarkable insights and understanding, yielded no specific overarching proposals for reform and reorganisation. Mayhew fixed upon the formation of the outcast poor, Booth upon its reduction.

But to give Mayhew his due, his best work was completed before political and economic changes and the erosion in orthodox economics had begun to influence social theory. Booth's work, by contrast, is best viewed as part of the reconstruction process that followed the displacement of classical economics. Positivism, along with Liberalism and Idealism, brought a new optimism to the possibilities of working-class advance. An industrial system of unlimited potential, and a working population capable of being made rational moral beings, presented possibilities for progress that had earlier seemed unimaginable. Mayhew was possessed, however, of a faith in the possibility of improvement. Social inquiry and social action were bent towards the creation of self-disciplined citizens from unrestrained low-lives. He was able, moreover, to identify specific flaws in the industrial system which could be tackled successfully to ameliorate the plight of the deserving poor. His commitment, for example, to the cause of the ballast-heavers was sincere and practically expressed.

VI
The Selection

The selection is taken, with one exception, from the four-volume edition published in 1861-2 by Griffin, Bohn and Company, which includes in volumes I and II the items originally printed in 1851 and 1852, in volume III some of the letters to the *Morning Chronicle* and interviews with street entertainers conducted in 1856, and in volume IV material largely provided by other investigators. The single exception is the material included here in Section 10 which is taken from the bound edition of the two-penny weekly in 1851–2. The Answers to Correspondents were omitted from the 1861–2 edition.

In presenting this selection from Mayhew's monumental *London Labour and the London Poor* in the compass of one paper-bound volume, we have inevitably had to shed a good deal of the original four-volume work. Although 'cutting' the text has proved very painful to us as editors, it could be that the end result will benefit and even please the reader. Perhaps we have been able to prevent this 'good material being buried by its bad dressing'.[86] While the serious Mayhew scholar will still return to the original versions of 1851 and 1861, the general reader, the teacher and the student should find here the materials of most interest and use to them.

If there is one aspect of Mayhew's work of which the general reader is aware, it is his 'characters'. These interviews, prefaced as they are by masterly pen-portraits and presented as they are with consummate skill, have been the subject of much scholarly study. The persons of mudlarks and musicians, costermongers and crossing-sweepers, prostitutes and patterers have become familiar to generations of readers. But, as indicated above, there is much more to Mayhew than this: the particular work represented here contains important analyses of the casual labour market, accounts of the history and conduct of individual occupations, descriptions of specific sites and of street-trading, insights into the life of various ethnic communities and recommendations for reform; the 'characters' were not simply included to provide a kaleidoscope of London street-life but themselves played a special part in Mayhew's survey. In this selection we have organised the materials so that all of these elements are well represented.

Within each section of our work the reader will find extracts especially pertinent to the highlighted topic. There is, however, a necessary overlap between the sections. For example, we have included in Section 3: Voices of the Poor a number of reported interviews – sufficient to give the reader a real flavour of this material and also to provide the basis of a study of Mayhew's interviewing technique, but the reader will find in many other sections additional interview material addressing specific problems such as that of casual labour or vagrancy. Similarly, almost every interview proffers some information on the domestic economy and on popular culture but the relevant sections include just a small selection of pertinent extracts. The reader is advised to use the Contents list and the relevant sections as their first ports of call.

Of course, in rearranging the sections, we run the risk of altering the balance and flavour of Mayhew's original work. We have taken various steps to avoid this danger. For example, we have included the contents lists for each of the four volumes and Mayhew's original preface. We have included a number of un-edited interviews, and have supplied above a table analysing the interviews in the work in order that the reader can see how our selection relates to the whole. We have added a number of the seldom printed *Answers to Correspondents,* which convey a sense of the place of Mayhew's investigative work in the everyday consciousness of the Victorian 'chattering classes'. Some of the original maps and illustrations are included to show how Mayhew pioneered the use of social mapping, daguerreotypes and photographs in the service of social investigation. Also, we have favoured lengthy extracts rather than short 'snippets' and this has enabled us to capture some of the rambling, repetitive and journalistic flavour of Mayhew's prose. This can hinder the reader's enjoyment but it also permits us to see Mayhew the investigative journalist, warts and all.

The selections have been arranged under broad modern headings. Each selection is prefaced by an elucidatory headnote, designed to place the extract in the context of Mayhew's original and to explain any difficult points. In some cases we have also included further explanatory headnotes but, in general, we have preferred to allow Mayhew to speak for himself. Editorial material is set in italics throughout. The wording of Mayhew's original headings and subheadings has frequently been retained but set to clarify the text. We have indicated ellipses within the extracts by the use of [. . .]. As a further aid we have included information to facilitate finding the extract within the 1861–2 edition. Additional annotation has been kept to a minimum but important aids have been provided: a list of Mayhew's stated written authorities in the 1851 edition; a detailed contents list; and a short bibliography of useful works on Mayhew.

NOTES

1 P. J. Keating (1971), *The Working Classes in Victorian Fiction,* London; H. S. Nelson, 'Dickens' "Our Mutual Friend" and Henry Mayhew's "London Labour and the London Poor"' in *Nineteenth Century Fiction,* 20, 1965, pp.207–222.

2 It continues, 'This will not only keep the work from being soiled, but enable Mr Mayhew to answer the inquiries of his several Correspondents.'

3 Henry Mayhew and John Binny (1862), *The Criminal Prisons of London.*

4 Karel Williams (1981), *From Pauperism to Poverty,* London, p.238.

5 Henry Mayhew (1861), *London Labour and the London Poor,* 4 vols, Griffin, Bohn and Co. (hereafter *LL&LP*), II, p.28.

6 This was republished in facsimile by Dover Publications in 1968.

7 His interview with the *Telescope Exhibitor* was conducted after October 13 1856: 'The night of the eclipse of the moon (the 13th October 1856), when it was so well seen in London, I took 1*l.* 1*d.* at 1*d.* each." *LL&LP,* III, p.83.

8 Caliban Edition (1980), *Morning Chronicle Survey of Labour and the Poor* (hereafter *Morning Chronicle Survey*), with an introduction by Peter Razzell, I, p.40.

9 Karel Williams, *From Pauperism to Poverty,* p.247; Anne Humpherys (1977), *Travels into the Poor Man's Country,* Athens, Georgia, p.49.

10 *Morning Chronicle,* 18 October 1849.

11 See below for more on Mayhew's use of sources.

12 *LL&LP,* I, p.xv; this statement also appeared in the 1851 edition.

13 See *Morning Chronicle Survey,,* I, pp.34, 36.

14 Henry Mayhew and John Binny (1862), *The Criminal Prisons of London,* pp.454–5

15 *LL&LP,* II, pp.441–2.

16 Answers to Correspondents, Nos. 6 and 9; Edward Thompson, 'Mayhew and the *Morning Chronicle',* in E.P. Thompson and E. Yeo (1971) (eds), *The Unknown Mayhew* (pb edition 1973), pp.46–7.

17 Henry Mayhew (1864), *German Life and Manners,* 2 vols, London, 1, p.118.

18 Problems of double-counting make approximation essential; 700 represents a highly conservative estimate to compensate for double-counting.

19 *LL&LP,* I, p.113.

20 He did, however, present such analyses of some of his collective interviews. It is probable, however, that this was because the collective interviews were organised for a different purpose – that of the ballast-heavers' wives, for instance, being arranged to provide grist to Mayhew's mill when giving evidence to the House of Commons regarding the abuses of the truck system and simply serving a dual purpose when used in *LL&LP.*

21 See Introduction, pp.xxvi, xxvii.

22 (mudlark) *LL&LP,* II, pp.256–8; (thieves) *LL&LP,* I, pp.418–23; (crossing-sweepers) *LL&LP,* II, pp.494–507; (periodicals) *LL&LP,* I, p.291; (box-maker) *LL&LP,* III, p.226.

23 *Morning Chronicle Survey,* I, p.111.

24 Eileen Yeo, 'Mayhew as Social Investigator' in E. P. Thompson and E. Yeo (1971) (eds), *The Unknown Mayhew* (pb edition 1973), p.71; Anne Humpherys (1977), *Travels into the Poor Man's Country,* Athens, Georgia, p.40.

25 *LL&LP,* I, Preface, p.xvi.

26 Evidence of Henry Mayhew, *Second Report of Select Committee of the House of Commons on Transportation* 1856 (296), XVII. qq.3504, 3742.

27 *LL&LP*, II, p.170.
28 *Morning Chronicle Survey*, I, p.170.
29 *Morning Chronicle Survey*, I, pp.170, 199–202.
30 *Morning Chronicle Survey*, II, pp.89, 93.
31 See Raphael Samuel (1973), 'Mayhew and Labour Historians', *Bulletin of the Society for the Study of Labour History*, No. 26, pp.47–52.
32 *LL&LP*, II, p.464.
33 *LL&LP*, III, p.234.
34 *LL&LP*, II, p.162.
35 Answers to Correspondents, No.50, 22 November 1851.
36 Answers to Correspondents, No.14, 15 March 1851.
37 *Morning Chronicle Survey*, I, pp.51–63.
38 Mayhew's criminological writings have not received systematic treatment from historians of crime or from students of social theory; the former are either uncritically enthusiastic or cautious and dismissive; the latter unaware of the possibilities for further inquiry.
39 *LL&LP*, III, pp.430–9.
40 J.B. Say, for example, is sometimes cited for his social observation rather than his economic theory. There are also references to Wakefield's work on co-operation, though it is not clear whether he read them in the original or at second hand in J. S. Mill's *Principles of Political Economy*, pp.116–7. See Appendix 3 for a full list of those Mayhew mentions in the text of *LL&LP*.
41 Answers to Correspondents, No.22, 27 September 1851.
42 Answers to Correspondents, No.10, 15 February 1851.
43 Henry Mayhew (1851), *Low Wages*, pp.36–51.
44 Answers to Correspondents, No.16, 29 March 1851.
45 The psychologistic approach is well illustrated by Anne J. Kershen (1993), 'Henry Mayhew and Charles Booth: Men of their Times?' in G. Alderman and C. Holmes (eds), *Outsiders and Outcasts: Essays in Honour of William J. Fishman*, London: Duckworth, p.100; the methodologically-centred approach is exemplified in the work of Karel Williams, *From Pauperism to Poverty*, London, pp.237–77.
46 Karel Williams, *From Pauperism to Poverty*, London, pp.257–8. It should be noted, though, that Mayhew did sometimes attempt to locate the theory of overwork outside the skilled trades: see, for example, *LL&LP*, II, pp.216-60, 297–338.
47 Gareth Stedman Jones (1984), 'The Labours of Henry Mayhew, "Metropolitan Correspondent"', *London Journal, 10 (1)*, 1984, pp.80–5.
48 *LL&LP*, II, p.236. On Mill's view of Chalmers, see John Stuart Mill (1909), *Principles of Political Economy*, W. J. Ashley (ed.), p.75.
49 Answers to Correspondents, No.11, 22 February 1851.
50 *LL&LP*, I, p.2.
51 Christopher Herbert (1991), *Culture and Anomie: Ethnographic Imagination in the Nineteenth Century*, Chicago and London, p.208 ff.
52 See Appendix 3 (Mayhew's authorities), which indicates that Mayhew wished to be seen to be conversant with contemporary work in this area.
53 *Morning Chronicle Survey*, I, p.52.
54 Answers to Correspondents, No.9.
55 *Morning Chronicle Survey*, III, pp.43–4.
56 Henry Mayhew and John Binny (1862), *The Criminal Prisons of London*, p.408.
57 *Morning Chronicle Survey*, IV, p.135; also in *Morning Chronicle Survey*, III, p.35.
58 Henry Mayhew and John Binny (1862), *The Criminal Prisons of London*, p.454.
59 On Mandeville's social thought see the excellent assessment by M. M. Goldsmith (1985), *Private Vices, Public Benefits*, Cambridge.
60 Mayhew, *Criminal Prisons of London*, pp.455–6.
61 *LL&LP*, III, pp.432–3.
62 On Mayhew and Evangelical effort, see E. P. Thompson (1967), 'The Political Education of Henry Mayhew', *Victorian Studies, 11*, pp.23–30. Quotation from Henry Mayhew and John Binny (1862), *The Criminal Prisons of London*, p.390.
63 Henry Mayhew and John Binny (1862), *The Criminal Prisons of London*, p.421.
64 Henry Mayhew and John Binny (1862), *The Criminal Prisons of London*, pp.421–2.

65 *Morning Chronicle Survey*, III, pp.42–3.
66 Henry Mayhew and John Binny (1862), *The Criminal Prisons of London*, p.431.
67 *Morning Chronicle Survey*, IV, p.135; Henry Mayhew and John Binny (1862), *The Criminal Prisons of London*.
68 See Anne Humpherys (1977), *Travels into the Poor Man's Country*, Athens, Georgia, p.70.
69 *LL&LP*, I, p.207.
70 Anne Humpherys (1977), *Travels into the Poor Man's Country*, Athens, Georgia, pp. 135–44. The 'scientific' status of Mayhew's work has, however, been vigorously contested: see Gertrude Himmelfarb (1984), *The Idea of Poverty, England in the Early Industrial Age*, 1985 pb edition, pp.312–62.
71 Anne Humpherys (1977), *Travels into the Poor Man's Country*, Athens, Georgia, p.221.
72 *LL&LP*, III, p.314.
73 *LL&LP*, III, p.316.
74 *LL&LP*, I, p.62.
75 'It is impossible to obtain any definite statistics on this part of the subject. Not one in every ten of the contractors keeps any account of the amount [of dust] that comes into the "yard" . . . I have, however, endeavoured to check the preceding estimate in the following manner . . . ' *LL&LP*, II, p.170.
76 *LL&LP*, II, p.464.
77 Huntington Library, San Marino, Ca: FU 607, Henry Mayhew to Frederick James Furnivall, 4 May 1852; the minutes of evidence appear to be missing.
78 Huntington Library, San Marino, Ca. HM 10774, Henry Mayhew to A.L., 18 April 1857
79 Answers to Correspondents, No.9
80 See review of Henry Mayhew, 'The Wonders of Science or Young Humphrey Davy' in *The Athenaeum* (15 December 1855), p.1464; also review of 'The Boyhood of Martin Luther' in *The Athenaeum* (30 May 1863), p.714.
81 *The Athenaeum* (19 December, 1857), pp.1581–2.
82 See unsigned review of *LL&LP* in *The Athenaeum* (15 November 1851), pp.1199–201.
83 *LL&LP*, III, pp.373-4.
84 *Select Committee on Transportation*, q.3516.
85 In his conflict with the Ragged School Union in 1850 Mayhew had argued in favour of a state-assisted scheme of educational and industrial training 'connected with a plan of systematic emigration which would secure honest employment in other lands for those who cannot find it here', *Morning Chronicle Survey*, IV, p.78.
86 BLPES, Passfield Papers, Beatrice Webb's (Manuscript) Diary, August 1887.

MAYHEW'S PREFACE
[to the 1861 edition]

The present volume is the first of an intended series, which it is hoped will form, when complete, a cyclopædia of the industry, the want, and the vice of the great metropolis.

It is believed that the book is curious for many reasons:

It surely may be considered curious as being the first attempt to publish the history of a people, from the lips of the people themselves – giving a literal description of their labour, their earnings, their trials, and their sufferings, in their own 'unvarnished' language; and to portray the condition of their homes and their families by personal observation of the places, and direct communion with the individuals.

It may be considered curious also as being the first commission of inquiry into the state of the people undertaken by a private individual, and the first 'blue book' ever published in twopenny numbers.

It is curious, moreover, as supplying information concerning a large body of persons, of whom the public had less knowledge than of the most distant tribes of the earth – the government population returns not even numbering them among the inhabitants of the kingdom; and as adducing facts so extraordinary, that the traveller in the undiscovered country of the poor must, like Bruce, until his stories are corroborated by after investigators, be content to lie under the imputation of telling such tales, as travellers are generally supposed to delight in.

Be the faults of the present volume what they may, assuredly they are rather shortcomings than exaggerations, for in every instance the author and his coadjutors have sought to understate, and most assuredly never to exceed the truth. For the omissions, the author would merely remind the reader of the entire novelty of the task – there being no other similar work in the language by which to guide or check his inquiries. When the following leaves are turned over, and the two or three pages of information derived from books contrasted with the hundreds of pages of facts obtained by positive observation and investigation, surely some allowance will be made for the details which may still be left for others to supply. Within the last two years some thousands of the humbler classes of society must have been seen and visited with the especial view of noticing their condition and learning their histories; and it is but right that the truthfulness of the poor generally should be made known; for though checks have been usually adopted, the people have been mostly found to be astonishingly correct in their statements, – so much so indeed, that the attempts at deception are certainly the exceptions rather than the rule. Those persons who, from an ignorance of the simplicity of the honest poor, might be inclined to think otherwise, have, in order to be convinced of the justice of the above remarks, only to consult the details given in the present volume, and to perceive the extraordinary agreement in the statements of all the vast number of individuals who have been seen at different times, and who cannot possibly have been supposed to have been acting in concert.

The larger statistics, such as those of the quantities of fish and fruit, &c., sold in London, have been collected from tradesmen connected with the several markets, or from the wholesale merchants belonging to the trade specified – gentlemen to whose courtesy and co-operation I am indebted for much valuable information, and whose names, were I at liberty to publish them, would be an indisputable guarantee for the facts advanced. The other statistics have been obtained in the same manner – the best authorities having been invariably consulted on the subject treated of.

It is right that I should make special mention of the assistance I have received in the compilation of the present volume from Mr Henry Wood and Mr Richard Knight (late of the City Mission), gentlemen who have been engaged with me from nearly the commencement of my inquiries, and to whose hearty co-operation both myself and the public are indebted for a large increase of knowledge. Mr Wood, indeed, has contributed so large a proportion of the contents of the present volume that he may fairly be considered as one of its authors.

The subject of the Street-Folk will still require another volume, in order to complete it in that comprehensive manner in which I am desirous of executing the modern history of this and every other portion of the people. There still remain – the Street-Buyers, the Street-Finders, the Street-Performers, the Street-Artisans, and the Street-Labourers, to be done, among the several classes of street-people; and the Street Jews, the Street Italians and Foreigners, and the Street Mechanics, to be treated of as varieties of the order. The present volume refers more particularly to the Street-Sellers, and includes special accounts of the Costermongers and the Patterers (the two broadly-marked varieties of street tradesmen), the Street Irish, the Female Street-Sellers, and the Children Street-Sellers of the metropolis.

My earnest hope is that the book may serve to give the rich a more intimate knowledge of the sufferings, and the frequent heroism under those sufferings, of the poor – that it may teach those who are beyond temptation to look with charity on the frailties of their less fortunate brethren – and cause those who are in 'high places', and those of whom much is expected, to bestir themselves to improve the condition of a class of people whose misery, ignorance, and vice, amidst all the immense wealth and great knowledge of 'the first city in the world', is, to say the very least, a national disgrace to us.

HENRY MAYHEW
[from a daguerrotype by Beard]

I

STREET–FOLK

The street sellers, as described by Mayhew, led lives that were so different from those of his readers as to require a special explanatory framework to render them intelligible. Their restless nomadic lifestyle, material condition, distinctive subculture, their hatred of authority, their amusements, appearance, language, education, personal and social relations all demanded comment and analysis. For this purpose Mayhew turned to contemporary ethnography and travel literature. The idea that the wandering costermonger community represented an arrested form of social development both in its culture and in individual physiognomy was borrowed from J. C. Pritchard (1786-1848), a leading ethnographer and author of the popular text The Natural History of Mankind. *From the Africanist Andrew Smith (1797-1872) Mayhew acquired the idea of the coexistence of civilised and backward elements and applied it to the situation of the costermongers. The progress of the nation and solution of the social problem, readers were reminded, depended on the extent to which the civilising influences could be brought to bear upon the unsettled, outcast and dangerous classes.*

THE LONDON COSTERMONGER

'Here Pertaters! Kearots and turnups! fine Brockello-o-o!'

[from a daguerrotype by Beard]

Of wandering tribes in general
[*volume i. pp.1,2*]

Of the thousand millions of human beings that are said to constitute the population of the entire globe, there are − socially, morally, and perhaps even physically considered − but two distinct and broadly marked races, viz., the wanderers and the settlers − the vagabond and the citizen − the nomadic and the civilised tribes. Between these two extremes, however, ethnologists recognise a mediate variety, partaking of the attributes of both. There is not only the race of hunters and manufacturers − those who live by shooting and fishing, and those who live by producing − but, say they, there are also the herdsmen, or those who live by tending and feeding what they consume.

Each of these classes has its peculiar and distinctive physical as well as moral characteristics. 'There are in mankind,' says Dr Pritchard, 'three principal varieties in the form of the head and other physical characters. Among the rudest tribes of men − the hunters and savage inhabitants of forests, dependent for their supply of food on the accidental produce of the soil and the chase − a form of head is prevalent which is mostly distinguished by the term '*prognathous*', indicating a prolongation or extension forward of the jaws. A second shape of the head belongs principally to such races as wander with their herds and flocks over vast plains; these nations have broad lozenge-shaped faces (owing to the great development of the cheek bones), and pyramidal skulls. The most civilised races, on the other hand − those who live by the arts of cultivated life, − have a shape of the head which differs from both of those above mentioned. The characteristic form of the skull among these nations may be termed oval or elliptical.'

These three forms of head, however, clearly admit of being reduced to two broadly-marked varieties, according as the bones of the face or those of the skull are more highly developed. A greater relative development of the jaws and cheek bones, says the author of the *Natural History of Man*, indicates a more ample extension of the organs subservient to sensation and the animal faculties. Such a configuration is adapted to the wandering tribes; whereas, the greater relative development of the bones of the skull – indicating as it does a greater expansion of the brain, and consequently of the intellectual faculties – is especially adapted to the civilised races or settlers, who depend mainly on their knowledge of the powers and properties of things for the necessaries and comforts of life.

Moreover it would appear, that not only are all races divisible into wanderers and settlers, but that each civilised or settled tribe has generally some wandering horde intermingled with, and in a measure preying upon, it.

According to Dr Andrew Smith, who has recently made extensive observations in South Africa, almost every tribe of people who have submitted themselves to social laws, recognising the rights of property and reciprocal social duties, and thus acquiring wealth and forming themselves into a respectable caste, are surrounded by hordes of vagabonds and outcasts from their own community. Such are the Bushmen and Sonquas of the Hottentot race – the term '*sonqua*' meaning literally *pauper*. But a similar condition in society produces similar results in regard to other races; and the Kafirs have their Bushmen as well as the Hottentots – these are called *Fingoes* – a word signifying wanderers, beggars, or outcasts. The Lappes seem to have borne a somewhat similar relation to the Finns; that is to say, they appear to have been a wild and predatory tribe who sought the desert like the Arabian Bedouins, while the Finns cultivated the soil like the industrious Fellahs.

But a phenomenon still more deserving of notice, is the difference of speech between the Bushmen and the Hottentots. The people of some hordes, Dr Andrew Smith assures us, vary their speech designedly, and adopt new words, with the intent of rendering their ideas unintelligible to all but the members of their own community. For this last custom a peculiar name exists, which is called '*cuze-cat*'. This is considered as greatly advantageous in assisting concealment of their designs.

Here, then, we have a series of facts of the utmost social importance. (1) There are two distinct races of men, viz.: – the wandering and the civilised tribes; (2) to each of these tribes a different form of head is peculiar, the wandering races being remarkable for the development of the bones of the face, as the jaws, cheek-bones, &c., and the civilised for the development of those of the head; (3) to each civilised tribe there is generally a wandering horde attached; (4) such wandering hordes have frequently a different language from the more civilised portion of the community, and that adopted with the intent of concealing their designs and exploits from them.

It is curious that no-one has as yet applied the above facts to the explanation of certain anomalies in the present state of society among ourselves. That we, like the Kafirs, Fellahs, and Finns, are surrounded by wandering hordes – the 'Sonquas' and the 'Fingoes' of this country – paupers, beggars, and outcasts, possessing nothing but what they acquire by depredation from the industrious, provident, and civilised portion of the community; – that the heads of these nomads are remarkable for the greater development of the jaws and cheekbones rather than those of the head; – and that they have a secret language of their own – an English '*cuze-cat*' or 'slang' as it is called – for the concealment of their designs: these are points of coincidence so striking that, when placed before the mind, make us marvel that the analogy should have remained thus long unnoticed.

The resemblance once discovered, however, becomes of great service in enabling us to use the moral characteristics of the nomad races of other countries, as a means of comprehending the more readily those of the vagabonds and outcasts of our own. Let us therefore, before entering upon the subject in hand, briefly run over the distinctive, moral, and intellectual features of the wandering tribes in general.

The nomad then is distinguished from the civilised man by his repugnance to regular and continuous labour – by his want of providence in laying up a store for the future – by his inability to perceive consequences ever so slightly removed from immediate apprehension – by his passion for stupefying herbs and roots, and, when possible, for intoxicating fermented liquors – by his extra-ordinary powers of enduring privation – by his comparative insensibility to pain – by an immoderate love of gaming, frequently risking his own personal liberty upon a single cast – by his love of libidinous dances – by the pleasure he experiences in witnessing the suffering of sentient creatures – by his delight in warfare and all perilous sports – by his desire for vengeance – by the looseness of his notions as to property – by the absence of chastity among his women, and his disregard of female honour – and lastly, by his vague sense of religion – his rude idea of a Creator, and utter absence of all appreciation of the mercy of the Divine Spirit.

Srange to say, despite its privations, its dangers, and its hardships, those who have once adopted the savage and wandering mode of life, rarely abandon it. There are countless examples of white men adopting all the usages of the Indian hunter, but there is scarcely one example of the Indian hunter or trapper adopting the steady and regular habits of civilised life; indeed, the various missionaries who have visited nomad races have found their labours utterly unavailing, so long as a wandering life continued, and have succeeded in bestowing the elements of civilisation, only on those compelled by circumstances to adopt a settled habitation.

Wandering tribes in this country
[*volume i. pp.2,3*]

The nomadic races of England are of many distinct kinds – from the habitual vagrant – half-beggar, half-thief – sleeping in barns, tents, and casual wards – to the mechanic on tramp, obtaining his bed and supper from the trade societies in the different towns, on his way to seek work. Between these two extremes there are several mediate varieties – consisting of pedlars, showmen, harvest-men, and all that large class who live by either selling, showing, or doing something through the country. These are, so to speak, the rural nomads – not confining their wanderings to any one particular locality, but ranging often from one end of the land to the other. Besides these, there are the urban and suburban wanderers, or those who follow some itinerant occupation in and round about the large towns. Such are, in the metropolis more particularly, the pickpockets – the beggars – the prostitutes – the street-sellers – the street-performers – the cabmen – the coachmen – the watermen – the sailors and such like. In each of these classes – according as they partake more or less of the purely vagabond, doing nothing whatsoever for their living, but moving from place to place preying upon the earnings of the more industrious portion of the community, so will the attributes of the nomad tribes be found to be more or less marked in them. Whether it be that in the mere act of wandering, there is a greater determination of blood to the surface of the body, and consequently a less quantity sent to the brain, the muscles being thus nourished at the expense of the mind, I leave physiologists to say. But certainly be the physical cause what it may, we must all allow that in each of the classes above-mentioned, there is a greater development of the animal than of the intellectual or moral nature of man, and that they are all more or less distinguished for their high cheek-bones and protruding jaws – for their use of a slang language – for their lax ideas of property – for their general improvidence – their repugnance to continuous labour – their disregard of female honour – their love of cruelty – their pugnacity – and their utter want of religion.

Of the number of costermongers and other street-folk
[*volume i. pp.4–6*]

The number of costermongers, – that it is to say, of those street-sellers attending the London 'green' and fish markets, – appears to be, from the best data at my command, now 30,000 men, women, and children. The census of 1841 gives only 2,045 'hawkers, hucksters, and pedlars' in the metropolis, and no costermongers or street-sellers, or street-performers at all. This number is absurdly small, and its absurdity is accounted for by the fact that not one in twenty of the costermongers, or of the people with whom they lodged, troubled themselves to fill up the census returns – the majority of them being unable to read and write, and others distrustful of the purpose for which the returns were wanted.

The costermongers frequenting Spitalfields-market average all the year through from 700 to 1,000 each market-day. They come from all parts, as far as Edmonton, Edgeware, and Tottenham; Highgate, Hampstead, and even from Greenwich and Lewisham. Full one-third of the produce of this market is purchased by them.

The number of costermongers attending the Borough-market is about 250 during the fruit season, after which time they decrease to about 200 per market morning. About one-sixth of the produce that comes into this market is purchased by the costermongers. One gentleman informed me, that the salesmen might shut up their shops were it not for these men. 'In fact,' said another, 'I don't know what would become of the fruit without them.'

The costers at Billingsgate-market, daily, number from 3,000 to 4,000 in winter, and about 2,500 in summer. A leading salesman told me that he would rather have an order from a costermonger than a fishmonger; for the one paid ready money, while the other required credit. The same gentleman assured me, that the costermongers bought excellent fish, and that very largely. They themselves aver that they purchase half the fish brought to Billingsgate – some fish trades being entirely in their hands. I ascertained, however, from the authorities at Billingsgate, and from experienced salesmen, that of the quantity of fish conveyed to that great mart, the costermongers bought one third; another third was sent into the country; and another disposed of to the fishmongers, and to such hotel-keepers, or other large purchasers, as resorted to Billingsgate.

The salesmen at the several markets all agreed in stating that no trust was given to the costermongers. 'Trust them!' exclaimed one, 'Oh, certainly, as far as I can see them.'

Now, adding the above figures together, we have the subjoined sum for the gross number of

Costermongers attending the London markets

Billingsgate-market	3,500
Covent-garden	4,000
Spitalfields	1,000
Borough	250
Leadenhall	100
	9,350

Besides these, I am credibly informed, that it may be assumed there are full 1,000 men who are unable to attend market, owing to the dissipation of the previous night; another 1,000 are absent owing to their having 'stock on hand', and so requiring no fresh purchases; and further, it may be estimated that there are at least 2,000 boys in London at work for costers, at half profits, and who consequently have no occasion to visit the markets. Hence, putting these numbers together, we arrive at the conclusion that there are in London upwards of 13,000 street-sellers, dealing in fish, fruit, vegetables, game, and poultry alone. To be on the safe side, however, let us assume the number of London costermongers to be 12,000, and that one half of these are married and have two children (which from all accounts appears to be about the proportion); and then we have 30,000 for the sum total of men, women, and children dependent on 'costermongering' for their subsistence.

Large as this number may seem, still I am satisfied it is rather within than beyond the truth. In order to convince myself of its accuracy, I caused it to be checked in several ways. In the first place, a survey was made as to the number of stalls in the streets of London – forty-six miles of the principal thoroughfares were travelled over, and an account taken of the 'standings'. Thus it was found that there were upon an average upwards of fourteen stalls to the mile, of which five-sixths were fish- and fruit-stalls. Now, according to the Metropolitan Police Returns, there are 2,000 miles of street throughout London, and calculating that the stalls through the whole of the metropolis run upon an average only four to the mile, we shall thus find that there are 8,000 stalls altogether in London; of these we may reckon that at least 6,000 are fish and fruit-stalls. I am informed, on the best authority, that twice as many costers 'go rounds' as have standings; hence we come to the conclusion that there are 18,000 itinerant and stationary street-sellers of fish, vegetables, and fruit, in the metropolis; and reckoning the same proportion of wives and children as before, we have thus 45,000 men, women, and children, obtaining a living in this manner. Further, 'to make assurance doubly sure', the street-markets throughout London were severally visited, and the number of street-sellers at each taken down on the spot. These gave a grand total of 3,801, of which number two-thirds were dealers in fish, fruit, and vegetables; and reckoning that twice as many costers again were on their rounds, we thus make the total number of London costermongers to be 11,403, or calculating men, women, and children, 34,209. It would appear, therefore, that if we estimate the gross number of individuals subsisting on the sale of fish, fruit, and vegetables, in the streets of London, at between thirty and forty thousand, we shall not be very wide of the truth.

But, great as is this number, still the costermongers are only a portion of the street-folk. Besides these, there are, as we have seen, many other large classes obtaining their livelihood in the streets. The street musicians, for instance, are said to number 1,000, and the old clothesmen the same. There are supposed to be at the least 500 sellers of water-cresses; 200 coffee-stalls; 300 cats-meat men; 250 ballad-singers; 200 play-bill sellers; from 800 to 1,000 bone-grubbers and mud-larks; 1,000 crossing-sweepers; another thousand chimney-sweeps, and the same number of turncocks and lamp-lighters; all of whom, together with the street-performers and showmen, tinkers, chair, umbrella, and clock-menders, sellers of bonnet-boxes, toys, stationery, songs, last dying-speeches, tubs, pails, mats, crockery, blacking, lucifers, corn-salves, clothes-pegs, brooms, sweetmeats, razors, dog-collars, dogs, birds, coals, sand, – scavengers, dustmen, and others, make up, it may be fairly assumed, full thirty thousand adults, so that, reckoning men, women, and children, we may truly say that there are upwards of fifty thousand individuals, or about a fortieth-part of the entire population of the metropolis getting their living in the streets.

Now of all modes of obtaining subsistence, that of street-selling is the most precarious. Continued wet weather deprives those who depend for their bread upon the number of people frequenting the public thoroughfares of all means of living; and it is painful to think of the hundreds belonging to this class in the the metropolis who are reduced to starvation by three or four days successive rain. Moreover, in the winter, the street-sellers of fruit and vegetables are cut off from the ordinary means of gaining their livelihood, and, consequently, they have to suffer the greatest privations at a time when the severity of the season demands the greatest amount of physical comforts. To expect that the increased earnings of the summer should be put aside as a provision against the deficiencies of the winter, is to expect that a precarious occupation should beget provident habits, which is against the nature of things, for it is always in those callings which are the most uncertain, that the greatest amount of improvidence and intemperance are found to exist. It is not the well-fed man, be it observed, but the starving one that is in danger of surfeiting himself.

Moreover, when the religious, moral, and intellectual degradation of the great majority of these fifty thousand people is impressed upon us, it becomes positively appalling to contemplate the vast amount of vice, ignorance and want, existing in these days in the very heart of our land. The public have but to read the following plain unvarnished account of the habits, amusements, dealings, education, politics, and religion of the London coster-mongers in the nineteenth century, and then to say whether they think it safe – even if it be thought fit – to allow men, women, and children to continue in such a state.

Of the varieties of street-folk in general, and costermongers in particular

[*volume i. pp.6,7*]

Among the street-folk there are many distinct characters of people – people differing as widely from each in tastes, habits, thoughts and creed, as one nation from another. Of these the costermongers form by far the largest and certainly the mostly broadly marked class. They appear to be a distinct race – perhaps, originally, of Irish extraction – seldom associating with any other of the street-folks, and being all known to each other. The 'patterers', or the men who cry the last dying-speeches, &c. in the street, and those who help off their wares by long harrangues in the public thoroughfares, are again a separate class. These, to use their own term, are 'the aristocracy of the street-sellers', despising the costers for their ignorance, and boasting that they live by their intellect. The public, they say, do not expect to receive from them an equivalent for their money – they pay to hear them talk. Compared with the costermongers, the patterers are generally an educated class, and among them are some classical scholars, one clergyman, and many sons of gentlemen. They appear to be the counterparts of the old mountebanks or street-doctors. As a body they seem far less improvable than the costers, being more 'knowing' and less impulsive. The street-performers differ again from those; these appear to possess many of the characteristics of the lower class of actors, viz., a strong desire to excite admiration, an indisposition to pursue any settled occupation, a love of the tap-room, though more for the society and display than for the drink connected with it, a great fondness for finery and predilection for the performance of dexterous or dangerous feats. Then there are the street mechanics, or artisans – quiet, melancholy, struggling men, who, unable to find any regular employment at their own trade, have made up a few things, and taken to hawk them in the streets, as the last shift of independence. Another distinct class of streetfolk are the blind people (mostly musicians in a rude way), who, after the loss of their eyesight, have sought to keep themselves from the workhouse by some little excuse for alms-seeking. These, so far as my experience goes, appear to be a far more deserving class than is usually supposed – their affliction, in most cases, seems to have chastened them and to have given a peculiar religious cast to their thoughts.

Such are the several varieties of street-folk, intellectually considered – looked at in a national point of view, they likewise include many distinct people. Among them are to be found the Irish fruit-sellers; the Jew clothesmen; the Italian organ boys, French singing women, the German brass bands, the Dutch buy-a-broom girls, the Highland bagpipe players, and the Indian crossing-sweepers – all of whom I here shall treat of in due order.

The costermongering class or order has also its many varieties. These appear to be in the following proportions: – One-half of the entire class are costermongers proper, that is to say, the calling with them is hereditary, and perhaps has been so for many generations; while the other half is composed of three-eighths Irish, and one-eighth mechanics, tradesmen, and Jews.

Under the term 'costermonger' is here included only such 'street-sellers' as deal in fish, fruit, and vegetables, purchasing their goods at the wholesale 'green' and fish markets. Of these some carry on their business at the same stationary stall or 'standing' in the street, while others go on 'rounds'. The itinerant costermongers, as contradistinguished from the stationary street-fishmongers and greengrocers, have in many instances regular rounds, which they go daily, and which extend from two to ten miles. The longest are those which embrace a suburban part; the shortest are through streets thickly peopled by the poor, where duly to 'work' a single street consumes, in some instances, an hour. There are also 'chance' rounds. Men 'working' these carry their wares to any part in which they hope to find customers. The costermongers, moreover, diversify their labours by occasionally going on a country round, travelling on these excursions, in all directions, from thirty to ninety and even a hundred miles from the metropolis. Some, again, confine their callings chiefly to the neighbouring races and fairs.

Of all the characteristics attending these diversities of traders, I shall treat severally. I may here premise, that the regular or 'thorough-bred costermongers', repudiate the numerous persons who sell only nuts or oranges in the streets, whether at a fixed stall, or any given locality, or who hawk them through the thoroughfares or parks. They repudiate also a number of Jews, who confine their street-trading to the sale of 'coker-nuts' on Sundays, vended from large barrows. Nor do they rank with themselves the individuals who sell tea and coffee in the streets, or such condiments as peas-soup, sweetmeats, spice-cakes, and the like; those articles not being purchased at the markets. I often heard all such classes called 'the illegitimates'.

Habits and amusements of costermongers
[*volume i. pp. 11-16*]

I find it impossible to separate these two headings; for the habits of the costermonger are not domestic. His busy life is passed in the markets or the streets, and as his leisure is devoted to the beer-shop, the dancing-room, or the theatre, we must look for his habits to his demeanour at those places. Home has few attractions to a man whose life is a street-life. Even those who are influenced by family ties and affections, prefer to 'home' – indeed that word is rarely mentioned among them – the conversation, warmth, and merriment of the beer-shop, where they can take their ease among their 'mates'. Excitement or amusement are indispensable to uneducated men. Of beer-shops resorted to by costermongers, and principally supported by them, it is computed that there are 400 in London.

Those who meet first in the beer-shop talk over the state of trade and of the markets, while the later comers enter at once into what may be styled the serious business of the evening – amusement.

Business topics are discussed in a most peculiar style. One man takes the pipe from his mouth and says, 'Bill made a doogheno hit this morning.' 'Jem,' says another, to a man just entering, 'you'll stand a top o' reeb?' 'On,' answers Jem, 'I've had a trosseno tol, and have been doing dab.' For an explanation of what may be obscure in this dialogue, I must refer my readers to my remarks concerning the language of the class. If any strangers are present, the conversation is still further clothed in slang, so as to be unintelligible even to the partially initiated. The evident puzzlement of any listener is of course gratifying to the costermonger's vanity, for he feels that he possesses a knowledge peculiarly his own.

Among the in-door amusements of the costermonger is card-playing, at which many of them are adepts. The usual games are all-fours, all-fives, cribbage, and put. Whist is known to a few, but is never played, being considered dull and slow. Of short whist they have not heard; 'but,' said one, whom I questioned on the subject, 'if it's come into fashion, it'll soon be among us.' The play is usually for beer, but the game is rendered exciting by bets both among the players and the lookers-on. 'I'll back Jem for a yanepatine,' says one. 'Jack for a gen,' cries another. A penny is the lowest sum laid, and five shillings generally the highest, but a shilling is not often exceeded. 'We play fair among ourselves,' said a costermonger to me – 'aye, fairer than the aristocrats – but we'll take in anybody else.' Where it is known that the landlord will not supply cards, 'a sporting coster' carries a pack or two with him. The cards played with have rarely been stamped; they are generally dirty, and sometimes almost illegible, from long handling and spilled beer. Some men will sit patiently for hours at these games, and they watch the dealing round of the dingy cards intently, and without the attempt – common among politer gamesters – to appear indifferent, though they bear their losses well. In a full room of card-players, the groups are all shrouded in tobacco-smoke, and from them are heard constant sounds – according to the games they are engaged in – of 'I'm low, and Ped's high', 'Tip and me's game', 'Fifteen four and a flush of five'. I may remark it is curious that costermongers, who can neither read nor write, and who have no knowledge of the multiplication table, are skilful in all the intric-acies and calculations of cribbage. There is not much quarrelling over the cards, unless strangers play with them, and then the coster-mongers all take part one with another, fairly or unfairly.

It has been said that there is a close resemblance between many of the characteristics of a very high class, socially, and a very low class. Those who remember the disclosures on a trial a few years back, as to how men of rank and wealth passed their leisure in card-playing – many of their lives being one continued leisure –

can judge how far the analogy holds when the card-passion of the costermongers is described.

'Shove-halfpenny' is another game played by them; so is 'Three up'. Three halfpennies are thrown up, and when they fall all 'heads' or all 'tails', it is a mark; and the man who gets the greatest number of marks out of a given amount – three, or five, or more – wins. 'Three-up' is played fairly among the costermongers; but is most frequently resorted to when strangers are present to 'make a pitch' – which is, in plain words, to cheat any stranger who is rash enough to bet upon them. 'This is the way, sir,' said an adept to me; 'bless you, I can make them fall as I please. If I'm playing with Jo, and a stranger bets with Jo, why, of course, I make Jo win.' This adept illustrated his skill to me by throwing up three half-pennies, and, five times out of six, they fell upon the floor, whether he threw them nearly to the ceiling or merely to his shoulder, all heads or all tails. The halfpence were the proper current coins – indeed, they were my own; and the result is gained by a peculiar position of the coins on the fingers, and a peculiar jerk in the throwing. There was an amusing manifestation of the pride of art in the way in which my obliging informant displayed his skill.

'Skittles' is another favourite amusement, and the costermongers class themselves among the best players in London. The game is always for beer, but betting goes on.

A fondness for 'sparring' and 'boxing' lingers among the rude members of some classes of the working men, such as the tanners. With the great majority of the costermongers this fondness is still as dominant as it was among the 'higher classes', when boxers were the pets of princes and nobles. The sparring among the costers is not for money, but for beer and 'a lark' – a convenient word covering much mischief. Two out of every ten landlords, whose houses are patronised by these lovers of 'the art of self-defence', supply gloves. Some charge 2*d.* a night for their use; others only 1*d.* The sparring seldom continues long, sometimes not above a quarter of an hour; for the costermongers, though excited for a while, weary of sports in which they cannot personally participate, and in the beer-shops only two spar at a time, though fifty or sixty may be present. The shortness of the duration of this pastime may be one reason why it seldom leads to quarrelling. The stake is usually a 'top of reeb', and the winner is the man who gives the first 'noser'; a bloody nose however is required to show that the blow was veritably a noser. The costermongers boast of their skill in pugilism as well as at skittles. 'We are all handy with our fists,' said one man, 'and are matches, aye, and more than matches, for anybody but reg'lar boxers. We've stuck to the ring, too, and gone reg'lar to the fights, more than any other men.'

'Twopenny-hops' are much resorted to by the costermongers, men and women, boys and girls. At these dances decorum is sometimes, but not often, violated. 'The women,' I was told by one man, 'doesn't show their necks as I've seen the ladies do in them there pictures of high life in the shop-winders, or on the stage. Their Sunday gowns, which is their dancing gowns, ain't made that way.' At these 'hops' the clog-hornpipe is often danced, and sometimes a collection is made to ensure the performance of a first-rate professor of that dance; sometimes, and more frequently, it is volunteered gratuitously. The other dances are jigs, 'flash jigs' – hornpipes in fetters – a dance rendered popular by the success of the acted *Jack Sheppard* – polkas, and country-dances, the last-mentioned being generally demanded by the women. Waltzes are as yet unknown to them. Sometimes they do the 'pipe-dance'. For this a number of tobacco-pipes, about a dozen, are laid close together on the floor, and the dancer places the toe of his boot between the different pipes, keeping time with the music. Two of the pipes are arranged as a cross, and the toe has to be inserted between each of the angles, without breaking them. The numbers present at these 'hops' vary from 30 to 100 of both sexes, their ages being from 14 to 45, and the female sex being slightly predominant as to the proportion of those in attendance. At these 'hops' there is nothing of the leisurely style of dancing – half a glide and half a skip – but vigorous, laborious capering. The hours are from half-past eight to twelve, sometimes to one or two in the morning, and never later than two, as the costermongers are early risers. There is sometimes a good deal of drinking; some of the young girls being often pressed to drink, and frequently yielding to the temptation. From 1*l.* to 7*l.* is spent in drink at a hop; the youngest men or lads present spend the most, especially in that act of costermonger politeness – 'treating the gals'. The music is always a fiddle, sometimes with the addition of a harp and a cornopean. The band is provided by the costermongers, to whom the assembly is confined; but during the present and the last year, when the costers' earnings have been less than the average, the landlord has provided the harp, whenever that instrument has added to the charms of the fiddle. Of one use to which these 'hops' are put I have given an account, under the head of 'Marriage'.

The other amusements of this class of the community are the theatre and the penny concert, and their visits are almost entirely confined to the galleries of the theatres on the Surrey-side – the Surrey, the Victoria, the Bower Saloon, and (but less frequently) Astley's. Three times a week is an average attendance at theatres and dances by the more prosperous costermongers. The most intelligent man I met with among them gave me the following account. He classes himself with the many, but his tastes are really those of an educated man: – 'Love and murder suits us best, sir; but within these few years I think there's a great deal more liking for deep tragedies among us. They set men a thinking; but then we all consider them too long. Of *Hamlet* we can make neither end nor side; and nine out of ten of us – ay, far more than that – would like it to be confined to the ghost scenes, and the funeral, and the killing off at the last. *Macbeth* would be better liked, if it was only the witches and the fighting. The high words in a tragedy we call jaw-breakers, and say we can't tumble to that barrikin. We always stay to the last, because we've paid for it all, or very few costers would see a tragedy out if any money was returned to those leaving after two or three acts. We are fond of music. Nigger music was very much liked among us, but it's stale now. Flash songs are liked, and sailors' songs, and patriotic songs. Most costers – indeed, I can't call to mind an exception – listen very quietly to songs that they don't in the least understand. We have among us translations of the patriotic French songs. "Mourir pour la patrie" is very popular, and so is the "Marseillaise". A song to take hold of us must have a good chorus.' 'They like something, sir, that is worth hearing,' said one of my informants, 'such as "The Soldier's Dream", "The Dream of Napoleon", or "I 'ad a dream – an 'appy dream".'

The songs in ridicule of Marshal Haynau, and in laudation of Barclay and Perkin's draymen, were and are very popular among the costers; but none are more popular than Paul Jones – 'A noble commander, Paul Jones was his name'. Among them the chorus of 'Britons never shall be slaves', is often rendered 'Britons always shall be slaves'. The most popular of all songs with the class, however, is 'Duck-legged Dick', of which I give the first verse.

> 'Duck-legged Dick had a donkey,
> And his lush loved much for to swill,
> One day he got rather lumpy,
> And got sent seven days to the mill.
>
> His donkey was taken to the green-yard,
> A fate which he never deserved.
> Oh! it was such a regular mean yard,
> That alas! the poor moke got starved.
>
> Oh! bad luck can't be prevented,
> Fortune she smiles or she frowns,
> He's best off that's contented,
> To mix, sirs, the ups and the downs.'

Their sports are enjoyed the more if they are dangerous and require both courage and dexterity to succeed in them. They prefer, if crossing a bridge, to climb over the parapet, and walk along on the stone coping. When a house is building, rows of coster lads will climb up the long ladders, leaning against the unslated roof, and then slide down again, each one resting on the other's shoulders. A peep show with a battle scene is sure of its coster audience, and a favourite pastime is fighting with cheap theatrical swords. They are, however, true to each other, and should a coster, who is the hero of his court, fall ill and go to a hospital, the whole of the inhabitants of his quarter will visit him on the Sunday, and take him presents of various articles so that 'he may live well'.

Among the men, rat-killing is a favourite sport. They will enter an old stable, fasten the door and then turn out the rats. Or they will find out some unfrequented yard, and at night time build up a pit with apple-case boards, and lighting up their lamps, enjoy the sport. Nearly every coster is fond of dogs. Some fancy them greatly, and are proud of making them fight. If when out working, they see a handsome stray, whether he is a 'toy' or 'sporting' dog, they whip him up – many of the class not being *very* particular whether the animals are stray or not.

Their dog fights are both cruel and frequent. It is not uncommon to see a lad walking with the trembling legs of a dog shivering under a bloody handkerchief, that covers the bitten and wounded body of an animal that has been figuring at some 'match'. These fights take place on the sly – the tap-room or back-yard of a beer-shop, being generally chosen for the purpose. A few men are let into the secret, and they attend to bet upon the winner, the police being carefully kept from the spot.

Pigeons are 'fancied' to a large extent, and are kept in lath cages on the roofs of the houses. The lads look upon a visit to the Red-house, Battersea, where the pigeon-shooting takes place, as a great treat. They stand without the hoarding that encloses the ground, and watch for the wounded pigeons to fall, when a violent scramble takes place among them, each bird being valued at $3d.$ or $4d.$ So popular has this sport become, that some boys take dogs with them trained to retrieve the birds, and two Lambeth costers attend regularly after their morning's work with their guns, to shoot those that escape the 'shots' within.

A good pugilist is looked up to with great admiration by the costers, and fighting is considered to be a necessary part of a boy's education. Among them cowardice in any shape is despised as being degrading and loathsome, indeed the man who would avoid a fight is scouted by the whole of the court he lives in. Hence it is important for a lad and even a girl to know how to 'work their fists well' – as expert boxing is called among them. If a coster man or woman is struck they are obliged to fight. When a quarrel takes place between two boys, a ring is formed, and the men urge them on to have it out, for they hold that it is a wrong thing to stop a battle, as it causes bad blood for life; whereas, if the lads fight it out they shake hands and forget all about it. Everybody practises fighting, and the man who has the largest and hardest muscle is spoken of in terms of the highest commendation. It is often said in admiration of such a man that 'he could muzzle half a dozen bobbies before breakfast'.

To serve out a policeman is the bravest act by which a coster-monger can distinguish himself. Some lads have been imprisoned upwards of a dozen times for this offence; and are consequently looked upon by their companions as martyrs. When they leave prison for such an act, a subscription is often got up for their benefit. In their continual warfare with the force, they resemble many savage nations, from the cunning and treachery they use. The lads endeavour to take the unsuspecting 'crusher' by surprise, and often crouch at the entrance of a court until a policeman passes, when a stone or a brick is hurled at him, and the youngster immediately disappears. Their love of revenge, too, is extreme – their hatred being in no way mitigated by time; they will wait for months, following a policeman who has offended or wronged them, anxiously looking out for an opportunity of paying back the injury. One boy, I was told, vowed vengeance against a member of the force, and for six months never allowed the man to escape his notice. At length, one night, he saw the policeman in a row outside a public-house, and running into the crowd kicked him savagely, shouting at the same time: 'Now, you b—, I've got you at last.' When the boy heard that his persecutor was injured for life, his joy was very great, and he declared the twelvemonth's imprisonment he was sentenced to for the offence to be 'dirt cheap'. The whole of the court where the lad resided sympathised with the boy, and vowed to a man, that had he escaped, they would have subscribed a pad or two of dry herrings, to send him into the country until the affair had blown over, for he had shown himself a 'plucky one'.

It is called 'plucky' to bear pain without complaining. To flinch from expected suffering is scorned, and he who does so is sneered at and told to wear a gown, as being more fit to be a woman. To show a disregard for pain, a lad, when without money, will say to his pal, 'Give us a penny, and you may have a punch at my nose.' They also delight in tattooing their chests and arms with anchors, and figures of different kinds. During the whole of this painful operation, the boy will not flinch, but laugh and joke with his admiring companions, as if perfectly at ease.

Gambling of costermongers
[*volume i. pp.16–18*]
It would be difficult to find in the whole of this numerous class, a youngster who is not – what may be safely called – a desperate gambler. At the age of fourteen this love of play first comes upon

the lad, and from that time until he is thirty or so, not a Sunday passes but he is at his stand on the gambling ground. Even if he has no money to stake, he will loll away the morning looking on, and so borrow excitement from the successes of others. Every attempt made by the police, to check this ruinous system, has been unavailing, and has rather given a gloss of daring courage to the sport, that tends to render it doubly attractive.

If a costermonger has an hour to spare, his first thought is to gamble away the time. He does not care what he plays for, so long as he can have a chance of winning something. Whilst waiting for a market to open, his delight is to find out some pieman and toss him for his stock, though, by so doing, he risks his market-money and only chance of living, to win that which he will give away to the first friend he meets. For the whole week the boy will work untiringly, spurred on by the thought of the money to be won on the Sunday. Nothing will damp his ardour for gambling, the most continued ill-fortune making him even more reckless than if he were the luckiest man alive.

Many a lad who had gone down to the gambling ground, with a good warm coat upon his back and his pocket well filled from the Saturday night's market, will leave it at evening penniless and coatless, having lost all his earnings, stock-money, and the better part of his clothing. Some of the boys, when desperate with 'bad luck', borrow to the utmost limit of their credit; then they mortgage their 'King's-man' or neck-tie, and they will even change their cord trousers, if better than those of the winner, so as to have one more chance at the turn of fortune. The coldest winter's day will not stop the Sunday's gathering on the river-side, for the heat of play warms them in spite of the sharp wind blowing down the Thames. If the weather be wet, so that the half-pence stick to the ground, they find out some railway-arch or else a beer-shop, and having filled the tap-room with their numbers, they muffle the table with handkerchiefs, and play secretly. When the game is very exciting, they will even forget their hunger, and continue to gamble until it is too dark to see, before they think of eating. One man told me, that when he was working the races with lemonade, he had often seen in the centre of a group, composed of costers, thimble-riggers and showmen, as much as 100*l.* on the ground at one time, in gold and silver. A friend of his, who had gone down in company with him, with a pony-truck of toys, lost in less than an hour his earnings, truck, stock of goods, and great-coat. Vowing to have his revenge next time, he took his boy on his back, and started off on the tramp to London, there to borrow sufficient money to bring down a fresh lot of goods on the morrow, and then gamble away his earnings as before.

It is perfectly immaterial to the coster with whom he plays, whether it be a lad from the Lambeth potteries, or a thief from the Westminster slums. Very often, too, the gamblers of one coster-monger district, will visit those of another, and work what is called 'a plant' in this way. One of the visitors will go beforehand, and, joining a group of gamblers, commence tossing. When sufficient time has elapsed to remove all suspicion of companionship, his mate will come up and commence betting on each of his pal's throws with those standing round. By a curious quickness of hand, a coster can make the toss tell favourably for his wagering friend, who meets him after the play is over in the evening, and shares the spoil.

The spots generally chosen for the Sunday's sport are in secret places, half-hidden from the eye of the passers, where a scout can give quick notice of the approach of the police: in the fields about King's-cross, or near any unfinished railway buildings. The Mint, St George's-fields, Blackfriars'-road, Bethnal-green, and Maryle-bone, are all favourite resorts. Between Lambeth and Chelsea, the shingle on the left side of the Thames is spotted with small rings of lads, half-hidden behind the barges. One boy (of the party) is always on the look out, and even if a stranger should advance, the cry is given of 'Namous' or 'Kool Eslop'. Instantly the money is whipped-up and pocketed, and the boys stand chattering and laughing together. It is never difficult for a coster to find out where the gambling parties are, for he has only to stop the first lad he meets, and ask him where the 'erht pu' or 'three up' is going on, to discover their whereabouts.

If during the game a cry of 'Police!' should be given by the looker-out, instantly a rush at the money is made by anyone in the group, the costers preferring that a stranger should have the money rather than the policeman. There is also a custom among them, that the ruined player should be started again by a gift of 2*d*. in every shilling lost, or, if the loss is heavy, a present of four or five shillings is made; neither is it considered at all dishonourable for the party winning to leave with the full bloom of success upon him.

That the description of one of these Sunday scenes might be more truthful, a visit was paid to a gambling-ring close to ——. Although not twenty yards distant from the steam-boat pier, yet the little party was so concealed among the the coal-barges, that not a head could be seen. The spot chosen was close to a small narrow court, leading from the street to the water-side, and here the lad on the look-out was stationed. There were about thirty young fellows, some tall strapping youths, in the costers' cable-cord costume, – others, mere boys, in rags, from the potteries, with their clothes stained with clay. The party was hidden from the river by the black dredger-boats on the beach; and it was so arranged, that should the alarm be given, they might leap into the coal-barges, and hide until the intruder had retired. Seated on some oars stretched across two craft, was a mortar-stained brick-layer, keeping a look-out towards the river, and acting as a sort of umpire in all disputes. The two that were tossing had been playing together since early morning; and it was easy to tell which was the loser, by the anxious-looking eye and compressed lip. He was quarrelsome too; and if the crowd pressed upon him, he would jerk his elbow back savagely, saying, 'I wish to C——t you'd stand backer.' The winner, a short man, in a mud-stained canvas jacket, and a week's yellow beard on his chin, never spake a word beyond his 'heads', or 'tails'; but his cheeks were red, and the pipe in his mouth was unlit, though he puffed at it.

In their hands they each held a long row of halfpence, extending to the wrist, and topped by shillings and half-crowns. Nearly everyone round had coppers in his hands, and bets were made and taken as rapidly as they could be spoken. 'I lost a sov. last night in less than no time,' said one man, who, with his hands in his pockets, was looking on; 'never mind – I musn't have no wenson this week, and try again next Sunday.'

The boy who was losing was adopting every means to 'bring back his luck again'. Before crying, he would toss up a halfpenny three times, to see what he should call. At last, with an oath, he pushed aside the boys round him, and shifted his place, to see what that would do; it had a good effect, for he won toss after toss in a curiously fortunate way, and then it was strange to watch his mouth gradually relax and his brows unknit. His opponent was a little startled, and passing his fingers through his dusty hair, said, with a stupid laugh, 'Well, I never see the likes.' The betting also began to shift. 'Sixpence Ned wins!' cried three or four; 'Sixpence he loses!' answered another; 'Done!' and up went the halfpence. 'Halfa-crown Joe loses!' – 'Here you are,' answered Joe, but he lost again. 'I'll try you a "gen" [shilling],' said a coster; 'And a "rouf yenap" [fourpence],' added the other. 'Say a "exes" [sixpence].' – 'Done!' and the betting continued, till the ground was spotted with silver and halfpence.

'That's ten bob he's won in five minutes,' said Joe (the loser), looking round with a forced smile; but Ned (the winner) never spake a word, even when he gave any change to his antagonist; and if he took a bet, he only nodded to the one that offered it, and threw down his money. Once, when he picked up more than a sovereign from the ground, that he had won in one throw, a washed sweep, with a black rim round his neck, said, 'There's a hog!' but there wasn't even a smile at the joke. At last Joe began to feel angry, and stamping his foot till the water squirted up from the beach, cried, 'It's no use; luck's set in him – he'd muck a thousand!' and so he shifted his ground, and betted all round on the chance of better fortune attending the movement. He lost again, and someone bantering said, 'You'll win the shine-rag, Joe,' meaning that he would be 'cracked up', or ruined, if he continued.

When one o'clock struck, a lad left, saying, he was 'going to get an inside lining [dinner]'. The sweep asked him what he was going to have. 'A two-and-half plate, and a ha'p'orth of smash [a plate of soup and a ha'p'orth of mashed potatoes],' replied the lad, bounding into the court. Nobody else seemed to care for his dinner, for all stayed to watch the gamblers.

Every now and then someone would go up the court to see if the lad watching for the police was keeping a good look-out; but the boy never deserted his post, for fear of losing his threepence. If he had, such is the wish to protect the players felt by every lad, that even whilst at dinner, one of them, if he saw a policeman pass, would spring up and rush to the gambling ring to give notice.

When the tall youth, 'Ned', had won nearly all the silver of the group, he suddenly jerked his gains into his coat-pocket, and saying, 'I've done,' walked off, and was out of sight in an instant. The surprise of the loser and all around was extreme. They looked at the court where he had disappeared, then at one another, and at last burst out into one expression of disgust. 'There's a scurf!' said one; 'He's a regular scab,' cried another; and a coster declared that he was 'a trosseno, and no mistake'. For although it is held to be fair for the winner to go whenever he wishes, yet such conduct is never relished by the losers.

It was then determined that 'they would have him to rights' the next time he came to gamble; for everyone would set at him, and win his money, and then 'turn up', as he had done.

The party was then broken up, the players separating to wait for the new-comers that would be sure to pour in after dinner.

The 'Vic. Gallery'

[*volume i. pp.18–20*]

On a good attractive night, the rush of costers to the threepenny gallery of the Coburg (better known as the 'Vic') is peculiar and almost awful.

The long zig-zag staircase that leads to the pay box is crowded to suffocation at least an hour before the theatre is opened; but, on the occasion of a piece with a good murder in it, the crowd will frequently collect as early as three o'clock in the afternoon. Lads stand upon the broad wooden bannisters about 50 feet from the ground, and jump on each others' backs, or adopt any expedient they can think of to obtain a good place.

The walls of the well-staircase having a remarkably fine echo, and the wooden floor of the steps serving as a sounding board, the shouting, whistling, and quarrelling of the impatient young costers is increased tenfold. If, as sometimes happens, a song with a chorus is started, the ears positively ache with the din, and when the chant has finished it seems as though a sudden silence had fallen on the people. To the centre of the road, and all round the door, the mob is in a ferment of excitement, and no sooner is the money-taker at his post than the most frightful rush takes place, everyone heaving with his shoulder at the back of the person immediately in front of him. The girls shriek, men shout, and a nervous fear is felt lest the massive staircase should fall in with the weight of the throng, as it lately did with the most terrible results. If a hat tumbles from the top of the staircase, a hundred hands snatch at it as it descends. When it is caught a voice roars above the tumult, 'All right, Bill, I've got it' – for they all seem to know one another – 'Keep us a pitch and I'll bring it.'

To anyone unaccustomed to be pressed flat it would be impossible to enter with the mob. To see the sight in the gallery it is better to wait until the first piece is over. The ham-sandwich men and pig-trotter women will give you notice when the time is come, for with the first clatter of the descending footsteps they commence their cries.

There are few grown-up men that go to the 'Vic' gallery. The generality of the visitors are lads from about twelve to three-and-twenty, and though a few black-faced sweeps or whitey-brown dustmen may be among the throng, the gallery audience consists mainly of costermongers. Young girls, too, are very plentiful, only one-third of whom now take their babies, owing to the new regulation of charging half-price for infants. At the foot of the staircase stands a group of boys begging for the return checks, which they sell again for $1\frac{1}{2}d.$ or $1d.$, according to the lateness of the hour.

At each step up the well-staircase the warmth and stench increase, until by the time one reaches the gallery doorway, a furnace-heat rushes out through the entrance that seems to force you backwards, whilst the odour positively prevents respiration. The mob on the landing, standing on tiptoe and closely wedged together, resists any civil attempt at gaining a glimpse of the stage, and yet a coster lad will rush up, elbow his way into the crowd, then jump up on to the shoulders of those before him, and suddenly disappear into the body of the gallery.

The gallery at 'the Vic' is one of the largest in London. It will hold from 1,500 to 2,000 people, and runs back to so great a distance, that the end of it is lost in shadow, excepting where the little gas-jets, against the wall, light up the two or three faces around them. When the gallery is well packed, it is usual to see piles of boys on each others shoulders at the back, while on the partition boards, dividing off the slips, lads will pitch themselves, despite the spikes.

As you look up the vast slanting mass of heads from the upper boxes, each one appears on the move. The huge black heap, dotted with faces, and spotted with white shirt sleeves, almost pains the eye to look at, and should a clapping of hands commence, the twinkling nearly blinds you. It is the fashion with the mob to take off their coats; and the cross-braces on the backs of some, and the bare shoulders peeping out of the ragged shirts of others, are the only variety to be found. The bonnets of the 'ladies' are hung over the iron railing in front, their numbers nearly hiding the panels, and one of the amusements of the lads in the back seats consists in pitching orange peel or nutshells into them, a good aim being rewarded with a shout of laughter.

When the orchestra begins playing, before 'the gods' have settled into their seats, it is impossible to hear a note of music. The puffed-out cheeks of the trumpeters, and the raised drumsticks tell you that the overture has commenced, but no tune is to be heard, an occasional burst of the full band being caught by gushes, as if a high wind were raging. Recognitions take place every moment, and 'Bill Smith' is called to in a loud voice from one side, and a shout in answer from the other asks 'What's up?' Or family secrets are revealed, and 'Bob Triller' is asked where 'Sal' is, and replies amid a roar of laughter, that she is 'a-larning the pynanney'.

By-and-by a youngster, who has come in late, jumps up over the shoulders at the door, and doubling himself into a ball, rolls down over the heads in front, leaving a trail of commotion for each one as he passes aims a blow at the fellow. Presently a fight is sure to begin, and then everyone rises from his seat whistling and shouting; three or four pairs of arms fall to, the audience waving their hands till the moving mass seems like microscopic eels in paste. But the commotion ceases suddenly on the rising of the curtain, and then the cries of 'Silence!' 'Ord-a-a-r!' 'Ord-a-a-r!' make more noise than ever.

The 'Vic' gallery is not to be moved by touching sentiment. They prefer vigorous exercise to any emotional speech. 'The Child of the Storm's' declaration that she would share her father's 'death or imprisonment as her duty', had no effect at all, compared with the split in the hornpipe. The shrill whistling and brayvos that followed the tar's performance showed how highly it was relished, and one 'god' went so far as to ask 'how it was done'. The comic actor kicking a dozen Polish peasants was encored, but the grand banquet of the Czar of all the Russias only produced merriment, and a request that he would 'give them a bit' was made directly the Emperor took the willow-patterned plate in his hand. All affecting situations were sure to be interrupted by cries of 'orda-a-r', and the lady begging for her father's life was told to 'speak up old gal'; though when the heroine of the 'dummestic dreamer' (as they call it) told the general of all the Cossack forces 'not to be a fool', the uproar of approbation grew greater than ever – and when the lady turned up her swan's-down cuffs, and seizing four Russian soldiers shook them successively by the collar, then the enthusiasm knew no bounds, and the cries of 'Bray-vo Vincent! Go it my tulip!' resounded from every throat.

Altogether the gallery audience do not seem to be of a gentle nature. One poor little lad shouted out in a crying tone, 'that he couldn't see', and instantly a dozen voices demanded 'that he should be thrown over'.

Whilst the pieces are going on, brown, flat bottles are frequently raised to the mouth, and between the acts a man with a tin can, glittering in the gas-light, goes round crying, 'Port-a-a-a-r! who's for port-a-a-a-r.' As the heat increased the faces grew bright red, every bonnet was taken off, and ladies could be seen wiping the perspiration from their cheeks with the play-bills.

No delay between the pieces will be allowed, and should the interval appear too long, someone will shout out – referring to the curtain – 'Pull up that there winder blind!' or they will call to the orchestra, saying, 'Now then you catgut-scrapers! Let's have a ha'purth of liveliness.' Neither will they suffer a play to proceed until they have a good view of the stage, and 'Higher the blue', is constantly shouted, when the sky is too low, or 'Light up the moon', when the transparency is rather dim.

The dances and comic songs, between the pieces, are liked better than anything else. A highland fling is certain to be repeated, and a stamping of feet will accompany the tune, and a shrill whistling, keep time through the entire performance.

But the grand hit of the evening is always when a song is sung to which the entire gallery can join in chorus. Then a deep silence prevails all through the stanzas. Should any burst in before his time, a shout of 'orda-a-r' is raised, and the intruder put down by a thousand indignant cries. At the proper time, however, the throats of the mob burst forth in all their strength. The most deafening noise breaks out suddenly, while the cat-calls keep up the tune, and an imitation of a dozen Mr Punches squeak out the words. Some actors at the minor theatres make a great point of this, and in the bill upon the night of my visit, under the title of 'There's a good time coming, boys', there was printed, 'assisted by the most numerous and effective chorus in the metropolis – ' meaning the whole of the gallery. The singer himself started the mob, saying, 'Now then, the Exeter Hall touch if you please gentlemen,' and beat time with his hand, parodying M. Jullien with his baton. An 'angcore' on such occasions is always demanded, and, despite a few murmurs of 'change it to "Duck-legged Dick"', invariably insisted on.

The politics of costermongers – policemen
[*volume i. p.*20]

The notion of the police is so intimately blended with what may be called the politics of the costermongers that I give them together.

The politics of these people are detailed in a few words – they are nearly all Chartists. 'You might say, sir,' remarked one of my informants, 'that they *all* were Chartists, but as it's better you should rather be under than over the mark, say *nearly* all.' Their ignorance, and their being impulsive, makes them a dangerous class. I am assured that in every district where the costermongers are congregated, one or two of the body, more intelligent than the others, have great influence over them; and these leading men are all Chartists, and being industrious and not unprosperous persons, their pecuniary and intellectual superiority cause them to be regarded as oracles. One of these men said to me: 'The costers think that working-men know best, and so they have confidence in us. I like to make men discontented, and I will make them discontented while the present system continues, because it's all for the middle and the moneyed classes, and nothing, in the way of rights, for the poor. People fancy when all's quiet that all's stagnating. Propagandism is going on for all that. It's when all's quiet that the seed's a growing. Republicans and Socialists are pressing their doctrines.'

The costermongers have very vague notions of an aristocracy; they call the more prosperous of their own body 'aristocrats'. Their notions of an aristocracy of birth or wealth seem to be formed on their opinion of the rich, or reputed rich salesmen with whom they deal; and the result is anything but favourable to the nobility.

Concerning free-trade, nothing, I am told, can check the coster-mongers' fervour for a cheap loaf. A Chartist costermonger told me that he knew numbers of costers who were keen Chartists without understanding anything about the six points.

The costermongers frequently attend political meetings, going there in bodies of from six to twelve. Some of them, I learned, could not understand why Chartist leaders exhorted them to peace and quietness, when they might as well fight it out with the police at once. The costers boast, moreover, that they stick more together in any 'row' than any other class. It is considered by them a reflection on the character of the thieves that they are seldom true to one another.

It is a matter of marvel to many of this class that people can live without working. The ignorant costers have no knowledge of 'property', or 'income', and conclude that the non-workers all live out of the taxes. Of the taxes generally they judge from their knowledge that tobacco, which they account a necessary of life, pays 3s. per lb. duty.

As regards the police, the hatred of a costermonger to a 'peeler' is intense, and with their opinion of the police, all the more ignorant unite that of the governing power. 'Can you wonder at it, sir,' said a costermonger to me, 'that I hate the police? They drive us about, we must move on, we can't stand here, and we can't pitch there. But if we're cracked up, that is if we're forced to go into the Union (I've known it both at Clerkenwell and the City of London workhouses), why the parish gives us money to buy a barrow, or a shallow, or to hire them, and leave the house and start for ourselves: and what's the use of that, if the police won't let us sell our goods? – Which is right, the parish or the police?'

To thwart the police in any measure the costermongers readily aid one another. One very common procedure, if the policeman has seized a barrow, is to whip off a wheel, while the officers have gone for assistance; for a large and loaded barrow requires two men to convey it to the green-yard. This is done with great dexterity; and the next step is to dispose of the stock to any passing costers, or to any 'standing' in the neighbourhood, and it is honestly accounted for. The policemen, on their return, find an empty, and unwheelable barrow, which they must carry off by main strength, amid the jeers of the populace.

I am assured that in case of a political riot every 'coster' would seize his policeman.

Marriage and concubinage of costermongers
[*volume i. pp.20,21*]
Only one-tenth – at the outside one-tenth – of the couples living together and carrying on the costermongering trade, are married. In Clerkenwell parish, however, where the number of married couples is about a fifth of the whole, this difference is easily accounted for, as in Advent and Easter the incumbent of that parish marries poor couples without a fee. Of the rights of 'legitimate' or 'illegitimate' children the costermongers understand nothing, and account it a mere waste of money and time to go through the ceremony of wedlock when a pair can live together, and be quite as well regarded by their fellows, without it. The married women associate with the unmarried mothers of families without the slightest scruple. There is no honour attached to the marriage state, and no shame to concubinage. Neither are the unmarried women less faithful to their 'partners' than the married; but I understand that, of the two classes, the unmarried betray the most jealousy.

As regards the fidelity of these women I was assured that, 'in anything like good times', they were rigidly faithful to their husbands or paramours; but that, in the worst pinch of poverty, a departure from this fidelity – if it provided a few meals or a fire – was not considered at all heinous. An old costermonger, who had been mixed up with other callings, and whose prejudices were certainly not in favour of his present trade, said to me, 'What I call the working girls, sir, are as industrious and as faithful a set as can well be. I'm satisfied that they're more faithful to their mates than other poor working women. I never knew one of these working girls do wrong that way. They're strong, hearty, healthy girls, and keep clean rooms. Why, there's numbers of men leave their stock-money with their women, just taking out two or three shillings to gamble with and get drunk upon. They sometimes take a little drop themselves, the women do, and get beaten by their husbands for it, and hardest beaten if the man's drunk himself. They're sometimes beaten for other things too, or for nothing at all. But they seem to like the men better for their beating them. I never could make that out.' Notwithstanding this fidelity, it appears that the 'larking and joking' of the young, and sometimes of the middle-aged people, among themselves, is anything but delicate. The unmarried separate as seldom as the married. The fidelity characterising the women does not belong to the men.

The dancing-rooms are the places where matches are made up. There the boys go to look out for 'mates', and sometimes a match is struck up the first night of meeting, and the couple live together forthwith. The girls at these dances are all the daughters of costermongers, or of persons pursuing some other course of street life. Unions take place when the lad is but 14. Two or three out of 100 have their female helpmates at that early age; but the female is generally a couple of years older than her partner. Nearly all the costermongers form such alliances as I have described, when both parties are under twenty. One reason why these alliances are contracted at early ages is, that when a boy has assisted his father, or anyone engaging him, in the business of a costermonger, he knows that he can borrow money, and hire a shallow or a barrow – or he may have saved 5s. – 'and then if the father vexes him or snubs him,' said one of my informants, 'he'll tell his father to go to h—ll, and he and his gal will start on their own account.'

Most of the costermongers have numerous families, but not those who contract alliances very young. The women continue working down to the day of their confinement.

'Chance children', as they are called, or children unrecognised by any father, are rare among the young women of the costermongers.

Religion of costermongers
[volume i. pp.21,22]
An intelligent and trustworthy man, until very recently actively engaged in costermongering, computed that not 3 in 100 costermongers had ever been in the interior of a church, or any place of worship, or knew what was meant by Christianity. The same person gave me the following account, which was confirmed by others.

'The costers have no religion at all, and very little notion, or none at all, of what religion or a future state is. Of all things they hate tracts. They hate them because the people leaving them never give them anything, and as they can't read the tract – not one in forty – they're vexed to be bothered with it. And really what is the use of giving people reading before you've taught them to read? Now, they respect the City Missionaries, because they read to them – and the costers will listen to reading when they don't understand it – and because they visit the sick, and sometimes give oranges and such like to them and the children. I've known a City Missionary buy a shilling's worth of oranges of a coster, and give them away to the sick and the children – most of them belonging to the costermongers – down the court, and that made him respected there. I think the City Missionaries have done good. But I'm satisfied that if the costers had to profess themselves of some religion tomorrow, they would all become Roman Catholics, every one of them. This is the reason: London costers live very often in the same courts and streets as the poor Irish, and if the Irish are sick, be sure there comes to them the priest, the Sisters of Charity – they *are* good women – and some other ladies. Many a man that's not a Catholic, has rotted and died without any good person near him. Why, I lived a good while in Lambeth, and there wasn't one coster in 100, I'm satisfied, knew so much as the rector's name, – though Mr Dalton's a very good man. But the reason I was telling you of, sir, is that the costers reckon that religion's the best that gives the most in charity, and they think the Catholics do this. I'm not a Catholic myself, but I believe every word of the Bible, and have the greater belief that it's the word of God because it teaches democracy. The Irish in the courts get sadly chaffed by the others about their priests, – but they'll die for the priest. Religion is a regular puzzle to the costers. They see people come out of church and chapel, and as they're mostly well dressed, and there's very few of their own sort among the church-goers, the costers somehow mix up being religious with being respectable, and so they have a queer sort of feeling about it. It's a mystery to them. It's shocking when you come to think of it. They'll listen to any preacher that goes among them; and then a few will say – I've heard it often – "A b—y fool, why don't he let people go to h—ll their own way?" There's another thing that makes the costers think so well of the Catholics. If a Catholic coster – there's only very few of them – is "cracked up" [penniless], he's often started again, and the others have a notion that it's through some chapel-fund. I don't know whether it is so or not, but I know the cracked-up men are started again, if they're Catholics. It's still the stranger that the regular costermongers, who are nearly all Londoners, should have such respect for the Roman Catholics, when they have such a hatred of the Irish, whom they look upon as intruders and underminers.' – 'If a missionary came among us with plenty of money,' said another costermonger, 'he might make us all Christians or Turks, or anything he liked.' Neither the Latter-day Saints, nor any similar sect, have made converts among the costermongers.

Of the uneducated state of costermongers
[*volume i. p.22*]
I have stated elsewhere, that only about one in ten of the regular costermongers is able to read. The want of education among both men and women is deplorable, and I tested it in several instances. The following statement, however, from one of the body, is no more to be taken as representing the ignorance of the class generally, than are the clear and discriminating accounts I received from intelligent costermongers to be taken as representing the intelligence of the body.

The man with whom I conversed, and from whom I received the following statement, seemed about thirty. He was certainly not ill-looking, but with a heavy cast of countenance, his light blue eyes having little expression. His statements, or opinions, I need hardly explain, were given both spontaneously in the course of conversation, and in answer to my questions. I give them almost verbatim, omitting oaths and slang:

'Well, times is bad, sir,' he said, 'but it's a deadish time. I don't do so well at present as in middlish times, I think. When I served the Prince of Naples, not far from here [I presume that he alluded to the Prince of Capua], I did better and times was better. That was five years ago, but I can't say to a year or two. He was a good customer, and was wery fond of peaches. I used to sell them to him, at 12s. the plasket when they was new. The plasket held a dozen, and cost me 6s. at Covent-garden – more sometimes;

but I didn't charge him more when they did. His footman was a black man, and a ignorant man quite, and his housekeeper was a Englishwoman. He was the Prince o' Naples, was my customer; but I don't know what he was like, for I never saw him. I've heard that he was the brother of the king of Naples. I can't say where Naples is, but if you was to ask at Euston-square, they'll tell you the fare there and the time to go it in. It may be in France for anything I know may Naples, or in Ireland. Why don't you ask at the square? I went to Croydon once by rail, and slept all the way without stirring, and so you may to Naples for anything I know. I never heard of the Pope being a neighbour of the King of Naples. Do you mean living next door to him? But I don't know nothing of the King of Naples, only the prince. I don't know what the Pope is. Is he any trade? It's nothing to me, when he's no customer of mine. I have nothing to say about nobody that ain't no customers. My crabs is caught in the sea, in course. I gets them at Billingsgate. I never saw the sea, but it's salt-water, I know. I can't say whereabouts it lays. I believe it's in the hands of the Billingsgate salesmen – all of it? I've heard of shipwrecks at sea, caused by drownding, in course. I never heard that the Prince of Naples was ever at sea. I like to talk about him, he was such a customer when he lived near here.' [Here he repeated his account of the supply of peaches to his Royal Highness.] 'I never was in France, no, sir, never. I don't know the way. Do you think I could do better there? I never was in the Republic there. What's it like? Bonaparte? Oh yes; I've heard of him. He was at Waterloo. I didn't know he'd been alive now and in France, as you ask me about him. I don't think you're larking, sir. Did I hear of the French taking possession of Naples, and Bonaparte making his brother-in-law king? Well, I didn't, but it may be true, because I served the Prince of Naples, what was the brother of the king. I never heard whether the Prince was the king's older brother or his younger. I wish he may turn out his older if there's property coming to him, as the oldest has the first turn; at least so I've heard – first come, first served. I've worked the streets and the courts at all times. I've worked them by moonlight, but you couldn't see the moonlight where it was busy. I can't say how far the moon's off us. It's nothing to me, but I've seen it a good bit higher than St Paul's. I don't know nothing about the sun. Why do you ask? It must be nearer than the moon for it's warmer, – and if they're both fire, that shows it. It's like the tap-room grate and that bit of a gas-light; to compare the two is. What was St Paul's that the moon was above? A church, sir; so I've heard. I never was in a church. Oh yes, I've heard of God; he made heaven and earth; I never heard of his making the sea; that's another thing, and you can best learn about that at Billingsgate. [He seemed to think that the sea was an appurtenance of Billingsgate.] Jesus Christ? Yes. I've heard of him. Our Redeemer? Well, I only wish I could redeem my Sunday togs from my uncle's.'

Another costermonger, in answer to inquiries, said: 'I 'spose you think us 'riginal coves that you ask. We're not like Methusalem, or some such swell's name [I presume that Malthus was meant], as wanted to murder children afore they was born, as I once heerd lectured about – we're nothing like that.'

Another on being questioned, and on being told that the information was wanted for the press, replied: 'The press? I'll have nothing to say to it. We are oppressed enough already.'

That a class numbering 30,000 should be permitted to remain in a state of almost brutish ignorance is a national disgrace. If the London costers belong especially to the 'dangerous classes', the danger of such a body is assuredly an evil of our own creation; for the gratitude of the poor creatures to anyone who seeks to give them the least knowledge is almost pathetic.

Language of costermongers
[volume i. pp.23,24]
The slang language of the costermongers is not very remarkable for originality of construction; it possesses no humour: but they boast that it is known only to themselves [. . .] The *root* of the costermonger tongue, so to speak, is to give the words spelt backward, or rather pronounced rudely backward, – for in my present chapter the language has, I believe, been reduced to orthography for the first time. With this backward pronunciation, which is very arbitrary, are mixed words reducible to no rule and seldom referrable to any origin, thus complicating the mystery of this unwritten tongue; while any syllable is added to a proper slang word, at the discretion of the speaker.

Slang is acquired very rapidly, and some costermongers will converse in it by the hour. The women use it sparingly; the girls more than the women; the men more than the girls; and the boys most of all. [. . .]

Speaking of this language, a costermonger said to me: 'The Irish can't tumble to it anyhow; the Jews can tumble better, but we're *their* masters. Some of the young salesmen at Billingsgate understand us, – but only at Billingsgate; and they think they're uncommon clever, but they're not quite up to the mark. The police don't understand us at all. It would be a pity if they did.' [. . .]

The costermonger's oaths, I may conclude, are all in the vernacular; nor are any of the common salutes, such as 'How d'you do?' or 'Good-night' known to their slang.

Kennetseeno	Stinking;
	(applied principally to the quality of fish).
Flatch kanurd	Half-drunk.
Flash it	Show it;
	(in cases of bargains offered).
On doog	No good.
Cross chap	A thief.
Showfulls	Bad money;
	(seldom in the hands of costermongers).
I'm on to the deb	I'm going to bed.
Do the tightner	Go to dinner.
Nommus	Be off.
Tol	Lot, Stock, or Share.

[. . .]

Of the nicknames of costermongers
[*volume i. p.24*]

Like many rude, and almost all wandering communities, the costermongers, like the cabmen and pickpockets, are hardly ever known by their real names; even the honest men among them are distinguished by some strange appellation. Indeed, they are all known one to another by nicknames, which they acquire either by some mode of dress, some remark that has ensured costermonger applause, some peculiarity in trading, or some defect or

singularity in personal appearance. Men are known as 'Rotten
Herrings', 'Spuddy' (a seller of bad potatoes, until beaten by
the Irish for his bad wares), 'Curly' (a man with a curly head),
'Foreigner' (a man who had been in the Spanish-Legion), 'Brassy'
(a very saucy person), 'Gaffy' (once a performer), 'The One-eyed
Buffer', 'Jawbreaker', 'Pine-apple Jack', 'Cast-iron Poll' (her head
having been struck with a pot without injury to her), 'Whilky',
'Blackwall Poll' (a woman generally having two black eyes),
'Lushy Bet', 'Dirty Sall' (the costermongers generally objecting to
dirty women), and 'Dancing Sue'.

Of the education of costermongers' children
[*volume i. p.24*]
I have used the heading of 'Education', but perhaps to say 'non-
education' would be more suitable. Very few indeed of the costermongers' children are sent even to the ragged schools; and if they
are, from all I could learn, it is done more that the mother may be
saved the trouble of tending them at home, than from any desire
that the children shall acquire useful knowledge. Both boys and
girls are sent out by their parents in the evening to sell nuts,
oranges, &c., at the doors of the theatres, or in any public place, or
'round the houses' (a stated circuit from their place of abode).
This trade they pursue eagerly for the sake of 'bunts', though
some carry home the money they take, very honestly. The
costermongers are kind to their children, 'perhaps in a rough way,
and the women make regular pets of them very often.' One
experienced man told me, that he had seen a poor costermonger's
wife – one of the few who could read – instructing her children
in reading; but such instances were very rare. The education of
these children is such only as the streets afford; and the streets
teach them, for the most part – and in greater or lesser degrees –
acuteness – a precocious acuteness – in all that concerns their
immediate wants, business, or gratifications; a patient endurance
of cold and hunger; a desire to obtain money without working for
it; a craving for the excitement of gambling; an inordinate love of
amusement; and an irrepressible repugnance to any settled in-
door industry.

The literature of costermongers

[*volume i. pp.25–26*]

We have now had an inkling of the London costermonger's
notions upon politics and religion. We have seen the brutified state
in which he is allowed by society to remain, though possessing the
same faculties and susceptibilities as ourselves – the same power to
perceive and admire the forms of truth, beauty, and goodness, as
even the very highest in the state. We have witnessed how,
instinct with all the elements of manhood and beasthood, the
qualities of the beast are principally developed in him, while those
of the man are stunted in their growth. It now remains for us to
look into some other matters concerning this curious class of
people, and, first, of their literature.

It may appear anomalous to speak of the literature of an uneducated body, but even the costermongers have their tastes for
books. They are very fond of hearing anyone read aloud to them,
and listen very attentively. One man often reads the Sunday paper
of the beer-shop to them, and on a fine summer's evening a
costermonger, or any neighbour who has the advantage of being 'a
schollard', reads aloud to them in the courts they inhabit. What they
love best to listen to – and, indeed, what they are most eager for –
are Reynolds's periodicals, especially the *Mysteries of the Court*.
'They've got tired of Lloyd's blood-stained stories,' said one man,
who was in the habit of reading to them, 'and I'm satisfied that, of
all London, Reynolds is the most popular man among them. They
stuck to him in Trafalgar-square, and would again. They all say he's
"a trump", and Feargus O'Connor's another trump with them.'

One intelligent man considered that the spirit of curiosity
manifested by costermongers, as regards the information or excitement derived from hearing stories read, augured well for the
improvability of the class.

Another intelligent costermonger, who had recently read some
of the cheap periodicals to ten or twelve men, women, and boys,
all costermongers, gave me an account of the comments made by
his auditors. They had assembled, after their day's work or their
rounds, for the purpose of hearing my informant read the last
number of some of the penny publications.

'The costermongers,' said my informant, 'are very fond of
illustrations. I have known a man, what couldn't read, buy a

periodical what had an illustration, a little out of the common way perhaps, just that he might learn from someone, who *could* read, what it was all about. They have all heard of Cruikshank, and they think everything funny is by him – funny scenes in a play and all. His "Bottle" was very much admired.' [. . .]

Tracts they will rarely listen to, but if any persevering man *will* read tracts, and state that he does it for their benefit and improvement, they listen without rudeness, though often with evident unwillingness. 'Sermons or tracts,' said one of their body to me, 'gives them the 'orrors.' Costermongers purchase, and not unfrequently, the first number of a penny periodical, 'to see what it's like.' [. . .]

Of the costermongers' capital
[*volume i. p.29*]
The costermongers, though living by buying and selling, are seldom or never capitalists. It is estimated that not more than one-fourth of the entire body trade upon their own property. Some borrow their stock-money, others borrow the stock itself, others again borrow the donkey-carts, barrows, or baskets, in which their stock is carried round, whilst others borrow even the weights and measures by which it is meted out.

The reader, however uninformed he may be as to the price the poor usually have to pay for any loans they may require, doubtlessly need not be told that the remuneration exacted for the use of the above-named commodities is not merely confined to the legal 5*l.* per centum per annum; still many of even the most 'knowing' will hardly be able to credit the fact that the ordinary rate of interest in the costermongers' moneymarket amounts to 20 per cent. per week, or no less than 1040*l.* a year, for every 100*l.* advanced.

But the iniquity of this usury in the present instance is felt, not so much by the costermongers themselves, as by the poor people whom they serve; for, of course, the enormous rate of interest must be paid out of the profits on the goods they sell, and consequently added to the price, so that coupling this overcharge with the customary short allowance – in either weight or measure, as the case may be – we can readily perceive how cruelly the poor are defrauded, and how they not only get often too little for what they do, but have as often to pay too much for what they buy.

Of the 'slang' weights and measures

[*volume i. p.32,33*]

All counterfeit weights and measures, the costermongers call by the appropriate name of 'slang'. 'There are not half so many slangs as there was eighteen months ago,' said a 'general dealer' to me. 'You see, sir, the letters in the *Morning Chronicle* set people a-talking, and some altered their way of business. Some was very angry at what was said in the articles on the street-sellers, and swore that costers was gentlemen, and that they'd smash the men's noses that had told you, sir, if they knew who they were. There's plenty of costers wouldn't use slangs at all, if people would give a fair price; but you see the boys will try it on for their bunts, and how is a man to sell fine cherries at 4*d*. a pound that cost him 3½*d*., when there's a kid alongside of him a-selling his "tol" at 2*d*. a pound, and singing it out as bold as brass? So the men slangs it, and cries "2*d*. a pound", and gives half-pound, as the boy does; which brings it to the same thing. We doesn't 'dulterate our goods like the tradesmen – that is, the regular hands doesn't. It wouldn't be easy, as you say, to 'dulterate cabbages or oysters; but we deals fair to all that's fair to us – and that's more than many a tradesman does, for all their juries.'

The slang quart is a pint and a half. It is made precisely like the proper quart; and the maker, I was told, 'knows well enough what it's for, as it's charged, new, 6*d*. more than a true quart measure; but it's nothing to him, as he says, what it's for, so long as he gets his price.' The slang quart is let out at 2*d*. a day – 1*d*. extra being charged 'for the risk'. The slang pint holds in some cases three-fourths of the just quantity, having a very thick bottom; others hold only half a pint, having a false bottom half-way up. These are used chiefly in measuring nuts, of which the proper quantity is hardly ever given to the purchaser; 'but then,' it was often said, or implied to me, the 'price is all the lower, and people just brings it on themselves, by wanting things for next to nothing; so it's all right; it's people's own faults.' The hire of the slang pint is 2*d*. per day.

The scales used are almost all true, but the weights are often beaten out flat to look large, and are 4, 5, 6, or even 7 oz. deficient in a pound, and in the same relative proportion with other weights. The charge is 2*d*., 3*d*., and 4*d*. a day for a pair of scales and a set of slang weights.

The wooden measures – such as pecks, half pecks, and quarter pecks – are not let out slang, but the bottoms are taken out by the costers, and put in again half an inch or so higher up. 'I call this,' said a humorous dealer to me, 'slop-work, or the cutting-system.'

One candid costermonger expressed his perfect contempt of slangs, as fit only for bunglers, as he could always 'work slang' with a true measure. 'Why, I can cheat any man,' he said. 'I can manage to measure mussels so as you'd think you got a lot over, but there's a lot under measure, for I holds them up with my fingers and keep crying, "Mussels! full measure, live mussels!" I can do the same with peas. I delight to do it with stingy aristocrats. We don't work slang in the City. People know what they're a buying on there. There's plenty of us would pay for an inspector of weights; I would. We might do fair without an inspector, and make as much if we only agreed one with another.'

Of the boys of the costermongers, and their bunts
[*volume i. pp.33,34*]
But there are still other 'agents' among the costermongers, and these are the 'boys' deputed to sell a man's goods for a certain sum, all over that amount being the boys' profit or 'bunts'. Almost every costermonger who trades through the streets with his barrow is accompanied by a boy. The ages of these lads vary from ten to sixteen, there are few above sixteen, for the lads think it is then high time for them to start on their own account. These boys are useful to the man in 'calling', their shrill voices being often more audible than the loudest pitch of an adult's lungs. Many persons, moreover, I am assured, prefer buying of a boy, believing that if the lad did not succeed in selling his goods he would be knocked about when he got home; others think that they are safer in a boy's hands, and less likely to be cheated; these, however, are equally mistaken notions. The boys also are useful in pushing at the barrow, or in drawing it along by tugging at a rope in front. Some of them are the sons of the costermongers; some go round to the costermongers' abodes and say: 'Will you want me tomorrow?' 'Shall I come and give you a lift?' The parents of the lads thus at large are, when they have parents, either unable to support them, or, if able, prefer putting their money to other uses (such as drinking); and so the lads have

to look out for themselves, or, as they say, 'pick up a few half-pence and a bit of grub as we can.' Such lads, however, are the smallest class of costermongering youths; and are sometimes called 'cas'alty boys', or 'nippers'.

The boys – and nearly the whole of them – soon become very quick, and grow masters of slang, in from six weeks to two or three months. 'I suppose,' said one man familiar with their character, 'they'd learn French as soon, if they was thrown into the way of it. They must learn slang to live, and as they have to wait at markets every now and then, from one hour to six, they associate one with another and carry on conversations in slang about the 'penny gaffs' (theatres), criticising the actors; or may be they toss the pieman, if they've got any ha'pence, or else they chaff the passers by. The older ones may talk about their sweethearts; but they always speak of them by the name of "nammow" (girls).

'The boys are severe critics too' (continued my informant) 'on dancing. I heard one say to another; "What do you think of Johnny Millicent's new step?" for they always recognise a new step, or they discuss the female dancer's legs, and not very decently. At other times the boys discuss the merits or demerits of their masters, as to who feeds them best. I have heard one say, "Oh, ain't Bob stingy? We have bread and cheese!" Another added; "*We* have steak and beer, and I've the use of Bill's [the master's] "baccy box".'

Some of these lads are paid by the day, generally from 2*d*. or 3*d*. and their food, and as much fruit as they think fit to eat, as by that they soon get sick of it. They generally carry home fruit in their pockets for their playmates, or brothers, or sisters; the coster-mongers allow this, if they are satisfied that the pocketing is not for sale. Some lads are engaged by the week, having from 1*s*. to 1*s*. 6*d*., and their food when out with their employer. Their lodging is found only in a few cases, and then they sleep in the same room with their master and mistress. Of master or mistress, however, they never speak, but of Jack and Bet. They behave respectfully to the women, who are generally kind to them. They soon desert a very surly or stingy master; though such a fellow could get fifty boys next day if he wanted them, but not lads used to the trade, for to these he's well known by their talk one with another, and they soon tell a man his character very plainly – 'very plainly indeed, sir, and to his face too,' said one.

Some of these boys are well beaten by their employers; this they put up with readily enough, if they experience kindness at the hands of the man's wife; for, as I said before, parties that have never thought of marriage, if they live together, call one another husbands and wives.

In 'working the country' these lads are put on the same footing as their masters, with whom they eat, drink, and sleep [. . .]

Education of the 'coster-lads'
[*volume i. pp.35,36*]
Among the costers the term education is (as I have already intimated) merely understood as meaning a complete knowledge of the art of 'buying in the cheapest market and selling in the dearest'. There are few lads whose training extends beyond this. The father is the tutor, who takes the boy to the different markets, instructs him in the art of buying, and when the youth is perfect on this point, the parent's duty is supposed to have been performed. Nearly all these boys are remarkable for their precocious sharpness. To use the words of one of the class, 'these young ones are as sharp as terriers, and learns every dodge of business in less than half no time. There's one I knows about three feet high, that's up to the business as clever as a man of thirty. Though he's only twelve years old he'll chaff down a peeler so uncommon severe, that the only way to stop him is to take him in charge!'

It is idle to imagine that these lads, possessed of a mental acuteness almost wonderful, will not educate themselves in vice, if we neglect to train them to virtue. At their youthful age, the power of acquiring knowledge is the strongest, and some kind of education is continually going on. If they are not taught by others, they will form their own characters – developing habits of dissipation, and educing all the grossest passions of their natures, and learning to indulge in the gratification of every appetite without the least restraint.

As soon as a boy is old enough to shout well and loudly, his father takes him into the streets. Some of these youths are not above seven years of age, and it is calculated that not more than one in a hundred has ever been to a school of any kind. The boy walks with the barrow, or guides the donkey, shouting by turns with the father, who, when the goods are sold, will as a reward, let him ride home on the tray. The lad attends all markets with his father, who teaches him his business and shows him his tricks of trade; 'for,' said a coster, 'a governor in our line leaves the knowledge of all his dodges to his son, jist as the rich coves do their tin.'

The life of a coster-boy is a very hard one. In summer he will have to be up by four o'clock in the morning, and in winter he is never in bed after six. When he has returned from market, it is generally his duty to wash the goods and help dress the barrow. About nine he begins his day's work, shouting whilst the father pushes; and as very often the man has lost his voice, this share of the labour is left entirely to him. When a coster has regular customers, the vegetables or fish are all sold by twelve o'clock, and in many coster families the lad is then packed off with fruit to hawk in the streets. When the work is over, the father will perhaps take the boy to a public-house with him, and give him part of his beer. Sometimes a child of four or five is taken to the tap-room, especially if he be pretty and the father proud of him. 'I have seen,' said a coster to me, 'a baby of five year old reeling drunk in a tap-room. His governor did it for the lark of the thing, to see him chuck hisself about – sillyfied like.'

The love of gambling soon seizes upon the coster boy. Youths of about twelve or so will as soon as they can get away from work go to a public-house and play cribbage for pints of beer, or for a pint a corner. They generally continue playing till about midnight, and rarely – except on a Sunday – keep it up all night.

It ordinarily happens that when a lad is about thirteen, he quarrels with his father, and gets turned away from home. Then he is forced to start for himself. He knows where he can borrow stock-money and get his barrow, for he is as well acquainted with the markets as the oldest hand at the business, and children may often be seen in the streets under-selling their parents. 'How's it possible,' said a woman, 'for people to live when there's their own son at the end of the court a-calling his goods as cheap again as we can afford to sell ourn.'

If the boy is lucky in trade, his next want is to get a girl to keep home for him. I was assured, that it is not at all uncommon for a lad of fifteen to be living with a girl of the same age, as man and wife. It creates no disgust among his class, but seems rather to give him a position among such people. Their courtship does not take long when once the mate has been fixed upon. The girl is invited to 'raffles', and treated to 'twopenny hops', and half-pints of beer. Perhaps a silk neck handkerchief – a 'King's-man' is given as a present; though some of the lads will, when the arrangement has been made, take the gift back again and wear it themselves. The boys are very jealous, and if once made angry behave with great brutality to the offending girl. A young fellow of about sixteen told me, as he seemed to grow angry at the very thought, 'If I seed my gal a-talking to another chap I'd fetch her sich a punch of the nose as should plaguy quick stop the whole business.' Another lad informed me, with a knowing look, 'that the gals – it was a rum thing now he come to think on it – axully liked a feller for walloping them. As long as the bruises hurted, she was always thinking on the cove as gived 'em her.' After a time, if the girl continues faithful, the young coster may marry her; but this is rarely the case, and many live with their girls until they have grown to be men, or perhaps they may quarrel the very first year, and have a fight and part.

These boys hate any continuous work. So strong is this objection to continuity that they cannot even remain selling the same article for more than a week together. Moreover none of them can be got to keep stalls. They must be perpetually on the move – or to use their own words 'they like a roving life'. They all of them delight in dressing 'flash' as they call it. If a 'governor' was to try and 'palm off' his old cord jacket upon the lad that worked with him, the boy wouldn't take it. 'It's too big and seedy for me,' he'd say, 'and I ain't going to have your leavings.' They try to dress like the men, with large pockets in their cord jackets and plenty of them. Their trowsers too must fit tight at the knee, and their boots they like as good as possible. A good 'King's-man', a plush skull cap, and a seam down the trowsers are the great points of ambition with the coster-boys.

The life of a coster-lad
[*volume i. pp.39,40*]

One lad that I spoke to gave me as much of his history as he could remember. He was a tall stout boy, about sixteen years old, with a face utterly vacant. His two heavy lead-coloured eyes stared unmeaningly at me, and, beyond a constant anxiety to keep his front lock curled on his cheek, he did not exhibit the slightest trace of feeling. He sank into his seat heavily and of a heap, and when once settled down he remained motionless, with his mouth open and his hands on his knees – almost as if paralysed. He was dressed in all the slang beauty of his class, with a bright red handkerchief and unexceptionable boots.

'My father,' he told me in a thick unimpassioned voice, 'was a waggoner, and worked the country roads. There was two on us at home with mother, and we used to play along with the boys of our court, in Golding-lane, at buttons and marbles. I recollects nothing more than this – only the big boys used to cheat like bricks and thump us if we grumbled – that's all I recollects of my infancy, as you calls it. Father I've heard tell died when I was three and brother only a year old. It was worse luck for us! – Mother was so easy with us. I once went to school for a couple of weeks, but the cove used to fetch me a wipe over the knuckles with his stick, and as I wasn't going to stand that there, why you see I ain't no great schollard. We did as we liked with mother, she was so precious easy, and I never learned anything but playing buttons and making leaden "bonces", that's all,' [here the youth laughed slightly] 'Mother used to be up and out very early washing in families – anything for a living. She was a good mother to us. We was left at home with the key of the room and some bread and butter for dinner. Afore she got into work – and it was a goodish long time – we was shocking hard up, and she pawned nigh everything. Sometimes, when we had'nt no grub at all, the other lads, perhaps, would give us some of their bread and butter, but often our stomachs used to ache with the hunger, and we would cry when we was werry far gone. She used to be at work from six in the morning till ten o'clock at night, which was a long time for a child's belly to hold out again, and when it was dark we would go and lie down on the bed and try and sleep until she came home with the food. I was eight year old then.

'A man as know'd mother, said to her, "Your boy's got nothing to do, let him come along with me and yarn a few ha'pence," and so I became a coster. He gave me 4d. a morning and my breakfast. I worked with him about three year, until I learnt the markets, and then I and brother got baskets of our own, and used to keep mother. One day with another, the two on us together could make 2s. 6d. by selling greens of a morning, and going round to the publics with nuts of a evening, till about ten o'clock at night. Mother used to have a bit of fried meat or a stew ready for us when we got home, and by using up the stock as we couldn't sell, we used to manage pretty tidy. When I was fourteen I took up with a girl. She lived in the same house as we did, and I used to walk out of a night with her and give her half-pints of beer at the publics. She were about thirteen, and used to dress werry nice, though she weren't above middling pretty. Now I'm working for another man as gives me a shilling a week, victuals, washing, and lodging, just as if I was one of the family.

'On a Sunday I goes out selling, and all I yarns I keeps. As for going to church, why, I can't afford it – besides, to tell the truth, I don't like it well enough. Plays, too, ain't in my line much; I'd sooner go to a dance – it's more livelier. The "penny gaffs" is rather more in my style; the songs are out and out, and makes our gals laugh. The smuttier the better, I thinks; bless you! the gals likes it as much as we do. If we lads ever has a quarrel, why, we fights for it. If I was to let a cove off once, he'd do it again; but I never give a lad a chance, so long as I can get anigh him. I never heard about Christianity, but if a cove was to fetch me a lick of the head, I'd give it him again, whether he was a big 'un or a little 'un. I'd precious soon see a henemy of mine shot afore I'd forgive him – where's the use? Do I understand what behaving to your neighbour is? – In coorse I do. If a feller as lives next me wanted a basket of mine as I wasn't using, why, he might have it; if I was working it though, I'd see him further! I can understand that all as lives in a court is neighbours; but as for policemen, they're nothing to me, and I should like to pay 'em all off well. No; I never heerd about this here creation you speaks about. In coorse God Almighty made the world, and the poor bricklayers' labourers built the houses arterwards – that's my opinion; but I can't say, for I've never been in no schools, only always hard at work, and knows nothing about it. I have heerd a little about our Saviour, – they seem to say he were a goodish kind of a man; but if he says as how a cove's to forgive a feller as hits you, I should say he know'd nothing about it. In coorse the gals the lads goes and lives with thinks our walloping 'em werry cruel of us, but we don't. Why don't we? – why, because we don't. Before father died, I used sometimes to say my prayers, but after that mother was too busy getting a living to mind about my praying. Yes, I knows! – in the Lord's prayer they says, "Forgive us our trespasses, as we forgives them as trespasses agin us." It's a very good thing, in coorse, but no costers can't do it.'

Of the 'penny gaff'
[*volume i. pp.40–42*]

In many of the thoroughfares of London there are shops which have been turned into a kind of temporary theatre (admission one penny), where dancing and singing take place every night. Rude pictures of the performers are arranged outside, to give the front a gaudy and attractive look, and at night-time coloured lamps and transparencies are displayed to draw an audience. These places are called by the costers 'penny gaffs'; and on a Monday night as many as six performances will take place, each one having its two hundred visitors.

It is impossible to contemplate the ignorance and immorality of so numerous a class as that of the costermongers, without wishing to discover the cause of their degradation. Let anyone curious on this point visit one of these penny shows, and he will wonder that any trace of virtue and honesty should remain among the people. Here the stage, instead of being the means for illustrating a moral precept, is turned into a platform to teach the cruellest debauchery. The audience is usually composed of children so young, that these dens become the school-rooms where the guiding morals of a life are picked up; and so precocious are the little things, that the girl of nine will, from constant attendance at such places, have learnt to understand the filthiest sayings, and laugh at them as loudly as the grown-up lads around her. What notions can the young female form of marriage and chastity, when the penny theatre rings with applause at the performance of a scene whose sole point turns upon the pantomimic imitation of the unrestrained indulgence of the most corrupt appetites of our nature? How can the lad learn to check his hot passions and think honesty and virtue admirable, when the shouts around him impart a glory to a descriptive song so painfully corrupt, that it can only have been made tolerable by the most habitual excess? The men who preside over these infamous places know too well the failings of their audiences. They know that these poor children require no nicely-turned joke to make the evening pass merrily, and that the filth they utter needs no double meaning to veil its obscenity. The show that will provide the most unrestrained debauchery will have the most crowded benches; and to gain this point, things are acted and spoken that it is criminal even to allude to.

Not wishing to believe in the description which some of the more intelligent of the costermongers had given of these places, it was thought better to visit one of them, so that all exaggeration might be avoided. One of the least offensive of the exhibitions was fixed upon.

The 'penny gaff' chosen was situated in a broad street near Smithfield; and for a great distance off, the jingling sound of music was heard, and the gas-light streamed out into the thick night air as from a dark lantern, glittering on the windows of the houses opposite, and lighting up the faces of the mob in the road, as on an illumination night. The front of a large shop had been entirely removed, and the entrance was decorated with paintings of the 'comic singers', in their most 'humourous' attitudes. On a table against the wall was perched the band, playing what the costers call 'dancing tunes' with great effect, for the hole at the money-taker's box was blocked up with hands tendering the penny. The crowd without was so numerous, that a policeman was in attendance to preserve order, and push the boys off the pavement – the music having the effect of drawing them insensibly towards the festooned green-baize curtain.

The shop itself had been turned into a waiting-room, and was crowded even to the top of the stairs leading to the gallery on the first floor. The ceiling of this 'lobby' was painted blue, and spotted with whitewash clouds, to represent the heavens; the boards of the trap-door, and the laths that showed through the holes in the plaster, being all of the same colour. A notice was here posted, over the canvas door leading into the theatre, to the effect that 'LADIES AND GENTLEMEN TO THE FRONT PLACES MUST PAY TWOPENCE.'

The visitors, with a few exceptions, were all boys and girls, whose ages seemed to vary from eight to twenty years. Some of the girls – though their figures showed them to be mere children – were dressed in showy cotton-velvet polkas, and wore dowdy feathers in their crushed bonnets. They stood laughing and joking with the lads, in an unconcerned, impudent manner, that was almost appalling. Some of them, when tired of waiting, chose their partners, and commenced dancing grotesquely, to the admiration of the lookers-on, who expressed their approbation in obscene terms, that, far from disgusting the poor little women, were received as compliments, and acknowledged with smiles and coarse repartees. The boys clustered together, smoking their pipes, and laughing at each other's anecdotes, or else jingling halfpence in time with the tune, while they whistled an accompaniment to it. Presently one of the performers, with a gilt crown on his well-greased locks, descended from the staircase, his fleshings covered by a dingy dressing-gown, and mixed with the mob, shaking hands with old acquaintances. The 'comic singer', too, made his appearance among the throng – the huge bow to his cravat, which nearly covered his waistcoat, and the red end to his nose, exciting neither merriment nor surprise.

To discover the kind of entertainment, a lad near me and my companion was asked 'if there was any flash dancing'. With a knowing wink the boy answered, 'Lots! show their legs and all, prime!' and immediately the boy followed up his information by a request for a 'yennep' to get a 'tib of occabot'. After waiting in the lobby some considerable time, the performance inside was concluded, and the audience came pouring out through the canvas door. As they had to pass singly, I noticed them particularly. Above three-fourths of them were women and girls, the rest consisting chiefly of mere boys – for out of about two hundred persons I counted only eighteen men. Forward they came, bringing an overpowering stench with them, laughing and yelling as they pushed their way through the waiting-room. One woman carrying a sickly child with a bulging forehead, was reeling drunk, the saliva running down her mouth as she stared about her with a heavy fixed eye. Two boys were pushing her from side to side, while the poor infant slept, breathing heavily, as if stupefied, through the din. Lads jumping on girls' shoulders, and girls laughing hysterically from being tickled by the youths behind them, everyone shouting and jumping, presented a mad scene of frightful enjoyment.

When these had left, a rush for places by those in waiting began, that set at defiance the blows and strugglings of a lady in spangles who endeavoured to preserve order and take the checks. As time

was a great object with the proprietor, the entertainment within
began directly the first seat was taken, so that the lads without,
rendered furious by the rattling of the piano within, made the
canvas partition bulge in and out, with the strugglings of those
seeking admission, like a sail in a flagging wind.

To form the theatre, the first floor had been removed; the
whitewashed beams however still stretched from wall to wall. The
lower room had evidently been the warehouse, while the upper
apartment had been the sitting-room, for the paper was still on the
walls. A gallery, with a canvas front, had been hurriedly built up,
and it was so fragile that the boards bent under the weight of
those above. The bricks in the warehouse were smeared over with
red paint, and had a few black curtains daubed upon them. The
coster-youths require no very great scenic embellishment, and
indeed the stage – which was about eight feet square – could
admit of none. Two jets of gas, like those outside a butcher's shop,
were placed on each side of the proscenium, and proved very
handy for the gentlemen whose pipes required lighting. The band
inside the 'theatre' could not compare with the band without. An
old grand piano, whose canvas-covered top extended the entire
length of the stage, sent forth its wiry notes under the be-ringed
fingers of a 'professor Wilkinsini', while another professional, with
his head resting on his violin, played vigorously, as he stared
unconcernedly at the noisy audience.

Singing and dancing formed the whole of the hour's performance, and, of the two, the singing was preferred. A young girl, of
about fourteen years of age, danced with more energy than grace,
and seemed to be well-known to the spectators, who cheered her
on by her Christian name. When the dance was concluded, the
proprietor of the establishment threw down a penny from the
gallery, in the hopes that others might be moved to similar acts of
generosity; but no-one followed up the offering, so the young lady
hunted after the money and departed. The 'comic singer', in a
battered hat and the huge bow to his cravat, was received with
deafening shouts. Several songs were named by the costers, but the
'funny gentleman' merely requested them 'to hold their jaws', and
putting on a 'knowing' look, sang a song, the whole point of
which consisted in the mere utterance of some filthy word at the
end of each stanza. Nothing, however, could have been more

successful. The lads stamped their feet with delight; the girls screamed with enjoyment. Once or twice a young shrill laugh would anticipate the fun – as if the words were well known – or the boys would forestall the point by shouting it out before the proper time. When the song was ended the house was in a delirium of applause. The canvas front to the gallery was beaten with sticks, drum-like, and sent down showers of white powder on the heads in the pit. Another song followed, and the actor knowing on what his success depended, lost no opportunity of increasing his laurels. The most obscene thoughts, the most disgusting scenes were coolly described, making a poor child near me wipe away the tears that rolled down her eyes with the enjoyment of the poison. There were three or four of these songs sung in the course of the evening, each one being encored, and then changed. One written about 'Pine-apple rock', was the grand treat of the night, and offered greater scope to the rhyming powers of the author than any of the others. In this, not a single chance had been missed; ingenuity had been exerted to its utmost lest an obscene thought should be passed by, and it was absolutely awful to behold the relish with which the young ones jumped to the hideous meaning of the verses.

There was one scene yet to come, that was perfect in its wickedness. A ballet began between a man dressed up as a woman, and a country clown. The most disgusting attitudes were struck, the most immoral acts represented, without one dissenting voice. If there had been any feat of agility, any grimacing, or, in fact, anything with which the laughter of the uneducated classes is usually associated, the applause might have been accounted for; but here were two ruffians degrading themselves each time they stirred a limb, and forcing into the brains of the childish audience before them thoughts that must embitter a lifetime, and descend from father to child like some bodily infirmity.

When I had left, I spoke to a better class costermonger on this saddening subject. 'Well, sir, it is frightful,' he said, 'but the boys will have their amusements. If their amusements is bad they don't care; they only wants to laugh, and this here kind of work does it. Give 'em better singing and better dancing, and they'd go, if the price was as cheap as this is. I've seen, when a decent concert was given at a penny, as many as four thousand costers present, behaving themselves as quietly and decently as possible. Their wives and children was with 'em, and no audience was better conducted. It's all stuff talking about them preferring this sort of thing. Give 'em good things at the same price, and I know they will like the good, better than the bad.'

My own experience with this neglected class goes to prove, that if we would really lift them out of the moral mire in which they are wallowing, the first step must be to provide them with wholesome amusements. The misfortune, however, is, that when we seek to elevate the character of the people, we give them such mere dry abstract truths and dogmas to digest, that the uneducated mind turns with abhorrence from them. We forget how we ourselves were originally won by our emotions to the consideration of such subjects. We do not remember how our own tastes have been formed, nor do we, in our zeal, stay to reflect how the tastes of a people generally are created; and, consequently, we cannot perceive that a habit of enjoying any matter whatsoever can only be induced in the mind by linking with it some æsthetic affection. The heart is the mainspring of the intellect, and the feelings the real educers and educators of the thoughts. As games with the young destroy the fatigue of muscular exercise, so do the sympathies stir the mind to action without any sense of effort. It is because 'serious' people generally object to enlist the emotions in the education of the poor, and look upon the delight which arises in the mind from the mere perception of the beauty of sound, motion, form, and colour – or from the apt association of harmonious or incongruous ideas – or from the sympathetic operation of the affections; it is because, I say, the zealous portion of society look upon these matters as 'vanity', that the amusements of the working-classes are left to venal traders to provide. Hence, in the low-priced entertainments which necessarily appeal to the poorer, and, therefore, to the least educated of the people, the proprietors, instead of trying to develop in them the purer sources of delight, seek only to gratify their audience in the coarsest manner, by appealing to their most brutal appetites. And thus the emotions, which the great Architect of the human mind gave us as the means of quickening our imaginations and refining our sentiments, are made the instruments of crushing every operation of the intellect and debasing our natures. It is idle and unfeeling to believe that the great majority of a people whose days are passed in excessive toil, and whose homes are mostly of an uninviting character, will forego all amusements, and consent to pass their evenings by their own firesides, reading tracts or singing hymns. It is folly to fancy that the mind, spent with the irksomeness of compelled labour, and depressed, perhaps, with the struggle to live by that labour after all, will not, when the work is over, seek out some place where at least it can forget its troubles or fatigues in the temporary pleasure begotten by some mental or physical stimulant. It is because we exact too much of the poor – because we, as it were, strive to make true knowledge and true beauty as forbidding as possible to the uneducated and unrefined, that they fly to their penny gaffs, their twopenny-hops, their beer-shops, and their gambling grounds for pleasures which we deny them, and which we, in our arrogance, believe it is possible for them to do without.

The experiment so successfully tried at Liverpool of furnishing music of an enlivening and yet elevating character at the same price as the concerts of the lowest grade, shows that the people may be won to delight in beauty instead of bestiality, and teaches us again that it is our fault to allow them to be as they are and not theirs to remain so. All men are compound animals, with many inlets of pleasure to their brains, and if one avenue be closed against them, why it but forces them to seek delight through another. So far from the perception of beauty inducing habits of gross enjoyment as 'serious' people generally imagine, a moment's reflection will tell us that these very habits are only the necessary consequences of the non-development of the æsthetic faculty; for the two assuredly cannot co-exist. To cultivate the sense of the beautiful is necessarily to inculcate a detestation of the sensual. Moreover, it is impossible for the mind to be accustomed to the contemplation of what is admirable without continually mounting to higher and higher forms of it – from the beauty of nature to that of thought – from thought to feeling, from feeling to action, and lastly to the fountain of all goodness – the great munificent Creator of the sea, the mountains, and the flowers – the stars, the sunshine, and the rainbow – the fancy, the reason, the love and the heroism of man and womankind – the instincts of the beasts – the glory of the angels – and the mercy of Christ.

Of the coster-girls

[*volume i. pp.43–45*]

The costermongers, taken as a body, entertain the most imperfect idea of the sanctity of marriage. To their undeveloped minds it merely consists in the fact of a man and woman living together, and sharing the gains they may each earn by selling in the street. The father and mother of the girl look upon it as a convenient means of shifting the support of their child over to another's exertions; and so thoroughly do they believe this to be the end and aim of matrimony, that the expense of a church ceremony is considered as a useless waste of money, and the new pair are received by their companions as cordially as if every form of law and religion had been complied with.

The notions of morality among these people agree strangely, as I have said, with those of many savage tribes – indeed, it would be curious if it were otherwise. They are a part of the nomads of England, neither knowing nor caring for the enjoyments of home. The hearth, which is so sacred a symbol to all civilised races as being the spot where the virtues of each succeeding generation are taught and encouraged, has no charms to them. The tap-room is the father's chief abiding place; whilst to the mother the house is only a better kind of *tent*. She is away at the stall, or hawking her goods from morning till night, while the children are left to play away the day in the court or alley, and pick their morals out of the gutter. So long as the limbs gain strength the parent cares for nothing else. As the young ones grow up, their only notions of wrong are formed by what the policeman will permit them to do. If we, who have known from babyhood the kindly influences of a home, require, before we are thrust out into the world to get a living for ourselves, that our perceptions of good and evil should be quickened and brightened (the same as our perceptions of truth and falsity) by the experience and counsel of those who are wiser and better than ourselves – if, indeed, it needed a special creation and example to teach the best and strongest of us the law of right, how bitterly must the children of the street-folk require tuition, training, and advice, when from their very cradles (if, indeed, they ever knew such luxuries) they are doomed to witness in their parents, whom they naturally believe to be their superiors, habits of life in which passion is the sole rule of action, and where

THE COSTER-GIRL

'Apples! An 'aypenny a lot, apples!'

[from a daguerrotype by Beard]

every appetite of our animal nature is indulged in without the least restraint.

I say thus much because I am anxious to make others feel, as I do myself, that we are the culpable parties in these matters. That they poor things should do as they do is but human nature – but that we should allow them to remain thus destitute of every blessing vouchsafed to ourselves – that we should willingly share what we enjoy with our brethren at the Antipodes, and yet leave those who are nearer and who, therefore, should be dearer to us, to want even the commonest moral necessaries is a paradox that gives to the zeal of our Christianity a strong savour of the chicanery of Cant.

The costermongers strongly resemble the North American Indians in their conduct to their wives. They can understand that it is the duty of the woman to contribute to the happiness of the man, but cannot feel that there is a reciprocal duty from the man to the woman. The wife is considered as an inexpensive servant, and the disobedience of a wish is punished with blows. She must work early and late, and to the husband must be given the proceeds of her labour. Often when the man is in one of his drunken fits – which sometimes last two or three days continuously – she must by her sole exertions find food for herself and him too. To live in peace with him, there must be no murmuring, no tiring under work, no fancied cause for jealousy – for if there be, she is either beaten into submission or cast adrift to begin life again – as another's leavings.

The story of one coster girl's life may be taken as a type of the many. When quite young she is placed out to nurse with some neighbour, the mother – if a fond one – visiting the child at certain periods of the day, for the purpose of feeding it, or sometimes, knowing the round she has to make, having the infant brought to her at certain places, to be 'suckled'. As soon as it is old enough to go alone, the court is its play-ground, the gutter its school-room, and under the care of an elder sister the little one passes the day, among children whose mothers like her own are too busy out in the streets helping to get the food, to be able to mind the family at home. When the girl is strong enough, she in her turn is made to assist the mother by keeping guard over the younger children, or, if there be none, she is lent out to carry about a baby, and so made to add to the family income by gaining her sixpence weekly. Her time is from the earliest years fully occupied; indeed, her parents cannot afford to keep her without doing and getting *something*. Very few of the children receive the least education. 'The parents,' I am told, 'never give their minds to learning, for they say, "What's the use of it? That won't yarn a gal a living." ' Everything is sacrificed – as, indeed, under the circumstances it must be – in the struggle to live – aye! and to live *merely*. Mind, heart, soul, are all absorbed in the belly. The rudest form of animal life, physiologists tell us, is simply a locomotive stomach. Verily, it would appear as if our social state had a tendency to make the highest animal sink into the lowest.

At about seven years of age the girls first go into the streets to sell. A shallow basket is given to them, with about two shillings for stock-money, and they hawk, according to the time of year, either oranges, apples, or violets; some begin their street education with the sale of water-cresses. The money earned by this means is strictly given to the parents. Sometimes – though rarely – a girl who has been unfortunate during the day will not dare to return home at night, and then she will sleep under some dry arch or about some market, until the morrow's gains shall ensure her a safe reception and shelter in her father's room.

The life of the coster-girls is as severe as that of the boys. Between four and five in the morning they have to leave home for the markets, and sell in the streets until about nine. Those that have more kindly parents, return then to breakfast, but many are obliged to earn the morning's meal for themselves. After breakfast, they generally remain in the streets until about ten o'clock at night; many having nothing during all that time but one meal of bread and butter and coffee, to enable them to support the fatigue of walking from street to street with the heavy basket on their heads. In the course of a day, some girls eat as much as a pound of bread, and very seldom get any meat, unless it be on a Sunday.

There are many poor families that, without the aid of these girls, would be forced into the workhouse. They are generally of an affectionate disposition, and some will perform acts of marvellous heroism to keep together the little home. It is not at all unusual for mere children of fifteen to walk their eight or ten miles a day, carrying a basket of nearly two hundred weight on their heads. A journey to Woolwich and back, or to the towns near London, is often undertaken to earn the 1s. 6d. their parents are anxiously waiting for at home.

Very few of these girls are married to the men they afterwards live with. Their courtship is usually a very short one; for, as one told me, 'the life is such a hard one, that a girl is ready to get rid of a *little* of the labour at any price.' The coster-lads see the girls at market, and if one of them be pretty, and a boy take a fancy to her, he will make her bargains for her, and carry her basket home. Sometimes a coster working his rounds will feel a liking for a wench selling her goods in the street, and will leave his barrow to go and talk with her. A girl seldom takes up with a lad before she is sixteen, though some of them, when barely fifteen or even fourteen, will pair off. They court for a time, going to raffles and 'gaffs' together, and then the affair is arranged. The girl tells her parents 'she's going to keep company with so-and-so,' packs up what things she has, and goes at once, without a word of remonstrance from either father or mother. A furnished room, at about 4s. a week, is taken, and the young couple begin life. The lad goes out as usual with his barrow, and the girl goes out with her basket, often working harder for her lover than she had done for her parents. They go to market together, and at about nine o'clock her day's selling begins. Very often she will take out with her in the morning what food she requires during the day, and never return home until eleven o'clock at night.

The men generally behave very cruelly to the girls they live with. They are as faithful to them as if they were married, but they are jealous in the extreme. To see a man talking to their girl is sufficient to ensure the poor thing a beating. They sometimes ill-treat them horribly – most unmercifully indeed – nevertheless the girls say they cannot help loving them still, and continue working for them, as if they experienced only kindness at their hands. Some of the men are gentler and more considerate in their treatment of them, but by far the larger portion are harsh and merciless. Often when the Saturday night's earnings of the two have been large, the man will take the entire money, and as soon as the Sunday's dinner is over, commence drinking hard, and continue drunk for two or three days together, until the funds are entirely exhausted. The women never gamble; they say, 'it gives them no excitement.' They prefer, if they have a spare moment in the evening, sitting near the fire making up and patching their clothes. 'Ah, sir,' said a girl to me, 'a neat gown does a deal with a man; he always likes a girl best when everybody else likes her too.' On a Sunday they clean their room for the week and go for a treat, if they can persuade their young man to take them out in the afternoon, either to Chalk Farm or Battersea Fields – 'where there's plenty of life.' [. . .]

As a type of the more prudent class of coster-girls, I would cite the following narrative received from the lips of a young woman in answer to a series of questions.

The life of a coster-girl
[*volume i. pp.45,46*]
[. . .]
The one I fixed upon was a fine-grown young woman of eighteen. She had a habit of curtseying to every question that was put to her. Her plaid shawl was tied over the breast, and her cotton-velvet bonnet was crushed in with carrying her basket. She seemed dreadfully puzzled where to put her hands, at one time tucking them under her shawl, warming them at the fire, or measuring the length of her apron, and when she answered a question she invariably addressed the fireplace. Her voice was husky from shouting apples.

'My mother has been in the streets selling all her lifetime. Her uncle learnt her the markets and she learnt me. When business grew bad she said to me, "Now you shall take care on the stall, and I'll go and work out charing." The way she learnt me the markets was to judge of the weight of the baskets of apples, and then said she, "Always bate 'em down, a'most a half." I always liked the street-life very well, that was if I was selling. I have mostly kept a stall myself, but I've known gals as walk about with apples, as have told me that the weight of the baskets is sich that the neck cricks, and when the load is took off, it's just as if you'd a stiff neck, and the head feels as light as a feather. The gals begins working very early at our work; the parents makes them go out when a'most babies. There's a little gal, I'm sure she an't more than half-past seven, that stands selling water-cresses next my stall, and mother was saying, "Only look there, how that little one has to get her living afore she a'most knows what a penn'orth means."

'There's six on us in family, and father and mother makes eight. Father used to do odd jobs with the gas-pipes in the streets, and when work was slack we had very hard times of it. Mother always liked being with us at home, and used to manage to keep us employed out of mischief – she'd give us an old gown to make into pinafores for the children and such like! She's been very good to us, has mother, and so's father. She always liked to hear us read to her whilst she was washing or such like! and then we big ones had to learn the little ones. But when father's work got slack, if she had no employment charing, she'd say, "Now I'll go and buy a bushel of apples," and then she'd turn out and get a penny that way. I suppose by sitting at the stall from nine in the morning till the shops shuts up – say ten o'clock at night, I can earn about 1s. 6d. a day. It's all according to the apples – whether they're good or not – what we makes. If I'm unlucky, mother will say, "Well, I'll go out tomorrow and see what I can do;" and if I've done well, she'll say, "Come you're a good hand at it; you've done famous." Yes, mother's very fair that way. Ah! there's many a gal I knows whose back has to suffer if she don't sell her stock well; but, thank God! I never get more than a blowing up. My parents is very fair to me.

'I dare say there ain't ten out of a hundred gals what's living with men, what's been married Church of England fashion. I know plenty myself, but I don't, indeed, think it right. It seems to me that the gals is fools to be 'ticed away, but, in coorse, they needn't go without they likes. This is why I don't think it's right. Perhaps a man will have a few words with his gal, and he'll say, "Oh! I ain't obligated to keep her!" and he'll turn her out: and then where's that poor gal to go? Now, there's a gal I knows as came to me no later than this here week, and she had a dreadful swole face and a awful black eye; and I says, "Who's done that?" and she says, says she, "Why, Jack" – just in that way; and then she says, says she, "I'm going to take a warrant out tomorrow." Well, he gets the warrant that same night, but she never appears again him, for fear of getting more beating. That don't seem to me to be like married people ought to be. Besides, if parties is married, they ought to bend to each other; and they won't, for sartain, if they're only living together. A man as is married is obligated to keep his wife if they quarrels or not; and he says to himself, says he, "Well, I may as well live happy, like." But if he can turn a poor gal off, as soon as he tires of her, he begins to have noises with her, and then gets quit of her altogether. Again, the men takes the money of the gals, and in coorse ought to treat 'em well – which they don't. This is another reason: when the gal is in the family way, the lads mostly sends them to the workhouse to lay in, and only goes sometimes to take them a bit of tea and shuggar; but, in coorse, married men wouldn't behave in such likes to their poor wives. After a quarrel, too, a lad goes and takes up with another young gal, and that isn't pleasant for the first one. The first step to ruin is them places of "penny gaffs", for they hears things there as oughtn't to be said to young gals. Besides, the lads is very insinivating, and after leaving them places will give a gal a drop of beer, and make her half tipsy, and then they makes their arrangements. I've often heerd the boys boasting of having ruined gals, for all the world as if they was the first noblemen in the land.

'It would be a good thing if these sort of goings on could be stopped. It's half the parents' fault; for if a gal can't get a living, they turns her out into the streets, and then what's to become of her? I'm sure the gals, if they was married, would be happier, because they couldn't be beat worse. And if they was married, they'd get a nice home about 'em; whereas, if they's only living together, they takes a furnished room. I'm sure, too, that it's a bad plan; for I've heerd the gals themselves say, "Ah! I wish I'd never seed Jack" (or Tom, or whatever it is); "I'm sure I'd never be half so bad but for him."

'Only last night father was talking about religion. We often talks about religion. Father has told me that God made the world, and I've heerd him talk about the first man and woman as was made and lived – it must be more than a hundred years ago – but I don't like to speak on what I don't know. Father, too, has told me about our Saviour what was nailed on a cross to suffer for such poor people as we is. Father has told us, too, about his giving a great many poor people a penny loaf and a bit of fish each, which proves him to have been a very kind gentleman. The Ten Commandments was made by him, I've heerd say, and he performed them too among other miracles. Yes! this is part of what our Saviour tells us. We are to forgive everybody, and do nobody no injury. I don't think I could forgive an enemy if she injured me very much; I'm sure I don't know why I couldn't, unless it is that I'm poor, and never learnt to do it. If a gal stole my shawl and didn't return it back or give me the value on it, I couldn't forgive her; but if she told me she lost it off her back, I shouldn't be so hard on her. We poor gals ain't very religious, but we are better than the men. We all of us thanks God for everything – even for a fine day; as for sprats, we always says they're God's blessing for the poor, and thinks it hard of the Lord Mayor not to let 'em come in afore the ninth of November, just because he wants to dine off them – which he always do. Yes, we knows for certain that they eats plenty of sprats at the Lord Mayor's "blanket". They say in the Bible that the world was made in six days: the beasts, the birds, the fish, and all – and sprats was among them in coorse. There was only one house at that time as was made, and that was the Ark for Adam and Eve and their family. It seems very wonderful indeed how all this world was done so quick. I should have thought that England alone would have took double the time; shouldn't you, sir? But then it says in the Bible, God Almighty's a just and true God, and in coorse time would be nothing to him. When a good person is dying, we says, "The Lord has called upon him, and he must go," but I can't think what it means, unless it is that an angel comes – like when we're a-dreaming – and tells the party he's wanted in heaven. I know where heaven is; it's above the clouds, and they're placed there to prevent us seeing into it. That's where all the good people go, but I'm afeerd' – she continued solemnly – 'there's very few costers among the angels – 'specially those as deceives poor gals.

'No, I don't think this world could well go on for ever. There's a great deal of ground in it, certainly, and it seems very strong at present; but they say there's to be a flood on the earth, and earthquakes, and that will destroy it. The earthquake ought to have took place some time ago, as people tells me, but I never heerd any more about it. If we cheats in the streets, I know we shan't go to Heaven; but it's very hard upon us, for if we didn't cheat we couldn't live, profits is so bad. It's the same with the shops, and I suppose the young men there won't go to Heaven neither; but if people won't give the money, both costers and tradesmen must cheat, and that's very hard. Why, look at apples! customers want them for less than they cost us, and so we are forced to shove in bad ones as well as good ones; and if we're to suffer for that, it does seem to me dreadful cruel.'

Curious and extravagant as this statement may perhaps appear to the uninitiated, nevertheless it is here given as it was spoken; and it was spoken with an earnestness that proved the poor girl looked upon it as a subject, the solemnity of which forced her to be truthful.

Of the homes of the costermongers
[*volume i. pp.47,48*]

The costermongers usually reside in the courts and alleys in the neighbourhood of the different street-markets. They themselves designate the locality where, so to speak, a colony of their people has been established, a 'coster district', and the entire metropolis is thus parcelled out, almost as systematically as if for the purposes of registration. These costermonger districts are as follows, and are here placed in the order of the numerical importance of the residents:

The New-cut (Lambeth)	Ratcliffe-highway
Whitecross-street	Lisson-grove
Leather-lane	Petticoat- and Rosemary-lane
The Brill, Somers' Town	Marylebone-lane
Whitechapel	Oxford-street
Camberwell	Rotherhithe
Walworth	Deptford
Peckham	Dockhead
Bermondsey	Greenwich
The Broadway, Westminster	Commercial-road (East)
Shoreditch	Poplar
Paddington and Edgeware-road	Limehouse
Tottenham-court-road	Bethnal-green
Drury-lane	Hackney-road
Old-street-road	Kingsland
Clare-market	Camden Town

The homes of the costermongers in these places may be divided into three classes; firstly, those who, by having a regular trade or by prudent economy, are enabled to live in comparative ease and plenty; secondly, those who, from having a large family or by imprudent expenditure, are, as it were, struggling with the world; and thirdly, those who for want of stock-money, or ill success in trade are nearly destitute.

The first home I visited was that of an old woman, who with the assistance of her son and girls, contrived to live in a most praise-worthy and comfortable manner. She and all her family were teetotallers, and may be taken as a fair type of the thriving costermonger.

As I ascended a dark flight of stairs, a savoury smell of stew grew stronger at each step I mounted. The woman lived in a large airy room on the first floor ('the drawing-room' as she told me laughing at her own joke), well lighted by a clean window, and I found her laying out the savoury-smelling dinner looking most temptingly clean. The floor was as white as if it had been newly planed, the coke fire was bright and warm, making the lid of the tin saucepan on it rattle up and down as the steam rushed out. The wall over the fire-place was patched up to the ceiling with little square pictures of saints, and on the mantel-piece, between a row of bright tumblers and wine glasses filled with odds and ends, stood glazed crockeryware images of Prince Albert and M. Jullien. Against the walls, which were papered with 'hangings' of four different patterns and colours, were hung several warm shawls, and in the band-box, which stood on the stained chest of drawers, you could tell that the Sunday bonnet was stowed safely away from the dust. A turn-up bedstead thrown back, and covered with a many-coloured patch-work quilt, stood opposite to a long dresser with its mugs and cups dangling from the hooks, and the clean blue plates and dishes ranged in order at the back. There were a few bushel baskets piled up in one corner, 'but the apples smelt so,' she said, 'they left them in a stable at night.'

By the fire sat the woman's daughter, a pretty meek-faced grey-eyed girl of sixteen, who 'was home nursing for a cold'. 'Steve' [her boy] I was informed, was out working. With his help, the woman assured me, she could live very comfortably – 'God be praised!' and when he got the barrow he was promised, she gave me to understand, that their riches were to increase past reckoning. Her girl too was to be off at work as soon as sprats came in. 'It's on Lord Mayor's-day they comes in,' said a neighbour who had rushed up to see the strange gentleman, 'they says he has 'em on his table, but I never seed 'em. They never gives us the pieces, no not even the heads,' and everyone laughed to their utmost. The good old dame was in high spirits, her dark eyes sparkling as she spoke about her 'Steve'. The daughter in a little time lost her bashfulness, and informed me 'that one of the Polish refugees was a-courting Mrs M— , who had given him a pair of black eyes.'

On taking my leave I was told by the mother that their silver gilt Dutch clock – with its glass face and blackleaded weights – 'was the best one in London, and might be relied on with the greatest safety.'

As a specimen of the dwellings of the struggling costers, the following may be cited:

The man, a tall, thick-built, almost good-looking fellow, with a large fur cap on his head, lived with his family in a front kitchen, and as there were, with his mother-in-law, five persons, and only one bed, I was somewhat puzzled to know where they could *all* sleep. The barrow standing on the railings over the window, half shut out the light, and when anyone passed there was a momentary shadow thrown over the room, and a loud rattling of the iron gratings above that completely prevented all conversation. When I entered, the mother-in-law was reading aloud one of the threepenny papers to her son, who lolled on the bed, that with its curtains nearly filled the room. There was the usual attempt to make the fireside comfortable. The stone sides had been well whitened, and the mantelpiece decorated with its small tin trays, tumblers, and a piece of looking-glass. A cat with a kitten were seated on the hearth-rug in front. 'They keeps the varmint away,' said the woman, stroking the 'puss', 'and gives a look of home.' By the drawers were piled up four bushel baskets, and in a dark corner near the bed stood a tall measure full of apples that scented the room. Over the head, on a string that stretched from wall to wall, dangled a couple of newly-washed shirts, and by the window were two stone barrels, for lemonade, when the coster visited the fairs and races.

Whilst we were talking, the man's little girl came home. For a poor man's child she was dressed to perfection; her pinafore was clean, her face shone with soap, and her tidy cotton print gown had clearly been newly put on that morning. She brought news that 'Janey' was coming home from auntey's, and instantly a pink cotton dress was placed by the mother-in-law before the fire to air. (It appeared that Janey was out at service, and came home once a week to see her parents and take back a clean frock.) Although these people were living, so to speak, in a cellar, still every endeavour had been made to give the home a look of comfort. The window, with its paper-patched panes, had a clean calico blind. The side-table was dressed up with yellow jugs and cups and saucers, and the band-boxes had been stowed away on the flat top of the bedstead. All the chairs, which were old fashioned mahogany ones, had sound backs and bottoms.

Of the third class, or the very poor, I chose the following 'type' out of the many others that presented themselves. The family here lived in a small slanting-roofed house, partly stripped of its tiles. More than one half of the small leaden squares of the first-floor window were covered with brown paper, puffing out and crackling in the wind, while through the greater part of the others were thrust out ball-shaped bundles of rags, to keep out the breeze. The panes that did remain were of all shapes and sizes, and at a distance had the appearance of yellow glass, they were so stained with dirt. I opened a door with a number chalked on it, and groped my way up a broken tottering staircase.

It took me some time after I had entered the apartment before I could get accustomed to the smoke that came pouring into the room from the chimney. The place was filled with it, curling in the light, and making everything so indistinct that I could with difficulty see the white mugs ranged in the corner-cupboard, not three yards from me. When the wind was in the north, or when it rained, it was always that way, I was told, 'but otherwise,' said an old dame about sixty, with long grisly hair spreading over her black shawl, 'it is pretty good for that.'

On a mattress, on the floor, lay a pale-faced girl – 'eighteen years old last twelfth-cake day' – her drawn-up form showing in the patch-work counterpane that covered her. She had just been confined, and the child had died! A little straw, stuffed into an old tick, was all she had to lie upon, and even that had been given up to her by the mother until she was well enough to work again. To shield her from the light of the window, a cloak had been fastened up slantingly across the panes; and on a string that ran along the wall was tied, amongst the bonnets, a clean nightcap – 'against the doctor came,' as the mother, curtseying, informed me. By the side of the bed, almost hidden in the dark shade, was a pile of sieve baskets, crowned by the flat shallow that the mother 'worked' with.

The room was about nine feet square, and furnished a home for three women. The ceiling slanted like that of a garret, and was the colour of old leather, excepting a few rough white patches, where the tenants had rudely mended it. The white light was easily seen through the laths, and in one corner a large patch of the paper looped down from the wall. One night the family had been startled from their sleep by a large mass of mortar – just where the roof bulged in – falling into the room. 'We never want rain water,' the woman told me, 'for we can catch plenty just over the chimney-place.'

They had made a carpet out of three or four old mats. They were 'obligated to it, for fear of dropping anything through the boards into the donkey stables in the parlour underneath. But we only pay ninepence a week rent,' said the old woman, 'and mustn't grumble.'

The only ornament in the place was on the mantel-piece – an old earthenware sugar-basin, well silvered over, that had been given by the eldest girl when she died, as a remembrance to her mother. Two cracked tea-cups, on their inverted saucers, stood on each side, and dressed up the fire-side into something like tidiness. The chair I sat on was by far the best out of the three in the room, and that had no back, and only half its quantity of straw.

The parish, the old woman told me, allowed her 1s. a week and two loaves. But the doctor ordered her girl to take sago and milk, and she was many a time sorely puzzled to get it. The neighbours helped her a good deal, and often sent her part of their unsold greens; – even if it was only the outer leaves of the cabbages, she was thankful for them. Her other girl – a big-boned wench, with a red shawl crossed over her bosom, and her black hair parted on one side – did all she could, and so they lived on. 'As long as they kept out of the "big house" [the workhouse] she would not complain.'

I never yet beheld so much destitution borne with so much content. Verily the acted philosophy of the poor is a thing to make those who write and preach about it hide their heads.

Of the dress of the costermongers
[*volume i. pp.51,52*]
[. . .]

The costermonger's ordinary costume partakes of the durability of the warehouseman's, with the quaintness of that of the stable-boy. A well-to-do 'coster', when dressed for the day's work, usually wears a small cloth cap, a little on one side. A close-fitting worsted tie-up skull-cap is very fashionable, just now, among the class, and ringlets at the temples are looked up to as the height of elegance. Hats they never wear – excepting on Sunday – on account of their baskets being frequently carried on their heads. Coats are seldom indulged in; their waistcoats, which are of a broad-ribbed cord-uroy, with fustian back and sleeves, being made as long as a groom's, and buttoned up nearly to the throat. If the corduroy be of a light sandy colour, then plain brass, or sporting buttons, with raised fox's or stag's heads upon them – or else black bone-buttons, with a flower-pattern – ornament the front; but if the cord be of a dark rat-skin hue, then mother-of-pearl buttons are preferred. Two large pockets – sometimes four – with huge flaps or lapels, like those in a shooting-coat, are commonly worn. If the costermonger be driving a good trade and have his set of regular customers, he will sport a blue cloth jacket, similar in cut to the cord ones above described; but this is looked upon as an extravagance of the highest order, for the slime and scales of the fish stick to the sleeves and shoulders of the garment, so as to spoil the appearance of it in a short time. The fashionable stuff for trousers, at the present, is a dark-coloured 'cable cord', and they are made to fit tightly at the knee and swell gradually until they reach the boot, which they nearly cover. Velveteen is now seldom worn, and knee-breeches are quite out of date. Those who deal wholly in fish wear a blue serge apron, either hanging down or tucked up round their waist. The costermonger, however, prides himself most of all upon his neckerchief and boots. Men, women, boys and girls, all have a passion for these articles. The man who does not wear his silk neckerchief – his 'King's-man' as it is called – is known to be in desperate circumstances; the inference being that it has gone to supply the morning's stock-money. A yellow flower on a green ground, or a red and blue pattern, is at present greatly in vogue. The women wear their kerchiefs tucked-in under their gowns, and the men have theirs wrapped loosely round the neck, with the ends hanging over their waistcoats. Even if a costermonger has two or three silk handkerchiefs by him already, he seldom hesitates to buy another, when tempted with a bright showy pattern hanging from a Field-lane door-post.

The costermonger's love of a good strong boot is a singular prejudice that runs throughout the whole class. From the father to the youngest child, all will be found well shod. So strong is their predilection in this respect, that a costermonger may be immediately known by a glance at his feet. He will part with everything rather than his boots, and to wear a pair of second-hand ones, or 'translators' (as they are called), is felt as a bitter degradation by them all. Among the men, this pride has risen to such a pitch, that many will have their upper-leathers tastily ornamented, and it is not uncommon to see the younger men of this class with a heart or a thistle, surrounded by a wreath of roses, worked below the instep, on their boots. The general costume of the women or girls is a black velveteen or straw bonnet, with a few ribbons or flowers, and almost always a net cap fitting closely to the cheek. The silk 'King's-man' covering their shoulders, is sometimes tucked into the neck of the printed cotton-gown, and sometimes the ends are brought down outside to the apron-strings. Silk dresses are never worn by them – they rather despise such articles. The petticoats are worn short, ending at the ankles, just high enough to show the whole of the much-admired boots. Coloured, or 'illustrated', shirts, as they are called, are especially objected to by the men.

On the Sunday no costermonger will, if he can possibly avoid it, wheel a barrow. If a shilling be an especial object to him, he may, perhaps, take his shallow and head-basket as far as Chalk-farm, or some neighbouring resort; but even then he objects strongly to the Sunday-trading. They leave this to the Jews and Irish, who are always willing to earn a penny – as they say.

The prosperous coster *will* have his holiday on the Sunday, and, if possible, his Sunday suit as well – which usually consists of a rough beaver hat, brown Petersham, with velvet facings of the same colour, and cloth trousers, with stripes down the side. The women, generally, manage to keep by them a cotton gown of a bright showy pattern, and a new shawl. As one of the craft said to me – 'Costers likes to see their gals and wives look lady-like when they takes them out.' Such of the costers as are not in a flourishing way of business, seldom make any alteration in their dress on the Sunday.

There are but five tailors in London who make the garb proper to costermongers; one of these is considered somewhat 'slop', or as a coster called him, a 'springer-up'.

This springer-up is blamed by some of the costermongers, who condemn him for employing women at reduced wages. A whole court of costermongers, I was assured, would withdraw their custom from a tradesman, if one of their body, who had influence among them, showed that the tradesman was unjust to his work-people. The tailor in question issues bills after the following fashion. I give one verbatim, merely withholding the address for obvious reasons:

ONCE TRY YOU'LL COME AGAIN
Slap-up Tog and out-and-out Kicksies Builder

Mr — nabs the chance of putting his customers awake, that he has just made his escape from Russia, not forgetting to clap his mawleys upon some of the right sort of Ducks, to make single and double backed Slops for gentlemen in black, when on his return home he was stunned to find one of the top manufacturers of Manchester had cut his lucky and stepped off to the Swan Stream, leaving behind him a valuable stock of Moleskins, Cords, Velveteens, Plushes, Swandowns, &c., and I having some ready in my kick, grabbed the chance, and stepped home with my swag, and am now safe landed at my crib. I can turn out toggery of every description very slap up, at the following low prices for

Ready Gilt – Tick being no go

Upper Benjamins, built on a downey plan, a monarch to half a finnuff. Slap up Velveteen Togs, lined with the same, 1 pound 1 quarter and a peg. Moleskin ditto, any colour, lined with the same, 1 couter. A pair of Kerseymere Kicksies, any colour, built very slap up, with the artful dodge, a canary. Pair of stout Cord ditto, built in the 'Melton Mowbray' style, half a sov. Pair of very good broad Cord ditto, made very saucy, 9 bob and a kick. Pair of long sleeve Moleskin, all colours, built hanky-spanky, with a double fakement down the side and artful buttons at bottom, half a monarch. Pair of stout ditto, built very serious, 9 times. Pair of out-and-out fancy sleeve Kicksies, cut to drop down on the trotters, 2 bulls. Waist Togs, cut long, with moleskin back and sleeves, 10 peg. Blue Cloth ditto, cut slap, with pearl buttons, 14 peg. Mud Pipes, Knee Caps, and Trotter Cases, built very low.

A decent allowance made to Seedy Swells, Tea Kettle Purgers, Head Robbers, and Flunkeys out of Collar.

N.B. Gentlemen finding their own Broady can be accommodated.

Of the diet and drink of costermongers
[*volume i. p.52*]

It is less easy to describe the diet of costermongers than it is to describe that of many other of the labouring classes, for their diet, so to speak, is an 'out-door diet'. They breakfast at a coffee-stall, and (if all their means have been expended in purchasing their stock, and none of it be yet sold) they expend on the meal only 1*d*., reserved for the purpose. For this sum they can procure a small cup of coffee, and two 'thin' (that is to say two thin slices of bread and butter). For dinner – which on a week-day is hardly ever eaten at the costermonger's abode – they buy 'block ornaments', as they call the small, dark-coloured pieces of meat exposed on the cheap butchers' blocks or counters. These they cook in a tap-room; half a pound costing 2*d*. If time be an object, the coster buys a hot pie or two; preferring fruit-pies when in season, and next to them meat-pies. 'We never eat eel-pies,' said one man to me, 'because we know they're often made of large dead eels. *We*, of all people, are not to be had that way. But the haristocrats eats 'em and never knows the difference.' I did not hear that these men had any repugnance to meat-pies; but the use of the dead eel happens to come within the immediate knowledge of the costermongers, who are, indeed, its purveyors. Saveloys, with a pint of beer, or a glass of 'short' (neat gin) is with them another common week-day dinner. The costers make all possible purchases of street-dealers, and pride themselves in thus 'sticking to their own'. On Sunday, the costermonger, when not 'cracked up', enjoys a good dinner at his own abode. This is always a joint – most frequently a shoulder or half-shoulder of mutton – and invariably with 'lots of good taturs baked along with it'. In the quality of their potatoes these people are generally particular.

The costermonger's usual beverage is beer, and many of them drink hard, having no other way of spending their leisure but in drinking and gambling. It is not unusual in 'a good time', for a costermonger to spend 12s. out of every 20s. in beer and pleasure.

I ought to add, that the 'single fellows', instead of living on 'block ornaments' and the like, live, when doing well, on the best fare, at the 'spiciest' cook-shops on their rounds, or in the neighbourhood of their residence.

There are some families of costermongers who have persevered in carrying out the principles of teetotalism. One man thought there might be 200 individuals, including men, women, and children, who practised total abstinence from intoxicating drinks. These parties are nearly all somewhat better off than their drinking companions. The number of teetotallers amongst the costers, however, was more numerous three or four years back.

Of the earnings of costermongers
[*volume i. pp.54,55*]
The earnings of the costermonger – the next subject of inquiry that, in due order, presents itself – vary as much as in more fashionable callings, for he is greatly dependent on the season, though he may be little affected by London being full or empty.

Concurrent testimony supplied me with the following estimate of their earnings. I cite the average earnings (apart from any charges or drawbacks), of the most staple commodities:

In January and February the costers generally sell fish. In these months the wealthier of the street fishmongers, or those who can always command 'money to go to market', enjoy a kind of monopoly. The wintry season renders the supply of fish dearer and less regular, so that the poorer dealers cannot buy 'at first hand', and sometimes cannot be supplied at all; while the others monopolise the fish, more or less; and will not sell it to any of the other street-dealers until a profit has been realised out of their own regular customers, and the demand partially satisfied. 'Why, I've known one man sell 10l. worth of fish – most of it mackerel – at his stall in Whitecross-street,' said a costermonger to me, 'and all in one snowy day, in last January. It was very stormy at that time, and fish came in unregular, and he got a haul. I've known him sell 2l. worth in an hour, and once 2l. 10s. worth, for I then helped at his stall. If people has dinner parties they must have fish, and gentlemen's servants came to buy. The *average* earnings however of those that 'go rounds' in these months are computed not to exceed 8s. a week; Monday and Saturday being days of little trade in fish.

'March is dreadful,' said an itinerant fish seller to me; 'we don't average, I'm satisfied, more nor 4s. a week. I've had my barrow idle for a week sometimes – at home every day, though it had to be paid for, all the same. At the latter end of March, if it's fine, it's 1s. a week better, because there's flower roots in – "all a-growing", you know, sir. And that lasts until April, and we then make above 6s. a week. I've heard people say when I've cried "all a-growing" on a fine-ish day, "Aye, now summer's a-coming." I wish you may get it, says I to myself; for I've studied the seasons.'

In May the costermonger's profit is greater. He vends fresh fish – of which there is a greater supply and a greater demand, and the fine and often not very hot weather ensures its freshness – and he sells dried herrings and 'roots' (as they are called) such as wall-flowers and stocks. The average earnings then are from 10s. to 12s. a week.

In June, new potatoes, peas, and beans tempt the costermongers' customers, and then his earnings rise to 1l. a week. In addition to this 1l., if the season allow, a costermonger at the end of the week, I was told by an experienced hand, 'will earn an extra 10s. if he has anything of a round.' 'Why, I've cleared thirty shillings myself,' he added, 'on a Saturday night.'

In July cherries are the principal article of traffic, and then the profit varies from 4s. to 8s. a day, weather permitting, or 30s. a week on a low average. On my inquiry if they did not sell fish in that month, the answer was, 'No, sir; we pitch fish to the — ; we stick to cherries, strawberries, raspberries, and ripe currants and gooseberries. Potatoes is getting good and cheap then, and so is peas. Many a round's worth a crown every day of the week.'

In August, the chief trading is in Orleans plums, green-gages, apples and pears, and in this month the earnings are from 5s. to 6s. a day. (I may here remark that the costermongers care little to deal in either vegetables or fish, 'when the fruit's in', but they usually carry a certain supply of vegetables all the year round, for those customers who require them.)

In September apples are vended, and about 2s. 6d. a day made.

In October 'the weather gets cold,' I was told, 'and the apples gets fewer, and the day's work's over at four; we then deals most in fish, such as soles; there's a good bit done in oysters, and we may make 1s. or 1s. 6d. a day, but it's uncertain.'

In November fish and vegetables are the chief commodities, and then from 1s. to 1s. 6d. a day is made; but in the latter part of the month an extra 6d. or 1s. a day may be cleared, as sprats come in and sell well when newly introduced.

In December the trade is still principally in fish, and 12d. or 18d. a day is the costermonger's earnings. Towards the close of the month he makes rather more, as he deals in new oranges and lemons, holly, ivy, &c., and in Christmas week he makes 3s. or 4s. a day.

These calculations give an average of about 14s. 6d. a week, when a man pursues his trade regularly. One man calculated it for me at 15s. average the year through – that is supposing, of course, that the larger earnings of the summer are carefully put by to eke out the winter's income. This, I need hardly say, is never done. Prudence is a virtue which is comparatively unknown to the London costermongers. They have no knowledge of savings-banks; and to expect that they themselves should keep their money by them untouched for months (even if they had the means of so doing) is simply to expect impossibilities – to look for the continued withstanding of temptation among a class who are unused to the least moral or prudential restraint.

Some costers, I am told, make upwards of 30s. a week all the year round; but allowing for cessations in the street-trade, through bad weather, neglect, ill-health, or casualty of any kind, and taking the more prosperous costers with the less successful – the English with the Irish – the men with the women – perhaps 10s. a week may be a fair average of the earnings of the entire body the year through.

These earnings, I am assured, were five years ago at least 25 per cent higher; some said they made half as much again: 'I can't make it out how it is,' said one man, 'but I remember that I could go out and sell twelve bushel of fruit in a day, when sugar was dear, and now, when sugar's cheap, I can't sell three bushel on the same round. Perhaps we want thinning.'

Such is the state of the working-classes, say all the costers, they have little or no money to spend. 'Why, I can assure you,' declared one of the parties from whom I obtained much important inform-ation, 'there's my missis – she sits at the corner of the street with fruit. Eight years ago she would have taken 8s. out of that street on a Saturday, and last Saturday week she had one bushel of apples, which cost 1s. 6d. She was out from ten in the morning till ten at night, and all she took that day was 1s. 7½ d. Go to whoever you will, you will hear much upon the same thing.' Another told me, 'The costers are often obliged to sell the things for what they gave for them. The people haven't got money to lay out with them – they tell us so; and if they are poor we must be poor too. If we can't get a profit upon what goods we buy with our stock-money, let it be our own or anybody's else, we are compelled to live upon it, and when that's broken into, we must either go to the work-house or starve. If we go to the workhouse, they'll give us a piece of dry bread, and abuse us worse than dogs.' Indeed, the whole course of my narratives shows how the costers generally – though far from universally – complain of the depressed state of their trade. The following statement was given to me by a man who, for twelve years, had been a stall-keeper in a street-market. It shows to what causes he (and I found others express similar opinions) attributes the depression:

'I never knew things so bad as at present – never! I had six prime cod-fish, weighing 15lbs. to 20lbs. each, yesterday and the day before, and had to take two home with me last night, and lost money on the others – besides all my time, and trouble, and expense. I had 100 herrings, too, that cost 3s. – prime quality, and I only sold ten out of them in a whole day. I had two pads of soles, sir, and lost 4s. – that is one pad – by them. I took only 4s. the first day I laid in this stock, and only 2s. 6d. the next; I then had to sell for anything I could get, and throw some away. Yet, people say mine's a lazy, easy life. I think the fall off is owing to meat being so cheap, 'cause people buy that rather than my goods, as they think there's more stay in it. I'm afeard things will get worse too.' (He then added by way of *sequitur*, though it is difficult to follow the reasoning,) 'If this here is free trade, then to h— with it, I say!'

Of the capital and income of the costermongers
[*volume i. p.56*]
[. . .]
Concerning the income of the entire body of costermongers in the metropolis, I estimate the earnings of the 10,000 costermongers, taking the average of the year, at 10s. weekly. My own observation, the result of my inquiries, confirmed by the opinion of some of the most intelligent of the costermongers, induce me to adopt this amount. It must be remembered, that if some costermongers do make 30s. a week through the year, others will not earn a fourth of it, and hence many of the complaints and sufferings of the class. Then there is the drawback in the sum paid for 'hire', 'interest', &c., by numbers of these people; so that it appears to me, that if we assume the income of the entire body – including Irish and English – to be 15s. a week per head in the summer, and 5s. a week each in the winter, as the two extremes, or a mean of 10s. a week all the year through, we shall not be far out either way. The aggregate earnings of the London costermongers, at this rate, are 5,000l. per week, or 260,000l. yearly. Reckoning that 30,000 individuals have to be supported out of this sum, it gives an average of 3s. 4d. a week per head. [. . .]

Of the providence and improvidence of costermongers
[*volume i. pp.56,57*]
The costermongers, like all wandering tribes, have generally no foresight; only an exceptional few are provident – and these are mostly the more intelligent of the class – though some of the very ignorant do occasionally save. The providence of the more intelligent costermonger enables him in some few cases to become 'a settled man', as I have before pointed out. He perhaps gets to be the proprietor of a coal-shed, with a greengrocery and potato business attached to it; and with the usual trade in oysters and ginger-beer. He may too, sometimes, have a sum of money in the savings-bank, or he may invest it in the purchase of a lease of the premises he occupies, or expend it in furnishing the rooms of his house to let them out to single-men lodgers; or he may become an usurer, and lend out his money to his less provident brethren at 1040l. per cent. per annum; or he may purchase largely at the markets, and engage youths to sell his surplus stock at half profits.

The provident costermonger, who has thus 'got on in the world', is rarely speculative. He can hardly be induced to become a member of a 'building' or 'freehold land' society, for instance. He has been accustomed to an almost *immediate* return for his outlays, and distrusts any remote or contingent profit. A regular costermonger – or anyone who has been a regular costermonger, in whatever trade he may be afterwards engaged – generally dies intestate, let his property be what it may; but there is seldom any dispute as to the disposition of his effects: the widow takes possession of them, as a matter of course. If there be grown-up children, they may be estranged from home, and not trouble their heads about the matter; or, if not estranged, an amicable arrangement is usually come to. The costermongers' dread of all courts of law, or of anything connected with the law, is only second to their hatred of the police.

The more ignorant costermonger, on the other hand, if he be of a saving turn, and have no great passion for strong drink or gaming, is often afraid to resort to the simple modes of investment which I have mentioned. He will rather keep money in his pocket; for, though it does not fructify there, at least it is safe. But this is only when provided with a donkey or pony 'what suits'; when not so provided, he will 'suit himself' forthwith. If, however, he have saved a little money, and have a craving after gambling or amusements, he is sure at last to squander it that way. Such a man, without any craving for drink or gaming, will often continue to pay usuriously for the hire of his barrow, not suspecting that he is purchasing it over and over and over again, in his weekly payments. To suggest to him that he might place his money in a bank, is to satisfy him that he would be 'had' in some way or other, as he believes all banks and public institutions to be connected with government, and the taxes, and the police. Were anyone to advise a man of this class – and it must be remembered that I am speaking of the *ignorant* costers – to invest a spare 50*l*. (supposing he possessed it) in the 'three per cents', it would but provoke a snappish remark that he knew nothing about them, and would have nothing to do with them; for he would be satisfied that there was 'some cheatery at the bottom'. If he could be made to understand what is meant by 3*l*. per centum per annum, he would be sure to be indignant at the robbery of giving only 7½*d*. for the use of 1*l*. for a whole year!

I may state, in conclusion, that a costermonger of the class I have been describing, mostly objects to give change for a five-pound note; he will sooner give credit – when he knows 'the party' – than change, even if he have it. If, however, he feels compelled, rather than offend a regular customer, to take the note, he will not rest until he has obtained sovereigns for it at a neighbouring innkeeper's, or from some tradesman to whom he is known. 'Sovereigns,' said one man, and not a very ignorant man, to me, 'is something to lay hold on; a note ain't.'

Moreover, should one of the more ignorant, having tastes for the beer-shop, &c., meet with 'a great haul', or save 5*l.* by some continuous industry (which he will most likely set down as 'luck'), he will spend it idly or recklessly in dissipation and amusement, regardless of the coming winter, whatever he may have suffered during the past. Nor, though they know, from the bitterest experience, that their earnings in the winter are not half those of the rest of the year, and that they are incapacitated from pursuing their trade in bad weather, do they endeavour to make the extra gains of their best time mitigate the want of the worst.

Of the costermongers in bad weather and during the cholera
[*volume i. pp.57,58*]

'Three wet days,' I was told by a clergyman, who is now engaged in selling stenographic cards in the streets, 'will bring the greater part of 30,000 street-people to the brink of starvation.' This statement, terrible as it is, is not exaggerated. The average number of wet days every year in London is, according to the records of the Royal Society, 161 – that is to say, rain falls in the metropolis more than three days in each week, and very nearly every other day throughout the year. How precarious a means of living then must street-selling be!

When a costermonger cannot pursue his outdoor labour, he leaves it to the women and children to 'work the public-houses', while he spends his time in the beer-shop. Here he gambles away his stock-money oft enough, 'if the cards or the luck runs agin him'; or else he has to dip into his stock-money to support himself and his family. He must then borrow fresh capital at any rate of interest to begin again, and he begins on a small scale. If it be in the cheap and busy seasons, he may buy a pad of soles for

2s. 6d., and clear 5s. on them, and that 'sets him a-going again, and then he gets his silk handkerchief out of pawn, and goes as usual to market.'

The sufferings of the costermongers during the prevalence of the cholera in 1849, were intense. Their customers generally relinquished the consumption of potatoes, greens, fruit, and fish; indeed, of almost every article on the consumption of which the costermongers depend for their daily bread. Many were driven to apply to the parish; 'many had relief and many hadn't,' I was told. Two young men, within the knowledge of one of my informants, became professional thieves, after enduring much destitution. It does not appear that the costermongers manifested any personal dread of the visitation of the cholera, or thought that their lives were imperilled: 'We weren't a bit afraid,' said one of them, 'and, perhaps, that was the reason so few costers died of the cholera. I knew them all in Lambeth, I think, and I knew only one die of it, and he drank hard. Poor Waxy! he was a good fellow enough, and was well known in the Cut. But it was a terrible time for us, sir. It seems to me now like a shocking dream. Fish I couldn't sell a bit of; the people had a perfect dread of it – all but the poor Irish, and there was no making a crust out of them. They had no dread of fish, however; indeed, they reckon it a religious sort of living, living on fish, – but they *will* have it dirt cheap. We were in terrible distress all that time.'

Of the costermongers' raffles
[*volume i. p.58*]
In their relief of the sick, if relief it is to be called, the costermongers resort to an exciting means; something is raffled, and the proceeds given to the sufferer. This mode is common to other working-classes; it partakes of the excitement of gambling, and is encouraged by the landlords of the houses to which the people resort. The landlord displays the terms of the raffle in his bar a few days before the occurrence, which is always in the evening. The raffle is not confined to the sick, but when anyone of the class is in distress – that is to say, without stock-money, and unable to borrow it – a raffle for some article of his is called at a public-house in the neighbourhood. Cards are printed, and distributed among his mates. The article, let it be whatever it may – perhaps

a handkerchief – is put up at 6*d*. a member, and from twenty to forty members are got, according as the man is liked by his 'mates', or as he has assisted others similarly situated. The paper of every raffle is kept by the party calling it, and before he puts his name down to a raffle for another party, he refers to the list of subscribers to his raffle, in order to see if the person ever assisted him. Raffles are very 'critical things, the pint pots fly about wonderful some-times' – to use the words of one of my informants. The party calling the raffle is expected to take the chair, if he can write down the subscribers' names. One who had been chairman at one of these meetings assured me that on a particular occasion, having called a 'general dealer' to order, the party very nearly split his head open with a quart measure. If the hucksters know that the person calling the raffle is 'down', and that it is necessity that has made him call it, they will not allow the property put up to be thrown for. 'If you was to go to the raffle tonight, sir,' said one of them to me, many months ago, before I became known to the class, 'they'd say to one another directly you come in, "Who's this here swell? What's he want?" And they'd think you were a "cad", or else a spy, come from the police. But they'd treat you civilly, I'm sure. Some very likely would fancy you was a fast kind of a gentleman, come there for a lark. But you need have no fear, though the pint pots *does* fly about sometimes.'

[. . .]

Of the tricks of costermongers
[*volume i. p.61*]
I shall now treat of the tricks of trade practised by the London costermongers. Of these the costers speak with as little reserve and as little shame as a fine gentleman of his peccadilloes. 'I've boiled lots of oranges,' chuckled one man, 'and sold them to Irish hawkers, as wasn't wide awake, for stunning big uns. The boiling swells the oranges and so makes 'em look finer ones, but it spoils them, for it takes out the juice. People can't find that out though until it's too late. I boiled the oranges only a few minutes, and three or four dozen at a time.' Oranges thus prepared will not keep, and any unfortunate Irishwoman, tricked as were my informant's customers, is astonished to find her stock of oranges turn

dark-coloured and worthless in forty-eight hours. The fruit is 'cooked' in this way for Saturday night and Sunday sale – times at which the demand is the briskest. Some prick the oranges and express the juice, which they sell to the British wine-makers.

Apples cannot be dealt with like oranges, but they are mixed. A cheap red-skinned fruit, known to costers as 'gawfs', is rubbed hard, to look bright and feel soft, and is mixed with apples of a superior description. 'Gawfs are sweet and sour at once,' I was told, 'and fit for nothing but mixing.' Some foreign apples, from Holland and Belgium, were bought very cheap last March, at no more than 16d. a bushel, and on a fine morning as many as fifty boys might be seen rubbing these apples, in Hooper-street, Lambeth. 'I've made a crown out of a bushel of 'em on a fine day,' said one sharp youth. The larger apples are rubbed sometimes with a piece of woollen cloth, or on the coat skirt, if that appendage form part of the dress of the person applying the friction, but most frequently they are rolled in the palms of the hand. The smaller apples are thrown to and fro in a sack, a lad holding each end. 'I wish I knew how the shopkeepers manage *their* fruit,' said one youth to me; 'I should like to be up to some of their moves; they do manages their things so plummy.'

Cherries are capital for mixing, I was assured by practical men. They purchase three sieves of indifferent Dutch, and one sieve of good English cherries, spread the English fruit over the inferior quality, and sell them as the best. Strawberry pottles are often half cabbage leaves, a few tempting strawberries being displayed on the top of the pottle. 'Topping up,' said a fruit dealer to me, 'is the principal thing, and we are perfectly justified in it. You ask any coster that knows the world, and he'll tell you that all the salesmen in the markets tops up. It's only making the best of it.' Filberts they bake to make them look brown and ripe. Prunes they boil to give them a plumper and finer appearance. The latter trick, however, is not unusual in the shops.

The more honest costermongers will throw away fish when it is unfit for consumption; less scrupulous dealers, however, only throw away what is utterly unsaleable; but none of them fling away the dead eels, though their prejudice against such dead fish prevents their indulging in eel-pies. The dead eels are mixed with the living, often in the proportion of 20 lb. dead to 5 lb. alive, equal quantities of each being accounted very fair dealing. 'And after all,' said a street fish dealer to me, 'I don't know why dead eels should be objected to; the aristocrats don't object to them. Nearly all fish is dead before it's cooked, and why not eels? Why not eat them when they're sweet, if they're ever so dead, just as you eat fresh herrings? I believe it's only among the poor and among our chaps, that there's this prejudice. Eels die quickly if they're exposed to the sun.'

Herrings are made to look fresh and bright by candle-light, by the lights being so disposed 'as to give them,' I was told, 'a good reflection. Why I can make them look splendid; quite a pictur. I can do the same with mackerel, but not so prime as herrings.'

There are many other tricks of a similar kind detailed in the course of my narrative. We should remember, however, that *shopkeepers* are not immaculate in this respect.

MINORITIES

Victorian London was a cosmopolitan city of great ethnic, religious and cultural diversity. There were German sugar bakers in Whitechapel, Italians in Saffron Hill, exile communities in Soho and lascar and black settlements in the riverside districts of the East End. The Jews of East London, the oldest non-Christian community and the most organised of immigrant minorities, attracted Mayhew's attention as did the larger and more diffuse Irish community. At the time of Mayhew's survey the Irish were considered a major influence upon the social problem. Forty years later the Jews arriving from Eastern Europe would occupy the same position. Blacks in Victorian London were as yet hardly noticed. Mayhew encountered them not through distinctive settlement patterns but as individuals engaged in street occupations. Their life histories, as recorded by him, may nevertheless be revealing of the situation of minorities in the Metropolis.

HINDOO TRACT SELLER

[from a daguerrotype by Beard]

MINORITIES

Of the street-Irish
[*volume i. pp.104–118*]

The Irish street-sellers are both a numerous and peculiar class of people. It therefore behoves me, for the due completeness of this work, to say a few words upon their numbers, earnings, condition, and mode of life.

The number of Irish street-sellers in the metropolis has increased greatly of late years. One gentleman, who had every means of being well-informed, considered that it was not too much to conclude, that, within these five years, the numbers of the poor Irish people who gain a scanty maintenance, or what is rather a substitute for a maintenance, by trading, or begging, or by carrying on the two avocations simultaneously in the streets of London, had been doubled in number.

I found among the English costermongers a general dislike of the Irish. In fact, next to a policeman, a genuine London coster-monger hates an Irishman, considering him an intruder. Whether there be any traditional or hereditary ill-feeling between them, originating from a clannish feeling, I cannot ascertain. The coster-mongers whom I questioned had no knowledge of the feelings or prejudices of their predecessors, but I am inclined to believe that the prejudice is modern, and has originated in the great influx of Irishmen and women, intermixing, more especially during the last five years, with the costermonger's business. [. . .]

Of the Irish street-sellers, at present, it is computed that there are, including men, women, and children, upwards of 10,000. Assuming the street-sellers attending the London fish and green markets to be, with their families, 30,000 in number, and 7 in every 20 of these to be Irish, we shall have rather more than the total above given. Of this large body three-fourths sell only fruit, and more especially nuts and oranges; indeed, the orange-season is called the 'Irishman's harvest'. The others deal in fish, fruit, and vegetables, but these are principally men. Some of the most wretched of the street-Irish deal in such trifles as lucifer-matches, water-cresses, &c.

I am informed that the great mass of these people have been connected, in some capacity or other, with the culture of the land in Ireland. The mechanics who have sought the metropolis from the sister kingdom have become mixed with their respective handicrafts in England, some of the Irish – though only a few – taking rank with the English skilled labourers. The greater part of the Irish artisans who have arrived within the last five years are to be found among the most degraded of the tailors and shoemakers who work at the East-end for the slop-masters.

A large class of the Irish who were agricultural labourers in their country are to be found among the men working for bricklayers, as well as among the dock-labourers and excavators, &c. Wood chopping is an occupation greatly resorted to by the Irish in London. Many of the Irish, however, who are not regularly employed in their respective callings, resort to the streets when they cannot obtain work otherwise.

The Irish women and girls who sell fruit, &c., in the streets, depend almost entirely on that mode of traffic for their subsistence. They are a class not sufficiently taught to avail themselves of the ordinary resources of women in the humbler walk of life. Unskilled at their needles, working for slop employers, even at the commonest shirt-making, is impossible to them. Their ignorance of household work, moreover (for such description of work is unknown in their wretched cabins in many parts of Ireland), incapacitates them in a great measure for such employments as 'charing', washing, and ironing, as well as from regular domestic employment. Thus there seems to remain to them but one thing to do – as, indeed, was said to me by one of themselves – viz., 'to sell for a ha'pinny the three apples which cost a farruthing.'

Very few of these women (nor, indeed, of the men, though rather more of them than the women) can read, and they are mostly all wretchedly poor; but the women present two characteristics which distinguish them from the London coster-women generally – they are chaste, and, unlike the 'coster girls', very seldom form any connection without the sanction of the marriage ceremony. They are, moreover, attentive to religious observances.

The majority of the Irish street-sellers of both sexes beg, and often very eloquently, as they carry on their trade; and I was further assured, that, but for this begging, some of them might starve outright.

The greater proportion of the Irish street-sellers are from Leinster and Munster, and a considerable number come from Connaught.

Of the causes which have made the Irish turn costermongers
[*volume i. pp.105,106*]

Notwithstanding the prejudices of the English costers, I am of opinion that the Irishmen and women who have become coster-mongers, belong to a better class than the Irish labourers. The Irishman may readily adapt himself, in a strange place, to labour, though not to trade; but these costers are – or the majority at least are – poor persevering traders enough.

The most intelligent and prosperous of the street-Irish are those who have 'risen' – for so I heard it expressed – 'into regular costers'. The untaught Irishman's capabilities, as I have before remarked, with all his powers of speech and quickness of appre-hension, are far less fitted for 'buying in the cheapest market and selling in the dearest' than for mere physical employment. Hence those who take to street-trading for a living seldom prosper in it, and three-fourths of the street-Irish confine their dealings to such articles as are easy of sale, like apples, nuts, or oranges, for they are rarely masters of purchasing to advantage, and seem to know little about tale or measure, beyond the most familiar quantities. Com-pared with an acute costermonger, the mere apple-seller is but as the labourer to the artisan.

One of the principal causes why the Irish costermongers have increased so extensively of late years, is to be found in the fact that the labouring classes (and of them chiefly the class employed in the culture of land), have been driven over from 'the sister Isle' more thickly for the last four or five years than formerly. Several circumstances have conspired to effect this. First, they were driven over by the famine, when they could not procure, or began to fear that soon they could not procure, food to eat. Secondly, they were forced to take refuge in this country by the evictions, when their landlords had left them no roof to shelter them in their own. (The shifts, the devices, the plans, to which numbers of these poor creatures had recourse, to raise the means of quitting Ireland for England – or for anywhere – will present a very remarkable chapter at some future period.) Thirdly, though the better class of small farmers who have emigrated from Ireland, in hopes of 'bettering themselves', have mostly sought the shores of North America, still some who have reached this country have at last settled into street-sellers. And, fourthly, many who have come over here only for the harvest have been either induced or compelled to stay.

Another main cause is, that the Irish, as labourers, can seldom obtain work all the year through, and thus the ranks of the Irish street-sellers are recruited every winter by the slackness of certain periodic trades in which they are largely employed – such as hodmen, dock-work, excavating, and the like. They are, therefore, driven by want of employment to the winter sale of oranges and nuts. These circumstances have a doubly malefic effect, as the increase of costers accrues in the winter months, and there are consequently the most sellers when there are the fewest buyers.

Moreover, the cessation of work in the construction of railways, compared with the abundance of employment which attracted so many to this country during the railway mania, has been another fertile cause of there being so many Irish in the London streets.

The prevalence of Irish women and children among street-sellers is easily accounted for – they are, as I said before, unable to do anything else to eke out the means of their husbands or parents. A needle is as useless in their fingers as a pen.

Bitterly as many of these people suffer in this country, grievous and often eloquent as are their statements, I met with *none* who did not manifest repugnance at the suggestion of a return to Ireland. If asked why they objected to return, the response was usually in the form of a question: 'Shure thin, sir, and what good could I do there?' Neither can I say that I heard any of these people express any love for their country, though they often spoke with great affection of their friends.

From an Irish costermonger, a middle-aged man, with a physiognomy best known as 'Irish', and dressed in corduroy trousers, with a loose great-coat, far too big for him, buttoned about him, I had the following statement:

'I had a bit o' land, yer honor, in County Limerick. Well, it wasn't just a farrum, nor what ye would call a garden here, but my father lived and died on it – glory be to God! – and brought up me and my sister on it. It was about an acre, and the taties was well known to be good. But the sore times came, and the taties was afflicted, and the wife and me – I have no childer – hadn't a bite nor a sup, but wather to live on, and an igg or two. I filt the famine a-comin'. I saw people a-feedin' on the wild green things, and as I had not such a bad take, I got Mr — (he was the head master's agent) to give me 28s. for possission in quietness, and I sould some poultry I had – their iggs was a blessin' to keep the life in us – I sould them in Limerick for 3s. 3d. – the poor things – four of them. The furnithur' I sould to the nabors, for somehow about 6s. It's the thruth I'm ay-tellin' of you, sir, and there's 2s. owin' of it still, and will be a perpitual loss. The wife and me walked to Dublin, though we had betther have gone by the "long say", but I didn't understand it thin, and we got to Liverpool. Then sorrow's the taste of worruk could I git, beyant oncte 3s. for two days' harrud porthering, that broke my back half in two. I was tould I'd do betther in London, and so, glory be to God! I have – perhaps I have. I knew Mr — , he porthers at Covent-garden, and I made him out, and hilped him in any long distance of a job. As I'd been used to farrumin' I thought it good raison I should be a costermonger, as they call it here. I can read and write too. And some good Christian – the heavens light him to glory when he's gone! – I don't know who he was – advanced me 10s. – or he gave it me, so to spake, through Father — [a Roman Catholic priest].' We earrun what keeps the life in us. I don't go to markit, but buy of a fair dealin' man – so I count him – though he's harrud sometimes. I can't till how many Irishmen is in the thrade. There's many has been brought down to it by the famin' and the changes. I don't go much among the English street-dalers. They talk like haythens. I never miss mass on a Sunday, and they don't know what the blissed mass manes. I'm almost glad I have no childer, to see how they're raired here. Indeed, sir, they're not raired at all – they run wild. They haven't the fear of God or the saints. They'd hang a praste – glory be to God! they would.'

How the street-Irish displanted the Jews in the orange trade
[*volume i. pp.106,107*]

The Jews, in the streets, while acting as costermongers, never 'worked a barrow', nor dealt in the more ponderous and least profitable articles of the trade, such as turnips and cabbages. They however had, at one period, the chief possession of a portion of the trade which the 'regular hands' do not consider proper costermongering, and which is now chiefly confined to the Irish – viz. orange selling.

The trade was, not many years ago, confined almost entirely to the Jew boys, who kept aloof from the vagrant lads of the streets, or mixed with them only in the cheap theatres and concert-rooms. A person who had had great experience at what was, till recently, one of the greatest 'coaching inns', told me that, speaking within his own recollection and from his own observation, he thought the sale of oranges was not so much in the hands of the Jew lads until about forty years back. The orange monopoly, so to speak, was established by the street-Jews, about 1810, or three or four years previous to that date, when recruiting and local soldiering were at their height, and when a great number of the vagabond or 'roving' population, who in one capacity or other now throng the streets, were induced to enlist. The young Jews never entered the ranks of the army. The streets were thus in a measure cleared for them, and the itinerant orange-trade fell almost entirely into their hands. Some of the young Jews gained, I am assured, at least 100*l*. a year in this traffic. The numbers of country people who hastened to London on the occasion of the Allied Sovereigns' visit in 1814 – many wealthy persons then seeing the capital for the first time – afforded an excellent market to these dealers.

Moreover, the perseverance of the Jew orange boys was not to be overcome; they would follow a man who even looked encouragingly at their wares for a mile or two. The great resort of these Jew dealers – who eschewed night-work generally, and left the theatre-doors to old men and women of all ages – was at the coaching inns; for year by year, after the peace of 1815, the improvement of the roads and the consequent increase of travellers to London, progressed.

About 1825, as nearly as my informant could recollect, these keen young traders began to add the sale of other goods to their oranges, pressing them upon the notice of those who were leaving or visiting London by the different coaches. So much was this the case, that it was a common remark at that time, that no-one could reach or leave the metropolis, even for the shortest journey, without being expected to be in urgent want of oranges and lemons, black-lead pencils, sticks of sealing-wax, many-bladed pen-knives, pocket-combs, razors, strops, braces, and sponges. To pursue the sale of the last-mentioned articles – they being found, I presume, to be more profitable – some of the street-Jews began to abandon the sale of oranges and lemons; and it was upon this, that the trade was 'taken up' by the wives and children of the Irish bricklayers' labourers, and of other Irish work-people then resident in London. The numbers of Irish in the metropolis at that time began to increase rapidly; for twenty years ago, they resorted numerously to England to gather in the harvest, and those who had been employed in contiguous counties during the autumn, made for London in the winter. 'I can't say they were well off, sir,' said one man to me, 'but they liked bread and herrings, or bread and tea – better than potatoes without bread at home.' From 1836 to 1840, I was informed, the Irish gradually superseded the Jews in the fruit traffic about the coaching-houses. One reason for this was, that they were far more eloquent, begging pathetically, and with many benedictions on their listeners. The Jews never begged, I was told; 'they were merely traders.' Another reason was, that the Irish, men or lads, who had entered into the fruit trade in the coach-yards, would not only sell and beg, but were ready to 'lend a hand' to any over-burthened coach-porter. This the Jews never did, and in that way the people of the yard came to encourage the Irish to the prejudice of the Jews. At present, I understand that, with the exception of one or two in the city, no Jews vend oranges in the streets, and that the trade is almost entirely in the hands of the Irish.

Another reason why the Irish could supersede and even under-sell the Jews and regular costermongers was this, as I am informed on excellent authority: Father Mathew, a dozen years back, made temperance societies popular in Ireland. Many of the itinerant Irish, especially the younger classes, were 'temperance men'. Thus the Irish could live as sparely as the Jew, but they did not, like him, squander any money for the evening's amusement, at the concert or the theatre.

I inquired what might be the number of the Jews plying, so to speak, at the coaching inns, and was assured that it was less numerous than was generally imagined. One man computed it at 300 individuals, all under 21; another at only 200; perhaps the mean, or 250, might be about the mark. The number was naturally considered greater, I was told, because the same set of street traders were seen over and over again. The Jews knew when the coaches were to arrive and when they started, and they would hurry, after availing themselves of a departure, from one inn – the Belle Sauvage, Ludgate-hill, for instance – to take advantage of an arrival at another – say the Saracen's Head, Snow-hill. Thus they appeared everywhere, but were the same individuals.

I inquired to what calling the youthful Jews, thus driven from their partially monopolised street commerce, had devoted themselves, and was told that even when the orange and hawking trade was at the best, the Jews rarely carried it on after they were twenty-two or twenty-three, but that they then resorted to some more wholesale calling, such as the purchase of nuts or foreign grapes, at public sales. At present, I am informed, they are more thickly than ever engaged in these trades, as well as in two new avocations, that have been established within these few years – the sale of the Bahama pineapples and of the Spanish and Portuguese onions.

About the Royal Exchange, Jew boys still hawk pencils, etc., but the number engaged in this pursuit throughout London is not, as far as I can ascertain, above one-eighth – if an eighth – of what it was even twelve years ago.

Of the religion of the street-Irish
[volume i. pp.107,108]
Having now given a brief sketch as to how the Irish people have come to form so large a proportion of the London street-sellers, I shall proceed, as I did with the English costermongers, to furnish the reader with a short account of their religious, moral, intell-ectual, and physical condition, so that he may be able to contrast the habits and circumstances of the one class with those of the other. First, of the religion of the Irish street-folk.

Almost all the street-Irish are Roman Catholics. Of course I can but speak generally; but during my inquiry I met with only two who said they were Protestants, and when I came to converse with them, I found out that they were partly ignorant of, and partly indifferent to, any religion whatever. An Irish Protestant gentleman said to me: 'You may depend upon it, if ever you meet any of my poor countrymen who will not talk to you about religion, they either know or care nothing about it; for the religious spirit runs high in Ireland, and Protestants and Catholics are easily led to converse about their faith.'

I found that *some* of the Irish Roman Catholics – but they had been for many years resident in England, and that among the poorest or vagrant class of the English – had become indifferent to their creed, and did not attend their chapels, unless at the great fasts or festivals, and this they did only occasionally. One old stall-keeper, who had been in London nearly thirty years, said to me: 'Ah! God knows, sir, I ought to attend mass every Sunday, but I haven't for a many years, barrin' Christmas-day and such times. But I'll thry and go more rigular, plase God.' This man seemed to resent, as a sort of indignity, my question if he ever attended any other place of worship. 'Av coorse not!' was the reply.

One Irishman, also a fruit-seller, with a well-stocked barrow, and without the complaint of poverty common among his class, entered keenly into the subject of his religious faith when I introduced it. He was born in Ireland, but had been in England since he was five or six. He was a good-looking, fresh-coloured man, of thirty or upwards, and could read and write well. He spoke without bitterness, though zealously enough. 'Perhaps, sir, you are a gintleman connected with the Protistant clargy,' he asked, 'or a missionary?' On my stating that I had no claim to either character, he resumed: 'Will, sir, it don't matther. All the worruld may know my riligion, and I wish all the worruld was of my riligion, and betther min in it than I am; I do, indeed. I'm a Roman Catholic, sir;' [here he made the sign of the cross] 'God be praised for it! Oh yis, I know all about Cardinal Wiseman. It's the will of God, I feel sure, that he's to be 'stablished here, and it's no use ribillin' against that. I've nothing to say against Protistints. I've heard it said, "It's best to pray for them." The street-people that call thimselves Protistants are no riligion at all at all. I serruve Protistant gintlemen and ladies too, and sometimes they talk to me kindly about religion. They're good custhomers, and I have no doubt good people. I can't say what their lot may be in another worruld for not being of the true faith. No, sir, I'll give no opinions – none.'

This man gave me a clear account of his belief that the Blessed Virgin (he crossed himself repeatedly as he spoke) was the mother of our Lord Jesus Christ, and was a mediator with our Lord, who was God of heaven and earth – of the duty of praying to the holy saints – of attending mass – ('but the priest,' he said, 'won't exact too much of a poor man, either about that or about fasting') – of going to confession at Easter and Christmas times, at the least – of receiving the body of Christ, 'the rale prisince', in the holy sacrament – of keeping all God's commandments – of purgatory being a purgation of sins – and of heaven and hell. I found the majority of those I spoke with, at least as earnest in their faith, if they were not as well instructed in it as my informant, who may be cited as an example of the better class of street-sellers.

Another Irishman – who may be taken as a type of the less informed, and who had been between two and three years in England, having been disappointed in emigrating to America with his wife and two children – gave me the following account, but not without considering and hesitating. He was a very melancholy looking man, tall and spare, and decently clad. He and his family were living upon 8d. a day, which he earned by sweeping a crossing. He had been prevented by ill health from earning 2l., which he could have made, he told me, in harvest time, as a store against winter. He had been a street-seller, and so had his wife; and she would be so again as soon as he could raise 2s. to buy her a stock of apples. He said, touching his hat at each holy name – 'Sure, yis, sir, I'm a Roman Cartholic, and go to mass every Sunday. Jesus Christ? Oh yis,' [hesitating, but proceeding readily after a word of prompting], 'he is the Lord our Saviour, and the Son of the Holy Virgin. The blessed saints? Yis, sir, yis. The praste prays for them. I – I mane prays to them. Oh yis. I pray to them mysilf ivery night for a blissin', and to rise me out of my misery. No, sir, I can't say I know what the mass is about. I don't know what I'm prayin' for thin, only that it's right. A poor man, that can neither read nor write – I wish I could and I might do betther – can't understand it; it's all in Latin. I've heard about Cardinal

Wiseman. It'll do us no good sir; it'll only set people more against us. But it ain't poor min's fault.'

As I was anxious to witness the religious zeal that characterises these people, I obtained permission to follow one of the priests as he made his rounds among his flock. Everywhere the people ran out to meet him. He had just returned to them I found, and the news spread round, and women crowded to their door-steps, and came creeping up from the cellars through the trap-doors, merely to curtsey to him. One old crone, as he passed, cried, 'You're a good father, Heaven comfort you,' and the boys playing about stood still to watch him. A lad, in a man's tail coat and a shirt-collar that nearly covered in his head – like the paper round a bouquet – was fortunate enough to be noticed, and his eyes sparkled, as he touched his hair at each word he spoke in answer. At a conversation that took place between the priest and a woman who kept a dry fish-stall, the dame excused herself for not having been up to take tea 'with his rivirince's mother lately, for thrade had been so bisy, and night was the fullest time'. Even as the priest walked along the street, boys running at full speed would pull up to touch their hair, and the stall-women would rise from their baskets; while all noise – even a quarrel – ceased until he had passed by. Still there was no look of fear in the people. He called them all by their names, and asked after their families, and once or twice the 'father' was taken aside and held by the button while some point that required his advice was whispered in his ear.

The religious fervour of the people whom I saw was intense. At one house that I entered, the woman set me marvelling at the strength of her zeal, by showing me how she contrived to have in her sitting-room a sanctuary to pray before every night and morning, and even in the day, 'when she felt weary and lonesome'. The room was rudely enough furnished, and the only decent table was covered with a new piece of varnished cloth; still before a rude print of our Saviour there were placed two old plated candlesticks, pink, with the copper shining through; and here it was that she told her beads. In her bed-room, too, was a coloured engraving of the 'Blessed Lady', which she never passed without curtseying to.

Of course I detail these matters as mere facts, without desiring to offer any opinion here, either as to the benefit or otherwise of the creed in question. As I had shown how the English costermonger neither had nor knew any religion whatever, it became my duty to give the reader a view of the religion of the Irish street-sellers. In order to be able to do so as truthfully as possible, I placed myself in communication with those parties who were in a position to give me the best information on the subject. The result is given above, in all the simplicity and impartiality of history.

Of the education, literature, amusements and politics of the street-Irish
[*volume i. pp.108,109*]

These several heads have often required from me lengthened notices, but as regards the class I am now describing they may be dismissed briefly enough. The majority of the street-Irish whom I saw were unable to read, but I found those who had no knowledge of reading – (and the same remark applies to the English street-sellers as well) – regret their inability, and say, 'I wish I could read, sir; I'd be better off now.' On the other hand, those who had a knowledge of reading and writing, said frequently enough, 'Why, yes, sir, I can read and write, but it's been no good to me,' as if they had been disappointed in their expectations as to the benefits attendant upon scholarship. I am inclined to think, however, that a greater anxiety exists among the poor generally, to have some schooling provided for their children, than was the case a few years back. One Irishman attributed this to the increased number of Roman Catholic schools, 'for the more schools there are,' he said, 'the more people think about schooling their children.'

The literature, or reading, of the street-Irish is, I believe, confined to Roman Catholic books, such as the *Lives of the Saints*, published in a cheap form; one, and only one, I found with the *Nation* newspaper. The very poor have no leisure to read. During three days spent in visiting the slop-workers at the East end of the town, not so much as the fragment of a leaf of a book was seen.

The amusements of the street-Irish are not those of the English costermongers – though there are exceptions, of course, to the remark. The Irish fathers and mothers do not allow their daughters, even when they possess the means, to resort to the 'penny gaffs' or the 'twopenny hops', unaccompanied by them. Some of the men frequent the beer-shops, and are inveterate drinkers and smokers too. I did not hear of any amusements popular among, or much resorted to, by the Irishmen, except dancing parties at one another's houses, where they jig and reel furiously. They frequent raffles also, but the article is often never thrown for, and the evening is spent in dancing.

I may here observe – in reference to the statement that Irish parents will not expose their daughters to the risk of what they consider corrupt influences – that when a young Irishwoman *does* break through the pale of chastity, she often becomes, as I was assured, one of the most violent and depraved of, perhaps, the most depraved class.

Of politics, I think, the street-Irish understand nothing, and my own observations in this respect were confirmed by a remark made to me by an Irish gentleman: 'Their politics are either a dead letter, or the politics of their priests.'

The homes of the street-Irish
[*volume i. pp.109–111*]
In almost all of the poorer districts of London are to be found 'nests of Irish' – as they are called – or courts inhabited solely by the Irish costermongers. These people form separate colonies, rarely visiting or mingling with the English costers. It is curious, on walking through one of these settlements, to notice the manner in which the Irish deal among themselves – street-seller buying of street-seller. Even in some of the smallest courts there may be seen stalls of vegetables, dried herrings, or salt cod, thriving, on the associative principle, by mutual support.

The parts of London that are the most thickly populated with Irish lie about Brook-street, Ratcliff-cross, down both sides of the Commercial Road, and in Rosemary-lane, though nearly all the 'coster-districts' cited at p.47,* have their Irish settlements – Cromer-street, Saffron-hill and King-street, Drury-lane, for instance, being thickly peopled with the Irish; but the places I have mentioned above are peculiarly distinguished, by being almost entirely peopled by visitors from the sister isle.

The same system of immigration is pursued in London as in America. As soon as the first settler is thriving in his newly chosen country, a certain portion of his or her earnings are carefully

* This page reference is to volume i of Mayhew's four-volume edition.

hoarded up, until they are sufficient to pay for the removal of another member of the family to England; then one of the friends left 'at home' is sent for; and thus by degrees the entire family is got over, and once more united.

Perhaps there is no quarter of London where the habits and habitations of the Irish can be better seen and studied than in Rosemary-lane, and the little courts and alleys that spring from it on each side. Some of these courts have other courts branching off from them, so that the locality is a perfect labyrinth of 'blind alleys'; and when once in the heart of the maze it is difficult to find the path that leads to the main-road. As you walk down 'the lane', and peep through the narrow openings between the houses, the place seems like a huge peep-show, with dark holes of gateways to look through, while the court within appears bright with the daylight; and down it are seen rough-headed urchins running with their feet bare through the puddles, and bonnetless girls, huddled in shawls, lolling against the door-posts. Sometimes you see a long narrow alley, with the houses so close together that opposite neighbours are talking from their windows; while the ropes, stretched zig-zag from wall to wall, afford just room enough to dry a blanket or a couple of shirts, that swell out drops-ically in the wind.

I visited one of the paved yards round which the Irish live, and found that it had been turned into a complete drying-ground, with shirts, gowns, and petticoats of every description and colour. The buildings at the end were completely hidden by 'the things', and the air felt damp and chilly, and smelt of soap-suds. The gutter was filled with dirty grey water emptied from the wash-tubs, and on the top were the thick bubbles floating about under the breath of the boys 'playing at boats' with them.

It is the custom with the inhabitants of these courts and alleys to assemble at the entrance with their baskets, and chat and smoke away the morning. Every court entrance has its little group of girls and women, lolling listlessly against the sides, with their heads uncovered, and their luxuriant hair fuzzy as oakum. It is peculiar with the Irish women that – after having been accustomed to their hoods – they seldom wear bonnets, unless on a long journey. Nearly all of them, too, have a thick plaid shawl, which they keep on all the day through, with their hands covered under it. At the

mouth of the only thoroughfare deserving of the name of street –
for a cart could just go through it – were congregated about thirty
men and women, who rented rooms in the houses on each side
of the road. Six women, with baskets of dried herrings, were
crouching in a line on the kerb-stone with the fish before them;
their legs were drawn up so closely to their bodies that the shawl
covered the entire figure, and they looked very like the podgy
'tombolers' sold by the Italian boys. As all their wares were alike, it
was puzzling work to imagine how, without the strongest opposition, they could each obtain a living. The men were dressed in
long-tail coats, with one or two brass buttons. One old dame, with
a face wrinkled like a dried plum, had her cloak placed over her
head like a hood, and the grisly hair hung down in matted hanks
about her face, her black eyes shining between the locks like those
of a Skye terrier; beside her was another old woman smoking a
pipe so short that her nose reached over the bowl.

After looking at the low foreheads and long bulging upper lips of
some of the group, it was pleasant to gaze upon the pretty faces of
the one or two girls that lolled against the wall. Their black hair,
smoothed with grease, and shining almost as if 'japanned', and
their large grey eyes with the thick dark fringe of lash, seemed out
of place among the hard features of their companions. It was only
by looking at the short petticoats and large feet you could assure
yourself that they belonged to the same class.

In all the houses that I entered were traces of household care and
neatness that I had little expected to have seen. The cupboard
fastened in the corner of the room, and stocked with mugs and
cups, the mantelpiece with its images, and the walls covered with
showy-coloured prints of saints and martyrs, gave an air of comfort
that strangely disagreed with the reports of the cabins in 'ould
Ireland'. As the doors to the houses were nearly all of them kept
open, I could, even whilst walking along, gain some notion of the
furniture of the homes. In one house that I visited there was a
family of five persons, living on the ground floor and occupying
two rooms. The boards were strewn with red sand, and the front
apartment had three beds in it, with the printed curtains drawn
closely round. In a dark room, at the back, lived the family itself.
It was fitted up as a parlour, and crowded to excess with chairs
and tables, the very staircase having pictures fastened against the

wooden partition. The fire, although it was midday, and a warm autumn morning, served as much for light as for heat, and round it crouched the mother, children, and visitors, bending over the flame as if in the severest winter time. In a room above this were a man and woman lately arrived in England. The woman sat huddled up in a corner smoking, with the husband standing over her in, what appeared at first, a menacing attitude; I was informed, however, that they were only planning for the future. This room was perfectly empty of furniture, and the once white-washed walls were black, excepting the little square patches which showed where the pictures of the former tenants had hung. In another room, I found a home so small and full of furniture, that it was almost a curiosity for domestic management. The bed, with its chintz curtains looped up, filled one end of the apartment, but the mattress of it served as a long bench for the visitors to sit on. The table was so large that it divided the room in two, and if there was one picture there must have been thirty – all of 'holy men', with yellow glories round their heads. The window-ledge was dressed out with crockery, and in a tumbler were placed the beads. The old dame herself was as curious as her room. Her shawl was fastened over her large frilled cap. She had a little 'button' of a nose, with the nostrils entering her face like bullet holes. She wore over her gown an old pilot coat, well-stained with fish slime, and her petticoats being short, she had very much the appearance of a Dutch fisherman or stage smuggler.

Her story was affecting – made more so, perhaps, by the emotional manner in which she related it. Nine years ago 'the father' of the district – 'the Blissed Lady guard him!' – had found her late at night, rolling in the gutter, and the boys pelting her with orange-peel and mud. She was drunk – 'the Lorrud pass by her' – and when she came to, she found herself in the chapel, lying before the sanctuary, 'under the shadow of the holy cross'. Watching over her was the 'good father', trying to bring back her consciousness. He spoke to her of her wickedness, and before she left she took the pledge of temperance. From that time she prospered, and the 1s. 6d. the 'father' gave her 'had God's blissin' in it', for she became the best-dressed woman in the court, and in less than three years had 15l. in the savings' bank, 'the father – Heaven chirish him' – keeping her book for her, as he did for other poor people. She also

joined 'the Association of the Blissed Lady', (and bought herself
the dress of the order, 'a beautiful grane vilvit, which she had now,
and which same cost her 30s.'), and then she was secure against
want in old age and sickness. But after nine years prudence and
comfort, a brother of hers returned home from the army, with a
pension of 1s. a day. He was wild, and persuaded her to break her
pledge, and in a short time he got all her savings from her and
spent every penny. She couldn't shake him off, 'for he was the
only kin she had on airth', and 'she must love her own flish and
bones'. Then began her misery. 'It plased God to visit her ould
limbs with aches and throubles, and her hips swole with the
cowld,' so that she was at last forced into a hospital, and all that was
left of her store was 'aten up by sufferin's.' This, she assured me, all
came about by the 'good father's' leaving that parish for another
one, but now he had returned to them again, and, with his help
and God's blessing, she would yet prosper once more.

Whilst I was in the room, the father entered, and 'old Norah',
half-divided between joy at seeing him and shame at 'being again a
beggar', laughed and wept at the same time. She stood wiping her
eyes with the shawl, and groaning out blessings on 'his rivirince's
hid', begging of him not 'to scould her for she was a wake
woman'. The renegade brother was had in to receive a lecture
from 'his rivirince'. A more sottish idiotic face it would be difficult
to imagine. He stood with his hands hanging down like the paws
of a dog begging, and his two small eyes stared in the face of the
priest, as he censured him, without the least expression even of
consciousness. Old Norah stood by, groaning like a bagpipe, and
writhing while the father spoke to her 'own brother', as though
every reproach were meant for her.

The one thing that struck me during my visit to this neighbourhood, was the apparent listlessness and lazy appearance of the
people. The boys at play were the only beings who seemed to have
any life in their actions. The women in their plaid shawls strolled
along the pavements, stopping each friend for a chat, or joining
some circle, and leaning against the wall as though utterly deficient
in energy. The men smoked, with their hands in their pockets,
listening to the old crones talking, and only now and then grunting
out a reply when a question was directly put to them. And yet it is
curious that these people, who here seemed as inactive as negroes,

will perform the severest bodily labour, undertaking tasks that the English are almost unfitted for.

To complete this account, I subjoin a brief description of the lodging-houses resorted to by the Irish immigrants on their arrival in this country.

Irish lodging-houses for immigrants
[*volume i. pp.111–113*]

Often an Irish immigrant, whose object is to settle in London, arrives by the Cork steamer without knowing a single friend to whom he can apply for house-room or assistance of any kind. Sometimes a whole family is landed late at night, worn out by sickness and the terrible fatigues of a three days' deck passage, almost paralysed by exhaustion, and scarcely able to speak English enough to inquire for shelter till morning.

If the immigrants, however, are bound for America, their lot is very different. Then they are consigned to some agent in London, who is always on the wharf at the time the steamer arrives, and takes the strangers to the homes he has prepared for them until the New York packet starts. During the two or three days' necessary stay in London, they are provided for at the agent's expense, and no trouble is experienced by the travellers. A large provision-merchant in the city told me that he often, during the season, had as many as 500 Irish consigned to him by one vessel, so that to lead them to their lodgings was like walking at the head of a regiment of recruits.

The necessities of the immigrants in London have caused several of their countrymen to open lodging-houses in the courts about Rosemary-lane; these men attend the coming in of the Cork steamer, and seek for customers among the poorest of the poor, after the manner of touters to a sea-side hotel.

The immigrants' houses are of two kinds – clean and dirty. The better class of Irish lodging-houses almost startle one by the comfort and cleanliness of the rooms; for after the descriptions you hear of the state in which the deck passengers are landed from the Irish boats, their clothes stained with the manure of the pigs, and drenched with the spray, you somehow expect to find all the accommodations disgusting and unwholesome. But one in particular, that I visited, had the floor clean, and sprinkled with red sand, while the windows were sound, bright, and transparent. The hobs of the large fire-place were piled up with bright tin pots, and the chimney piece was white and red with the china images ranged upon it. In one corner of the principal apartment there stood two or three boxes still corded up, and with bundles strung to the sides, and against the wall was hung a bunch of blue cloaks, such as the Irishwomen wear. The proprietor of the house, who was dressed in a grey tail-coat and knee-breeches, that had somewhat the effect of a footman's livery, told me that he had received seven lodgers the day before, but six were men, and they were all out seeking for work. In front of the fire sat a woman, bending over it so close that the bright cotton gown she had on smelt of scorching. Her feet were bare, and she held the soles of them near to the bars, curling her toes about with the heat. She was a short, thick-set woman, with a pair of wonderfully muscular arms crossed over her bosom, and her loose rusty hair streaming over her neck. It was in vain that I spoke to her about her journey, for she wouldn't answer me, but kept her round, open eyes fixed on my face with a wild, nervous look, following me about with them everywhere.

Across the room hung a line, with the newly-washed and well-patched clothes of the immigrants hanging to it, and on a side-table were the six yellow basins that had been used for the men's breakfasts. During my visit, the neighbours, having observed a strange gentleman enter, came pouring in, each proferring some fresh bit of news about their newly-arrived countrymen. I was nearly stunned by half-a-dozen voices speaking together, and telling me how the poor people had been four days 'at say', so that they were glad to get near the pigs for 'warrumth', and instructing me as to the best manner of laying out the sum of money that it was supposed I was about to shower down upon the immigrants.

In one of the worst class of lodging-houses I found ten human beings living together in a small room. The apartment was entirely devoid of all furniture, excepting an old mattress rolled up against the wall, and a dirty piece of cloth hung across one corner, to screen the women whilst dressing. An old man, the father of five out of the ten, was seated on a tea-chest, mending shoes, and the other men were looking on with their hands in their pockets. Two girls and a woman were huddled together on the floor in front of the fire, talking in Irish. All these people seemed to be utterly devoid of energy, and the men moved about so lazily that I couldn't help asking some of them if they had tried to obtain work. Everyone turned to a good-looking young fellow lolling against the wall, as if they expected him to answer for them. 'Ah, sure, and that they have,' was the reply; 'it's the docks they have tried, worrus luck.' The others appeared struck with the truthfulness of the answer, for they all shook their heads, and said, 'Sure an' that's thruth, anyhow.' Here my Irish guide ventured an observation, by remarking solemnly, 'It's no use tilling a lie;' to which the whole room assented, by exclaiming altogether, 'Thrue for you, Norah.' The chosen spokesman then told me, 'They paid half-a-crown a week for the room, and that was as much as they could earrun, and it was starruve they should if the neighbours didn't hilp them a bit.' I asked them if they were better off over here than when in Ireland, but could get no direct answer, for my question only gave rise to a political discussion. 'There's plenty of food over here,' said the spokesman, addressing his companions as much as myself, 'plenty of 'taties – plenty of mate – plenty of porruk.' 'But where the use,' observed my guide, 'if there's no money to buy 'em wid?' to which the audience muttered, 'Thrue for you again, Norah;' and so it went on, each one pleading poverty in the most eloquent style.

After I had left, the young fellow who had acted as spokesman followed me into the street, and taking me into a corner, told me that he was a 'sailor by thrade, but had lost his "rigisthration-ticket", or he'd have got a berruth long since, and that it was all for 3s. 6d. he wasn't at say.'

Concerning the number of Irish immigrants, I have obtained the following information:

The great influx of the Irish into London was in the year of the famine, 1847–8. This cannot be better shown than by citing the returns of the number of persons admitted into the Asylum for the Houseless Poor, in Playhouse-yard, Cripplegate. These returns I obtained for fourteen years, and the average number of admissions of the applicants from all parts during that time was 8,794 yearly. Of these, the Irish averaged 2,455 yearly, or considerably more than a fourth of the whole number received. The total number of applicants thus sheltered in the fourteen years was 130,625, of which the Irish numbered 34,378. The smallest number of Irish (men, women, and children) admitted, was in 1834–5, about 300; in 1846–7, it was as many as 7,576, while in 1847–8, it was 10,756, and in 1848–9, 5,068.

But it was into Liverpool that the tide of immigration flowed the strongest, in the calamitous year of the famine. 'Between the 13th Jan., and the 13th Dec., both inclusive,' writes Mr Rushton, the Liverpool magistrate, to Sir G. Grey, on the 21st April last, '296,231 persons landed in this port [Liverpool] from Ireland. Of this vast number, about 130,000 emigrated to the United States; some 50,000 were passengers on business; and the remainder (161,231), mere paupers, half-naked and starving, landed, for the most part, during the winter, and became, immediately on landing, applicants for parochial relief. You already know the immediate results of this accumulation of misery in the crowded town of Liverpool; of the cost of relief at once rendered necessary to prevent the thousands of hungry and naked Irish perishing in our streets; and also of the cost of the pestilence which generally follows in the train of famine and misery such as we then had to encounter. . . . Hundreds of patients perished, notwithstanding all efforts made to save them; and ten Roman Catholic and one Protestant clergyman, many parochial officers, and many medical men, who devoted themselves to the task of alleviating the sufferings of the wretched, died in the discharge of these high duties.'

Great numbers of these people were, at the same time, also conveyed from Ireland to Wales, especially to Newport. They were brought over by coal-vessels as a return cargo – a living ballast – 2s. 6d. being the highest fare, and were huddled together like pigs. The manager of the Newport tramp-house has stated concerning these people, 'They don't live long, diseased as they are. They are very remarkable; they will eat salt by basons-full, and drink a great quantity of water after. I have frequently known those who could not have been hungry eat cabbage-leaves and other refuse from the ash-heap.'

It is necessary that I should thus briefly allude to this matter, as there is no doubt that some of these people, making their way to London, soon became street-sellers there, and many of them took to the business subsequently, when there was no employment in harvesting, hop-picking, &c. Of the poor wretches landed at

Liverpool, many (Mr Rushton states) became beggars, and many thieves. Many, there is no doubt, tramped their way to London, sleeping at the 'casual wards' of the Unions on their way; but I believe that of those who had become habituated to the practice of beggary or theft, few or none would follow the occupation of street-selling, as even the half-passive industry of such a calling would be irksome to the apathetic and dishonest.

Of the immigration, direct by the vessels trading from Ireland to London, there are no returns such has have been collected by Mr Rushton for Liverpool, but the influx is comparatively small, on account of the greater length and cost of the voyage. During the last year I am informed that 15,000 or 16,000 passengers were brought from Ireland to London direct, and, in addition to these, 500 more were brought over from Cork in connection with the arrangements for emigration to the United States, and consigned to the emigration agent here. Of the 15,500 (taking the mean between the two numbers above given) 1,000 emigrated to the United States. It appears, on the authority of Mr Rushton, that even in the great year of the immigration, more than one-sixth of the passengers from Ireland to Dublin came on business. It may, then, be reasonable to calculate that during last year one-fourth at least of the passengers to London had the same object in view, leaving about 10,000 persons who have either emigrated to British North America, Australia, &c., or have resorted to some mode of subsistence in the metropolis or the adjacent parts. Besides these there are the numbers who make their way up to London, tramping it from the several provincial ports – namely, Liverpool, Bristol, Newport, and Glasgow. Of these I have no means of forming any estimate, or of the proportion who adopt street-selling on their arrival here – all that can be said is, that the influx of Irish into the street-trade every year must be very considerable. I believe, however, that only those who 'have friends in the line' resort to street-selling on their arrival in London, though all may make it a resource when other endeavours fail. The great immigration into London is from Cork, the average cost of a deck passage being 5s. The immigrants direct to London from Cork are rarely of the poorest class.

Of the diet, drink and expense of living of the street-Irish
[volume i. pp.113,114]

The diet of the Irish men, women, and children, who obtain a livelihood (or what is so designated) by street-sale in London, has, I am told, on good authority, experienced a change. In the lodging-houses that they resorted to, their breakfast, two or three years ago, was a dish of potatoes – two, three, or four lbs., or more, in weight – for a family. Now half an ounce of coffee (half chicory) costs ½ *d.*, and that, with the half or quarter of a loaf, according to the number in family, is almost always their breakfast at the present time. When their constant diet was potatoes, there were frequent squabbles at the lodging-houses – to which many of the poor Irish on their first arrival resort – as to whether the potato-pot or the tea-kettle should have the preference on the fire. A man of superior intelligence, who had been driven to sleep and eat occasionally in lodging-houses, told me of some dialogues he had heard on these occasions: 'It's about three years ago,' he said, 'since I heard a bitter old Englishwoman say, "To — with your 'taty-pot; they're only meat for pigs." "Sure, thin," said a young Irish-man – he was a nice 'cute fellow – "sure, thin, ma'am, I should be afther offering you a taste." I heard that myself, sir. You may have noticed, that when an Irishman doesn't get out of temper, he never loses his politeness, or rather his blarney.'

The dinner, or second meal of the day – assuming that there has been a breakfast – ordinarily consists of cheap fish and potatoes. Of the diet of the poor street-Irish I had an account from a little Irishman, then keeping an oyster-stall, though he generally sold fruit. In all such details I have found the Irish far more commun-icative than the English. Many a poor untaught Englishman will shrink from speaking of his spare diet, and his trouble to procure that; a reserve, too, much more noticeable among the men than the women. My Irish informant told me he usually had his breakfast at a lodging-house – he preferred a lodging-house, he said, on account of the warmth and the society. Here he boiled half an ounce of coffee, costing a ½ *d.* He purchased of his land-lady the fourth of a quartern loaf (1¼ *d.* or 1½ *d.*), for she generally cut a quartern loaf into four for her single men lodgers, such as himself, clearing sometimes a farthing or two thereby. For dinner, my informant boiled at the lodging-house two or three lbs. of potatoes, costing usually 1d. or 1½ d., and fried three, or four herrings, or as many as cost a penny. He sometimes mashed his potatoes, and spread over them the herrings, the fatty portion of which flavoured the potatoes, which were further flavoured by the roes of the herrings being crushed into them. He drank water to this meal, and the cost of the whole was 2d. or 2½ d. A neighbouring stall-keeper attended to this man's stock in his absence at dinner, and my informant did the same for him in his turn. For 'tea' he expended 1d. on coffee, or 1½ d. on tea, being a 'cup' of tea, or 'half-pint of coffee', at a coffee-shop. Sometimes he had a halfpenny-worth of butter, and with his tea he ate the bread he had saved from his breakfast, and which he had carried in his pocket. He had no butter to his breakfast, he said, for he could not buy less than a pennyworth about where he lodged, and this was too dear for one meal. On a Sunday morning however he generally had butter, sometimes joining with a fellow-lodger for a pennyworth; for his Sunday dinner he had a piece of meat, which cost him 2d. on the Saturday night. Supper he dispensed with, but if he felt much tired he had a half-pint of beer, which was three farthings 'in his own jug', before he went to bed, about nine or ten, as he did little or nothing late at night, except on Saturday. He thus spent 4½ d. a day for food, and reckoning 2½ d. extra for somewhat better fare on a Sunday, his board was 2s. 10d. a week. His earnings he computed at 5s., and thus he had 2s. 2d. weekly for other expenses. Of these there was 1s. for lodging; 2d. or 3d. for washing (but this not every week); ½ d. for a Sunday morning's shave; 1d. 'for his religion' (as he worded it); and 6d. for 'odds and ends', such as thread to mend his clothes, a piece of leather to patch his shoes, worsted to darn his stockings, &c. He was subject to rheumatism, or 'he might have saved a trifle of money'. Judging by his methodical habits, it was probable he had done so. He had nothing of the eloquence of his countrymen, and seemed indeed of rather a morose turn.

A family boarding together live even cheaper than this man, for more potatoes and less fish fall to the share of the children. A meal too is not unfrequently saved in this manner: If a man, his wife, and two children, all go out in the streets selling, they breakfast before starting, and perhaps agree to re-assemble at four o'clock. Then the wife prepares the dinner of fish and potatoes, and so tea is dispensed with. In that case the husband's and wife's board would be 4*d*. or 4½ *d*. a day each, the children's 3*d*. or 3½ *d*. each, and giving 1½ *d*. extra to each for Sunday, the weekly cost is 10*s*. 3*d*. Supposing the husband and wife cleared 5*s*. a week each, and the children each 3*s*., their earnings would be 16*s*. The balance is the surplus left to pay rent, washing, firing, and clothing.

From what I can ascertain, the Irish street-seller can always live at about half the cost of the English costermonger; the Englishman must have butter for his bread, and meat at no long intervals, for he 'hates fish more than once a week'. It is by this spareness of living, as well as by frequently importunate and mendacious begging, that the street-Irish manage to save money.

The diet I have spoken of is *generally*, but not universally, that of the poor street-Irish; those who live differently, do not, as a rule, incur greater expense.

It is difficult to ascertain in what proportion the Irish street-sellers consume strong drink, when compared with the consumption of the English costers; as a poor Irishman, if questioned on that or any subject, will far more frequently shape his reply to what he thinks will please his querist and induce a trifle for himself, than answer according to the truth. The landlord of a large public-house, after inquiring of his assistants, that his opinions might be checked by theirs, told me that in one respect there was a marked difference between the beer-drinking of the two people. He considered that in the poor streets near his house there were residing quite as many Irish street-sellers and labourers as English, but the instances in which the Irish conveyed beer to their own rooms, as a portion of their meals, was not as 1 in 20 compared with the English: 'I have read your work, sir,' he said, 'and I know that you are quite right in saying that the costermongers go for a good Sunday dinner. I don't know what my customers are except by their appearance, but I do know that many are costermongers, and by the best of all proofs, for I have bought fish, fruit, and vegetables of them. Well, now, we'll take a fine Sunday in spring or summer, when times are pretty good with them; and, perhaps, in the ten minutes after my doors are opened at one on the Sunday, there are 100 customers for their dinner-beer. Nearly three-quarters of these are working men and their wives, working either in the streets, or at their indoor trades, such as tailoring. But among the number, I'm satisfied, there are not more than two Irishmen. There may be three or four Irishwomen, but one of my barmen tells me he knows that two of them – very well-behaved and good-looking women – are married to Englishmen. In my opinion the proportion, as to Sunday dinner-beer, between English and Irish, may be two or three in 70.'

An Irish gentleman and his wife, who are both well acquainted with the habits and condition of the people in their own country, informed me, that among the classes who, though earning only scant incomes, could not well be called 'impoverished', the use of beer, or even of small ale – known, now or recently – as 'Thunder's thruppeny', was very unfrequent. Even in many 'independent' families, only water is drunk at dinner, with punch to follow. This shows the accuracy of the information I derived from Mr — (the innkeeper), for persons unused to the drinking of malt liquor in their own country are not likely to resort to it afterwards, when their means are limited. I was further informed, that reckoning the teetotallers among the English street-sellers at 300, there are 600 among the Irish – teetotallers too, who, having taken the pledge, under the sanction of their priests, and looking upon it as a religious obligation, keep it rigidly.

The Irish street-sellers who frequent the gin-palaces or public-houses, drink a pot of beer, in a company of three or four, but far more frequently, a quartern of gin (very seldom whisky) oftener than do the English. Indeed, from all I could ascertain, the Irish street-sellers, whether from inferior earnings, their early training, or the restraints of their priests, drink less beer, by one-fourth, than their English brethren, but a larger proportion of gin. 'And you must bear this in mind, sir,' I was told by an innkeeper, 'I had rather have twenty poor Englishmen drunk in my tap-room than a couple of poor Irishmen. They'll quarrel with anybody – the Irish will – and sometimes clear the room by swearing they'll "use their knives, by Jasus"; and if there's a scuffle they'll kick like devils, and scratch, and bite, like women or cats, instead of using their fists. I wish all the drunkards were teetotallers, if it were only to be rid of them.'

Whisky, I was told, would be drunk by the Irish, in preference to gin, were it not that gin was about half the price. One old Irish fruit-seller – who admitted that he was fond of a glass of gin – told me that he had not tasted whisky for fourteen years, 'becase of the price'. The Irish, moreover, as I have shown, live on stronger and coarser food than the English, buying all the rough (bad) fish, for, to use the words of one of my informants, they look to quantity more than quality; this may account for their preferring a stronger and fiercer stimulant by way of drink.

Of the resources of the street-Irish as regards 'stock-money', sickness, burials, &c.
[volume i. pp. 114, 115]

It is not easy to ascertain from the poor Irish themselves how they raise their stock-money, for their command of money is a subject on which they are not communicative, or, if communicative, not truthful. 'My opinion is,' said an Irish gentleman to me, 'that some of these poor fellows would declare to God that they hadn't the value of a halfpenny, even if you heard the silver chink in their pockets.' It is certain that they never, or very rarely, borrow of the usurers like their English brethren.

The more usual custom is, that if a poor Irish street-seller be in want of 5s., it is lent to him by the more prosperous people of his court – bricklayers' labourers, or other working men – who club 1s. a piece. This is always repaid. An Irish bricklayer, when in full work, will trust a needy countryman with some article to pledge, on the understanding that it is to be redeemed and returned when the borrower is able. Sometimes, if a poor Irishwoman need 1s. to buy oranges, four others – only less poor than herself, because not utterly penniless – will readily advance 3d. each. Money is also advanced to the deserving Irish through the agency of the Roman Catholic priests, who are the medium through whom charitable persons of their own faith exercise good offices. Money, too, there is no doubt, is often advanced out of the priest's own pocket.

On all the kinds of loans with which the poor Irish are aided by their countrymen, no interest is ever charged. 'I don't like the Irish,' said an English costermonger to me; 'but they do stick to one another far more than we do.'

The Irish costers hire barrows and shallows like the English, but, if they 'get on' at all, they will possess themselves of their own vehicles much sooner than an English costermonger. A quick-witted Irishman will begin to ponder on his paying 1s. 6d. a week for the hire of a barrow worth 20s., and he will save and hoard until a pound is at his command to purchase one for himself; while an obtuse English coster (who will yet buy cheaper than an Irishman) will probably pride himself on his cleverness in having got the charge for his barrow reduced, in the third year of its hire, to 1s. a week the twelvemonth round!

In cases of sickness the mode of relief adopted is similar to that of the English. A raffle is got up for the benefit of the Irish sufferer, and, if it be a bad case, the subscribers pay their money without caring what trifle they throw for, or whether they throw at all. If sickness continue and such means as raffles cannot be persevered in, there is one resource from which a poor Irishman never shrinks – the parish. He will apply for and accept parochial relief without the least sense of shame, a sense which rarely deserts an Englishman who has been reared apart from paupers. The English costers appear to have a horror of the Union. If the Irishman be taken into the workhouse, his friends do not lose sight of him. In case of his death, they apply for, and generally receive his body, from the parochial authorities, undertaking the expence of the funeral, when the body is duly 'waked'. 'I think there's a family contract among the Irish,' said a costermonger to me; 'that's where it is.'

The Irish street-folk are, generally speaking, a far more provident body of people than the English street-sellers. To save, the Irish will often sacrifice what many Englishmen consider a necessary, and undergo many a hardship.

From all I could ascertain, the saving of an Irish street-seller does not arise from any wish to establish himself more prosperously in his business, but for the attainment of some cherished project, such as emigration. Some of the objects, however, for which these struggling men hoard money, are of the most praiseworthy character. They will treasure up halfpenny after halfpenny, and continue to do so for years, in order to send money to enable their wives and children, and even their brothers and sisters, when in the depth of distress in Ireland, to take shipping for England. They will save to be able to remit money for the relief of their aged parents in Ireland. They will save to defray the expense of their marriage, an expense the English costermonger so frequently dispenses with – but they will not save to preserve either themselves or their children from the degradation of a workhouse; indeed they often, with the means of independence secreted on their persons, apply for parish relief, and that principally to save the expenditure of their own money. Even when detected in such an attempt at extortion an Irishman betrays no passion, and hardly manifests any emotion – he has speculated and failed. Not one of them but has a positive genius for begging – both the taste and the faculty for alms-seeking developed to an extraordinary extent.

Of the amount 'saved' by the patience of the poor Irishmen, I can form no conjecture.

Of the history of some Irish street-sellers
[*volume i. pp.115–117*]
In order that the following statements might be as truthful as possible, I obtained permission to use the name of a Roman Catholic clergyman, to whom I am indebted for much valuable information touching this part of my subject.

A young woman, of whose age it was not easy to form a conjecture, her features were so embrowned by exposure to the weather, and perhaps when I saw her a little swollen from cold, gave me the following account as to her living. Her tone and manner betrayed indifference to the future, caused perhaps by ignorance – for uneducated persons I find are apt to look on the future as if it must needs be but a repetition of the present, while the past in many instances is little more than a blank to them. This young woman said, her brogue being little perceptible, though she spoke thickly:

'I live by keepin' this fruit stall. It's a poor livin' when I see how others live. Yes, in thruth, sir, but it's thankful I am for to be able to live at all, at all; troth is it, in these sore times. My father and mother are both did. God be gracious to their sowls! They was evicted. The family of us was. The thatch of the bit o' home was tuk off above our hids, and we were lift to the wide worruld – yis, indeed, sir, and in the open air too. The rint wasn't paid and it couldn't be paid, and so we had to face the wither. It was a sorrowful time. But God was good, and so was the neighbours. And when we saw the praste, he was a frind to us. And we came to this counthry, though I'd always heard it called a black counthry. Sure, an' there's much in it to indhure. There's goin's on it, sir, that the praste, God rewarrud him! wouldn't like to see. There's bad ways. I won't talk about thim, and I'm sure you are too much of a gintlemin to ask me; for if you know Father — , that shows you are the best of gintlemin, sure. It was the eviction that brought us here. I don't know about where we was just; not in what county; nor parish. I was so young whin we lift the land. I belave I'm now 19, perhaps only 18,' [she certainly looked much older, but I have often noticed that of her class] 'I can't be more, I think, for sure an it's only 5 or 6 years since we left Watherford and come to Bristol. I'm sure it was Watherford, and a beautiful place it is, and I know it was Bristol we come to. We walked all the long way to London. My parints died of the cholera, and I live with mysilf, but my aunt lodges me and sees to me. She sills in the sthreets too. I don't make 7d. a day. I may make 6d. There's a good many young payple I know is now sillin' in the streets becase they was evicted in their own counthry. I suppose they had no where ilse to come to. I'm nivir out of a night. I sleep with my aunt, and we keep to oursilves sure. I very sildom taste mate, but perhaps I do oftener than before we was evicted — glory be to God.'

One Irish street-seller I saw informed me that she was a 'widdy wid three childer'. Her husband died about four years since. She had then five children, and was near her confinement with another. Since the death of her husband she had lost three of her children; a boy about twelve years died of stoppage on his lungs, brought on, she said, through being in the streets, and shouting so loud 'to get sale of the fruit'. She has been in Clare-street, Clare-market, seven years with a fruit stall. In the summer she sells green fruit, which she purchases at Covent-garden. When the nuts, oranges, &c., come in season, she furnishes her stall with that kind of fruit, and continues to sell them until the spring salad comes in. During the spring and summer her weekly average income is about 5s., but the remaining portion of the year her income is not more than 3s. 6d. weekly, so that taking the year through, her average weekly income is about 4s. 3d.; out of this she pays 1s. 6d. a week rent, leaving only 2s. 9d. a week to find necessary comforts for herself and family. For fuel the children go to the market and gather up the waste walnuts, bring them home and dry them, and these, with a pennyworth of coal and coke, serve to warm their chilled feet and hands. They have no bedstead, but in one corner of a room is a flock bed upon the floor, with an old sheet, blanket, and quilt to cover them at this inclement season. There is neither chair nor table; a stool serves for the chair, and two pieces of board upon some baskets do duty for a table, and an old penny tea-canister for a candlestick. She had parted with every article of furniture to get food for her family. She received nothing from the parish, but depended upon the sale of her fruit for her living.

The Irishmen who are in this trade are also very poor; and I learned that both Irishmen and Irishwomen left the occupation now and then, and took to begging, as a more profitable calling, often going begging this month and fruit-selling the next. This is one of the causes which prompt the London costermongers' dislike of the Irish. 'They'll beg themselves into a meal, and work us out of one,' said an English coster to me. Some of them are, however, less 'poverty-struck' (a word in common use among the costermongers); but these for the most part are men who have been in the trade for some years, and have got regular 'pitches'.

The woman who gave me the following statement seemed about twenty-two or twenty-three. She was large-boned, and of heavy figure and deportment. Her complexion and features were both coarse, but her voice had a softness, even in its broadest brogue, which is not very frequent among poor Irishwomen. The first sentence she uttered seems to me tersely to embody a deplorable history of the poverty of a day. It was between six and seven in the evening when I saw the poor creature.

'Sure, thin, sir, it's thrippince I've taken today, and tuppince is to pay for my night's lodgin'. I shall do no more good tonight, and shall only stay in the cowld, if I stay in it, for nothing. I'm an orphand, sir,' [she three or four times alluded to this circumstance] 'and there's nobody to care for me but God, glory be to his name! I came to London to join my brother, that had come over and did will, and he sint for me, but whin I got here I couldn't find him in it anyhow. I don't know how long that's ago. It may be five years; it may be tin; but' [she added, with the true eloquence of beggary] 'sure, thin, sir, I had no harrut to keep count, if I knew how. My father and mother wasn't able to keep me, nor to keep thimsilves in Ireland, and so I was sint over here. They was counthry payple. I don't know about their landlorrud. They died not long afther I came here. I don't know what they died of, but sure it was of the will of God, and they hadn't much to make them love this worruld; no more have I. Would I like to go back to my own counthry? Will, thin, what would be the use? I sleep at a lodging-house, and it's a dacint place. It's mostly my own counthrywomen that's in it; that is, in the women's part. I pay 1s. a week, that's 2d. a night, for I'm not charged for Sundays. I live on brid, and 'taties and salt, and a herrin' sometimes. I niver taste beer, and not often tay, but I sit here all day, and I feel the hunger this day and that day. It goes off though, if I have nothin' to ate. I don't know why, but I won't deny the goodness of God to bring such a thing about. I have lived for a day on a pinny, sir: a ha'pinny for brid, and a ha'pinny for a herrin', or two herrin's for a ha'pinny, and 'taties for the place of brid. I've changed apples for a herrin' with a poor man, God rewarrud him. Sometimes I make on to 6d. a day, and sometimes I have made 1s. 6d., but I think that I don't make 5d. a day – arrah, no, thin, sir! one day with the other, and I don't worruk on Sunday, not often. If I've no mate to ate, I'd rather rist. I never miss mass on a Sunday. A lady gives me a rag sometimes, but the bitther time's comin'. If I was sick I don't know what I'd do, but I would sind for the praste, and he'd counsil me. I could read a little once, but I can't now.'

Of the Irish 'refuse'-sellers
[*volume i. pp.117,118*]

There still remains to be described one branch of the Irish street-trade which is peculiar to the class – viz., the sale of 'refuse', or such fruit and vegetables as are damaged, and suited only to the very poorest purchasers.

In assorting his goods, a fruit-salesman in the markets generally throws to one side the shrivelled, dwarfish, or damaged fruit – called by the street-traders the 'specks'. If the supply to the markets be large, as in the pride of the season, he will put his several kinds of specks in separate baskets. At other times all kinds are tossed together, and sometimes with an admixture of nuts and walnuts. The Irish women purchase these at a quarter, or within a quarter, of the regular price, paying from 6d. to 1s. a bushel for apples; 9d. to 1s. 6d. for pears; 1s. 6d. to 2s. 6d. for plums. They are then sorted into halfpenny-worths for sale on the stalls. Among the refuse is always a portion of what is called 'tidy' fruit, and this occupies the prominent place in the 'halfpenny lots' – for they are usually sold

at a halfpenny. Sometimes, too, a salesman will throw in among
the refuse a little good fruit, if he happen to have it over, either
gratuitously or at the refuse price; and this, of course, is always
made the most conspicuous on the stalls. Of other fruits, perhaps,
only a small portion is damaged, from over-ripeness, or by the
aggression of wasps and insects, the remainder being very fine, so
that the retail 'lots' are generally cheap. The sellers aim at 'half
profits', or cent. per cent.

The 'refuse' trade in fruit – and the refuse-trade is mainly
confined to fruit – is principally in the hands of the Irish. The
persons carrying it on are nearly all middle-aged and elderly
women. I once or twice saw a delicate and pretty-looking girl
sitting with the old 'refuse' women; but I found that she was not a
'regular hand', and only now and then 'minded the stall' in her
mother's absence. She worked with her needle, I was told.

Of the women who confine themselves to this trade there are
never less than twenty, and frequently thirty. Sometimes, when
the refuse is very cheap and very abundant, as many as 100 fruit-
sellers, women and girls, will sell it in halfpenny-worths, along
with better articles. These women also sell refuse dry-fruit, purchased in Duke's-place, but only when they cannot obtain green-
fruit, or cannot obtain it sufficiently. All is sold at stalls, as these
dealers seem to think that if it were hawked, the police might look
too inquisitively at a barrow stocked with refuse. The refuse-sellers
buy at all the markets. The poorer street-sellers, whose more staple
trade is in oranges or nuts, are *occasional* dealers in it.

Perhaps the regular refuse-buyers are not among the very
poorest class, as their sale is tolerably quick and certain, but
with the usual drawbacks of wet weather. They make, I was told,
from 4d. to 1s. a day the year round, or perhaps 7d. or 8d. a day,
Sunday included. They are all Roman Catholics, and resort to
the street-sale after mass. They are mostly widows, or women
who have reached middle-age, unmarried. Some are the wives
of street-sellers. Two of their best pitches are on Saffron-hill
and in Petticoat-lane. It is somewhat curious to witness these
women sitting in a line of five or six, and notwithstanding their
natural garrulity, hardly exchanging a word one with another.
Some of them derive an evident solace from deliberate puffs
at a short black pipe.

A stout, healthy-looking woman of this class said: 'Sure thin, sir, I've sat and sould my bit of fruit in this place, or near it, for twinty year and more, as is very well known indeed, is it. I could make twice the money twenty year ago that I can now, for the boys had the ha'pinnies more thin than they has now, more's the pity. The childer is my custhomers, very few beyant – such as has only a ha'pinny now and thin, God hilp them. They'll come a mile from any parrut, to spind it with such as me, for they know it's chape we sill! Yis, indeed, or they'll come with a fardin either, for it's a ha'pinny lot we'll split for them any time. The boys buys most, but they're dridful tazes. It's the patience of the divil must be had to dale wid the likes of thim. They was dridful about the Pope, but they've tired of it now. Oh no, it wasn't the boys of my counthry that demaned themselves that way. Well, I make 4d. some days, and 6d. some, and 1s. 6d. some, and I have made 3s. 6d., and I have made nothing. Perhaps I make 5s. or 6s. a week rigular, but I'm established and well-known you see.'

The quantity of refuse at the metropolitan 'green' markets varies with the different descriptions of fruit. Of apples it averages one-twentieth, and of plums and greengages one-fifteenth, of the entire supply. With pears, cherries, gooseberries, and currants, however, the damaged amounts to one-twelfth, while of straw-berries and mulberries it reaches as high as one-tenth of the aggregate quantity sent to market.

The Irish street-sellers, I am informed, buy full two-thirds of all the refuse, the other third being purchased by the lower class of English costermongers – 'the illegitimates', as they are called. We must not consider the sale of the damaged fruit so great an evil as it would, at the first blush, appear, for it constitutes perhaps the sole luxury of poor children, as well as of the poor themselves, who, were it not for the halfpenny and farthing lots of the refuse-sellers, would doubtlessly never know the taste of such things.

[. . .]

The street-Jews

[*volume ii. pp.115–132*]

Although my present inquiry relates to London life in London streets, it is necessary that I should briefly treat of the Jews generally, as an integral, but distinct and peculiar part of street-life. [. . .]

In what estimation the street-, and, incidentally, all classes of Jews are held at the present time, will be seen in the course of my remarks; and in the narratives to be given. I may here observe, however, that among some the dominant feeling against the Jews on account of their faith still flourishes, as is shown by the following statement: A gentleman of my acquaintance was one evening, about twilight, walking down Brydges-street, Covent-garden, when an elderly Jew was preceding him, apparently on his return from a day's work, as an old clothesman. His bag accidentally touched the bonnet of a dashing woman of the town, who was passing, and she turned round, abused the Jew, and spat at him, saying with an oath: 'You old rags humbug! You can't do that!' – an allusion to a vulgar notion that Jews have been unable to do more than *slobber*, since spitting on the Saviour.

The number of Jews now in England is computed at 35,000. This is the result at which the Chief Rabbi arrived a few years ago, after collecting all the statistical information at his command. Of these 35,000, more than one-half, or about 18,000, reside in London. I am informed that there may now be a small increase to this population, but only small, for many Jews have emigrated – some to California. A few years ago – a circumstance mentioned in my account of the street-sellers of jewellery – there were a number of Jews known as 'hawkers', or 'travellers', who traverse every part of England selling watches, gold and silver pencil-cases, eye-glasses, and all the more portable descriptions of jewellery, as well as thermometers, barometers, telescopes, and microscopes. This trade is now little pursued, except by the stationary dealers; and the Jews who carried it on, and who were chiefly foreign Jews, have emigrated to America. The foreign Jews who, though a fluctuating body, are always numerous in London, are included in the computation of 18,000; of this population two-thirds reside in the city, or the streets adjacent to the eastern boundaries of the city.

Of the trades and localities of the street-Jews
[*volume ii, pp. 117–119*]

The trades which the Jews most affect, I was told by one of themselves, are those in which, as they describe it, 'there's a chance'; that is, they prefer a trade in such commodity as is not subjected to a fixed price, so that there may be abundant scope for speculation, and something like a gambler's chance for profit or loss. In this way, Sir Walter Scott has said, trade has 'all the fascination of gambling, without the moral guilt'; but the absence of moral guilt in connection with such trading is certainly dubious.

The wholesale trades in foreign commodities which are now principally or solely in the hands of the Jews, often as importers and exporters, are, watches and jewels, sponges – fruits, especially green fruits, such as oranges, lemons, grapes, walnuts, cocoa-nuts, &c., and dates among dried fruits – shells, tortoises, parrots and foreign birds, curiosities, ostrich feathers, snuffs, cigars, and pipes; but cigars far more extensively at one time.

The localities in which these wholesale and retail traders reside are mostly at the East-end – indeed the Jews of London, as a congregated body, have been, from the times when their numbers were sufficient to institute a 'settlement' or 'colony', peculiar to themselves, always resident in the eastern quarter of the metropolis.

Of course a wealthy Jew millionaire – merchant, stock-jobber, or stock-broker – resides where he pleases – in a villa near the Marquis of Hertford's in the Regent's-park, a mansion near the Duke of Wellington's in Piccadilly, a house and grounds at Clapham or Stamford-hill; but these are exceptions. The quarters of the Jews are not difficult to describe. The trading-class in the capacity of shopkeepers, warehousemen, or manufacturers, are the thickest in Houndsditch, Aldgate, and the Minories, more especially as regards the 'swagshops' and the manufacture and sale of wearing apparel. The wholesale dealers in fruit are in Duke's-place and Pudding-lane (Thames-street), but the superior retail Jew fruiterers – some of whose shops are remarkable for the beauty of their fruit – are in Cheapside, Oxford-street, Piccadilly, and most of all in Covent-garden market. The inferior jewellers (some of whom deal with the first shops) are also at the East-end, about Whitechapel, Bevis-marks, and Houndsditch; the wealthier goldsmiths and watchmakers having, like other tradesmen of the class, their shops in the superior thoroughfares. The great congregation of working watchmakers is in Clerkenwell, but in that locality there are only a few Jews. The Hebrew dealers in second-hand garments, and second-hand wares generally, are located about Petticoat-lane, the peculiarities of which place I have lately described. The manufacturers of such things as cigars, pencils, and sealing-wax, the wholesale importers of sponge, bristles and toys, the dealers in quills and in 'looking-glasses', reside in large private-looking houses, when display is not needed for purposes of business, in such parts as Maunsell-street, Great Prescott-street, Great Ailie-street, Leman-street, and other parts of the eastern quarter known as Goodman's-fields. The wholesale dealers in foreign birds and shells, and in the many foreign things known as 'curiosities', reside in East Smithfield, Ratcliffe-highway, High-street (Shadwell), or in some of the parts adjacent to the Thames. In the long range of river-side streets, stretching from the Tower to Poplar and Blackwall, are Jews, who fulfil the many capacities of slop-sellers, &c., called into exercise by the requirements of seafaring people on their return from or commencement of a voyage. A few Jews keep boarding-houses for sailors in Shadwell and Wapping. Of the localities and abodes of the poorest of the Jews I shall speak hereafter.

Concerning the street-trades pursued by the Jews, I believe there is not at present a single one of which they can be said to have a monopoly; nor in any one branch of the street-traffic are there so many of the Jew traders as there were a few years back.

This remarkable change is thus to be accounted for. Strange as the fact may appear, the Jew has been undersold in the streets, and he has been beaten on what might be called his own ground – the buying of old clothes. The Jew boys, and the feebler and elder Jews, had, until some twelve or fifteen years back, almost the monopoly of orange and lemon street-selling, or street-hawking. The costermonger class had possession of the theatre doors and the approaches to the theatres; they had, too, occasionally their barrows full of oranges; but the Jews were the daily, assiduous, and itinerant street-sellers of this most popular of foreign, and perhaps of all, fruits. In their hopes of sale they followed any one a mile if encouraged, even by a few approving glances. The great theatre of this traffic was in the stage-coach yards in such inns as the Bull and Mouth (St Martin's-le-Grand), the Belle Sauvage (Ludgate-hill), the Saracen's Head (Snow-hill), the Bull (Aldgate), the Swan-with-two-Necks (Lad-lane, City), the George and Blue Boar (Holborn), the White Horse (Fetter-lane), and other such places. They were seen too, 'with all their eyes about them,' as one informant expressed it, outside the inns where the coaches stopped to take up passengers – at the White Horse Cellar in Piccadilly, for instance, and the Angel and the (now defunct) Peacock in Islington. A commercial traveller told me that he could never leave town by any 'mail' or 'stage' without being besieged by a small army of Jew boys, who most pertinaciously offered him oranges, lemons, sponges, combs, pocket-books, pencils, sealing-wax, paper, many-bladed pen-knives, razors, pocket-mirrors, and shaving-boxes – as if a man could not possibly quit the metropolis without requiring a stock of such commodities. In the whole of these trades, unless in some degree in sponges and blacklead-pencils, the Jew is now out-numbered or displaced.

I have before alluded to the underselling of the Jew boy by the Irish boy in the street-orange trade; but the characteristics of the change are so peculiar, that a further notice is necessary. It is curious to observe that the most assiduous, and hitherto the most successful of street-traders, were supplanted, not by a more per-severing or more skilful body of street-sellers, but simply by a more *starving* body. [. . .]

The Irish boy could live *harder* than the Jew – often in his own country he subsisted on a stolen turnip a day; he could lodge harder – lodge for 1*d*. a night in any noisome den, or sleep in the open air, which is seldom done by the Jew boy; he could dispense with the use of shoes and stockings – a dispensation at which his rival in trade revolted; he drank only water, or if he took tea or coffee, it was as a meal, and not merely as a beverage; to crown the whole, the city-bred Jew boy required some evening recre-ation, the penny or twopenny concert, or a game at draughts or dominoes; but this the Irish boy, country bred, never thought of, for *his* sole luxury was a deep sleep, and, being regardless or ignorant of all such recreations, he worked longer hours, and so sold more oranges, than his Hebrew competitor. Thus, as the Munster or Connaught lad could live on less than the young denizen of Petticoat-lane, he could sell at smaller profit, and did so sell, until gradually the Hebrew youths were displaced by the Irish in the street orange trade.

It is the same, or the same in a degree, with other street-trades, which were at one time all but monopolised by the Jew adults. Among these were the street-sale of spectacles and sponges. The prevalence of slop-work and slop-wages, and the frequent diffi-culty of obtaining properly-remunerated employment – the pinch of want, in short – have driven many mechanics to street-traffic; so that the numbers of street-traffickers have been augmented, while no small portion of the new comers have adopted the more knowing street avocations, formerly pursued only by the Jews.

[. . .]

Of the Jew old-clothes men
[*volume ii. pp.119–121*]
Fifty years ago the appearance of the street-Jews, engaged in the purchase of second-hand clothes, was different to what it is at the present time. The Jew then had far more of the distinctive garb and aspect of a foreigner. He not unfrequently wore the gabardine, which is never seen now in the streets, but some of the long loose frock coats worn by the Jew clothes' buyers resemble it. At that period, too, the Jew's long beard was far more distinctive than it is in this hirsute generation.

In other respects the street-Jew is unchanged. Now, as during the last century, he traverses every street, square, and road, with the monotonous cry, sometimes like a bleat, of 'Clo'! Clo'!' On this head, however, I have previously remarked, when describing the street-Jew of a hundred years ago.

In an inquiry into the condition of the old-clothes dealers a year and a half ago, a Jew gave me the following account. He told me, at the commencement of his statement, that he was of opinion that his people were far more speculative than the Gentiles, and therefore the English liked better to deal with them. 'Our people,' he said, 'will be out all day in the wet, and begrudge themselves a bit of anything to eat till they go home, and then, may be, they'll gamble away their crown, just for the love of speculation.' My informant, who could write or speak several languages, and had been 50 years in the business, then said, 'I am no bigot; indeed I do not care where I buy my meat, so long as I can get it. I often go into the Minories and buy some, without looking to how it has been killed, or whether it has a seal on it or not.'

He then gave me some account of the Jewish children, and the number of men in the trade, which I have embodied under the proper heads. The itinerant Jew clothes man, he told me, was generally the son of a former old-clothes man, but some were cigar-makers, or pencil-makers, taking to the clothes business, when those trades were slack; but that nineteen out of twenty had been born to it. If the parents of the Jew boy are poor, and the boy a sharp lad, he generally commences business at ten years of age, by selling lemons, or some trifle in the streets, and so, as he expressed it, the boy 'gets a round', or street-connection, by becoming known to the neighbourhoods he visits. If he sees a servant, he will, when selling his lemons, ask if she have any old shoes or old clothes, and offer to be a purchaser. If the clothes should come to more than the Jew boy has in his pocket, he leaves what silver he has as 'an earnest upon them', and then seeks some regular Jew clothes man, who will advance the purchase money. This the old Jew agrees to do upon the understanding that he is to have 'half Rybeck', that is, a moiety of the profit, and then he will accompany the boy to the house, to pass his judgment on the goods, and satisfy himself that the stripling has not made a blind bargain, an error into which he very rarely falls. After this he goes with the lad to Petticoat-lane, and there they share whatever money the clothes may bring over and above what has been paid for them. By such means the Jew boy gets his knowledge of the old-clothes business; and so quick are these lads generally, that in the course of two months they will acquire sufficient experience in connection with the trade to begin dealing on their own account. There are some, he told me, as sharp at 15 as men of 50.

'It is very seldom,' my informant stated, 'very seldom indeed, that a Jew clothes man takes away any of the property of the house he may be called into. I expect there's a good many of 'em,' he continued, for he sometimes spoke of his co-traders as if they were not of his own class, 'is fond of cheating – that is, they won't mind giving only 2s. for a thing that's worth 5s. They are fond of money, and will do almost anything to get it. Jews are perhaps the most money-loving people in all England. There are certainly some old-clothes men who will buy articles at such a price that they must know them to have been stolen. Their rule, however, is to ask no questions, and to get as cheap an article as possible. A Jew clothes man is seldom or never seen in liquor. They gamble for money, either at their own homes or at public-houses. The favourite games are tossing, dominoes, and cards.

[...]

'They seldom go to synagogue, and on a Sunday evening have card parties at their own houses. They seldom eat anything on their rounds. The reason is, not because they object to eat meat killed by a Christian, but because they are afraid of losing a "deal", or the chance of buying a lot of old clothes by delay. They are generally too lazy to light their own fires before they start of a morning, and nineteen out of twenty obtain their breakfasts at the coffee-shops about Houndsditch.

'When they return from their day's work they have mostly some stew ready, prepared by their parents or wife. If they are not family men they go to an eating-house. This is sometimes a Jewish house, but if no-one is looking they creep into a Christian "cook-shop", not being particular about eating "tryfer" – that is, meat which has been killed by a Christian. Those that are single generally go to a neighbour and agree with him to be boarded on the Sabbath; and for this the charge is generally about 2s. 6d. On a Saturday there's cold fish for breakfast and supper; indeed, a Jew would pawn the shirt off his back sooner than go without fish then; and in holiday-time he will have it, if he has to get it out of the stones. It is not reckoned a holiday unless there's fish.'

'Forty years ago I have made as much as 5l. in a week by the purchase of old clothes in the streets,' said a Jew informant. 'Upon an average then, I could earn weekly about 2l. But now things are different. People are more wide awake. Every one knows the value of an old coat now-a-days. The women know more than the men. The general average, I think, take the good weeks with the bad throughout the year, is about 1l. a week; some weeks we get 2l., and some scarcely nothing.'

I was told by a Jewish professional gentleman that the account of the *spirit* of gambling prevalent among his people was correct, but the amounts said to be staked, he thought, rare or exaggerated.

The Jew old-clothes men are generally far more cleanly in their habits than the poorer classes of English people. Their hands they always wash before their meals, and this is done whether the party be a strict Jew or 'Meshumet', a convert, or apostate from Judaism. Neither will the Israelite ever use the same knife to cut his meat that he previously used to spread his butter, and he will not even put his meat on a plate that has had butter on it; nor will he use for his soup the spoon that has had melted butter in it. This objection to mix butter with meat is carried so far, that, after partaking of the one, Jews will not eat of the other for the space of two hours. The Jews are generally, when married, most exemplary family men. There are few fonder fathers than they are, and they will starve themselves sooner than their wives and children should want. Whatever their faults may be, they are good fathers, husbands, and sons. Their principal characteristic is their extreme love of money; and, though the strict Jew does not trade himself on the Sabbath, he may not object to employ either one of his tribe, or a Gentile, to do so for him.

The capital required for commencing in the old-clothes line is generally about 1l. This the Jew frequently borrows, especially after holiday-time, for then he has generally spent all his earnings, unless he be a provident man. When his stock-money is exhausted, he goes either to a neighbour or to a publican in the vicinity, and borrows 1l. on the Monday morning, 'to strike a light with,' as he calls it, and agrees to return it on the Friday evening, with 1l. interest for the loan. This he always pays back. If he was to sell the coat off his back he would do this, I am told, because to fail in so doing would be to prevent his obtaining any stock-money for the future. With this capital he starts on his rounds about eight in the morning, and I am assured he will frequently begin his work without tasting food, rather than break into the borrowed stock-money. Each man has his particular walk, and never interferes with that of his neighbour; indeed, while upon another's beat he will seldom cry for clothes. Sometimes they go 'half Rybeck' together – that is, they will share the profits of the day's business, and when they agree to do this the one will take one street, and the other another. The lower the neighbourhood the more old clothes are there for sale. At the east end of the town they like the neighbourhoods frequented by

THE JEW OLD–CLOTHES MAN

'CLO', CLO', CLO'.'

[from a daguerrotype by Beard]

sailors, and there they purchase of the girls and the women the sailors' jackets and trowsers. But they buy most of the Petticoat-lane, the Old-Clothes Exchange, and the marine-store dealers; for as the Jew clothes man never travels the streets by night-time, the parties who then have old clothes to dispose of usually sell them to the marine-store or second-hand dealers over-night, and the Jew buys them in the morning. The first thing that he does on his rounds is to seek out these shops, and see what he can pick up there. A very great amount of business is done by the Jew clothes man at the marine-store shops at the west as well as at the east end of London.

At the West-end the itinerant clothes men prefer the mews at the back of gentlemen's houses to all other places, or else the streets where the little tradesmen and small genteel families reside. My informant assured me that he had once bought a Bishop's hat of his lordship's servant for 1s. 6d. on a Sunday morning.

These traders, as I have elsewhere stated, live at the East-end of the town. The greater number of them reside in Portsoken Ward, Houndsditch; and their favourite localities in this district are either Cobb's-yard, Roper's-building, or Wentworth-street. They mostly occupy small houses, about 4s. 6d. a week rent, and live with their families. They are generally sober men. It is seldom that a Jew leaves his house and owes his landlord money; and if his goods should be seized the rest of his tribe will go round and collect what is owing.

The rooms occupied by the old-clothes men are far from being so comfortable as those of the English artisans whose earnings are not superior to the gains of these clothes men. Those which I saw had all a littered look; the furniture was old and scant, and the apartment seemed neither shop, parlour, nor bed-room. For domestic and family men, as some of the Jew old-clothes men are, they seem very indifferent to the comforts of a home.

[. . .]

I am informed that of the Jew old-clothes men there are now only from 500 to 600 in London; at one time there might have been 1,000. Their average earnings may be something short of 20s. a week in second-hand clothes alone; but the gains are difficult to estimate.

Of a Jew street-seller
[*volume ii. p.122*]

An elderly man, who, at the time I saw him, was vending spectacles, or bartering them for old clothes, old books, or any second-hand articles, gave me an account of his street-life, but it presented little remarkable beyond the not unusual vicissitudes of the lives of those of his class.

He had been in every street-trade, and had on four occasions travelled all over England, selling quills, sealing-wax, pencils, sponges, braces, cheap or superior jewellery, thermometers, and pictures. He had sold barometers in the mountainous parts of Cumberland, sometimes walking for hours without seeing man or woman. '*I liked it then*,' he said, '*for I was young and strong, and didn't care to sleep twice in the same town*. I was afterwards in the old-clothes line. I buy a few odd hats and light things still, but I'm not able to carry heavy weights, as my breath is getting rather short.' [I find that the Jews generally object to the more laborious kinds of street-traffic.] 'Yes, I've been twice to Ireland, and sold a good many quills in Dublin, for I crossed over from Liverpool. Quills and wax were a great trade with us once; now it's quite different. I've had as much as 60*l*. of my own, and that more than half-a-dozen times, but all of it went in speculations. Yes, some went in gambling. I had a share in a gaming-booth at the races, for three years. Oh, I dare say that's more than 20 years back; but we did very little good. There was such fees to pay for the tent on a race-ground, and often such delays between the races in the different towns, and bribes to be given to the town-officers – such as town-sergeants and chief constables, and I hardly know who – and so many expenses altogether, that the profits were mostly swamped. Once at Newcastle races there was a fight among the pitmen, and our tent was in their way, and was demolished almost to bits. A deal of the money was lost or stolen. I don't know how much, but not near so much as my partners wanted to make out. I wasn't on the spot just at the time. I got married after that, and took a shop in the second-hand clothes line in Bristol, but my wife died in child-bed in less than a year, and the shop didn't answer; so I got sick of it, and at last got rid of it. Oh, I work both the country and London still. I shall take a turn into Kent in a day or two. I suppose I clear between 10*s*. and 20*s*. a week in anything, and as I've only myself, I do middling, and am ready for another chance if any likely speculation offers. I lodge with a relation, and sometimes live with his family. No, I never touch any meat but "Coshar". I suppose my meat now costs me 6d. or 7d. a day, but it has cost me ten times that – and 2d. for beer in addition.'

I am informed that there are about 50 adult Jews (besides old-clothes men) in the streets selling fruit, cakes, pencils, spectacles, sponge, accordions, drugs, &c.

Of the Jew-boy street-sellers
[*volume ii. pp.122,123*]

I have ascertained, and from sources where no ignorance on the subject could prevail, that there are now in the streets of London, rather more than 100 Jew-boys engaged principally in fruit and cake-selling in the streets. Very few Jewesses are itinerant street-sellers. Most of the older Jews thus engaged have been street-sellers from their boyhood. The young Jews who ply in street-callings, however, are all men in matters of traffic, almost before they cease, in years, to be children. In addition to the Jew-boy street-sellers above enumerated, there are from 50 to 100, but usually about 50, who are occasional, or 'casual' street-traders, vending for the most part cocoa-nuts and grapes, and confining their sales chiefly to the Sundays.

On the subject of the street-Jew boys, a Hebrew gentleman said to me: 'When we speak of street-Jew boys, it should be understood, that the great majority of them are but little more conversant with or interested in the religion of their fathers, than are the costermonger boys of whom you have written. They are Jews by the accident of their birth, as others in the same way, with equal ignorance of the assumed faith, are Christians.'

I received from a Jew-boy the following account of his trading pursuits and individual aspirations. There was somewhat of a thickness in his utterance, otherwise his speech was but little distinguishable from that of an English street-boy. His physiognomy was decidedly Jewish, but not of the handsomer type. His hair was light-coloured, but clean, and apparently well brushed, without being oiled, or, as I heard a street-boy style it, 'greased'; it was long, and he said his aunt told him it 'wanted cutting sadly'; but he 'liked it that way'; indeed, he kept dashing his curls from his eyes, and back from his temples, as he was conversing, as if he were somewhat vain of doing so. He was dressed in a corduroy suit, old but not ragged, and wore a tolerably clean, very coarse, and altogether buttonless shirt, which he said 'was made for one bigger than me, sir.' He had bought it for 9*d*. in Petticoat-lane, and accounted it a bargain, as its wear would be durable. He was selling sponges when I saw him, and of the commonest kind, offering a large piece for 3*d*., which (he admitted) would be rubbed to bits in no time. This sponge, I should mention, is frequently 'dressed' with sulphuric acid, and an eminent surgeon informed me that on his servant attempting to clean his black dress coat with a sponge that he had newly bought in the streets, the colour of the garment, to his horror, changed to a bright purple. The Jew-boy said:

'I believe I'm twelve. I've been to school, but it's long since, and my mother was very ill then, and I was forced to go out in the streets to have a chance. I never was kept to school. I can't read; I've forgot all about it. I'd rather now that I could read, but very likely I could soon learn if I could only spare time, but if I stay long in the house I feel sick; it's not healthy. Oh no, sir, inside or out it would be all the same to me, just to make a living and keep my health. I can't say how long it is since I began to sell, it's a good long time; one must do something. I could keep myself now, and do sometimes, but my father − I live with him (my mother's dead) is often laid up. Would you like to see him, sir? He knows a deal. No, he can't write, but he can read a little. Can I speak Hebrew? Well, I know what you mean. Oh no, I can't. I don't go to synagogue; I haven't time. My father goes, but only sometimes; so he says, and he tells me to look out, for we must both go by-and-by.' [I began to ask him what he knew of Joseph, and others recorded in the Old Testament, but he bristled up, and asked if I wanted to make a Meshumet (a convert) of him?] 'I have sold all sorts of things,' he continued, 'oranges, and lemons, and sponges, and nuts, and sweets. I should like to have a real good ginger-beer fountain of my own; but I must wait, and there's many in the trade. I only go with boys of my own sort. I sell to all sorts of boys, but that's nothing. Very likely they're Christians, but that's nothing to me. I don't know what's the difference between a Jew and Christian, and I don't want to talk about it. The Meshumets are never any good. Anybody will tell you that. Yes, I like music and can sing a bit. I get to a penny and sometimes a two-penny concert. No, I haven't been to Sussex Hall – I know where it is – I shouldn't understand it. You get in for nothing, that's one thing. I've heard of Baron Rothschild. He has more money than I could count in shillings in a year. I don't know about his wanting to get into parliament, or what it means; but he's sure to do it or anything else, with his money. He's very charitable, I've heard. I don't know whether he's a German Jew, or a Portegee, or what. He's a cut above me, a precious sight. I only wish he was my uncle. I can't say what I should do if I had his money. Perhaps I should go a-travelling, and see everything everywhere. I don't know how long the Jews have been in England; always perhaps. Yes, I know there's Jews in other countries. This sponge is Greek sponge, but I don't know where it's grown, only it's in foreign parts. Jerusalem! Yes, I've heard of it. I'm of no tribe that I know of. I buy what I eat about Petticoat-lane. No, I don't like fish, but the stews, and the onions with them is beautiful for two-pence; you may get a pennorth. The pickles – cowcumbers is best – are stunning. But they're plummiest with a bit of cheese or anything cold – that's my opinion, but you may think different. Pork! Ah! No, I never touched it; I'd as soon eat a cat; so would my father. No, sir, I don't think pork smells nice in a cook-shop, but some Jew boys, as I knows, thinks it does. I don't know why it shouldn't be eaten, only that it's wrong to eat it. No, I never touched a ham-sandwich, but other Jew boys have, and laughed at it, I know.

'I don't know what I make in a week. I think I make as much on one thing as on another. I've sold strawberries, and cherries, and gooseberries, and nuts and walnuts in the season. Oh, as to what I make, that's nothing to nobody. Sometimes 6d. a day, sometimes 1s.; sometimes a little more, and sometimes nothing. No, I never sells inferior things if I can help it, but if one hasn't stock-money one must do as one can, but it isn't so easy to try it on. There was a boy beaten by a woman not long since for selling a big pottle of strawberries that was rubbish all under the toppers. It was all strawberry leaves, and crushed strawberries, and such like. She wanted to take back from him the two-pence she'd paid for it, and got hold of his pockets and there was a regular fight, but she didn't get a farthing back though she tried her very hardest, 'cause he slipped from her and hooked it. So you see it's dangerous to try it on.' [This last remark was made gravely enough, but the lad told of the feat with such manifest glee, that I'm inclined to believe that he himself was the culprit in question.] 'Yes, it was a Jew boy it happened to, but other boys in the streets is just the same. Do I like the streets? I can't say I do, there's too little to be made in them. *No, I wouldn't like to go to school, nor to be in a shop, nor be anybody's servant but my own.* Oh, I don't know what I shall be when I'm grown up. I shall take my chance like others.'

Of the pursuits, dwellings, traffic, etc., of the Jew-boy street-sellers
[*volume ii. pp. 123, 124*]

To speak of the street Jew-boys as regards their traffic, manners, haunts, and associations, is to speak of the same class of boys who may not be employed regularly in street-sale, but are the comrades of those who are; a class, who, on any cessation of their employment in cigar manufactories, or indeed any capacity, will apply themselves temporarily to street-selling, for it seems to these poor and uneducated lads a sort of natural vocation.

These youths, *uncontrolled* or *incontrollable* by their parents (who are of the lowest class of the Jews, and who often, I am told, care little about the matter, so long as the child can earn his own maintenance), frequently in the evenings, after their day's work, resort to coffee-shops, in preference even to a cheap concert-room. In these places they amuse themselves as men might do in a tavern where the landlord leaves his guests to their own caprices. Sometimes one of them reads aloud from some exciting or degrading book, the lads who are unable to read listening with all the intentness with which many of the uneducated attend to any one reading. The reading is, however, not unfrequently interrupted by rude comments from the listeners. If a newspaper be read, the 'police', or 'crimes', are mostly the parts preferred. But the most approved way of passing the evening, among the Jew-boys, is to play at draughts, dominoes, or cribbage, and to bet on the play. Draughts and dominoes are unpractised among the costermonger boys, but some of the young Jews are adepts in those games.

[. . .]

The dwellings of boys such as these are among the worst in London, as regards ventilation, comfort, or cleanliness. They reside in the courts and recesses about Whitechapel and Petticoat-lane, and generally in a garret. If not orphans they usually dwell with their father. I am told that the care of a mother is almost indispensable to a poor Jew-boy, and having that care he seldom becomes an outcast. The Jewesses and Jew-girls are rarely itinerant street-sellers – not in the proportion of one to twelve, compared with the men and boys; in this respect therefore the street Jews differ widely from the English costermongers and the street Irish, nor are the Hebrew females even stall-keepers in the same proportion.

[. . .]

The callings of which the Jew-boys have the monopoly are not connected with the sale of any especial article, but rather with such things as present a variety from those ordinarily offered in the streets, such as cakes, sweetmeats, fried fish, and (in the winter) elder wine. The cakes known as 'boolers' – a mixture of egg, flour, and candied orange or lemon peel, cut very thin, and with a slight colouring from saffron or something similar – are now sold principally, and used to be sold exclusively, by the Jew-boys. Almond cakes (little round cakes of crushed almonds) are at present vended by the Jew-boys, and their sponge biscuits are in demand. All these dainties are bought by the street-lads of the Jew pastry-cooks. The difference in these cakes, in their sweetmeats, and their elder wine, is that there is a dash of spice about them not ordinarily met with. It is the same with the fried fish, a little spice or pepper being blended with the oil. In the street-sale of pickles the Jews have also the monopoly; these, however, are seldom hawked, but generally sold from windows and door-steads. The pickles are cucumbers or gherkins, and onions – a large cucumber being 2d., and the smaller 1d. and ½d.

The faults of the Jew lad are an eagerness to make money by any means, so that he often grows up a cheat, a trickster, a receiver of stolen goods, though seldom a thief, for he leaves that to others. He is content to profit by the thief's work, but seldom steals himself, however he may cheat.

[. . .]

Of the street Jewesses and street Jew-girls
[*volume ii. pp.124,125*]

I have mentioned that the Jewesses and the young Jew-girls, compared with the adult Jews and Jew-boys, are not street-traders in anything like the proportion which the females were found to bear to the males among the Irish street-folk and the English costermongers. There are, however, a few Jewish females who are itinerant street-sellers as well as stall-keepers, in the proportion, perhaps, of one female to seven or eight males. The majority of the street Jew-girls whom I saw on a round were accompanied by boys who were represented to be their brothers, and I have little doubt such was the facts, for these young Jewesses, although often pert and ignorant, are not unchaste. Of this I was assured by a medical gentleman who could speak with sufficient positiveness on the subject.

Fruit is generally sold by these boys and girls together, the lad driving the barrow, and the girl inviting custom and handing the purchases to the buyers. In tending a little stall or a basket at a regular pitch, with such things as cherries or strawberries, the little Jewess differs only from her street-selling sisters in being a brisker trader. The stalls, with a few old knives or scissors, or odds and ends of laces, that are tended by the Jew-girls in the streets in the Jewish quarters (I am told there are not above a dozen of them) are generally near the shops and within sight of their parents or friends. One little Jewess, with whom I had some conversation, had not even heard the name of the Chief Rabbi, the Rev. Dr Adler, and knew nothing of any distinction between German and Portuguese Jews; she had, I am inclined to believe, never heard of either. I am told that the whole, or nearly the whole, of these young female traders reside with parents or friends, and that there is among them far less than the average number of runaways. One Jew told me he thought that the young female members of his tribe did not tramp with the juveniles of the other sex – no, not in the proportion of one to a hundred in comparison, he said with a laugh, with 'young women of the Christian persuasion'. My informant had means of knowing this fact, as although still a young man, he had traversed the greater part of England hawking perfumery, which he had abandoned as a bad trade. A wireworker, long familiar with tramping and going into the country –

a man upon whose word I have every reason to rely – told me that he could not remember a single instance of his having seen a young Jewess 'travelling' with a boy.

There are a few adult Jewesses who are itinerant traders, but very few. I met with one who carried on her arm a not very large basket, filled with glass wares; chiefly salt-cellars, cigar-ash plates, blue glass dessert plates, vinegar-cruets, and such like. The greater part of her wares appeared to be blue, and she carried nothing but glass. She was a good-looking and neatly-dressed woman. She peeped in at each shop-door, and up at the windows of every private house, in the street in which I met her, crying, 'Clo', old clo'!' She bartered her glass for old clothes, or bought the garments, dealing principally in female attire, and almost entirely with women. She declined to say anything about her family or her circumstances, except that she had nothing that way to complain about, but – when I had used some names I had authority to make mention of – she said she would, with pleasure, tell me all about her trade, which she carried on rather than do nothing. 'When I hawk,' she said with an English accent, her face being unmistakeably Jewish, 'I hawk only good glass, and it can hardly be called hawking, as I swop it for more than I sell it. I always ask for the mistress, and if she wants any of my glass we come to a bargain if we can. Oh, it's ridiculous to see what things some ladies – I suppose they must be called ladies – offer for my glass. Children's green or blue gauze veils, torn or faded, and not worth picking up, because no use whatever; old ribbons, not worth dyeing, and old frocks, not worth washing. People say, "as keen as a Jew", but ladies can't think we're very keen when they offer us such rubbish. I do most at the middle kind of houses, both shops and private. I sometimes give a little money for such a thing as a shawl, or a fur tippet, as well as my glass – but only when I can't help it – to secure a bargain. Sometimes, but not often, I get the old thing and a trifle for my glass. Occasionally I buy outright. I don't do much, there's so many in the line, and I don't go out regularly. I can't say how many women are in my way – very few; Oh, I do middling. I told you I had no complaints to make. I don't calculate my profits or what I sell. My family do that and I don't trouble myself.'

Of the synagogues and the religion of the street- and other Jews
[*volume ii. pp.125,126*]

The Jews in this country are classed as 'Portuguese' and 'German'. Among them are no distinctions of tribes, but there is of rites and ceremonies, as is set forth in the following extract (which shows also the mode of government) from a Jewish writer: 'The Spanish and Portuguese Congregation of Jews, who are also called Sephardin (from the word Sepharad, which signifies Spain in Hebrew), are distinct from the German and Polish Jews in their ritual service. The prayers both daily and for the Sabbath materially differ from each other, and the festival prayers differ still more. Hence the Portuguese Jews have a distinct prayer-book, and the German Jews likewise.

'The fundamental laws are equally observed by both sects, but in the ceremonial worship there exists numerous differences. The Portuguese Jews eat some food during the Passover, which the German Jews are prohibited doing by some Rabbis, but their authority is not acknowledged by the Portuguese Rabbis. Nor are the present ecclesiastical authorities in London of the two sects the same. The Portuguese Jews have their own Rabbis, and the German have their own. The German Jews are much more numerous than the Portuguese; the chief Rabbi of the German Jews is the Rev. Dr Nathan Marcus Adler, late Chief Rabbi of Hanover, who wears no beard, and dresses in the German costume. The presiding Rabbi of the Portuguese Jews is the Rev. David Meldola, a native of Leghorn; his father filled the same office in London. Each chief Rabbi is supported by three other Rabbis, called Dayamin, which signifies in Hebrew "Judges". Every Monday and Thursday the Chief Rabbi of the German Jews, Dr Adler, supported by his three colleagues, sits for two hours in the Rabbinical College (Beth Hamedrash), Smith's-buildings, Leadenhall-street, to attend to all applications from the German Jews, which may be brought before him, and which are decided according to the Jewish law. Many disputes between Jews in religious matters are settled in this manner; and if the Lord Mayor or any other magistrate is told that the matter has already been settled by the Jewish Rabbi he seldom interferes. This applies only to civil and not to criminal cases. The Portuguese Jews have their own hospital and their own schools. Both congregations have their representatives in the Board of Deputies of British

Jews, which board is acknowledged by government, and is triennial. Sir Moses Montefiore, a Jew of great wealth, who distinguished himself by his mission to Damascus, during the persecution of the Jews in that place, and also by his mission to Russia, some years ago, is the President of the Board. All political matters, calling for communications with government, are within the province of that useful board.'

The Jews have eight synagogues in London, besides some smaller places which may perhaps, adopting the language of another church, be called synagogues of ease. The great synagogue in Duke's-place (a locality of which I have often had to speak) is the largest, but the new synagogue, St Helen's, Bishopgate, is the one which most betokens the wealth of the worshippers. It is rich with ornaments, marble, and painted glass; the pavement is of painted marble, and presents a perfect round, while the ceiling is a half dome. There are besides these the Hamburg Synagogue, in Fen-church-street; the Portuguese Synagogue, in Bevis-marks; two smaller places, in Cutler-street and Gun-yard, Houndsditch, known as Polish Synagogues; the Maiden-lane (Covent-garden), Synagogue; the Western Synagogue, St Alban's-place, Pall-mall; and the West London Synagogue of British Jews, Margaret-street, Cavendish-square. The last-mentioned is the most aristocratic of the synagogues. The service there is curtailed, the ritual abbreviated, and the days of observance of the Jewish festival reduced from two to one. This alteration is strongly protested against by the other Jews, and the practices of this synagogue seem to show a yielding to the exactions or requirements of the wealthy. [. . .]

The synagogues are not well attended, the congregations being smaller in proportion to the population than those of the Church of England. Neither, during the observance of the Jewish worship, is there any especial manifestation of the service being regarded as of a sacred and divinely-ordained character. There is a buzzing talk among the attendants during the ceremony, and an absence of seriousness and attention. Some of the Jews, however, show the greatest devotion, and the same may be said of the Jewesses, who sit apart in the synagogues, and are not required to attend so regularly as the men.

I should not have alluded to this absence of the solemnities of devotion, as regards the congregations of the Hebrews, had I not heard it regretted by Hebrews themselves. 'It is shocking,' one said. Another remarked, 'To attend the synagogue is looked upon too much as a matter of business; but perhaps there is the same spirit in some of the Christian churches.'

As to the street-Jews, religion is little known among them, or little cared for. They are indifferent to it – not to such a degree, indeed, as the costermongers, for they are not so ignorant a class – but yet contrasting strongly in their neglect with the religious intensity of the majority of the Roman Catholic Irish of the streets. [. . .]

Among the Jews I conversed with – and of course only the more intelligent understood, or were at all interested in, the question – I heard the most contemptuous denunciation of all converts from Judaism. One learned informant, who was by no means blind to the short-comings of his own people, expressed his conviction that no Jew had ever been really *converted*. He had abandoned his faith from interested motives. On this subject I am not called upon to express any opinion, and merely mention it to show a prevalent feeling among the class I am describing.

The street-Jews, including the majority of the more prosperous and most numerous class among them, the old-clothes men, are far from being religious in feeling, or well versed in their faith, and are, perhaps, in that respect on a level with the mass of the members of the Church of England; I say of the Church of England, because of that church the many who do not profess religion are usually accounted members.

[. . .]

Of the politics, literature, and amusements of the Jews
[*volume ii. pp.126,127*]

Perhaps there is no people in the world, possessing the average amount of intelligence in busy communities, who care so little for politics as the general body of the Jews. The wealthy classes may take an interest in the matter, but I am assured, and by those who know their countrymen well, that even with them such a quality as patriotism is a mere word. This may be accounted for in a great measure, perhaps, from an hereditary feeling. The Jew could hardly be expected to love a land, or to strive for the promotion of its general welfare, where he felt he was but a sojourner, and where he was at the best but tolerated and often proscribed. But this feeling becomes highly reprehensible when it extends – as I am assured it does among many of the rich Jews – to their own people, for whom, apart from conventionalities, say my informants, *they care nothing whatever*, for so long as they are undisturbed in money-getting at home, their brethren may be persecuted all over the world, while the rich Jew merely shrugs his shoulders. [. . .]

I was told by a Hebrew gentleman (a professional man) that so little did the Jews themselves care for 'Jewish emancipation', that he questioned if one man in ten, actuated solely by his own feelings, would trouble himself to walk the length of the street in which he lived to secure Baron Rothschild's admission into the House of Commons. This apathy, my informant urged with perfect truth, in nowise affected the merits of the question, though he was convinced it formed a great obstacle to Baron Rothschild's success; 'for governments,' he said, 'won't give boons to people who don't care for them; and, though this is called a boon, I look upon it as only a right.'

When such is the feeling of the comparatively wealthier Jews, no-one can wonder that I found among the Jewish street-sellers and old-clothes men with whom I talked on the subject – and their more influential brethren gave me every facility to prosecute my inquiry among them – a perfect indifference to, and nearly as perfect an ignorance of, politics. Perhaps no men buy so few newspapers, and read them so little, as the Jews generally. The street-traders, when I alluded to the subject, said they read little but the 'Police Reports'.

Among the body of the Jews there is little love of Literature. They read far less (let it be remembered I have acquired all this information from Jews themselves, and from men who could not be mistaken in the matter), and are far less familiar with English authorship, either historical or literary, than are the poorer English artisans. Neither do the wealthiest classes of the Jews care to foster literature among their own people. One author, a short time ago, failing to interest the English Jews, to promote the publication of his work, went to the United States, and his book was issued in Philadelphia, the city of Quakers!

The amusements of the Jews – and here I speak more especially of the street or open-air traders – are the theatres and concert rooms. The City of London Theatre, the Standard Theatre, and other playhouses at the East-end of London, are greatly resorted to by the Jews, and more especially by the younger members of the body, who sometimes constitute a rather obstreperous gallery. The cheap concerts which they patronise are generally of a superior order, for the Jews are fond of music, and among them have been many eminent composers and performers, so that the trash and jingle which delights the costermonger class would not please the street Jew-boys; hence their concerts are superior to the general run of cheap concerts, and are almost always 'got up' by their own people.

Sussex-hall, in Leadenhall-street, is chiefly supported by Israelites; there the 'Jews' and General Literary and Scientific Institution' is established, with reading-rooms and a library; and there lectures, concerts, &c., are given as at similar institutions. Of late, on every Friday evening, Sussex-hall has been thrown open to the general public, without any charge for admission, and lectures have been delivered gratuitously, on literature, science, art, and general sub-jects, which have attracted crowded audiences. The lecturers are chiefly Jews, but the lectures are neither theological nor sectarian. The lecturers are Mr M. H. Bresslau, the Rev. B. H. Ascher, Mr J. L. Levison (of Brighton), and Mr Clarke, a merchant in the City, a Christian, whose lectures are very popular among the Jews. The behaviour of the Jew attendants, and the others, the Jews being the majority, is decorous. They seem 'to like to receive information', I was told; and a gentleman connected with the hall argued that this attention showed a readiness for proper instruction, when given in an attractive form, which favoured the opinion that the young Jews, when not thrown in childhood into the vortex of money-making, were very easily teachable, while their natural quickness made them both ready and willing to be taught.

[. . .]

Of the charities, schools, and education of the Jews
[volume ii, pp. 127,130]
The Jewish charities are highly honourable to the body, for they allow none of their people to live or die in a parish workhouse. It is true that among the Jews in London there are many individuals of immense wealth; but there are also many rich Christians who

care not one jot for the need of their brethren. It must be borne in mind also, that not only do the Jews voluntarily support their own poor and institutions, but they contribute – compulsorily it is true – their quota to the support of the English poor and church; and, indeed, pay their due proportion of all the parliamentary or local imposts. This is the more honourable and the more remarkable among the Jews, when we recollect their indisputable greed of money.

If a Jew be worn out in his old age, and unable to maintain himself, he is either supported by the contributions of his friends, or out of some local or general fund, or provided for in some asylum, and all this seems to be done with a less than ordinary fuss and display, so that the recipient of the charity feels himself more a pensioner than a pauper.

The Jews' Hospital, in the Mile-end Road, is an extensive building, into which feeble old men and destitute children of both sexes are admitted. Here the boys are taught trades, and the girls qualified for respectable domestic service. The Widows' Home, in Duke-street, Aldgate, is for poor Hebrew widows. The Orphan Asylum, built at the cost of Mr A. L. Moses, and supported by subscription, now contains 14 girls and 3 boys; a school is attached to the asylum, which is in the Tenter Ground, Goodman's-fields. The Hand-in-Hand Asylum, for decayed old people, men and women, is in Duke's-place, Aldgate. There are likewise alms-houses for the Jews, erected also by Mr A. L. Moses, at Mile-end, and other alms-houses, erected by Mr Joel Emanuel, in Wellclose-square, near the Tower. There are, further, three institutions for granting marriage dowers to fatherless children; an institution in Bevis-marks, for the burial of the poor of the congregation; 'Beth Holim', a house for the reception of the sick poor, and of poor lying-in women belonging to the congregation of the Spanish and Portuguese Jews; 'Magasim Zobim', for lending money to aid apprenticeships among boys, to fit girls for good domestic service, and for helping poor children to proceed to foreign parts, when it is believed that the change will be advantageous to them; and 'Noten Lebem Larcebim', to distribute bread to the poor of the congregation on the day preceding the Sabbath.

I am assured that these institutions are well-managed, and that, if the charities are abused by being dispensed to undeserving objects, it is usually with the knowledge of the managers, who often let the abuse pass, as a smaller evil than driving a man to theft or subjecting him to the chance of starvation. One gentleman, familiar with most of these establishments, said to me with a laugh, 'I believe, if you have had any conversation with the gentlemen who manage these matters, you will have concluded that they are not the people to be imposed upon very easily.'

There are seven Jewish schools in London, four in the city, and three at the West-end, all supported by voluntary contributions. [. . .]

Notwithstanding these means of education, the body of the poorer, or what in other callings might be termed the working-classes, are not even tolerably well educated; they are indifferent to the matter. With many, the multiplication table seems to constitute what they think the acme of all knowledge needful to a man. The great majority of the Jew-boys, in the street, cannot read. A smaller portion can read, but so imperfectly that their ability to read detracts nothing from their ignorance. So neglectful or so necessitous (but I heard the ignorance attributed to neglect far more frequently than necessity) are the poorer Jews, and so soon do they take their children away from school, 'to learn and do something for themselves', and so irregular is their attendance, on the plea that the time cannot be spared, and the boy must do something for himself, that many children leave the free-schools not only about as ignorant as when they entered them, but almost with an incentive to continued ignorance; for they knew nothing of reading, except that to acquire its rudiments is a pain, a labour, and a restraint. On some of the Jew-boys the vagrant spirit is strong; they will be itinerants, if not wanderers, – though this is a spirit in no way confined to the Jew-boys.

[. . .]

I shall now proceed to set forth an account of the sums yearly subscribed for purposes of education and charity by the Jews.

The Jews' Free School in Spitalfields is supported by voluntary contributions to the amount of about 1200*l.* yearly. To this sum a few Christians contribute, as to some, other Hebrew institutions (which I shall specify), while Jews often are liberal supporters of Christian public charities – indeed, some of the wealthier Jews are looked upon by the members of their own faith as inclined to act more generously where Christian charities, with the prestige of high aristocratic and fashionable patronage, are in question, than towards their own institutions. To the Jews' Free School the Court of Common Council of the Corporation of London lately granted 100*l.*, through the exertions of Mr Benjamin S. Phillips, of Newgate-street, a member of the court. The Baroness Lionel de Rothschild (as I have formerly stated of the late Baroness) supplies clothing for the scholars. The school is adapted for the reception of 1,200 boys and girls in equal proportion; about 900 is the average attendance.

The Jews' Infant School in Houndsditch, with an average attendance approaching 400, is similarly supported at a cost of from 800*l.* to 1,000*l.* yearly.

The Orphan Asylum School, in Goodman's-fields, receives a somewhat larger support, but in the expenditure is the cost of an asylum (before mentioned, and containing 22 inmates). The funds are about 1,500*l.* yearly. Christians subscribe to this institution also – Mr Frederick Peel, M.P., taking great interest in it. The attendance of pupils is from 300 to 400.

It might be tedious to enumerate the other schools, after having described the principal; I will merely add, therefore, that the yearly contributions to each are from 700*l.* to 1,000*l.*, and the pupils taught in each from 200 to 400. Of these further schools there are four already specified.

The Jews' Hospital, at Mile End, is maintained at a yearly cost of about 3,000*l.*, to which Christians contribute, but not to a twentieth of the amount collected. The persons benefited are worn-out old men, and destitute children, while the number of almspeople is from 150 to 200 yearly.

The other two asylums, &c., which I have specified, are maintained at a cost of about 800*l.* each, as a yearly average, and the Almshouses, three in number, at about half that sum. The persons relieved by these last-mentioned institutions number about 250, two-thirds, or thereabouts, being in the asylums.

The Loan Societies are three: the Jewish Ladies Visiting and Benevolent Loan Society; the Linusarian Loan Society (why called Linusarian a learned Hebrew scholar could not inform me, although he had asked the question of others); and the Magasim Zobim (the Good Deeds), a Portuguese Jews' Loan Society.

The business of these three societies is conducted on the same principle. Money is lent on personal or any security approved by the managers, and no interest is charged to the borrower. The amount lent yearly is from 600*l.* to 700*l.* by each society, the whole being repaid and with sufficient punctuality; a few weeks' 'grace' is occasionally allowed in the event of illness or any unforeseen event. The Loan Societies have not yet found it necessary to proceed against any of their debtors; my informant thought this forbearance extended over six years.

[. . .]

I have before spoken of a Board of Deputies, in connection with the Jews, and now proceed to describe its constitution. It is not a parliament among the Jews, I am told, nor a governing power, but what may be called a directing or regulating body. It is authorised by the body of Jews, and recognised by her Majesty's Government, as an established corporation, with powers to treat and determine on matters of civil and political policy affecting the condition of the Hebrews in this country, and interferes in no way with religious matters. It is neither a metropolitan nor a local nor a detached board, but, as far as the Jews in England may be so described, a national board. This board is elected triennially. The electors are the 'seat-holders' in the Jewish synagogues; that is to say, they belong to the class of Jews who promote the support of the synagogues by renting seats, and so paying towards the cost of those establishments.

There are in England, Ireland, and Scotland, about 1,000 of these seat-holders exercising the franchise, or rather entitled to exercise it, but many of them are indifferent to the privilege, as is often testified by the apathy shown on the days of election. Perhaps three-fourths of the privileged number may vote. The services of the representatives are gratuitous, and no qualification is required, but the elected are usually the leading metropolitan Jews. The proportion of the electors voting is in the ratio of the deputies elected. London returns 12 deputies; Liverpool, 2; Manchester, 2; Birmingham, 2; Edinburgh, Dublin (the only places in either Scotland or Ireland returning deputies), Dover, Portsmouth, Southampton, Plymouth, Canterbury, Norwich, Swansea, Newcastle-on-Tyne, and two other places (according to the number of seat-holders), each one deputy, thus making up the number to 30. On election days the attendance, as I have said, is often small, but fluctuating according to any cause of excitement, which, however, is but seldom.

The question which has of late been discussed by this Board, and which is now under consideration, and negotiation with the Education Commissioners of her Majesty's Privy Council, is the obtaining a grant of money in the same proportion as it has been granted to other educational establishments. Nothing has as yet been given to the Jewish schools, and the matter is still undetermined.

With religious or sacerdotal questions the Board of Deputies does not, or is not required to meddle; it leaves all such matters to the bodies or tribunals I have mentioned. Indeed the deputies concern themselves only with what may be called the public interests of the Jews, both as a part of the community and as a distinct people. The Jewish institutions, however, are not an exception to the absence of unanimity among the professors of the same creeds, for the members of the Reform Synagogue in Margaret-street, Cavendish-square, are not recognised as entitled to vote, and do not vote, accordingly, in the election of the Jewish deputies. Indeed, the Reform members, whose synagogue was established eight years ago, were formally excommunicated by a declaration of the late Chief Rabbi, but this seems now to be regarded as a mere matter of form, for the members have lately partaken of all the rites to which orthodox Jews are entitled.

[. . .]

The Negro crossing-sweeper, who had lost both his legs
[volume ii, pp. 490–498]

This man sweeps a crossing in a principal and central thoroughfare when the weather is cold enough to let him walk; the colder the better, he says, as it 'numbs his stumps like'. He is unable to follow this occupation in warm weather, as his legs feel 'just like corns', and he cannot walk more than a mile a day. Under these circumstances he takes to begging, which he thinks he has a perfect right to do, as he has been left destitute in what is to him almost a strange country, and has been denied what he terms 'his rights'. He generally sits while begging; dressed in a sailor shirt and trousers, with a black necker-chief round his neck, tied in the usual nautical knot. He places before him the placard which is given beneath, and never moves a muscle for the purpose of soliciting charity. He always appears scrupulously clean.

I went to see him at his home early one morning – in fact, at half-past eight, but he was not then up. I went again at nine, and found him prepared for my visit in a little parlour, in a dirty and rather disreputable alley running out of a court in a street near Brunswick-square. The negro's parlour was scantily furnished with two chairs, a turn-up bedstead, and a sea-chest. A few odds and ends of crockery stood on the sideboard, and a kettle was singing over a cheerful bit of fire. The little man was seated on a chair, with his stumps of legs sticking straight out. He showed some amount of intelligence in answering my questions. We were quite alone, for he sent his wife and child – the former a pleasant-looking 'half-caste', and the latter the cheeriest little crowing, smiling 'piccaninny' I have ever seen – he sent them out into the alley, while I conversed with himself.

His life is embittered by the idea that he has never yet had 'his rights' – that the owners of the ship in which his legs were burnt off have not paid him his wages (of which, indeed, he says, he never received any but the five pounds which he had in advance before starting), and that he has been robbed of 42*l.* by a grocer in Glasgow. How true these statements may be it is almost impossible to say, but from what he says, some injustice seems to have been done him by the canny Scotchman, who refuses him his 'pay', without which he is determined 'never to leave the country'.

'I was on that crossing,' he said, 'almost the whole of last winter. It was very cold, and I had nothing at all to do; so, as I passed there, I asked the gentleman at the baccer-shop, as well as the gentleman at the office, and I asked at the boot-shop, too, if they would let me sweep there. The policeman wanted to turn me away, but I went to the gentleman inside the office, and he told the policeman to leave me alone. The policeman said first, "You must go away," but I said, "I couldn't do anything else, and he ought to think it a charity to let me stop."

'I don't stop in London very long, though, at a time; I go to Glasgow, in Scotland, where the owners of the ship in which my legs were burnt off live. I served nine years in the merchant service and the navy. I was born in Kingston, in Jamaica; it is an English place, sir, so I am counted as not a foreigner. I'm different from them Lascars. I went to sea when I was only nine years old. The owners is in London who had that ship. I was cabin-boy; and after I had served my time I became cook, or when I couldn't get the place of cook I went before the mast. I went as head cook in 1851, in the *Madeira* barque; she used to be a West Indy trader, and to trade out when I belonged to her. We got down to 69 south of Cape Horn; and there we got almost froze and perished to death. That is the book what I sell.'

The 'Book' (as he calls it) consists of eight pages, printed on paper the size of a sheet of note paper; it is entitled –

BRIEF SKETCH OF THE LIFE OF
EDWARD ALBERT!
A native of Kingston, Jamaica

Showing the hardships he underwent and the sufferings
he endured in having both legs amputated.

HULL:
W. HOWE, PRINTER

It is embellished with a portrait of a black man, which has evidently been in its time a comic 'nigger' of the Jim-Crow tobacco-paper kind, as is evidenced by the traces of a tobacco-pipe, which has been unskilfully erased.

The 'Book' itself is concocted from an affidavit made by Edward Albert before 'P. Mackinlay, Esq., one of Her Majesty's Justices of the Peace for the country [so it is printed] of Lanark.'

I have seen the affidavit, and it is almost identical with the statement in the 'book', excepting in the matter of grammar, which has rather suffered on its road to Mr Howe, the printer.

The following will give an idea of the matter of which it is composed:

In February, 1851, I engaged to serve as cook on board the barque *Madeira*, of Glasgow, Captain J. Douglas, on her voyage from Glasgow to California, thence to China, and thence home to a port of discharge in the United Kingdom. I signed articles, and delivered up my register-ticket as a British seaman, as required by law. I entered the service on board the said vessel, under the said engagement, and sailed with that vessel on the 18th of February, 1851. I discharged my duty as cook on board the said vessel, from the date of its having left the Clyde, until June the same year, in which month the vessed rounded Cape Horne, at that time my legs became frost-bitten, and I became in consequence unfit for duty.

In the course of the next day after my limbs became affected, the master of the vessel, and mate, took me to the ship's oven, in order, as they said, to cure me; the oven was hot at the time, a fowl that was roasting therein having been removed in order to make room for my feet, which was put into the oven; in consequence of the treatment, my feet burst through the intense swelling, and mortification ensued.

The vessel called, six weeks after, at Valpariso, and I was there taken to an hospital, where I remained five months and a half. Both my legs were amputated three inches below my knees soon after I went to the hospital at Valpariso. I asked my master for my wages due to me, for my service on board the vessel, and demanded my register-ticket; when the captain told me I should not recover, that the vessel could not wait for me, and that I was a dead man, and that he could not discharge a dead man; and that he also said, that as I had no friends there to get my money, he would only put a little money into the hands of the consul, which would be applied in burying me. On being discharged from the hospital I called on the consul, and was informed by him that master had not left any money.

I was afterwards taken on board one of her Majesty's ships, the *Driver*, Captain Charles Johnston, and landed at Portsmouth; from thence I got a passage to Glasgow, ware I remained three months. Upon supplic-ation to the register-office for seamen, in London, my register-ticket has been forwarded to the Collector of Customs, Glasgow; and he his ready to deliver it to me upon obtaining the authority of the Justices of the Peace, and I recovered the same under the 22nd section of the General Merchant Seaman's Act. Declares I cannot write.

(Signed) DAVID MACKINLAY, J. P.

The Justices having considered the foregoing information and declar-ation, finds that Edward Albert, therein named the last-register ticket, sought to be covered under circumstances which, so far as he was concerned, were unavoidable, and that no fraud was intended or committed by him in reference thereto, therefore authorised the Collector and Comptroller of Customs at the port of Glasgow to deliver to the said Edward Albert the register-ticket, sought to be recovered by him all in terms of 22nd section of the General Merchant Seamen's Act.

(Signed) DAVID MACKINLAY, J.P.

Glasgow, Oct. 6th, 1852.

Register Ticket, No. 512, 652, age 25 years.

'I could make a large book of my sufferings, sir, if I liked,' he said, 'and I will disgrace the owners of that ship as long as they don't give me what they owe me.

'I will never leave England or Scotland until I get my rights; but they says money makes money, and if I had money I could get it. If they would only give me what they owe me, I wouldn't ask anybody for a farthing, God knows, sir. I don't know why the master put my feet in the oven; he said to cure me: the agony of pain I was in was such, he said, that it must be done.

'The loss of my limbs is bad enough, but it's still worse when you can't get what is your rights, nor anything for the sweat that they worked out of me.

'After I went down to Glasgow for my money I opened a little coffee-house; it was called "Uncle Tom's Cabin". I did very well. The man who sold me tea and coffee said he would get me on, and I had better give my money to him to keep safe, and he used to put it away in a tin box which I had given four-and-sixpence for. He advertised my place in the papers, and I did a good business. I had the place open a month, when he kept all my savings – two-and-forty pounds – and shut up the place, and denied me of it, and I never got a farthing.

'I declare to you I can't describe the agony I felt when my legs were burst; I fainted away over and over again. There was four men came; I was lying in my hammock, and they moved the fowl that was roasting, and put my legs in the oven. There they held me for ten minutes. They said it would take the cold out; but after I came out the cold caught 'em again, and the next day they swole up as big round as a pillar, and burst, and then like water come out. No man but God knows what I have suffered and went through.

'By the order of the doctor at Valparaiso, the sick patients had to come out of the room I went into; the smell was so bad I couldn't bear it myself – it was all mortification – they had to use chloride o' zinc to keep the smell down. They tried to save one leg, but the mortification was getting up into my body. I got better after my legs were off.

'I was three months good before I could turn, or able to lift up my hand to my head. I was glad to move after that time, it was a regular relief to me; if it wasn't for good attendance, I should not have lived. You know they don't allow tobaccer in a hospital, but I had it; it was the only thing I cared for. The Reverend Mr Armstrong used to bring me a pound a fortnight; he used to bring it regular. I never used to smoke before; they said I never should recover, but after I got the tobaccer it seemed to soothe me. I was five months and a half in that place.

'Admiral Moseley, of the *Thetis* frigate, sent me home; and the reason why he sent me home was, that after I came well, I called on Mr Rouse, the English consul, and he sent me to the boarding-house, till such time as he could find a ship to send me home in. I was there about two months, and the boarding-master, Jan Pace, sent me to the consul.

'I used to get about a little, with two small crutches, and I also had a little cart before that, on three wheels; it was made by a man in the hospital. I used to lash myself down in it. That was the best thing I ever had – I could get about best in that.

'Well, I went to the consul, and when I went to him, he says, "I can't pay your board; you must beg and pay for it;" so I went and told Jan Pace, and he said, "If you had stopped here a hundred years, I would not turn you out;" and then I asked Pace to tell me where the Admiral lived. "What do you want with him?" says he. I said, "I think the Admiral must be higher than the consul." Pace slapped me on the back. Says he, "I'm glad to see you've got the pluck to complain to the Admiral."

'I went down at nine o'clock the next morning, to see the Admiral. He said, "Well, Prince Albert, how are you getting on?" So I told him I was getting on very bad; and then I told him all about the consul; and he said, as long as he stopped he would see me righted, and took me on board his ship, the *Thetis*; and he wrote to the consul, and said to me, "If the consul sends for you, don't you go to him; tell him you have no legs to walk, and he must walk to you."

'The consul wanted to send me back in a merchant ship, but the Admiral wouldn't have it, so I came in the *Driver*, one of Her Majesty's vessels. It was the 8th of May, 1852, when I got to Portsmouth.

'I stopped a little while – about a week – in Portsmouth. I went to the Admiral of the dockyard, and he told me I must go to the Lord Mayor of London. So I paid my passage to London, saw the Lord Mayor, who sent me to Mr Yardley, the magistrate, and he advertised the case for me, and I got four pounds fifteen shillings, besides my passage to Glasgow. After I got there, I went to Mr Symee, a Custom-house officer (he'd been in the same ship with me to California); he said, "Oh, gracious, Edward, how have you lost your limbs!" and I burst out a-crying. I told him all about it. He advised me to go to the owner. I went there; but the police-man in London had put my name down as Robert Thorpe, which was the man I lodged with; so they denied me.

'I went to the shipping office, where they reckonised me; and I went to Mr Symee again, and he told me to go before the Lord Mayor (a Lord Provost they call him in Scotland), and make an affidavit; and so, when they found my story was right, they sent to London for my seaman's ticket; but they couldn't do anything, because the captain was not there.

'When I got back to London, I commenced sweeping the crossin', sir. I only sweep it in the winter, because I can't stand in the summer. Oh, yes, I feel my feet still: it is just as if I had them sitting on the floor, now. I feel my toes moving, like as if I had 'em. I could count them, the whole ten, whenever I work my knees. I had a corn on one of my toes, and I can feel it still, particularly at the change of weather.

'Sometimes I might get two shillings a day at my crossing, some-times one shilling and sixpence, sometimes I don't take above six-pence. The most I ever made in one day was three shillings and sixpence, but that's very seldom.

'I am a very steady man. I don't drink what money I get; and if I had the means to get something to do, I'd keep off the streets.

'When I offered to go to the parish, they told me to go to Scotland, to spite the men who owed me my wages.

'Many people tell me I ought to go to my country; but I tell them it's very hard – I didn't come here without my legs – I lost them, as it were, in this country; but if I had lost them in my own country, I should have been better off. I should have gone down to the magistrate every Friday, and have taken my ten shillings.

'I went to the Merchant Seaman's Fund, and they said that those who got hurted before 1852 have been getting the funds, but those who were hurted after 1852 couldn't get nothing – it was stopped in '51, and the merchants wouldn't pay any more, and don't pay any more.

'That's scandalous, because, whether you're willing or not, you must pay two shillings a-month (one shilling a-month for the hospital fees, and one shilling a-month to the Merchant Seaman's Fund), out of your pay.

'I am married: my wife is the same colour as me, but an English-woman. I've been married two years. I married her from where she belonged, in Leeds. I couldn't get on to do anything without her. Sometimes she goes out and sells things – fruit, and so on – but she don't make much. With the assistance of my wife, if I could get my money, I would set up in the same line of business as before, in a coffee-shop. If I had three pounds I could do it: it took well in Scotland. I am not a common cook, either; I am a pastrycook. I used to make all the sorts of cakes they have in the shops. I bought the shapes, and tins, and things to make them proper.

'I'll tell you how I did – there was a kind of apparatus; it boils water and coffee, and the milk and the tea, in different depart-ments; but you couldn't see the divisions – the pipes all ran into one tap, like. I've had a sixpence and a shilling for people to look at it: it cost me two pound ten.

'Even if I had a coffee-stall down at Covent-garden, I should do; and, besides, I understand the making of eel-soup. I have one child, – it is just three months and a week old. It is a boy, and we call it James Edward Albert. James is after my grandfather, who was a slave.

'I was a little boy when the slaves in Jamaica got their freedom: the people were very glad to be free; they do better since, I know, because some of them have got property, and send their children to school. There's more Christianity there than there is here. The public-house is close shut on Saturday night, and not opened till Monday morning. No fruit is allowed to be sold in the street. I am a Protestant. I don't know the name of the church, but I goes down to a new-built church, near King's-cross. I never go in, because of my legs; but I just go inside the door; and sometimes when I don't go, I read the Testament I've got here: in all my sickness I took care of that.

'There are a great many Irish in this place. I would like to get away from it, for it is a very disgraceful place, – it is an awful, awful place altogether. I haven't been in it very long, and I want to get out of it; it is not fit.

'I pay one-and-sixpence rent. If you don't go out and drink and carouse with them, they don't like it; they make use of bad language – they chaff me about my misfortune – they call me "Cripple"; some says "Uncle Tom", and some says "Nigger"; but I never takes no notice of 'em at all.' [. . .]

The Negro cook

[*volume iii, p. 421*]

The poor fellow who gave me the following narrative was a coloured man, with the regular negro physiognomy, but with nothing of the lighthearted look they sometimes present. His only attire was a sadly soiled shirt of coarse striped cotton, an old handkerchief round his neck, old canvas trousers, and shoes. 'I am twenty,' he said, in good English, 'and was born in New York. My father was a very dark negro, but my mother was white. I was sent to school, and can read a little, but can't write. My father was coachman to a gentleman. My mother spoke Dutch chiefly; she taught it to my father. She could speak English, and always did to me. I worked in a gentleman's house in New York, cleaning knives and going errands. I was always well treated in New York, and by all sorts of people. Some of the "rough-uns" in the streets would shout after me as I was going to church on a Sunday night. At church I couldn't sit with the white people. I didn't think that any hardship. I saved seven dollars by the time I was sixteen, and then I went to sea as a cabin-boy on board the *Elizabeth*, a brigantine. My first voyage was to St John's, New Brunswick, with a cargo of corn and provisions. My second voyage was to Boston. After that I was raised to be cook. I had a notion I could cook well. I had cooked on shore before, in a gentleman's house, where I was shown cooking. Pretty many of the cooks in New York are coloured people – the men more than the women. The women are chiefly chambermaids. There was a vacancy, I was still in the *Elizabeth*, when the cook ran away. He was in a bother with the captain about wasting tea and sugar. We went some more voyages, and I then got engaged as cook on board a new British ship, just off the stocks, at St John's, New Brunswick, the *Jessica*. About four months ago I came in her to Liverpool, where we were all paid off. We were only engaged for the run. I received 5*l*. I paid 2*l*. 10*s*. to my boarding mistress for two months' board. It was 5*s*. and extras a week. I laid out the rest in clothes. I had a job in Liverpool, in loading hay. I was told I had a better chance for a ship in London. I tramped it all the way, selling some of my clothes to start me. I had 6*s*. to start with, and got to London with hardly any clothes, and no money. That's two months back, or nearly so. I couldn't find a ship. I never begged, but I stood on the highways, and some persons gave me twopences and pennies. I was often out all night, perishing. Sometimes I slept under the butchers' stalls in Whitechapel. I felt the cold very bitter, as I was used to a hot climate chiefly. Sometimes I couldn't feel my feet. A policeman told me to come here, and I was admitted. I want to get a ship. I have a good character as a cook; my dishes were always relished; my pea-soup was capital, and so was my dough and pudding. I often wished for them when I was starving.' [He showed his white teeth, smiling as he spoke.] 'Often under the Whitechapel stalls I was so frozen up I could hardly stir in the morning. I was out all the night before Christmas that it snowed. That was my worst night, I think, and it was my first. I couldn't walk, and hardly stand, when the morning came. I have no home to go to.'

3

VOICES OF THE POOR
The Employed and the Destitute

Mayhew divided the occupations of the street people into rough categories such as sellers, buyers, finders or collectors, cleansers and so forth. Here we present a selection of the material he collected from interviews which preserve to some extent the balance of the entire work. Mayhew is well-known for his 'characters' and there is certainly a temptation to include the more colourful among them — the clown, the piper, the street fire-king, for example. Women and children often seem to have been more garrulous than adult males and the reports of Mayhew's conversations with them are frequently, as a result, more detailed. Nevertheless, we have selected 'voices' from a wide range of occupations and from adult males and females as well as children and have resisted the temptation to over-represent the Barnum & Bailey element (who appear in this volume under the heading 'Culture and belief'). Further interview material appears in other sections of the book: for instance, in those treating 'casual labour' and 'minorities'.

THE STREET-SELLER OF NUTMEG-GRATERS

[from a daguerrotype by Beard]

Street-sellers of 'wet' fish
[*volume i. pp.62–78*]

The railways had brought supplies of cheap 'wet' fish and shellfish to London in great quantities. As a result fish, especially herring, was part of the staple diet of poor families from October to May. After this time the fishmonger would sell mackerel (from May to late July) and then rely on sales of 'dried' fish such as haddock and red herring. In the better streets of the suburbs the season extended to cover the sale of salmon from late May to July. Everywhere 'wet' fish was sold in the morning; after noon the fishmonger might sell pickled fish, for example, to race-goers; at night the leftover fish from the morning was sold cheap. At the bottom end of the trade were fishmongers who sold sprats or shellfish.

[*volume i. p.62*]
The rooms of the very neediest of our needy metropolitan population, always smell of fish; most frequently of herrings. So much so, indeed, that to those who, like myself, have been in the habit of visiting their dwellings, the smell of herrings, even in comfortable homes, savours from association so strongly of squalor and wretchedness, as to be often most oppressive. The volatile oil of the fish seems to hang about the walls and beams of the rooms for ever. Those who have experienced the smell of fish only in a well-ordered kitchen, can form no adequate notion of this stench, in perhaps a dilapidated and ill-drained house, and in a rarely-cleaned room; and I have many a time heard both husband and wife – one couple especially, who were 'sweating' for a gorgeous clothes' emporium – say that they had not time to be clean.

The costermonger supplies the poor with every kind of fish, for he deals, usually, in every kind when it is cheap. [. . .]

Street-sellers of 'wet' fish
[*volume i. pp.68,69*]

Concerning the sale of 'wet' or fresh fish, I had the following account from a trustworthy man, of considerable experience and superior education:

'I have sold "wet fish" in the streets for more than fourteen years,' he said; 'before that I was a gentleman, and was brought up a gentleman, if I'm a beggar now. I bought fish largely in the north of England once, and now I must sell it in the streets of London. Never mind talking about that, sir; there's some things won't bear talking about. There's a wonderful difference in the streets since I knew them first; I could make a pound then, where I can hardly make a crown now. People had more money, and less meanness then. I consider that the railways have injured me, and all wet fish-sellers, to a great extent. Fish now, you see, sir, comes in at all hours, so that nobody can calculate on the quantity that will be received – nobody. That's the mischief of it; we are afraid to buy, and miss many a chance of turning a penny. In my time, since railways were in, I've seen cod-fish sold at a guinea in the morning that were a shilling at noon; for either the wind and the tide had served, or else the railway fishing-places were more than commonly supplied, and there was a glut to London. There's no trade requires greater judgment than mine – none whatever. Before the railways – and I never could see the good of them – the fish came in by the tide, and we knew how to buy, for there would be no more till next tide. Now, we don't know. I go to Billingsgate to buy my fish, and am very well known to Mr — and Mr — [mentioning the names of some well-known salesmen]. The Jews are my ruin there now. When I go to Billingsgate, Mr — will say, or rather, I will say to him, "How much for this pad of soles?" He will answer, "Fourteen shillings." "Fourteen shillings!" I say, "I'll give you seven shillings – that's the proper amount;" then the Jew-boys – none of them twenty that are there – ranged about will begin; and one says, when I bid 7s., "I'll give 8s.," "nine," says another, close on my left; "ten," shouts another, on my right, and so they go offering on; at last Mr — says to one of them, as grave as a judge, "Yours, sir, at 13s.," but it's all gammon. The 13s. buyer isn't a buyer at all, and isn't required to pay a farthing, and never touches the goods. It's all done to keep up the price to poor fishmen, and so to poor buyers that are our customers in the streets. Money makes money, and it don't matter how. Those Jew-boys – I dare say they're the same sort as once sold oranges about the streets – are paid, I know 1s. for spending three or four hours that way in the cold and wet. My trade has been injured, too, by the great increase of Irish costermongers; for an Irishman will starve out an Englishman any day; besides if a tailor can't live by his trade, he'll take to fish, or fruit and cabbages. The month of May is a fine season for plaice, which is bought very largely by my customers. Plaice are sold at ½ d. and 1 d. a piece. It is a difficult fish to manage, and in poor neighbourhoods an important one to manage well. The old hands make a profit out of it; new hands a loss. There's not much cod or other wet fish sold to the poor, while plaice is in. My customers are poor men's wives – mechanics, I fancy. They want fish at most unreasonable prices. If I could go and pull them off a line flung off Waterloo-bridge, and no other expense, I couldn't supply them as cheap as they expect them. Very cheap fish-sellers lose their customers, through the Billingsgate bummarees, for they have pipes, and blow up the cod-fish, most of all, and puff up their bellies till they are twice the size, but when it comes to table, there's hardly to say any fish at all. The Billingsgate authorities would soon stop it, if they knew all I know. They won't allow any roguery, or any trick, if they only come to hear of it. These bummarees have caused many respect-able people to avoid street-buying, and so fair traders like me are injured. I've nothing to complain of about the police. Oft enough, if I could be allowed ten minutes longer on a Saturday night, I could get through all my stock without loss. About a quarter to twelve I begin to halloo away as hard as I can, and there's plenty of customers that lay out never a farthing till that time, and then they can't be served fast enough, so they get their fish cheaper than I do. If any halloos out that way sooner, we must all do the same. Anything rather than keep fish over a warm Sunday. I have kept mine in ice; I haven't opportunity now, but it'll keep in a cool place this time of year. I think there's as many sellers as buyers in the streets, and there's scores of them don't give just weight or measure. I wish there was good moral rules in force, and every-body gave proper weight. I often talk to street-dealers about it. I've given them many a lecture; but they say they only do what

plenty of shopkeepers do, and just get fined and go on again, without being a pin the worse thought of. They are abusive sometimes, too; I mean the street-sellers are, because they are ignorant. I have no children, thank God, and my wife helps me in my business. Take the year through, I clear from 10s. to 12s. every week. That's not much to support two people. Some weeks I earn only 4s. – such as in wet March weather. In others I earn 18s. or 1l. November, December, and January are good months for me. I wouldn't mind if they lasted all the year round. I'm often very badly off indeed – very badly; and the misery of being hard up, sir, is not when you're making a struggle to get out of your trouble; no, nor to raise a meal off herrings that you've given away once, but when your wife and you's sitting by a grate without a fire, and putting the candle out to save it, a-planning how to raise money. "Can we borrow there?" "Can we manage to sell if we can borrow?" "Shall we get from very bad to the parish?" Then, perhaps, there's a day lost, and without a bite in our mouths trying to borrow. Let alone a little drop to give a body courage, which perhaps is the only good use of spirit after all. That's the pinch, sir. When the rain you hear outside puts you in mind of drownding!'
[. . .]

Street-sellers of sprats
[*volume i. pp.69–71*]
Sprats – one of the cheapest and most grateful luxuries of the poor – are generally introduced about the 9th of November. Indeed 'Lord Mayor's day' is sometimes called 'sprat day'. They continue in about ten weeks. They are sold at Billingsgate by the 'toss', or 'chuck', which is about half a bushel, and weighs from 40 lbs. to 50 lbs. The price varies from 1s. to 5s. Sprats are, this season, pronounced remarkably fine. 'Look at my lot sir,' said a street-seller to me; 'they're a heap of new silver,' and the bright shiny appearance of the glittering little fish made the comparison not inappropriate. In very few, if in any, instances does a coster-monger confine himself to the sale of sprats, unless his means limit him to that one branch of the business. A more prosperous street-fishmonger will sometimes detach the sprats from his stall, and his wife, or one of his children will take charge of them. Only a few sprat-sellers are itinerant, the fish being usually sold by stationary

street-sellers at 'pitches'. One who worked his sprats through the streets, or sold them from a stall as he thought best, gave me the following account. He was dressed in a newish fustian-jacket, buttoned close up his chest, but showing a portion of a clean cotton shirt at the neck, with a bright-coloured coarse hand-kerchief round it; the rest of his dress was covered by a white apron. His hair, as far as I could see it under his cloth cap, was carefully brushed, and (it appeared) as carefully oiled. At the first glance I set him down as having been a gentleman's servant. He had a somewhat deferential, though far from cringing manner with him, and seemed to be about twenty-five or twenty-six – he thought he was older, he said, but did not know his age exactly.

'Ah! sir,' he began, in a tone according with his look, 'sprats is a blessing to the poor. Fresh herrings is a blessing too, and sprats is young herrings, and is a blessing in 'portion' [for so he pronounced what seemed to be a favourite word with him, 'proportion']. 'It's only four years – yes, four, I'm sure of that – since I walked the streets starving, in the depth of winter, and looked at the sprats, and said, I wish I could fill my belly off you. Sir, I hope it was no great sin, but I could hardly keep my hands from stealing some and eating them raw. If they make me sick, thought I, the police'll take care of me, and that'll be something. While these thoughts was a passing through my mind, I met a man who was a gentle-man's coachman; I knew him a little formerly, and so I stopped him and told him who I was, and that I hadn't had a meal for two days. "Well, by G——," said the coachman, "you look like it, why I shouldn't have known you. Here's a shilling." And then he went on a little way, and then stopped, and turned back and thrust 3½ d. more into my hand, and bolted off. I've never seen him since. But I'm grateful to him in the same 'portion [proportion] as if I had. After I'd had a penn'orth of bread and a penn'orth of cheese, and half-a-pint of beer, I felt a new man, and I went to the party as I'd longed to steal the sprats from, and told him what I'd thought of. I can't say what made me tell him, but it turned out for good. I don't know much about religion, though I can read a little, but may be that had something to do with it.' The rest of the man's narrative was – briefly told – as follows. He was the only child of a gentleman's coachman His father had deserted his mother and him, and gone abroad, he believed, with some family. His mother, however, took care of him until her death, which happened 'when he was a little turned thirteen, he had heard, but could not remember the year'. After that he was 'a helper and a jobber in different stables', and 'anybody's boy', for a few years, until he got a footman's, or rather footboy's place, which he kept above a year. After that he was in service, in and out of different situations, until the time he specified, when he had been out of place for nearly five weeks, and was starving. His master had got in difficulties, and had gone abroad; so he was left without a character. 'Well, sir,' he continued, 'the man as I wanted to steal the sprats from, says to me, says he, "Poor fellow; I know what a hempty belly is myself – come and have a pint." And over that there pint, he told me, if I could rise 10s. there might be a chance for me in the streets, and he'd show me how to do. He died not very long after that, poor man. Well, after a little bit, I managed to borrow 10s. of Mr — (I thought of him all of a sudden). He was butler in a family that I had lived in, and had a charitable character, though he was reckoned very proud. But I plucked up a spirit, and told him how I was off, and he said, "Well, I'll try you," and he lent me 10s., which I paid him back, little by little, in six or eight weeks; and so I started in the costermonger line, with the advice of my friend, and I've made from 5s. to 10s., sometimes more, a week, at it ever since. The police don't trouble me much. They is civil to me in 'portion [proportion] as I am civil to them. I never mixed with the costers but when I've met them at market. I stay at a lodging-house, but it's very decent and clean, and I have a bed to myself, at 1s. a week, for I'm a regular man. I'm on sprats now, you see, sir, and you'd wonder, sometimes, to see how keen people looks to them when they're new. They're a blessing to the poor, in 'portion [proportion] of course. Not twenty minutes before you spoke to me, there was two poor women came up – they was sickly-looking, but I don't know what they was – perhaps shirt-makers – and they says to me, says they, "Show us what a penny plateful is." "Sart'nly, ladies," says I. Then they whispered together, and at last one says, says she, "We'll have two platefuls." I told you they was a blessing to the poor, sir – 'specially to such as them, as lives all the year round on bread and tea. But it's not only the poor as buys; others in 'portion [proportion]. When they're new they're a treat to everybody. I've sold them to poor working men, who've said,

"I'll take a treat home to the old 'oman and the kids; they dotes on sprats." Gentlemen's servants is very fond of them, and mechanics comes down – such as shoemakers in their leather aprons, and sings out, "Here, old sprats, give us two penn'orth."' [. . .]

Street-sellers of shell-fish
[*volume i. pp.71,72*]
I had the following account from an experienced man. He lived with his mother, his wife, and four children, in one of the streets near Gray's-inn-lane. The street was inhabited altogether by people of his class, the women looking sharply out when a stranger visited the place. On my first visit to this man's room, his wife, who is near her confinement, was at dinner with her children. The time was quarter to 12. The meal was tea, and bread with butter very thinly spread over it. On the wife's bread was a small piece of pickled pork, covering about one-eighth of the slice of a quartern loaf cut through. In one corner of the room, which is on the ground floor, was a scantily-covered bed. A few dingy-looking rags were hanging up to dry in the middle of the room, which was littered with baskets and boxes, mixed up with old furniture, so that it was a difficulty to stir. The room (although the paper, covering the broken panes in the window, was torn and full of holes) was most oppressively close and hot, and there was a fetid smell, difficult to sustain, though it was less noticeable on a subsequent call. I have often had occasion to remark that the poor, especially those who are much subjected to cold in the open air, will sacrifice much for heat. The adjoining room, which had no door, seemed littered like the one where the family were. The walls of the room I was in were discoloured and weather-stained. The only attempt at ornament was over the mantel-shelf, the wall here being papered with red and other gay-coloured papers, that once had been upholsterer's patterns.

On my second visit, the husband was at dinner with the family, on good boiled beef and potatoes. He was a small-featured man, with a head of very curly and long black hair, and both in mien, manners, and dress, resembled the mechanic far more than the costermonger. He said:

'I've been twenty years and more, perhaps twenty-four, selling shell-fish in the streets. I was a boot-closer when I was young, and

have made my 20s. and 30s., and sometimes 40s., and then sometimes not 10s. a week; but I had an attack of rheumatic-fever, and
lost the use of my hands for my trade. The streets hadn't any great
name, as far as I knew, then, but as I couldn't work, it was just a
choice between street-selling and starving, so I didn't prefer the
last. It was reckoned degrading to go into the streets – but I
couldn't help that. I was astonished at my success when I first
began, and got into the business – that is into the understanding of
it – after a week, or two, or three. Why, I made 3l. the first week
I knew my trade, properly; yes, I cleared 3l.! I made, not long after,
5l. a week – but not often. I was giddy and extravagant. Indeed, I
was a fool, and spent my money like a fool. I could have brought
up a family then like a gentleman – I send them to school as it is –
but I hadn't a wife and family then, or it might have been better;
it's a great check on a man, is a family. I began with shell-fish, and
sell it still; very seldom anything else. There's more demand for
shells, no doubt, because it's far cheaper, but then there's so many
more sellers. I don't know why exactly. I suppose it's because poor
people go into the streets when they can't live other ways, and
some do it because they think it's an idle life; but it ain't. Where I
took 35s. in a day at my stall – and well on to half of it profit – I
now take 5s. or 6s., or perhaps 7s., in the day and less profit on that
less money. I don't clear 3s. a day now, take the year through. I
don't keep accounts, but I'm certain enough that I average about
15s. a week the year through, and my wife has to help me to make
that. She'll mind the stall, while I take a round sometimes. I sell all
kinds of shell-fish, but my great dependence is on winkles. I don't
do much in lobsters. Very few speculate in them. The price varies
very greatly. What's 10s. a score one day may be 25s. the next. I
sometimes get a score for 5s. or 6s., but it's a poor trade, for 6d. is
the top of the tree, with me, for a price to a seller. I never get
more. I sell them to mechanics and tradesmen. I do more in pound
crabs. There's a great call for ha'porths and pennorths of lobster
or crab, by children; that's their claws. I bile them all myself, and
buy them alive. I can bile twenty in half an hour, and do it over a
grate in a back-yard. Lobsters don't fight or struggle much in the
hot water, if they're properly packed. It's very few that knows
how to bile a lobster as he should be biled. I wish I knew any way
of killing lobsters before biling them. I can't kill them without

THE OYSTER–STALL

'Penny a lot, Oysters! Penny a lot!'

[*from a daguerrotype by Beard*]

smashing them to bits, and that won't do at all. I kill my crabs before I bile them. I stick them in the throat with a knife and they're dead in an instant. Some sticks them with a skewer, but they kick a good while with the skewer in them. It's a shame to torture anything when it can be helped. If I didn't kill the crabs they'd shed every leg in the hot water; they'd come out as bare of claws as this plate. I've known it oft enough, as it is; though I kill them uncommon quick, a crab will be quicker and shed every leg – throw them off in the moment I kill them, but that doesn't happen once in fifty times. Oysters are capital this season, I mean as to quality, but they're not a good sale. I made 3*l.* a week in oysters, not reckoning anything else, eighteen or twenty years back. It was easy to make money then; like putting down one sovereign and taking two up. I sold oysters then oft enough at 1*d.* a piece. Now I sell far finer at three a penny and five for 2*d.* People can't spend money in shell-fish when they haven't got any. They say that fortune knocks once at every man's door. I wish I'd opened my door when he knocked at it.'

This man's wife told me afterwards, that last winter, after an attack of rheumatism, all their stock-money was exhausted, and her husband sat day by day at home almost out of his mind; for nothing could tempt him to apply to the parish, and 'he would never have mentioned his sufferings to me,' she said; 'he had too much pride.' The loan of a few shillings from a poor costermonger enabled the man to go to market again, or he and his family would now have been in the Union.

[. . .]

Street-sellers of fruit and vegetables
[*volume i. pp.79–104*]

Fruit sold in the streets was divided into 'green' fruit (which was fresh and had to be consumed immediately) and 'dried' fruit (which could be sold out of season). Fruit was generally sold by the costermongers from their barrows although, especially in the suburbs, there were peripatetic vendors who sold from their baskets. Oranges, chestnuts and walnuts were not sold by the costermongers but by a 'lower class' of vendor. Costermongers also sold a wide variety of vegetables. Costermongers who dealt in fruit usually restricted their business to fruit year-round; vegetable costers, on the other hand, usually also sold fish and were known as 'general dealers'. The 'general dealers' organised their trade according to what was in season: sprats, plaice, soles, mackerel, haddock and red herring until the very early summer; gooseberries, cherries, plums, apples and pears in the summer; vegetables in the autumn and winter. Some moved their barrows from place to place but about 632 costers had stalls in fixed locations.

[refer to chapter 1 for further material on the costermongers.]

Superior or 'aristocratic' vegetable–sellers
[*volume i. pp.92,93*]
In designating these dealers I use a word not uncommon among the costermongers. These aristocratic sellers, who are not one in twenty, or perhaps in twenty-five, of the whole body of coster-mongers, are generally men of superior manners and better dressed than their brethren. The following narrative, given to me by one of the body, shows the nature of the trade:

'It depends a good deal upon the season and the price, as to what I begin with in the "haristocratic" way. My rounds are always in the suburbs. I sell neither in the streets, nor squares in town. I like it best where there are detached villas, and best of all where there are kept mistresses. They are the best of all customers to men like me. We talk our customers over among ourselves, and generally know who's who. One way by which we know the kept ladies is, they never sell cast-off clothes, as some ladies do, for new potatoes or early peas. Now, my worst customers, as to price, are the ladies – or gentlemen – they're both of a kidney – what keeps fashionable schools. *They* are the people to drive a bargain, but then they buy largely. Some buy entirely of costermongers. There's one gent. of a school-keeper buys so much and knows so well what o'clock it is, that I'm satisfied he saves many a pound a year by buying of us 'stead of the greengrocers.

'Perhaps I begin the season in the haristocratic way, with early lettuces for salads. I carry my goods in handsome baskets, and sometimes with a boy, or a boy and a girl, to help me. I buy my lettuces by the score [of heads] when first in, at 1s. 6d., and sell them at 1½ d. each, which is 1s. profit on a score. I have sold twenty, and I once sold thirty score, that way in a day. The profit on the thirty was 2l. 5s., but out of that I had to pay three boys, for I took three with me, and our expenses was 7s. But you must consider, sir, that this is a precarious trade. Such goods are delicate, and spoil if they don't go off. I give credit sometimes, if anybody I know says he has no change. I never lost nothing.

'Then there's grass [asparagus], and that's often good money. I buy all mine at Covent-garden, where it's sold in bundles, according to the earliness of the season, at from 5s. to 1s., containing from six to ten dozen squibs [heads]. These you have to take home, untie, cut off the scraggy ends, trim, and scrape, and make them level. Children help me to do this in the court where I live. I give them a few ha'pence, though they're eager enough to do it for nothing but the fun. I've had 10s. worth made ready in half an hour.

'Well, now, sir, about grass, there's not a coster in London, I'm sure, ever tasted it; and how it's eaten puzzles us.' I explained the manner in which asparagus was brought to table. 'That's the ticket, is it, sir? Well, I was once at the Surrey, and there was some mac-aroni eaten on the stage, and I thought grass was eaten in the same way, perhaps; swallowed like one o'clock [rather a favourite comparison among the costers].'

'I have the grass − it's always called, when cried in the streets, "Spar-row gra-ass" − tied up in bundles of a dozen, twelve to a dozen, or one over, and for these I never expect less than 6d. For a three or four dozen lot, in a neat sieve, I ask 2s. 6d., and never take less than 1s. 3d. I once walked thirty-five miles with grass, and have oft enough been thirty miles. I made 7s. or 8s. a day by it, and next day or two perhaps nothing, or maybe had but one customer. I've sold half-crown lots, on a Saturday night, for a sixpence; and it was sold some time back at 2d. a bundle, in the New-cut, to poor people. I dare say some as bought it had been maidservants and understood it. I've raffled 5s. worth of grass in the parlour of a respectable country inn of an evening.

'The costers generally buy new potatoes at 4s. to 5s. the bushel, and cry them at "three-pound-tuppence"; but I've given 7s. a bushel, for choice and early, and sold them at 2d. a pound. It's no great trade, for the bushel may weigh only 50 lb., and at 2d. a pound that's only 8s. 4d. The schools don't buy at all until they're 1d. the pound, and don't buy in any quantity until they're 1s. 6d. the 25 lb. One day a school 'stonished me by giving me 2s. 6d. for 25 lb., which is the general weight of the half bushel. Perhaps the master had taken a drop of something short that morning. The schools are dreadful screws, to be sure.

'Green peas, early ones, I don't buy when they first come in, for then they're very dear, but when they're 4s. or 3s. 6d. a bushel, and that's pretty soon. I can make five pecks of a bushel. Schools don't touch peas 'till they're 2s. a bushel.

'Cowcumbers were an aristocratic sale. Four or five years ago they were looked upon, when first in, and with a beautiful bloom upon them, as the finest possible relish. But the cholera came in 1849, and everybody – 'specially the women – thought the cholera was in cowcumbers, and I've known cases, foreign and English, sent from the Borough-market for manure.

'I sell a good many mushrooms. I sometimes can pick up a cheap lot at Covent-garden. I make them up in neat sieves of three dozen to eight dozen according to size, and I have sold them at 4s. the sieve, and made half that on each sieve I sold. They are down to 1s. or 1s. 6d. a sieve very soon.

'Green walnuts for pickling I sell a quantity of. One day I sold 20s. worth – half profit – I got them so cheap, but that was an exception. I sold them cheap too. One lady has bought a bushel and a half at a time. For walnut catsup the refuse of the walnut is used; it's picked up in the court, where I've got children or poor fellows for a few ha'pence or a pint of beer to help me to peel the walnuts.'

Of the character of the street-stalls
[volume i. p.99]
[. . .]
The other means adopted by the street-sellers for the exhibition of their various goods at certain 'pitches' or fixed localities are as follows. Straw bonnets, boys' caps, women's caps, and prints, are generally arranged for sale in large umbrellas, placed 'upside down'. Haberdashery, with rolls of ribbons, edgings, and lace, some street-sellers display on a stall; whilst others have a board at the edge of the pavement, and expose their wares upon it as tastefully as they can. Old shoes, patched up and well blacked, ready for the purchaser's feet, and tin ware, are often ranged upon the ground, or, where the stock is small, a stall or table is used.

Many stationary street-sellers use merely baskets, or trays, either supported in their hand, or on their arm, or else they are strapped round their loins, or suspended round their necks. These are mostly fruit-women, watercress, blacking, congreves, sheep's-trotters, and ham-sandwich sellers.

Many stationary street-sellers stand on or near the bridges; others near the steam-packet wharfs or the railway terminuses; a great number of them take their pitch at the entrance to a court, or at the corners of streets; and stall-keepers with oysters stand opposite the doors of public-houses.

It is customary for a street-seller who wants to 'pitch' in a new locality to solicit the leave of the housekeeper, opposite whose premises he desires to place his stall. Such leave obtained, no other course is necessary.

A fruit-stall keeper
[*volume i. pp.99, 100*]

I had the following statement from a woman who has 'kept a stall' in Marylebone, at the corner of a street, which she calls 'my corner', for 38 years. I was referred to her as a curious type of the class of stall-keepers, and on my visit, found her daughter at the 'pitch'. This daughter had all the eloquence which is attractive in a street-seller, and so, I found, had her mother when she joined us. They are profuse in blessings; and on a bystander observing, when he heard the name of these street-sellers, that a jockey of that name had won the Derby lately, the daughter exclaimed, 'To be sure he did; he's my own uncle's relation, and what a lot of money came into the family! Bless God for all things, and bless everybody! Walnuts, sir, walnuts, a penny a dozen! Wouldn't give you a bad one for the world, which is a great thing for a poor 'oman for to offer to do.' The daughter was dressed in a drab great-coat, which covered her whole person. When I saw the mother, she carried a similar great-coat, as she was on her way to the stall; and she used it as ladies do their muffs, burying her hands in it. The mother's dark-coloured old clothes seemed, to borrow a description from Sir Walter Scott, flung on with a pitchfork. These two women were at first very suspicious, and could not be made to understand my object in questioning them; but after a little while, the mother became not only communicative, but garrulous, conversing – with no small impatience at any interruption – of the doings of the people in her neighbourhood. I was accompanied by an intelligent costermonger, who assured me of his certitude that the old woman's statement was perfectly correct, and I found moreover from other inquiries that it was so.

'Well, sir,' she began, 'what is it that you want of me? Do I owe you anything? There's half-pay officers about here for no good; what is it you want? Hold your tongue, you young fool,' [to her daughter, who was beginning to speak] 'what do you know about it?' On my satisfying her that I had no desire to injure her, she continued, to say after spitting, a common practice with her class, on a piece of money 'for luck': 'Certainly, sir, that's very proper and good. Aye, I've seen the world – the town world and the country. I don't know where I was born; never mind about that – it's nothing to nobody. I don't know nothing about my father and mother; but I know that afore I was eleven I went through the country with my missis. She was a smuggler. I didn't know then what smuggling was – bless you, sir, I didn't; I knew no more nor I know who made that lamp-post. I didn't know the taste of the stuff we smuggled for two years – didn't know it from small beer; I've known it well enough since, God knows. My missis made a deal of money that time at Deptford Dockyard. The men wasn't paid and let out till twelve of a night – I hardly mind what night it was, days was so alike then – and they was our customers till one, two, or three in the morning – Sunday morning, for anything I know. I don't know what my missis gained; something jolly, there's not a fear of it. She was kind enough to me. I don't know how long I was with missis. After that I was a-hopping, and made my 15s. regular at it, and a-haymaking; but I've had a pitch at my corner for thirty-eight year – aye! turned thirty-eight. It's no use asking me what I made at first – I can't tell; but I'm sure I made more than twice as much as my daughter and me makes now, the two of us. I wish people that thinks we're idle now were with me for a day. I'd teach them. I don't – that's the two of us don't – make 15s. a week now, nor the half of it, when all's paid. D——d if I do. The d——d boys take care of that.' Here I had a statement of the boys' tradings, similar to what I have given. 'There's "Canterbury" has lots of boys, and they bother me. I can tell, and always could, how it is with working men. When mechanics is in good work, their children has halfpennies to spend with me. If they're hard up, there's no halfpennies. The pennies go to a loaf or to buy a candle. I might have saved money once, but had a misfortunate family. My husband? Oh, never mind about him. D——n him. I've been a widow many years. My son – it's nothing how many children I have – is married; he had the care of an ingine. But he lost it from ill health. It was in a feather-house, and the flue got down his throat, and coughed him; and so he went into the country, 108 miles off, to his wife's mother. But his wife's mother got her living by wooding, and other ways, and couldn't help him or his wife; so he left, and he's with me now. He has a job sometimes with a greengrocer. at 6d. a day and a bit of grub; a little bit – very. I must shelter him. I couldn't turn him out. If a Turk I knew was in distress, and I had only half a loaf, I'd give him half of that, if he was ever such a Turk – I would, sir! Out of 6d. a day, my son – poor fellow, he's only twenty-seven! – wants a bit of 'baccy and a pint of beer. It 'ud be unnatural to oppose that, wouldn't it, sir? He frets about his wife, that's staying with her mother, 108 miles off; and about his little girl; but I tell him to wait, and he may have more little girls. God knows, they come when they're not wanted a bit. I joke and say all my old sweethearts is dying away. Old Jemmy went off sudden. He lent me money sometimes, but I always paid him. He had a public once, and had some money when he died. I saw him the day afore he died. He was in bed, but wasn't his own man quite; though he spoke sensible enough to me. He said, said he, "Won't you have half a quartern of rum, as we've often had it?" "Certainly, Jemmy," says I, "I came for that very thing." Poor fellow! his friends are quarrelling now about what he left. It's 56l. they say, and they'll go to law very likely, and lose every thing. There'll be no such quarrelling when I die, unless it is for the pawn-tickets. I get a meal now, and got a meal afore; but it was a better meal then, sir. Then look at my expenses. I was a customer once. I used to buy, and plenty such did, blue cloth aprons, opposite Drury-lane theatre: the very shop's there still, but I don't know what it is now; I can't call to mind. I gave 2s. 6d. a yard, from twenty to thirty years ago, for an apron, and it took two yards, and I paid 4d. for making it, and so an apron cost 5s. 4d. – that wasn't much thought of in those times. I used to be different off then. I never go to church; I used to go when I was a little child at Sevenoaks. I suppose I was born somewhere thereabouts. I've forgot what the inside of a church is like. There's no costermongers ever go to church, except the rogues of them, that wants to appear good. I buy my fruit at Covent-garden. Apples is now 4s. 6d. a bushel there. I may make twice that in selling them; but a bushel may last me two, three, or four days.'

[. . .]

The London flower-girls
[*volume i. pp.130–144*]

Mayhew explained that it was difficult to estimate the number of flower girls because few were dedicated solely to flower selling; when oranges were cheap they would turn instead to selling fruit; costermongers sent their children out some days to sell flowers and on others to sell watercress or onions. On Sundays there were perhaps 400 young people (aged between 6 and 20) selling flowers but on weekdays about 200. Girls outnumbered boys by 8 to 1. The girls could be divided into two broad groups: older girls who used flower selling to solicit custom for prostitution; young girls who depended upon the trade to support themselves and their parents.

Of two orphan flower-girls
[*volume i. pp.135,136*]
Of these girls the elder was fifteen and the younger eleven. Both were clad in old, but not torn, dark print frocks, hanging so closely, and yet so loosely, about them as to show the deficiency of under-clothing; they wore old broken black chip bonnets. The older sister (or rather half-sister) had a pair of old worn-out shoes on her feet, the younger was barefoot, but trotted along, in a gait at once quick and feeble – as if the soles of her little feet were impervious, like horn, to the roughness of the road. The elder girl has a modest expression of countenance, with no pretensions to prettiness except in having tolerably good eyes. Her complexion was somewhat muddy, and her features somewhat pinched. The younger child had a round, chubby, and even rosy face, and quite a healthful look. [. . .]

They lived in one of the streets near Drury-lane. They were inmates of a house, not let out as a lodging-house, in separate beds, but in rooms, and inhabited by street-sellers and street-labourers. The room they occupied was large, and one dim candle lighted it so insufficiently that it seemed to exaggerate the dimensions. The walls were bare and discoloured with damp. The furniture consisted of a crazy table and a few chairs, and in the centre of the room was an old four-post bedstead of the larger size. This bed was occupied nightly by the two sisters and their brother, a lad just turned thirteen. In a sort of recess in a corner of the room was the decency of an old curtain – or something equivalent, for I could hardly see in the dimness – and behind this was, I presume, the bed of the married couple. The three children paid 2s. a week for the room, the tenant an Irishman out of work paying 2s. 9d., but the furniture was his, and his wife aided the children in their trifle of washing, mended their clothes, where such a thing was possible, and such like. The husband was absent at the time of my visit, but the wife seemed of a better stamp, judging by her appearance, and by her refraining from any direct, or even indirect, way of begging, as well as from the 'Glory be to Gods!' 'the heavens be your honour's bed!' or 'it's the thruth I'm telling of you sir,' that I so frequently meet with on similar visits.

The elder girl said, in an English accent, not at all garrulously, but merely in answer to my questions: 'I sell flowers, sir; we live almost on flowers when they are to be got. I sell, and so does my sister, all kinds, but it's very little use offering any that's not sweet. I think it's the sweetness as sells them. I sell primroses, when they're in, and violets, and wall-flowers, and stocks, and roses of different sorts, and pinks, and carnations, and mixed flowers, and lilies of the valley, and green lavender, and mignonette (but that I do very seldom), and violets again at this time of the year, for we get them both in spring and winter.' [They are forced in hot-houses for winter sale, I may remark.] 'The best sale of all is, I think, moss-roses, young moss-roses. We do best of all on them. Primroses are good, for people say: "Well, here's spring again to a certainty." Gentlemen are our best customers. I've heard that they buy flowers to give to the ladies. Ladies have sometimes said: "A penny, my poor girl, here's three-halfpence for the bunch." Or they've given me the price of two bunches for one; so have gentlemen. I never had a rude word said to

me by a gentleman in my life. No, sir, neither lady nor gentleman
ever gave me 6d. for a bunch of flowers. I never had a sixpence
given to me in my life – never. I never go among boys, I know
nobody but my brother. My father was a tradesman in Mitchels-
town, in the County Cork. I don't know what sort of a tradesman
he was. I never saw him. He was a tradesman I've been told. I was
born in London. Mother was a charwoman, and lived very well.
None of us ever saw a father.' [It was evident that they were
illegitimate children, but the landlady had never seen the mother,
and could give me no information.] 'We don't know anything
about our fathers. We were all "mother's children". Mother died
seven years ago last Guy Faux day. I've got myself, and my brother
and sister a bit of bread ever since, and never had any help but from
the neighbours. I never troubled the parish. Oh yes, sir, the neighbours is all poor people, very poor, some of them. We've lived with
her' [indicating her landlady by a gesture] 'these two years, and off
and on before that. I can't say how long.' 'Well, I don't know
exactly,' said the landlady, 'but I've had them with me almost all the
time, for four years, as near as I can recollect; perhaps more. I've
moved three times, and they always followed me.' In answer to my
inquiries the landlady assured me that these two poor girls were
never out of doors all the time she had known them after six at
night. 'We've always good health. We can all read.' Here the three
somewhat insisted upon proving to me their proficiency in reading,
and having produced a Roman Catholic book, the *Garden of Heaven*,
they read very well. 'I put myself,' continued the girl, 'and I put my
brother and sister to a Roman Catholic school – and to ragged
schools – but *I* could read before mother died. My brother can
write, and I pray to God that he'll do well with it. I buy my flowers
at Covent Garden; sometimes, but very seldom, at Farringdon. I
pay 1s. for a dozen bunches, whatever flowers are in. Out of every
two bunches I can make three, at 1d. a piece. Some-times one or
two over in the dozen, but not so often as I would like. We make
the bunches up ourselves. We get the rush to tie them with for
nothing. We put their own leaves round these violets [she produced
a bunch]. The paper for a dozen costs a penny; sometimes only a
halfpenny. The two of us doesn't make less than 6d. a day, unless it's
very ill luck. But religion teaches us that God will support us, and if
we make less we say nothing. We do better on oranges in March or

April, I think it is, than on flowers. Oranges keep better than flowers you see, sir. We make 1s. a day, and 9d. a day, on oranges, the two of us. I wish they was in all the year. I generally go St John's-wood way, and Hampstead and Highgate way with my flowers. I can get them nearly all the year, but oranges is better liked than flowers, I think. I always keep 1s. stock-money, if I can. If it's bad weather, so bad that we can't sell flowers at all, and so if we've had to spend our stock-money for a bit of bread, she [the landlady] lends us 1s., if she has one, or she borrows one of a neighbour, if she hasn't, of if the neighbours hasn't it, she borrows it at a dolly-shop [the illegal pawnshop]. There's 2d. a week to pay for 1s. at a dolly, and perhaps an old rug left for it; if it's very hard weather, the rug must be taken at night time, or we are starved with the cold. It sometimes has to be put into the dolly again next morning, and then there's 2d. to pay for it for the day. We've had a frock in for 6d., and that's a penny a week, and the same for a day. We never pawned anything; we have nothing they would take in at the pawnshop. We live on bread and tea, and sometimes a fresh herring of a night. Sometimes we don't eat a bit all day when we're out; sometimes we take a bit of bread with us, or buy a bit. My sister can't eat taturs; they sicken her. I don't know what emigrating means.' I informed her and she continued: 'No, sir, I wouldn't like to emigrate and leave brother and sister. If they went with me I don't think I should like it, not among strangers. I think our living costs us 2s. a week for the two of us; the rest goes in rent. That's all we make.'

The brother earned from 1s. 6d. to 2s. a week, with an occasional meal, as a costermonger's boy. Neither of them ever missed mass on a Sunday.

Of the life of a flower-girl [who had kept 'loose' company] [volume i. p.136]

Some of these girls are, as I have stated, of an immoral character, and some of them are sent out by their parents to make out a livelihood by prostitution. One of this class, whom I saw, had come out of prison a short time previously. She was not nineteen, and had been sentenced about a twelvemonth before to three months' imprisonment with hard labour, 'for heaving her shoe,' as she said, 'at the Lord Mayor, to get a comfortable lodging, for she was tired of being about the streets.' After this she was locked up for breaking the lamps in the street. She alleged that her motive for this was a belief that by committing some such act she might be able to get into an asylum for females. She was sent out into the streets by her father and mother, at the age of nine, to sell flowers. Her father used to supply her with the money to buy the flowers, and she used to take the proceeds of the day's work home to her parents. She used to be out frequently till past midnight, and seldom or never got home before nine. She associated only with flower-girls of loose character. The result may be imagined. She could not state positively that her parents were aware of the manner in which she got the money she took home to them. She supposes that they must have imagined what her practices were. He used to give her no supper if she 'didn't bring home a good bit of money'. Her father and mother did little or no work all this while. They lived on what she brought home. At thirteen years old she was sent to prison (she stated) 'for selling combs in the street' (it was winter, and there were no flowers to be had). She was incarcerated fourteen days, and when liberated she returned to her former practices. The very night that she came home from gaol her father sent her out into the streets again. She continued in this state, her father and mother living upon her, until about twelve months before I received this account from her, when her father turned her out of his house, because she didn't bring home money enough. She then went into Kent, hop-picking, and there fell in with a beggar, who accosted her while she was sitting under a tree. He said, 'You have got a very bad pair of shoes on; come with me, and you shall have some better ones.' She consented, and walked with him into the village close by, where they stood out in the middle of the streets, and the man began addressing the people, 'My kind good Christians, me and my poor wife here is ashamed to appear before you in the state we are in.' She remained with this person all the winter, and travelled with him through the country, begging. He was a beggar by trade. In the spring she returned to the flower-selling, but scarcely got any money either by that or other means. At last she grew desperate, and wanted to get back to prison. She broke the lamps outside the Mansion-house, and was sentenced to fourteen days' imprisonment. She had been out of prison nearly three weeks when I saw her, and was in training to go into an asylum. She was sick and tired, she said, of her life.

The street-sellers of fried fish
[*volume i. pp. 165–170*]

Fried fish was sold on the street; it was estimated that between 250 and 350 plied this trade. It was not, however, the stallholders' regular fare: many sold fried fish only on Saturday nights and Monday nights or just on an occasional basis. Most fried fish sellers were men and boys and the few women who were engaged in the trade were either wives or daughters of men in the business. Very few Irish were involved in the trade. Mayhew explains that the fish were washed, gutted and trimmed before being fried in a flour and water batter in pale rape oil in ordinary frying pans. The sale took place on 'rounds' or at the stalls. By far the biggest sale took place in the public houses, where fish and bread were served for 1d. Itinerants offered the fish from trays lined with clean newsprint and with a salt-box available. The fried fish sellers often lived in garrets because the odour made them unpopular lodgers and neighbours.

'Fishy' the trader in fried fish
[*volume i. pp. 169, 170*]

The man who gave me the following information was well-looking, and might be about 45 or 50. He was poorly dressed, but his old brown surtout fitted him close and well, was jauntily buttoned up to his black satin stock, worn, but of good quality; and, altogether, he had what is understood among a class as 'a *betterly* appearance about him'. His statement, as well as those of the other vendors of provisions, is curious in its details of public-house vagaries.

'I've been in the trade,' he said, 'seventeen years. Before that, I was a gentleman's servant, and I married a servant-maid, and we had a family, and, on that account, couldn't, either of us, get a situation, though we'd good characters. I was out of employ for seven or eight months, and things was beginning to go to the pawn for a living; but at last, when I gave up any hope of getting into a gentleman's service, I raised 10s., and determined to try something else. I was persuaded, by a friend who kept a beer-shop, to sell oysters at his door. I took his advice, and went to Billingsgate for the first time in my life, and bought a peck of oysters for 2s. 6d. I was dressed respectable then – nothing like the mess and dirt I'm in now;' [I may observe, that there was no dirt about him] 'and so the salesman laid it on, but I gave him all he asked. I know a deal better now. I'd never been used to open oysters, and I couldn't do it. I cut my fingers with the knife slipping all over them, and had to hire a man to open for me, or the blood from my cut fingers would have run upon the oysters. For all that, I cleared 2s. 6d. on that peck, and I soon got up to the trade, and did well; till, in two or three months, the season got over, and I was advised, by the same friend, to try fried fish. That suited me. I've lived in good families, where there was first-rate men-cooks, and I know what good cooking means. I bought a dozen plaice; I forget what I gave for them, but they were dearer then than now. For all that, I took between 11s. and 12s. the first night – it was Saturday – that I started; and I stuck to it, and took from 7s. to 10s. every night, with more, of course, on Saturday, and it was half of it profit then. I cleared a good mechanic's earnings at that time – 30s. a week and more. Soon after, I was told that, if agreeable, my wife could have a stall with fried fish, opposite a wine-vaults just opened, and she made nearly half as much as I did on my rounds. I served the public-houses, and soon got known. With some landlords I had the privilege of the parlour, and tap-room, and bar, when other tradesmen have been kept out. The landlords will say to me still: "*You* can go in, Fishy." Somehow, I got the name of "Fishy" then, and I've kept it ever since. There was hospitality in those days. I've gone into a room in a public-house, used by mechanics, and one of them has said: "I'll stand fish round, gentlemen"; and I've supplied fifteen penn'orths. Perhaps he was a stranger, such a sort of customer, that wanted to be agreeable. Now, it's more likely I hear: "Jack, lend us a penny to buy a bit of fried"; and then Jack says: "You be d—d! Here, lass, let's have another pint." The insults and difficulties I've had in the public-house trade is dreadful. I once sold 16d. worth to three rough-looking fellows I'd never seen before, and they seemed hearty, and asked me to drink with them, so I took a pull; but they wouldn't pay me when I asked, and I waited a goodish bit before I did ask. I thought, at first, it was their fun, but I waited from four to seven, and I found it was no fun. I felt upset, and ran out and told the policeman, but he said it was only a debt, and he couldn't interfere. So I ran to the station, but the head man there said the same, and told me I should hand over the fish with one hand, and hold out the other hand for my money. So I went back to the public-house, and asked for my money – and there was some mechanics that knew me there then – but I got nothing but " — you's!" and one of 'em used most dreadful language. At last, one of the mechanics said: "Muzzle him, Fishy, if he won't pay." He was far bigger than me, him that was one in debt; but my spirit was up, and I let go at him and gave him a bloody nose, and the next hit I knocked him backwards, I'm sure I don't know how, on to a table; but I fell on him, and he clutched me by the coat-collar – I was respectable dressed then – and half smothered me. He tore the back of my coat, too, and I went home like Jim Crow. The potman and the others parted us, and they made the man give me 1s., and the waiter paid me the other 4d., and said he'd take his chance to get it – but he never got it. Another time I went into a bar, and there was a ball in the house, and one of the ball gents came down and gave my basket a kick without ever a word, and started the fish; and in a scuffle – he was a little fellow, but my master – I had this finger put out of joint – you can see that, sir, still – and was in the hospital a week from an injury to my leg; the tiblin bone [the tibia] was hurt, the doctors said. I've had my tray kicked over for a lark in a public-house, and a scramble for my fish, and all gone, and no help and no money for me. The landlords always prevent such things, when they can, and interfere for a poor man; but then it's done sudden, and over in an instant. That sort of thing wasn't the worst. I once had some powdery stuff flung sudden over me at a parlour door. My fish fell off, for I jumped, because I felt blinded, and what became of them I don't know; but I aimed at once for home – it was very late – and had to feel my way almost like a blind man. I can't tell what I suffered. I found it was something black, for I kept rubbing my face with my apron, and could just tell it came away black. I let myself in with my latch, and my wife was in bed, and I told her to get up and look at my face and get some water, and she thought I was joking, as she was half asleep; but when she got up and got a light, and a glass, she screamed, and said I looked such a shiny image; and so I did, as well as I could see, for it was black lead – such as they use for grates – that was flung on me. I washed it off, but it wasn't easy, and my face was sore days after. I had a respectable coat on then, too, which was greatly spoiled, and no remedy at all. I don't know who did it to me. I heard someone say: "You're served out beautiful." It's men that calls themselves gentlemen that does such things. I know the style of them then – it was eight or ten years ago; they'd heard of Lord — , and his goings on. That way it's better now, but worse, far, in the way of getting a living. I dare say, if I had dressed in rough corderoys, I shouldn't have been larked at so much, because they might have thought I was a regular coster, and a fighter; but I don't like that sort of thing – I like to be decent and respectable, if I can.

'I've been in the "fried" trade ever since, except about three months that I tried the sandwiches. I didn't do so well in them, but it was a far easier trade; no carrying heavy weights all the way from Billingsgate: but I went back to the fried. Why now, sir, a good week with me – and I've only myself in the trade now [he was a widower] – is to earn 12s., a poor week is 9s.; and there's as many of one as of the other. I'm known to sell the best of fish, and to cook it in the best style. I think half of us, take it round and round for a year, may earn as much as I do, and the other half about half as much. I think so. I might have saved money, but for a family. I've only one at home with me now, and he really *is* a good lad. My customers are public-house people that want a relish or a sort of supper with their beer, not so much to drinkers. I sell to tradesmen, too; 4d. worth for tea or supper. Some of them send to my place, for I'm known. The Great Exhibition can't be any difference to me. I've a regular round. I used to sell a good deal to women of the town, but I don't now. They haven't the money, I believe. Where I took 10s. of them, eight or ten years ago, I now take only 6d. They may go for other sorts of relishes now; I can't say. The worst of my trade is, that people must have as big penn'orths when fish is dear as when its cheap. I never sold a piece of fish to an Italian boy in my life, though they're Catholics. Indeed, I never saw an Italian boy spend a halfpenny in the streets on anything.'

A working man told me that he often bought fried fish, and accounted it a good to men like himself. He was fond of fried fish to his supper; he couldn't buy half so cheap as the street-sellers, perhaps not a quarter; and, if he could, it would cost him 1d. for dripping to fry the fish in, and he got it ready, and well fried, and generally good, for 1d.

Subsequent inquiries satisfied me that my informant was correct as to his calculations of his fellows' earnings, judging from his own. The price of plaice at Billingsgate is from ½ d. to 2d. each, according to size (the fried fish purveyors never calculate by the weight), ¾ d. being a fair average. A plaice costing 1d. will now be fried into four pieces, each 1d.; but the addition of bread, cost of oil, &c., reduces the 'fried' peoples' profits to rather less than cent. per cent. Soles and the other fish are, moreover, 30 per cent. dearer than plaice. As 150 sellers make as much weekly as my informant, and the other 150 half that amount, we have an average yearly earning of 27l. 6s. in one case, and of 13l. 13s. in the other. Taking only 20l. a year as a medium earning, and adding 90 per cent. for profit, the outlay on the fried fish supplied by London street-sellers is 11,400l.

The street-sellers of baked potatoes
[volume i. pp.173–175]

The baked potato trade, as carried out in the streets, was but fifteen years old at the time of the Great Exhibition. It continued for six months out of the year, from August to April. About 300 people were engaged in the trade. The potatoes were selected for size, cleaned by the huckster, and taken to the baker's for cooking. The baker charged 9d. a cwt for this service which took about an hour and a half. The huckster collected the baked potatoes and carried them home in a green baize-covered basket; then they were placed in a half-lidded can which stood on four legs and they were kept hot by a boiler of hot water. Many people purchased the potatoes to keep their hands warm. Gentlefolk bought them but 'the working classes are the greatest purchasers'. When the season was over the hucksters turned to selling strawberries, raspberries and anything else in season.

A baked potato vendor
[volume i. p.174,175]
[. . .] One of my informants, who had been a bricklayer's labourer, said that after the season he always looked out for work among the bricklayers, and this kept him employed until the baked potato season came round again.

'When I first took to it,' he said, 'I was very badly off. My master had no employment for me, and my brother was ill, and so was my wife's sister, and I had no way of keeping 'em, or myself either.

The labouring men are mostly out of work in the winter time, so I spoke to a friend of mine, and he told me how he managed every winter, and advised me to do the same. I took to it, and have stuck to it ever since. The trade was much better then. I could buy a hundred-weight of potatoes for 1s. 9d. to 2s. 3d., and there were fewer to sell them. We generally use to a cwt. of potatoes three-quarters of a pound of butter – tenpenny salt butter is what we buy – a pennyworth of salt, a pennyworth of pepper, and five pennyworth of charcoal. This, with the baking, 9d., brings the expenses to just upon 7s. 6d. per cwt., and for this our receipts will be 12s. 6d., thus leaving about 5s. per cwt. profit.' Hence the average profits of the trade are about 30s. a week – 'and more to some,' said my informant. A man in Smithfield-market, I am credibly informed, clears at the least 3l. a week. On the Friday he has a fresh basket of hot potatoes brought to him from the baker's every quarter of an hour. Such is his custom that he has not even time to take money, and his wife stands by his side to do so.

Another potato-vendor who shifted his can, he said, 'from a public-house where the tap dined at twelve,' to another half-a-mile off, where it 'dined at one, and so did the parlour,' and afterwards to any place he deemed best, gave me the following account of his customers:

'Such a day as this, sir [Jan. 24], when the fog's like a cloud come down, people looks very shy at my taties, very; they've been more suspicious ever since the taty rot. I thought I should never have rekivered it; never, not the rot. I sell most to mechanics – I was a grocer's porter myself before I was a baked taty – for their dinners, and they're on for good shops where I serves the taps and parlours, and pays me without grumbling, like gentlemen. Gentlemen does grumble though, for I've sold to them at private houses when they've held the door half open as they've called me – aye, and ladies too – and they've said, "Is *that* all for 2d.?" If it'd been a peck they'd have said the same, I know. Some customers is very pleasant with me, and says I'm a blessing. One always says he'll give me a ton of taties when his ship comes home, 'cause he can always have a hot murphy to his cold saveloy, when tin's short. He's a harness-maker, and the railways has injured him. There's Union-street and there's Pearl-row, and there's Market-street, now – they're all off the Borough-road – if I go there at ten at night or so, I can sell 3s.

worth, perhaps, 'cause they know me, and I have another baked taty to help there sometimes. They're women that's not reckoned the best in the world that buys there, but they pay me. I know why I got my name up. I had luck to have good fruit when the rot was about, and they got to know me. I only go twice or thrice a week, for it's two miles from my regular places. I've trusted them sometimes. They've said to me, as modest as could be, "Do give me credit, and 'pon my word you shall be paid; there's a dear!" I am paid mostly. Little shopkeepers is fair customers, but I do best for the taps and the parlours. Perhaps I make 12s. or 15s. a week – I hardly know, for I've only myself and keep no 'count – for the season; money goes one can't tell how, and 'specially if you drinks a drop, as I do sometimes. Foggy weather drives me to it, I'm so worritted; that is, now and then, you'll mind, sir.'

There are, at present, 300 vendors of hot baked potatoes getting their living in the streets of London, each of whom sell, upon an average, ¾ cwt. of potatoes daily. The average takings of each vendor is 6s. a day; and the receipts of the whole number throughout the season (which lasts from the latter end of September till March inclusive), a period of 6 months, is 14,000l.

A capital is required to start in this trade, as follows: can, 2l.; knife, 3d.; stock-money, 8s.; charge for baking 100 potatoes, 1s.; charcoal, 4d.; butter, 2d.; salt, 1d., and pepper, 1d.; altogether, 2l. 9s. 11d. The can and knife is the only property described as fixed, stock-money, &c., being daily occurring, amounts to 75l. during the season.

[. . .]

The cats'- and dogs'-meat dealers
[*volume i. pp. 181–183*]

The cats' and dogs' meat dealers or 'carriers' purchased their meat from the knackers' (or horse slaughterers') yards at twenty locations in London. Mayhew gives a detailed account of the knackers' business, including the sources of horse carcasses for the trade and the uses to which the meat and bones were put. The 'carriers' collected the meat in the mornings and then took it around town on a specified 'walk', dealing directly with the public.

There were at least 1,000 such carriers - men, women and boys; most had failed to make a living in any other employment and they had a bad reputation as drunkards. The slaughtermen made a good living but the dealers made little profit.

A cats'-meat carrier
[*volume i. p.183*]
'My father was a baker by trade,' said a carrier to me, 'but through an enlargement of the heart he was obliged to give up working at his trade; leaning over the trough increased his complaint so severely, that he used to fall down, and be obliged to be brought home. This made him take to the cats' and dogs' meat trade, and he brought me up to it. I do pretty comfortably. I have a very good business, having been all my life at it. If it wasn't for the bad debts I should do much better; but some of the people I trust leave the houses, and actually take in a double quantity of meat the day before. I suppose there is at the present moment as much as 20*l.* owing to me that I never expect to see a farthing of.'

The generality of the dealers wear a shiny hat, black plush waistcoat and sleeves, a blue apron, corduroy trousers, and a blue and white spotted handkerchief round their necks. Some, indeed, will wear two and three handkerchiefs round their necks, this being fashionable among them. A great many meet every Friday afternoon in the donkey-market, Smithfield, and retire to a public-house adjoining, to spend the evening.

A 'cats' meat carrier' who supplied me with information was more comfortably situated than any of the poorer classes that I have yet seen. He lived in the front room of a second floor, in an open and respectable quarter of the town, and his lodgings were the perfection of comfort and cleanliness in an humble sphere. It was late in the evening when I reached the house. I found the 'carrier' and his family preparing for supper. In a large morocco leather easy chair sat the cats' meat carrier himself; his 'blue apron and black shiny hat' had disappeared, and he wore a 'dress' coat and a black satin waistcoat instead. His wife, who was a remarkably pretty woman, and of very attractive manners, wore a 'Dolly Varden' cap, placed jauntily at the back of her head, and a drab merino dress. The room was cosily carpeted, and in one corner stood a mahogany 'crib' with cane-work sides, in which one of the children was asleep. On the table was a clean white table-cloth, and the room was savoury with the steaks, and mashed potatoes that were cooking on the fire. Indeed, I have never yet seen greater comfort in the abodes of the poor. The cleanliness and wholesomeness of the apartment were the more striking from the unpleasant associations connected with the calling.

It is believed by one who has been engaged at the business for 25 years, that there are from 900 to 1,000 horses, averaging 2 cwt. of meat each – little and big – boiled down every week; so that the quantity of cats' and dogs' meat used throughout London is about 200,000 lbs. per week, and this, sold at the rate of 2½ d. per lb., gives 2,000l. a week for the money spent in cats' and dogs' meat, or upwards of 100,000l. a year, which is at the rate of 100l.-worth sold annually by each carrier. The profits of the carriers may be estimated at about 50l. each per annum.

The capital required to start in this business varies from 1l. to 2l. The stock-money needed is between 5s. and 10s. The barrow and basket, weights and scales, knife and steel, or blackstone, cost about 2l. when new, and from 15s. to 4s. second-hand.

Street-sellers of drinkables (coffee)
[*volume i. pp.183–186*]

The sale of tea and coffee at street stalls was, according to Mayhew's informants, relatively unusual until after 1842. By the time he wrote there were more than 300 stalls selling coffee, mainly run by women. Coffee mixed with ground chicory and with carrots was cheap and popular. Because it was not an essential part of the diet, purchasers tended to be reasonably well off. Coffee-stall-keepers stood at the corner of the street on the main thoroughfares and near the markets. The coffee stalls did brisk business in the early mornings. They consisted of spring barrows, bearing a table or a trestle on which stood several cans of coffee kept hot by a charcoal burner. Bread and butter, sliced currant cake, watercress, hard boiled eggs and ham sandwiches were also on sale and mugs were provided. Such stalls also served people abroad at night.

THE LONDON COFFEE–STALL

[from a daguerrotype by Beard]

A coffee-vendor in a small way of business

[*volume i. p.185,186*]

[. . .]

The class of persons usually belonging to the business have been either cab-men, policemen, labourers, or artisans. Many have been bred to dealing in the streets, and brought up to no other employment, but many have taken to the business owing to the difficulty of obtaining work at their own trade. The generality of them are opposed to one another. I asked one in a small way of business what was the average amount of his profits, and his answer was:

'I usually buy 10 ounces of coffee a night. That costs, when good, 1s. 0½ d. With this I should make five gallons of coffee, such as I sell in the street, which would require 3 quarts of milk, at 3d. per quart, and 1½ lb. of sugar, at 3½ d. per lb., there is some at 3d. This would come to 2s. 2¾ d.; and, allowing 1¼ d. for a quarter of a peck of charcoal to keep the coffee hot, it would give 2s. 4d. for the cost of five gallons of coffee. This I should sell out at about 1½ d. per pint; so that the five gallons would produce me 5s., or 2s. 8d. clear. I generally get rid of one quartern loaf and 6 oz. of butter with this quantity of coffee, and for this I pay 5d. the loaf and 3d. the butter, making 8d.; and these I make into twenty-eight slices at ½ d. per slice; so the whole brings me in 1s. 2d., or about 6d. clear. Added to this, I sell a 4 lb. cake, which costs me 3½ d. per lb. 1s. 2d. the entire cake; and this in twenty-eight slices, at 1d. per slice, would yield 2s. 4d., or 1s. 2d. clear; so that altogether my clear gains would be 4s. 4d. upon an expenditure of 2s. 2d. – say 200 per cent.'

This is said to be about the usual profit of the trade. Sometimes they give credit. One person assured me he trusted as much as 9½ d. that morning, and out of that he was satisfied there was 4d., at least, he should never see. Most of the stalls are stationary, but some are locomotive. Some cans are carried about with yokes, like milk-cans, the mugs being kept in a basket. The best district for the night-trade is the City, and the approaches to the bridges. There are more men and women, I was told, walking along Cheapside, Aldersgate-street, Bishopsgate-street, and Fleet-street. In the latter place a good trade is frequently done between twelve at night and two in the morning. For the morning trade the best districts are the Strand, Oxford-street, City-road, New-road (from one end to the other), the markets, especially Covent-garden, Billingsgate, Newgate, and the Borough. There are no coffee-stalls in Smith-field. The reason is that the drovers, on arriving at the market, are generally tired and cold, and prefer sitting down to their coffee in a warm shop rather than drink it in the open street. The best days for coffee-stalls are market mornings, viz. Tuesday, Thursday, and Saturday. On these days the receipts are generally half as much again as those of the other mornings. The best time of the year for the business is the summer. This is, I am told, because the workpeople and costermongers have more money to spend. Some stall-keepers save sufficient to take a shop, but these are only such as have a 'pitch' in the best thoroughfares. One who did a little business informed me that he usually cleared, including Sunday, 14s. − last week his gains were 15s.; the week before that he could not remember. He is very frequently out all night, and does not earn sixpence. This is on wet and cold nights, when there are few people about. His is generally the night-trade. The average weekly earnings of the trade, throughout the year, are said to be 1l. The trade, I am assured by all, is overstocked. They are half too many, they say. 'Two of us,' to use their own words, 'are eating one man's bread.' 'When coffee in the streets first came up, a man could go and earn,' I am told, 'his 8s. a night at the very lowest; but now the same class of men cannot earn more than 3s.' Some men may earn comparatively a large sum, as much as 38s. or 2l., but the generality of the trade cannot make more than 1l. per week, if so much. The following is the statement of one of the class:

'I was a mason's labourer, a smith's labourer, a plasterer's labourer, or a bricklayer's labourer. I was, indeed, a labouring man. I could not get employment. I was for six months without any employ-ment. I did not know which way to support my wife and child (I have only one child). Being so long out of employment, I saw no other means of getting a living but out of the streets. I was almost starving before I took to it − that I certainly was. I'm not ashamed of telling anybody that, because it's true, and I sought for a livelihood wherever I could. Many said they wouldn't do such a thing as keep a coffee-stall, but I said I'd do anything to get a bit of bread honestly. Years ago, when I was a boy, I used to go out selling water-cresses, and apples, oranges, and radishes, with a barrow, for my landlord; so I thought, when I was thrown out of employment, I would take to selling coffee in the streets. I went to a tinman, and paid him 10s. 6d. (the last of my savings, after I'd been four or five months out of work) for a can, I didn't care how I got my living so long as I could turn an honest penny. Well; I went on, and knocked about, and couldn't get a pitch anywhere; but at last I heard that an old man, who had been in the habit of standing for many years at the entrance of one of the markets, had fell ill; so, what did I do, but I goes and pops into his pitch, and there I've done better than ever I did afore. I get 20s. now where I got 10s. one time; and if I only had such a thing as 5l. or 10l., I might get a good living for life. I cannot do half as much as the man that was there before me. He used to make his coffee down there, and had a can for hot water as well; but I have but one can to keep coffee and all in; and I have to borrow my barrow, and pay 1s. a week for it. If I sell my can out, I can't do any more. The struggle to get a living is so great, that, what with one and another in the coffee-trade, it's only those as can get good "pitches" that can get a crust at it.'

As it appears that each coffee-stall keeper on an average clears 1l. a week, and his takings may be said to be at least double that sum, the yearly street expenditure for tea, coffee, &c., amounts to 31,200l. The quantity of coffee sold annually in the streets appears to be about 550,000 gallons.

To commence as a coffee-stall keeper in a moderate manner requires about 5l. capital. The truck costs 2l., and the other utensils and materials 3l. The expense of the cans is near upon 16s. each. The stock-money is a few shillings. [. . .]

Sellers of hot-cross buns

[volume i. pp.201,202]

Perhaps no cry – though it is only for one morning – is more familiar to the ears of a Londoner, than that of 'One-a-penny, two-a-penny, hot-cross buns', on Good Friday. [. . .]

The sellers of the Good Friday buns are principally boys, and they are of mixed classes – costers' boys, boys habitually and boys occasionally street-sellers, and boys street-sellers for that occasion only. One great inducement to embark in the trade is the hope of raising a little money for the Greenwich Fair of the following Monday.

I am informed that 500 persons are employed on Good Friday in the streets of London in the sale of hot-cross buns, each itinerant selling upon the day's average six dozen halfpenny, and seven dozen penny buns, for which he will take 12s. 6d. (his profits being 3d. in the shilling or 3s. 1½ d.). One person informed me that last Good Friday he had sold during the day forty dozen penny buns, for which he received 50s.

The bun-selling itinerants derive their supplies principally from the wholesale pastry-cooks, and, in a less degree, from the small bakers and pastry-cooks, who work more for 'the trade' than themselves. The street hot-cross bun trade is less than it was seven or eight years ago, as the bakers have entered into it more freely, and send round for orders: so that the itinerants complain that they have lost many a good customer. One informant (a master pastry-cook, who had been in the business nearly fifty years) said to me: 'Times are sadly altered to what they were when I was a boy. Why I have known my master to bake five sacks of flour in nothing but hot-cross buns, and that is sufficient for 20,000 buns,' (one sack of flour being used for 4,000 buns, or 500 lbs. of raw material to the same quantity of buns). The itinerants carry their baskets slung on their arm, or borne upon the head. A flannel or green baize is placed at the bottom of the basket and brought over the buns, after which a white cloth is spread over the top of the baize, to give it a clean appearance.

A vendor of 'hot-cross buns' has to provide himself with a basket, a flannel (to keep the buns warm), and a cloth, to give a clean appearance to his commodities. These articles, if bought for the purpose, cost – basket, 2s. 6d.; flannel and cloth, 2s.; stock-money, average, 5s. (largest amount 15s., smallest 2s. 6d.); or about 10s. in all.

There is expended in one day, in hot-cross buns purchased in the London streets, 300l., and nearly 100,000 buns thus bought.

The Chelsea buns are now altogether superseded by the Bath and Alexander's buns. ' People,' the street-sellers say, 'want so much for their money.' There are now but two Chelsea bun-houses; the one at Pimlico, and the other at Chelsea. The principal times Chelsea buns were sold in the streets was Good Friday, Easter, and Whitsuntide; and, with the exception of Good Friday, the great sales were at Greenwich Fair, and then they were sold with other cakes and sweetmeats. I am informed that twenty years ago there was one man, with a rich musical voice, who sold these buns, about Westminster principally, all the year round; his cry – which was one of the musical ones – was, 'One-a-penny, two-a-penny, hot Chelsea buns! Burning hot! smoking hot! r-r-r-reeking hot! hot Chelsea buns!'

The muffin-man
[volume i. pp.202,203]

The street-sellers of muffins and crumpets rank among the old street-tradesmen. It is difficult to estimate their numbers, but they were computed for me at 500, during the winter months. They are for the most part boys, young men, or old men, and some of them infirm. There are a few girls in the trade, but very few women.

The ringing of the muffin-man's bell – attached to which the pleasant associations are not a few – was prohibited by a recent Act of Parliament, but the prohibition has been as inoperative as that which forbad the use of a drum to the costermonger, for the muffin bell still tinkles along the streets, and is rung vigorously in the suburbs. The sellers of muffins and crumpets are a mixed class, but I am told that more of them are the children of bakers, or worn-out bakers, than can be said of any other calling. The best sale is in the suburbs. 'As far as I know, sir,' said a muffin-seller, 'it's the best Hackney way, and Stoke Newington, and Dalston, and Balls Pond, and Islington; where the gents that's in banks – the steady coves of them – goes home to their teas, and the missuses has muffins to welcome them; that's my opinion.'

I did not hear of any street-seller who made the muffins or crumpets he vended. Indeed, he could not make the small quantity required, so as to be remunerative. The muffins are bought of the bakers, and at prices to leave a profit of 4d. in 1s. Some bakers give thirteen to the dozen to the street-sellers whom they know. The muffin-man carries his delicacies in a basket, wherein they are well swathed in flannel, to retain the heat: 'People likes them warm, sir,' an old man told me, 'to satisfy them they're fresh, and they almost always are fresh; but it can't matter so much about their being warm, as they have to be toasted again. I only wish good butter was a sight cheaper, and that would make the muffins go.

Butter's half the battle.' The basket and flannels cost the muffin-man 2s. 6d. or 3s. 6d. His bell stands him in from 4d. to 2s., 'according as the metal is'. The regular price of good-sized muffins from the street-sellers is a halfpenny each; the crumpets are four a penny. Some are sold cheaper, but these are generally smaller, or made of inferior flour. Most of the street-sellers give thirteen, and some even fourteen to the dozen, especially if the purchase be made early in the day, as the muffin-man can then, if he deem it prudent, obtain a further supply.

A sharp London lad of fourteen, whose father had been a journeyman baker, and whose mother (a widow) kept a small chandler's shop, gave me the following account:

'I turns out with muffins and crumpets, sir, in October, and continues until it gets well into the spring, according to the weather. I carries a fust-rate article; werry much so. If you was to taste 'em, sir, you'd say the same. If I sells three dozen muffins at ½d. each, and twice that in crumpets, it's a werry fair day, werry fair; all beyond that is a *good* day. The profit on the three dozen and the others is 1s., but that's a great help, really a wonderful help, to mother, for I should be only mindin' the shop at home. Perhaps I clears 4s. a week, perhaps more, perhaps less; but that's about it, sir. Some does far better than that, and some can't hold a candle to it. If I has a hextra day's sale, mother'll give me 3d. to go to the play, and that hencourages a young man, you know, sir. If there's any unsold, a coffee-shop gets them cheap, and puts 'em off cheap again next morning. My best customers is genteel houses, 'cause I sells a genteel thing. I likes wet days best, 'cause there's werry respectable ladies what don't keep a servant, and they buys to save themselves going out. We're a great conwenience to the ladies, sir – a great conwenience to them as likes a slap-up tea. I have made 1s. 8d. in a day; that was my best. I once took only 2½d. – I don't know why – that was my worst. The shops don't love me – I puts their noses out. Sunday is no better day than others, or werry little. I can read, but wish I could read easier.'

Calculating 500 muffin-sellers, each clearing 4s. a week, we find 300l. a week expended on the metropolitan street sale of muffins; or, in the course of twenty weeks, 2,000l. Five shillings, with the price of a basket, &c., which is about 3s. 6d. more, is the capital required for a start.

Street-orators
[*volume i. pp.213–251*]

Mayhew describes the 'patterers' (formerly known as mountebanks), who use their 'patter' to help sell their wares of stationery, literature, etc. 'We are the haristocracy of the streets . . . People don't pay us for what we gives 'em, but only to hear us talk. We live like yourself, sir, by the hexercise of our hintellects – we by talking, and you by writing,' said one who told penny fortunes with a bottle. Standing patterers had a pitch from which they could sell nostrums and street wonders. Some used boards to advertise their wares. Others sold straws and provided with them pornographic materials. Others recited and commented upon current events. Closely allied to them were the 'chaunters' who sang the contents of the papers they sold.

These traffickers constitute the principal street-sellers of literature, or 'paper-workers', of the 'pattering' class. [. . .]

Of running patterers
[*volume i. pp.221,222*]
Few of the residents in London – but chiefly those in the quieter streets – have not been aroused, and most frequently in the evening, by a hurly-burly on each side of the street. An attentive listening will not lead any one to an accurate knowledge of what the clamour is about. It is from a 'mob' or 'school' of the running patterers (for both those words are used), and consists of two, three, or four men. All these men state that the greater the noise they make, the better is the chance of sale, and better still when the noise is on each side of a street, for it appears as if the vendors were proclaiming such interesting or important intelligence, that they were vying with one another who should supply the demand which must ensue. It is not possible to ascertain with any certitude what the patterers are so anxious to sell, for only a few leading words are audible. One of the cleverest of running patterers repeated to me, in a subdued tone, his announcements of murders. The words 'Murder', 'Horrible', 'Barbarous', 'Love', 'Mysterious', 'Former Crimes', and the like, could only be caught by the ear, but there was no announcement of anything like 'particulars'. If, however, the 'paper' relate to any well-known criminal, such as

Rush, the name is given distinctly enough, and so is any new or pretended fact. The running patterers describe, or profess to describe, the contents of their papers as they go rapidly along, and they seldom or ever stand still. They usually deal in murders, seductions, crim.-cons., explosions, alarming accidents, 'assassinations', deaths of public characters, duels, and love-letters. But popular, or notorious, murders are the 'great goes'. The running patterer cares less than other street-sellers for bad weather, for if he 'work' on a wet and gloomy evening, and if the work be 'a cock', which is a fictitious statement or even a pretended fictitious statement, there is the less chance of any one detecting the ruse. But of late years no new 'cocks' have been printed, excepting for temporary purposes, such as I have specified as under its appropriate head in my account of 'Death and Fire-Hunters'.* Among the old stereotyped 'cocks' are love-letters. One is well known as 'The Husband caught in a Trap', and being in an epistolary form sub-serves any purpose: whether it be the patterer's aim to sell the 'Love Letters' of any well-known person, such as Lola Montes, or to fit them for a local (pretended) scandal, as the 'Letters from a Lady in this neighbourhood to a Gentleman not 100 miles off '.

The street-buyers
[*volume ii. pp.103–115*]

Mayhew's introduction to the subject
[. . .] It is usually the lot of a poor person who has been driven to the streets, or has adopted such a life when an adult, to *sell* trifling things – such as are light to carry and require a small outlay – in advanced age. Old men and women totter about offering lucifer-matches, boot and stay-laces, penny memorandum books, and such like. But the elder portion of the street-folk I have now to speak of do not sell, but buy. The street-seller commends his wares, their cheapness, and excellence. The same sort of man, when a buyer, depreciates everything offered to him, in order to ensure a cheaper bargain, while many of the things thus obtained find their way into street-sale, and are then as much commended

* Not reproduced in this edition.

for cheapness and goodness, as if they were the stock-in-trade of an acute slop advertisement-monger, and this is done sometimes by the very man who, when a buyer, condemned them as utterly valueless. But this is common to all trades.

Street-buyers of rags and bones
[*volume ii. pp.104–108*]

Traders in these items were not unprosperous; the poor people who picked up rags and bones in the street were not buyers but finders. Street-buyers had barrows, and sometimes donkeys and carts, and bought the rags and bones. They were particularly to be seen in the suburbs such as Croydon, Deptford, Greenwich and Woolwich. They called especially upon the servants of the wealthy. Finders of rags and bones sometimes bought their supplies also. Some bartered toys with poor children who had found bones in the street.

The rag-and-bone man
[*volume ii. pp.105,106*]

A street-buyer of the class I have described, upon presenting himself at any house, offers to buy rags, broken metal, or glass, and for rags especially there is often a serious bargaining, and some-times, I was told by an itinerant street-seller, who had been an ear-witness, a little joking not of the most delicate kind. For coloured rags these men give ½ d. a pound, or 1d. for three pounds; for inferior white rags ½ d. a pound, and up to 1½ d.; for the best, 2d. the pound. It is common, however, and even more common, I am assured, among masters of the old rag and bottle shops, than among street-buyers, to announce 2d. or 3d., or even as much as 6d., for the best rags, but, somehow or other, the rags taken for sale to those buyers never are of the best. To offer 6d. a pound for rags is ridiculous, but such an offer may be seen at some rag-shops, the figure '6', perhaps, crowning a painting of a large plum-pudding, as a representation of what may be a Christmas result, merely from the thrifty preservation of rags, grease, and dripping. Some of the street-buyers, when working the suburbs or the country, attach a similar 'illustration' to their barrows or carts. I saw the winter placard of one of these men, which he was reserving for a country excursion as far as Rochester, 'when the plum-pudding time was a-coming'. In this pictorial advertisement a man and woman, very florid and full-faced, were on the point of enjoying a huge plum-pudding, the man flourishing a large knife, and looking very hospitable. On a scroll which issued from his mouth were the words: 'From our rags! The best prices given by — — , of London.' The woman in like manner exclaimed: 'From dripping and house fat! The best prices given by — — , of London.'

This man told me that at some times, both in town and country, he did not buy a pound of rags in a week. He had heard the old hands in the trade say, that 20 or 30 years back they could 'gather' (the word generally used for buying) twice and three times as many rags as at present. My formant attributed this change to two causes, depending more upon what he had heard from experienced street-buyers than upon his own knowledge. At one time it was common for a mistress to allow her maidservant to 'keep a rag-bag', in which all refuse linen, &c., was collected for sale for the servant's behoof; a privilege now rarely accorded. The other cause was that working-people's wives had less money at their command now than they had formerly, so that instead of gathering a good heap for the man who called on them periodically, they ran to a marine store-shop and sold them by one, two, and three pennyworths at a time. This related to all the things in the street-buyer's trade, as well as to rags.

'I've known this trade ten years or so,' said my informant, 'I was a costermonger before that, and I work coster-work now in the summer, and buy things in the winter. Before Christmas is the best time for second-hand trade. When I set out on a country round – and I've gone as far as Guildford and Maidstone, and St Alban's – I lays in as great a stock of glass and crocks as I can raise money for, or as my donkey or pony – I've had both, but I'm working a ass now – can drag without distressing him. I swops my crocks for anythink in the second-hand way, and when I've got through them I buys outright, and so works my way back to London. I bring back what I've bought in the crates and hampers I've had to pack the crocks in. The first year as I started I got hold of a few very tidy rags, coloured things mostly. The Jew I sold 'em to when I got home again gave me more than I expected. Oh Lord no, not more than I asked! He told me, too, that he'd buy any more I might have, as they was wanted at some town not very far off, where there was a call for them for patching quilts. I haven't heard of a call for any that way since. I get less and less rags every year, I think. Well, I can't say what I got last year; perhaps about two stone. No, none of them was woollen. They're things as people's seldom satisfied with the price for, is rags. I've bought muslin window curtains or frocks as was worn, and good for nothink but rags, but there always seems such a lot, and they weighs so light and comes to so little, that there's sure to be grumbling. I've sometimes bought a lot of old clothes, by the lump, or I've swopped crocks for them, and among them there's frequently been things as the Jew in Petticoat-lane, what I sells them to, has put o' one side as rags. If I'd offered to give rag prices, them as I got 'em of would have been offended, and have thought I wanted to cheat. When you get a lot at one go, and 'specially if it's for crocks, you must make the best of them. This for that, and t'other for t'other. I stay at the beer-shops and little inns in the country. Some of the landlords looks very shy at one, if you're a stranger, acause, if the police detectives is after anythink, they go as hawkers, or barrowmen, or somethink that way.' [This statement as to the police is correct; but the man did not know how it came to his knowledge; he had 'heard of it'. he believed.] 'I've very seldom slept in a common lodging-house. I'd rather sleep on my barrow.' [I have before had occasion to remark the aversion of the coster-monger class to sleep in low lodging-houses. These men, almost always, and from the necessities of their calling, have rooms of their own in London; so that, I presume, they hate to sleep in public, as the accommodation for repose in many a lodging-house may very well be called. At any rate the costermongers, of all classes of street-sellers, when on their country excursions, resort the least to the lodging-houses.] 'The last round I had in the country, as far as Reading and Pangbourne, I was away about five weeks, I think, and came back a better man by a pound; that was all. I mean I had 30 shillings' worth of things to start with, and when I'd got back, and turned my rags, and old metal, and things into money, I had 50s. To be sure Jenny [the ass] and me lived well all the time, and I bought a pair of half-boots and a pair of stockings at Reading, so it weren't so bad. Yes, sir, there's nothing I likes better than a turn into the country. It does one's health good, if it don't turn out so well for profits as it might.' [. . .]

Street-sellers of second-hand articles
[*volume ii. pp.5–47*]

Mayhew described the recycling trade in some detail. He subdivided it into: sellers of old metal articles (such as cutlery, tools, candle-sticks, fire-irons, grate bottoms); sellers of old linen, cotton and wool (such as stocking-legs for re-footing or old sheeting for use as towels); sellers of old glass and crockery (such as bottles, pans, pitchers, wash hand basins); street sellers of miscellaneous items (such as musical instruments, baskets, stuffed birds, pictures, chess and draught boards); sellers of old clothes (including male, female, juvenile and infant attire). Such sales took place both in shops and from stalls and barrows. The shops include the well-known marine store shops on the Ratcliff Highway (and here Mayhew quotes 'Mr Dickens, one of the most minute and truthful of observers' [ii. pp.24–25].)

Seller of second-hand metal-wares
[*volume ii. pp.11,12*]

An experienced man in the business, who thought he was 'turned 50, or somewhere about that', gave me the following account of his trade, his customers, &c.

'I've been in most street-trades,' he said, 'and was born to it, like, for my mother was a rag-gatherer – not a bad business once – and I helped her. I never saw my father, but he was a soldier, and it's supposed lost his life in foreign parts. No, I don't remember ever having heard what foreign parts, and it don't matter. Well, perhaps, this is about as tidy a trade for a bit of bread as any that's going now. Perhaps selling fish may be better, but that's to a man what knows fish well. I can't say I ever did. I'm more a dab at cooking it.' [with a laugh] 'I like a bloater best on what's an Irish gridiron. Do you know what that is, sir? I know, though I'm not Irish, but I married an Irish wife, and as good a woman as ever was a wife. It's done on the tongs, sir, laid across the fire, and the bloater's laid across the tongs. Some says it's best turned and turned very quick on the coals themselves, but the tongs is best, for you can raise or lower.' [My informant seemed interested in his account of this and other modes of cookery, which I need not detail.] 'This is really a very trying trade. Oh, I mean it tries a man's patience so. Why, it was in Easter week a man dressed like a gentleman – but I don't think he was a real gentleman – looked out some bolts, and a hammer head, and other things, odds and ends, and they came to 10*d*. He said he'd give 6*d*. "Sixpence!" says I; "why, d'you think I stole 'em?" "Well," says he, "if I didn't think you'd stole 'em, I shouldn't have come to *you*." I don't think he was joking. Well, sir, we got to high words, and I said, "Then I'm d—d if you have them for less than 1*s*." And a bit of a crowd began to gather, they was most boys, but the p'liceman came up, as slow as you please, and so my friend flings down 1*s*., and puts the things in his pocket and marches off, with a few boys to keep him company. That's the way one's temper's tried. Well, it's hard to say what sells best. A latch-lock and keys goes off quick. I've had them from 2*d*. to 6*d*.; but it's only the lower-priced things as sells now in any trade. Bolts is a fairish stock, and so is all sorts of tools. Well, not saws so much as such things as screwdrivers, or hammers, or choppers, or tools that if they're rusty people can clean up theirselves. Saws ain't so easy to manage; bed-keys is good. No, I don't clean the metal up unless it's very bad; I think things don't sell so well that way. People's jealous that they're just done up on purpose to deceive, though they may cost only 1*d*. or 2*d*. There's that cheese-cutter now, it's getting rustier and there'll be very likely a better chance to sell it. This is how it is, sir, I know. You see if a man's going to buy old metal, and he sees it all rough and rusty, he says to himself, "Well, there's no gammon about it; I can just see what it is." Then folks like to clean up a thing theirselves, and it's as if it was something made from their own cleverness. That was just my feeling, sir, when I bought old metals for my own use, before I was in the trade, and I goes by that. Oh, working people's by far my best customers. Many of 'em's very fond of jobbing about their rooms or their houses, and they come to such as me. Then a many has fancies for pigeons, or rabbits, or poultry, or dogs, and they mostly make up the places for them their-selves, and as money's an object, why them sort of fancy people buys hinges, and locks, and screws, and hammers, and what they want of me. A clever mechanic can turn his hand to most things that he wants for his own use. I know a shoemaker that makes beautiful rabbit-hutches and sells them along with his prize cattle, as I calls his great big long-eared rabbits. Perhaps I take 2*s*. 6*d*. or 3*s*. a day, and it's about half profit. Yes, this time of the year I make good 10*s*. 6*d*. a week, but in winter not 1*s*. a day. That would be very poor pickings for two people to live on, and I can't do without my drop of beer, but my wife has constant work with a first-rate laundress at Mile End, and so we rub on, for we've no family living.'

This informant told me further of the way in which the old metal stocks sold in the streets were provided; but that branch of the subject relates to street-buying. Some of the street-sellers, however, buy their stocks of the shopkeepers.

I find a difficulty in estimating the number of the second-hand metal-ware street-sellers. Many of the stalls or barrows are the property of the marine-store shopkeepers, or old metal dealers (marine stores being about the only things the marine-store men do not sell), and these are generally placed near the shop, being indeed a portion of its contents out of doors. Some of the marine-store men (a class of traders, by the by, not superior to street-sellers, making no 'odious' comparison as to the honesty of the two), when they have purchased largely – the refuse iron for instance after a house has been pulled down – establish two or three pitches in the street, confiding the stalls or barrows to their wives and children. I was told by several in the trade that there were 200 old-metal-sellers in the streets, but from the best information at my command not more than 50 appear to be strictly street-sellers, unconnected with shopkeeping. Estimating a weekly receipt, per individual, of 15s. (half being profit), the yearly street outlay among this body alone amounts to 1950l. [. . .]

The 'pure'-finders
[volume ii. pp.142–145]

Dogs' dung was called 'pure' because of its cleansing and purefying prop-erties. The men and women engaged in collecting dogs' dung from the streets had been known as 'pure'-finders for about thirty years, when Mayhew wrote. There were between 200 and 300 finders. (Before this time, it had been an almost wholly-female occupation and the women had been known as 'bunters' because they were primarily rag-gatherers.) Mayhew believed that most were former mechanics and small tradesmen who had fallen on bad times. The 'pure'-finders sold their 'pure' to the thirty or so tanyards in Bermondsey. These tanyards had their own regular 'pure' finders. Some

*earned as much as 15s. a week while others were hard put to earn 3s.
Traditionally the finders carried a basket with a handle for purposes of
collection and wore a black leather glove on one hand to scoop up the 'pure';
more and more the glove was dispensed with and the finders resorted to
washing their hands instead. Women 'pure'-finders often retained their
interest in collecting rags and wore aprons with capacious pockets to stow
these away.*

A female 'pure'-finder
[*volume ii. pp.143–145*]

In the wretched locality already referred to as lying between the
Docks and Rosemary-lane, redolent of filth and pregnant with
pestilential diseases, and whither all the outcasts of the metropolitan population seem to be drawn, either in the hope of finding
fitting associates and companions in their wretchedness (for there
is doubtlessly something attractive and agreeable to them in such
companionship), or else for the purpose of hiding themselves and
their shifts and struggles for existence from the world, – in this
dismal quarter, and branching from one of the many narrow lanes
which interlace it, there is a little court with about half-a-dozen
houses of the very smallest dimensions, consisting of merely two
rooms, one over the other. Here in one of the upper rooms (the
lower one of the same house being occupied by another family and
apparently *filled* with little ragged children), I discerned, after considerable difficulty, an old woman, a 'pure'-finder. When I opened
the door the little light that struggled through the small window,
the many broken panes of which were stuffed with old rags, was
not sufficient to enable me to perceive who or what was in the
room. After a short time, however, I began to make out an old
chair standing near the fire-place, and then to discover a poor old
woman resembling a bundle of rags and filth stretched on some
dirty straw in the corner of the apartment. The place was bare
and almost naked. There was nothing in it except a couple of old
tin kettles and a basket, and some broken crockeryware in the
recess of the window. To my astonishment I found this wretched
creature to be, to a certain extent, a 'superior' woman; she could
read and write well, spoke correctly, and appeared to have been a
person of natural good sense, though broken up with age, want,
and infirmity, so that she was characterised by all that dull and

hardened stupidity of manner which I have noticed in the class. She made the following statement:

'I am about 60 years of age. My father was a milkman, and very well off; he had a barn and a great many cows. I was kept at school till I was thirteen or fourteen years of age; about that time my father died, and then I was taken home to help my mother in the business. After a while things went wrong; the cows began to die, and mother, alleging she could not manage the business herself, married again. I soon found out the difference. Glad to get away, anywhere out of the house, I married a sailor, and was very comfortable with him for some years, as he made short voyages, and was often at home, and always left me half his pay. At last he was pressed, when at home with me, and sent away; I forget now where he was sent to, but I never saw him from that day to this. The only thing I know is that some sailors came to me four or five years after, and told me that he deserted from the ship in which he had gone out, and got on board the *Neptune*, East Indiaman, bound for Bombay, where he acted as boatswain's mate; some little time afterwards, he had got intoxicated while the ship was lying in harbour, and, going down the side to get into a bumboat, and buy more drink, he had fallen overboard and was drowned. I got some money that was due to him from the India House, and, after that was all gone, I went into service, in the Mile-end Road. There I stayed for several years, till I met my second husband, who was bred to the water, too, but as a waterman on the river. We did very well together for a long time, till he lost his health. He became paralysed like, and was deprived of the use of all one side, and nearly lost the sight of one of his eyes; this was not very conspicuous at first, but when we came to get pinched, and to be badly off, then any one might have seen that there was something the matter with his eye. Then we parted with everything we had in the world; and, at last, when we had no other means of living left, we were advised to take to gathering "Pure". At first I couldn't endure the business; I couldn't bear to eat a morsel, and I was obliged to discontinue it for a long time. My husband kept at it though, for he could do that well enough, only he couldn't walk as fast as he ought. He couldn't lift his hands as high as his head, but he managed to work under him, and so put the Pure in the basket. When I saw that he, poor fellow, couldn't make enough to keep us both, I took heart and went out again, and used to gather more than he did; that's fifteen years ago now; the times were good then, and we used to do very well. If we only gathered a pail-full in the day, we could live very well; but we could do much more than that, for there wasn't near so many at the business then, and the Pure was easier to be had. For my part I can't tell where all the poor creatures have come from of late years; the world seems growing worse and worse every day. They have pulled down the price of Pure, that's certain; but the poor things must do some-thing, they can't starve while there's anything to be got. Why, no later than six or seven years ago, it was as high as 3s. 6d. and 4s. a pail-full, and a ready sale for as much of it as you could get; but now you can only get 1s. and in some places 1s. 2d. a pail-full; and, as I said before, there are so many at it, that there is not much left for a poor old creature like me to find. The men that are strong and smart get the most, of course, and some of them do very well, at least they manage to live. Six years ago, my husband complained that he was ill, in the evening, and lay down in the bed – we lived in Whitechapel then – he took a fit of coughing, and was smothered in his own blood. Oh dear,' [the poor old soul here ejaculated] 'what troubles I have gone through! I had eight children at one time, and there is not one of them alive now. My daughter lived to 30 years of age, and then she died in childbirth, and, since then, I have had nobody in the wide world to care for me – none but myself, all alone as I am. After my husband's death I couldn't do much, and all my things went away, one by one, until I've nothing but bare walls, and that's the reason why I was vexed at first at your coming in, sir. I was yesterday out all day, and went round Aldgate, Whitechapel, St George's East, Stepney, Bow, and Bromley, and then came home; after that, I went over to Bermondsey, and there I got only 6d. for my pains. To-day I wasn't out at all; I wasn't well; I had a bad headache, and I'm so much afraid of the fevers that are all about here – though I don't know why I should be afraid of them – I was lying down, when you came, to get rid of my pains. There's such a dizziness in my head now, I feel as if it didn't belong to me. No, I have earned no money today. I have had a piece of dried bread that I steeped in water to eat. I haven't eat anything else today; but, pray, sir, don't tell anybody of it. I could never bear the thought of going into the "great house" [workhouse]; I'm so used to the air, that I'd sooner die in the street, as many I know have done. I've known several of our people, who have sat down in the street with their basket alongside them, and died. I knew one not long ago, who took ill just as she was stooping down to gather up the Pure, and fell on her face; she was taken to the London Hospital, and died at three o'clock in the morning. I'd sooner die like them than be deprived of my liberty, and be prevented from going about where I liked. No, I'll never go into the workhouse; my master is kind to me' [the tanner whom she supplies]. 'When I'm ill, he sometimes gives me a sixpence; but there's one gentleman has done us great harm, by forcing so many into the business. He's a Poor Law guardian, and when any poor person applies for relief, he tells them to go and gather Pure, and that he'll buy it of them (for he's in the line), and so the parish, you see, don't have to give anything, and that's one way that so many have come into the trade of late, that the likes of me can do little or no good at it. Almost every one I've ever known engaged at Pure-finding were people who were better off once. I knew a man who went by the name of Brown, who picked up Pure for years before I went to it; he was a very quiet man; he used to lodge in Blue Anchor-yard, and seldom used to speak to anybody. We two used to talk together sometimes, but never much. One morning he was found dead in his bed; it was of a Tuesday morning, and he was buried about 12 o'clock on the Friday following. About 6 o'clock on that afternoon, three or four gentlemen came searching all through this place, looking for a man named Brown, and offering a reward to any who would find him out; there was a whole crowd about them when I came up. One of the gentlemen said that the man they wanted had lost the first finger of his right hand, and then I knew that it was the man that had been buried only that morning. Would you believe it, Mr Brown was a real gentleman all the time, and had a large estate, of I don't know how many thousand pounds, just left him, and the lawyers had advertised and searched everywhere for him, but never found him, you may say, till he was dead. We discovered that his name was not Brown; he had only taken that name to hide his real one, which, of course, he did not want any one to know. I've often thought of him, poor man, and all the misery he might have been spared, if the good news had only come a year or two sooner.' [. . .]

The mud-larks
[*volume ii. pp. 155–158*]

Mud-larks were a variety of river-finder who worked on the shore. The name came from their wading through the mud up to their waists to collect items such as coals, old-iron, copper nails, rope and bones, left by the tide, which were a source of cheap fuel for the poor. Boys, girls, and old men and women, engaged in this occupation, and most lived in alleyways near the river from Vauxhall Bridge to Woolwich. Oftentimes they sold tools that they found to seamen in exchange for biscuits and meat. The boy mud-larks sometimes spent the remainder of their time (when the tide was in) opening cab doors for gentry at the cabstands. Some of this group also attended ragged schools in the evenings.

A child mud-lark
[*volume ii. pp. 155–157*]

At one of the stairs in the neighbourhood of the pool, I collected about a dozen of these unfortunate children; there was not one of them over twelve years of age, and many of them were but six. It would be almost impossible to describe the wretched group, so motley was their appearance, so extraordinary their dress, and so stolid and inexpressive their countenances. Some carried baskets, filled with the produce of their morning's work, and others old tin kettles with iron handles.

Some, for want of these articles, had old hats filled with the bones and coals they had picked up; and others, more needy still, had actually taken the caps from their own heads, and filled them with what they had happened to find. The muddy slush was dripping from their clothes and utensils, and forming a puddle in which they stood. There did not appear to be among the whole group as many filthy cotton rags to their backs as, when stitched together, would have been sufficient to form the material of one shirt. [. . .]

On questioning one, he said his father was a coal-backer; he had been dead eight years; the boy was nine years old. His mother was alive; she went out charing and washing when she could get any such work to do. She had 1s. a day when she could get employment, but that was not often; he remembered once to have had a pair of shoes, but it was a long time since. 'It is very cold in winter,' he said, 'to stand in the mud without shoes,' but he did not mind it in summer. He had been three years mud-larking, and supposed he should remain a mud-lark all his life. What else could he be, for there was nothing else that he knew *how* to do? Some days he earned 1*d*., and some days 4*d*.; he never earned 8*d*. in one day, that would have been a 'jolly lot of money'. He never found a saw or a hammer, he 'only wished' he could, they would be glad to get hold of them at the dolly's. He had been one month at school before he went mud-larking. Some time ago he had gone to the ragged school; but he no longer went there, for he forgot it. He could neither read nor write, and did not think he could learn if he tried 'ever so much'. He didn't know what religion his father and mother were, nor did know what religion meant. God was God, he said. He had heard he was good, but didn't know what good he was to him. He thought he was a Christian, but he didn't know what a Christian was. He had heard of Jesus Christ once, when he went to a Catholic chapel, but he never heard tell of who or what he was, and didn't 'particular care' about knowing. His father and mother were born in Aberdeen, but he didn't know where Aberdeen was. London was England, and England, he said, was in London, but he couldn't tell in what part. He could not tell where he would go to when he died, and didn't believe any one could tell *that*. Prayers, he told me, were what people said to themselves at night. *He* never said any, and didn't know any; his mother sometimes used to speak to him about them, but he could never learn any. His mother didn't go to church or to chapel, because she had no clothes. All the money he got he gave to his mother, and she bought bread with it, and when they had no money they lived the best way they could.

Such was the amount of intelligence manifested by this unfortunate child. [. . .]

As an illustration of the doctrines I have endeavoured to enforce throughout this publication, I cite the following history of one of the above class. It may serve to teach those who are still sceptical as to the degrading influence of circumstances upon the poor, that many of the humbler classes, if placed in the same easy position as ourselves, would become, perhaps, quite as 'respectable' members of society.

The lad of whom I speak was discovered by me now nearly two years ago 'mud-larking' on the banks of the river near the docks. He was a quick, intelligent little fellow, and had been at the business, he told me, about three years. He had taken to mud-larking, he said, because his clothes were too bad for him to look for anything better. He worked every day, with 20 or 30 boys, who might all be seen at day-break with their trowsers tucked up, groping about, and picking out the pieces of coal from the mud on the banks of the Thames. He went into the river up to his knees, and in searching the mud he often ran pieces of glass and long nails into his feet. When this was the case, he went home and dressed the wounds, but returned to the river-side directly, 'for should the tide come up,' he added, 'without my having found something, why I must starve till next low tide.' In the very cold weather he and his other shoeless companions used to stand in the hot water that ran down the river side from some of the steam-factories, to warm their frozen feet.

The experiences of a juvenile mud-lark
[*volume ii. pp.157,158*]
[. . .] At first he found it difficult to keep his footing in the mud, and he had known many beginners fall in. He came to my house, at my request, the morning after my first meeting with him. It was the depth of winter, and the poor little fellow was nearly destitute of clothing. His trousers were worn away up to his knees, he had no shirt, and his legs and feet (which were bare) were covered with chilblains. On being questioned by me he gave the following account of his life:

He was fourteen years old. He had two sisters, one fifteen and the other twelve years of age. His father had been dead nine years. The man had been a coal-whipper, and, from getting his work from one of the publican employers in those days, had become a confirmed drunkard. When he married he held a situation in a warehouse, where his wife managed the first year to save 4*l*. 10*s*. out of her husband's earnings; but from the day he took to coal-whipping she had never saved one halfpenny, indeed she and her children were often left to starve. The man (whilst in a state of intoxication) had fallen between two barges, and the injuries he received had been so severe that he had lingered in a helpless state for three years before his death. After her husband's decease the poor woman's neigh-bours subscribed 1*l*. 5*s*. for her; with this sum she opened a greengrocer's shop, and got on very well for five years.

When the boy was nine years old his mother sent him to the Red Lion school at Green-bank, near Old Gravel-lane, Ratcliffe-highway; she paid 1*d.* a week for his learning. He remained there for a year; then the potato-rot came, and his mother lost upon all she bought. About the same time two of her customers died 30*s.* in her debt; this loss, together with the potato-disease, completely ruined her, and the whole family had been in the greatest poverty from that period. Then she was obliged to take all her children from their school, that they might help to keep themselves as best they could. Her eldest girl sold fish in the streets, and the boy went to the river-side to 'pick up' his living. The change, however, was so great that shortly afterwards the little fellow lay ill eighteen weeks with the ague. As soon as the boy recovered his mother and his two sisters were 'taken bad' with a fever. The poor woman went into the 'Great House', and the children were taken to the Fever Hospital. When the mother returned home she was too weak to work, and all she had to depend on was what her boy brought from the river. They had nothing to eat and no money until the little fellow had been down to the shore and picked up some coals, selling them for a trifle. 'And hard enough he had to work for what he got, poor boy,' said his mother to me on a future occasion, sobbing; 'still he never complained, but was quite proud when he brought home enough for us to get a bit of meat with; and when he has sometimes seen me down-hearted, he has clung round my neck, and assured me that one day God would see us cared for if I would put my trust in Him.' As soon as his mother was well enough she sold fruit in the streets, or went out washing when she could get a day's work.

The lad suffered much from the pieces of broken glass in the mud. Some little time before I met with him he had run a copper nail into his foot. This lamed him for three months, and his mother was obliged to carry him on her back every morning to the doctor. As soon, however, as he could 'hobble' (to use his mother's own words) he went back to the river, and often returned (after many hours' hard work in the mud) with only a few pieces of coal, not enough to sell even to get them a bit of bread. One evening, as he was warming his feet in the water that ran from a steam-factory, he heard some boys talking about the ragged school in High-street, Wapping.

'They was saying what they used to learn there,' added the boy. 'They asked me to come along with them for it was great fun. They told me that all the boys used to be laughing and making game of the master. They said they used to put out the gas and chuck the slates all about. They told me, too, that there was a good fire there, so I went to have a warm and see what it was like. When I got there the master was very kind to me. They used to give us tea-parties, and to keep us quiet they used to show us the magic lantern. I soon got to like going there, and went every night for six months. There was about 40 or 50 boys in the school. The most of them was thieves, and they used to go thieving the coals out of barges along shore, and cutting the ropes off ships, and going and selling it at the rag-shops. They used to get $\frac{3}{4}d$. a lb. for the rope when dry, and $\frac{1}{2}d$. when wet. Some used to steal pudding out of shops and hand it to those outside, and the last boy it was handed to would go off with it. They used to steal bacon and bread sometimes as well. About half of the boys at the school was thieves. Some had work to do at ironmongers, lead-factories, engineers, soap-boilers, and so on, and some had no work to do and was good boys still. After we came out of school at nine o'clock at night, some of the bad boys would go a-thieving, perhaps half-a-dozen and from that to eight would go out in a gang together. There was one big boy of the name of C— ; he was 18 years old, and is in prison now for stealing bacon; I think he is in the House of Correction. This C— used to go out of school before any of us, and wait outside the door as the other boys came out. Then he would call the boys he wanted for his gangs on one side, and tell them where to go and steal. He used to look out in the daytime for shops where things could be "prigged", and at night he would tell the boys to go to them. He was called the captain of the gangs. He had about three gangs altogether with him, and there were from six to eight boys in each gang. The boys used to bring what they stole to C— , and he used to share it with them. I belonged to one of the gangs. There were six boys altogether in my gang; the biggest lad, that knowed all about the thieving, was the captain of the gang I was in, and C— was captain over him and over all of us.

'There was two brothers of them; you seed them, sir, the night you first met me. The other boys, as was in my gang, was B— B—, and B— L— , and W— B— , and a boy we used to call "Tim"; these, with myself, used to make up one of the gangs, and we all of us used to go a-thieving every night after school-hours. When the tide would be right up, and we had nothing to do along shore, we used to go thieving in the daytime as well. It was B— B— , and B— L— , as first put me up to go thieving; they took me with them, one night, up the lane [New Gravel-lane], and I see them take some bread out of a baker's, and they wasn't found out; and, after that, I used to go with them regular. Then I joined C—'s gang; and, after that, C— came and told us that his gang could do better than ourn, and he asked us to join our gang to his'n, and we did so. Sometimes we used to make 3s. or 4s. a day; or about 6d. apiece. While waiting outside the school-doors, before they opened, we used to plan up where we would go thieving after school was over. I was taken up once for thieving coals myself, but I was let go again.'

I was so much struck with the boy's truthfulness of manner, that I asked him, would he really lead a different life, if he saw a means of so doing? He assured me he would, and begged me earnestly to try him. Upon his leaving me, 2s. were given him for his trouble. This small sum (I afterwards learned) kept the family for more than a fortnight. The girl laid it out in sprats (it being then winter-time); these she sold in the streets.

I mentioned the fact to a literary friend, who interested himself in the boy's welfare; and eventually succeeded in procuring him a situation at an eminent printer's. The subjoined letter will show how the lad conducted himself while there.

Whitefriars, April 22, 1850

Messrs. Bradbury and Evans beg to say that the boy J. C. has conducted himself in a very satisfactory manner since he has been in their employment.

The same literary friend took the girl into his service. She is in a situation still, though not in the same family.

The boy now holds a good situation at one of the daily newspaper offices. So well has he behaved himself, that, a few weeks since, his wages were increased from 6s. to 9s. per week. His mother (owing to the boy's exertions) has now a little shop, and is doing well.

This simple story requires no comments, and is narrated here in the hope that it may teach many to know how often the poor boys reared in the gutter are thieves, merely because society forbids them being honest lads. [. . .]

Scavengers
[*volume ii. pp.205–278*]

Street-sweepers belonged, in Mayhew's view, to a category of 'orderlies' or cleansers. Others in this category were dustmen, nightmen and rubbish-carters. Street-sweepers, or 'scavagers', were divided into regular workers and casual workers. The former worked in gangs with gang-leaders for contractors. There were also carmen who took around their horses and carts to gather up the debris that had been swept by the gangs. The division in labour between gangsmen, gangs-leaders and carmen was reflected in rates of pay. There were also those who were only casual workers.

A 'regular scavager'
[*volume ii. pp.224,225*]

The following statement of his business, his sentiments, and, indeed, of the subjects which concerned him, or about which he was questioned, was given to me by a street-sweeper, so he called himself, for I have found some of these men not to relish the appellation of 'scavager'. He was a short, sturdy, somewhat red-faced man, without anything particular in his appearance to distinguish him from the mass of mere labourers, but with the sodden and sometimes dogged look of a man contented in his ignorance, and – for it is not a very uncommon case – rather proud of it.

'I don't know how old I am,' he said – I have observed, by the by, that there is not any excessive vulgarity in these men's tones or accent so much as grossness in some of their expressions – 'and I can't see what that consarns anyone, as I's old enough to have a jolly rough beard, and so can take care of myself. I should think so. My father was a sweeper, and I wanted to be a waterman, but father – he hasn't been dead long – didn't like the thoughts on it, as he said they was all drownded one time or 'nother; so I ran away and tried my hand as a Jack-in-the-water, but I was starved back in a week, and got a h— of a clouting. After that I sifted a bit in a dust-yard, and helped in any way; and I was sent to help at and larn honey-pot and other pot making, at Deptford; but honey-pots was a great thing in the business. Master's foreman married a relation of mine, some way or other. I never tasted honey, but I've heered it's like sugar and butter mixed. The pots was often wanted to look like foreign pots; I don't know nothing what was meant by it; some b— dodge or other. No, the trade didn't suit me at all, master, so I left. I don't know why it didn't suit me; cause it didn't. Just then, father had hurt his hand and arm, in a jam again' a cart, and so, as I was a big lad, I got to take his place, and gave every satisfaction to Mr — . Yes, he was a contractor and a great man. I can't say as I knows how contracting's done; but it's a bargain atween man and man. So I got on. I'm now looked on as a stunning good workman, I can tell you.

'Well, I can't say as I thinks sweeping the streets is hard work. I'd rather sweep two hours than shovel one. It tires one's arms and back so, to go on shovelling. You can't change, you see, sir, and the same parts keeps getting gripped more and more. Then you must mind your eye, if you're shovelling slop into a cart, perticler so; or some feller may run off with a complaint that he's been splashed o' purpose. *Is* a man ever splashed o' purpose? No, sir, not as I knows on, in coorse not. [Laughing] Why should he?

'The streets must be done as they're done now. It always was so, and will always be so. Did I ever hear what London streets were like a thousand years ago? It's nothing to me, but they must have been like what they is now. Yes, there was always streets, or how was people that has tin to get their coals taken to them, and how was the public-houses to get their beer? It's talking nonsense, talking that way, a-asking sich questions.' [As the scavager seemed likely to lose his temper, I changed the subject of conversation.]

'Yes,' he continued, 'I have good health. I never had a doctor but twice; once was for a hurt, and the t'other I won't tell on. Well, I think nightwork's healthful enough, but I'll not say so much for it as you may hear some on 'em say. I don't like it, but I do it when I's obligated under a necessity. It pays one as over-work; and werry like more one's in it, more one may be suited. I reckon no men works harder nor sich as me. Oh, as to poor journeymen tailors and sich like, I knows they're stunning badly off, and many of their masters is the hardest of beggars. I have a nephew as works for a Jew slop, but I don't reckon that work; anybody might do it. You think not, sir? Werry well, it's all the same. No, I won't say as I could make a veskit, but I've sowed my own buttons on to one afore now.

'Yes, I've heered on the Board of Health. They've put down some night-yards, and if they goes on putting down more, what's to become of the night-soil? I can't think what they're up to; but if they don't touch wages, it may be all right in the end on it. I don't know that them there consarns does touch wages, but one's naterally afeard on 'em. I could read a little when I was a child, but I can't now for want of practice, or I might know more about it. I yarns my money gallows hard, and requires support to do hard work, and if wages goes down, one's strength goes down. I'm a man as understands what things belongs. I was once out of work, through a mistake, for a good many weeks, perhaps five or six or more; I larned then what short grub meant. I got a drop of beer and a crust sometimes with men as I knowed, or I might have dropped in the street. What did I do to pass my time when I was out of work? Sartinly the days seemed wery long; but I went about and called at dust-yards, till I didn't like to go too often; and I met men I know'd at tap-rooms, and spent time that way, and axed if there was any openings for work. I've been out of collar odd weeks now and then, but when this happened, I'd been on slack work a goodish bit, and was bad for rent three weeks and more. My rent was 2s. a week then; its 1s. 9d. now, and my own traps.

'No, I can't say I was sorry when I was forced to be idle that way, that I hadn't kept up my reading, nor tried to keep it up, because I couldn't then have settled down my mind to read; I know I couldn't. I likes to hear the paper read well enough, if I's resting; but old Bill, as often wolunteers to read, has to spell the hard words so, that one can't tell what the devil he's reading about. I never heers anything about books; I never heered of *Robinson Crusoe*, if it wasn't once at the Wic. [Victoria Theatre]; I think there was some sich a name there. He lived on a deserted island, did he, sir, all by his-self? Well, I think, now you mentions it, I have heered on him. But one needn't believe all one heers, whether out of books or not. I don't know much good that ever anybody as I knows ever got out of books; they're fittest for idle people. Sartinly I've seen working people reading in coffee-shops; but they might as well be resting theirselves to keep up their strength. Do I think so? I'm sure on it, master. I sometimes spends a few browns a-going to the play; mostly about Christmas. It's werry fine and grand at the Wic., that's the place I goes to most; both the pantomimers and t'other things is werry stunning. I can't say how much I spends a year in plays; I keeps no account; perhaps 5s. or so in a year, including expenses, sich as beer, when one goes out after a stopper on the stage. I don't keep no accounts of what I gets, or what I spends, it would be no use; money comes and it goes, and it often goes a d—d sight faster than it comes; so it seems to me, though I ain't in debt just at this time.

'I never goes to any church or chapel. Sometimes I hasn't clothes as is fit, and I s'pose I couldn't be admitted into sich fine places in my working dress. I was once in a church, but felt queer, as one does in them strange places, and never went again. They're fittest for rich people. Yes, I've heered about religion and about God Almighty. *What* religion have I heered on? Why, the regular religion. I'm satisfied with what I knows and feels about it, and that's enough about it. I came to tell you about trade and work, because Mr — told me it might do good; but religion hasn't nothing to do with it. Yes, Mr —'s a good master, and a religious man; but I've known masters as didn't care a d—n for religion, as good as him; and so you see it comes to much the same thing. I cares nothing about politics neither; but I'm a chartist.

'I'm not a married man. I was a-going to be married to a young woman as lived with me a goodish bit as my housekeeper,' [this he said very demurely] 'but she went to the hopping to yarn a few shillings for herself, and never came back. I heered that she'd taken up with an Irish hawker, but I can't say as to the rights on it. Did I fret about her? Perhaps not; but I was wexed.

'I'm sure I can't say what I spends my wages in. I sometimes makes 12s. 6d. a week, and sometimes better than 21s. with night-work. I suppose grub costs 1s. a day, and beer 6d.; but I keeps no accounts. I buy ready-cooked meat; often cold b'iled beef, and eats it at any tap-room. I have meat every day; mostly more than once a day. Wegetables I don't care about, only ingans and cabbage, if you can get it smoking hot, with plenty of pepper. The rest of my tin goes for rent and baccy and togs, and a little drop of gin now and then.'

Omnibus drivers and conductors
[*volume iii. pp.336–347*]

Mr Shillibeer started the first horse-drawn omnibus on 4th July 1829 from the Bank to the Yorkshire Stingo in competition with the 'short stages'. Shillibeers, as they came to be known, offered cheap, clean and punctual transport. George Shillibeer withdrew from the metropolitan trade in early 1834 and left the business to his competitors. Proprietors, drivers, conductors, time-keepers, odd-men and watermen were the occupations associated with this branch of transport in London. There were approximately 7,000 drivers and conductors in the period surrounding the Great Exhibition. Drivers were well paid (circa 34s. a week) and drawn from tradespeople, gentlemen's servants and, occasionally, artisans; they were largely literate married men with families; their wives rarely worked and their children were generally sent to school. Conductors or 'cads' had to be literate as a condition of employment and they had to bring with them good character references. Few were married men. A conductor earned 4s. a day, which he deducted directly from the fares he took.

An omnibus driver
[*volume iii. pp.344,345*]

[. . .] They are strong and healthy men, for their calling requires both strength and health. Each driver (as well as the time-keeper and conductor) is licensed, at a yearly cost to him of 5s. From a driver I had the following statement:

'I have been a driver fourteen years. I was brought up as a builder, but had friends that was using horses, and I sometimes assisted them in driving and grooming when I was out of work. I got to like that sort of work, and thought it would be better than my own business if I could get to be connected with a 'bus; and I had friends, and first got employed as a time-keeper; but I've been a driver for fourteen years. I'm now paid by the week, and not by

CAB-DRIVER
[*from a photograph*]

the box. It's a fair payment, but we must live well. It's hard work is mine; for I never have any rest but a few minutes, except every other Sunday, and then only two hours; that's the time of a journey there and back. If I was to ask leave to go to church, and then go to work again, I know what answer there would be – "You can go to church as often as you like, and we can get a man who doesn't want to go there." The cattle I drive are equal to gentlemen's carriage-horses. One I've driven five years, and I believe she was worked five years before I drove her. It's very hard work for the horses, but I don't know that they are over-worked in 'buses. The starting after stopping is the hardest work for them; it's such a terrible strain. I've felt for the poor things on a wet night, with a 'bus full of big people. I think that it's a pity that anybody uses a bearing rein. There's not many uses it now. It bears up a horse's head, and he can only go on pulling, pulling up a hill, one way. Take off his bearing rein, and he'll relieve the strain on him by bearing down his head, and flinging his weight on the collar to help him pull. If a man had to carry a weight up a hill on his back, how would he like to have his head tied back? Perhaps you may have noticed Mr —'s horses pull the 'bus up Holborn Hill. They're tightly borne up; but then they are very fine animals, fat and fine: there's no such cattle, perhaps, in a London 'bus – leastways there's none better – and they're borne up for show. Now, a jib-horse won't go in a bearing rein, and will without it. I've seen that myself; so what can be the use of it? It's just teasing the poor things for a sort of fashion. I must keep exact time at every place where a time-keeper's stationed. Not a minute's excused – there's a fine for the least delay. I can't say that it's often levied; but still we are liable to it. If I've been blocked, I must make up for the block by galloping; and if I'm seen to gallop, and anybody tells our people, I'm called over the coals. I must drive as quick with a thunder-rain pelting in my face, and the roads in a muddle, and the horses starting – I can't call it shying, I have 'em too well in hand, – at every flash, just as quick as if it was a fine hard road, and fine weather. It's not easy to drive a 'bus; but I can drive, and must drive, to an inch: yes, sir, to half an inch. I know if I can get my horses' heads through a space, I can get my splinter-bar through. I drive by my pole, making it my centre. If I keep it fair in the centre, a carriage must follow, unless it's slippery weather, and then there's no calculating. I saw the first 'bus start in 1829. I heard the first 'bus called a Punch-and-Judy carriage, 'cause you could see the people inside without a frame. The shape was about the same as it is now, but bigger and heavier. A 'bus changes horses four or five times a day, according to the distance. There's no cruelty to the horses, not a bit, it wouldn't be allowed. I fancy that 'buses now pay the proprietors well. The duty was 2d. a mile, and now it's 1d. Some companies save twelve guineas a week by the doing away of toll-gates. The 'stablishing the three-pennies – the short uns – has put money in their pockets. I'm an unmarried man. A 'bus driver never has time to look out for a wife. Every horse in our stables has one day's rest in every four; but it's no rest for the driver.'

An omnibus conductor
[*volume iii. pp.345,346*]
From one of the conductors, a very intelligent man, I had the following statement:

'I am 35 or 36, and have been a conductor for six years. Before that I was a lawyer's clerk, and then a picture-dealer; but didn't get on, though I maintained a good character. I'm a conductor now, but wouldn't be long behind a 'bus if it wasn't from necessity. It's hard to get anything else to do that you can keep a wife and family on, for people won't have you from off a 'bus. The worst part of my business is its uncertainty, I may be discharged any day, and not know for what. If I did, and I was accused unjustly, I might bring my action; but it's merely, "You're not wanted." I think I've done better as a conductor in hot weather, or fine weather, than in wet; though I've got a good journey when it's come on showery, as people was starting for or starting from the City. I had one master, who, when his 'bus came in full in the wet, used to say, "This is prime. Them's God Almighty's customers; he sent them." I've heard him say so many a time. We get far more ladies and children, too, on a fine day; they go more a-shopping then, and of an evening they go more to public places. I pay over my money every night. It runs from 40s. to 4l. 4s., or a little more on extraordinary occasions. I have taken more money since the short uns were established. One day before that I took only 18s. There's three riders and more now, where there was two formerly at the higher rate. I never get to a public place, whether it's a chapel or a play-house, unless, indeed, I get a holiday, and that is once in two years. I've asked for a day's holiday and been refused. I was told I might take a week's holiday, if I liked, or as long as I lived. I'm quite ignorant of what's passing in the world, my time's so taken up. We only know what's going on from hearing people talk in the 'bus. I never care to read the paper now, though I used to like it. If I have two minutes to spare, I'd rather take a nap than anything else. We know no more politics than the backwoodsmen of America, because we haven't time to care about it. I've fallen asleep on my step as the 'bus was going on, and almost fallen off. I have often to put up with insolence from vulgar fellows, who think it fun to chaff a cad, as they call it. There's no help for it. Our masters won't listen to complaints: if we are not satisfied we can go. Conductors are a sober set of men. We must be sober. It takes every farthing of our wages to live well enough, and keep a wife and family. I never knew but one teetotaller on the road. He's gone off it now, and he looked as if he was going off altogether. The other day a teetotaller on the 'bus saw me take a drink of beer, and he began to talk to me about its being wrong; but I drove him mad with argument, and the passengers took part with me. I live one and a half mile off the place I start from. In summer I sometimes breakfast before I start. In winter, I never see my three children, only as they're in bed; and I never hear their voices, if they don't wake up early. If they cry at night it don't disturb me; I sleep so heavy after fifteen hours' work out in the air. My wife doesn't do anything but mind the family, and that's plenty to do with young children. My business is so uncertain. Why, I knew a conductor who found he had paid 6d. short – he had left it in a corner of his pocket; and he handed it over next morning, and was discharged for that – he was reckoned a fool. They say the sharper the man the better the 'busman. There's a great deal in understanding the business, in keeping a sharp look-out for people's hailing, and in working the time properly. If the conductor's slow the driver can't get along; and if the driver isn't up to the mark the conductor's bothered. I've always kept time except once, and that was in such a fog, that I had to walk by the horses' heads with a link, and could hardly see my hand that held the link; and after all I lost my 'bus, but it was all safe and right in the end. We're licensed now in Scotland-yard. They're far civiller there than in Lancaster-place. I hope, too, they'll be more particular in granting licenses. They used to grant them day after day, and I believe made no inquiry. It'll be better now. I've never been fined: if I had I should have to pay it out of my own pocket. If you plead guilty it's 5s. If not, and it's very hard to prove that you did display your badge properly if the City policeman — there's always one on the look-out for us — swears you didn't, and summons you for that: or, if you plead not guilty, because you weren't guilty, you may pay 1l. I don't know of the checks now; but I know there are such people. A man was discharged the other day because he was accused of having returned three out of thirteen short. He offered to make oath he was correct; but it was of no use — he went.'

Carmen and porters
[volume iii. pp.357–367]

Mayhew associated these two groups of men with the carrying trade. Carmen he divided into two categories: public and private. He saw them as a category of servant. There were about 207 master-carmen, 12 of whom had licences to ply their trade from official stands in the city. Many of these were quite large employers. Those without licences used horse-drawn spring carriages to effect house removals. Others ran excursions, for example to Hampton Court and back, for twenty to thirty people at a time. This class of carman generally combined his trade with some other, such as that of greengrocer, grocer, chandler or dairyman. Porters, messengers and errand-boys were a much larger group, because they had no overheads. The census of 1841 gave a figure of 24,092 in England alone, of whom 13,103 were in London. More than a fifth of the group were youths below the age of 20 engaged as errand boys. Porters had to be ticketed (licensed) to ply their trade.

Van driver

[*volume iii. pp.362–363*]

The behaviour of these excursionists is, from the concurrent testimony of the many van-proprietors and drivers whom I saw, most exemplary, and perhaps I shall best show this by at once giving the following statement from a very trustworthy man:

'I have been in the van-trade for twenty years, and have gone excursions for sixteen years. Hampton Court has the call for excursions in vans, because of free-trade in the palace: there's nothing to pay for admission. A party makes up an excursion, and one of them bargains with me, say for 2*l*. It shouldn't be a farthing less with such cattle as mine, and everything in agreement with it. Since I've known the trade, vans have increased greatly. I should say there's five now where there was one sixteen years ago, and more. There's a recommendable and a respectable behaviour amongst those that goes excursions. But now on an excursion there's hardly any drunkenness, or if there is, it's through the accident of a bad stomach, or something that way. The excursionists generally carry a fiddler with them, sometimes a trumpeter, or else some of them is master of an instrument as goes down. They generally sings, too, such songs as "There's a Good Time coming" and "The Brave Old Oak". Sometimes a nigger-thing, but not so often. They carry aways, I think, their own eatables and drinkables; and they take them on the grass very often. Last Whit-Monday I counted fifty vans at Hampton, and didn't see anybody drunk there. I reckoned them earlyish, and perhaps ten came after, at least; and every van would have twenty and more.' [Sixty vans would, at this moderate computation, convey 1,200 persons.] 'They walk through the Palace at Hampton, and sometimes dance on the grass after that, but not for long. It soon tires, dancing on the grass. A school often goes, or a club, or a society, or any party. I generally do Hampton Court in three hours with two horses. I reckon it's fourteen miles, or near that, from my place. If I go to High Beach there's the swings for the young ones, and the other merry-makings. At Rye House it's country enjoyment – mere looking about the real country. The Derby day's a great van-day. I'm sure I couldn't guess to one hundred – not, perhaps, to twice that – how many pleasure-vans go to the Derby. It's extra charge – 3*l*. 10*s*. for the van to Epsom and back. It's a long distance; but the Derby has a wonderful draw. I've taken all sorts of excursions, but it's working people that's our great support. They often smoke as they come back, though it's against my rules. They often takes a barrel of beer with them.'

Crossing-sweepers
[*volume ii. pp.465–507*]

Mayhew claimed that crossing-sweepers formed a large group among the London poor. A crossing-sweeper was normally an individual who regarded the 'calling' as 'the last chance left of obtaining an honest crust'. Little capital was involved to provide equipment; it was possible to solicit gratuities without being charged with begging; there was a possibility of establishing a regular clientèle of sympathetic benefactors in a given location. Mayhew tried to discover what 'right' an individual crossing-sweeper had to his patch. Sometimes a sweeper obtained the permission of the nearby inhabitants. In some cases, such as the banks, crossing-sweepers were employed to serve the clientèle. The police also protected the crossings against the encroachment of rivals. Crossing-sweepers were divided by Mayhew into various categories: casual, who did the job only on certain days of the week or who (like the boy sweepers) moved around from crossing to crossing, and regular, who had fixed positions on the corners of major streets and squares; male and female; able bodied and disabled; adult and juvenile. Many combined their callings with other casual jobs. Juveniles often worked in gangs.

The old dame who supports a pensioner
[*volume ii. pp.478,479*]

This old dame is remarkable from the fact of being the chief support of a poor deaf cripple, who is as much poorer than the crossing-sweeper as she is poorer than Mrs — in — street, who allows the sweeper sixpence a week. The crossing-sweeper is a rather stout old woman, with a carnying tone, and constant curtsey. She complains, in common with most of her class, of the present hard times, and reverts longingly to the good old days when people were more liberal than they are now, and had more to give. She says:

'I was on my crossing before the police was made, for I am not able to work, and only get helped by the people who knows me. Mr — , in the square, gives me a shilling a week; Mrs — , in — street, gives me sixpence (she has gone in the country now, but she has left it at the oil-shop for me); that's what I depinds upon, darlin', to help pay my rent, which is half-a-crown. My rent was three shillings, till the landlord didn't wish me to go, 'cause I was so punctual with my money. I give a corner of my room to a poor cretur, who's deaf as a beadle; she works at the soldiers' coats, and is a very good hand at it, and would earn a good deal of money if she had constant work. She owed as good as twelve shillings and sixpence for rent, poor thing, where she was last, and the landlord took all her goods except her bed; she's got that, so I give her a corner of my room for charity's sake. We must look to one another: she's as poor as a church mouse. I thought she would be company for me, still a deaf person is but poor company to one. She had that heavy sickness they call the cholera about five years ago, and it fell in her side and in the side of her head too – that made her deaf. Oh! she's a poor object. She has been with me since the month of February. I've lent her money out of my own pocket. I give her a cup of tea or a slice of bread when I see she hasn't got my. Then the people up-stairs are kind to her, and give her a bite and a sup.

'My husband was a soldier; he fought at the battle of Waterloo. His pension was ninepence a-day. All my family are dead, except my grandson, what's in New Orleans. I expect him back this very month that now we have: he gave me four pounds before he went, to carry me over the last winter.

'If the Almighty God pleases to send him back, he'll be a great help to me. He's all I've got left. I never had but two children in all my life.

'I worked in noblemen's houses before I was married to my husband, who is dead; but he came to be poor, and I had to leave my houses where I used to work.

'I took twopence-halfpenny yesterday, and threepence today; the day before yesterday I didn't take a penny. I never come out on Sunday; I goes to Rosomon-street Chapel. Last Saturday I made one shilling and sixpence; on Friday, sixpence. I dare say I make three shillings and sixpence a week, besides the one shilling and sixpence I gets allowed me. I am forced to make a do of it somehow, but I've no more strength left in me than this ould broom.'

Mary, who had been a serving-maid
[*volume ii. pp.479–481*]
She is to be found any day between eight in the morning and seven in the evening, sweeping away in a convulsive, jerky sort of manner, close to — Square, near the Foundling. She may be known by her pinched-up straw bonnet, with a broad, faded, almost colourless ribbon. She has weak eyes, and wears over them a brownish shade. Her face is tied up, because of a gathering which she has on her head. She wears a small, old plaid cloak, a clean checked apron, and a tidy printed gown.

She is rather shy at first, but willing and obliging enough withal; and she lives down Little — Yard, in Great — Street. The 'yard' is made like a mousetrap – small at the entrance, but amazingly large inside, and dilapidated though extensive.

Here are stables and a couple of blind alleys, nameless, or bearing the same name as the yard itself, and wherein are huddled more people than one could count in a quarter of an hour, and more children than one likes to remember, – dirty children, listlessly trailing an old tin baking-dish, or a worn-out shoe, tied to a piece of string; sullen children, who turn away in a fit of sleepy anger if spoken to; screaming children, setting all the parents in the 'yard' at defiance; and quiet children, who are arranging banquets of dirt in the reeking gutters.

The 'yard' is devoted principally to costermongers.

The crossing-sweeper lives in the top-room of a two-storeyed house, in the very depth of the blind alley at the end of the yard. She has not even a room to herself, but pays one shilling a week for the privilege of sleeping with a woman who gets her living by selling tapes in the streets.

'Ah!' says the sweeper, 'poor woman, she has a hard time of it; her husband is in the hospital with a bad leg – in fact, he's scarcely ever out. If you could hear that woman cough, you'd never forget it. She would have had to starve today if it hadn't been for a person who actually lent her a gown to pledge to raise her stock-money, poor thing.'

The room in which these people live has a sloping roof, and a small-paned window on each side. For furniture, there were two chairs and a shaky, three-legged stool, a deal table, and a bed rolled up against the wall – nothing else. In one corner of the room lay the last lump remaining of the seven pounds of coals. In another corner there were herbs in pans, and two water-bottles without their noses. The most striking thing in that little room was some crockery the woman had managed to save from the wreck of her things; among this, curiously enough, was a soup-tureen, with its lid not even cracked.

There was a piece of looking-glass – a small three-cornered piece – forming an almost equilateral triangle, – and the oldest, and most rubbed and worn-out piece of a mirror that ever escaped the dustbin.

The fireplace was a very small one, and on the table were two or three potatoes and about one-fifth of a red herring, which the poor street-seller had saved out of her breakfast to serve for her supper. 'Take my solemn word for it, sir,' said the sweeper, 'and I wouldn't deceive you, that is all she will get besides a cup of weak tea when she comes home tired at night.'

The statement of this old sweeper is as follows:

'My name is Mary — . I live in — Yard. I live with a person of the name of — , in the back attic; she gets her living by selling flowers in pots in the street, but she is now doing badly. I pay her a shilling a week.

'My parents were Welsh. I was in service, or maid-of-all-work, till I got married. My husband was a seafaring man when I married him. After we were married, he got his living by selling memorandum-almanack books, and the like, about the streets. He was driven to that because he had no trade in his hand, and he was obliged to do something for a living. He did not make much, and over-exertion, with want of nourishment, brought on a paralytic stroke. He had the first fit about two years before he had the second; the third fit, which was the last, he had on the Monday, and died on the Wednesday week. I have two children still living. One of them is married to a poor man, who gets his living in the streets; but as far as lays in his power he makes a good husband and father. My other daughter is living with a niece of mine, for I can't keep her, sir; she minds the children.

'My father was a journeyman shoemaker. He was killed; but I cannot remember how – I was too young. I can't recollect my mother. I was brought up by an uncle and aunt till I was able to go to service. I went out to service at five, to mind children under a nurse, and I was in service till I got married. I had a great many situations; you see, sir, I was forced to keep in place, because I had nowhere to go to, my uncle and aunt not being able to keep me. I was never in noblemen's families, only trades-people's. Service was very hard, sir, and so I believe it continues.

'I am fifty-five years of age, and I have been on the crossing fourteen years; but just now it is very poor work indeed. Well, if I wishes for bad weather, I'm only like other people, I suppose. I have no regular customers at all; the only one I had left has lost his senses, sir. Mr H — , he used to allow us sixpence a week; but he went mad, and we don't get it now. By us, I mean the three crossing-sweepers in the square where I work.

'Indeed, I like the winter-time, for the families is in. Though the weather is more severe, yet you *do* get a few more ha'pence. I take more from the staid elderly people than from the young. At Christmas, I think I took about eleven shillings, but certainly not more. The most I ever made at that season was fourteen shillings. The worst about Christmas is, that those who give much then generally hold their hand for a week or two.

'A shilling a-day would be as much as I want, sir. I have stood in the square all day for a ha'penny, and I have stood here for nothing. One week with another, I make two shillings in the seven days, after paying for my broom. I have taken threepence ha'penny today. Yesterday – let me see – well, it was threepence ha'penny, too; Monday I don't remember; but Sunday I recollect – it was fippence ha'penny. Years ago I made a great deal more – nearly three times as much.

'I come about eight o'clock in the morning, and go away about six or seven; I am here every day. The boys used to come at one time with their brooms, but they're not allowed here now by the police.

'I should not think crossings worth purchasing, unless people made a better living on them than I do.'

I gave the poor creature a small piece of silver for her trouble, and asked her if that, with the threepence halfpenny, made a good day. She answered heartily – 'I should like to see such another day tomorrow, sir.

'Yes, winter is very much better than summer, only for the trial of standing in the frost and snow, but we certainly do get more then. The families won't be in town for three months to come yet. Ah! this neighbourhood is nothing to what it was. By God's removal, and by their own removal, the good families are all gone. The present families are not so liberal nor so wealthy. It is not the richest people that give the most. Tradespeople, and 'specially gentlefolks who have situations, are better to me than the nobleman who rides in his carriage.

'I always go to Trinity Church, Gray's-inn road, about two doors from the Welsh School – the Rev. Dr Witherington preaches there. I always go on Sunday afternoon and evening, for I can't go in the morning; I can't get away from my crossing in time. I never omit a day in coming here, unless I'm ill, or the snow is too heavy, or the weather too bad, and then I'm obligated to resign.

'I have no friends, sir, only my children; my uncle and aunt have been dead a long time. I go to see my children on Sunday, or in the evening, when I leave here.

'After I leave I have a cup of tea, and after that I go to bed; very frequently I'm in bed at nine o'clock. I have my cup of tea if I can anyway get it; but I'm forced to go without that sometimes.

'When my sight was better, I used to be very partial to reading; but I can't see the print, sir, now. I used to read the Bible, and the newspaper. Story-books I have read, too, but not many novels. Yes, *Robinson Crusoe* I know, but not *The Pilgrim's Progress*. I've heard of it; they tell me it is a very interesting book to read, but I never had it. We never have any ladies or Scripture-readers come to our lodgings; you see, we're so out, they might come a dozen times and not find us at home.

'I wear out three brooms in a week; but in the summer one will last a fortnight. I give threepence ha'penny for them; there are two-penny-ha'penny brooms, but they are not so good, they are liable to have their handles come out. It is very fatiguing standing so many hours; my legs aches with pain, and swells. I was once in Middlesex Hospital for sixteen weeks with my legs. My eyes have been weak from a child. I have got a gathering in my head from catching cold standing on the crossing. I had the fever this time twelvemonth. I laid a fortnight and four days at home, and seven weeks in the hospital. I took the diarrhœa after that, and was six weeks under the doctor's hands. I used to do odd jobs, but my health won't permit me now. I used to make two or three shillings a week by 'em, and get scraps and things. But I get no broken victuals now.

'I never get anything from servants; they don't get more than they know what to do with.

'I don't get a drop of beer once in a month.

'I don't know but what this being out may be the best thing, after all; for if I was at home all my time, it would not agree with me.'

Gander, 'captain' of the boy crossing-sweepers
[*volume ii. pp.499–501*]

Gander, the captain of the gang of boy crossing-sweepers, was a big lad of sixteen, with a face devoid of all expression, until he laughed, when the cheeks, mouth, and forehead instantly became crumpled up with a wonderful quantity of lines and dimples. His hair was cut short, and stood up in all directions, like the bristles of a hearth-broom, and was a light dust tint, matching with the hue of his complexion, which also, from an absence of washing, had turned to a decided drab, or what house-painters term a stone-colour.

He spoke with a lisp, occasioned by the loss of two of his large front teeth, which allowed the tongue as he talked to appear through the opening in a round nob like a raspberry.

The boy's clothing was in a shocking condition. He had no coat, and his blue-striped shirt was as dirty as a French-polisher's rags, and so tattered, that the shoulder was completely bare, while the sleeve hung down over the hand like a big bag.

From the fish-scales on the sleeves of his coat, it had evidently once belonged to some coster in the herring line. The nap was all worn off, so that the lines of the web were showing like a coarse carpet; and instead of buttons, string had been passed through holes pierced at the side.

Of course he had no shoes on, and his black trousers, which, with the grease on them, were gradually assuming a tarpaulin look, were fastened over one shoulder by means of a brace and bits of string.

During his statement, he illustrated his account of the tumbling backwards – the 'caten-wheeling' – with different specimens of the art, throwing himself about on the floor with an ease and almost grace, and taking up so small a space of the ground for the performance, that his limbs seemed to bend as though his bones were flexible like cane.

'To tell you the blessed truth, I can't say the last shilling I handled.'

'Don't you go a-believing on him,' whispered another lad in my ear, whilst Gander's head was turned: 'he took thirteenpence last night, he did.'

It was perfectly impossible to obtain from this lad any account of his average earnings. The other boys in the gang told me that he made more than any of them. But Gander, who is a thorough street-beggar, and speaks with a peculiar whine, and who, directly you look at him, puts on an expression of deep distress, seemed to have made up his mind, that if he made himself out to be in great want I should most likely relieve him – so he would not budge an inch from his twopence a-day, declaring it to be the maximum of his daily earnings.

'Ah,' he continued, with a persecuted tone of voice, 'if I had only got a little money, I'd be a bright youth! The first chance as I get of earning a few halfpence, I'll buy myself a coat, and be off to the country, and I'll lay something I'd soon be a gentleman then, and come home with a couple of pounds in my pocket, instead of never having ne'er a farthing, as now.'

One of the other lads here exclaimed, 'Don't go on like that there, Goose; you're making us out all liars to the gentleman.'

The old woman also interfered. She lost all patience with Gander, and reproached him for making a false return of his income. She tried to shame him into truthfulness, by saying, –

'Look at my Johnny – my grandson, sir, he's not a quarther the Goose's size, and yet he'll bring me home his shilling, or perhaps eighteenpence or two shillings – for shame on you, Gander! Now, did you make six shillings last week? – now, speak God's truth!'

'What! six shillings?' cried the Goose – 'six shillings!' and he began to look up at the ceiling, and shake his hands. 'Why, I never heard of sich a sum. I did once *see* a half-crown; but I don't know as I ever touched e'er a one.'

'Thin,' added the old woman, indignantly, 'it's because you're idle, Gander, and you don't study when you're on the crossing;

but lets the gintlefolk go by without ever a word. That's what it is, sir.'

The Goose seemed to feel the truth of this reproach, for he said with a sigh, 'I knows I am fickle-minded.'

He then continued his statement, –

'I can't tell how many brooms I use; for as fast as I gets one, it is took from me. God help me! They watch me put it away, and then up they comes and takes it. What kinds of brooms is the best? Why, as far as I am concerned, I would sooner have a stump on a dry day – it's lighter and handier to carry; but on a wet day, give me a new un.

'I'm sixteen, your honour, and my name's George Gandea, and the boys calls me "the Goose" in consequence; for it's a nickname they gives me, though my name ain't spelt with a *har* at the end, but with a *h'ay*, so that I ain't Gand*er* after all, but Gand*ea*, which is a sell for 'em.

'God knows what I am – whether I'm h'Irish or h'*I*talian, or what; but I was christened here in London, and that's all about it.

'Father was a bookbinder. I'm sixteen now, and father turned me away when I was nine year old, for mother had been dead before that. I was told my right name by my brother-in-law, who had my register. He's a sweep, sir, by trade, and I wanted to know about my real name when I was going down to the *Waterloo* – that's a ship as I wanted to get aboard as a cabin-boy.

'I remember the fust night I slept out after father got rid of me. I slept on a gentleman's door-step, in the winter, on the 15th January. I packed my shirt and coat, which was a pretty good one, right over my ears, and then scrunched myself into a door-way, and the policeman passed by four or five times without seeing on me.

'I had a mother-in-law at the time; but father used to drink, or else I should never have been as I am; and he came home one night, and says he, "Go out and get me a few ha'pence for breakfast," and I said I had never been in the streets in my life, and couldn't: and, says he, "Go out, and never let me see you no more," and I took him to his word, and have never been near him since.

'Father lived in Barbican at that time, and after leaving him, I used to go to the Royal Exchange, and there I met a boy of the name of Michael, and he first learnt me to beg, and made me run after people, saying, "Poor boy, sir – please give us a ha'penny to get a mossel of bread." But as fast as I got anythink, he used to take it away, and knock me about shameful; so I left him, and then I picked up with a chap as taught me tumbling. I soon larnt how to do it, and then I used to go tumbling after busses. That was my notion all along, and I hadn't picked up the way of doing it half an hour before I was after that game.'

'I took to crossings about eight year ago, and the very fust person as I asked, I had a fourpenny-piece give to me. I said to him, "Poor little Jack, yer honour," and, fust of all, says he, "I haven't got no coppers," and then he turns back and give me a fourpenny-bit. I thought I was made for life when I got that.

'I wasn't working in a gang then, but all by myself, and I used to do well, making about a shilling or ninepence a-day. I lodged in Church-lane at that time.

'It was at the time of the Shibition year [1851] as these gangs come up. There was lots of boys that came out sweeping, and that's how they picked up the tumbling off me, seeing me do it up in the Park, going along to the Shibition.

'The crossing at St Martin's Church was mine fust of all; and when the other lads come to it I didn't take no heed of 'em – only for that I'd have been a bright boy by now, but they carnied me over like; for when I tried to turn 'em off they'd say, in a carnying way, "Oh, let us stay on", so I never took no heed of 'em.

'There was about thirteen of 'em in my gang at that time.

'They made me cap'an over the lot – I suppose because they thought I was the best tumbler of 'em. They obeyed me a little. If I told 'em not to go to any gentleman, they wouldn't, and leave him to me. There was only one feller as used to give me a share of his money, and that was for larning him to tumble – he'd give a penny or twopence, just as he yearnt a little or a lot. I taught 'em all to tumble, and we used to do it near the crossing, and at night along the streets.

'We used to be sometimes together of a day, some a-running after one gentleman, and some after another; but we seldom kept together more than three or four at a time.

'I was the fust to introduce tumbling backards, and I'm proud of it – yes, sir, I'm proud of it. There's another little chap as I'm

larning to do it; but he ain't got strength enough in his arms like.'
('Ah!' exclaimed a lad in the room, 'he is a one to tumble, is
Johnny – go along the streets like anythink.')

'He is the King of the Tumblers,' continued Gander – 'King,
and I'm Cap'an.'

The old grandmother here joined in. 'He was taught by a
furreign gintleman, sir, whose wife rode at a circus. He used to
come here twice a-day and give him lessons in this here very
room, sir. That's how he got it, sir.'

'Ah,' added another lad, in an admiring tone, 'see him and the
Goose have a race! Away they goes, but Jacky will leave him a
mile behind.'

The history then continued: 'People liked the tumbling backards and forards, and it got a good bit of money at fust, but they is
getting tired with it, and I'm growing too hold, I fancy. It hurt me
awful at fust. I tried it fust under a railway arch of the Blackwall
Railway; and when I goes backards, I thought it'd cut my head
open. It hurts me if I've got a thin cap on.

'The man as taught me tumbling has gone on the stage. Fust he
went about with swords, fencing, in public-houses, and then he
got engaged. Me and him once tumbled all round the circus at the
Rotunda one night wot was a benefit, and got one-and-eightpence
a-piece, and all for only five hours and a half – from six to half-past
eleven, and we acting and tumbling, and all that. We had plenty of
beer, too. We was wery much applauded when we did it.

'I was the fust boy as ever did ornamental work in the mud of
my crossings. I used to be at the crossing at the corner of Regent-
suckus; and that's the wery place where I fust did it. The wery
fust thing as I did was a hanker [anchor] – a regular one, with
turn-up sides and a rope down the centre, and all. I sweeped it
away clean in the mud in the shape of the drawing I'd seen. It
paid well, for I took one-and-ninepence on it. The next thing I
tried was writing "God save the Queen"; and that, too, paid
capital, for I think I got two bob. After that I tried We Har [V. R.]
and a star, and that was a sweep too. I never did no flowers, but
I've done imitations of laurels, and put them all round the
crossing, and very pretty it looked, too, at night. I'd buy a
farthing candle and stick it over it, and make it nice and comfortable, so that the people could look at it easy. Whenever I see

a carriage coming I used to douse the glim and run away with it, but the wheels would regularly spile the drawings, and then we'd have all the trouble to put it to rights again, and that we used to do with our hands.

'I fust learnt drawing in the mud from a man in Adelaide-street, Strand; he kept a crossing, but he only used to draw 'em close to the kerb-stone. He used to keep some soft mud there, and when a carriage come up to the Lowther Arcade, after he'd opened the door and let the lady out, he would set to work, and by the time she come back he'd have some flowers, or a We Har, or whatever he liked, done in the mud, and underneath he'd write, "Please to remember honnest hindustry."

'I used to stand by and see him do it, until I'd learnt, and when I knowed, I went off and did it at my crossing.

'I was the fust to light up at night though, and now I wish I'd never done it, for it was that which got me turned off my crossing, and a capital one it was. I thought the gentlemen coming from the play would like it, for it looked very pretty. The policeman said I was destructing [obstructing] the thoroughfare, and making too much row there, for the people used to stop in the crossing to look, it were so pretty. He took me in charge three times on one night, cause I wouldn't go away; but he let me go again, till at last I thought he would lock me up for the night, so I hooked it.

'It was after this as I went to St Martin's Church, and I haven't done half as well there. Last night I took three-ha'pence; but I was larking, or I might have had more.'

As a proof of the very small expense which is required for the toilette of a crossing-sweeper, I may mention, that within a few minutes after Master Gander had finished his statement, he was in possession of a coat, for which he had paid the sum of fivepence.

When he brought it into the room, all the boys and the women crowded round to see the purchase.

'It's a very good un,' said the Goose. 'It only wants just taking up here and there; and this cuff putting to rights.' And as he spoke he pointed to tears large enough for a head to be thrust through.

'I've seen that coat before, sum'ares,' said one of the women; 'where did you get it?'

'At the chandly-shop,' answered the Goose.

The street where the boy-sweepers lodged
[*volume ii. pp.503,504*]

I was anxious to see the room in which the gang of boy crossing-sweepers lived, so that I might judge of their peculiar style of house-keeping, and form some notion of their principles of domestic economy.

I asked young Harry and 'the Goose' to conduct me to their lodgings, and they at once consented, 'the Goose' prefacing his compliance with the remark that 'it wern't such as genilmen had been accustomed to, but then I must take 'em as they was.'

The boys led me in the direction of Drury-lane; and before entering one of the narrow streets which branch off like the side-bones of a fish's spine from that long thoroughfare, they thought fit to caution me that I was not to be frightened, as nobody would touch me, for all was very civil.

The locality consisted of one of those narrow streets which, were it not for the paved cart-way in the centre would be called a court. Seated on the pavement at each side of the entrance was a costerwoman with her basket before her, and her legs tucked up mysteriously under her gown into a round ball, so that her figure resembled in shape the plaster tumblers sold by the Italians. These women remained as inanimate as if they had been carved images, and it was only when a passenger went by that they gave signs of life, by calling out in a low voice, like talking to themselves, 'Two for three haarpence – herrens', – 'Fine hinguns'.

The street itself is like the description given of thoroughfares in the East. Opposite neighbours could not exactly shake hands out of window, but they could talk together very comfortably; and, indeed, as I passed along, I observed several women with their arms folded up like a cat's paws on the sill, and chatting with their friends over the way.

Nearly all the inhabitants were costermongers, and, indeed, the narrow cartway seemed to have been made just wide enough for a truck to wheel down it. A beershop and a general store, together with a couple of sweeps, – whose residences were distinguished by a broom over the door, – formed the only exceptions to the street-selling class of inhabitants.

As I entered the place, it gave me the notion that it belonged to a distinct coster colony, and formed one large hawkers' home; for everybody seemed to be doing just as he liked, and I was stared at as if condered an intruder. Women were seated on the pavement, knitting, and repairing their linen; the doorways were filled up with bonnetless girls, who wore their shawls over their head, as the Spanish women do their mantillas; and the youths in corduroy and brass buttons, who were chatting with them, leant against the walls as they smoked their pipes, and blocked up the pavement, as if they were the proprietors of the place. Little children formed a convenient bench out of the kerbstone; and a party of four men were seated on the footway, playing with cards which had turned to the colour of brown paper from long usage, and marking the points with chalk upon the flags.

The parlour-windows of the houses had all of them wooden shutters, as thick and clumsy-looking as a kitchen flap-table, the paint of which had turned to the dull dirt-colour of an old slate. Some of these shutters were evidently never used as a security for the dwelling, but served only as tables on which to chalk the accounts of the day's sales.

Before most of the doors were costermongers' trucks – some standing ready to be wheeled off, and others stained and muddy with the day's work. A few of the costers were dressing up their barrows, arranging the sieves of waxy-looking potatoes – and others taking the stiff herrings, browned like a meerschaum with the smoke they had been dried in, from the barrels beside them, and spacing them out in pennyworths on their trays.

You might guess what each costermonger had taken out that day by the heap of refuse swept into the street before the doors. One house had a blue mound of mussel-shells in front of it – another, a pile of the outside leaves of broccoli and cabbages, turning yellow and slimy with bruises and moisture.

Hanging up beside some of the doors were bundles of old strawberry pottles, stained red with the fruit. Over the trap-doors to the cellars were piles of market-gardeners' sieves, ruddled like a sheep's back with big red letters. In fact, everything that met the eye seemed to be in some way connected with the coster's trade.

From the windows poles stretched out, on which blankets, petticoats, and linen were drying; and so numerous were they, that they reminded me of the flags hung out at a Paris fête. Some of the sheets had patches as big as trap-doors let into their centres;

and the blankets were – many of them – as full of holes as a pigeon-house.

As I entered the court, a 'row' was going on; and from a first-floor window a lady, whose hair sadly wanted brushing, was haranguing a crowd beneath, throwing her arms about like a drowning man, and in her excitement thrusting her body half out of her temporary rostrum as energetically as I have seen Punch lean over his theatre.

'The willin dragged her,' she shouted, 'by the hair of her head, at least three yards into the court – the willin! and then he kicked her, and the blood was on his boot.'

It was a sweep who had been behaving in this cowardly manner; but still he had his defenders in the women around him. One with very shiny hair, and an Indian kerchief round her neck, answered the lady in the window, by calling her a 'd—d old cat'; whilst the sweep's wife rushed about, clapping her hands together as quickly as if she was applauding at a theatre, and styled somebody or other 'an old wagabones as she wouldn't dirty her hands to fight with'.

This 'row' had the effect of drawing all the lodgers to the windows – their heads popping out as suddenly as dogs from their kennels in a fancier's yard.

The boy-sweepers' room
[*volume ii. pp.504,505*]

The room where the boys lodged was scarcely bigger than a coach-house; and so low was the ceiling, that a fly-paper suspended from a clothes-line was on a level with my head, and had to be carefully avoided when I moved about.

One corner of the apartment was completely filled up by a big four-post bedstead, which fitted into a kind of recess as perfectly as if it had been built to order.

The old woman who kept this lodging had endeavoured to give it a homely look of comfort, by hanging little black-framed pictures, scarcely bigger than pocket-books, on the walls. Most of these were sacred subjects, with large yellow glories round the heads; though between the drawing representing the bleeding heart of Christ, and the Saviour bearing the Cross, was an illustration of a red-waistcoated sailor smoking his pipe. The Adoration of the Shepherds, again, was matched on the other side of the fireplace by a portrait of Daniel O'Connell.

A chest of drawers was covered over with a green baize cloth, on which books, shelves, and clean glasses were tidily set out.

Where so many persons (for there were about eight of them, including the landlady, her daughter, and grandson) could all sleep, puzzled me extremely.

The landlady wore a frilled nightcap, which fitted so closely to the skull, that it was evident she had lost her hair. One of her eyes was slowly recovering from a blow, which, to use her own words, 'a blackgeyard gave her'. Her lip, too, had suffered in the encounter, for it was swollen and cut.

'I've a nice flock-bid for the boys,' she said, when I inquired into the accommodation of her lodging-house, 'where three of them can slape aisy and comfortable.'

'It's a large bed, sir,' said one of the boys, 'and a warm covering over us; and you see it's better than a regular lodging-house; for, if you want a knife or a cup, you don't have to leave something on it till it's returned.'

The old woman spoke up for her lodgers, telling me that they were good boys, and very honest; 'for,' she added, 'they pays me rig'lar ivery night, which is threepence.'

The only youth as to whose morals she seemed to be at all doubtful was 'the Goose', 'for he kept late hours, and sometimes came home without a penny in his pocket.'

Flushermen
[*volume ii. pp.427–431*]

Flushing the sewers was introduced in London by Mr John Rose in about 1847. An inspector reported on the condition of the sewer; then flushermen entered the sewers and loosened the deposits with shovels and rakes; then dammed up water was flushed through the sewer to remove the debris. The flushermen worked as members of subcontracted gangs.

The flusherman who had been a seaman
[*volume ii. pp.430,431*]

'I don't think flushing work disagrees with my husband,' said a flusherman's wife to me, 'for he eats about as much again at that work as he did at the other.' 'The smell underground is sometimes

very bad,' said the man, 'but then we generally take a drop of
rum first, and something to eat. It wouldn't do to go into it on an
empty stomach, 'cause it would get into our inside. But in some
sewers there's scarcely any smell at all. *Most of the men are healthy
who are engaged in it; and when the cholera was about many used to ask us
how it was we escaped.*'

The following statement contains the history of an individual
flusherman:

'I was brought up to the sea,' he said, 'and served on board
a man-of-war, the *Racer*, a 16-gun brig, laying off Cuba, in the
West Indies, and there-away, watching the slavers. I served seven
years. We were paid off in '43 at Portsmouth, and a friend got me
into the *shores*. It was a great change from the open sea to a close
shore – great; and I didn't like it at all at first. But it suits a married
man, as I am now, with a family, much better than being a seaman,
for a man aboard a ship can hardly do his children justice in their
schooling and such like. Well, I didn't much admire going down
the man-hole at first – the "man-hole" is a sort of iron trap-door
that you unlock and pull up; it leads to a lot of steps, and so you
get into the *shore* – but one soon gets accustomed to anything.
I've been at flushing and *shore* work now since '43, all but eleven
weeks, which was before I got engaged.

'We work in gangs from three to five men.' [Here I had an
account of the process of flushing, such as I have given.] 'I've been
carried off my feet sometimes in the flush of a *shore*. Why, today,'
[a very rainy and windy day, Feb. 4] 'it came down Baker-street,
when we flushed it, 4 foot plomb. It would have done for a mill-
dam. One couldn't smoke or do anything. Oh, yes, we can have a
pipe and a chat now and then in the *shore*. The tobacco checks the
smell. No, I can't say I felt the smell very bad when I first was in a
shore. I've felt it worse since. I've been made innocent drunk like
in a *shore* by a drain from a distiller's. That happened me first in
Vine-street *shore*, St Giles's, from Mr Rickett's distillery. It came
into the *shore* like steam. No, I can't say it tasted like gin when you
breathed it – only intoxicating like. It was the same in Whitechapel from Smith's distillery. One night I was forced to leave off
there, the steam had such an effect. I was falling on my back,
when a mate caught me. The breweries have something of the
same effect, but nothing like so strong as the distilleries. It comes

into the *shore* from the brewers' places in steam. I've known such a steam followed by bushels of grains; ay, sir, cart-loads washed into the *shore*.

'Well, I never found anything in a *shore* worth picking up but once a half-crown. That was in the Buckingham Palace sewer. Another time I found 16*s*. 6*d*., and thought that was a haul; but every bit of it, every coin, shillings and sixpences and joeys, was bad – all smashers. Yes, of course it was a disappointment, naturally so. That happened in Brick-lane *shore*, Whitechapel. Oh, somebody or other had got frightened, I suppose, and had shied the coins down into the drains. I found them just by the chapel there.'

A second man gave me the following account of his experience in flushing:

'You remember, sir, that great storm on the 1st August, 1848. I was in three *shores* that fell in – Conduit-street and Foubert's-passage, Regent-street. There was then a risk of being drowned in the *shores*, but no lives were lost. All the house-drains were blocked about Carnaby-market – that's the Foubert's-passage *shore* – and the poor people was what you might call houseless. We got in up to the neck in water in some places, 'cause we had to stoop, and knocked about the rubbish as well as we could, to give a way to the water. The police put up barriers to prevent any carts or carriages going that way along the streets. No, there was no lives lost in the *shores*. One man was so overcome that he was falling off into a sort of sleep in Milford-lane *shore*, but was pulled out. I helped to pull him. He was as heavy as lead with one thing or other – wet, and all that. Another time, six or seven year ago, Whitechapel High-street *shore* was almost choked with butchers' offal, and we had a great deal of trouble with it.'

[. . .] 'The sewers generally swarms with rats,' said another man. 'I runs away from 'em; I don't like 'em. They in general gets away from us; but in case we comes to a stunt end where there's a wall and no place for 'em to get away, and we goes to touch 'em, they fly at us. They're some of 'em as big as good-sized kittens. One of our men caught hold of one the other day by the tail, and he found it trying to release itself, and the tail slipping through his fingers; so he put up his left hand to stop it, and the rat caught hold of his finger, and the man's got an arm now as big as his thigh.' [I heard from several that there had been occasionally battles among the rats, one with another.]

'Why, sir,' said one flusherman, 'as to the number of rats, it ain't possible to say. There hasn't been a census [laughing] taken of them. But I can tell you this – I was one of the first flushermen when flushing came in general – I think it was before Christmas, 1847, under Mr Roe – and there was cart-loads and cart-loads of drowned rats carried into the Thames. It was in a West Strand *shore* that I saw the most. I don't exactly remember which, but I think Northumberland-street. By a block or a hitch of some sort, there was, I should say, just a bushel of drowned rats stopped at the corner of one of the gates, which I swept into the next stream. I see far fewer drowned rats now than before the *shores* was flushed. They're not so plenty, that's one thing. Perhaps, too, they may have got to understand about flushing, they're that 'cute, and manage to keep out of the way. About Newgate-market was at one time the worst for rats. Men couldn't venture into the sewers then, on account of the varmint. It's bad enough still, I hear, but I haven't worked in the City for a few years.'

Cesspool-sewermen
[*volume ii. pp.433–449*]

After 1830 it became an indictable offence for a newly erected house not to have a cesspool which drained directly into a sewer. Such private cesspools were emptied at the expense of the owner. There were also public cesspools in courts, alleys and places into which the refuse from all the houses drained. The charge for cleansing these public cesspools was defrayed out of the rates. There were two methods of cleansing: by pump and hose (hydraulic method) into the sewers; by shovel and tube (manual labour) into carts which hauled the refuse to a distant night-yard. The hydraulic method was introduced to London in the winter of 1847. Gangs of five (four men under the direction of a ganger) performed the work. One problem with this system was that the refuse became sewage and was pumped straight into the Thames from which London drew its drinking water.

A cesspool-sewerman's statement

[*volume ii. pp.448,449*]

I give the following brief and characteristic statement, which is peculiar in showing the habitual *restlessness* of the mere labourer. My informant was a stout, hale-looking man, who had rarely known illness. All these sort of labourers (nightmen included) scout the notion of the cholera attacking *them*!

'Work, sir? Well, I think I do know what work is, and has known it since I was a child; and then I was set to help at the weaving. My friends were weavers at Norwich, and 26 years ago, until steam pulled working men down from being well paid and well off, it was a capital trade. Why, my father could sometimes earn 3*l*. at his work as a working weaver; there was money for ever then; now 12*s*. a week is, I believe, the tip-top earnings of his trade, but *I didn't like the confinement or the close air in the factories*, and so, when I grew big enough, I went to ground-work in the city [so he frequently called Norwich]; I call ground-work such as digging drains and the like. Then I 'listed into the Marines. *Oh, I hardly know what made me*; men does foolish things and don't know why; it's human natur. I'm sure it wasn't the bounty of 3*l*. that tempted me, for I was doing middling, and sometimes had night-work as well as ground-work to do. I was then sent to Sheerness and put on board the *Thunderer* man-of-war, carrying 84 guns, as a marine. She sailed through the Straits [of Gibraltar], and was three years and three months blockading the Dardanelles and cruising among the islands. I never saw anything like such fortifications as at the Dardanelles; why, there was mortars there as would throw a ton weight. No, I never heard of their having been fired. Yes, we sometimes got leave for a party to go ashore on one of the islands. They called them Greek islands, but I fancy as how it was Turks near the Dardanelles. Oh yes, the men on the islands was civil enough to us; they never spoke to us, and we never spoke to them. The sailors sometimes, and indeed the lot of us, would have bits of larks with them, laughing at 'em and taking sights at 'em and suchlike. Why, I've seen a fine-dressed Turk, one of their grand gentlemen there, when a couple of sailors has each been taking a sight at him, and dancing the shuffle along with it, make each on 'em a low bow, as solemn as could be. Perhaps he thought it was a way of being civil in our country! I've seen some of the head ones stuck over with so many knives, and cutlasses, and belts, and pistols, and things, that he looked like a cutler's shop window. We were ordered home at last, and after being some months in barracks, which I didn't relish at all, were paid off at Plymouth. Oh, a barrack life's anything but pleasant, but I've done with it. After that I was eight years and a quarter a gentleman's servant, coachman, or anything [in Norwich], and then got tired of that and came to London, and got to ground and new sewer-work, and have been on the sewers above five years. Yes, I prefer the sewers to the Greek islands. I was one of the first set as worked a pump. There was a great many spectators; I dare say as there was 40 skientific gentlemen. I've been on the sewers, flushing and pumping, ever since. The houses we clean out, all says it's far the best plan, ours is. "Never no more nightmen," they say. You see, sir, our plan's far less trouble to the people in the house, and there's no smell, least I never found no smell, and it's cheap, too. In time the nightmen'll disappear; in course they must, there's so many new dodges comes up, always some one of the working classes is a being ruined. If it ain't steam, it's something else as knocks the bread out of their mouths quite as quick.'

Chimney-sweeps
[*volume ii. pp.338–378*]

The title 'sweep' covered a number of categories of worker. Master Chimney Sweeps were divided into three types: large or high masters who employed between two and ten men and two boys and had horses and carts; small or low masters who employed, usually, two men; single-handed masters who did all the work themselves. Within each type there were two subdivisions: 'greenuns' or 'leeks' who had not yet served their time; 'knullers' or 'queriers' who solicited custom by knocking on the doors of houses. There were also journeymen, climbing men and, illegally, climbing boys. There were well over one thousand men and boys employed in the trade in London. Payment was either in money or in money and kind or simply in kind. There were no trade societies but the sweeps met in public houses.

A 'knuller' or 'querier'
[*volume ii. pp.377,378*]

Another knuller (to whom I was referred by a master who occassionally employed him as a journeyman) gave me the following account. He was 'doing just middling' when I saw him, he said, but his look was that of a man who had known privations, and the soot actually seemed to bring out his wrinkles more fully, although he told me he was only between 40 and 50 years old; he believed he was not 46.

'I was hard brought up, sir,' he said; 'ay, them as'll read your book – I mean them readers as is well to do – cannot fancy how hard. Mother was a widow; father was nobody knew where; and, poor woman, she was sometimes distracted that a daughter she had before her marriage went all wrong. She was a washerwoman, and slaved herself to death. She died in the house [workhouse] in Birmingham. I can read and write a little. I was sent to a charity school, and when I was big enough I was put 'prentice to a gunsmith at Birmingham. I'm master of the business generally, but my perticler part is a gun lock-filer. No, sir, I can't say as ever I liked it; nothing but file file all day. I used to wish I was like the free bits o' boys that used to beg steel filings of me for their fifth of November fireworks. I never could bear confinement. It's made me look older than I ought, I know, but what can a poor man do? No, I never cared much about drinking. I worked in an iron-foundry when I was out of my time. I had a relation that was foreman there. Perhaps it might be that, among all the dust and heat and smoke and stuff, that made me a sweep at last, for I was then almost or quite as black as a sweep.

'Then I come up to London; ay, that must be more nor 20 years back. Oh, I came up to better myself, but I couldn't get work either at the gun-makers – and I fancy the London masters don't like Birmingham hands – nor at the iron-foundries, and the iron-foundries is nothing in London to what they is in Staffordshire and Warwickshire; nothing at all, they may say what they like. Well, sir, I soon got very bad off. My togs was hardly to call togs. One night – and it was a coldish night, too – I slept in the park, and was all stiff and shivery next morning. As I was wandering about near the park, I walked up a street near the Abbey – King-street, I think it is – and there was a picture outside a public-house, and a writing of men wanted for the East India Company's Service. I went there again in the evening, and there was soldiers smoking and drinking up and down, and I 'listed at once. I was to have my full bounty when I got to the depôt – Southampton I think they called it. Somehow I began to rue what I'd done. Well, I hardly can tell you why. Oh, no; I don't say I was badly used; not at all. But I had heard of snakes and things in the parts I was going to, and I gently hooked it. I was a navvy on different rails after that, but I never was strong enough for that there work, and at last I couldn't get any more work to do. I came back to London; well, sir, I can't say, as you ask, why I came to London 'stead of Birmingham. I seemed to go natural like. I could get nothing to do, and Lord! what I suffered! I once fell down in the Cut from hunger, and I was lifted into Watchorn's, and he said to his men, "Give the poor fellow a little drop of brandy, and after that a biscuit; the best things he can have." He saved my life, sir. The people at the bar – they see'd it was no humbug – gathered 7d. for me. A penny a-piece from some of Maudslay's men, and a halfpenny from a gent. that hadn't no other change, and a poor woman as I was going away slipt a couple of trotters into my hand.

'I slept at a lodging-house, then, in Baldwin's-gardens when I had money, and one day in Gray's Inn-lane I picked up an old gent that fell in the middle of the street, and might have been run over. After he'd felt in all his pockets, and found he was all right, he gave me 5s. I knew a sweep, for I sometimes slept in the same house, in King-street, Drury-lane; and he was sick, and was going to the big house. And he told me all about his machines, that's six or seven years back, and said if I'd pay 2s. 6d. down, and 2s. 6d. a week, if I couldn't pay more, I might have his machine for 20s. I took it at 17s. 6d., and paid him every farthing. That just kept him out of the house, but he died soon after.

'Yes, I've been a sweep ever since. I've had to shift as well as I could. I don't know that I'm what you call a Nuller, or a Querier. Well, if I'm asked if I'm anybody's man, I don't like to say "no", and I don't like to say "yes"; so I says nothing if I can help it. Yes, I call at houses to ask if anything's wanted. I've got a job that way sometimes. If they took me for anybody's man, I can't help that.

I lodge with another sweep which is better off nor I am, and pay him 2s. 9d. a week for a little stair-head place with a bed in it. I think I clear 7s. a week, one week with another, but that's the outside. I never go to church or chapel. I've never got into the way of it. Besides, I wouldn't be let in, I s'pose, in my togs. I've only myself. I can't say I much like what I'm doing, but what can a poor man do?'

Ballast-heavers and coal-whippers
[volume iii. pp.265–288]

The interviews with the ballast-heavers and their wives are especially intriguing because ballast-heaving represents one of the few instances when we know that Mayhew intervened to support reform of working conditions. Coal-whipping involved the removal of cargoes of coal from the ships to barges. Ballast-heaving supplied the now-emptied coal ships with a ballast of sand, dredged from the floor of the Thames. They also unloaded ballast from other ships which came to London to collect coal. Traditionally both coal-whippers and ballast-heavers waited in public-houses or shops on shore until coal-ship captains were ready to employ a gang: the captain paid the publican, and the publican paid the coal-whipper or ballast-heaver. While they waited the men drank and had often 'consumed' most of their wages before they received them. The publicans divided the men into 'constants' (who were first served when gangs were sought) and 'stragglers'. The 'constants' were expected, in return, to spend their spare time in the public-house and even to lodge there. Quite recently a Coal-whippers' Office had been established which corrected this abuse with regard to the coal-whippers; the ballast-heavers, however, were still prisoners of the system. Mayhew explicitly stated that his intention in publishing the details of these 'iniquities' was that he would be 'at least instrumental in putting an end to a most vile and wicked plan for the degradation and demoralisation of our fellow-creatures.' [iii. p.272]

The meeting of the ballast-heavers' wives

[volume iii. pp.285–288]

[. . .] It is the wife and children who are the real sufferers from the intemperance of the working man; and being anxious to give the public some idea of the amount of misery entailed upon these poor creatures by the compulsory and induced drunkenness of the husbands, I requested as many as could leave their homes to meet me at the British and Foreign School, in Shakespeare-walk, Shadwell. The meeting consisted of the wives of ballast-heavers and coal-whippers. The wives of the coal-whippers had come there to contrast their present state with their past, with a view of showing the misery they had endured when their husbands were under the same thraldom to the publican as the ballast-heavers are now, and the comparative happiness which they have experienced since they were freed from it. They had attended unsolicited, in the hope, by making their statements public, of getting for the ballast-heavers the same freedom from the control of the publican which the coal-whippers had obtained.

The meeting consisted of the wives of ballast-heavers and coal-whippers, thirty-one were present. Of the thirty-one, nine were the wives of coal-whippers, the remaining twenty-two the wives of ballast-heavers. Many others, who had expressed a desire to attend, were prevented by family cares and arrangements; but, small as the meeting was comparatively, it afforded a very fair representation of the circumstances and characters of their husbands. For instance, those who were coal-whippers' wives appeared comfortable and 'well to do'. They wore warm gowns, had on winter-bonnets and clean tidy caps underneath; the ballast-heavers' wives, on the contrary, were mostly ragged, dejected, and anxious-looking.

An endeavour was made to ascertain in the first instance how many children each person had. This was done by questioning them separately; and from the answers it appeared that they all had families. Eight had one child each, the rest varied from two to eight, and one woman stated that she had twelve children, all of whom were living, but that only four resided now with her and her husband. Five had infants in their arms, and several had children sick, either at home or in some hospital.

In the next place the ballast-heavers' wives were asked whether their husbands worked under publicans. 'All of them,' was the

reply, 'work under publicans;' and, said one, 'Worse luck for us' –
a sentiment that was very warmly concurred in by all the rest.

This fact having been specifically ascertained from each woman,
we proceeded to inquire from them separately how much their
husbands earned, and how much of their earnings was spent at the
publicans' houses through which they obtained work, or where
they were paid.

'My husband,' said the first woman, 'works under a publican,
and I know that he earns now 12s. or 13s. a week, but he brings
home to me only half-a-crown, and sometimes not so much. He
spends all the rest at a public-house where he gets his jobs, and
often comes home drunk.'

'My husband,' exclaimed the second, 'will sometimes get from
24s. to 28s. a week, but I never see anything the likes o' that
money from him. He spends it at the publican's. And when he has
earned 24s. he will sometimes bring home only 2s. or 2s. 6d. We
are badly off, you may be sure, when the money goes in this way.
But my husband cannot help spending it, for he is obliged to get
his jobs at the public-house.'

'Last week,' interposed another, 'we had not one penny coming
into our house; and the week before – which was Christmas
week – my husband got two jobs which would come, he told me,
to 8s. or 9s. if he had brought it all home; but he only brought me
1s. This was all the money I had to keep me and my five children
for the whole week; and I'm sure I don't know how we got
through. This is all owing to the public-house. And when we go
to fetch our husbands at eleven or twelve o'clock at night they
shut us out, and say they are not there, though we know very
well they are inside in a back place. My husband has been kept in
that back place many a time till two or three in the morning –
then he has been turned out and come home drunk, without 6d.
in his pocket, though the same day he has received 8s. or 9s. at the
same public-house.'

'They go to the public-house,' added another woman, 'to get
jobs, and to curry favour they spend their money there, because if
they did not spend their money they would never get a job. The
men who will drink the greatest quantity of money will get the
most jobs. This leaves their families and their wives miserable, and
I am sure me and my poor family are miserable enough.'

'But this,' interposed a quiet, elderly woman, 'is the beginning of the tenth week, in all of which my husband has only had four jobs, and all I have received of him during that time is 1s. 3d. a week, and we stand in 2s. 6d. a week rent. I am sure I don't know how we get along. But our publicans are very civil, for my husband works for two. Still, if he does not drink a good part of it away we know very well he will get no more work.'

'It is very little,' said a female with an infant in her arms, 'that my husband earns; and of what little he does earn he does not fetch much to me. He got one job last week, heaving 45 tons, and he fetched me home 1s. 6d. for it. I was then in lodgings at 1s. 6d. a week, but I could not afford them, but now I'm in lodgings at 9d. a week. This week he has no work yet. In Christmas week my man told me he earned 25s., and I believe he did, but he only fetched me home 8s. or 9s. on Saturday. My husband works for a publican, and it was at his house he spent his money. One day last week he asked the publican to give him a job, and he said, "I cannot give you a job, for there is nothing against you on the slate but 1s.," and so he got none there. My infant is six weeks old today, and this woman by me [appealing to the female next to her] knows well it is the truth that I tell – that for two nights in last week my child and myself were obliged to go to bed breadless. We had nothing neither of those two days. It was the same in one night the week before Christmas, though my husband received that night 8s., but all was spent at the public-house. On Christmas night we could not get any supper. We had no money, and I took the gown off my back and pawned it for 2s. to provide something for us to eat. I have nothing else to say but this – that whatever my husband earns I get little or nothing of it, for it goes to the public-house where he gets his jobs.'

An infirm woman, approaching fifty years of age, who spoke in a tone of sorrowful resignation, said, 'We have had very little money coming in of late. My husband has been very bad for ten weeks back. He throws up blood; I suppose he has strained himself too much. All the money I have had for six weeks to keep us both has been 8s. If he was earning money he would bring it to me.'

Another woman, 'Not without the publican's allowance, I am sure.'

The first woman, 'No; the publican's allowance would be taken off; but the publican, you see, must have a little – I do not know how much it is, but they must have something if they give us their jobs.'

This woman was here asked if her husband ever came home drunk?

'Yes,' she replied; 'many a time he comes home drunk; but he must have the drink to get the jobs.'

A number of other women having made statements confirmatory of the above:

'Do you think,' the meeting was asked, 'your husbands would be sober as well as industrious men if they could be got away from the public house system of employment and payment of wages?'

'God Almighty bless you!' exclaimed one woman, 'they would love us and their families all the better for it! We should all be much the better for it.'

'And so say all of us!' was the next and perfectly unanimous exclamation.

'If we could see that day,' said one who had spoken before, 'our families would have little to complain of.'

Another added, 'The night-houses ought to be closed. That would be one good thing.'

Some enquiries were then made as to whether these poor women were ill-treated by their husbands when they came home in a state of intoxication. There was a good deal of hesitation before any answers could be obtained. At last one woman said, 'her husband did certainly beat her, of course; but then,' she added, 'he did not know what he was doing.'

'I,' said another, 'should not know what it was to have an angry word with my husband if he was always sober. He is a quiet man – very, when the drink is out of him; but we have many words together when he is tipsy; and – ' she stopped without completing the sentence.

Several others gave similar testimony; and many declared that it was the public-house system which led their husbands to drink.

One woman here said that the foremen of gangs, as well as the publican, helped to reduce the ballast-heaver's earnings; for they gave work to men who took lodgings from them, though they did not occupy them.

This was confirmed by another woman, who spoke with great warmth upon the subject. She said that married men who could not afford to spend with the publican and lodge with the foremen in the manner pointed out, would be sure to have no work. Other men went straight from one job to another, while her own husband and other women's husbands had been three or four weeks without lifting a shovelful of ballast. She considered this was very hard on men who had families.

A question was here asked, whether any women were present whose husbands, in order to obtain work, were obliged to pay for lodgings which they did not use?

One immediately rose and said, 'They do it regularly at a publican's in Wapping; and I know the men that have paid for them have had six jobs together, when my husband has had none for weeks.' 'There are now,' added another, 'fourteen at that very place who never lodge there, though they are paying for lodgings.'

They were next asked, who had suffered from want owing to their husbands drinking their earnings, as described at the public-houses in question?

'Starvation has been my lot,' said one. 'And mine,' added another. 'My children,' said a third, 'have often gone to bed at night without breaking their fast the whole length of the day.' 'And mine,' said one, 'have many a time gone without a bit or sup of anything all the day, through their father working for the publican.'

'I cannot,' exclaimed the next, 'afford my children a ha'porth of milk a-day.'

'Many a time,' said one, who appeared to be very much moved, 'have I put my four children to bed, when the only meal they have had the whole day has been 1 lb. of bread; but it's of no use opening my mouth.'

'I,' said the last, 'have been in London twenty-seven years, and during that time I can safely say I have never taken myself a single glass of spirits or anything else; but in that time I have suffered the martyrdom of forty years – all through my husband and the public-house. I have two children who bring me in, one of them 2s. 6d. and the other 6s. 6d. a week, which is all we have, for my husband gets nearly nothing. If he could bring his earnings home, instead of spending them at a public-house, we should be very comfortable.'

These questions led to one concerning the late-hour system at the public-houses frequented by the ballast-heavers.

'I often go for my husband,' said one, 'at one or two o'clock in the morning, after I know he has been paid; but they have kept him in a back apartment away from me, till I have threatened to smash the windows if they did not let him out. I threatened to smash the windows because my children were wanting the money for bread, which he was spending there. If our husbands were inclined to come home sober there is little chance, for they have cards and bagatelle to keep them till they become heady, and when they are become heady, there is nothing left for their families – then the publicans kick our poor men out, and lock the doors.'

This statement was confirmed, and after several other persons had described their feelings, –

The coal-whippers' wives were asked whether or not their condition and that of their families had been improved since the system of carrying on the trade had been altered by the Legislature?

The answer was a most decisive affirmative. Their husbands, they said, used to spend all, or very nearly all, their earnings with the publicans; but now, when they got a good ship, they brought home the greatest part of their earnings, which was sufficient to make their families comfortable. Their husbands had become quite different men. They used to ill-treat them when they were paid at a public-house – very much so, because of the drink; but now they were very much altered, because they were become sober men to what they were. None were now distressed to provide for their families, and if there was plenty of work they would be quite happy. The improvement, one woman said, must be very great, otherwise there would not be so many institutions and benefit societies, pension societies, and schools for their children.

This declaration was very warmly applauded by the wives of the ballast-heavers. They declared that similar measures would produce similar benefits in their case, and they hoped the day would soon come when they should be secure in the enjoyment of them.

So terminated the proceedings.

Asylum for the Houseless Poor
[*volume iii. pp.428,429*]

Mayhew used the detailed records of this philanthropic agency – a refuge for the destitute which stood between them and the workhouse – to construct his report. About four hundred people appear to have found relief within the Asylum, situated in Playhouse Yard, Blackfriars. Mayhew was eager to draw a sharp distinction between the professional vagabonds who thronged the streets of London and the honest, unemployed workmen. His reporting of the interviews at the Asylum reveals his deep respect for the latter class.

The Asylum for the Houseless Poor
[*volume iii. p.417*]

There is a world of wisdom to be learnt at the Asylum for the Houseless Poor. Those who wish to be taught in this, the severest school of all, should pay a visit to Playhouse-yard, and see the homeless crowds gathered about the Asylum, waiting for the first opening of the doors, with their bare feet, blue and ulcerous with the cold, resting for hours on the ice and snow in the streets, and the bleak stinging wind blowing through their rags. To hear the cries of the hungry, shivering children, and the wrangling of the greedy men, scrambling for a bed and a pound of dry bread, is a thing to haunt one for life. There are 400 and odd creatures utterly destitute – mothers with infants at their breasts – fathers with boys holding by their side – the friendless – the penniless – the shirtless, shoeless, breadless, homeless; in a word, the very poorest of this the very richest city in the world.

The Asylum for the Houseless is the confluence of the many tides of poverty that, at this period of the year, flow towards the metropolis. It should be remembered that there are certain callings, which yield a subsistence to those who pursue them only at particular seasons. Brickmakers, agricultural labourers, garden-women, and many such vocations, are labours that admit of being performed only in the summer, when indeed, the labourer has the fewest wants to satisfy. The privations of such classes, then, come at a period when even the elements conspire to make their destitution more terrible. Hence, restless with want, they wander in hordes across the land, making, in vain hope, for London, as the great emporium of wealth — the market of the world. But London is as overstocked with hands as every other nook and corner of the country. And then the poor creatures, far away from home and friends, find at last to their cost, that the very privations they were flying from pursue them here with a tenfold severity. I do not pretend to say that all found within the walls of these asylums are such as I have described; many, I know, trade upon the sympathy of those who would ease the sufferings of the destitute labourers, and they make their appearance in the metropolis at this especial season. Winter is the beggar's harvest. That there are hundreds of professional vagabonds drawn to London at such a time, I am well aware; but with them come the unemployed workmen. We must not, therefore, confound one with the other, nor let our indignation at the vagabond who will not work, check our commiseration for the labourer or artisan who cannot get work to do. [. . .]

A homeless painter
[*volume iii. pp.417–419*]

A homeless painter gave me the following statement. His appearance presented nothing remarkable. It was merely that of the poor artisan. There was nothing dirty or squalid about him:

'I was brought up a painter,' he said, 'and I am now 27. I served my apprenticeship in Yorkshire, and stayed two years after my term was out with the same master. I then worked in Liverpool, earning but little through illness, and working on and off as my health permitted. I got married in Liverpool, and went with my wife to Londonderry, in Ireland, of which place she was a native. There she died of the cholera in 1847. I was very ill with diarrhœa myself. We lived with her friends, but I got work, though wages are very low there. I never earned more than 2s. 6d. a-day there. I have earned 5s. 6d. a-day in Liverpool, but in Londonderry provisions are very cheap — the best meat at 4d. a-pound. It was an advantage to me being an Englishman. English workmen seem to be preferred in Ireland, so far as I can tell, and I have worked in Belfast and Coleraine, and a short time in Dublin, as well as in Londonderry. I came back to Liverpool early in 1848, and got work, but was again greatly distressed through sickness. I then had to travel the country again, getting a little employment at

Hemel Hempstead, and St Alban's, and other places about, for I aimed at London, and at last I got to London. That was in November, 1848. When in the country I was forced to part with my clothes. I had a beautiful suit of black among them. I very seldom got even a trifle from the painters in the country towns; sometimes 2*d*. or 3*d*. from a master. In London I could get no work, and my shirts and my flannel-shirts went to keep me. I stayed about a month, and having nothing left, was obliged to start for the country. I got a job at Luton, and at a few other places. Wages are very low. I was always a temperate man. Many a time I have never tasted drink for a week together, and this when I had money in my pocket, for I had 30*l*. when I got married. I have, too the character of being a good workman. I returned to London again three weeks back, but could find no work. I had again to part with any odd things I had. The last I parted with was my stopping-knife and diamond, for I can work as a glazier and plumber; country painters often can – I mean those apprenticed in the country. I have no clothes but what I have on. For the last ten days, I declare solemnly, I have had nothing but what I picked up in the streets. I picked up crusts that I saw in the streets, put out on the steps by the mistresses of the houses for the poor like myself. I got so weak and ill that I had to go to King's College Hospital, and they gave me medicine which did me good. I often had to walk the streets all night. I was so perished I could hardly move my limbs. I never asked charity, I can't; but I could have eaten anything. I longed for the fried fish I saw; yes, I was ravenous for that, and such like though I couldn't have touched it when I had money, and was middling well off. Things are so different in the country that I couldn't fancy such meat. I was brought to that pitch, I had the greatest mind to steal something to get into prison, where, at any rate, I said to myself, I shall have some food and shelter. I didn't – I thought better of it. I hoped something might turn up next day; besides, it might have got into the papers, and my friends might have seen it, and I should have felt I disgraced them, or that they would think so, because they couldn't know my temptations and my sufferings. When out all night, I used to get shelter, if I could, about Hungerford-market, among the straw. The cold made me almost dead with sleep; and when obliged to move, I couldn't walk at first, I could only crawl along. One night I had a penny given me, all I had gotten in five bitter nights in the streets. For that penny I got half a pint of coffee; it made me sick, my stomach was so weak. On Tuesday I asked a policeman if he couldn't recommend me to some workhouse, and he told me to come here, and I was admitted, and was very thankful to get under shelter.'

A homeless carpenter
[*volume iii. pp.419,420*]

The next was a carpenter, a tall, fine-built man, with a pleasing expression of countenance. He was dressed in a flannel jacket and fustian trousers, with the peculiar little side-pocket for his foot-rule, that told you of his calling. He was about 40 years of age, and had the appearance, even in his destitution, of a most respectable mechanic. It is astonishing to mark the difference between the poor artisan and the labourer. The one seems alive to his poverty, and to feel it more acutely than the other. The labourer is more accustomed to 'rough it', as it is called; but the artisan, earning better wages, and used to better ways, appears among the houseless poor as a really pitiable character. Carpenters are among the classes of mechanics in which there appears to be the greatest amount of destitution, and I selected this man as a fair average specimen of the body. He said:

'I have been out of work nearly three months. I have had some little work in the mean time, an odd job or two at intervals, but nothing regular. When I am in full work, on day work, I can make 5s. a-day in London; but the masters very generally wishes the men to take piece-work, and that is the cause of men's work being cut down as it is, because men is obliged to take the work as they offers. I could get about 30s. a week when I had good employ-ment. I had no one but myself to keep out of my earnings. I have saved something when I have been on day-work; but then it went again as soon as I got to piece-work. This is generally the case with the carpenters. The last job I had was at Cobham, in Surrey, doing joiners' work, and business with my master got slack, and I was discharged. Then I made my way to London, and have been about from place to place since then, endeavouring to get work from every one that I knew or could get recommended to. But I have not met with any success. Well, sir, I have been obliged to part with all I had, even to my tools; though they're not left for much. My tools are pawned for 12s., and my clothes are all gone. The last I had to part with was my rule and chalk-line, and them I left for a night's lodging. I have no other clothes but what you see me in at present. There are a vast many carpenters out of work, and like me. It is now three weeks since the last of my things went, and after that I have been about the streets, and gone into bakers' shops, and asked for a crust. Sometimes I have got a penny out of the tap-room of a public-house. It's now more than a fortnight since I quitted my lodgings. I have been in the Asylum eight nights. Before that, I was out in the streets for five nights together. They were very cold nights; yes, very.' [The man shivered at the recollection.] 'I walked up one street, and down another. I sometimes got under a doorway, but it was impossible to stand still long, it was so cruel cold. The sleet was coming down one night, and freezed on my clothes as it fell. The cold made me stiff more than sleepy. It was next day that I felt tired; and then, if I came to sit down at a fireside, I should drop asleep in a minute. I tried, when I was dead-beat, to get into St Giles's union, but they wouldn't admit me. Then the police sent me up to another union: I forget the name, but they refused me. I tried at Lambeth, and there I was refused. I don't think I went a day without some small bit of bread. I begged for it. But when I walked from St Alban's to London, I was two days without a bit to put in my mouth. I never stole, not a particle, from any person, in all my trials. I was brought up honest, and, thank God, I have kept so all my life. I would work willingly, and am quite capable: yes, and I would do my work with all my heart, but it's not to be got at.'

This the poor fellow said with deep emotion; and, indeed, his whole statement appeared in every way worthy of credit. I heard afterwards that he had offered to 'put up the stairs of two houses' at some man's own terms, rather than remain unemployed. He had told the master that his tools were in pawn, and promised, if they were taken out of pledge for him, to work for his bare food. He was a native of Somerset, and his father and mother were both dead. [. . .]

A homeless tailor

[*volume iii. pp.422,423*]

Then came a tailor, a young man only twenty-one years old, habited in a black frock-coat, with a plaid shawl twisted round his neck. His eyes were full and expressive, and he had a look of intelligence superior to any that I had yet seen. He told a story which my inquiries into the 'slop trade' taught me was 'ower true'.

'I have been knocking about for near upon six weeks,' he replied, in answer to my inquiries. 'I was working at the slop-trade at the West-end. I am a native of Scotland. I was living with a sweater. I used to board and lodge with him entirely. At the week's end I was almost always in debt with him − at least he made it out so. I had very often to work all night, but let me slave as hard as I might I never could get out of debt with the sweater. There were often as many as six of us there, and we slept two together in each bed. The work had been slack for some time, and he gave me employment till I worked myself out of his debt, and then he turned me into the streets. I had a few clothes remaining, and these soon were sold to get food and lodging. I lived on my other coat and shirts for a week or two, and at last all was gone, and I was left entirely destitute. Then I had to pace the streets all day and night. The two nights before I came here I never tasted food nor lay down to rest. I had been in a four-penny lodging before then, but I couldn't raise even that; and I knew it was no good going there without the money. You must pay before you go to bed at those places. Several times I got into a doorway, to shelter from the wind and cold, and twice I was roused by the policeman, for I was so tired that I fell asleep standing against a shop near the Bank. What with hunger and cold, I was in a half-stupid state. I didn't know what to do: I was far from home and my mother. I have not liked to let her know how badly I was off.' [The poor lad's eyes flooded with tears at the recollection of his parent.] 'I thought I had better steal something, and then at least I should have a roof over my head. Then I thought I'd make away with myself. I can't say how; it was a sort of desperation; and I was so stupid with cold and want, that I can hardly remember what I thought. All I wanted was to be allowed to sit down on some doorstep and die; but the police did not allow this. In the daytime I went up and lay about the parks most part of the day, but I couldn't sleep then; I hardly know why, but I'd been so long without food, that I couldn't rest. I have purposely kept from writing to my mother. It would break her heart to know my sufferings. She has been a widow this ten years past. She keeps a lodging-house in Leith, and has two children to support. I have been away eight months from her. I came to London from a desire to see the place, and thinking I could better my situation. In Edinburgh, I had made my 1*l.* a week regularly; often more, and seldom less. When I came to London, a woman met me in the street, and asked me if I wasn't a tailor? On my replying in the affirmative, she informed me if I would come and work for her husband, I should have good wages, and live with her and her husband, and they would make me quite comfortable. I didn't know she was the wife of a sweater at that time. It was a thing I had never heard of in Edinburgh. After that time, I kept getting worse and worse off, working day and night, and all Sunday, and still always being in debt to them I worked for. Indeed, I wish I had never left home. If I could get back, I'd go in a moment. I have worked early and late, in the hope of accumulating money enough to take me home again, but I could not even get out of debt, much more save, work as hard as I would.'

I asked if he would allow me to see some letters of his mother's, as vouchers for the truth of his story, and he produced a small packet, from which, with his permission, I copied the following:

MY DEAR SON, – I have this moment received your letter. I was happy to hear from you, and trust you are well. Think of that God who has carried you in safety over the mighty deep. We are all much as you left us. I hope you will soon write. Ever believe me,

Your affectionate mother,

— —

This was the first letter written after his absence from home. Since then his mother, who is aged and rheumatic (his letters vouched for this), had been unable to write a line. His brother, a lad of 16, says, in one of his letters, –

I am getting on with my Greek, Hebrew, Latin, and French, only I am terribly ill off for want of books. My mother was saying that you would be bringing me a first-rate present from London. I think the most appropriate present you can bring me will be a Greek and English, or a Hebrew and English Lexicon; or some Hebrew, Greek, or Latin book.

A letter from his sister, a girl of 18, ran as follows:

MY DEAR BROTHER, – I take this opportunity of writing you, as you wrote that you would like to have a letter from me. I am very sorry you have been ill, but I hope you are keeping better. I trust also that affliction will be the means of leading you only more closely to the only true source of happiness. Oh, my dear brother, you are still young, and God has told us in His word, that those who seek Him early shall find Him. My dear brother, we get many a sad and solemn warning to prepare to meet our God: and oh! my dear brother, 'what is a man profited, if he shall gain the whole world and lose his own soul?'

The last letter was dated the 5th of December last, and from his brother:

We received your kind letter [it ran] this instant, and we hasten to answer it. It has given my mother and me great relief to hear from you, as my mother and I were very miserable about you, thinking you were ill. We trust you will take care of yourself, and not get any more cold. We hope you will be able to write on receipt of this, and let us know how you are, and when we may expect you home, as we have daily expected you since the month of October.

These letters were shown to me at my request, and not produced by the young man himself, so that it was evident they were kept by the youth with no view of being used by him as a means of inducing charity; indeed, the whole manner of the young man was such as entirely precluded suspicion. On my asking whether he had any other credentials as to character, he showed me a letter from a Scotch minister, stating that 'he had been under his charge, and that from his conduct he had been led to form a favourable opinion of his talents and moral character; and that he believed him to be a deserving, industrious young man.' [. . .]

4

THE LONDON LABOUR MARKET AND
THE CASUAL LABOUR PROBLEM

Poverty and the organisation of the labour market went hand in glove. In a brilliant and original analysis, Mayhew showed how insufficiency of employment contributed to the misery of the unskilled, to the subversion of the skilled and to the growth of the dangerous classes. Mayhew calculated that, of a workforce of around 4.5 million people, there was regular and constant work for under a half, with 1.5 million employed only half the time and the remaining 1.5 million wholly unemployed, subsisting upon an occasional day's work by the displacement of others. Mayhew showed how the size of the casual labour force was influenced by the seasonality of production due to changes in fashion, shifts in demand, the interruption of production due to weather and trade factors, etc. He showed, too, how the over-supply of surplus labour was influenced by adjustments to work organisation, hiring arrangements and wage payment systems and by changes in the volume of labour due to a decrease either in demand or the means of supply.

THE LONDON SCAVAGER

[from a daguerrotype by Beard]

THE LONDON LABOUR MARKET AND
THE CASUAL LABOUR PROBLEM

Casual labour

[*volume ii. pp.297–323*]

The subject of casual labour is one of such vast importance in connection with the welfare of a nation and its people, and one of which the causes as well as consequences seem to be so utterly ignored by economical writers and unheeded by the public, that I purpose here saying a few words upon the matter in general, with the view of enabling the reader the better to understand the difficulties that almost all unskilled and many skilled labourers have to contend with in this country.

By *casual* labour I mean such labour as can obtain only *occasional* as contradistinguished from *constant* employment. In this definition I include all classes of workers, literate and illiterate, skilled and unskilled, whose professions, trades, or callings expose them to be employed temporarily rather than continuously, and whose incomes are in a consequent degree fluctuating, casual, and uncertain.

In no country in the world is there such an extent, and at the same time such a diversity, of casual labour as in Great Britain. This is attributable to many causes – commercial and agricultural, natural and artificial, controllable and uncontrollable.

I will first show what are the causes of casual labour, and then point out its effects.

The causes of casual labour may be grouped under two heads:

1. *The Brisk and Slack Seasons, and Fit Times*, or periodical increase and decrease of work in certain occupations.

2. *The Surplus Hands* appertaining to the different trades.

First, as to the briskness or slackness of employment in different occupations. This depends in different trades on different causes, among which may be enumerated –

(a) The weather.
(b) The seasons of the year.
(c) The fashion of the day.
(d) Commerce and accidents.

I shall deal with each of these causes *seriatim*.

(a) The labour of thousands is influenced by the *weather*; it is suspended or prevented in many instances by stormy or rainy weather; and in some few instances it is promoted by such a state of things.

Among those whose labour cannot be executed on *wet days*, or executed but imperfectly, and who are consequently deprived of their ordinary means of living on such days, are – paviours, pipe-layers, bricklayers, painters of the exteriors of houses, slaters, fishermen, watermen (plying with their boats for hire), the crews of the river steamers, a large body of agricultural labourers (such as hedgers, ditchers, mowers, reapers, ploughmen, thatchers, and gardeners), costermongers and all classes of street-sellers (to a great degree), street-performers, and showmen.

With regard to the degree in which agricultural (or indeed in this instance woodland) labour may be influenced by the weather, I may state that a few years back there had been a fall of oaks on an estate belonging to Col. Cradock, near Greta-bridge, and the poor people, old men and women, in the neighbourhood, were selected to strip off the bark for the tanners, under the direction of a person appointed by the proprietor: for this work they were paid by the basket-load. The trees lay in an open and exposed situation, and the rain was so incessant that the 'barkers' could scarcely do any work for the whole of the first week, but kept waiting under the nearest shelter in the hopes that it would 'clear up'. In the first week of this employment nearly one-third of the poor persons, who had commenced their work with eagerness, had to apply for some temporary parochial relief. A rather curious instance this, of a parish suffering from the casualty of a very humble labour, and actually from the attempt of the poor to earn money, and do work prepared for them.

On the other hand, some few classes may be said to be benefited by the rain which is impoverishing others: these are cabmen (who are the busiest on *showery* days), scavagers, umbrella-makers, clog and patten-makers. I was told by the omnibus people that their vehicles filled better in hot than in wet weather.

But the labour of thousands is influenced also by the *wind*; an easterly wind prevailing for a few days will throw out of employment 20,000 dock labourers and others who are dependent on the shipping for their employment; such as lumpers, corn-porters, timber-porters, ship-builders, sail-makers, lightermen, watermen, and, indeed, almost all those who are known as "long-shoremen". The same state of things prevails at Hull, Bristol, Liverpool, and all our large ports.

Frost, again, is equally inimical to some labourers' interests; the frozen-out market-gardeners are familiar to almost everyone, and indeed all those who are engaged upon the land may be said to be deprived of work by severely cold weather.

In the weather alone, then, we find a means of starving thousands of our people. Rain, wind, and frost are many a labourer's natural enemies, and to those who are fully aware of the influence of 'the elements' upon the living and comforts of hundreds of their fellow-creatures, the changes of weather are frequently watched with a terrible interest. I am convinced that, altogether, a wet day deprives not less than 100,000, and probably nearer 200,000 people, including builders, bricklayers, and agricultural labourers, of their ordinary means of subsistence, and drives the same number to the public-houses and beer-shops (on this part of the subject I have collected some curious facts); thus not only decreasing their income, but positively increasing their expenditure, and that, perhaps, in the worst of ways.

Nor can there be fewer dependent on the winds for their bread. If we think of the vast number employed either directly or indirectly at the various ports of this country, and then remember that at each of these places the prevalence of a particular wind must prevent the ordinary arrival of shipping, and so require the employment of fewer hands, we shall have some idea of the enormous multitude of men in this country who can be starved by 'a nipping and an eager air'. If in London alone there are 20,000 people deprived of food by the prevalence of an easterly wind (and I had the calculation from one of the principal officers of the St Katherine Dock Company), surely it will not be too much to say that throughout the country there are not less than 50,000 people whose living is thus precariously dependent.

Altogether I am inclined to believe, that we shall not be over the truth if we assert there are between 100,000 and 200,000 individuals and their families, or half a million of people, dependent on the elements for their support in this country.

But this calculation refers to those classes only who are deprived of a certain number of *days'* work by an alteration of the weather, a cause that is essentially *ephemeral* in its character. The other series of natural events influencing the demand for labour in this country are of a more *continuous* nature – the stimulus and the depression enduring for weeks rather than days. I allude to the *second* of the four circumstances above-mentioned as inducing briskness or slackness of employment in different occupations, viz.:

(b) The seasons.

These are the seasons of the year, and not the arbitrary seasons of fashion, of which I shall speak next.

The following classes are among those exposed to the uncertainty of employment, and consequently of income, from the above cause, since it is only in particular seasons that particular works, such as buildings, will be undertaken, or that open-air pleasure excursions will be attempted: carpenters, builders, brickmakers, painters, plasterers, paper-hangers, rubbish-carters, sweeps, and riggers and lumpers, the latter depending mainly on the arrival of the timber ships to the Thames (and this, owing to the ice in the Baltic Sea and in the river St Lawrence, &c., takes place only at certain seasons of the year), coal-whippers and coal-porters (the coal trade being much brisker in winter), market-porters, and those employed in summer in steam-boat, railway, van, and barge excursions.

Then there are the casualties attending agricultural labour, for, although the operations of nature are regular 'even as the seed time follows the harvest', there is, almost invariably, a smaller employment of labour after the completion of the haymaking, the sheep-shearing, and the grain-reaping labours.

For the hay and corn harvests it is well known that there is a periodical immigration of Irishmen and women, who clamour for the *casual* employment; others, again, leave the towns for the same purpose; the same result takes place also in the fruit and pea-picking season for the London green-markets; while in the winter such people return some to their own country, and some to form a large proportion of the casual class in the metropolis. A tall Irishman of about 34 or 35 (whom I had to see when treating of the religion of the street Irish) leaves his accustomed crossing-sweeping at all or most of the seasons I have mentioned, and returns to it for the winter at the end of October; while his wife and children are then so many units to add to the casualties of the street sale of apples, nuts, and onions, by over-stocking the open-air markets.

The autumnal season of hop-picking is the grand rendezvous for the vagrancy of England and Ireland, the stream of London vagrancy flowing freely into Kent at that period, and afterwards flowing back with increased volume. Men, women, and children are attracted to the hop harvest. The season is over in less than a month, and then the casual labourers engaged in it (and they are nearly all casual labourers) must divert their industry, or their endeavours for a living, into other channels, swelling the amount of casualty in unskilled work or street-trade.

Numerically to estimate the influence of the seasons on the labour-market of this country is almost an overwhelming task. Let us try, however: there are in round numbers one million agricultural labourers in this country; saying that in the summer four labourers are employed for every three in the winter, there would be 250,000 people and their families, or say 1,000,000 of individuals, deprived of their ordinary subsistence in the winter time; this, of course, does not include those who come from Ireland to assist at the harvest-getting – how many these may be I have no means of ascertaining. Added to these there are the natural vagabonds, whom I have before estimated at another hundred thousand, and who generally help at the harvest work or the fruit or hop-picking.

Then there are the carpenters, who are 163,000 in number; the builders, 9,200; the brickmakers, 18,000; the painters, 48,200; the coal-whippers, 9,200; the coal-miners, 110,000; making altogether 350,000 people, and estimating that for every four hands employed in the brisk season, there are only three required in the slack, we have 80,000 more families, or 300,000 people, deprived of their living by the casualty of labour; so that if we assert that there are, at the least, including agricultural labourers, 1,250,000 people thus deprived of their usual means of living, we shall not be very wide of the truth.

The next cause of the briskness or slackness of different employments is –

(c) Fashion.

The London fashionable season is also the parliamentary season, and is the 'briskest' from about the end of February to the middle of July.

The workmen most affected by the aristocratic, popular, or general fashions, are –

Tailors, ladies' habit-makers, boot and shoe-makers, hatters, glovers, milliners, dress-makers, mantua-makers, drawn and straw bonnet-makers, artificial flower-makers, plumassiers, stay-makers, silk and velvet weavers, saddlers, harness-makers, coach-builders, cabmen, job-coachmen, farriers, livery stable keepers, poulterers, pastry-cooks, confectioners, &c., &c.

The above-mentioned classes may be taken, according to the Occupation Abstract of the last Census, at between 500,000 and 600,000; and, assuming the same ratio as to the difference of employment between the brisk and the slack seasons of the trades, or, in other words, that 25 per cent less hands are required at the slack than at the brisk time of these trades, we have another 150,000 people, who, with their families, may be estimated altogether at say 500,000, who are thrown out of work at a certain season, and have to starve on as best they can for at least three months in the year.

The last-mentioned of the causes inducing briskness or slackness of employment are –

(d) Commerce and Accidents.

Commerce has its periodical fits and starts. The publishers, for instance, have their season, generally from October to March, as people read more in winter than in summer; and this arrangement immediately effects the printers and book-binders; there is no change, however, as regards the newspapers and periodicals. Again, the early importation to this country of the new foreign fruits gives activity to the dock and wharf labourers and porters and carmen. Thus the arrival here, generally in autumn, of the nut, chestnut, and grape (raisin) produce of Spain; of the almond crops in Portugal, Spain, and Barbary; the date harvest in Morocco, and different parts of Africa; the orange gathering in Madeira, and in St Michael's, Terceira, and other islands of the Azores; the fig harvest from the Levant; the plum harvest of the south of France; the currant picking of Zante, Ithaca, and other Ionian Islands; – all these events give an activity, as new fruit is always most saleable, to the traders in these southern productions; and more shopmen, shop-porters, wharf labourers, and assistant lightermen are required – casually required – for the time.

I was told by a grocer, with a country connection, and in a large way of business, that for three weeks or a month before Christmas he required the aid of four fresh hands, a shopman, an errand-boy, and two porters (one skilled in packing), for whom he had nothing to do after Christmas. If in the wide sweep of London trade there be 1,000 persons, including the market salesmen, the retail butchers, the carriers, &c., so circumstanced, then 4,000 men are *casually* employed, and for a very brief time.

The brief increase of the carrying business generally about Christmas, by road, water, or railway, is sufficiently indicated by the foregoing account.

The employment, again, in the cotton and woollen manufacturing districts may be said to depend for its briskness on commerce rather than on the seasons.

Accidents, or extraordinary social events, promote casual labour and then depress it. Often they depress without having promoted it.

During the display of the Great Exhibition, there were some thousands employed in the different capacities of police, packing, cleaning, porterage, watching, interpreting, door-keeping and money-taking, cab-regulating, &c.; and after the close of the Exhibition how many were retained? Thus the Great Exhibition fostered casual, or uncertain labour. Foreign revolutions, moreover, affect the trade of England: speculators become timid and will not embark in trade or in any proposed undertaking; the foreign import and export trades are paralysed; and fewer clerks and fewer labourers are employed. Home political agitations, also, have the same effect. [. . .] Labour is affected also by the death of a member of the royal family, and the hurried demand for general mourning, but in a very small degree to what was once the case. A West-end tailor employing a great number of hands did not receive a single order for mourning on the death of Queen Adelaide; while on the demise of the Princess Charlotte (in 1817) thousands of operative tailors, throughout the three kingdoms, worked day and night, and for double wages, on the general mourning. Gluts in the markets, an increase of heavy bankruptcies and 'panics', such as were experienced in the money market in 1825–6, and again in 1846, with the failure of banks and merchants, likewise have the effect of augmenting the mass of casual labour; for capitalists and employers, under such circumstances, expend as little as possible in wages or employment until the storm blows over. Bad harvests have a similar depressing effect.

There are also the consequences of changes of taste. The abandonment of the fashions of gentlemen's wearing swords, as well as embroidered garments, flowing periwigs, large shoe-buckles, all reduced able artisans to poverty by depriving them of work. So it was, when, to carry on the war with France, Mr Pitt introduced a tax on hair powder. Hundreds of hair-dressers were thrown out of employment, many persons abandoning the fashion of wearing powder rather than pay the tax. There are now city gentlemen, who can remember that when clerks, they had sometimes to wait two or three hours for 'their turn' at a barber's shop on a Sunday morning; for they could not go abroad until their hair was dressed and powdered, and their queues trimmed to the due standard of fashion. So it has been, moreover, in modern times in the substitution of silk for metal buttons, silk hats for stuff, and in the supersedence of one material of dress by another.

These several causes, then, which could only exist in a community of great wealth and great poverty, have rendered, and are continually rendering, the labour market uncertain and over-stocked; to what extent they do and have done this, it is, of course, almost impossible to say *precisely*; but, ever with the strongest disposition to avoid exaggeration, we may assert that there are in this country no less than 125,000 families, or 500,000 people, who depend on the weather for their food; 300,000 families, or 1,250,000 people, who can obtain employment only at particular seasons; 150,000 more families, or 500,000 people, whose trade depends upon the fashionable rather than the natural seasons, are thrown out of work at the cessation of the brisk time of their business; and, perhaps, another 150,000 of families, or 500,000 people, dependent on the periodical increase and decrease of commerce, and certain social and political accidents which tend to cause a greater or less demand for labour. Altogether we may assert, with safety, that there are at the least 725,000 families, or three millions of men, women, and children, whose means of living, far from being certain and constant, are of a precarious kind, depending either upon the rain, the wind, the sunshine, the caprice of fashion, or the ebbings and flowings of commerce.

But there is a still more potent cause at work to increase the amount of *casual* labour in this country. Thus far we have proceeded on the assumption that at the brisk season of each trade there is full employment for all; but this is far from being the case in the great majority, if not the whole, of the instances above cited. In almost all occupations there is in this country a *superfluity of labourers*, and this alone would tend to render the employment of a vast number of the hands of a casual rather than a regular character. In the generality of trades the calculation is that one-third of the hands are fully employed, one-third partially, and one-third unemployed throughout the year. This, of course, would be the case if there were twice too many work-people; for suppose the number of work-people in a given trade to be 6,000, and the work sufficient to employ (fully) only half the quantity, then, of course, 2,000 might be occupied their whole time, 2,000 more might have work sufficient to occupy them half their time, and the remaining 2,000 have no work at all; or the whole 4,000 might, on the average, obtain three months' employment out of the twelve; and this is frequently the case. Hence we see that a surplusage of hands in a trade tends to change the employment of the great majority from a state of constancy and regularity into one of casualty and precariousness.

Consequently it becomes of the highest importance that we should endeavour to ascertain what are the circumstances inducing a surplusage of hands in the several trades of the present day. A *surplusage of hands* in a trade may proceed from three different causes, viz.:

1. The alteration of the hours, rate, or mode of working, or else the term of hiring.

2. The increase of the hands themselves.

3. The decrease of the work.

Each of these causes is essentially distinct; in the first case there is neither an increase in the number of hands nor a decrease in the quantity of work, and yet a surplusage of labourers is the consequence, for it is self-evident that if there be work enough in a given trade to occupy 6,000 men all the year round, labouring twelve hours per day for six days in the week, the same quantity of work will afford occupation to only 4,000 men, or one-third less, labouring between fifteen and sixteen hours per diem for seven days in the week. The same result would, of course, take place, if the workman were made to labour one-third more quickly, and so to get through one-third more work in the same time (either by increasing their interest in their work, by the invention of a new tool, by extra supervision, or by the subdivision of labour, &c., &c.); the same result would, of course, ensue as if they laboured one-third longer hours, viz., one-third of the hands must be thrown out of employment. So, again, by altering the *mode or form of work*, as by producing on the large scale, instead of the small, a smaller number of labourers are required to execute the same amount of work; and thus (if the market for such work be necessarily limited) a surplusage of labourers is the result. Hence we see that the alteration of the hours, rate, or mode of working may tend as positively to overstock a country with labourers as if the labourers themselves had unduly increased.

But this, of course, is on the assumption that both the quantity of work and the number of hands remain the same. The next of the three causes, above mentioned as inducing a surplusage of hands, is that which arises from a positive *increase in the number of labourers*, while the quantity of work remains the same or increases at a less rate than the labourers; and the third cause is, where the surplusage of labourers arises not from any alteration in the number of hands, but from a positive *decrease in the quantity of work*.

These are distinctions necessary to be borne clearly in mind for the proper understanding of this branch of the subject.

In the first case both the number of hands and the quantity of work remain the same, but the term, rate, or mode of working is changed.

In the second, hours, rate, or mode of working remain the same, as well as the quantity of work, but the number of hands is increased.

And in the third case, neither the number of hands nor the hours, rate, or mode of working is supposed to have been altered, but the work only to have decreased.

The surplusage of hands will, of course, be the same in each of these cases.

I will begin with the first, viz., that which induces a surplusage of labourers in a trade by enabling fewer hands to get through the ordinary amount of work. This is what is called the 'economy of labour'.

There are, of course, only three modes of economising labour, or causing the same quantity of work to be done by a smaller number of hands.

1st. By causing the men to work *longer*.

2nd. By causing the men to work *quicker*, and so get through more work in the same time.

3rd. By *altering the mode of work*, or hiring, as in the 'large system of production', where fewer hands are required; or the custom of temporary hirings, where the men are retained only so long as their services are needed, and discharged immediately afterwards.

First, of that mode of economising labour which depends on an *increase of either the ordinary hours or days for work*. This is what is usually termed over-work and Sunday-work, both of which are largely creative of surplus hands. The hours of labour in mechanical callings are usually twelve, two of them devoted to meals, or 72 hours (less by the permitted intervals) in a week. In the course of my inquiries for the *Chronicle*, I met with slop cabinet-makers, tailors, and milliners who worked sixteen hours and more daily, their toil being only interrupted by the necessity of going out, if small masters, to purchase materials, and offer the goods for sale; or, if journeymen in the slop trade, to obtain more work and carry what was completed to the master's shop. They worked on Sundays also; one tailor told me that the coat he worked at on the previous Sunday was for the Rev. Mr — , who 'little thought it', and these slop-workers rarely give above a few minutes to a meal. Thus they toil 40 hours beyond the hours usual in an honourable trade (112 hours instead of 72), in the course of a week, or between three and four days of the regular hours of work of the six working days. In other words, two such men will in less than a week accomplish work which should occupy three men a full week; or 1,000 men will execute labour fairly calculated to employ 1,500 at the least. A paucity of employment is thus caused among the general body, by this system of over-labour decreasing the share of work accruing to the several operatives, and so adding to surplus hands.

Of over-work, as regards excessive labour, both in the general and fancy cabinet trade, I heard the following accounts, which different operatives concurred in giving; while some represented the labour as of longer duration by at least an hour, and some by two hours, a day, than I have stated.

The labour of the men who depend entirely on 'the slaughter-houses' for the purchase of their articles is usually seven days a week the year through. That is, seven days – for Sunday-work is all but universal – each of 13 hours, or 91 hours in all; while the established hours of labour in the 'honourable trade' are six days of the week, each of 10 hours, or 60 hours in all. Thus 50 per cent is added to the extent of the production of low-priced cabinet-work, merely from 'over-hours'; but in some cases I heard of 15 hours for seven days in the week, or 105 hours in all.

Concerning the hours of labour in this trade, I had the following minute particulars from a garret-master who was a chair-maker:

'I work from six every morning to nine at night; some work till ten. My breakfast at eight stops me for ten minutes. I can break-fast in less time, but it's a rest; my dinner takes me say twenty minutes at the outside; and my tea, eight minutes. All the rest of the time I'm slaving at my bench. How many minutes' rest is that, sir? Thirty-eight; well, say three-quarters of an hour, and that allows a few sucks at a pipe when I rest; but I can smoke and work too. I have only one room to work and eat in, or I should lose more time. Altogether I labour 14 hours every day, and I must work on Sundays – at least 40 Sundays in the year. One may as well work as sit fretting. But on Sundays I only work till it's dusk, or till five or six in summer. When it's dusk I take a walk. I'm not well-dressed enough for a Sunday walk when it's light, and I can't wear my apron on that day very well to hide patches. But there's eight hours that I reckon I take up every week one with another, in dancing about to the slaughterers. I'm satisfied that I work very nearly 100 hours a week the year through; deducting the time taken up by the slaughterers, and buying stuff – say eight hours a week – it gives more than 90 hours a week for my work, and there's hundreds labour as hard as I do, just for a crust.'

The East-end turners generally, I was informed, when inquiring into the state of that trade, labour at the lathe from six o'clock in the morning till eleven and twelve at night, being 18 hours' work per day, or 108 hours per week. They allow themselves two hours for their meals. It takes them, upon an average, two hours more every day fetching and carrying their work home. Some of the East-end men work on Sundays, and not a few either, said my informant. 'Sometimes I have worked hard,' said one man, 'from six one morning till four the next, and scarcely had any time to take my meals in the bargain. I have been almost suffocated with the dust flying down my throat after working so many hours upon such heavy work too, and sweating so much. It makes a man drink where he would not.'

This system of over-work exists in the 'slop' part of almost every business – indeed, it is the principal means by which the cheap trade is maintained. Let me cite from my letters in the *Chronicle* some more of my experience on this subject. As regards the London mantua-makers, I said: 'The workwomen for good shops that give fair, or tolerably fair wages, and expect good work, can make six average-sized mantles in a week, *working from ten to twelve hours a day*; but the slop-workers, by toiling from thirteen to sixteen hours a day, will make *nine* such sized mantles in a week. In a season of twelve weeks 1,000 workers for the slop-houses and warehouses would at this rate make 108,000 mantles, or 36,000 more than workers for the fair trade. Or, to put it in another light, these slop-women, by being compelled, in order to live, to work such over-hours as inflict lasting injury on the health, supplant, by their over-work and over-hours, the labour of 500 hands, working the regular hours.'

The following are the words of a chamber-master, working for the cheap shoe trade:

'From people being obliged to work twice the hours they once *did* work, or that in reason they *ought* to work, a ghut of hands is the consequence, and the masters are led to make reductions in the wages. They take advantage of our poverty and lower the wages, so as to undersell each other, and command business. My daughters have to work fifteen hours a day that we may make a bare living. They seem to have no spirit and no animation in them; in fact, such very hard work takes the youth out of them. They have no time to enjoy their youth, and, with all their work, they can't present the respectable appearance they ought.' 'I' (interposed my informant's wife) 'often feel a faintness and oppression from my hard work, as if my blood did not circulate.'

The better class of artisans denounce the system of Sunday working as the most iniquitous of all the impositions. They object to it, not only on moral and religious grounds, but economically also. 'Every 600 men employed on the Sabbath,' say they, 'deprive 100 individuals of a week's work. Every six men who labour seven days in the week must necessarily throw one other man out of employ for a whole week. The seventh man is thus deprived of his fair share of work by the overtoiling of the other six.' This Sunday working is a necessary consequence of the cheap slop-trade. The workmen cannot keep their families by their six days' labour, and therefore they not only, under that system, get less wages and do more work, but by their extra labour throw so many more hands out of employment.

Here then, in the over-work of many of the trade, we find a vast cause of surplus hands, and, consequently, of casual labour; and that the work in these trades has not proportionately increased is proven by the fact of the existence of a superfluity of workmen.

Let us now turn our attention to the *second* of the causes above cited, viz., *the causing of men to work quicker*, and so to accomplish more in the same time. There are several means of attaining this end; it may be brought about either (a) by making the workman's gains depend directly on the quantity of work executed by him, as by the substitution of piece-work for day-work; (b) by the omission of certain details or parts necessary for the perfection of the work; (c) by decreasing the workman's pay, and so increasing the necessity for him to execute a greater quantity of work in order to obtain the same income; (d) by increasing the supervision, and encouraging a spirit of emulation among the workpeople; (e) by dividing the labour into a number of simple and minute processes, and so increasing the expertness of the labourers; (f) by the invention of some new tool or machine for expediting the operations of the workman.

I shall give a brief illustration of each of these causes *seriatim*, showing how they tend to produce a surplusage of hands in the trades to which they are severally applied. And first, as to *making the workman's gains depend directly on the quantity of work executed by him.*

Of course there are but two direct modes of paying for labour – either by the day or by the piece. Over-work by day-work is effected by means of what is called the 'strapping system' (as described in the *Morning Chronicle* in my letter upon the carpenters and joiners), where a whole shop are set to race over their work in silence one with another, each striving to outdo the rest, from the knowledge that anything short of extraordinary exertion will be sure to be punished with dismissal. Over-work by piece-work, on the other hand, is almost a necessary consequence of that mode of payment – for where men are paid by the quantity they do, of course it becomes the interest of a workman to do more than he otherwise would.

'Almost all who work by the day, or for a fixed salary, that is to say, those who labour for the gain of others, not for their own, have,' it has been well remarked, 'no interest in doing more than the smallest quantity of work that will pass as a fulfilment of the mere terms of their engagement. Owing to the insufficient interest which day labourers have in the result of their labour, there is a natural tendency in such labour to be extremely inefficient – a tendency only to be overcome by vigilant superintendence on the part of the persons who are interested in the result. The "master's eye" is notoriously the only security to be relied on. But superintend them as you will, day labourers are so much inferior to those who work by the piece, that, as was before said, the latter system is practised in all industrial occupations where the work admits of being put out in definite portions, without involving the necessity of too troublesome a surveillance to guard against inferiority (or scamping) in the execution.' But if the labourer at piece-work is made to produce a greater quantity than at day-work, and this solely by connecting his own interest with that of his employer, how much more largely must the productiveness of workmen be increased when labouring wholly on their own account! Accordingly it has been invariably found that when-ever the operative unites in himself the double function of capitalist and labourer, as the 'garret-master' in the cabinet trade, and the 'chamber-master' in the shoe trade, making up his own materials or working on his own property, his productiveness, single-handed, is considerably greater than can be attained even under the large system of production, where all the arts and appliances of which extensive capital can avail itself are brought into operation.

As regards the increased production by *omitting certain details necessary for the due perfection of the work*, it may be said that 'scamping' adds at least 200 per cent. to the productions of the cabinet-maker's trade. I ascertained, in the course of my previous inquiries, several cases of this over-work from scamping, and adduce two. A very quick hand, a little master, working, as he called it, 'at a slaughtering pace', for a warehouse, made 60 plain writing-desks in a week of 90 hours; while a first-rate workman, also a quick hand, made 18 in a week of 70 hours. The scamping hand said he must work at the rate he did to make 14s. a week from a slaughter-house; and so used to such style of work had he become, that, though a few years back he did West-end work in the best style, he could not now make eighteen desks in a week, if compelled to finish them in the style of excellence displayed in the work of the journeyman employed for the honourable trade. Perhaps, he added, he couldn't make them in that style at all. The frequent use of rosewood veneers in the fancy cabinet, and their occasional use in the general cabinet trade gives, I was told, great facilities for scamping. If in his haste the scamping hand injure the veneer, or if it have been originally faulty, he takes a mixture of gum shellac and 'colour' (colour being a composition of Venetian red and lamp black), which he has ready by him, rubs it over the damaged part, smooths it with a slightly-heated iron, and so blends it with the colour of the rosewood that the warehouseman does not detect the flaw. In the general, as contradistinguished from the fancy, cabinet trade I found the same ratio of 'scamping'. A good workman in the better-paid trade made a four-foot mahogany chest of drawers in five days, working the regular hours, and receiving, at piece-work price, 35s. A scamping hand made five of the same size in a week, and had time to carry them for sale to the warehouses, wait for their purchase or refusal, and buy material. But for the necessity of doing this the scamping hand could have made seven in the 91 hours of his week, though of course in a very inferior manner. 'They would hold together for a time,' I was assured, 'and that was all; but the slaughterer cared only to have them viewly and cheap.' These two cases exceed the average, and I have cited them to show what can be done under the scamping system.

We now come to the *increased rate of working induced by a reduction of the ordinary rate of remuneration of the workman.* Not only is it true that over-work makes under-pay, but the converse of the proposition is equally true, that under-pay makes over-work – that is to say, it is true of those trades where the system of piece-work or small mastership admits of the operative doing the utmost amount of work that he is able to accomplish; for the workman in such cases seldom or never thinks of reducing his expenditure to his income, but rather of increasing his labour, so as still to bring his income, by extra production, up to his expenditure. Hence we find that, as the wages of a trade descend, so do the labourers extend their hours of work to the utmost possible limits – they not only toil earlier and later than before, but the Sunday becomes a work-day like the rest (amongst the 'sweaters' of the tailoring trade Sunday labour, as I have shown, is almost universal); and when the hours of work are carried to the extreme of human industry, then more is sought to be done in a given space of time, either by the employment of the members of their own family, or apprentices, upon the inferior portion of the work, or else by 'scamping it'. 'My employer,' I was told by a journeyman tailor working for the Messrs. Nicoll, 'reduces my wages one-third, and the consequence is, I put in two stitches where I used to give three.' 'I must work from six to eight, and later,' said a pembroke-table-maker to me, 'to get 18s. now for my labour, where I used to get 54s. a week – that's just a third. I could in the old times give my children good schooling and good meals. Now children have to be put to work very young. I have four sons working for me at present. Not only, therefore, does any stimulus to extra production make over-work, and over-work make under-pay; but under-pay, by becoming an additional provocative to increased industry, again gives rise in its turn to over-work. Hence we arrive at a plain unerring law – *over-work makes under-pay and under-pay makes over-work.*

But the above means of increasing the rate of working refer solely to those cases where the extra labour is induced by making it the *interest* of the workman so to do. The other means of extra production is *by stricter supervision of journeymen, or those paid by the day.* The shops where this system is enforced are termed 'strapping-shops', as indicative of establishments where an undue quantity of work is expected from a journeyman in the course of the day. Such shops, though not directly making use of cheap labour (for the wages paid in them are generally of the higher rate), still, by exacting more work, may of course be said, in strictness, to encourage the system now becoming general, of less pay and inferior skill. These strapping establishments sometimes go by the name of 'scamping shops', on account of the time allowed for the manufacture of the different articles not being sufficient to admit of good workmanship.

Concerning this '*strapping*' system I received the following extra-ordinary account from a man after his heavy day's labour. Never in all my experience had I seen so sad an instance of over-work. The poor fellow was so fatigued that he could hardly rest in his seat. As he spoke he sighed deeply and heavily, and appeared almost spirit-broken with excessive labour:

'I work at what is called a strapping shop,' he said, 'and have worked at nothing else for these many years past in London. I call "strapping" doing as much work as a human being or a horse possibly can in a day, and that without any hanging upon the collar, but with the foreman's eyes constantly fixed upon you, from six o'clock in the morning to six o'clock at night. The shop in which I work is for all the world like a prison; the silent system is as strictly carried out there as in a model gaol. If a man was to ask any common question of his neighbour, except it was connected with his trade, he would be discharged there and then. If a journeyman makes the least mistake, he is packed off just the same.

A man working at such places is almost always in fear; for the most trifling things he's thrown out of work in an instant. And then the quantity of work that one is forced to get through is positively awful; if he can't do a plenty of it, he don't stop long where I am. No-one would think it was possible to get so much out of blood and bones. No slaves work like we do. At some of the strapping shops the foreman keeps continually walking about with his eyes on all the men at once. At others the foreman is perched high up, so that he can have the whole of the men under his eye together. I suppose since I knew the trade that *a man does four times the work that he did formerly*. I know a man that's done four pairs of sashes in a day, and one is considered to be a good day's labour. What's worse than all, the men are every one striving one against the other. Each is trying to get through the work quicker than his neighbours. Four or five men are set the same job, so that they may be all pitted against one another, and then away they go every one striving his hardest for fear that the others should get finished first. They are all tearing along from the first thing in the morning to the last at night, as hard as they can go, and when the time comes to knock off they are ready to drop. I was hours after I got home last night before I could get a wink of sleep; the soles of my feet were on fire, and my arms ached to that degree that I could hardly lift my hand to my head. Often, too, when we get up of a morning, we are more tired than when we went to bed, for we can't sleep many a night; but we mustn't let our employers know it, or else they'd be certain we couldn't do enough for them, and we'd get the sack. So, tired as we may be, we are obliged to look lively, somehow or other, at the shop of a morning. If we're not beside our bench the very moment the bell's done ringing, our time's docked – they won't give us a single minute out of the hour. If I was working for a fair master, I should do nearly one-third, and sometimes a half, less work than I am now forced to get through, and, even to manage that much, I shouldn't be idle a second of my time. It's quite a mystery to me how they *do* contrive to get so much work out of the men. But they are very clever people. They know how to have the most out of a man, better than any one in the world. They are all picked men in the shop – regular "strappers", and no mistake. The most of them are five foot ten, and fine broad-shouldered, strong-backed fellows too – if they weren't they wouldn't have them. Bless you, they make no words with the men, they sack them if they're not strong enough to do all they want; and they can pretty soon tell, the very first shaving a man strikes in the shop, what a chap is made of. Some men are done up at such work – quite old men and grey with spectacles on, by the time they are forty. I have seen fine strong men, of 36, come in there and be bent double in two or three years. They are most all countrymen at the strapping shops. If they see a great strapping fellow, who they think has got some stuff about him that will come out, they will give him a job directly. We are used for all the world like cab or omnibus horses. Directly they've had all the work out of us, we are turned off, and I am sure, after my day's work is over, my feelings must be very much the same as one of the London cab horses. As for Sunday, it is *literally* a day of rest with us, for the greater part of us lay a-bed all day, and even that will hardly take the aches and pains out of our bones and muscles. When I'm done and flung by, of course I must starve.'

The next means of inducing a quicker rate of working, and so economising the number of labourers, is by the *division* and *sub-division of labour*. In perhaps all the skilled work of London, of the better sort, this is more or less the case; it is the case in a much smaller degree in the country.

The nice subdivision makes the operatives perfect adepts in their respective branches, working at them with a greater and a more assured facility than if their care had to be given to the whole work, and in this manner the work is completed in less time, and consequently by fewer hands.

In illustration of the extraordinary increased productiveness induced by the division of labour, I need only cite the well-known cases:

'It is found,' says Mr Mill, 'that the productive power of labour is increased by carrying the separation further and further; by breaking down more and more every process of industry into parts, so that each labourer shall confine himself to an even smaller number of simple operations. And thus, in time, arise those remarkable cases of what is called the division of labour, with which all readers on subjects of this nature are familiar. Adam Smith's illustration from pin-making, though so well-known, is so much to the point, that I will venture once more to transcribe it.

"The business of making a pin is divided into eighteen distinct operations. One man draws out the wire, another straightens it, a third cuts it, a fourth points it, and a fifth grinds it at the top for receiving the head; to make the head requires two or three distinct operations; to put it on, is a peculiar business; to whiten the pins is another; it is even a trade by itself to put them into the paper. I have seen a small manufactory where ten men only were employed, and where some of them, consequently, performed two or three distinct operations. But though they were very poor, and therefore but indifferently accommodated with the necessary machinery, they could, when they exerted themselves, make among them about twelve pounds of pins in a day. There are in a pound upwards of 4,000 pins of a middling size.

' "Those ten persons, therefore, could make among them upwards of 48,000 pins in a day. Each person, therefore, making a tenth part of 48,000 pins, might be considered as making 4,800 pins in a day. But if they had all wrought separately and independently, and without any of them having been educated to this peculiar business, they certainly could not each of them have made 20, perhaps not one pin in a day." '

M. Say furnishes a still stronger example of the effects of division of labour, from a not very important branch of industry certainly, the manufacture of playing cards. 'It is said by those engaged in the business, that each card, that is, a piece of pasteboard of the size of the hand, before being ready for sale, does not undergo fewer than 70 operations, every one of which might be the occupation of a distinct class of workmen. And if there are not 70 classes of workpeople in each card manufactory, it is because the division of labour is not carried so far as it might be; because the same workman is charged with two, three, or four distinct operations. The influence of this distribution of employment is immense. I have seen a card manufactory where thirty workmen produced daily 15,500 cards, being above 500 cards for each labourer; and it may be presumed that if each of these workmen were obliged to perform all the operations himself, even supposing him a practised hand, he would not, perhaps, complete two cards in a day; and the 30 workmen, instead of 15,500 cards, would make only 60.'

One great promoter of the decrease of manual labour is to be found in the economy of labour from a very different cause to any

I have pointed out as tending to the increase of surplus hands and casual labour, viz., *to the use of machinery*.

In this country the use of machinery has economised the labour both of man and horse to a greater extent than is known in any other land, and that in nearly all departments of commerce or traffic. The total estimated machine power in the kingdom is 600,000,000 of human beings, and this has been all produced within the last century. In agriculture, for example, the threshing of the corn was the peasant's work of the later autumn and of a great part of the winter, until towards the latter part of the last century. The harvest was hardly considered complete until the corn was threshed by the peasants. On the first introduction of the threshing machines, they were demolished in many places by the country labourers, whose rage was excited to find that their winter's work, instead of being regular, had become *casual*.

But the use of these machines is now almost universal. It would, of course, be the height of absurdity to say that threshing machines could possibly increase the number of threshers, even as the reaping machines cannot possibly increase the number of reapers; their effect is rather to displace the greater number of labourers so engaged, and hence indeed the 'economy' of them. It is not known what number of men were, at any time, employed in threshing corn. Their displacement was gradual, and in some of the more remote parts of the provinces, the flails of the threshers may be heard still, but if a threshing machine – for they are of different power – do the work, as has been stated, of six labourers, the economisation or displacement of manual labour is at once shown to be the economisation and displacement of the whole labour (for a season) of a country side; thus increasing surplus hands.

In other matters – in the unloading vessels by cranes, in *all* branches of manufactures, and even in such minor matters as the grinding of coffee berries, and the cutting and splitting of wood for lucifer matches, an immense amount of manual labour has been minimised, economised, or displaced by steam machinery. On my inquiry into the condition of the London sawyers, I found that the labour of 2,000 men had been displaced by the steam saw-mills of the metropolis alone. At one of the largest builder's I saw machines for making mortises and tenons, for sticking mouldings, and, indeed, performing all the operations of the carpenter – one such machine doing the work, perhaps, of a hundred men. I asked the probable influence that such an instrument was likely to have on the men? 'Ruin them all,' was the laconic reply of the superintendent of the business! Within the last year casks have been made by machinery – a feat that the coopers declared impossible. Wheels, also, have been lately produced by steam. I need, however, as I have so recently touched upon the subject, do no more than call attention to the information I have given concerning the use of machinery in lieu of human labour. It is there shown that if the public street-sweeping were effected, throughout the metropolis, by the machines, nearly 196 of the 275 manual labourers, now scavaging for the parish contractors, would be thrown out of work, and deprived of 7438*l.*, out of their joint earnings, in the year.

It is the fashion of political economists to insist on the general proposition that machinery increases the demand for labour, rather than decreases it; when they write unguardedly, however, they invariably betray a consciousness that the benefits of machinery to manual labourers are not quite so invariable as they would otherwise make out. [. . .]

It must, then, be admitted that machinery, *in some cases at least*, does displace manual labour, and so tend to produce a surplusage of labourers, even as over-work, Sunday-work, scamping-work, strapping-work, piece-work, minutely-divided work, &c., have the same effect so long as the quantity of work to be done remains unaltered. *The extensibility of the market* is the one circumstance which determines whether the economy of labour produced by these means is a blessing or a curse to the nation. To apply mechanical power, the division of labour, the large system of production, or indeed any other means of enabling a less number of labourers to do the same amount of work *when the quantity of work to be done is limited in its nature*, as, for instance, the threshing of corn, the sawing of wood, &c., is necessarily to make either paupers or criminals of those who were previously honest independent men, living by the exercise of their industry in that particular direction. Economise your labour one-half, in connection with a particular article, and you must sell twice the quantity of that article or displace a certain number of the labourers; that is to say, suppose it requires 400 men to produce 4,000 commodities in a given time, then, if you enable 200 men to produce the same quantity in the same time, you must get rid of 8,000 commodities, or deprive a certain number of labourers of their ordinary means of living. Indeed, the proposition is almost self-evident, though generally ignored by social philosophers: economise your labour at a greater rate than you expand your markets, and you must necessarily increase your paupers and criminals in precisely the same ratio. 'The division of labour,' says Mr Mill, following Adam Smith, 'is limited by the extent of the market. If by the separation of pin-making into ten distinct employments 48,000 pins can be made in a day, this separation will only be advisable if the number of accessible consumers is such as to require every day something like 48,000 pins. If there is a demand for only 25,000, the division of labour can be advantageously carried out to the extent which will every day produce that smaller number.' Again, as regards the large system of production, the same authority says, 'the possibility of substituting the large system of production for the small depends, of course, on the extent of the market. The large system can only be advantageous when a large amount of business is to be done; it implies, therefore, either a populous and flourishing community, or a great opening for exportation.' But these are mere glimmerings of the broad incontrovertible principle, that *the economisation of labour at a greater rate than the expansion of the markets, is necessarily the cause of surplus labour in a community*.

The effect of machinery in depriving the families of agricultural labourers of their ordinary sources of income is well established. 'Those countries,' writes Mr Thornton, 'in which the class of agricultural labourers is most depressed, have all one thing in common. Each of them was formerly the seat of a flourishing manufacture carried on by the cottagers at their own homes, which has now decayed or been withdrawn to other situations. Thus, in Buckinghamshire and Bedfordshire, the wives and children of labouring men had formerly very profitable occupation in making lace; during the last war a tolerable lace-maker, working eight hours a day, could easily earn 10s. or 12s. a week; the profits of this employment have been since so much reduced by the use of machinery, that a pillow lace-maker must now work twelve hours daily to earn 2s. 6d. a week.'

The last of the conditions above cited, as causing the same or a greater amount of work to be executed with a less quantity of labour, is *the large system of production*. Mr Babbage and Mr Mill have so well and fully pointed out 'the economy of labour' effected in this manner. [. . .]

We now come to the last-mentioned of the circumstances inducing a surplusage of labourers, and, consequently, augmenting the amount of casual labour throughout the kingdom, viz., by *altering the mode of hiring the labourers*. [. . .]

Formerly the mode of hiring farm-labourers was by the year, so that the employer was bound to maintain the men when unemployed. But now weekly hirelings and even journey-work, or hiring by the day, prevail, and the labourers being paid mere subsistence-money only when wanted are necessitated to become either paupers or thieves when their services are no longer required. It is, moreover, this change from yearly to weekly and daily hirings, and the consequent discarding of men when no longer wanted, that has partly caused the immense mass of surplus labourers, who are continually vagabondising through the country, begging or stealing as they go – men for whom there is but some two or three weeks' work (harvesting. hop-picking, and the like) throughout the year. [. . .]

Mr Thornton says, 'until recently it had been common for farm servants, even when married and living in their own cottages, to take their meals with their master; and, what was of more consequence, in every farm-house, many unmarried servants, of both sexes, were lodged, as well as boarded. The latter, therefore, even if ill paid, might be tolerably housed and fed, and many of them fared, no doubt, much better than they could have done if they had been left to provide for themselves, with treble their actual wages.'

Formerly throughout the kingdom – and it is a custom *still* prevalent in some parts, more especially in the north – single men and women seeking engagements as farm-servants, congregated at what were called the 'Hirings', held usually on the three successive market days which were nearest to May-day and Martinmas-day. The hiring was thus at two periods of the year, but the engagement was usually for the twelvemonth. By the concurrent consent, however, of master and servant, when the hiring took place, either side might terminate it at the expiration of the six months, by giving due notice; or a further hiring for a second twelvemonth could be legally effected without the necessity of again going to the hirings. The servants, even before their term of service had expired, could attend a hiring (generally held under the authority of the town's charter) as a matter of right; the master and mistress having no authority to prevent them. The Market Cross was the central point for the holding of the hirings, and the men and women, the latter usually the most numerous, stood in rows around the cross. The terms being settled, the master or mistress gave the servant 'a piece of money', known as a 'god's penny' (the 'handsel penny'), the offer and acceptance of this god's penny being a legal ratification of the agreement, without any other step. In the old times such engagements had almost always (as shown in the term 'God's penny') a character of religious obligation. At the earliest period, the hirings were held in the church-yards; afterwards by the Market Cross.

I have spoken of this matter more in the past than the present tense, for the system is greatly changed as regards the male farm-servant, though little as regards the female. Now the male farm-labourers, instead of being hired for a specific term, are more generally hired by week, by job, or by day; indeed, even 'half-a-day's' work is known. At one period it was merely the married country labourers, residing in their own cottages, who were temporarily engaged, but it is now the general body, married and unmarried, old and young, with a few exceptions. Formerly the farmer was bound to find work for six or twelve months (for both terms existed) for his hired labourers. If the land did not supply it, still the man must be maintained, and be paid his full wages when due. By such a provision, the labour and wage of the hired husbandman were regular and rarely *casual*; but this arrangement is now seldom entered into, and the hired husbandman's labour is consequently generally casual and rarely regular. This principle of hiring labourers only for so long as they are wanted, as contra-distinguished from the '*principle of natural equity*', spoken of by Blackstone, which requires that 'the servant shall serve and the master maintain him *throughout all the revolutions of the respective seasons, as well when there is work to be done as when there is not*', has been the cause, perhaps, of more casual labour and more

pauperism and crime, in this country, than, perhaps, any other of
the antecedents before mentioned. The harvest is now collected
solely by casual labourers, by a horde of squalid immigrants, or
the tribe of natural and forced vagabonds who are continually
begging or stealing their way throughout the country; our hops
are picked, our fruit and vegetables gathered by the same precarious bands – wretches who, perhaps, obtain some three months'
harvest labour in the course of the year. The ships at our several
ports are discharged by the same 'casual hands', who may be seen
at our docks scrambling like hounds for the occasional bit of
bread that is vouchsafed to them; there numbers loiter throughout the day, even on the chance of an hour's employment; for the
term of hiring has been cut down to the finest possible limits, so
that the labourer may not be paid for even a second longer than
he is wanted. And since he gets only bare subsistence money
when employed, 'What,' we should ask ourselves, 'must be his
lot when unemployed?'

I now come to consider the circumstances causing an undue
increase of the labourers in a country. Thus far we have proceeded
on the assumption that both the quantity of work to be done and
the number of hands to do it remained stationary, and we have
seen that by the mere alteration of the time, rate, and mode of
working, a vast amount of surplus, and, consequently, casual
labour may be induced in a community. We have now to
ascertain how, still assuming the quantity of work to remain
unaltered, the same effect may be brought about by an undue
increase of the number of labourers.

There are many means by which the number of labourers may
be increased besides that of a positive increase of the people.
These are –

1. By the undue increase of apprentices.
2. By drafting into the ranks of labour those who should be
otherwise engaged, as women and children.
3. By the importation of labourers from abroad.
4. By the migration of country labourers to towns, and so
overcrowding the market in the cities.
5. By the depression of other trades.
6. By the undue increase of the people themselves.

Each and every of the first-mentioned causes are as effective a circumstance for the promotion of surplus labour, as even the positive extension of the population of the country.

Let me begin with the undue increase of a trade by means of *apprentices*.

This is, perhaps, one of the chief aids to the cheap system. For it is principally by apprentice labour that the better masters, as well as workmen, are undersold, and the skilled labourer consequently depressed to the level of the unskilled. But the great evil is, that the cheapening of goods by this means causes an undue increase in the trade. The apprentices grow up and become labourers, and so the trade is glutted with workmen, and casual labour is the consequence.

This apprentice system is the great bane of the printer's trade. Country printers take an undue number of boys to help them cheap; these lads grow up, and then, finding wages in the provinces depressed through this system of apprentice labour, they flock to the towns, and so tend to glut the labour market, and consequently to increase the number of casual hands.

One cause of the increased surplus and casual labour in such trades as dressing-case, work-box, writing-desk-making and other things in the fancy cabinet trade (among the worst trades even in Spitalfields and Bethnal Green), shoemaking, and especially of women and children's shoes, is the taking of many apprentices by small masters (supplying the great warehouses). As journey-work is all but unknown in the slop fancy cabinet trade, an apprentice, when he has 'served his time', must start on his own account in the same wretched way of business, or become a casual labourer in some unskilled avocation, and this is one way in which the hands surely, although gradually, increase beyond the demand. It is the same with the general slop cabinet-maker's trade in the same parts. The small masters supply the 'slaughter-houses', the linen-drapers, &c., who sell cheap furniture; they work in the quickest and most scamping manner, and do more work (which is nearly all done on the chance of sale), as they must confine themselves to one branch. The slop chair-makers cannot make tables, nor the slop table-makers, chairs; nor the chiffonier and drawer-makers, bedsteads; for they have not been taught. Even if they knew the method, and *could* accomplish other work, the want of practice would compel them to do it slowly, and the slop mechanic can never afford to work slowly. Such classes of little masters, then, to meet the demand for low-priced furniture, rear their sons to the business, and frequently take apprentices, to whom they pay small amounts. The hands so trained (as in the former instances) are not skilled enough to work for the honourable trade, so that they can only adopt the course pursued by their parents, or masters, before them. Hence a rapid, although again gradual, increase of surplus hands; or hence a resort to some unskilled labour, to be wrought casually. This happens too, but in a smaller degree, in trades which are not slop, from the same cause. Concerning the *apprentice system* in the boot and shoe trade, when making my inquiries into the condition of the London workmen, I received the following statements:

'My employer had seven apprentices when I was with him; of these, two were parish apprentices (I was one), and the other five from the Refuge for the Destitute, at Hoxton. With each Refuge boy he got 5*l*. and three suits of clothes, and a kit [tools]. With the parish boys of Covent-garden and St Andrew's, Holborn, he got 5*l*. and two suits of clothes, reckoning what the boy wore as one. My employer was a journeyman, and by having all us boys he was able to get up work very cheap, though he received good wages for it. We boys had no allowance in money, only board, lodging, and clothing. The board was middling, the lodging was too, and there was nothing to complain about in the clothing. He was severe in the way of flogging. I ran away six times myself, but was forced to go back again, as I had no money and no friend in the world. When I first ran away I complained to Mr — the magistrate, and he was going to give me six weeks. He said it would do me good; but Mr — interfered, and I was let go. I don't know what he was going to give me six weeks for, unless it was for having a black eye that my master had given me with the stirrup. Of the seven only one served his time out. He let me off two years before my time was up, as we couldn't agree. The mischief of taking so many apprentices is this: the master gets money with them from the parish, and can feed them much as he likes as to quality and quantity; and if they run away soon, the master's none the worse, for he's got the money; and so boys are sent out to turn vagrants when they run away, as such boys have no friends. Of us seven boys (at the wages our employer got) one could earn 19*s*., another 15s., another 12s., another 10s., and the rest not less than 8s. each, for all worked sixteen hours a day – that's 4l. 8s. a week for the seven, or 225l. 10s. a year. You must recollect I reckon this on nearly the best wages in the women's trade. My employer you may call a sweater, and he made money fast, though he drank a good deal. We seldom saw him when he was drunk; but he did pitch into us when he was getting sober. Look how easily such a man with apprentices can undersell others when he wants to work as cheap as possible for the great slop warehouses. They serve haberdashers so cheap that oft enough it's starvation wages for the same shops.'

Akin to the system of using a large number of apprentices is that of *employing boys and girls* to displace the work of men, at the less laborious parts of the trade.

'It is probable,' said a working shoemaker to me, 'that, independent of apprentices, 200 additional hands are added to our already over-burdened trade yearly. Sewing boys soon learn the use of the knife. Plenty of poor men will offer to finish them for a pound and a month's work; and men, for a few shillings and a few weeks' work, will teach other boys to sew. There are many of the wives of chamber-masters teach girls entirely to make children's work for a pound and a few months' work, and there are many in Bethnal-green who have learnt the business in this way. These teach some other members of their families, and then actually set up in business in opposition to those who taught them, and in cutting offer their work for sale at a much lower rate of profit; and shopkeepers in town and country, having circulars sent to solicit custom, will have their goods from a warehouse that will serve them cheapest; then the warehouseman will have them cheap from the manufacturer; and he in his turn cuts down the wages of the work-people, who fear to refuse offers at the warehouse price, knowing the low rate at which chamber-masters will serve the warehouse.'

As in all trades where lowness of wages is the rule, the boy system of labour prevails among the cheap cabinet-workers. It prevails, however, among the garret-masters, by very many of them having one, two, three or four youths to help them, and so the number of boys thus employed through the whole trade is considerable. This refers principally to the general cabinet trade.

In the fancy trade the number is greater, as the boys' labour is more readily available; but in this trade the greatest number of apprentices is employed by such warehousemen as are manufacturers, as some at the East-end are, or rather by the men that they constantly keep at work. Of these men, one has now eight and another fourteen boys in his service, some apprenticed, some merely 'engaged and dischargeable at pleasure'. A sharp boy, in six or eight months, becomes 'handy'; but four out of five of the workmen thus brought up can do nothing well but their own particular branch, and that only well as far as celerity in production is considered.

It is these boys who are put to make, or as a master of the better class distinguished to me, not to make but to put together, ladies' work-boxes at 5d. a piece, the boy receiving 2½ d. a box. 'Such boxes,' said another workman, 'are nailed together; there's no dove-tailing, nothing of what I call work, or workmanship, as you say, about them, but the deal's nailed together, and the veneer's dabbed on, and if the deal's covered, why the thing passes. The worst of it is, that people don't understand either good work or good wood. Polish them up and they look well. Besides – and that's another bad thing, for it encourages bad work – there's no stress on a lady's work-box, as on a chair or a sofa, and so bad work lasts far too long, though not half so long as good; in solids especially, if not in veneers.'

To such a pitch is this demand for children's labour carried, that there is a market in Bethnal-green, where boys and girls stand twice a week to be hired as binders and sewers. Hence it will be easily understood that it is impossible for the skilled and grown artisan to compete with the labour of mere children, who are thus literally brought into the market to undersell him!

Concerning this market for boys and girls, in Bethnal-green, I received, during my inquiries into the boot and shoe trade, the following statements from shopkeepers on the spot:

'Mr H— has lived there sixteen years. The market-days are Monday and Tuesday mornings, from seven to nine. The ages of persons who assemble there vary from ten to twenty, and they are often of the worst character, and a decideded nuisance to the inhabitants. A great many of both sexes congregate together, and most market days there are three females to one male. They consist of sewing boys, shoe-binders, winders for weavers, and girls for all kinds of slop needle-work, girls for domestic work, nursing children, &c. No one can testify, for a fact, that they [the females] are prostitutes; but, by their general conduct, they are fit for anything. The market, some years since, was held at the top of Abbey-street; but, on account of the nuisance, it was removed to the other end of Abbey-street. When the schools were built, the nuisance became so intolerable that it was removed to a railway arch in White-street, Bethnal-green. There are two policemen on market mornings to keep order, but my informant says they require four to maintain anything like subjection.'

But *family work, or the conjoint labour of a workman's wife and children*, is an equally extensive cause of surplus and casual labour.

A small master, working, perhaps, upon goods to be supplied at the lowest rates to wholesale warehousemen, will often contribute to this result by the way in which he brings up his children. It is less expensive to him to teach them his own business, and he may even reap a profit from their labour, than to have them brought up to some other calling. I met with an instance of this in an inquiry among the toy-makers. A maker of common toys brought up five children to his own trade, for boys and girls can be made useful in such labour at an early age. His business fell off rapidly, which he attributed to the great and numerous packages of cheap toys imported from Germany, Holland, and France, after the lowering of the duty by Sir Robert Peel's tariff. The chief profit to the toy-maker was derived from the labour, as the material was of trifling cost. He found, on the change in his trade, that he could not employ all his family. His fellow tradesmen, he said, were in the same predicament; and thus surplus hands were created, so leading to casualty in labour.

'The system which has, I believe, the worst effect on the women's trade in the boot and shoe business throughout England is,' I said in the *Morning Chronicle*, 'chamber-mastering. There are between 300 and 400 chamber-masters. Commonly the man has a wife, and three or four children, ten years old or upwards. The wife cuts out the work for the binders, the husband does the knife-work, the children sew with uncommon rapidity. The husband, when the work is finished at night, goes out with it, though wet and cold, and perhaps hungry – his wife and children waiting his return. He returns sometimes, having sold his work at cost price, or not cleared 1s. 6d. for the day's labour of himself and family. In the winter, by this means, the shopkeepers and warehouses can take the advantage of the chamber-master, buying the work at their own price. By this means haberdashers' shops are supplied with boots, shoes, and slippers; they can sell women's boots at 1s. 9d. per pair; shoes, 1s. 3d. per pair; children's 6d., 8d., and 9d. per pair, getting a good profit, having bought them of the poor chamber-master for almost nothing, and he glad to sell them at any price, late at night, his children wanting bread, and he having walked about for hours, in vain trying to get a fair price for them; thus, women and children labour as well as husbands and fathers, and, with their combined labours, they only obtain a miserable living.'

The labour of the wife, and indeed the whole family – family work, as it is called – is attended with the same evil to a trade, introducing a large supply of fresh hands to the labour market, and so tending to glut with workpeople each trade into which they are introduced, and thus to increase the casual labour, and decrease the earnings of the whole.

'The only means of escape from the inevitable poverty,' I said in the same letters, 'which sooner or later overwhelms those in connection with the cheap shoe trade, seems to the workmen to be by the employment of his whole family as soon as his children are able to be put to the trade – and yet this only increases the very depression that he seeks to avoid. I give the statement of such a man residing in the suburbs of London, and working with three girls to help him:

' "I have known the business," he said, "many years, but was not brought up to it. I took it up because my wife's father was in the trade, and taught me. I was a weaver originally, but it is a bad business, and I have been in this trade seventeen years. Then I had only my wife and myself able to work. At that time my wife and I, by hard work, could earn 1l. a week; on the same work we could not now earn 12s. a week. As soon as the children grew old enough the falling off in the wages compelled us to put them to work one by one – as soon as a child could make threads. One began to do that between eight and nine. I have had a large family, and with very hard work too. We have had to lie on straw oft enough. Now, three daughters, my wife, and myself work together, in chamber-mastering; the whole of us may earn, one week with another, 28s. a week, and out of that I have eight to support. Out of that 28s. I have to pay for grindery and candles, which cost me 1s. a week the year through. I now make children's shoes for the wholesale houses and anybody. About two years ago I travelled from Thomas-street, Bethnal-green, to Oxford-street, 'on the hawk'. I then positively had nothing in my inside, and in Holborn I had to lean against a house, through weakness from hunger. I was compelled, as I could sell nothing at that end of the town, to walk down to Whitechapel at ten at night. I went into a shop near Mile-end turn-pike, and the same articles [children's patent leather shoes] that I received 8s. a dozen for from the wholesale houses, I was compelled to sell to the shopkeeper for 6s. 6d. This is a very frequent case – very frequent – with persons circumstanced as I am, and so trade is injured and only some hard man gains by it." '

Here is the statement of a worker at 'fancy cabinet' work on the same subject:

'The most on us has got large families. We put the children to work as soon as we can. My little girl began about six, but about eight or nine is the usual age.' *'Oh, poor little things,' said the wife, 'they are obliged to begin the very minute they can use their fingers at all.'* 'The most of the cabinet-makers of the East-end have from five to six in family, and they are generally all at work for them. The small masters mostly marry when they are turned of 20. You see our trade's coming to such a pass, that unless a man has children to help him he can't live at all. *I've worked more than a month together, and the longest night's rest I've had has been an hour and a quarter; aye, and I've been up three nights a week besides.* I've had my children lying ill, and been obliged to wait on them into the bargain. You see, we couldn't live if it wasn't for the labour of our children, though it makes 'em – poor little things! – old people long afore they are growed up.'

'Why, I stood at this bench,' said the wife, 'with my child, only ten years of age, from four o'clock on Friday morning till ten minutes past seven in the evening, without a bit to eat or drink. I never sat down a minute from the time I began till I finished my work, and then I went out to sell what I had done. I walked all the way from here [Shoreditch] down to the Lowther Arcade, to get rid of the articles.' *Here she burst out in a violent flood of tears, saying, 'Oh, sir, it is hard to be obliged to labour from morning till night as we do, all of us, little ones and all, and yet not be able to live by it either.*

'And you see the worst of it is, this here children's labour is of such value now in our trade, that there's more brought into the business every year, so that it's really for all the world like breeding slaves. Without my children I don't know how we should be able to get along.'

'There's that little thing,' said the man, pointing to the girl ten years of age before alluded to, as she sat at the edge of the bed, 'why she works regularly every day from six in the morning till ten at night. She never goes to school. We can't spare her. There's schools enough about here for a penny a week, but we could not afford to keep her without working. If I'd ten more children I should be obliged to employ them all the same way, and there's hundreds and thousands of children now slaving at this business. There's the M—s; they have a family of eight, and the youngest to the oldest of all works at the bench; and the oldest ain't fourteen. I'm sure, of the 2,500 small masters in the cabinet line, you may safely say that 2,000 of them, at the very least, has from five to six in family, *and that's upwards of 12,000 children that's been put to the trade since prices has come down.* Twenty years ago I don't think there was a child at work in our business; and I am sure there is not a small master now whose whole family doesn't assist him. But what I want to know is, what's to become of the 12,000 children when they're growed up, and come regular into the trade? Here are all my young ones growing up without being taught anything but a business that I know they must starve at.'

In answer to my inquiry as to what dependence he had in case of sickness, 'Oh, bless you,' he said, 'there's nothing but the parish for us. I did belong to a Benefit Society about four years ago, but I couldn't keep up my payments any longer. I was in the society above five-and-twenty year, and then was obliged to leave it after all. I don't know of one as belongs to any Friendly Society, and I don't think there is a man as can afford it in our trade now. They must all go to the workhouse when they're sick or old.'

The following is from a journeyman tailor, concerning the employment of women in his trade:

'When I first began working at this branch, there were but very few females employed in it: a few white waistcoats were given out to them, under the idea that women would make them cleaner than men – and so indeed they can. But since the last five years the sweaters have employed females upon cloth, silk, and satin waistcoats as well, and before that time the idea of a woman making a cloth waistcoat would have been scouted. But since the increase of the puffing and the sweating system, masters and sweaters have sought everywhere for such hands as would do the work below the regular ones. Hence the wife has been made to compete with the husband, and the daughter with the wife: they all learn the waistcoat business, and must all get a living. If the man will not reduce the price of his labour to that of the female, why he must remain unemployed; and if the full-grown woman will not take the work at the same price as the young girl, why she must remain without any. The female hands, I can confidently state, have been sought out and introduced to the business by the sweaters, from a desire on their part continually to ferret out hands who will do the work cheaper than others. The effect that this continual reduction has had upon me is this: Before the year 1844 I could live comfortably, and keep my wife and children (I had five in family) by my own labour. My wife then attended to her domestic and family duties; but since that time, owing to the reduction in prices, she has been compelled to resort to her needle, as well as myself, for her living.' [On the table was a bundle of crape and bombazine ready to be made up into a dress.] 'I cannot afford now to let her remain idle – that is, if I wish to live, and keep my children out of the streets, and pay my way. My wife's earnings are, upon an average, 8s. per week. She makes dresses. I never would teach her to make waistcoats, because I knew the introduction of female hands had been the ruin of my trade. With the labour of myself and wife now I can only earn 32s. a week, and six years ago I could make my 36s. If I had a daughter I should be obliged to make her work as well, and then probably, with the labour of the three of us, we could make up at the week's end as much money, as, up to 1844, I could get by my own single hands. My wife, since she took to dressmaking, has become sickly from over-exertion. Her work, and her domestic and family duties altogether, are too much for her. Last night I was up all night with her, and was compelled to call in a female to attend her as well. The over-exertion now necessary for us to maintain a decent appearance, has so ruined her constitution that she is not the same woman as she was. In fact, ill as she is, she has been compelled to rise from her bed to finish a mourning-dress against time, and I myself have been obliged to give her a helping-hand, and turn to at women's work in the same manner as the women are turning to at men's work.'

'The cause of the serious decrease in our trade,' said another tailor to me, 'is the employment given to workmen at their own homes; or, in other words, to the "sweaters". The sweater is the greatest evil to us; as the sweating system increases the number of hands to an almost incredible extent – wives, sons, daughters, and extra women, all working "long days" – that is, labouring from sixteen to eighteen hours per day, and Sundays as well. I date the decrease in the wages of the workman from the introduction of piece-work and giving out garments to be made off the premises of the master; for the effect of this was, that the workman making the garment, knowing that the master could not tell whom he got to do his work for him, employed women and children to help him, and paid them little or nothing for their labour. This was the beginning of the sweating system. The workmen gradually became transformed from journeymen into "middlemen", living by the labour of others. Employers soon began to find that they could get garments made at a less sum than the regular price, and those tradesmen who were anxious to force their trade, by underselling their more honourable neighbours, readily availed themselves of this means of obtaining cheap labour. The consequence was, that the sweater sought out where he could get the work done the cheapest, and so introduced a fresh stock of hands into the trade. Female labour, of course, could be had cheaper than male, and the sweater readily availed himself of the services of women on that account. Hence the males who had formerly been employed upon the garments were thrown out of work by the females, and obliged to remain unemployed, unless they would reduce the price of their work to that of the women. It cannot, therefore, be said that the reduction of prices originally arose from there having been more workmen than there was work for them to do. There was no superabundance of hands until female labour was generally introduced – and even if the workmen had increased 25 per cent. more than what they were twenty years back, still that extra number of hands would be required now to make the same number of garments, owing to the work put into each article being at least one-fourth more than formerly. So far from the trade being over-stocked with male hands, if the work were confined to the men or the masters' premises, there would not be sufficient hands to do the whole.'

According to the last Census (1841, G.B.), out of a population of 18,720,000 the proportions of the people occupied and un-occupied were as follows:

Occupied	7,800,000
Unoccupied (including women and children),	10,920,000

Of those who were occupied the following were the proportions:

Engaged in productive employments [*]	5,350,000
Engaged in non-productive employments	2,450,000

Of those who were engaged in productive employments, the proportion (in round numbers) ran as follows:

Men	3,785,000
Women	660,000
Boys and girls	905,000

Here, then, we find nearly one-fifth, or 20 per cent., of our producers to be boys and girls, and upwards of 10 per cent. to be women. Such was the state of things in 1841. In order to judge of the possible and probable condition of the labour market of the country, if this introduction of women and children into the ranks of the labourers be persisted in, let us see what were the proportions of the 10,920,000 men, women, and children who ten years ago still remained unoccupied among us. The ratio was as follows:

Men	275,000
Women	3,570,000
Boys and girls	7,075,000

Here the unoccupied men are about 5 per cent. of the whole, the children nearly two-thirds, and the wives about one-third.

---

[*] I have here included those engaged in Trade and Commerce, and em-ployers as well as the employed among the *producers*.

Now it appears that out of say 19,000,000 people, 8,000,000 were, in 1841, occupied, and by far the greater number, 11,000,000, unoccupied.

Who were the remaining eleven millions, and what were they doing? They, of course, consisted principally of the unemployed wives and children of the eight millions of people before specified, three millions and a half of the number being females of twenty years of age and upwards, and seven millions being children of both sexes under twenty. Of these children, four millions, according to the 'age abstract', were under ten years, so that we may fairly assume that, at the time of taking the last census, *there were very nearly seven millions of wives and children of a workable age still unoccupied.* Let us suppose, then, that these seven millions of people are brought in competition with the five million producers. What is to be the consequence? If the labour market be overstocked at present with only five millions of people working for the support of nineteen millions (I speak according to the Census of 1841), what would it be if another seven millions were to be dragged into it? And if wages are low now, and employment is precarious on account of this, what will not both work and pay sink to when the number is again increased, and the people clamouring for employment are at least treble what they are at present? When the wife has been taught to compete for work with the husband, and son and daughter to undersell their own father, what will be the state of our labour market then?

But the labour of wives, and children, and apprentices, is not the only means of glutting a particular trade with hands. There is another system becoming every day more popular with our enterprising tradesmen, and this is the *importation of foreign labourers*. In the cheap tailoring this is made a regular practice. Cheap labour is regularly imported, not only from Ireland (the wives of sweaters making visits to the Emerald Isle for the express purpose), but small armies of working tailors, ready to receive the lowest pittance, are continually being shipped into this country. That this is no exaggeration let the following statement prove:

'I am a native of Pesth, having left Hungary about eight years ago. By the custom of the country I was compelled to travel three years in foreign parts, before I could settle in my native place. I went to Paris, after travelling about in the different countries of Germany. I stayed in Paris about two years. My father's wish was that I should visit England, and I came to London in June, 1847. I first worked for a West-end show shop – not *directly* for them, but through the person who is their middle-man getting work done at what rates he could for the firm, and obtaining the prices they allowed for making the garments. I once worked four days and a half for him, finding my own trimmings, &c., for 9s. For this my employer would receive 12s. 6d. He then employed 190 hands; he has employed 300. Many of those so employed set their wives, children, and others to work, some employing as many as five hands this way. The middleman keeps his carriage, and will give fifty guineas for a horse. I became unable to work from a pain in my back, from long sitting at my occupation. The doctor told me not to sit much, and so, as a countryman of mine was doing the same, I employed hands, making the best I could of their labour. I have now four young women (all Irish girls) so employed. Last week one of them received 4s., another 4s. 2d., the other two 5s. each. They find their board and lodging, but I find them a place to work in, a small room, the rent of which I share with another tailor, who works on his own account. There are not so many Jews come over from Hungary or Germany as from Poland. The law of travelling three years brings over many, but not more than it did. The revolutions have brought numbers this year and last. They are Jew tailors flying from Russian and Prussian Poland to avoid the conscription. I never knew any of these Jews go back again. *There is a constant communication among the Jews, and when their friends in Poland, and other places, learn they are safe in England, and in work and out of trouble, they come over too. I worked as a journeyman in Pesth, and got 2s. 6d. a week, my board and washing, and lodging, for my labour.* We lived well, everything being so cheap. The Jews come in the greatest number about Easter. They try to work their way here, most of them. Some save money here, but they never go back; if they leave England it is to go to America.'

The labour market of a particular place, however, comes to be overstocked with hands, not only from the introduction of an inordinate number of apprentices and women and children into the trade, as well as the importation of workmen from abroad, but the same effect is produced by *the migration of country labourers to towns*. This, as I have before said, is specially the case in the printer's and carpenter's trades, where the cheap provincial work is executed chiefly by apprentices, who, when their time is up, flock to the principal towns, in the hopes of getting better wages than can be obtained in the country, owing to the prevalence of the apprentice system of work in those parts. The London carpenters suffer greatly from what are called 'improvers', who come up to town to get perfected in their art, and work for little or no wages. The work of some of the large houses is executed mainly in this way; that of Mr Myers was, for instance, against whom the men lately struck.

But the unskilled labour of towns suffers far more than the skilled from the above cause.

The employment of unskilled labourers in towns is being constantly rendered more casual by the migrations from the country parts. The peasants, owing to the insufficiency of their wages, and the wretchedness of their dwellings and diet, in Wilts, Somerset, Dorset, and elsewhere, leave their native places without regret, and swell the sum of unskilled labour in towns. This is shown by the increase of population far beyond the excess of births over deaths in those counties where there are large manufacturing or commercial towns; whilst in purely agricultural counties the increase of population does not keep pace with the excess of births. 'Thus in Lancashire,' writes Mr Thornton, in his work on Over-Population, 'the increase of the population in the ten years ending in 1841, was 330,210, and in Cheshire, 60,919; whilst the excess of births was only 150,150 in the former, and 28,000 in the latter. In particular towns the contrast is still more striking. In Liverpool and Bristol the annual deaths actually exceed the births, so that these towns are only saved from depopulation by their rural recruits, yet the first increased the number of its inhabitants in ten years by more than one-third, and the other by more than one-sixth. In Manchester, the annual excess of births could only have added 19,390 to the population between 1831 and 1841; the actual increase was 68,375. The number of emigrants (immigrants) into Birmingham, during the same period, may, in the same way, be estimated at 40,000; into Leeds, at 8,000; into the metropolis, at 130,000. On the other hand, in Dorset, Somerset, and Devon, the actual addition to the population, in the same decennial period, was only 15,491, 31,802, and 39,253 respectively; although the excess of births over deaths in the same counties was about 20,000, 38,600, and 48,700.'

The unskilled labour market suffers, again, from the depression of almost any branch of skilled labour; for whatever branch of labour be depressed, and men so be deprived of a sufficiency of employment, one especial result ensues – the unskilled labour market is glutted. The skilled labourer, a tailor, for instance, may be driven to work for the wretched pittance of an East-end slop-tailor, but he cannot 'turn his hand' to any other description of skilled labour. He cannot say, 'I will make billiard-tables, or book-cases, or boots, or razors;' so that there is no resource for him but in unskilled labour. The Spitalfields weavers have often sought dock labour; the turners of the same locality, whose bobbins were once in great demand by the silk-winders, and for the fringes of upholsterers, have done the same; and in this way the increase of casual labour increases the poverty of the poor, and so tends directly to the increase of pauperism.

We have now seen what a vast number of surplus labourers may be produced by an extension of time, rate, or mode of working, as well as by the increase of the hands, by other means than by *the increase of the people themselves*. If, however, we are increasing our workers at a greater rate than we are increasing the means of work, the excess of workmen must, of course, remain unemployed. But are we doing this? [. . .]

Discarding, then, all conjectural results, and adhering solely to the returns of the censuses, we find that, according to the official numberings of the people *throughout the kingdom*, the increased rate of population is, in round numbers, 10 per cent. every ten years; that is to say, where 100 persons were living in the United Kingdom in 1821, there are 130 living in the present year of 1851. The average increase in England and Wales for the last 50 years may, however, be said to be 1.5 per cent. per annum, the population having doubled itself during that period.

How, then, does this rate of increase among the people, and consequently the labourers and artisans of the country, correspond with the rate of increase in the production of commodities, or, in plain English, the means of employment? This is the main inquiry.

The only means of determining the total amount of commodities produced, and consequently the quantity of work done in the country, is from official returns, submitted to the Parliament and the public as part of the 'revenue' of the kingdom. These afford a broad and accurate basis for the necessary statistics. [. . .]

The annual rate of increase among the population has been 0.9 per cent. From 1801 to 1841 the population of the kingdom at the outside cannot be said to have doubled itself. Yet the productions in cotton goods *were not less than ten times greater in 1851 than in 1801.* The increase in the use of wool from 1821 to 1851 was more than sixfold; that of the population, I may repeat, not two fold. In twenty years (1831 to 1851) the hides were more than doubled in amount as a means of production; in *fifty* years the population has not increased to the same amount. Can any one, then, contend that the labouring population has extended itself at a greater rate than the means of labour, or that the vast mass of surplus labour throughout the country is owing to the working classes having increased more rapidly than the means of employing them?

Thus, it is evident, that the means of labour have increased at a more rapid pace than the labouring population. But the increase in 'property' of the country, in that which is sometimes called the 'staple' property, being the assured possessions of the class of proprietors or capitalists, as well as in the profits, prove that, if the labourers of the country have been hungering for want of employment, at least the wealth of the nation has kept pace with the increase of the people, while the profits of trade have exceeded it.

AMOUNT OF THE PROPERTY AND INCOME OF GREAT BRITAIN

Year	Property assessed to Property-tax	Annual Profits of Trade
1815	£60,000,000	£37,000,000
1842	95,250,000	
1844		60,000,000
Increase	58 per cent.	62 per cent.
Annual rate of increase	1.7 per cent.	1.7 per cent.

Here, then, we find, that the property assessed to the property tax has increased 35,250,000*l.* in 27 years, from 1815 to 1842, or upwards of 1,000,000*l.* sterling a year; this is at the rate of 1.7 per cent. every year, whereas the population of Great Britain has increased at the rate of only 1.4 per cent. per annum. But the amount of assessment under the property tax, it should be borne in mind, does not represent the full value of the possessions, so that among this class of proprietors there is far greater wealth than the returns show.

As regards the annual profits of trade, the increase between the years 1815 and 1844 has been 23,000,000*l.* in 29 years. This is at the rate of 1.7 per cent. per annum, and the annual increase in the population of Great Britain is only 1.4 per cent. But the amount of the profits of trade is unquestionably greater than appears in the financial tables of the revenue of the country; consequently there is a greater increase of wealth over population than the figures indicate.

The above returns show the following results:

	Increase % per ann.
Population of the United Kingdom	0.9
Productions from	21 to 5
Exports	14
Imports	5
Shipping entering Ports	9
Property	1.7
Profits of trade	1.7

Far, very far indeed then, beyond the increase of the population, has been the increase of the wealth and work of the country.

And now, after this imposing array of wealth, let us contemplate the reverse of the picture: let us inquire if, while we have been increasing in riches and productions far more rapidly than we have been increasing in people and producers – let us inquire, I say, if we have been numerically increasing also in the sad long lists of paupers and criminals. Has our progress in poverty and crime been *pari passu*, or been more than commensurate in the rapidity of its strides?

TABLE SHOWING THE NUMBER OF PAUPERS
IN ENGLAND AND WALES

Years	Number of paupers relieved, quarters ending Lady-day	Numerical increase and decrease	Increase and decrease %
1840	1,199,529		
1841	1,299,048	+99,519	+8
1842	1,427,187	+128,139	+10
1843	1,539,490	+112,303	+8
1844	1,477,561	+938,071	+60
1845	1,470,970	−6,591	−0.4
1846	1,332,089	− 38,881	−3
1847	1,721,350	+389,261	+29
1848	1,876,541	+155,191	+ 9

Increase % from 1840 to 1848 = 56; Annual Increase, 7 %

Here, then, we have an increase of 56 per cent. in less than ten years, though the increase of the population of England and Wales, in the same time, was but 13 per cent.; and let it be remembered that the increase of upwards of 650,000 paupers, in nine years, has accrued since the New Poor Law has been in what may be considered full working; a law which many were confident would result in a diminution of pauperism, and which certainly cannot be charged with offering the least encouragement to it. Still in *nine* years, our poverty increases while our wealth increases, and our paupers grow nearly four times as quick as our people, while the profits on trade nearly double themselves in little more than a quarter of a century.

We now come to the records of criminality:

TABLE SHOWING THE INCREASE IN THE NUMBER OF CRIMINALS
IN ENGLAND AND WALES FROM 1805 TO 1850

	Annual average no. of criminals committed	Numerical increase	Decennial increase %	Annual increase %
1805	4,605			
1811	5,375	770	17	2.8
1821	9,783	4408	82	8.2
1831	15,318	5535	57	5.7
1841	22,305	6987	46	4.6
1850	27,814	5509	25	3.6

Increase % in the 43 years = 504; Annual Average Increase, 11.7 %

From these results – and such figures are facts, and therefore stubborn things – the people cannot be said to have increased beyond the wealth or the means of employing them, for it is evident that *we increase in poverty and crime as we increase in wealth, and in both far beyond our increase in numbers*. The above are the bare facts of the country – it is for the reader to explain them as he pleases.

As yet we have dealt with those causes of casual labour only which may induce a surplusage of labourers without any *decrease taking place in the quantity of work*. We have seen, first, how the number of the unemployed may be increased either by altering the hours, rate, or mode of working, or else by changing the term of hiring, and this while the number of labourers remains the same; and, secondly, we have seen how the same results may ensue from increasing the number of labourers, while the conditions of working and hiring are unaltered. Under both these circumstances, however, the actual quantity of work to be done in the country has been supposed to undergo no change whatever; and at present we have to point out not only how the amount of surplus, and, consequently, of casual labour, in the kingdom, may be increased by *a decrease of the work*, but also how the work itself may be made to decrease. To know the causes of the one we must ascertain the antecedents of the other. What, then, are the circumstances inducing a decrease in the quantity of work? And, consequently, what the circumstances inducing an increase in the amount of surplus and casual labour?

In the first place we may induce a large amount of casual labour *in particular districts*, not by decreasing the gross quantity of work required by the country, but by merely shifting the work into new quarters, and so decreasing the quantity in the ordinary localities. 'The west of England,' says Mr Dodd, in his account of the textile manufactures of Great Britain, 'was formerly, and continued to be till a comparatively recent period, the most important clothing district in England. The changes which the woollen manufacture, as respects both localisation and mode of management, has been and is now undergoing, are very remarkable. Some years ago the 'west of England cloths' were the test of excellence in this manufacture; while the productions of Yorkshire were deemed of a coarser and cheaper character. At present, although the western counties have not deteriorated in their product, the West Riding of Yorkshire has made giant strides, by which equal skill in every department has been attained; while the commercial advantages resulting from coal-mines, from water-power, from canals and railroads, and from vicinage to the eastern port of Hull and the western port of Liverpool, give to the West Riding a power which Gloucestershire and Somersetshire cannot equal. The steam-engine, too, and various machines for facilitating some of the manufacturing processes, have been more readily introduced into the former than into the latter; a circumstance which, even without reference to other points of comparison, is sufficient to account for much of the recent advance in the north.' [. . .]

But the work of particular localities may not only decrease, and the casual labour, in those parts, increase in the same proportion, by shifting it to other localities (either at home or abroad), even while the gross quantity of work required by the nation remains the same, but the quantity of work may be less than ordinary at *a particular time*, even while the same gross quantity annually required undergoes no change. This is the case in those periodical gluts which arise from over-production, in the cotton and other trades. The manufacturers, in such cases, have been increasing the supplies at a too rapid rate in proportion to the demand of the markets, so that, though there be no decrease in the requirements of the country, there ultimately accrues such a surplus of commodities beyond the wants and means of the people, that the manufacturers are compelled to stop producing until such time as the regular demand carries off the extra supply. And during all this time either the labourers have to work half-time at half-pay, or else they are thrown out of employment altogether.

Thus far we have proceeded in the assumption that the actual quantity of work required by the nation *does not decrease in the aggregate, but only in particular places or at particular times*, owing to a greater quantity than usual being done in other places or at other times. We have still to consider what are the circumstances which tend to *diminish the gross quantity of work required by the country*. To understand these we must know the conditions on which all work depends; these are simply the conditions of demand and supply, and hence to know what it is that regulates the demand for commodities, and what it is that regulates the supply of them, is also to know what it is that regulates the quantity of work required by the nation.

Let me begin with the decrease of work arising from a *decrease of the demand* for certain commodities. This decrease of demand may proceed from one of three causes:

1. An increase of cost.
2. A change of taste or fashion.
3. A change of circumstances.

The *increase of cost* may be brought about either by an increase in the expense of production or by a tax laid upon the article, as in the case of hair-powder, before quoted. Of the *change of taste or fashion*, as a means of decreasing the demand for a certain article of manufacture, and, consequently, of a particular form of labour, many instances have already been given. [. . .]

The decrease of work arising from a *change of circumstances* may be seen in the fluctuations of the iron trade; in the railway excitement the demand for labour in the iron districts was at least tenfold as great as it is at present, and so again with the demand for arms during war time; at such periods the quantity of work in that particular line at Birmingham is necessarily increased, while the contrary effects, of course, ensue immediately the requirements cease, and a large mass of surplus and casual hands is the result. It is the same with the soldiers themselves, as with the gun and sword makers; on the disbanding of certain portions of the army at the conclusion of a war, a vast amount of surplus labourers are poured into the country to compete with those already in work, and either to drag down their weekly earnings, or else, by obtaining casual employment in their stead, to reduce the gross quantity of work accruing to each, and so to render their incomes not only less in amount but less constant and regular. Within the last few weeks no less than 1,000 policemen employed during the Exhibition have been discharged, of course with a like result to the labour market.

The circumstances tending to *diminish the supply* of certain commodities, are –

1. Want of capital.
2. Want of materials.
3. Want of labourers.
4. Want of opportunity.

The *decrease of the quantity of capital* in a trade may be brought about by several means: it may be produced by a want of security felt among the moneyed classes, as at the time of revolutions, political agitations, commercial depressions, or panics; or it may be produced by a deficiency of enterprise after the bursting of certain commercial 'bubbles', or the decline of particular manias for speculation, as on the cessation of the railway excitement; so, again, it may be brought about by a failure of the ordinary produce of the year, as with bad harvests.

The *decrease of the quantity of materials*, as tending to diminish the supply of certain commodities, may be seen in the failure of the cotton crops, which, of course, deprive the cotton manufac-turers of their ordinary quantity of work. The same diminution in the ordinary supply of particular articles ensues when the men engaged in the production of them 'strike' either for an advance of wages, or more generally to resist the attempt of some cutting employer to reduce their ordinary earnings; and lastly, a like decrease of work necessarily ensues when the *opportunity of working is changed*. Some kinds of work, as we have already seen, depend on the weather – on either the wind, rain, or temper-ature; while other kinds can only be pursued at certain seasons of the year, as brick-making, building, and the like; hence, on the cessation of the opportunities for working in these trades, there is necessarily a great decrease in the quantity of work, and consequently a large increase in the amount of surplus and therefore casual labour.

We have now, I believe, exhausted the several causes of that vast national evil – casual labour. We have seen that it depends,

First, upon certain times and seasons, fashions and accidents, which tend to cause a periodical briskness or slackness in different employments;

And secondly, upon the number of surplus labourers in the country.

The circumstances inducing surplus labour we have likewise ascert-ained to be three.

1. An alteration in the hours, rate, or mode of working, as well as in the mode of hiring.
2. An increase of the hands.

3. A decrease of the work, either in particular places, at particular times, or in the aggregate, owing to a decrease either in the demand or means of supply.

Any one of these causes, it has been demonstrated, must necessarily tend to induce an over-supply of labourers and consequently a casualty of labour, for it has been pointed out that an over-supply of labourers does not depend *solely* on an increase of the workers beyond the means of working, but that a decrease of the ordinary quantity of work, or a general increase of the hours or rate of working, or an extension of the system of production, or even a diminution of the term of hiring, will also be attended with the same result – facts which should be borne steadily in mind by all those who would understand the difficulties of the times, and which the 'economists' invariably ignore.

On a careful revision of the whole of the circumstances before detailed, I am led to believe that there is considerable truth in the statement lately put forward by the working classes, that only one-third of the operatives of this country are fully employed, while another third are partially employed, and the remaining third wholly unemployed; that is to say, estimating the working classes as being between four and five millions in number, I think we may safely assert – considering how many depend for their employment on particular times, seasons, fashions, and accidents, and the vast quantity of over-work and scamp-work in nearly all the cheap trades of the present day, the number of women and children who are being continually drafted into the different handicrafts with the view of reducing the earnings of the men, the displacement of human labour in some cases by machinery, and the tendency to increase the division of labour, and to extend the large system of production beyond the requirements of the markets, as well as the temporary mode of hiring – all these things being considered, I say I believe we may safely conclude that, out of the four million five hundred thousand people who have to depend on their industry for the livelihood of themselves and families, there is (owing to the extraordinary means of economising labour which have been developed of late years, and the discovery as to how to do the work of the nation with fewer people) barely sufficient work for the regular employment of half of our labourers, so that only 1,500,000 are fully and constantly employed, while 1,500,000 more are employed only half their time, and the remaining 1,500,000 wholly unemployed, obtaining a day's work occasionally by the displacement of some of the others.

Adopt what explanation we will of this appalling deficiency of employment, one thing at least is certain: we cannot *consistently with the facts of the country*, ascribe it to an increase of the population beyond the means of labour; for we have seen that, while the people have increased during the last fifty years at the rate of 0.9 per cent. per annum, the wealth and productions of the kingdom have far exceeded that amount.

Of the casual labourers among the rubbish-carters
[*volume ii, pp. 323,324*]

The casual labour of so large a body of men as the rubbish-carters is a question of high importance, for it affects the whole unskilled labour market. And this is one of the circumstances distinguishing unskilled from skilled labour. Unemployed cabinet-makers, for instance, do not apply for work to a tailor; so that, with skilled labourers, only one trade is affected in the slack season by the scarcity of employment among its operatives. With unskilled labourers it is otherwise. If in the course of next week 100 rubbish-carters were from any cause to be thrown out of employment, and found an impossibility to obtain work at rubbish-carting, there would be 100 fresh applicants for employment among the brick-layer's-labourers, scavagers, nightmen, sewer-men, dock-workers, lumpers, &c. Many of the 100 thus unemployed would, of course, be willing to work at reduced wages merely that they might subsist; and thus the hands employed by the regular and 'honour-able' part of those trades are exposed to the risk of being under-worked, as regards wages, from the surplusage of labour in other unskilled occupations.

The employment of the rubbish-carters depends, in the first instance, upon the *season*. The services of the men are called into requisition when houses are being built or removed. In the one case, the rubbish-carters cart away the refuse earth; in the other they remove the old materials. The *brisk season* for the builders, and consequently for the rubbish-carters, is, as I heard several of them express it, 'when days are long'. From about the middle of April to the middle of October is the *brisk* season of the rubbish-carters, for during those six months more buildings are erected than in the winter half of the year. There is an advantage in fine weather in the masonry becoming *set*; and efforts are generally made to complete at least the carcase of a house before the end of October, at the latest.

I am informed that the difference in the employment of labourers about buildings is 30 per cent. – one builder estimated it at 50 per cent. – less in winter than in summer, from the circumstance of fewer buildings being then in the course of erection. It may be thought that, as rubbish-carters are employed frequently on the foundation of buildings, their business would not be greatly affected by the season or the weather. But the work is often more difficult in wet weather, the ground being heavier, so that a smaller extent of work only can be accomplished, compared to what can be done in fine weather; and an employer may decline to pay six days' wages for work in winter, which he might get done in five days in summer. If the men work by the piece or the load the result is the same; the rubbish-carter's employer has a smaller return, for there is less work to be charged to the customer, while the cost in keeping the horses is the same.

Thus it appears that under the most favourable circumstances about *one-fourth* of the rubbish-carters, even in the honourable trade, may be exposed to the evils of non-employment merely from the state of the weather influencing, more or less, the custom of the trade, and this even during the six months' employment out of the year; after which the men must find some other means of earning a livelihood.

There are, in round numbers, 850 operative rubbish-carters employed in the brisk season throughout the metropolis; hence 212 men, at this calculation, would be regularly deprived of work every year for six months out of the twelve. It will be seen, however, on reference to the table here given, that the average number of weeks each of the rubbish-carters is employed throughout the twelve months is far below 26; indeed many have but three and four weeks work out of the 52.

By an analysis of the returns I have collected on this subject I find the following to have been the actual term of employment for the several rubbish-carters in the course of last year:

Men		Employment in the year
9	had	39 weeks, or 9 months
214	had	26 weeks, or 6 months
4	had	20 weeks, or 5 months
10	had	18 weeks
28	had	16 weeks, or 4 months
8	had	14 weeks
353	had	13 weeks, or 3 months
4	had	12 weeks
34	had	10 weeks
29	had	9 weeks
38	had	8 weeks, or 2 months
38	had	6 weeks
27	had	5 weeks
45	had	4 weeks, or 1 month
15	had	3 weeks
856		

Hence about one-fourth of the trade appear to have been employed for six months, while upwards of one-half had work for only three months or less throughout the year – many being at work only three days in the week during that time.

The rubbish-carter is exposed to another casualty over which he can no more exercise control than he can over the weather; I mean to what is generally called *speculation*, or a rage for building. This is evoked by the state of the money market, and other causes upon which I need not dilate; but the effect of it upon the labourers I am describing is this: capitalists may in one year embark sufficient means in building speculations to erect, say 500 new houses, in any partic-ular district. In the following year they may not erect more than 200 (if any), and thus, as there is the same extent of unskilled labour in the market, the number of hands required is, if the trade be generally less speculative, less in one year than in its predecessor by the number of rubbish-carters required to work at the found-ations of 300 houses. Such a cause may be exceptional; but during the last ten years the inhabited houses in the five districts of the Registrar-General have increased to the extent of 45,000, or from 262,737 in 1841, to 307,722 in 1851. It appears, then, that the annual increase of our metropolitan houses, concluding that they increase in a reg-ular yearly ratio, is 4,500. Last year, however, as I am informed by an experienced builder, there were rather fewer buildings erected (he spoke only from his own observations and personal knowledge of the business) than the yearly average of the decennial term.

The casual and constant wages of the rubbish-carters may be thus detailed. The whole system of the labour, I may again state, must be regarded as *casual*, or – as the word imports in its derivation from the Latin *casus*, a chance – the labour of men who are occasionally employed. Some of the most respectable and industrious rubbish-carters with whom I met, told me they generally might make up their minds, though they might have excellent masters, to be six months of the year unemployed at rubbish-carting; this, too, is less than the average of this chance employment.

Calculating, then, the rubbish-carter's receipt of *nominal wages* at 18s., and his *actual wages* at 20s. in the honourable trade, I find the following amount to be paid.

By nominal wages, I have before explained, I mean what a man is *said* to receive, or has been *promised* that he shall be paid weekly. Actual wages, on the other hand, are what a man positively *receives*, there being sometimes additions in the form of perquisites or allowances; sometimes deductions in the way of fines and stoppages; the additions in the rubbish-carting trade appear to average about 2s. a week. But these *actual wages* are received only so long as the men are employed, that is to say, they are the *casual* rather than the *constant* earnings of the men working at a trade, which is essentially of an occasional or temporary character; the average employment at rubbish-carting being only three months in the year.

Let us see, therefore, what would be the constant earnings or income of the men working at the better-paid portion of the trade.

	£	s.	d.
The gross actual wages of ten rubbish-carters, casually employed for 39 weeks, at 20s. per week, amount to	390	0	0
The gross actual wages of 250 rubbish-carters, casually employed for 26 weeks, at 20s. per week	6,500	0	0
The gross actual wages of 360 rubbish-carters, casually employed for 13 weeks, at 20s. per week	4,600	0	0
Total gross actual wages of 620 of the better-paid rubbish-carters	11,490	0	0

But this, as I said before, represents only the casual wages of the better-paid operatives – that is to say, it shows the amount of money or money's worth that is positively received by the men while they are in employment. To understand what are the *constant* wages of these men, we must divide their gross casual earnings by 52, the number of weeks in the year: thus we find that the constant wages of the ten men who were employed for 39 weeks, were 15s. instead of 20s. per week – that is to say, their wages, equally divided throughout the year, would have yielded that constant weekly income. By the same reasoning, the 20s. per week casual wages of the 250 men employed for 26 weeks out of the 52, were equal to only 10s. constant weekly wages; and so the 360 men, who had 20s. per week casually for only three months in the year, had but 5s. a week constantly throughout the whole year. Hence we see the enormous difference there may be between a man's casual and his constant earnings at a given trade.

The next question that forces itself on the mind is, how do the rubbish-carters live when no longer employed at this kind of work?

When the slack season among rubbish-carters commences, nearly one-fifth of the operatives are discharged. These take to scavaging or dustman's work, as well as that of navigators, or, indeed, any form of unskilled labour, some obtaining full employ, but the greater part being able to 'get a job only now and then'. Those masters who keep their men on throughout the year are some of them large dust contractors, some carmen, some dairymen, and (in one or two instances in the suburbs, as at Hackney) small farmers. The dust-contractors and carmen, who are by far the more numerous, find employment for the men employed by them as rubbish-carters in the season, either at the dust-yard or carrying sand, or, indeed, carting any materials they may have to move – the wages to the men remaining the same; indeed such is the transient character of the rubbish-carting trade, that there are no masters or operatives who devote themselves solely to the business.

The effects of casual labour in general
[*volume ii, pp. 325–327*]
Having now pointed out the causes of casual labour, I proceed to set forth its effects.

All casual labour, as I have said, is necessarily *uncertain* labour; and wherever uncertainty exists, there can be no foresight or providence. Had the succession of events in nature been irregular, – had it been ordained by the Creator that similar causes under similar circumstances should not be attended with similar effects, – it would have been impossible for us to have had any knowledge of the future, or to have made any preparations concerning it. Had the seasons followed each other fitfully, – had the sequences in the external world been variable instead of invariable, and what are now termed 'constants' from the regularity of their succession been changed into inconstants, – what provision could even the most prudent of us have made? Where all was dark and unstable, we could only have guessed instead of reasoned as to what was to come; and who would have deprived himself of present enjoyments to avoid future privations, which could appear neither probable nor even possible to him? Providence, therefore, is simply the result of certainty, and whatever tends to increase our faith in the uniform sequences of outward events, as well as our reliance on the means we have of avoiding the evils connected with them, necessarily tends to make us more prudent. Where the means of sustenance and comfort are fixed, the human being becomes conscious of what he has to depend upon; and if he feel assured that such means may fail him in old age or in sickness, and be fully impressed with the *certainty* of suffering from either, he will immediately proceed to make some provision against the time of adversity or infirmity. If, however, his means be uncertain – abundant at one time, and deficient at another – a spirit of speculation or gambling with the future will be induced, and the individual get to believe in 'luck' and 'fate' as the arbiters of his happiness rather than to look upon himself as 'the architect of his fortunes' – trusting to 'chance' rather than his own powers and foresight to relieve him at the hour of necessity. The same result will necessarily ensue if, from defective reasoning powers, the ordinary course of nature be not sufficiently apparent to him, or if, being in good health, he grow too confident upon its continuance, and, either from this or other causes, is led to believe that death will overtake him before his powers of self-support decay.

The ordinary effects of uncertain labour, then, are to drive the labourers to improvidence, recklessness, and pauperism.

Even in the classes which we do not rank among labourers, as, for instance, authors, artists, musicians, actors, uncertainty or irregularity of employment and remuneration produces a spirit of wastefulness and carelessness. The steady and daily accruing gains of trade and of some of the professions form a certain and staple income; while in other professions, where a large sum may be realised at one time, and then no money be earned until after an interval, incomings are rapidly spent, and the interval is one of suffering. This is part of the very nature, the very essence, of the casualty of employment and the delay of remuneration. The past privation gives a zest to the present enjoyment; while the present enjoyment renders the past privation faint as a remembrance and unimpressive as a warning. 'Want of providence,' writes Mr Porter, 'on the part of those who live by the labour of their hands, and whose employments so often depend upon circumstances beyond their control, is a theme which is constantly brought forward by many whose lot in life has been cast beyond the reach of want. It is, indeed, greatly to be wished, for their own sakes, that the habit were general among the labouring classes of saving some part of their wages when fully employed, against less prosperous times; but it is difficult for those who are placed in circumstances of ease to *estimate the amount of virtue that is implied in this self-denial*. It must be a hard trial for one who has recently, perhaps, seen his family enduring want, to deny them the small amount of indulgences, which are, at the best of times, placed within their reach.' [. . .]

There can hardly be a stronger illustration of the blessing of constant and the curse of casual labour. We have competence and frugality as the results of one system; poverty and extravagance as the results of the other; and among the very same individuals.

In the evidence given by Mr Galloway, the engineer, before a parliamentary committee, he remarks, that 'when employers are competent to show their men that their business is *steady and certain*, and when men find that they are likely to have *permanent* employment, they have always *better habits and more settled notions*, which will make them *better men* and *better workmen*, and will produce great benefits to all who are interested in their employment.'

Moreover, even if payment be assured to a working man regularly, *but deferred for long intervals*, so as to make the returns lose all appearance of regularity, he will rarely be found able to resist the temptation of a tavern, and, perhaps, a long-continued carouse, or of some other extravagance to his taste, when he receives a month's dues at once. [. . .]

I may cite the following example as to the effects of uncertain earnings upon the household outlay of labourers who suffer from the casualties of employment induced by the season of the year. 'In the long fine days of summer, the little daughter of a working brickmaker,' I was told, 'used to order chops and other choice dainties of a butcher, saying, "Please, sir, father don't care for the price just a-now; but he must have his chops good; line-chops, sir, and tender, please – 'cause he's a brickmaker." In the winter, it was, "Oh please, sir, here's a fourpenny bit, and you must send father something cheap. He don't care what it is, so long as it's cheap. It's winter, and he hasn't no work, sir – 'cause he's a brickmaker."'

I have spoken of the tendency of casual labour to induce intemperate habits. In confirmation of this I am enabled to give the following account as to the increase of the sale of malt liquor in the metropolis *consequent upon wet weather*. [. . .]

The reason for this increased consumption is obvious; when the weather prevents workmen from prosecuting their respective callings in the open air, they have recourse to drinking, to pass away the idle time. Anyone who has made himself familiar with the habits of the working classes has often found them crowding a public-house during a hard rain, especially in the neighbourhood of new buildings, or any public open-air work. The street-sellers, themselves prevented from plying their trades outside, are busy in such times in the 'publics', offering for sale braces, belts, hose, tobacco-boxes, nuts of different kinds, apples, &c. A bargain may then be struck for so much and a half-pint of beer, and so the consumption is augmented by the trade in other matters. [. . .]

A censor of morals might say that these men should go home under such circumstances; but their homes may be at a distance, and may present no great attractions; the single men among them may have no homes, merely sleeping-places; and even the more prudent may think it advisable to wait awhile under shelter in hopes of the weather improving, so that they could resume their labour, and only an hour or so be deducted from their wages. Besides, there is the attraction to the labourer of the warmth, discussion, freedom, and excitement of the public-house. [. . .]

Of the scurf trade among the rubbish-carters
[*volume ii, pp. 327–335*]

Before proceeding to treat of the cheap or 'scurf' labourers among the rubbish-carters, I shall do as I have done in connection with the casual labourers of the same trade, say a few words on that kind of labour in general, both as to the means by which it is usually obtained and as to the distinctive qualities of the scurf or low-priced labourers; for experience teaches me that the mode by which labour is cheapened is more or less similar in all trades, and it will therefore save much time and space if I here – as with the casual labourers – give the general facts in connection with this part of my subject.

In the first place, then, there are but two direct modes of cheapening labour, viz.:

1. By making the workmen do *more* work for the *same* pay.
2. By making them do the *same* work for *less* pay.

The first of these modes is what is technically termed '*driving*', especially when effected by compulsory 'over-work'; and it is called the 'economy of labour' when brought about by more elaborate and refined processes, such as the division of labour, the large system of production, the invention of machinery, and the *temporary*, as contradistinguished from the *permanent*, mode of hiring.

Each of these modes of making workmen do *more* work for the *same* pay, can but have the same depressing effect on the labour market, for not only is the *rate* of remuneration (or ratio of the work to the pay) reduced when the operative is made to do a greater quantity of work for the same amount of money, but, unless the means of disposing of the extra products be proportionately increased, it is evident that just as many work-men must be displaced thereby as the increased term or rate of working exceeds the extension of the markets; that is to say, if

4,000 workpeople be made to produce each twice as much as formerly (either by extending the hours of labour or increasing their rate of labouring), then if the markets or means of disposing of the extra products be increased only one-half, 1,000 hands must, according to Cocker, be deprived of their ordinary employment; and these competing with those who are in work will immediately tend to reduce the wages of the trade generally, so that not only will the *rate* of wages be decreased, since each will have more work to do, but the actual earnings of the workmen will be diminished likewise.

Of the economy of labour itself, as a means of cheapening work, there is no necessity for me to speak here. It is, indeed, generally admitted, that to economise labour without proportionally extending the markets for the products of such labour, is to deprive a certain number of workmen of their ordinary means of living; and under the head of casual labour so many instances have been given of this principle that it would be wearisome to the reader were I to do other than allude to the matter at present. There are, however, several other means of causing a workman to do more than his ordinary quantity of work. These are:

1. By extra supervision when the workmen are paid by the day. Of this mode of increased production an instance has already been cited in the account of the strapping-shops given [pp.282–4].
2. By increasing the workman's interest in his work; as in piece-work, where the payment of the operative is made proportional to the quantity of work done by him. Of this mode examples have already been given [p.281].
3. By large quantities of work given out at one time; as in 'lump-work' and 'contract work'.
4. By the domestic system of work, or giving out materials to be made up at the homes of the workpeople.
5. By the middleman system of labour.
6. By the prevalence of small masters.
7. By a reduced rate of pay, as forcing operatives to labour both longer and quicker, in order to make up the same amount of income.

Of several of these modes of work I have already spoken, citing facts as to their pernicious influence upon the greater portion of those trades where they are found to prevail. I have already shown how, by extra supervision – by increased interest in the work – as well as by decreased pay, operatives can be made to do more work than they otherwise would, and so be the cause, unless the market be proportionately extended, of depriving some of their fellow-labourers of their fair share of employment. It now only remains for me to set forth the effect of those modes of employment which have not yet been described, viz., the domestic system, the middleman system, and the contract and lump system, as well as the small-master system of work.

Let me begin with the first of the last-mentioned modes of cheapening labour, viz., *the domestic system of work*.

I find, by investigation, that in trades where the system of working on the master's premises has been departed from, and a man is allowed to take his work home, there is invariably a tendency to cheapen labour. These home workers, whenever opportunity offers, will use other men's ill-paid labour, or else employ the members of their family to enhance their own profits.

The domestic system, moreover, naturally induces *over-work and Sunday-work, as well as tends to change journeymen into trading operatives, living on the labour of their fellow-workmen*. When the work is executed off the master's premises, of course there are neither definite hours nor days for labour; and the consequence is, the generality of home workers labour early and late, Sundays as well as week-days, availing themselves at the same time of the co-operation of their wives and children; thus the trade becomes overstocked with workpeople by the introduction of a vast number of new hands into it, as well as by the over-work of the men themselves who thus obtain employment. When I was among the tailors, I received from a journeyman to whom I was referred by the Trades' Society as the one best able to explain the causes of the decline of that trade, the following lucid account of the evils of this system of labour:

'The principal cause of the decline of our trade is the employ-ment given to workmen at their own homes, or, in other words, to the "sweaters". The sweater is the greatest evil in the trade; as the sweating system increases the number of hands to an almost incredible extent – wives, sons, daughters, and extra women, all working "long days" – that is, labouring from sixteen to eighteen hours per day, and Sundays as well. By this system two men obtain as much work as would give employment to three or four men working regular hours in the shop. Consequently, the sweater being enabled to get the work done by women and children at a lower price than the regular workman, obtains the greater part of the garments to be made, while men who depend upon the shop for their living are obliged to walk about idle. A greater quantity of work is done under the sweating system at a lower price. I consider that the decline of my trade dates from the change of day-work into piece-work. According to the old system, the journeyman was paid by the day, and consequently must have done his work under the eye of his employer. It is true that work was given out by the master before the change from day-work to piece-work was regularly acknowledged in the trade. But still it was morally impossible for work to be given out and not be paid by the piece. *Hence I date the decrease in the wages of the workman from the introduction of piece-work, and giving out garments to be made off the premises of the master.* The effect of this was, that the workman making the garment, knowing that the master could not tell whom he got to do his work for him, employed women and children to help him, and paid them little or nothing for their labour. This was the beginning of the sweating system. The workmen gradually became transformed from journeymen into "middlemen", living by the labour of others. Employers soon began to find that they could get garments made at a less sum than the regular price, and those tradesmen who were anxious to force their trade, by underselling their more honourable neighbours, readily availed themselves of this means of obtaining cheap labour.'

The *middleman system of work* is so much akin to the domestic system, of which, indeed, it is but a necessary result, that it forms a natural addendum to the above. Of this indirect mode of employing workmen, I said, in the *Chronicle*, when treating of the timber-porters at the docks:

'The middleman system is the one crying evil of the day. Whether he goes by the name of "sweater", "chamber-master", "lumper", or contractor, it is this *trading operative* who is the great means of reducing the wages of his fellow working men. To make a profit out of the employment of his brother operatives he must, of course, obtain a lower class and, consequently, cheaper labour. Hence it becomes a *business* with him to hunt out the lowest grades of working men – that is to say, those who are either morally or intellectually inferior in the craft – the drunken, the dishonest, the idle, the vagabond, and the unskilful; these are the instruments that he seeks for, because, these being unable to obtain employment at the regular wages of the sober, honest, industrious, and skilful portion of the trade, he can obtain their labour at a lower rate than what is usually paid. Hence drunkards, tramps, men without character or station, apprentices, children – all suit him. Indeed, the more degraded the labourers, the better they answer his purpose, for the cheaper he can get their work, and consequently the more he can make out of it.

' "Boy labour or thief labour," said a middleman, on a large scale, to me, "what do I care, so long as I can get my work done cheap?" That this *seeking out* of cheap and inferior labour really takes place, and is a necessary consequence of the middleman system, we have merely to look into the condition of any trade where it is extensively pursued. I have shown, in my account of the tailors' trade printed in the *Chronicle*, that the wives of the sweaters not only parade the streets of London on the look-out for youths raw from the country, but that they make periodical trips to the poorest provinces of Ireland, in order to obtain workmen at the lowest possible rate. I have shown, moreover, that foreigners are annually imported from the Continent for the same purpose, and that among the chamber-masters in the shoe trade, the child-market at Bethnal-green, as well as the workhouses, are continually ransacked for the means of obtaining a cheaper kind of labour. All my investigations go to prove, that it is chiefly by means of this middleman system that the wages of the working men are reduced. It is this contractor – this trading operative – who is invariably the prime mover in the reduction of the wages of his fellow-workmen. He uses the most degraded of the class as a means of underselling the worthy and skilful labourers, and of ultimately dragging the better down to the abasement of the worst. He cares not whether the trade to which he belongs is already overstocked with hands, for, be those hands as many as they may, and the ordinary wages of his craft down to bare subsistence point, it matters not a jot to him; he can live solely by reducing them still lower, and so he immediately sets about drafting or importing a fresh and cheaper stock into the trade. If men cannot subsist on lower prices, then he takes apprentices, or hires children; if women of chastity cannot afford to labour at the price he gives, then he has recourse to prostitutes; or if workmen of character and worth refuse to work at less than the ordinary rate, then he seeks out the moral refuse of the trade — those whom none else will employ; or else he flies, to find labour meet for his purpose, to the workhouse and the gaol. Backed by this cheap and refuse labour, he offers his work at lower prices, and so keeps on reducing and reducing the wages of his brethren, until all sink in poverty, wretchedness, and vice. Go where we will, look into whatever poorly-paid craft we please, we shall find this *trading operative*, this *middleman* or contractor, at the bottom of the degradation.'

The 'contract system' or 'lump work', as it is called, is but a corollary, as it were, of the foregoing; for it is an essential part of the middleman system, that the work should be obtained by the trading operative in large quantities, so that those upon whose labour he lives should be kept continually occupied, and the more, of course, that he can obtain work for, the greater his profit. When a quantity of work, usually paid for by the piece, is given out at one time, the natural tendency is for the piece-work to pass into lump-work; that is to say, if there be in a trade a number of distinct parts, each requiring, perhaps, from the division of labour, a distinct hand for the execution of it, or if each of these parts bear a different price, it is frequently the case that the master will contract with some one workman for the execution of the whole, agreeing to give a certain price for the job 'in the lump', and allowing the workman to get whom he pleases to execute it. This is the case with the piece-working masters in the coach-building trade; but it is not essential to the contract or lump system of work, that other hands should be employed; the main distinction between it and piece-work being that the work is given out in large quantities, and a certain allowance or reduction of price effected from that cause alone.

It is this contract or lump work which constitutes the great evil of the carpenter's, as well as of many other trades; and as in those crafts, so in this, we find that the lower the wages are reduced the greater becomes the number of trading operatives or middlemen.

For it is when workmen find the difficulty of living by their labour increased that they take to scheming and trading upon the labour of their fellows. In the slop trade, where the pay is the worst, these creatures abound the most; and so in the carpenter's trade, where the wages are the lowest – as among the speculative builders – there the system of contracting and sub-contracting is found in full force.

Of this contract or lump work, I received the following account from the foreman to a large speculating builder, when I was inquiring into the condition of the London carpenters:

'The way in which the work is done is mostly by letting and subletting. The masters usually prefer to let work, because it takes all the trouble off their hands. They know what they are to get for the job, and of course they let it as much under that figure as they possibly can, all of which is clear gain without the least trouble. How the work is done, or by whom, it's no matter to them, so long as they can make what they want out of the job, and have no bother about it. Some of our largest builders are taking to this plan, and a party who used to have one of the largest shops in London has within the last three years discharged all the men in his employ [he had 200 at least], and has now merely an office, and none but clerks and accountants in his pay. He has taken to letting his work out instead of doing it at home. The parties to whom the work is let by the speculating builders are generally working men, and these men in their turn look out for other working men, who will take the job cheaper than they will; and so I leave you, sir, and the public to judge what the party who really executes the work gets for his labour, and what is the quality of work that he is likely to put into it. The speculating builder generally employs an overlooker to see that the work is done sufficiently well to pass the surveyor. That's all he cares about. Whether it's done by thieves, or drunkards, or boys, it's no matter to him. The overlooker, of course, sees after the first party to whom the work is let, and this party in his turn looks after the several hands that he has sublet it to. The first man who agrees to the job takes it in the lump, and he again lets it to others in the piece. I have known instances of its having been let again a third time, but this is not usual. The party who takes the job in the lump from the speculator usually employs a foreman, whose duty it is to give out the materials and to make working drawings. The men to whom it is sublet only find labour, while the "lumper", or first contractor, agrees for both labour and materials. It is usual in contract work, for the first party who takes the job to be bound in a large sum for the due and faithful performance of his contract. He then, in his turn, finds out a sub-contractor, who is mostly a small builder, who will also bind himself that the work shall be properly executed, and there the binding ceases – those parties to whom the job is afterwards let, or sublet, employing foremen or overlookers to see that their contract is carried out. The first contractor has scarcely any trouble whatsoever; he merely engages a gentleman, who rides about in a gig, to see that what is done is likely to pass muster. The sub-contractor has a little more trouble; and so it goes on as it gets down and down. Of course I need not tell you that the first contractor, who does the *least* of all, gets the *most* of all; while the poor wretch of a working man, who positively executes the job, is obliged to slave away every hour, night after night, to get a bare living out of it; and this is the contract system.'

A tradesman, or a speculator, will contract, for a certain sum, to complete the skeleton of a house, and render it fit for habitation. He will sublet the flooring to some working joiner, who will, in very many cases, take it on such terms as to allow himself, by working early and late, the regular journeymen's wages of 30s. a week, or perhaps rather more. Now this sub-contractor cannot complete the work within the requisite time by his own unaided industry, and he employs men to assist him, often subletting again, and such assistant men will earn perhaps but 4s. a day. It is the same with the doors, the staircases, the balustrades, the window-frames, the room-skirtings, the closets; in short, all parts of the building.

The subletting is accomplished without difficulty. Old men are sometimes employed in such work, and will be glad of any re-muneration to escape the workhouse; while stronger workmen are usually sanguine that by extra exertion, 'though the figure is low, they may make a tidy thing out of it after all.' In this way labour is cheapened. 'Lump' work, 'piece' work, work by 'the job', are all portions of the contract system. The principle is the same. 'Here is this work to be done, what will you undertake to do it for?'

In number after number of the *Builder* will be found statements headed 'Blind Builders'. One firm, responding to an advertisement for 'estimates' of the building of a church, sends in an offer to execute the work in the best style for 5,000*l*. Another firm may offer to do it for somewhere about 3,000*l*. The first-mentioned firm would do the work well, paying the 'honourable' rate of wages. The under-working firm must resort to the scamping and subletting system I have alluded to. It appears that the building of churches and chapels, of all denominations, is one of the greatest encouragement to slop, or scamp, or under-paid work. The same system prevails in many trades with equally pernicious effects. [. . .]

The last mentioned of the several modes of cheapening labour is the *small-master system* of work, that is to say, the operatives taking to make up materials on their own account rather than for capitalist employers. In every trade where there are small masters, trades into which it requires but little capital to embark, there is certain to be a cheapening of labour. Such a man works himself, and to get work, to meet the exigencies of the rent and the demands of the collectors of the parliamentary and parochial taxes, he will often under-work the very journeymen whom he occasionally employs, doing 'the job' in such cases with the assistance of his family and apprentices, at a less rate of profit than the amount of journeymen's wages. [. . .]

The cause of the extraordinary decline of wages in the cabinet trade (even though the hands decreased and the work increased to an unprecedented extent) will be found to consist in the increase that has taken place within the last 20 years of what are called 'garret-masters' in the cabinet trade. These garret-masters are a class of small 'trade-working masters', the same as the 'chamber masters' in the shoe trade, supplying both capital and labour. They are in manufacture what 'the peasant proprietors' are in agriculture – their own employers and their own workmen. There is, however, this one marked distinction between the two classes – the garret-master cannot, like the peasant proprietor, *eat* what he produces; the consequence is, that he is obliged to convert each article into food immediately he manufactures it – no matter what the state of the market may be. The capital of the garret-master being generally sufficient to find him in materials for the manufacture of only one article at a time, and his savings being but barely enough for his subsistence while he is engaged in putting those materials together, he is compelled, the moment the work is completed, to part with it for whatever he can get. He cannot afford to keep it even a day, for to do so is generally to remain a day unfed. Hence, if the market be at all slack, he has to force a sale by offering his goods at the lowest possible price. What wonder, then, that the necessities of such a class of individuals should have created a special race of employers, known by the significant name of 'slaughter-house men' – or that these, being aware of the inability of the 'garret-masters' to hold out against any offer, no matter how slight a remuneration it affords for their labour, should continually lower and lower their prices, until the entire body of the competitive portion of the cabinet trade is sunk in utter destitution and misery? Moreover, it is well known how strong is the stimulus among peasant proprietors, or, indeed, any class working for themselves, to extra production. So it is, indeed, with the garret-masters; their industry is almost incessant, and hence a greater quantity of work is turned out by them, and continually forced into the market, than there would otherwise be. What though there be a brisk and a slack season in the cabinet-maker's trade as in the majority of others? – slack or brisk, the garret-masters must produce the same excessive quantity of goods. In the hope of extricating himself from his overwhelming poverty, he toils on, producing more and more – and yet the more he produces the more hopeless does his position become; for the greater the stock that he thrusts into the market, the lower does the price of his labour fall, until at last, he and his whole family work for less than half what he himself could earn a few years back by his own unaided labour.'

The small-master system of work leads, like the domestic system, with which, indeed, it is intimately connected, to the employment of wives, children, and apprentices, as a means of assistance and extra production – for as the prices decline so do the small masters strive by further labour to compensate for their loss of income.

Such, then, are the several modes of work by which labour is cheapened. There are, as we have seen, but two ways of *directly* effecting this, viz., first by making men do more work for the same pay, and secondly, by making them do the same work for less pay. The way in which men are made to do more, it has been pointed out, is, by causing them either to work longer or quicker, or else by employing fewer hands in proportion to the work; or engaging them only for such time as their services are required, and discharging them immediately afterwards. These constitute the several modes of economising labour, which lowers the rate of remuneration (the ratio of the pay to the work) rather than the pay itself. The several means by which this result is attained are termed 'systems of work, production, or engagement', and such are those above detailed.

Now it is a necessity of these several systems, though the actual amount of remuneration is not directly reduced by them, that a cheaper labour should be obtained for carrying them out. Thus, in contract or lump work, perhaps, the price may not be immediately lowered; the saving to the employer consisting chiefly in supervision, he having in such a case only one man to look to instead of perhaps a hundred. The contractor, or lumper, however, is differently situated; he, in order to reap any benefit from the contract, must, since he cannot do the whole work himself, employ others to help him, and to reap any benefit from the contract, this of course must be done at a lower price than he himself receives; so it is with the middleman system, where a profit is derived from the labour of other operatives; so, again, with the domestic system of work, where the several members of the family, or cheaper labourers, are generally employed as assistants; and even so is it with the small-master system, where the labour of apprentices and wives and children is the principal means of help. Hence the operatives adopting these several systems of work are rather the instruments by which cheap labour is obtained than the cheap labourers themselves. It is true that a sweater, a chamber master, or garret-master, a lumper or con-tractor, or a home worker, generally works cheaper than the ordinary operatives, but this he does chiefly by the cheap labourers he employs, and then, finding that he is able to under-work the rest of the trade, and that the more hands he employs the greater becomes his profit, he offers to do work at less than the usual rate. It is not a necessity of the system that the middleman operative, the domestic worker, the lumper, or garret-master should be himself underpaid, but simply that he should employ others who are so, and it is thus that such systems of work tend to cheapen the labour of those trades in which they are found to prevail. Who, then, are the cheap labourers? – who the individuals, by means of whose services the sweater, the smaller master, the lumper, and others, is enabled to under-work the rest of his trade? – what the general characteristics of those who, in the majority of handicrafts, are found ready to do the same work for less pay, and how are these usually distinguished from such as obtain the higher rate of remuneration?

The cheap workmen in all trades, I find, are divisible into three classes:

1. The unskilful.
2. The untrustworthy.
3. The inexpensive.

First, as regards the *unskilful*. Long ago it has been noticed how frequently boys were put to trades to which their tastes and temperaments were antagonistic. Gay, who in his quiet, unpretending style often elicited a truth, tells how a century and a half ago the generality of parents never considered for what business a boy was best adapted –

> But ev'n in infancy decree
> What this or t'other son shall be.

A boy thus brought up to a craft for which he entertains a dislike can hardly become a proficient in it. At the present time thousands of parents are glad to have their sons reared to any business which their means or opportunities place within their reach, even though the lad be altogether unsuited to the craft. The consequence is, that these boys often grow up to be unskilful workmen. There are technical terms for them in different trades, but perhaps the generic appellation is 'muffs'. Such workmen, however well conducted, can rarely obtain employment in a good shop at good wages, and are compelled, therefore, to accept second, third, and fourth-rate wages, and are often driven to slop-work.

Other causes may be cited as tending to form unskilful workmen: the neglect of masters or foremen, or their incapacity to teach apprentices; irregular habits in the learner; and insufficient practice during a master's paucity of employment. I am assured, moreover, that hundreds of mechanics yearly come to London *from the country parts*, whose skill is altogether inadequate to the demands of the 'honourable trade'. Of course, during the finishing of their education they can only work for inferior shops at inferior wages; hence another cause of cheap labour. Of this I will cite an instance: a bootmaker, who for years had worked for first-rate West-end shops, told me that when he came to London from a country town he was sanguine of success, because he knew that he was a *ready* man [a quick workman]. He very soon found out, however, he said, that as he aspired to do the best work, he 'had his business to learn all over again'; and until he attained the requisite skill, he worked for 'just what he could get': he was a cheap, because then an unskilful, labourer.

There is, moreover, the cheaper labour of *apprentices*, the great prop of many a slop-trader; for as such traders disregard all the niceties of work, as they disregard also the solidity and perfect finish of any work (finishing it, as it was once described to me, 'just to the eye'), a lad is soon made useful, and his labour remunerative to his master, as far as slop remuneration goes, which, though small in a small business, is wealth in a 'monster business'.

There are, again, the '*improvers*'. These are the most frequent in the dress-making and millinery business, as young women find it impossible to form a good connection among a wealthier class of ladies in any country town, unless the 'patronesses' are satisfied that their skill and taste have been perfected in London. In my inquiry (in the course of two letters in the *Morning Chronicle*) into the condition of the workwomen in this calling, I was told by a retired dressmaker, who had for upwards of twenty years carried on business in the neighbourhood of Grosvenor-square, that she had sometimes met with 'improvers' so tasteful and quick, from a good provincial tuition, that they had really little or nothing to learn in London. And yet their services were secured for one, and oftener for two years, merely for board and lodging, while others employed in the same establishment had not only board and lodging, but handsome salaries. The improver's, then, is generally a cheap labour, and often a very cheap labour too. The same form of cheap labour prevails in the carpenter's trade.

There is, moreover, the labour of *old men*. A tailor, for instance, who may have executed the most skilled work of his craft, in his old age, or before the period of old age, finds his eyesight fail him, – finds his tremulous fingers have not a full and rapid mastery of the needle, and he then labours, at greatly reduced rates of payment, on the making of soldiers' clothing – 'sanc-work', as it is called – or on any ill-paid and therefore ill-wrought labour.

The inferior, as regards the quality of the work, and under-paid class of *women*, in tailoring, for example, again, cheapen labour. It is cheapened, also, by the employment of *Irishmen* (in, perhaps, all branches of skilled or unskilled labour), and of *foreigners*, more especially of Poles, who are inferior workmen to the English, and who will work very cheap, thus supplying a low-price labour to those who seek it.

I may remark further, that if a first-rate workman be driven to slop-work, he soon loses his skill; he can only work slop; this has been shown over and over again, and so his labour becomes cheap in the mart.

2. Of *untrustworthy labour* (as a cause of cheap labour) I need not say much. It is obvious that a drunken, idle, or dishonest workman or workwoman, when pressed by want, will and must labour, not for the recompense the labour merits, but for whatever pittance an employer will accord. There is no reliance to be placed in him. Such a man cannot 'hold out' for terms, for he is perhaps starving, and it is known that 'he cannot be depended upon'. In the sweep's trade many of those who work at a lower rate than the rest of the trade are men who have lost their regular work by dishonesty.

3. The *inexpensive class* of workpeople are very numerous. They consist of three sub-divisions:
(a) Those who have been accustomed to a coarser kind of diet, and who, consequently, requiring less, can afford to work for less.
(b) Those who derive their subsistence from other sources, and who, consequently, do not live by their labour.
(c) Those who are in receipt of certain 'aids to their wages', or who have other means of living beside their work.

Of course these causes can alone have influence where the wages are minimised or reduced to the lowest ebb of subsistence, in which case they become so many means of driving down the price of labour still lower.

(a) Those who, being what is designated hard-reared, that is to say, accustomed to a scantier or coarser diet, and who, therefore, 'can do' with a less quantity or less expensive quality of food than the average run of labourers, can of course live at a lower cost, and so *afford* to work at a lower rate. Among such (unskilled) labourers are the peasants from many of the counties, who seek to amend their condition by obtaining employment in the towns. [. . .]

(b) Those who derive their subsistence from other sources can, of course, afford to work cheaper than those who have to live by their labour. To this class belongs the labour of wives and children, who, being supposed to be maintained by the toil of the husband, are never paid 'living wages' for what they do; and hence the misery of the great mass of needlewomen, widows, unmarried and friendless females, and the like, who, having none to assist them, are forced to starve upon the pittance they receive for their work. The labour of those who are in prisons, workhouses, and asylums, and who consequently have their subsistence found them in such places, as well as the work of prostitutes, who obtain their living by other means than work, all come under the category of those who can afford to labour at a lower rate than such as are condemned to toil for an honest living. It is the same with apprentices and 'improvers', for whose labour the instruction received is generally considered to be either a sufficient or partial recompense, and who consequently look to other means for their support. Under the same head, too, may be cited the labour of amateurs, that is to say, of persons who either are not, or who are too proud to acknowledge themselves, regular members of the trade at which they work. Such is the case with very many of the daughters of tradesmen, and of many who are considered *genteel* people. These young women, residing with their parents, and often in comfortable homes, at no cost to themselves, will, and do, undersell the regular needlewomen; the one works merely for pocket-money (often to possess herself of some article of finery), while the other works for what is called 'the bare life'.

(c) The last-mentioned class, or those who are in possession of what may be called 'aids to wages', are differently circumstanced. Such are the men who have other employment besides that for which they accept less than the ordinary pay, as is the case with those who attend at gentlemen's houses for one or two hours every morning, cleaning boots, brushing clothes, &c., and who, having the remainder of the day at their own disposal, can afford to work at any calling cheaper than others, because not solely dependent upon it for their living.

The army and navy pensioners (non-commissioned officers and privates) were, at one period, on the disbanding of the militia and other forces, a very numerous body, but it was chiefly the military pensioners whose position had an effect upon the labour of the country. The naval pensioners found employment as fishermen, or in some avocation connected with the sea. The military pensioners, however, were men who, after a career of soldiership, were not generally disposed to settle down into the drudgery of regular work, even if it were in their power to do so; and so, as they always had their pensions to depend upon, they were a sort of universal jobbers, and jobbed cheaply. At the present time, however, this means of cheap labour is greatly restricted, compared with what was the case, the number of the pensioners being considerably diminished. Many of the army pensioners turn the wheels for turners at present.

The allotment of gardens, which yield a partial support to the allottee, are another means of cheap labour. The allotment demands a certain portion of time, but is by no means a thorough employment, but merely an 'aid', and consequently a *means*, to low wages. Such a man has the advantage of obtaining his potatoes and vegetables at the cheapest rate, and so can afford to work cheaper than other men of his class. It was the same formerly with those who received 'relief' under the old Poor Law.

And even under the present system it has been found that the same practice is attended with the same result. In the Sixth Annual Report of the Poor Law Commissioners, 1840, at p.31, there are the following remarks on the subject:

'Whilst upon the subject of relief to widows in aid of wages, we must not omit to bring under your Lordship's notice an illustration of the *depressing effect* which is produced by the practice of giving relief in aid of wages to widows upon the earnings of females. Colonel A'Court states:

' "As regards females, the instance to which I have alluded presents itself in the Portsea Island Union, where, from the insufficiency of workhouse accommodation, as well as from benevolent feelings, small allowances of 1s. 6d. or 2s. a week are given to widows with or without small children, or to married women deserted by their husbands. *Having this certain income, however small, they are enabled to work at lower wages than those who do not possess this advantage.* The consequence is, that competition has enabled the shirt and stay manufacturers, who abound in the Union, and who furnish in great measure the London as well as many foreign markets with these articles of their trade, to get their work done at the extraordinary low prices of – stays, complete, 9*d.*; shirts, from 1*s.* to 1*s.* 6*d.* per dozen.

' "The women all declare that they cannot possibly, after working from twelve to fifteen hours per day, earn more than 1*s.* 6*d.* per week. The manufacturers assert that, by steady work, 4*s.* to 6*s.* a week may be earned under ordinary circumstances.

' "In the meantime *the demand for workwomen increases*, and it is by no means unusual to see hand-bills posted over the town requiring from 500 to 1,000 additional stitchers." '

Such, then, is the character of the cheap workers in all trades; go where we will, we shall find the low-priced labour of the trade to consist of either one or other of the three classes above-mentioned; while the means by which this labour is brought into operation will be generally by one of the 'systems of work' before specified. [. . .]

Skilled and unskilled
[*volume iii, pp. 221–231*]
Mayhew devoted particular attention to the situation of skilled workers. Socially aware, conversant with developments in their trade and excellent record keepers, they were a treasure both as informants and as a register of national progress. The decline in the position of self-supporting craftsmen was a matter of the deepest concern.

'Garret-masters'
[*volume iii, pp. 221–231*]
The cabinet-makers, socially as well as commercially considered, consist, like all other operatives, of two distinct classes, that is to say, of society and non-society men, or, in the language of political economy, of those whose wages are regulated by custom and those whose earnings are determined by competition. The former class

numbers between 600 and 700 of the trade, and the latter between 4,000 and 5,000. As a general rule I may remark, that I find the society-men of every trade comprise about one-tenth of the whole. Hence it follows, that if the non-society men are neither so skilful nor so well-conducted as the others, at least they are quite as important a body, from the fact that they constitute the main portion of the trade. The transition from the one class to the other is, however, in most cases, of a very disheartening character. The difference between the tailor at the West-end, working for better shops at the better prices, and the poor wretch starving at starvation wages for the sweaters and slop-shops at the East-end, has already been pointed out. The same marked contrast was also shown to exist between the society and non-society boot and shoemakers. The carpenters and joiners told the same story. There were found society men renting houses of their own – some paying as much as 70l. a-year – and the non-society men over-worked and underpaid, so that a few weeks' sickness reduced them to absolute pauperism. Nor, I regret to say, can any other tale be told of the cabinet-makers; except it be, that the competitive men in this trade are even in a worse position than any other. I have already portrayed to the reader the difference between the homes of the two classes – the comfort and well-furnished abodes of the one, and the squalor and bare walls of the other. But those who wish to be impressed with the social advantages of a fairly-paid class of mechanics should attend a meeting of the Wood-carvers' Society. On the first floor of a small private house in Tottenham-street, Tottenham-court-road, is, so to speak, the museum of the working men belonging to this branch of the cabinet-makers. The walls of the back-room are hung round with plaster casts of some of the choicest specimens of the arts, and in the front room the table is strewn with volumes of valuable prints and drawings in connection with the craft. Round this table are ranged the members of the society – some forty or fifty were there on the night of my attendance – discussing the affairs of the trade. Among the collection of books may be found, *The Architectural Ornaments and Decorations of Cottingham*, *The Gothic Ornaments* of Pugin, Tatham's *Greek Relics*, Raphael's *Pilaster Ornaments of the Vatican*, Le Pautre's *Designs*, and Baptiste's *Collection of Flowers*, large size; while among the casts are articles of the same choice description. The objects of this society are, in the words of the preface to the printed catalogue, 'to enable wood-carvers to co-operate for the advancement of their art, and by forming a collection of books, prints, and drawings, to afford them facilities for self-improvement; also, by the diffusion of information among its members, to assist them in the exercise of their art, as well as to enable them to obtain employment.' The society does not interfere in the regulation of wages in any other way than, by the diffusion of information among its members, to assist them in the exercise of their art, as well as to enable them to obtain employment; so that both employers and employed may, by becoming members, promote their own and each other's interests. The collection is now much enlarged, and with the additions that have been made to it, offers aid to the members which in many cases is invaluable. As a means of facilitating the use of this collection, the opportunities of borrowing from it have been made as general as possible. The meetings of the society are held at a place where attendance is unaccompanied by expense; and they are, therefore, says the preface, 'free from all objection on account of inducements to exceed the time required for business'. All this appears to be in the best possible taste, and the attention of the society being still directed to its improvement, assuredly gives the members, as they say, 'good reason to hope that it will become one of which the wood-carver may be proud, as affording valuable assistance, both in the design and execution of any style of wood-carving'. In the whole course of my investigations I have never experienced more gratification than I did on the evening of my visit to this society. The members all gave evidence, both in manner and appearance, of the refining character of their craft: and it was indeed a hearty relief from the scenes of squalor, misery, dirt, vice, ignorance, and discontent, with which these inquiries too frequently bring one into connection, to find one's self surrounded with an atmosphere of beauty, refinement, comfort, intelligence, and ease.

The public, generally, are deplorably misinformed as to the character and purpose of trade societies. The common impression is that they are combinations of working men, instituted and maintained solely with the view of exacting an exorbitant rate of wages from their employers, and that they are necessarily connected with strikes, and with sundry other savage and silly means of attaining this object. It is my duty, however, to make known that the rate of wages which such societies are instituted to uphold has, with but few exceptions, been agreed upon at a conference of both masters and men, and that in almost every case I find the members as strongly opposed to strikes, as a means of upholding them, as the public themselves. But at all events the maintenance of the standard rate of wages is not the sole object of such societies – the majority of them being organised as much for the support of the sick and aged as for the regulation of the price of labour; and even in those societies whose efforts are confined to the latter purpose alone, a considerable sum is devoted annually for the subsistence of their members when out of work. [. . .]

I have been thus explicit on the subject of trade societies in general, because I know there exists in the public mind a strong prejudice against such institutions, and because it is the fact of belonging to some such society which invariably distinguishes the better class of workmen from the worse. The competitive men, or cheap workers, seldom or never are members of any association, either enrolled or unenrolled. The consequence is, that when out of work, or disabled from sickness or old age, they are left to the parish to support. It is the slop-workers of the different trades – the cheap men or non-society hands – who constitute the great mass of paupers in this country. And here lies the main social distinction between the workmen who belong to societies and those who do not – the one maintain their own poor, the others are left to the mercy of the parish. [. . .]

Such, then, is the state of the society men belonging to the cabinet-makers' trade. These, as I before said, constitute that portion of the workmen whose wages are regulated by custom, and it now only remains for me to set forth the state of those whose earnings are determined by competition. [. . .] How [. . .] are we to explain the fact that, while the hands have decreased 33 per cent, and work increased at a considerable rate, wages a few years ago were 300 per cent better than they are at present? The solution of the problem will be found in the extraordinary increase that has taken place within the last 20 years of what are called 'garret-masters' in the cabinet trade. [See pages 331–2]

Another cause of the necessity of the garret-master to part with his goods as soon as made is the large size of the articles he manufactures, and the consequent cost of conveying them from slaughter-house to slaughter-house till a purchaser be found. For this purpose a van is frequently hired; and the consequence is, that he cannot hold out against the slaughterer's offer, even for an hour, without increasing the expense of carriage, and so virtually decreasing his gains. This is so well known at the slaughter-houses, that if a man, after seeking in vain for a fair remuneration for his work, is goaded by his necessities to call at a shop a second time to accept a price which he had previously refused, he seldom obtains what was first offered him. Sometimes when he has been ground down to the lowest possible sum, he is paid late on a Saturday night with a cheque, and forced to give the firm a liberal discount for cashing it. [. . .]

The decline which has taken place within the last twenty years in the wages of the operative cabinet-makers of London is so enormous, and, moreover, it seems so opposed to the principles of political economy, that it becomes of the highest importance in an inquiry like the present to trace out the circumstances to which this special depreciation is to be attributed. It has been before shown that the number of hands belonging to the London cabinet trade decreased between 1831 and 1841 33 per cent in comparison with the rest of the metropolitan population; and that, notwithstanding this falling off, the workman's wages in 1831 were at least 400 per cent better than they are at present, 20s. having formerly been paid for the making of articles for which now only 5s. are given. [. . .]

Here, then, we find that wages in the competitive portion of the cabinet trade – that is among the non-society hands – (the wages of the society men I have before explained are regulated, or rather fixed by custom) – were twenty years ago 400 per cent better in some cases, and in others no less than 900 per cent higher than they are at present, and this while the number of workmen has decreased as much as one-third relatively to the rest of the population. How, then, is this extraordinary diminution in the price of labour to be accounted for? Certainly not on the natural assumption that the quantity of work has declined in a still greater proportion than the number of hands to do it, for it has also been proved that the number of new houses built annually in the metropolis, and therefore the quantity of new furniture required has of late years increased very considerably.

In the cabinet trade, then, we find a collection of circumstances at variance with that law of supply and demand by which many suppose that the rate of wages is invariably determined. Wages, it is said, depend upon the demand and supply of labour; and it is commonly assumed that they cannot be affected by anything else. That they are, however, subject to other influence, the history of the cabinet trade for the last twenty years is a most convincing proof, for there we find, that while the quantity of work, or in other words, the demand for labour, has increased, and the supply decreased, wages, instead of rising, have suffered a heavy decline. By what means, then, is this reduction in the price of labour to be explained? What other circumstance is there affecting the remuneration for work, of which economists have usually omitted to take cognisance? The answer is, that wages depend as much on the distribution of labour as on the demand and supply of it. Assuming a certain quantity of work to be done, the amount of remuneration coming to each of the workmen engaged must, of course, be regulated, not only by the number of hands, but by the proportion of labour done by them respectively; that is to say, if there be work enough to employ the whole of the operatives for sixty hours a week, and if two-thirds of the hands are supplied with sufficient to occupy them ninety hours in the same space of time, then one-third of the trade must be thrown fully out of employment: thus proving that there may be surplus labour without any increase of the population. It may, therefore, be safely asserted, that any system of labour which tends to make the members of a craft produce a greater quantity of work than usual, tends at the same time to over-populate the trade as certainly as an increase of workmen. This law may be summed up briefly in the expression that over-work makes under-pay.

Hence the next point in the inquiry is as to the means by which the productiveness of operatives is capable of being extended. There are many modes of effecting this. Some of these have been long known to students of political economy, while others have been made public for the first time in these letters. Under the former class are included the division and co-operation of labour, as well as the 'large system of production'; and to the latter belongs 'the strapping system', by which men are made to get through four times as much work as usual, and which I have before described.

But the most effectual means of increasing the productiveness of labourers is found to consist, not in any system of supervision, however cogent, nor in any limitation of the operations performed by the work-people to the smallest possible number, nor in the apportionment of the different parts of the work to the different capabilities of the operatives, but in connecting the workman's interest directly with his labour; that is to say, by making the amount of his earnings depend upon the quantity of work done by him. This is ordinarily effected in manufacture by means of what is called piece-work. Almost all who work by the day, or for a fixed salary – that is to say, those who labour for the gain of others, not for their own – have, it has been well remarked, 'no interest in doing more than the smallest quantity of work that will pass as a fulfilment of the mere terms of their engagement.' Owing to the insufficient interest which day-labourers have in the result of their labour, there is a natural tendency in such labour to be extremely inefficient – a tendency only to be overcome by vigilant super-intendance (such as is carried on under the strapping system among the joiners) on the part of the persons who are interested in the result. The master's eye is notoriously the only security to be relied on. But superintend them as you will, day labourers are so much inferior to those who work by the piece, that, as we before said, the latter system is practised in all industrial occupations where the work admits of being put out in definite portions, without involv-ing the necessity of too troublesome a surveillance to guard against inferiority (or scamping) in the execution. But if the labourer at piece-work is made to produce a greater quantity than at day-work, and this solely by connecting his own interest with that of his employer, how much more largely must the productiveness of workmen be increased when labouring wholly on their own account! Accordingly, it has been invariably found, that whenever the operative unites in himself the double function of capitalist and labourer, making up his own materials or working on his own property, his productiveness single-handed is considerably greater than can be attained under the large system of production, where all the arts and appliances of which extensive capital can avail itself are brought into operation.

Of the industry of working masters or trading operatives in manufactures there are as yet no authentic accounts. We have, however, ample records concerning the indefatigability of their agricultural counterparts – the peasant-proprietors. [. . .] 'The industry of the small proprietor,' says Arthur Young, in his *Travels in France*, 'were so conspicuous and so meritorious, that no commendation would be too great for it. It was sufficient to prove that property in land is, of all others, the most active instigator to severe and incessant labour.' If, then, this principle of working for one's self has been found to increase the industry, and consequently the productiveness of labourers, to such an extent in agriculture, it is but natural that it should be attended with the same results in manufactures, and that we should find the small masters and the peasant-proprietors toiling longer and working quicker than labourers serving others rather than themselves. But there is an important distinction to be drawn between the produce of the peasant-proprietor and that of the small master. Toil as diligently as the little farmer may, since he cultivates the soil not for profit, but as a means of subsistence, and his produce contributes directly to his support, it follows that his comforts must be increased by his extra-production; or, in other words, that the more he labours, the more food he obtains. The small master, however, producing what he cannot eat, must carry his goods to market and exchange them for articles of consumption. Hence, by over-toil he lowers the market against himself; that is to say, the more he labours the less food he ultimately obtains.

But not only is it true that over-work makes under-pay, but the converse of the proposition is equally true, that under-pay makes over-work; that is to say, it is true of those trades where the system of piece-work or small mastership admits of the operative doing the utmost amount of work that he is able to accomplish, for the workman in such cases seldom or never thinks of reducing his expenditure to his income, but rather of increasing his labour, so as still to bring his income, by extra production, up to his expenditure. This brings us to another important distinction which it is necessary to make between the peasant-proprietor and the small master. The little farmer cannot increase his produce by devoting a less amount of labour to each of the articles; that is to say, he cannot scamp his work without diminishing his future stock. A given quantity of labour must be used to obtain a given amount of produce. None of the details can be omitted without a diminution of the result: scamp the ploughing and there will be a smaller crop. In manufactures, however, the result is very different. There one of the principal means of increasing the productions of a particular trade, and of the cabinet trade especially, is by decreasing the amount of work in each article. Hence, in such cases, all kinds of schemes and impositions are resorted to to make the unskilled labour equal to the skilled, and thus the market is glutted with slop productions till the honourable part of the trade, both workmen and employers, are ultimately obliged to resort to the same tricks as the rest.

[. . .]

I now come to the amount of capital required for an operative cabinet-maker to begin business on his own account.

To show the readiness with which any youth out of his time, as it is called, can start in trade as a garret cabinet master, I have learned the following particulars: This lad, when not living with his friends, usually occupies a garret, and in this he constructs a rude bench out of old materials, which may cost him 2s. If he be penniless when he ceases to be an apprentice, and can get no work as a journeyman, which is nearly always the case, for reasons I have before stated, he assists another garret-master to make a bedstead, perhaps; and the established garret-master carries two bedsteads instead of one to the slaughter-house. The lad's share of the proceeds may be about 5s.; and out of that, if his needs will permit him, he buys the article, and so proceeds by degrees. Many men, to start themselves, as it is called, have endured, I am informed, something like starvation most patiently. The tools are generally collected by degrees, and often in the last year of app-renticeship, out of the boy's earnings. They are seldom bought first-hand, but at the marine-store shops, or at the second-hand furniture brokers' in the New-cut. The purchaser grinds and sharpens them up at any friendly workman's where he can meet with the loan of a grindstone, and puts new handles to them himself out of pieces of waste wood; 10s. or even 5s. thus invested has started a man with tools, while 20s. has accomplished it in what might be considered good style. In some cases the friends of the boy, if they are not poverty-stricken, advance him from 40s. to 50s. to begin with, and he must then shift for himself.

When a bench and tools have been obtained, the young master buys such material as his means afford, and sets himself to work. If he has a few shillings to spare he makes himself a sort of bedstead, and buys a rug or a sheet and a little bedding. If he has not the means to do so he sleeps on shavings stuffed into an old sack. In some few cases he hires a bench alongside some other garret-master, but the arrangement of two or three men occupying one room for their labour is more frequent when the garrets where the men sleep are required for their wives' labour in any distinct business, or when the articles the men make are too cumbrous, like wardrobes, to be carried easily down the narrow stairs. [. . .]

The next point in this inquiry is concerning the industry and productiveness of this class of workmen. Of over-work, as regards excessive labour, and of over-production from scamped workmanship, I heard the following accounts which different operatives, both in the fancy and general cabinet trade concurred in giving, while some represented the labour as of longer duration by at least an hour, and some by two hours a day, than I have stated.

The labour of the men who depend entirely on the slaughter-houses for the purchase of their articles, with all the disadvantages that I described in a former letter, is usually seven days a week the year through. That is seven days – for Sunday-work is all but universal – each of 13 hours, or 91 hours in all, while the established hours of labour in the honourable trade are six days of the week, each of 10 hours, or 60 hours in all. Thus 50 per cent is added to the extent of the production of low-priced cabinet work merely from over-hours, but in some cases I heard of 15 hours for seven days in the week, or 105 hours in all. The exceptions to this continuous toil are from one to three hours once or twice in the week, when the workman is engaged in purchasing his material of a timber merchant, who sells it in small quantities, and from six to eight hours when he is employed in conveying his goods to a warehouse, or from warehouse to warehouse for sale. [. . .]

This excessive toil, however, is but one element of over-production. Scamping adds at least 200 per cent to the productions of the cabinet-maker's trade. [. . .]

I now come to show how this scamp work is executed, that is to say, by what helps or assistants when such are employed. As in all trades where lowness of wages is the rule, the apprentice system prevails among the cheap cabinet-workers. It prevails, however, among the garret-masters, by very many of them having one, two, three, or four apprentices, and so the number of boys thus employed through the whole trade is considerable. This refers principally to the general cabinet trade. In the fancy trade the number is greater, as the boys' labour is more readily available, but in this trade the greatest number of apprentices is employed by such warehousemen as are manufacturers, as some at the East-end are – or rather by the men that they constantly keep at work. Of these men one has now 8, and another 14 boys in his service, some apprenticed, some merely engaged and discharged at pleasure. A sharp boy, thus apprenticed, in six or eight months becomes handy, but four out of five of the workmen thus brought up can do nothing well but their own particular branch, and that only well as far as celerity in production is considered. [. . .]

Scavengers etc.
[*volume ii, pp. 217–220*]
The following case study presents a detailed account of the division of labour along with the mode and rates of payment, unemployment and average earnings of the operative scavengers, or scavagers, of London. Apart from its intrinsic interest, it underscores the contrast in living standards between the constant and casual hands and the devastating effects of climate on the quantity of work.

Scavengers
I have now to deal with what throughout the whole course of my inquiry into the state of London labour and the London poor I have considered the great object of investigation – the condition and characteristics of the working men; and what is more immediately the 'labour question', the relation of the labourer to his employer, as to rates of payment, modes of payment, hiring of labourers, constancy or inconstancy of work, supply of hands, the many points concerning wages, perquisites, family work, and parochial or club relief.

First, I shall give an account of the class employment, together with the labour season and earnings of the labourers, or 'economical' part of the subject. I shall then pass to the social points, concerning their homes, general expenditure, &c., and then to the more moral and intellectual questions of education, literature, politics, religion, marriage, and concubinage of the men and of their families. All this will refer, it should be remembered, only to the working scavagers in the honourable or better-paid trade; the cheaper labourers I shall treat separately as a distinct class; the details in both cases I shall illustrate with the statement of men of the class described.

The first part of this multifarious subject appertains to the division of labour. This in the scavaging trade consists rather of that kind of 'gang-work' which Mr Wakefield styles 'simple co-operation', or the working together of a number of people at the same thing, as opposed to 'complex co-operation', or the working together of a number at *different branches* of the same thing. Simple co-operation is of course the ruder kind; but even this, rude as it appears, is far from being barbaric. 'The savages of New Holland,' we are told, 'never help each other even in the most simple operations; and their condition is hardly superior – in some respects it is inferior – to that of the wild animals which they now and then catch.'

As an instance of the advantages of 'simple co-operation', Mr Wakefield tells us that 'in a vast number of simple operations performed by human exertion, it is quite obvious that two men working together will do more than four, or four times four men, each of whom should work alone. In the lifting of heavy weights, for example, in the felling of trees, in the gathering of much hay and corn during a short period of fine weather, in draining a large extent of land during the short season when such a work may be properly conducted, in the pulling of ropes on board ship, in the rowing of large boats, in some mining operations, in the erection of a scaffolding for a building, and in the breaking of stones for the repair of a road, so that the whole road shall always be kept in good repair – in all these simple operations, and thousands more, it is absolutely necessary that many persons should work together at the same time, in the same place, and in the same way.'

To the above instances of simple co-operation, or gang-working, as it may be briefly styled in Saxon English, Mr Wakefield might have added dock labour and scavaging.

The principle of complex co-operation, however, is not entirely unknown in the public cleansing trade. This business consists of as many branches as there are distinct kinds of refuse, and these appear to be four. There are (1) the wet and (2) the dry *house*-refuse (or dust and night-soil), and (3) the wet and (4) the dry *street*-refuse (or mud and rubbish); and in these four different branches of the one general trade the principle of complex co-operation is found commonly, though not invariably, to prevail.

The difference as to the class employments of the general body of public cleansers – the dustmen, street-sweepers, nightmen, and rubbish carters – seems to be this: any nightman will work as a dustman or scavager; but it is not all the dustmen and scavagers who will work as nightmen. The reason is almost obvious. The avocations of the dustman and the nightman are in some degree hereditary. A rude man provides for the future maintenance of his sons in the way which is most patent to his notice; he makes the boy share in his own labour, and grow up unfit for anything else.

The regular working scavagers are then generally a distinct class from the working dustmen, and are all paid by the week, while the dustmen are paid by the load. In very wet weather, when there is a great quantity of 'slop' in the streets, a dustman is often called upon to lend a helping hand, and sometimes when a working scavager is out of employ, in order to keep himself from want, he goes to a 'job of dust work', but seldom from any other cause.

In a parish where there is a crowded population, the dustman's labours consume, on an average, from six to eight hours a day. In scavagery, the average hours of daily work are twelve (Sundays of course excepted), but they sometimes extended to fifteen, and even sixteen hours, in places of great business traffic; while in very fine dry weather, the twelve hours may be abridged by two, three, four, or even more. Thus it is manifest that the consumption of time alone prevents the same working men being simultaneously dustmen and scavagers. In the more remote and quiet parishes, however, and under the management of the smaller contractors, the opposite arrangement frequently exists; the operative is a scavager one day, and a dustman the next. This is not the case in the busier districts, and with the large contractors, unless exceptionally, or on an emergency.

If the scavagers or dustmen have completed their street and house labours in a shorter time than usual, there is generally some sort of employment for them in the yards or wharfs of the contractors, or they may sometimes avail themselves of their leisure to enjoy themselves in their own way. In many parts, indeed, as I have shown, the street-sweeping must be finished by noon, or earlier.

Concerning the *division of labour*, it may be said, that the principle of complex co-operation in the scavaging trade exists only in its rudest form, for the characteristics distinguishing the labour of the working scavagers are far from being of that complicated nature common to many other callings.

As regards the act of sweeping or scraping the streets, the labour is performed by the *gangsman* and his *gang*. The gangsman usually loads the cart, and occasionally, when a number are employed in a district, acts as a foreman by superintending them, and giving directions; he is a working scavager, but has the office of overlooker confided to him, and receives a higher amount of wage than the others.

For the completion of the street-work there are the *one-horse carmen* and the *two-horse carmen*, who are also working scavagers, and so called from their having to load the carts drawn by one or two horses. These are the men who shovel into the cart the dirt swept or scraped to one side of the public way by the gang (some of it mere slop), and then drive the cart to its destination, which is generally their master's yard. Thus far only does the street-labour extend. The carmen have the care of the vehicles in cleaning them, greasing the wheels, and such like, but the horses are usually groomed by stablemen, who are not employed in the streets.

The division of labour, then, among the working scavagers, may be said to be as follows:

1st. The *ganger*, whose office it is to superintend the gang, and shovel the dirt into the cart.

2nd. The *gang*, which consists of from three to ten or twelve men, who sweep in a row and collect the dirt in heaps ready for the ganger to shovel into the cart.

3rd. The *carman* (one-horse or two-horse, as the case may be), who attends to the horse and cart, brushes the dirt into the ganger's shovel, and assists the ganger in wet sloppy weather in carting the dirt, and then takes the mud to the place where it is deposited.

There is only one *mode of payment* for the above labours pursued among the master scavagers, and that is by the week.

1st. The ganger receives a weekly salary of 18s. when working for an 'honourable' master; with a 'scurf', however, the ganger's pay is but 16s. a week.

2nd. The gang receive in a large establishment each 16s. per week, but in a small one they usually get from 14s. to 15s. a week. When working for a small master they have often, by working over-hours, to 'make eight days to the week instead of six'.

3rd. The one-horse carman receives 16s. a week in a large, and 15s. in a small establishment.

4th. The two-horse carman receives 18s. weekly, but is employed only by the larger masters.

On the [following] page I give a table on this point.

Some of these men are paid by the day, some by the week, and some on Wednesdays and Saturdays, perhaps in about equal proportions, the 'casuals' being mostly paid by the day, and the regular hands (with some exceptions among the scurfs) once or twice a week. The chance hands are sometimes engaged for a half day, and, as I was told, 'jump at a bob and a joey [1s. 4d.], or at a bob.' I heard of one contractor who not unfrequently said to any foreman or gangsman who mentioned to him the applications for work, 'Oh, give the poor devils a turn, if it's only for a day now and then.'

Piece-work, or, as the scavagers call it, 'by the load', *did* at one time prevail, but not to any great extent. The prices varied, according to the nature and the state of the road, from 2s. to 2s. 6d. the load. The system of piece-work was never liked by the men; it seems to have been resorted to less as a system, or mode of labour, than to insure assiduity on the part of the working scavagers, when a rapid street-cleansing was desirable. It was rather in the favour of the working man's individual emoluments than otherwise, as may be shown in the following way. In Battle-bridge, four men collect five loads in dry, and six men seven loads in wet weather. If the average piece hire be 2s. 3d. a load, it is 2s. 9¾d. for each of the five men's day's work; if 2s. 2d. a load, it is 2s. 8½d. (the regular wage,

TABLE SHOWING THE DIVISION OF LABOUR, MODE AND RATES OF PAYMENT, NATURE OF WORK PERFORMED, TIME UNEMPLOYED, AND AVERAGE EARNINGS OF THE OPERATIVE SCAVAGERS OF LONDON

Operative scavagers	Mode of payment	Rates of payment	Nature of work performed	Time unemployed during the year	Average casual (or constant) gains throughout the year
I. Manual Labourers					
A. Better paid					
Ganger	By the day	18s. weekly, + 2s. allowance	To load the cart and superintend the men	Not two days during the year	20s. per week
Carman (2 horse)	By the day	18s. weekly, and allowance	To take care of the horses, help load the cart, and take the dirt and slop to the dustyard	Seldom or never out of employment	20s. per week
Carman (1 horse)	By the day	16s. weekly, + 2s. allowance	To take care of the horses, help load the cart, and take the dirt and slop to the dustyard	Seldom or never out of employment	18s. per week
Sweepers	By the day	16s. weekly, + 2s. allowance	To sweep the district to which they are sent, and collect the dirt or slop ready for carting away	About three months during the year	13s. 6d. per week
B. Worse paid					
Ganger	By the day	16s. weekly, + 1s. allowance	To load the cart and superintend the men	Three months during the year	12s. 9d. per week
Carman	By the day	15s. weekly, + 1s. allowance	To take charge of the horse and cart, help load the cart, and take the dirt or slop to the dustyard	Three months during the year	12s. per week
Sweepers	By the day	15s. weekly, + 1s. allowance	To sweep the district, collect dirt or slop ready for carting off, work in the yard, and load the cart	Three months during the year	12s. per week
II. Machine men					
Carman	By the day	16s. weekly	To take charge of the horse and machine, collect the dirt and take it to the yard	Three months during the year	12s. per week
Sweepers	By the day	16s. weekly	To sweep where the machine cannot touch, work in the yard, and load the barges	Three months during the year	12s. per week
III. Parish men					
A. Out-door paupers					
1. Paid in money					
Married men	By the day	9s. weekly	Sweep the streets and courts belonging to the parish, and collect the dirt or slop ready for carting away	Six months during the year	4s. 6d. per week
Single men	By the day	6s. weekly	and collect the dirt or slop ready for carting away	Six months during the year	3s. per week
2. Paid part in kind					
Married men	By the day	6s. 9d. weekly; 3 quartern loaves	Sweep the streets and courts belonging to the parish, and collect the dirt or slop ready for carting away	Six months during the year	3s. 4½d. per week, + loaves
Single men	By the day	5s. weekly; 3 half-quartern loaves	Sweep the streets and courts belonging to the parish, and collect the dirt or slop ready for carting away	Six months during the year	2s. 6d. per week, + loaves
B. In-door paupers	All in kind	Food, lodging, clothes	ditto ditto ditto	....	Food, lodging, clothes
IV. Street orderlies					
Foreman/Ganger	By the day	15s. weekly	Superintend the men and see that their work is done well		
Sweepers	By the day	12s. weekly	Collect the dirt or slop ready for carting away		
Barrow men	By the day	....	Collect the dirt or slop ready for carting away		
Barrow boys	By the day	....	Collect the short dung as it gathers in the district to which they are appointed		

and an extra halfpenny); if 2*s*., it is 2*s*. 6*d*.; and if less (which has been paid), the day's wage is not lower than 2*s*. At the lowest rates, however, the men, I was informed, could not be induced to take the necessary pains, as they would struggle to 'make up half-a-crown'; while, if the streets were scavaged in a slovenly manner, the contractor was sure to hear from his friends of the parish that he was not acting up to his contract. I could not hear of any men now set to piece-work withing the precincts of the places specified in the table. This extra work and scamping work are the two great evils of the piece system.

In their payments to their men the contractors show a superiority to the practices of some traders, and even of some dock-companies: the men are never paid at public-houses; the payment, moreover, is always in money. One contractor told me that he would like all his men to be teetotallers, if he could get them, though he was not one himself.

But these remarks refer only to the nominal wages of the scavagers; and I find the nominal wages of operatives in many cases are widely different (either from some additions by way of perquisites, &c., or deductions by way of fines, &c., but oftener the latter) from the actual wages received by them. Again, the average wages, or gross yearly income of the casually-employed men, are very different from those of the constant hands; so are the gains of a particular individual often no criterion of the general or average earnings of the trade. Indeed I find that the several varieties of wages may be classified as follows:

1. *Nominal Wages*. – Those said to be paid in a trade.

2. *Actual Wages*. – Those *really* received, and which are equal to the nominal wages, *plus* the additions to, or *minus* the deductions from, them.

3. *Casual Wages*. – The earnings of the men who are only occasionally employed.

4. *Average Casual or Constant Wages*. – Those obtained throughout the year by such as are either occasionally or regularly employed.

5. *Individual Wages*. – Those of particular hands, whether belonging to the scurf or honourable trade, whether working long or short hours, whether partially or fully employed, and the like.

6. *General Wages*. – Or the *average* wages of the whole trade, constant or casual, fully or partially employed, honourable or scurf,

long and short hour men, &c., &c., all lumped together and the mean taken of the whole.

Now, in the preceding account of the working scavagers' mode and rate of payment I have spoken only of the nominal wages; and in order to arrive at their actual wages we must, as we have seen, ascertain what additions and what deductions are generally made to and from this amount. The deductions in the honourable trade are, as usual, inconsiderable.

All the *tools* used by operative scavagers are supplied to them by their employers – the tools being only brooms and shovels; and for this supply there are *no stoppages* to cover the expense.

Neither by *fines* nor by way of *security* are the men's wages reduced.

The *truck system*, moreover, is unknown, and has never prevailed in the trade. I heard of only one instance of an approach to it. A yard foreman, some years ago, who had a great deal of influence with his employer, had a chandler's-shop, managed by his wife, and it was broadly intimated to the men that they must make their purchases there. Complaints, however, were made to the contractor, and the foreman dismissed. One man of whom I inquired did not even know what the 'truck system' meant; and when informed, thought they were 'pretty safe' from it, as the contractor had nothing which he *could* truck with the men, and if 'he polls us hisself,' the man said, 'he's not likely to let anybody else do it.'

There are, moreover, no trade-payments to which the men are subjected; there are no trade-societies among the working men, no benefit nor sick clubs; neither do parochial relief and family labour characterise the regular hands in the honourable trade, although in sickness they may have no other resource.

Indeed, the working scavagers employed by the more honourable portion of the trade, instead of having any deductions made from their nominal wages, have rather additions to them in the form of perquisites coming from the public. These perquisites consist of allowances of beer-money, obtained in the same manner as the dustmen – not through the medium of their employers (though, to say the least, through their sufferance), but from the householders of the parish in which their labours are prosecuted.

The scavagers, it seems, are not required to sweep any places considered 'private', nor even to sweep the public foot-paths;

and when they *do* sweep or carry away the refuse of a butcher's premises, for instance – for, by law, the butcher is required to do so himself – they receive a gratuity. In the contract entered into by the city scavagers, it is expressly covenanted that no men employed shall accept gratuities from the householders; a condition little or not at all regarded, though I am told that these gratuities become less every year. I am informed also by an experienced butcher, who had at one time a private slaughter-house in the Borough, that, until within these six or seven years, he thought the scavagers, and even the dustmen, would carry away entrails, &c., in the carts, from the butcher's and the knacker's premises, for an allowance.

I cannot learn that the contractors, whether of the honourable or scurf trade, take any advantage of these 'allowances'. A working scavager receives the same wage, when he enjoys what I heard called in another trade 'the height of perquisites', or is employed in a locality where there are no such additions to his wages. I believe, however, that the contracting scavagers let their best and steadiest hands have the best perquisited work.

These perquisites, I am assured, average from 1s. to 2s. a week, but one butcher told me he thought 1s. 6d. might be rather too high an average, for a pint of beer (2d.) was the customary sum given, and that was, or ought to be, divided among the gang. 'In my opinion,' he said, 'there'll be no allowances in a year or two.' By the amount of these perquisites, then, the scavagers' gains are so far enhanced.

The wages, therefore, of an operative scavager in full employ, and working for the 'honourable' portion of the trade, may be thus expressed:

Nominal weekly wages	16s.
Perquisites in the form of allowances for beer from the public	2s.
Actual weekly wages	18s.

'Casual hands' among the scavengers
[*volume ii, pp. 220–224*]

Of the scavagers proper there are, as in all classes of unskilled labour, that is to say, of labour which requires no previous apprenticeship, and to which any one can 'turn his hand' on an emergency, two distinct orders of workmen, 'the *regulars* and *casuals*' to adopt the trade terms; that is to say, the labourers consist of those who have been many years at the trade, constantly employed at it, and those who have but recently taken to it as a means of obtaining a subsistence after their ordinary resources have failed. This mixture of *constant* and *casual* hands is, moreover, a necessary consequence of all trades which depend upon the seasons, and in which an additional number of labourers are required at different periods. Such is necessarily the case with dock labour, where an easterly wind prevailing for several days deprives *thousands of work*, and where the change from a foul to a fair wind causes an equally inordinate demand for workmen. The same temporary increase of employment takes place in the agricultural districts at harvesting time, and the same among the hop growers in the picking season; and it will be hereafter seen that there are the same labour fluctuations in the scavaging trade, a greater or lesser number of hands being required, of course, according as the season is wet or dry.

This occasional increase of employment, though a benefit in some few cases (as enabling a man suddenly deprived of his ordinary means of living to obtain 'a job of work' until he can 'turn himself round'), is generally a most alarming evil in a State. What are the casual hands to do when the extra employment ceases? Those who have paid attention to the subject of dock labour and the subject of casual labour in general, may form some notion of the vast mass of misery that must be generally existing in London. The subject of hop-picking again belongs to the same question. Here are thousands of the very poorest employed only for a few days in the year. What, the mind naturally asks, do they after their short term of honest independence has ceased? With dock labour the poor man's bread depends upon the very winds; in scavaging and in street life generally it depends upon the rain; and in market-gardening, harvesting, hop-picking, and the like, it depends upon the sunshine. How many thousands in this huge metropolis have to look immediately to the very elements for their bread, it is overwhelming to contemplate; and yet, with all this fitfulness of employment we wonder that an extended knowledge of reading and writing does not produce a decrease of crime! We should, however, ask ourselves whether men can stay their hunger with alphabets or grow fat on spelling books; and wanting employment, and consequently food, and objecting to the incarceration of the workhouse, can we be astonished – indeed is it not a natural law – that they should help themselves to the property of others?

Concerning the 'regular hands' of the contracting scavagers, it may, perhaps, be reasonable to compute that little short of one-half of them have been 'to the manner born'. The others are, as I have said, what these regular hands call 'casuals', or 'casualties'. As an instance of the peculiar mixture of the regular and casual hands in the scavaging trade, I may state that one of my in-formants told me he had, at one period, under his immediate direction, fourteen men, of whom the former occupations had been as follows:

- 7 Always scavagers (or dustmen, and six of them nightmen when required).
- 1 Pot-boy at a public-house (but only as a boy).
- 1 Stable-man (also nightman).
- 1 Formerly a pugilist, then a showman's assistant.
- 1 Navvy.
- 1 Ploughman (nightman occasionally).
- 2 Unknown, one of them saying, but gaining no belief, that he had once been a gentleman.

$\overline{14}$

In my account of the street orderlies will be given an interesting and elaborate statement of the former avocations, the habits, ex-penditure, &c., of a body of street-sweepers, 67 in number. This table will be found very curious, as showing what classes of men have been *driven* to street-sweeping, but it will not furnish a criterion of the character of the 'regular hands' employed by the contractors.

The 'casuals' or the 'casualties' (always called among the men 'cazzelties'), may be more properly described as men whose em-ployment is accidental, chanceful, or uncertain. The regular hands of the scavagers are apt to designate any new comer, even for a permanence, any sweeper not reared to or versed in the business, a casual ('cazzel'). I shall, however, here deal with the 'casual hands', not only as hands newly introduced into the trade, but as men of chanceful and irregular employment.

These persons are now, I understand, numerous in all branches of unskilled labour, willing to undertake or attempt any kind of work, but perhaps there is a greater tendency on the part of the surplus unskilled to turn to scavaging, from the fact that any broken-down man seems to account himself competent to sweep the streets.

To ascertain the number of these casual or outside labourers in the scavaging trade is difficult, for, as I have said, they are willing in their need to attempt any kind of work, and so may be 'casuals' in divers departments of unskilled labour.

I do not think that I can better approximate the number of casuals than by quoting the opinion of a contracting scavager familiar with his workmen and their ways. He considered that there were always nearly as many hands on the look-out for a job in the streets, as there were regularly employed at the business by the large contractors; this I have shown to be 262, let us estimate therefore the number of casuals at 200.

According to the table I have given at pp. 213, 214,* the number of men regularly or constantly employed at the metropolitan trade is as follows:

Scavagers employed by large contractors	262
Ditto small contractors	13
Ditto machines	25
Ditto parishes	218
Ditto street-orderlies	60
Total working scavagers in London	578

But the prior table given at pp. 186, 187,* shows the number of scavagers employed throughout the metropolis in wet and dry weather (*exclusive of the street-orderlies*) to be as follows:

Scavagers employed in wet weather	531
Ditto in dry weather	358
Difference	173

Hence it would appear that about one-third less hands are required in the dry than in the wet season of the year. The 170 hands, then, discharged in the dry season are the casually employed men, but the whole of these 170 are not turned adrift immediately they are no longer wanted, some being kept on 'odd

* Not reprinted in this edition

jobs' in the yard, &c.; nor can that number be said to represent the entire amount of the surplus labour in the trade, but only that portion of it which does obtain even casual employment. After much trouble, and taking the average of various statements, it would appear that the number of casualty or quantity of occasional surplus labour in the scavaging trade may be represented at between 200 and 250 hands.

The scavaging trade, however, is not, I am informed, so overstocked with labourers now as it was formerly. Seven years ago, and from that to ten, there were usually between 200 and 300 hands out of work; this was owing to there being a less extent of paved streets, and comparatively few contractors; the scavaging work, moreover, was 'scamped', the men, to use their own phrase, 'licking the work over any how', so that fewer hands were required. Now, however, the inhabitants are more particular, I am told, 'about the crooks and corners', and require the streets to be swept oftener. Formerly a gang of operative scavagers would only collect six loads of dirt a day, but now a gang will collect nine loads daily. The causes to which the surplus of labourers at present may be attributed are, I find, as follows: Each operative has to do nearly double the work to what he formerly did, the extra cleansing of the streets having tended not only to employ more hands, but to make each of those employed do more work. The result has, however been followed by an increase in the wages of the operatives; seven years ago the labourers received but 2s. a day, and the ganger 2s. 6d., but now the labourers receive 2s. 8d. a day, and the ganger 3s.

In the city the men have to work very long hours, sometimes as many as 18 hours a day without any extra pay. This practice of over-working is, I find, carried on to a great extent, even with those master scavagers who pay the regular wages. One man told me that when he worked for a certain large master, whom he named, he has many times been out at work 28 hours in the wet (saturated to the skin) without having any rest. This plan of overworking, again, is generally adopted by the small masters, whose men, after they have done a regular day's labour, are set to work in the yard, sometimes toiling 18 hours a day, and usually not less than 16 hours daily. Often so tired and weary are the men, that when they rise in the morning to pursue their daily labour, they feel as fatigued as when they went to bed. 'Frequently,' said one of my informants, 'have I gone to bed so worn out, that I haven't been able to sleep. However' (he added), 'there is the work to be done, and we must do it or be off.'

This system of over-work, especially in those trades where the quantity of work to be done is in a measure fixed, I find to be a far more influential cause of surplus labour than 'over-population'. The mere number of labourers in a trade is, *per se*, no criterion as to the quantity of labour employed in it; to arrive at this three things are required:

(1) The number of hands;
(2) The hours of labour;
(3) The rate of labouring;

for it is a mere point of arithmetic, that if the hands in the scavaging trade work 18 hours a day, there must be one-third less men employed than there otherwise would, or in other words one-third of the men who are in work must be thus deprived of it. This is one of the crying evils of the day, and which the economists, filled as they are with their over-population theories, have entirely overlooked.

There are 262 men employed in the Metropolitan Scavaging Trade; one-half of these at the least may be said to work 16 hours per diem instead of 12, or one-third longer than they should; so that if the hours of labour in this trade were restricted to the usual day's work, there would be employment for one-sixth more hands, or nearly 50 individuals extra.

The other causes of the present amount of surplus labour are –

The many hands thrown out of employment by the discontinuance of railway works.

A less demand for unskilled labour in agricultural districts, or a smaller remuneration for it.

A less demand for some branches of labour (as ostlers, &c.), by the introduction of machinery (applied to roads), or through the caprices of fashion.

It should, however, be remembered, that men often found their opinions of such causes on prejudices, or express them according to their class interests, and it is only a few employers of unskilled labourers who care to inquire into the antecedent circumstances of men who ask for work.

As regards the population part of the question, it cannot be said that the surplus labour of the scavaging trade is referable to any inordinate increase in the families of the men. Those who are married appear to have, on the average, four children, and about one-half of the men have no family at all. Early marriages are by no means usual. Of the casual hands, however, full three-fourths are married, and one-half have families.

There are not more than ten or a dozen Irish labourers who have taken to the scavaging, though several have 'tried it on'; the regular hands say that the Irish are too lazy to continue at the trade; but surely the labour of the hodman, in which the Irish seem to delight, is sufficient to disprove this assertion, be the cause what it may. About one-fourth of the scavagers entering the scavaging trade as casual hands have been agricultural labourers, and have come up to London from the several agricultural districts in quest of work; about the same proportion appear to have been connected with horses, such as ostlers, carmen, &c.

The *brisk and slack seasons* in the scavaging trade depend upon the state of the weather. In the depth of winter, owing to the shortness of the days, more hands are usually required for street cleansing; but a 'clear frost' renders the scavager's labour in little demand. In the winter, too, his work is generally the hardest, and the hardest of all when there is snow, which soon becomes mud in London streets; and though a continued frost is a sort of lull to the scavagers' labour, after 'a great thaw' his strength is taxed to the uttermost; and then, indeed, new hands have had to be put on. At the West-end, in the height of the summer, which is usually the height of the fashionable season, there is again a more than usual requirement of scavaging industry in wet weather; but perhaps the greatest exercise of such industry is after a series of the fogs peculiar to the London atmosphere, when the men cannot see to sweep. The table I have given shows the influence of the weather, as on wet days 531 men are employed, and on dry days only 358; this, however, does not influence the Street-Orderly system, as under it the men are employed every day, unless the weather make it an actual impossibility.

According to the rain table given at p. 202,* there would appear to be, on an average of 23 years, 178 wet days in London out of the

* Not reprinted in this edition

365, that is to say, about 100 in every 205 days are 'rainy ones'. The months having the greatest and least number of wet days are as follows:

	No. of days in the month in which rain falls
December	17
July, August, October	16
February, May, November	15
January, April	14
March, September	12
June	11

Hence it would appear that June is the least and December the most showery month in the course of the year; the greatest quantity of rain falling in any month is, however, in October, and the least quantity in March. The number of wet days, and the quantity of rain falling in each half of the year, may be expressed as follows:

	Total in no. of wet days	Total depth of rain falling (in inches)
The first six months in the year ending June there are	84	10
The second six months in the year ending December there are	93	14

Hence we perceive that the quantity of work for the scavagers would fluctuate in the first and last half of the year in the proportion of 10 to 14, which is very nearly in the ratio of 358 to 531, which are the numbers of hands given in the table,* as those employed in wet and dry weather throughout the metropolis.

If, then, the labour in the scavaging trade varies in the proportion of 5 to 7, that is to say, that 5 hands are required at one period and 7 at another to execute the work, the question consequently becomes, how do the 2 casuals who are discharged out of every 7 obtain their living when the wet season is over?

When a scavager is out of employ, he seldom or never applies to the parish; this he does, I am informed, only when he is fairly 'beaten out' through sickness or old age, for the men 'hate the thought of going to the big house' (the union workhouse). An unemployed operative scavager will go from yard to yard and offer

---

* 'Scavagers employed in wet weather', page 362.

his services to do anything in the dust trade or any other kind of employment in connection with dust or scavaging.

Generally speaking, an operative scavager who is casually employed obtains work at that trade for six or eight months during the year, and the remaining portion of his time is occupied either at rubbish-carting or brick-carting, or else he gets a job for a month or two in a dust-yard.

Many of these men seem to form a body of street-jobbers or operative labourers, ready to work at the docks, to be navvies (when strong enough), bricklayers' labourers, street-sweepers, carriers of trunks or parcels, window-cleaners, errand-goers, porters, and (occasionally) nightmen. Few of the class seem to apply themselves to trading, as in the costermonger line. They are the loungers about the boundaries of trading, but seldom take any onward steps. The street-sweeper of this week, a 'casual' hand, may be a rubbish-carter or a labourer about buildings the next, or he may be a starving man for days together, and the more he is starving with the less energy will he exert himself to obtain work: 'it's not in' a starving or ill-fed man to exert himself otherwise than what may be called *passively*; this is well known to all who have paid attention to the subject. The want of energy and carelessness begotten by want of food was well described by the tinman, at p. 355 in vol. i.

One casual hand told me that last year he was out of work altogether three months, and the year before not more than six weeks, and during the six weeks he got a day's work sometimes at rubbish-carting and sometimes at loading bricks. Their wives are often employed in the yards as sifters, and their boys, when big enough, work also at the heap, either in carrying off, or else as fillers-in; if there are any girls, one is generally left at home to look after the rest and get the meals ready for the other members of the family. If any of the children go to school, they are usually sent to a ragged school in the neighbourhood, though they seldom attend the school more than two or three times during the week.

The additional hands employed in wet weather are either men who at other times work in the yards, or such as have their 'turns' in street-sweeping, if not regularly employed. There appears, however, to be little of system in the arrangement. If more hands are wanted, the gangsman, who receives his orders from the contractor or the contractor's managing man, is told to put on so many new hands, and over-night he has but to tell any of the men at work that Jack, and Bob, and Bill will be wanted in the morning, and they, if not employed in other work, appear accordingly.

There is nothing, however, which can be designated a *labour market* appertaining to the trade. No 'house of call', no trade society. If men seek such employment, they must apply at the contractor's premises, and I am assured that poor men not unfrequently ask the scavagers whom they see at work in the streets where to apply 'for a job', and sometimes receive gruff or abusive replies. But though there is nothing like a labour market in the scavager's trade, the employers have not to 'look out' for men, for I was told by one of their foremen, that he would undertake, if necessary, which it never was, by a mere 'round of the docks', to select 200 new hale men, of all classes, and strong ones, too, if properly fed, who in a few days would be tolerable street-sweepers. It is a calling to which agricultural labourers are glad to resort, and a calling to which any labourer or any mechanic may resort, more especially as regards sweeping or scraping, apart from shovelling, which is regarded as something like the high art of the business.

We now come to estimate the earnings of the casual hands, whose yearly incomes must, of course, be very different from those of the regulars. The *constant* weekly wages of any workman are of course the average of his casual – and hence we shall find the wages of those who are *regularly* employed far exceed those of the *occasionally* employed men:

	£	s.	d.
Nominal yearly wages at scavaging for 25 weeks in the year, at 16s. per week	20	16	0
Perquisites for 26 weeks, at 2s.	2	12	0
Actual yearly wages at scavaging	23	8	0
Nominal and actual weekly wages at rubbish carting for 20 weeks in the year, at 12s.	12	0	0
Unemployed six weeks in the year	0	0	0
Gross yearly earnings	35	8	0
Average casual or constant weekly wages throughout the year		15	4½

Hence the difference between the earnings of the casual and the regular hand would appear to be one-sixth. But the great evil of all casual labour is the uncertainty of the income – for where there is the greatest chance connected with an employment, there is not only the greatest necessity for providence, but unfortunately the greatest tendency to improvidence. It is only when a man's income becomes regular and fixed that he grows thrifty, and lays by for the future; but where all is chance-work there is but little ground for reasoning, and the accident which assisted the man out of his difficulties at one period is continually expected to do the same good turn for him at another. Hence the casual hand, who passes the half of the year on 18s., and twenty weeks on 12s., and *six weeks on nothing*, lives a life of excess both ways – of excess of 'guzzling' when in work, and excess of privation when out of it – oscillating, as it were, between surfeit and starvation.

A man who had worked in an iron-foundry, but who had 'lost his work' (I believe through some misconduct) and was glad to get employment as a street-sweeper, as he had a good recommendation to a contractor, told me that 'the misery of the thing' was the want of regular work. 'I've worked,' he said, 'for a good master for four months an end at 2s. 8d. a day, and they were prime times. Then I hadn't a stroke of work for a fortnight, and very little for two months, and if my wife hadn't had middling work with a laundress we might have starved, or I might have made a hole in the Thames, for it's no good living to be miserable and feel you can't help yourself any how. We was sometimes half-starved, as it was. I'd rather at this minute have regular work at 10s. a week all the year round, than have chance-work that I could earn 20s. a week at. I once had 15s. in relief from the parish, and a doctor to attend us, when my wife and I was both laid up sick. Oh, there's no difference in the way of doing the work, whatever wages you're on for; the streets must be swept clean, of course. The plan's the same, and there's the same sort of management, any how.'

Coal-heavers and dock labourers

[*volume iii, pp. 233–243 and 300–310*]

*Casual labour not only affected the conditions and remuneration of labour,
it also created a distinctive culture which distanced the casual worker from
the regularly employed and well-paid craftsman. Mayhew is at his best in
describing the working environment and way of life of those who subsisted
below the breadline.*

Coal-heavers and -whippers

[*volume iii, pp. 233–243*]

The transition from the artisan to the labourer is curious in many
respects. In passing from the skilled operative of the West-end
to the unskilled workman of the eastern quarter of London,
the moral and intellectual change is so great, that it seems as if
we were in a new land, and among another race. The artisans
are almost to a man red-hot politicians. They are sufficiently
educated and thoughtful to have a sense of their importance
in the State. It is true they may entertain exaggerated notions
of their natural rank and position in the social scale, but at least
they have read, and reflected, and argued upon the subject, and
their opinions are entitled to consideration. The political character and sentiments of the working classes appear to me to be
a distinctive feature of the age, and they are a necessary consequence of the dawning intelligence of the mass. As their minds
expand, they are naturally led to take a more enlarged view of
their calling, and to contemplate their labours in relation to
the whole framework of society. They begin to view their class,
not as a mere isolated body of workmen, but as an integral
portion of the nation, contributing their quota to the general
welfare. If property has its duties as well as its rights; labour, on
the other hand, they say, has its rights as well as its duties. The
artisans of London seem to be generally well-informed upon
these subjects. That they express their opinions violently, and
often savagely, it is my duty to acknowledge; but that they are the
unenlightened and unthinking body of people that they are generally considered by those who never go among them, and who see
them only as 'the dangerous classes', it is my duty also to deny. So
far as my experience has gone, I am bound to confess, that I have

found the skilled labourers of the metropolis the very reverse, both morally and intellectually, of what the popular prejudice imagines them.

The unskilled labourers are a different class of people. As yet they are as unpolitical as footmen, and instead of entertaining violent democratic opinions, they appear to have no political opinions whatever; or, if they do possess any, they rather lead towards the maintenance of 'things as they are', than towards the ascendancy of the working people. I have lately been investigating the state of the coal-whippers, and these reflections are forced upon me by the marked difference in the character and sentiments of these people from those of the operative tailors. Among the latter class there appeared to be a general bias towards the six points of the Charter; but the former were extremely proud of their having turned out to a man on the 10th of April, 1848, and become special constables for the maintenance of law and order on the day of the great Chartist demonstration. As to which of these classes are the better members of the state, it is not for me to offer an opinion; I merely assert a social fact. The artisans of the metropolis are intelligent, and dissatisfied with their political position: the labourers of London appear to be the reverse; and in passing from one class to the other, the change is so curious and striking, that the phenomenon deserves at least to be recorded in this place.

The labourers, in point of numbers, rank second on the occupation-list of the metropolis. The domestic servants, as a body of people, have the first numerical position, being as many 168,000, while the labourers are less than one-third that number, or 50,000 strong. They, however, are nearly twice as many as the boot and shoemakers, who stand next upon the list, and muster 28,000 individuals among them; and they are more than twice as many as the tailors and breeches-makers, who are fourth in regard to their number, and count 23,500 persons. After these come the milliners and dressmakers, who are 20,000 in number. [. . .]

In the winter, the coal-whipper is occupied about five days out of eight, and about three days out of eight in the summer; so that, taking it all the year round, he is only about half of his time employed. As soon as a collier arrives at Gravesend, the captain sends the ship's papers up to the factor at the Coal Exchange, informing him of the quality and quantity of coal in the ship.

The captain then falls into some tier near Gravesend, and remains there until he is ordered nearer London by the harbour-master. When the coal is sold and the ship supplied with the coal-meter, the captain receives orders from the harbour-master to come up into the Pool, and take his berth in a particular tier. The captain, when he has moored his ship into the Pool as directed, applies at the Coal-whippers' Office, and 'the gang' next in rotation is sent to him.

There are upwards of 200 gangs of coal-whippers. The class, supernumeraries included, numbers about 2,000 individuals. The number of meters is 150; the consequence is, that more than one-fourth of the gangs are unprovided with meters to work with them. Hence there are upwards of fifty gangs (of nine men each) of coal-whippers, or altogether 450 men more than there is any real occasion for. The consequence is, that each coal-whipper is necessarily thrown out of employ one-quarter of his time by the excess of hands. The cause of this extra number of hands being kept on the books is, that when there is a glut of vessels in the river, the coal merchants may not be delayed in having their cargoes delivered from want of whippers. When such a glut occurs, the merchant has it in his power to employ a private meter; so that the 450 to 500 men are kept on the year through, merely to meet the particular exigency, and to promote the merchant's convenience. Did any good arise from this system to the public, the evil might be overlooked; but since, owing to the combination of the coal-factors, no more coals can come into the market than are sufficient to meet the demand *without lowering the price*, it is clear that the extra 450 or 500 men are kept on and allowed to deprive their fellow-labourers of one-quarter of their regular work as whippers, without any advantage to the public.

The coal-whippers, previous to the passing of the Act of Parliament in 1843, were employed and paid by the publicans in the neighbourhood of the river, from Tower-hill to Lime-house. Under this system, none but the most dissolute and intemperate obtained employment; in fact, the more intemperate they were the more readily they found work. The publicans were the relatives of the northern ship-owners; they mostly had come to London penniless, and being placed in a tavern by their relatives, soon became shipowners themselves. There were at that time seventy taverns on the north side of the Thames, below bridge, employing coal-whippers, and all of the landlords making fortunes out of the earnings of the people. When a ship came to be 'made up', that is, for the hands to be hired, the men assembled round the bar in crowds and began calling for drink, and outbidding each other in the extent of their orders, so as to induce the landlord to give them employment. If one called for beer, the next would be sure to give an order for rum; for he who spent most at the public-house had the greatest chance of employment. After being 'taken on', their first care was to put up a score at the public-house, so as to please their employer, the publican. In the morning before going to their work, they would invariably call at the house for a quartern of gin or rum; and they were obliged to take off with them to the ship 'a bottle', holding nine pots of beer, and that of the worst description, for it was the invariable practice among the publicans to supply the coal-whippers with the very worst articles at the highest prices. When the men returned from their work they went back to the public-house, and there remained drinking the greater part of the night, [so] that frequently, on the publican settling with them after leaving the ship, instead of having anything to receive, they were brought in several shillings in debt; this remained as a score for the next ship: in fact, it was only those who were in debt to the publican who were sure of employment on the next occasion. [. . .] The children of the coal-whippers were almost reared in the tap-room. [. . .]

My informant tells me that he has frequently seen as many as 100 men at one time fighting pell-mell at King James's-stairs, and the publican standing by to see fair play. [. . .]

The wives and families of the men at this time were in the greatest destitution, the daughters invariably became prostitutes, and the mothers ultimately went to swell the number of paupers at the union. This state of things continued till 1843, when, by the efforts of three of the coal-whippers, the Legislature was induced to pass an Act forbidding the system, and appointing Commissioners for the registration and regulation of coal-whippers in the port of London, and so establishing an office where the men were in future employed and paid. Under this Act, every man then following the calling of a coal-whipper was to be registered. For this registration 4d. was to be paid; and every man desirous of entering upon the same business had to pay the same sum, and to have his name registered. The employment is open to any labouring man; but every new hand, after registering himself, must work for twenty-one days on half-pay before he is considered to be 'broken in', and entitled to take rank and receive pay as a regular coal-whipper.

All the coal-whippers are arranged in gangs of eight whippers, with a basket-man or foreman. These gangs are numbered from 1 up to 218, which is the highest number at the present time. The basket-men, or foremen, enter their names in a rotation-book kept in the office, and as their names stand in that book so do they take their turn to clear the ship that is offered. On a ship being offered, a printed form of application, kept in the office, is filled up by the captain, in which he states the number of tons, the price, and time in which she is to be delivered. If the gang whose turn of work it is refuse the ship at the price offered, then it is offered to all the gangs, and if accepted by any other gang, the next in rotation may claim it as their right, before all others. In connection with the office there is a long hall, extending from the street to the water-side, where the men wait to take their turn. There is also a room called the basket-men's room, where the foremen of the gang remain in attendance. There is likewise a floating pier called a depot, which is used as a receptacle for the tackle with which the colliers are unloaded. This floating pier is fitted up with seats, where the men wait in the summer. The usual price at present for delivering the colliers is 8d. per ton; but in case of a less price being offered, and the gangs all refusing it, then the captain is at liberty to employ any hands he pleases. According to the Act, however, the owner or purchaser of the coals is at liberty to employ his own servants, provided they have been in his service fourteen clear days previous, and so have become what the Act terms *bona fide* servants. This is very often taken advantage of, for the purpose of obtaining labourers at a less price. One lighterman, who is employed by the gas companies to 'lighter' their coals to their various destinations, makes a practice of employing parties whom he calls the *bona fide* servants of the gas companies, to deliver the coals at a penny per ton less than the regular price. Besides this, he takes one man's pay to himself, and so stops one-tenth of the whole proceeds, thereby realising, as he boasts, the sum of 300l. per annum. Added to this, a relative of his keeps a beer-shop, where the '*bona fide* servants' spend the chief part of their earnings, thereby bringing back the old system, which was the cause of so much misery and destitution to the work-people.

According to the custom of the trade, the rate at which a ship is to be delivered is forty-nine tons per day, and if the ship cannot be delivered at that rate, owing to the merchant failing to send craft to receive the coals, then the coal-whippers are entitled to receive pay at the rate of forty-nine tons per day, for each day they are kept in the ship over and above the time allowed by the custom of the trade for the delivery of the coals. The merchants, however, if they should have failed to send craft, and so keep the men idle on the first days of the contract, can, by the by-laws of the Commissioners, compel the coal-whippers to deliver the ship at the rate of ninety-eight tons per day: the merchants surely should be made to pay for the loss of time to the men at the same rate. The wrong done by this practice is rendered more apparent by the conduct of the merchants during the brisk and slack periods. When there is a slack, the merchants are all anxious to get their vessels delivered as fast as they can, because coals are wanting, and are consequently at a high price; then the men are taxed beyond their power, and are frequently made to deliver 150 to 200 tons per day, or to do four days' work in one. On the contrary, when there is a glut of ships, and the merchants are not particularly anxious about the delivery of the coals, the men are left to idle away their time upon the decks for the first two or three days of the contract, and then forced to the same extra exertion for the last two or three days, in order to make up for the lost time of the merchant, and so save him from being put to extra expense by his own neglect. The cause of the injustice of these by-laws may be fairly traced to the fact of there being several coal-merchants among the Commissioners, who are entrusted with the formation of bye-laws and regulations of the trade. The coal-factors are generally ship-owners, and occasionally pit-owners; and when a glut of ships come in they combine together to keep up the prices, especially in the winter time, for they keep back the cargoes, and only offer such a number of ships as will not influence the market. Since the passing of the Act, establishing the Coal-whippers' Office, and thus taking the employment and pay of the men out of the hands of the publicans, so visible has been the improvement in the whole character of the labourers, that they have raised themselves in the respect of all who know them.

Within the last few years they have established a Benefit Society, and [. . .] a superannuation fund, out of which they allow 5s. per week to each member who is incapacitated from old age or accident. They are, at the present time, paying such pensions to twenty members. At the time of the celebrated Chartist demonstration, on the 10th of April, the coal-whippers were, I believe, the first class of persons who spontaneously offered their services as special constables. [. . .]

The men are liable to many accidents; some fall off the plank into the hold of the vessel, and are killed; others are injured by large lumps of coal falling on them; and, indeed, so frequent are these disasters, that the Commissioners have directed that the indivisible fraction which remains, after dividing the earnings of the men into nine equal parts, should be applied to the relief of the injured; and although the fund raised by these insignificant means amounts in the course of the year to 30l. or 40l., the whole is absorbed by the calamities.

[. . .] I then proceeded to visit one of the vessels in the river, so that I might see the nature of the labour performed. No-one on board the vessel [. . .] was previously aware of my visit or its object. I need not describe the vessel, as my business is with the London labourers in the coal trade. It is necessary, however, in order to show the nature of the labour of coal-whipping, that I should state that the average depth of coal in the hold of a collier, from ceiling to combing, is sixteen feet, while there is an additional seven feet to be reckoned for the basket-man's 'boom', which makes the height that the coals have to be raised by the whippers from twenty-three to thirty feet. The complement of a gang of coal-whippers is about nine. In the hold are four men, who relieve each other in filling a basket – only one basket being in use with coal. The labour of these four men is arduous: so exhausting is it in hot weather that their usual attire is found to be cumbrous, and they have often to work merely in their trousers or drawers. As fast as these four men in the hold fill the basket, which holds 1¼ cwt., four whippers draw it up. This is effected in a peculiar and, to a person unused to the contemplation of the process, really an impressive manner. The four whippers stand on the deck, at the foot of what is called 'a way'. This way resembles a short rude ladder: it is formed of four broken oars lashed lengthways, from four to five feet in height (giving a step from oar to oar of more than a foot), while the upright spars to which they are attached are called a 'derrick'. At the top of this 'derrick' is a 'gin', which is a revolving wheel, to which the ropes holding the basket, 'filled' and 'whipped', are attached. The process is thus one of manual labour with mechanical aid. The basket having been filled in the hold, the whippers correctly guessing the time for the filling – for they never look down into the hold – skip up the 'way', holding the ropes attached to the basket and the gin, and pulling the ropes at two skips, simultaneously, as they ascend. They thus hoist the loaded basket some height out of the hold, and, when hoisted so far, jump down, keeping exact time in their jump, from the topmost beam of the way on to the deck, so giving the momentum of their bodily weight to the motion communicated to the basket. While the basket is influenced by this motion and momentum, the basket-man, who is stationed on a plank flung across the hold, seizes the basket, runs on with it (the gin revolving) to 'the boom', and shoots the contents into the weighing-machine. The boom is formed of two upright poles, with a cross-pole attached by way of step, on to which the basket-man vaults, and rapidly reversing the basket, empties it. This process is very quickly effected, for if the basket-man did not avail himself of the swing of the basket, the feat would be almost beyond a man's strength, or, at least, he would soon be exhausted by it.

The machine is a large coal-scuttle or wooden box, attached to a scale connected with 2½ cwt. When the weight is raised by two deposits in the machine, which hangs over the side of the ship, it discharges it, by pulling a rope connected with it down a sliding wooden plane into the barge below. The machine holds 2½ cwt., and so the meter registers the weight of coal unladen. This process is not only remarkable for its celerity but for another characteristic. Sailors, when they have to 'pull away' together, generally time their pulling to some rude chant; their 'Yo, heave, yo', is thought not only to regulate but to mitigate the weight of their labour. The coal-whippers do their work in perfect silence: they do it indeed like work, and hard work, too. The basket-man and the meter are equally silent, so that nothing is heard but the friction of the ropes, the discharge of the coal from the basket into the machine, and from the machine into the barge. The usual amount of work done by the whippers in a day (but not as an average, one day with another) is to unload, or whip, ninety-eight tons! To whip one ton, sixteen basketfuls are required; so that to whip a single ton these men jump up and down 144 feet: for a day's work of ninety-eight tons, they jump up and down 13,088 feet, more in some instances; for in the largest ship the way has five steps, and ten men are employed. The coal-whippers, therefore, raise 1¼ cwt. very nearly four miles high, or twice as high as a balloon ordinarily mounts in the air: and, in addition to this, the coal-whippers themselves ascend very nearly 1½ mile perpendicularly in the course of the day. On some days they whip upwards of 150 tons – 200 have been whipped, when double this labour must be gone through. The ninety-eight tons take about seven hours. The basket-man's work is the most critical, and accidents, from his falling into the hold, are not very unfrequent. The complement of men for the unlading of a vessel is, as I have said, nine: four in the hold, four whippers, and the basket-man – the meter forms a tenth, but he acts independently of the others. They seldom work by candlelight, and, whenever possible, avoid working in very bad weather; but the merchant, as I have shown, has great power in regulating their labour for his own convenience. [. . .]

The coal-whippers all present the same aspect – they are all black. In summer, when the men strip more to their work, perspiration causes the coal-dust to adhere to the skin, and blackness is more than ever the rule. All about the ship partakes of the grimness of the prevailing hue. The sails are black; the gilding on the figure-head of the vessel becomes blackened, and the very visitor feels his complexion soon grow sable. The dress of the whippers is of every description; some have fustian jackets, some have sailors' jackets, some loose great coats, some Guernsey frocks. Many of them work in strong shirts, which once were white with a blue stripe: loose cotton neckerchiefs are generally worn by the whippers. All have black hair and black whiskers – no matter what the original hue; to the more stubbly beards and moustachios the coal-dust adheres freely between the bristles, and may even be seen, now and then, to glitter in the light amidst the hair. [. . .]

There are no specific hours for the payment of these men: they are entitled to their money as soon as their work is reported to be completed. Nothing can be better than the way in which the whippers are now paid. The basket-man enters the office of the pay-clerk of the coal commission at one door, and hands over an adjoining counter an amount of money he has received from the captain. The pay-clerk ascertains that the amount is correct. He then divides the sum into nine portions, and, touching a spring to open a door, he cries out for 'Gang such a number'. The nine men, who, with many others, are in attendance in rooms provided for them adjacent to the pay-office, appear immediately, and are paid off. I was present when nine whippers were paid for the discharge of 363½ tons. The following was the work done and the remuneration received:

	Day	Tons
Dec. 14th	1st	35
Dec. 15th	2nd	56
	Sunday intervenes	
Dec. 17th	3rd	84
Dec. 18th	4th	98
Dec. 19th	5th	90½
		363½

These 363½ tons, at 8*d*. per ton, realised to each man, for five days' work, 1*l*. 6*s*. 4¼*d*.; 10*s*. of which had been paid to each as subsistence money during the progress of the work. In addition to the work so paid to each, there was deducted a farthing in every shilling as office fees, to defray the expenses of the office. From this farthing reduction, moreover, the basket-man is paid 1½*d*. in the pound, as commission for bringing the money from the captain. Out of the sum to be divided on the occasion I specify there was an indivisible fraction of 1¼*d*. This, as it cannot be shared among nine men, goes to what is called 'The Fraction Fund', which is established for the relief of persons suffering from accidents on board coal-ships. These indivisible fractions realise between 30*l*. and 40*l*. yearly.

Connected with the calling of the whippers I may mention the existence of the purlmen. These are men who carry kegs of malt liquor in boats, and retail it afloat, having a license from the Waterman's Company to do so. In each boat is a small iron grating, containing a fire, so that any customer can have the chill off, should he require that luxury. The purlman rings a bell to announce his visit to the men on board. There are several purlmen, who keep rowing all day about the coal fleet; they are not allowed to sell spirits. In a fog the glaring of the fire in the purlmen's boats, discernible on the river, has a curious effect, nothing but the fire being visible. [. . .]

I then proceeded to take the statement of some of the different classes of the men. The first was a coal-whipper, whom the men had selected as one knowing more about their calling than the generality. He told me as follows:

'I am about forty, and am a married man with a family of six children. I worked under the old system, and that to my sorrow. If I had been paid in money, according to the work I then did, I could have averaged 30s. a week. Instead of receiving that amount in money, I was compelled to spend in drink 15s. to 18s. per week, when work was good; and the publican even then gave me the residue very grudgingly, and often kept me from eleven to twelve on Saturday night, before he would pay me. The consequences of this system were, that I had a miserable home to go to: I would often have faced Newgate as soon. My health didn't suffer, because I didn't drink the liquor I was forced to pay for. I gave most of it away. The liquors were beer, rum, and gin, all prepared the night before, adulterated shamefully for our consumption, as we dursn't refuse it, – dursn't even grumble. The condition of my poor wife and children was then most wretched. Now the thing is materially altered, thank God; my wife and children can go to chapel at certain times, when work is pretty good, and our things are not in pawn. By the strictest economy, I can do middling well – very well when compared with what things were. When the new system first came into operation, I felt almost in a new world. I felt myself a free man; I wasn't compelled to drink; my home assumed a better aspect, and keeps it still. Last Monday night I received 19s. 7d. for my work (five days) in the previous week. I shall now [Thursday] have to wait until Monday next before I can get to work at my business. Sometimes I get a job in idle times at the docks, or otherwise, and wish I could get more. I may make, one week with another, by odd jobs, 1s. a week. Perhaps for months I can't get a job. All that time I have no choice but to be idle. One week with another, the year through [at 8d. per ton], I may earn 14s. The great evil is the uncertainty of the work. We have all to take our rotation. This uncertainty has this effect upon many of the men – they are compelled to live on credit. One day a man may receive 19s., and be idle for eight days after. Consequently, we go to the dealer where we have credit. The chandler supplies me with bread, to be paid for next pay-day, charging me a halfpenny a loaf more. A man with a wife and family of six children, as I have, will consume sixteen or seventeen quartern loaves a week; consequently, he has to pay 8d. a week extra on account of the irregularity or uncertainty. My rotation would come much oftener but for the backing system and the "bonafides". I also pay the butcher from a halfpenny to a penny per pound extra for credit when my family requires meat, some- times a bit of mutton, sometimes a bit of beef. I leave that to the wife, who does it with economy. I this way pay the butcher 6d. a week extra. The additional cost to me of the other articles, cheese, butter, soap, &c., which I get on credit, will be 6d. a week. Al- together that will be 3l. 18s. a-year. My rent for a little house with two nice little rooms is 3s. per week; so that the extra charge for credit would just pay my rent. Many coal-whippers deal with tallymen for their wearing apparel, and have to pay enormous prices. I have had dealings with a tallyman, and suffered for it, but for all that I must make application for a supply of blankets from him for my family this winter. I paid him 45s. for wearing apparel – a shawl for my wife, some dresses for the children, a blanket, and other things. Their intrinsic value was 30s. Many of us – indeed most of us, if not all of us – are always putting things in and out of the pawnshops. I know I have myself paid more than 10s. a-year for interest to the pawnbroker. I know some of my fellow-workmen who pay nearly 5l. a-year. I once put in a coat that cost me 3l. 12s. I could only get 30s. on it. I was never able to redeem it, and lost it. The articles lost by the coal-whippers pledged at the pawnshop are three out of four. There are 2,000 coal-whippers, and I am sure that each has 50s. in pawn, making

5,000*l*. in a year. Interest may be paid on one half this amount, 2,500*l*. The other half of the property, at least, is lost. As the pawnbroker only advances one-third of the value, the loss in the forfeiture of the property is 7,500*l*., and in interest 2,500*l*., making a total of 10,000*l*. lost every year, greatly through the uncertainty of labour. A coal-whipper's life is one of debt and struggles – it is a round of relieving, paying, and credit. We very rarely have a halfpenny in the pocket when we meet our credit. If any system could possibly be discovered which would render our work and our earnings more certain, and our payments more frequent, it would benefit us as much as we have been benefited by the establishment of the office.'

I visited this man's cottage, and found it neat and tidy. His children looked healthy. The walls of the lower room were covered with some cheap prints; a few old books, well worn, as if well used, were to be seen; and everything evinced a man who was struggling bravely to rear a large family well on small means. I took the family at a disadvantage, moreover, as washing was going on. [. . .]

Dock labourers
[*volume iii, pp. 300,301*]

I shall now pass to the labourers at the docks. This transition I am induced to make, not because there is any affinity between the kinds of work performed at the two places; but because the docks constitute, as it were, a sort of home colony to Spitalfields, to which the unemployed weaver migrates in the hope of bettering his condition. From this it would be generally imagined that the work at the docks was either better paid, less heavy, or more easily, and therefore more regularly, obtained. So far from such being the fact, however, the labour at the docks appears to be not only more onerous, but doubly as precarious as that of weaving; while the average earnings of the entire class seems to be less. What, then, it will be asked, constitutes the inducement for the change? Why does the weaver abandon the calling of his life, and forsake an occupation that at least appears to have, and actually had in the days of better prices, a refining and intellectual tendency? Why does he quit his graceful art for the mere muscular labour of the human animal? This, we shall find, arises purely from a desire for some out-of-door employment. And it is a consequence of all skilled labour – since the acquirement of the skill is the result of long practice – that if the art to which the operative has been educated is abandoned, he must take to some unskilled labour as a means of subsistence. I pass, then, to the consideration of the incomings and condition of the dock-labourers of the metropolis, not because the class of labour is similar to that of weaving, but because the two classes of labourers are locally associated. I would rather have pursued some more systematic plan in my inquiries; but in the present state of ignorance as to the general occupation of the poor, system is impossible. I am unable to generalise, not being acquainted with the particulars; for each day's investigation brings me incidentally into contact with a means of living utterly unknown among the well-fed portion of society. All I can at present assert is, that the poor appear to admit of being classified according to their employments under three heads – artisans, labourers, and petty traders; the first class consisting of skilled, and the second of unskilled workmen; while the third comprises hawkers, costermongers, and such other small dealers, who are contradistinguished from the larger ones by bringing their wares to the consumer instead of leaving the consumer to seek the wares. Of the skilled workmen few are so poorly paid for their labour as not to obtain a sufficiency for the satisfaction of their wants. The amount of wages is generally considered above the sum required for the positive necessaries of life; that is to say, for appeasing an appetite or allaying a pain, rather than gratifying a desire. The class of Spitalfields weavers, however, appear to constitute a striking exception to the rule, from what cause I do not even venture to conjecture. But with the unskilled labourer the amount of remuneration is seldom much above subsistence-point, if it be not very frequently below it. Such a labourer, commercially considered, is, as it were, a human steam-engine, supplied with so much fuel in the shape of food, merely to set him in motion. If he can be made to perform the same amount of work with half the consumption, why a saving of one-half the expense is supposed to be effected. Indeed, the grand object in the labour-market of the present day appears to be to economise human fuel. If the living steam-engine can be made to work as long and as well with a less amount of coal, just so much the better is the result considered.

The dock-labourers are a striking instance of mere brute force with brute appetites. This class of labour is as unskilled as the power of a hurricane. Mere muscle is all that is needed; hence every human locomotive is capable of working there. All that is wanted is the power of moving heavy bodies from one place to another. Mr Stuart Mill tells us that labour in the physical world is always and solely employed in putting objects in motion; and assuredly, if this be the principle of physical labour, the docks exhibit the perfection of human action. Dock-work is precisely the office that every kind of man is fitted to perform, and there we find every kind of man performing it. Those who are unable to live by the occupation to which they have been educated, can obtain a living there without any previous training. Hence we find men of every calling labouring at the docks. There are decayed and bankrupt master-butchers, master-bakers, publicans, grocers, old soldiers, old sailors, Polish refugees, broken-down gentlemen, discharged lawyers' clerks, suspended government clerks, almsmen, pensioners, servants, thieves – indeed, every one who wants a loaf, and is willing to work for it. The London Dock is one of the few places in the metropolis where men can get employment without either character or recommendation, so that the labourers employed there are naturally a most incongruous assembly. Each of the docks employs several hundred hands to ship and discharge the cargoes of the numerous vessels that enter; and as there are some six or seven of such docks attached to the metropolis, it may be imagined how large a number of individuals are dependent on them for their subsistence. At a rough calculation, there must be at least 20,000 souls getting their living by such means.

The London Dock
[*volume iii, pp. 301–310*]
This immense establishment is worked by from one to three thousand hands, according as the business is either brisk or slack. Out of this number there are always 400 to 500 permanent labourers, receiving on an average 16s. 6d. per week, with the exception of coopers, carpenters, smiths, and other mechanics, who are paid the usual wages of those crafts. Besides these are many hundred – from 1,000 to 2,500 – casual labourers, who are

engaged at the rate of 2s. 6d. per day in the summer and 2s. 4d. in the winter months. Frequently, in case of many arrivals, extra hands are hired in the course of the day, at the rate of 4d. per hour. For the permanent labourers a recommendation is required; but for the casual labourers no character is demanded. The number of the casual hands engaged by the day depends, of course, upon the amount of work to be done; and I find that the total number of labourers in the dock varies from 500 to 3,000 and odd. On the 4th May, 1840, the number of hands engaged, both permanent and casual, was 2,794; on the 26th of the same month it was 3012; and on the 30th it was 1,189. These appear to be the extreme of the variation for that year: the fluctuation is due to a greater or less number of ships entering the dock. The lowest number of ships entering the dock in any one week last year was 29, while the highest number was 141. This rise and fall is owing to the prevalence of easterly winds, which serve to keep the ships back, and so make the business slack. Now, deducting the lowest number of hands employed from the highest number, we have no less than 1823 individuals who obtain so precarious a subsistence by their labour at the docks, that by the mere shifting of the wind; they may be all deprived of their daily bread. Calculating the wages at 2s. 6d. per day for each, the company would have paid 376l. 10s. to the 3,013 hands employed on the 26th of May 1849; while only 148l. 12s. 6d. would have been paid to the 1,189 hands engaged on the 30th of the same month. Hence, not only would 1,823 hands have been thrown out of employ by the chopping of the wind, but the labouring men dependent upon the business of the docks for their subsistence would in one day have been deprived of 227l. 17s. 6d. This will afford the reader some faint idea of the precarious character of the subsistence obtained by the labourers employed in this neighbourhood, and, consequently, as it has been well proved, that all men who obtain their livelihood by irregular employment are the most intemperate and improvident of all.

It will be easy to judge what may be the condition and morals of a class who today, as a body, may earn near upon 400l., and tomorrow only 150l. I had hoped to have been able to have shown the fluctuations m the total amount of wages paid to the dock-labourers for each week throughout the whole year; and so, by contrasting the comparative affluence and comfort of one week with the distress and misery of the other, to have afforded the reader some more vivid idea of the body of men who are performing, perhaps, the heaviest labour, and getting the most fickle provision of all. But still I will endeavour to impress him, with some faint idea of the struggle there is to gain the uncertain daily bread. Until I saw with my own eyes this scene of greedy despair, I could not have believed that there was so mad an eagerness to work, and so biting a want of it, among so vast a body of men. A day or two before I had sat at midnight in the room of the starving weaver; and as I heard him tell his bitter story, there was a patience in his misery that gave it more an air of heroism than desperation. But in the scenes I have lately witnessed the want has been positively tragic, and the struggle for life partaking of the sublime. The reader must first remember what kind of men the casual labourers generally are. They are men, it should be borne in mind, who are shut out from the usual means of life by the want of character. Hence, you are not astonished to hear from those who are best acquainted with the men, that there are hundreds among the body who are known thieves, and who go to the docks to seek a living; so that, if taken for any past offence, their late industry may plead for some little lenity in their punishment.

He who wishes to behold one of the most extraordinary and least-known scenes of this metropolis, should wend his way to the London Dock gates at half-past seven in the morning. There he will see congregated within the principal entrance masses of men of all grades, looks, and kinds. Some in half-fashioned surtouts burst at the elbows, with the dirty shirts showing through. Others in greasy sporting jackets, with red pimpled faces. Others in the rags of their half-slang gentility, with the velvet collars of their paletots worn through to the canvas. Some in rusty black, with their waistcoats fastened tight up to the throat. Others, again, with the knowing thieves' curl on each side of the jaunty cap: whilst here and there you may see a big-whiskered Pole, with his hands in the pockets of his plaited French trousers. Some loll outside the gates, smoking the pipe which is forbidden within; but these are mostly Irish.

Presently you know, by the stream pouring through the gates and the rush towards particular spots, that the 'calling foremen' have made their appearance. Then begins the scuffling and scrambling forth of countless hands high in the air, to catch the eye of him whose voice may give them work. As the foreman calls from a book the names, some men jump up on the backs of the others, so as to lift themselves high above the rest, and attract the notice of him who hires them. All are shouting. Some cry aloud his surname, some his Christian name, others call out their own names, to remind him that they are there. Now the appeal is made in Irish blarney – now in broken English. Indeed, it is a sight to sadden the most callous, to see thousands of men struggling for only one day's hire; the scuffle being made the fiercer by the knowledge that hundreds out of the number there assembled must be left to idle the day out in want. To look in the faces of that hungry crowd is to see a sight that must be ever remembered. Some are smiling to the foreman to coax him into remembrance of them; others, with their protruding eyes, eager to snatch at the hoped-for pass. For weeks many have gone there, and gone through the same struggle, the same cries; and have gone away, after all, without the work they had screamed for.

From this it might be imagined that the work was of a peculiarly light and pleasant kind, and so, when I first saw the scene, I could not help imagining myself. But, in reality, the labour is of that heavy and continuous character that you would fancy only the best fed could stand it. The work may be divided into three classes. 1. Wheel-work, or that which is moved by the muscles of the legs and weight of the body; 2. jigger, or winch-work, or that which is moved by the muscles of the arm. In each of these the labourer is stationary; but in the truck work, which forms the third class, the labourer has to travel over a space of ground greater or less in proportion to the distance which the goods have to be removed.

The wheel-work is performed somewhat on the system of the treadwheel, with the exception that the force is applied inside instead of outside the wheel. From six to eight men enter a wooden cylinder or drum, upon which are nailed battens, and the men laying hold of ropes commence treading the wheel round, occasionally singing the while, and stamping time in a manner that is pleasant, from its novelty. The wheel is generally about sixteen feet in diameter and eight to nine feet broad; and the six or eight men treading within it, will lift from sixteen to eighteen hundred weight, and often a ton, forty times in an hour, an average of twenty-seven feet high. Other men will get out a cargo of from 800 to 900 casks of wine, each cask averaging about five hundred weight, and being lifted about eighteen feet, in a day and a half. At trucking each man is said to go on an average thirty miles a–day, and two-thirds of that time he is moving 1½ cwt. at six miles and a half per hour.

This labour, though requiring to be seen to be properly understood, must still appear so arduous that one would imagine it was not of that tempting nature, that 3,000 men could be found every day in London desperate enough to fight and battle for the privilege of getting 2s. 6d. by it; and even if they fail in 'getting taken on' at the commencement of the day, that they should then retire to the appointed yard, there to remain hour after hour in the hope that the wind might blow them some stray ship, so that other gangs might be wanted, and the calling foreman seek them there. It is a curious sight to see the men waiting in these yards to be hired at 4d. per hour, for such are the terms given in the after part of the day. There, seated on long benches ranged against the wall, they remain, some telling their miseries and some their crimes to one another, whilst others doze away their time. Rain or sunshine, there can always be found plenty ready to catch the stray 1s. or 6d. worth of work. By the size of the shed, you can tell how many men sometimes remain there in the pouring rain, rather than run the chance of losing the stray hours' work. Some loiter on the bridges close by, and presently, as their practised eye or ear tells them that the calling foreman is in want of another gang, they rush forward in a stream towards the gate, though only six or eight at most can be hired out of the hundred or more that are waiting there. Again the same mad fight takes place as in the morning. There is the same jumping on benches, the same raising of hands, the same entreaties, and the same failure as before. It is strange to mark the change that takes place in the manner of the men when the foreman has left. Those that have been engaged go smiling to their labour. Indeed, I myself met on the quay just such a chuckling gang passing to their work. Those who are left behind give vent to their disappointment in abuse of him whom they had been supplicating and smiling at a few minutes before. Upon talking with some of the unsuccessful ones, they assured me that the men who had supplanted them had only gained their ends by bribing the foreman who had engaged them. This I made a point of inquiring into, and the deputy warehouse-keeper, of whom I sought the information, soon assured me, by the production of his book, that he himself was the person who chose the men, the foreman merely executing his orders: and this, indeed, I found to be the custom throughout the dock.

At four o'clock the eight hours' labour ceases, and then comes the paying. The names of the men are called out of the muster-book, and each man, as he answers to the cry, has half-a-crown given to him. So rapidly is this done that, in a quarter of an hour, the whole of the men have had their wages paid them. They then pour towards the gate. Here two constables stand, and as each man passes through the wicket, he takes his hat off, and is felt from head to foot by the dock-officers and attendant: and yet, with all the want, misery, and temptation, the millions of pounds of property amid which they work, and the thousands of pipes and hogsheads of wines and spirits about the docks, I am informed, upon the best authority, that there are on an average but thirty charges of drunkenness in the course of the year, and only eight of dishonesty every month. This may, perhaps, arise from the vigilance of the superintendents; but to see the distressed condition of the men who seek and gain employment in the London Dock, it appears almost incredible, that out of so vast a body of men, without means and without character, there should be so little vice or crime. There still remains one curious circumstance to be added in connection with the destitution of the dock-labourers. Close to the gate by which they are obliged to leave, sits on a coping-stone the refreshment man, with his two large canvas pockets tied in front of him, and filled with silver and copper, ready to give change to those whom he has trusted with their dinner that day until they were paid.

As the men passed slowly on in a double file towards the gate, I sat beside the victualler, and asked him what constituted the general dinner of the labourers. He told me that he supplied them with pea-soup, bread and cheese, saveloys, and beer. 'Some,' he said, 'had twice as much as others. Some had a pennyworth, some had eatables and a pint of beer; others, two pints, and others four, and some spend their whole half-crown in eating and drinking.'

This gave me a more clear insight into the destitution of the men who stood there each morning. Many of them, it was clear, came to the gate without the means of a day's meal, and, being hired, were obliged to go on credit for the very food they worked upon. What wonder, then, that the calling foreman should be often carried many yards away by the struggle and rush of the men around him seeking employment at his hands! One gentleman assured me that he had been taken off his feet and hurried a distance of a quarter of a mile by the eagerness of this impatient crowd around him.

Having made myself acquainted with the character and amount of the labour performed, I next proceeded to make inquiries into the condition of the labourers themselves, and thus to learn the average amount of their wages from so precarious an occupation. For this purpose, hearing that there were several cheap lodging-houses in the neighbourhood, I thought I should be better enabled to arrive at an average result by converging with the inmates of them, and thus endeavouring to elicit from them some such statements of their earnings at one time and at another, as would enable me to judge what was their average amount throughout the year. I had heard the most pathetic accounts from men in the waiting-yard; how they had been six weeks without a day's hire. I had been told of others who had been known to come there day after day in the hope of getting sixpence, and who lived upon the stray pieces of bread given to them in charity by their fellow-labourers. Of one person I was informed by a gentleman who had sought out his history in pure sympathy, from the wretchedness of the man's appearance. The man had once been possessed of 500l. a-year, and had squandered it all away; and through some act or acts that I do not feel myself at liberty to state, had lost caste, character, friends, and everything that could make life easy to him. From that time he had sunk and sunk in the world, until, at last, he had found him, with a lodging-house for his dwelling-place, the associate of thieves and pickpockets. His only means of living at this time was bones and rag-grubbing; and for this purpose the man would wander through the streets at three every morning, to see what little bits of old iron, or rag, or refuse bone he could find in the roads. His principal source of income I am informed, from such a source as precludes the possibility of doubt, was by picking up the refuse ends of cigars, drying them, and selling them at one-halfpenny per ounce, as tobacco, to the thieves with whom he lodged.

However, to arrive at a fair estimate as to the character and the earnings of labourers generally, I directed my guide, after the closing of the docks, to take me to one of the largest lodging-houses in the neighbourhood. The young man who was with me happened to know one of the labourers who was lodging there, and having called him out, I told him the object of my visit, and requested to be allowed to obtain information from the labourers assembled within. The man assented, and directing me to follow him, he led me through a narrow passage into a small room on the ground floor, in which sat, I should think, at least twenty or thirty of the most wretched objects I ever beheld. Some were shoeless – some coat-less, others shirt-less; and from all these came so rank and foul a stench, that I was sickened with a moment's inhalation of the fetid atmosphere. Some of the men were seated in front of a table, eating soup out of yellow basins. As they saw me enter, they gathered round me; and I was proceeding to tell them what information I wished to gather from them, when in swaggered a drunken man, in a white canvas suit, who announced himself as the landlord of the place, asking whether there had been a robbery in the house, that people should come in without saying 'with your leave' or 'by your leave'. I explained to him that I had mistaken the person who had introduced me for the proprietor of the house, when he grew very abusive, and declared I should not remain there. Some of the men, however, swore as lustily that I should; and after a time succeeded in pacifying him. He then bade me let him hear what I wanted, and I again briefly stated the object of my visit. I told him I wished to publish the state of the dock-labourers in the newspapers, on which the man burst into an ironical laugh, and vowed with an oath that *he* knowed me, and that the men were a set of b—y flats to be done in that way. 'I know who you are well enough,' he shouted. I requested to be informed for whom he took me. 'Take you for!' he cried; 'why, for a b—y spy! You come here from the Secretary of State, you know you do, to see how many men I've got in the house, and what kind they are.' This caused a great stir among the company, and I could see that I was mistaken for one of the detective police.

I was located in so wretched a court, and so far removed from the street, with a dead wall opposite, that I knew any atrocity might be committed there almost unheard: indeed, the young man who had brought me to the house had warned me of its dangerous character before I went; but, from the kind reception I had met with from other labourers, I had no fear. At last the landlord flung the door wide open, and shouted from his clenched teeth, 'By G— ! if you ain't soon mizzled, I'll crack your b—y skull open for you!' And so saying, he prepared to make a rush towards me, but was held back by the youth who had brought me to the place. I felt that it would be dangerous to remain; and rising, informed the man that I would not trouble him to proceed to extremities.

It was now so late that I felt it would be imprudent to venture into another such house that night; so, having heard of the case of a dock-labourer who had formerly been a clerk in a Government office, I made the best of my way to the place where he resided.

He lived in a top back-room in a small house, in another dismal court. I was told by the woman who answered the door to mount the steep stairs, as she shrieked out to the man's wife to show me a light. I found the man seated on the edge of a bed, with six young children grouped round him. They were all shoeless, and playing on the bed was an infant with only a shirt to cover it. The room was about 7 feet square, and, with the man and his wife, there were eight human creatures living in it. In the middle of the apartment, upon a chair, stood a washing-tub foaming with fresh suds, and from the white crinkled hands of the wife it was plain that I had interrupted her in her washing. On one chair, close by, was a heap of dirty linen, and on another was flung the newly-washed. There was a saucepan on the handful of fire, and the only ornaments on the mantelpiece were two flat-irons and a broken shaving-glass. On the table at which I took my notes there was the bottom of a broken ginger-beer bottle filled with soda. The man was without a coat, and wore an old tattered and greasy black satin waistcoat. Across the ceiling ran strings to hang clothes upon. On my observing to the woman that I supposed she dried the clothes in that room, she told me that they were obliged to do so, and it gave them all colds and bad eyes. On the floor was a little bit of matting, and on the shelves in the corner one or two plates. In answer to my questionings the man told me he had been a dock-labourer for five or six years. He was in Her Majesty's Stationery Office. When there he had 150*l*. a-year. Left through accepting a bill of exchange for 871*l*. He was suspended eight years ago, and had petitioned the Lords of the Treasury, but never could get any answer. After that he was out for two or three years, going about doing what he could get, such as writing letters. 'Then,' said the wife, 'you went into Mr What's-his-name's shop.' 'Oh, yes,' answered the man, 'I had six months' employment at Camberwell. I had 12*s*. a week and my board there.'

Before this they had lived upon their things. He had a good stock of furniture and clothing at that time. The wife used to go out for a day's work when she could get it. She used to go out shelling peas in the pea season – washing or charing – anything she could get to do. His father was a farmer, well to do. He should say the old man was worth a good bit of money, and he would have some property at his death.

'Oh, sir,' said the woman, 'we have been really very bad off indeed; sometimes without even food or firing in the depth of winter. It is not until recently that we have been to say very badly off, because within the last four years has been our worst trouble. We had a very good house – a seven-roomed house in Walworth – and well furnished and very comfortable. We were in business for ourselves before we went there. We were grocers, near Oxford-street. We lived there at the time when Aldis the pawnbroker's was burnt down. We might have done well if we had not given so much credit.'

'I've got,' said the husband, 'about 90*l*. owing me down there now. It's quite out of character to think of getting it. At Clerkenwell I got a job at a grocer's shop. The master was in the Queen's-bench Prison, and the mistress employed me at 12*s*. a week until he went through the Insolvent Debtors Court. When he passed the Court the business was sold, and of course he didn't want me after that. I've done nothing else but this dock-labouring work for this long time. Took to it first because I found there was no chance of anything else. The character with the bill transaction was very much against me: so, being unable to obtain employment in a wholesale house, or anywhere else, I applied to the docks. They require no character at all there. I think I may sometimes have had 7 or 8 days altogether. Then I was out for a fortnight or three weeks perhaps; and then we might get a day or two again, and on some occasion such a thing as – well, say July, August, September, and October. I was in work one year almost the whole of those months – three years ago I think that was. Then I did not get anything, excepting now and then, not more than about three days' work until the nest March; that was owing to the slack time. The first year I might say that I might have been employed about one-third of the time. The second year I was employed six months. The third year I was very unfortunate. I was laid up for three months with bad eyes and a quinsey in the throat, through working in an ice ship. I've scarcely had anything to do since then. That is nearly 18 months ago; and since then I have had casual employment, perhaps one, and sometimes two days a week. It would average 5s. a week the whole year. Within the last few weeks I have, through a friend, applied at a shipping-merchant's, and within the month I have had five days' work with them, and nothing else, except writing a letter, which I had 2d. for – that's all the employment I've met with myself. My wife has been at employment for the last three months, she has a place she goes to work at. She has 3s. a week for washing, for charing, and for mangling: the party my wife works for has a mangle, and I go sometimes to help; for if she has got 6d. worth of washing to do at home, than I go to turn the mangle for an hour instead of her – she's not strong enough.'

'We buy most bread,' said the wife, 'and a bit of firing, and I do manage on a Saturday night to get them a bit of meat for Sunday if I possibly can; but what with the soap, and one thing and another, that's the only day they do get a bit of meat, unless I've a bit given me. As for clothing, I'm sure I can't get them any unless I have that given me, poor little things.'

'Yes, but we have managed to get a little bread lately,' said the man. 'When bread was 11d. a loaf, that was the time when we was worse off. Of course we had the seven children alive then. We buried one only three months ago. She was an afflicted little creature for 16 or 17 months: it was one person's work to attend to her, and was very badly off for a few months then. We've known what it was sometimes to go without bread and coals in the depth of winter. Last Christmas two years we did so for the whole day, until the wife came home in the evening and brought it might be

6d. or 9d. according how long she worked. I was looking after them. I was at home ill. I have known us to sit several days and not have more than 6d. to feed and warm the whole of us for the whole of the day. We'll buy half-a-quartern loaf, that'll be 4½d. or sometimes 5d., and then we have a penny for coals, that would be pretty nigh all that we could have for our money. Sometimes we get a little oatmeal and make gruel. We had hard work to keep the children warm at all. What with their clothes and what we had, we did as well as we could. My children is very contented; give 'em bread, and they're as happy as all the world. That's one comfort. For instance, today we've had half a quartern loaf, and we had a piece left of last night's after I had come home. I had been earning some money yesterday. We had 3oz. of butter, and I had this afternoon a quarter of an oz. of tea and a pennyworth of sugar. When I was ill I've had two or three of the children round me at a time, fretting for want of food. That was at the time I was ill. A friend gave me half a sovereign to bury my child. The parish provided me with a coffin, and it cost me about 3s. besides. We didn't have her taken away from here, not as a parish funeral exactly. I agreed that if he would fetch it, and let it stand in an open space that he had got there, near his shop, until the Saturday which was the time, I would give the undertaker 3s. to let a man come with a pall to throw over the coffin, so that it should not be seen exactly it was a parish funeral. Even the people in the house don't know, not one of them, that it was buried in that way. I had to give 1s. 6d. for a pair of shoes before I could follow my child to the grave, and we paid 1s. 9d. for rent, all out of the half sovereign. I think there's some people at the docks a great deal worse off than us. I should say there's men go down there and stand at that gate from 7 to 12, and then they may get called in and earn 1s., and that only for two or three days in the week, after spending the whole of their time there.'

The scenes witnessed at the London Dock were of so painful a description, the struggle for one day's work – the scramble for twenty-four hours' extra-subsistence and extra-life were of so tragic a character, that I was anxious to ascertain if possible the exact number of individuals in and around the metropolis who live by dock labour. I have said that at one of the docks alone I found that 1823 stomachs would be deprived of food by the mere chopping of the breeze. 'It's an ill wind,' says the proverb, 'that blows nobody good;' and until I came to investigate the condition of the dock-labourer I could not have believed it possible that near upon 2,000 souls in one place alone lived, chameleon-like, upon the air, or that an easterly wind, despite the wise saw, could deprive so many of bread. It is indeed 'a nipping and an eager air'. That the sustenance of thousands of families should be as fickle as the very breeze itself; that the weathercock should be the index of daily want or daily ease to such a vast number of men, women, and children, was a climax of misery and wretchedness that I could not have imagined to exist; and since that I have witnessed such scenes of squalor, and crime, and suffering, as oppress the mind even to a feeling of awe.

The docks of London are to a superficial observer the very focus of metropolitan wealth. The cranes creak with the mass of riches. In the warehouses are stored goods that are as it were ingots of untold gold. Above and below ground you see piles upon piles of treasure that the eye cannot compass. The wealth appears as boundless as the very sea it has traversed. The brain aches in an attempt to comprehend the amount of riches before, above, and beneath it. There are acres upon acres of treasure, more than enough, one would fancy, to stay the cravings of the whole world, and yet you have but to visit the hovels grouped round about all this amazing excess of riches to witness the same amazing excess of poverty. If the incomprehensibility of the wealth rises to sublimity, assuredly the want that co-exists with it is equally incomprehensible and equally sublime. Pass from the quay and warehouses to the courts and alleys that surround them, and the mind is as bewildered with the destitution of the one place as it is with the superabundance of the other. Many come to see the riches, but few the poverty, abounding in absolute masses round the far-famed port of London.

According to the official returns, there belonged to this port on the 31st of December, 1842, very nearly 3,000 ships, of the aggregate burden of 600,000 tons. Besides that there were 239 steamers, of 50,000 tons burden; and the crews of the entire number of ships and steamers amounted to 35,000 men and boys. The number of British and foreign ships that entered the port of London during the same year was 6400 and odd, whose capacity was upwards of a million and a quarter of tons, and the gross amount of customs duly collected upon their cargoes was very nearly 12,000*l*. of money. So vast an amount of shipping and commerce, it has been truly said, was never concentrated in any other single port.

Now, against this we must set the amount of misery that co-exists with it. We have shown that the mass of men dependent for their bread upon the business of only one of the docks are, by the shifting of the breeze, occasionally deprived in one day of no less than 220*l*., the labourers at the London Dock earning as a body near upon 400*l*. today, and tomorrow scarcely 150*l*. These docks, however, are but one of six similar establishments – three being on the north and three on the south side of the Thames – and all employing a greater or less number of hands, equally dependent upon the winds for their subsistence. Deducting, then, the highest from the lowest number of labourers engaged at the London Dock – the extremes according to the books are under 500 and over 3,000 – we have as many as 2,500 individuals deprived of a day's work and a living by the prevalence of an easterly wind; and calculating that the same effect takes place at the other docks – the East and West India for instance, St Katherine's, Commercial, Grand Surrey, and East Country, to a greater or less extent, and that the hands employed to load and unload the vessels entering and quitting all these places are only four times more than those required at the London Dock, we have as many as 12,000 individuals or families whose daily bread is as fickle as the wind itself; whose wages, in fact, are one day collectively as much as 1,500*l*. and the next as low as 500*l*., so that 8,000 men are frequently thrown out of employ, while the earnings of the class today amount to 1,000*l*. less than they did yesterday.

It would be curious to take an average number of days that easterly winds prevail in London throughout the year, and so arrive at an estimate of the exact time that the above 8,000 men are unemployed in the course of twelve months. This would give us some idea of the amount of their average weekly earnings. By the labourers themselves I am assured that, taking one week with another, they do not gain 5*s*. weekly throughout the year. I have made a point of visiting and interrogating a large number of them, in order to obtain some definite information respecting the extent of their income, and have found in only one instance an account kept of the individual earnings. In that case the wages averaged within a fraction of 13s. per week, the total sum gained since the beginning of the year being 25l. odd. I should state, however, that the man earning thus much was pointed out to me as one of the most provident of the casual labourers, and one, moreover, who is generally employed. 'If it is possible to get work, he'll have it,' was said of him; 'there's not a lazy bone in his skin.' Besides this he had done a considerable quantity of piece-work, so that altogether the man's earnings might be taken as the very extreme made by the best kind of extra hands.

The man himself gives the following explanation as to the state of the labour-market at the London Dock. 'He has had a good turn of work,' he says, since he has been there. 'Some don't get half what he does. He's not always employed, excepting when the business is in anyway brisk, but when a kind of a slack comes the recommended men get the preference of the work, and the extras have nothing to do. This is the best summer he has had since he has been in London. Has had a good bit of piece-work. Obliged to live as he does because he can't depend on work. Isn't certain of the second day's work. He's paid off every night, and can't say whether or not they'll want him on the morrow.' The account of his wages was written in pencil on the cover of an old memorandum-book, and ran as follows:

	£. s. d.	£. s. d.
Earned by day-work from		
1st Jan. to 1st Aug. 1849	16 11 6	averaging 0 11 10 per week
By piece-work in August	5 5 8	averaging 1 6 5 per week
By day work from		
1st Sept. to 1st Oct.	3 8 7	averaging 0 17 1¾
Total . . .	25 5 9	averaging 0 12 9 per week

If, then, 13s. be the average amount of weekly earnings by the most provident, industrious, and fortunate of the casual labourers at the docks – and that at the best season – it may be safely asserted that the lowest grade of workmen there do not gain more than 6s. per week throughout the year. It should be remembered that the man himself says 'some don't get half what he does', and from a multiplicity of inquiries that I have made upon the subject this appears to be about the truth. Moreover, we should bear in mind that the average weekly wages of the dock-labourer, miserable as they are, are rendered even more wretched by the uncertain character of the work on which they depend. Were the income of the casual labourer at the docks 6s. per week from one year's end to another the workman would know exactly how much he had to subsist upon, and might therefore be expected to display some little providence and temperance in the expenditure of his wages. But where the means of subsistence occasionally rise to 15s. a week, and occasionally sink to nothing, it is absurd to look for prudence, economy, or moderation. Regularity of habits are incompatible with irregularity of income; indeed, the very conditions necessary for the formation of any habit whatsoever are, that the act or thing to which we are to become habituated should be repeated at frequent and regular intervals. It is a moral impossibility that the class of labourers who are only occasionally employed should be either generally industrious or temperate – both industry and temperance being habits produced by constancy of employment and uniformity of income. Hence, where the greatest fluctuation occurs in the labour, there, of course, will be the greatest idleness and improvidence; where the greatest want generally is, there we shall find the greatest occasional excess; where from the uncertainty of the occupation prudence is most needed, there, strange to say, we shall meet with the highest imprudence of all. 'Previous to the formation of a canal in the north of Ireland,' says Mr Porter, in *The Progress of the Nation*, 'the men were improvident even to recklessness. Such work as they got before came at uncertain intervals, the wages insufficient for the comfortable sustenance of their families were wasted at the whisky-shop, and the men appeared to be sunk in a state of hopeless degradation. From the moment, however, that work was offered to them which was constant in its nature and certain in its duration, men who before had been idle and dissolute were converted into sober, hard-working labourers, and proved themselves kind and careful husbands and fathers; and it is said that, notwithstanding the distribution of several hundred pounds weekly in wages, the whole of which must be considered as so much additional money placed in their hands, the consumption of whisky was absolutely and permanently diminished in the district. Indeed it is a fact worthy of notice, as illustrative of the tendency of the times of pressure, and consequently of deficient and uncertain employment, to increase spirit-drinking, that whilst in the year 1836 – a year of the greatest prosperity – the tax on British spirits amounted only to 2,390,000*l.*; yet, under the privations of 1841, the English poorer classes paid no less than 2,600,000*l* in taxes upon the liquor they consumed – thus spending upwards of 200,000*l.* more in drink at a time when they were less able to afford it, and so proving that a fluctuation in the income of the working-classes is almost invariably attended with an excess of improvidence in the expenditure. Moreover, with reference to the dock-labourers, we have been informed, upon unquestionable authority, that some years back there were near upon 220 ships waiting to be discharged in one dock alone; and such was the pressure of business then, that it became necessary to obtain leave of Her Majesty's Customs to increase the usual time of daily labour from eight to twelve hours. The men employed, therefore, earned 50 per cent more than they were in the habit of doing at the briskest times; but so far from the extra amount of wages being devoted to increase the comforts of their homes, it was principally spent in public-houses. The riot and confusion thus created in the neighbourhood were such as had never been known before, and indeed were so general among the workmen, that every respectable person in the immediate vicinity expressed a hope that such a thing as 'over-time' would never occur again.

It may then be safely asserted, that though the wages of the casual labourer at the docks average 5*s.* per week, still the weekly earnings are of so precarious and variable a nature, that when the time of the men is 'fully employed, the money which is gained over and above the amount absolutely required for subsistence is almost sure to be spent in intemperance, and that when there is little or no demand for their work, and their gains are consequently insufficient for the satisfaction of their appetites, they and those who depend upon their labour for their food must at least want, if not starve. The improvidence of the casual dock-labourer is due, therefore, not to any particular malformation of his moral constitution, but to the precarious character of his calling. His vices are the vices of ordinary human nature. Ninety-nine in every hundred similarly circumstanced would commit similar enormities. If the very winds could whistle away the food and firing of wife and children, I doubt much whether, after a week's or a month's privation, we should many of us be able to prevent ourselves from falling into the very same excesses.

It is consoling to moralise in our easy chairs, after a good dinner, and to assure ourselves that we should do differently. Self-denial is not very difficult when our stomachs are full and our backs are warm; but let us live a month of hunger and cold, and assuredly we should be as self-indulgent as they.

I have devoted some time to the investigation of the state of the casual labourers at the other docks, and shall now proceed to set forth the result of my inquiries.*

The problem of low wages
[*volume ii, pp. 253–257*]

Empirical inquiry raised doubts in Mayhew's mind about the explanations of poverty advanced by orthodox political economy. By the close of the survey Mayhew had broken with general theories of over-population but found nothing with which to replace them. Here he reviews the principal arguments and alternatives.

Review of the problem of low wages
In the first place, let us understand clearly what is meant by philanthropic labour, and how it is distinguished from pauper labour on the one hand, and self-supporting labour on the other. Self-supporting labour I take to be that form of work which returns not less, and generally something more, than is expended upon it. Pauper labour, on the other hand, is work to which the applicants for parish relief are 'set', not with a view to the profit to be derived from it, but partly as a test of their willingness to work, and partly as a means of employing the unemployed; while philanthropic labour is employment provided for the unemployed with the same disregard of profit as distinguishes pauper labour, but with a greater regard for the poor, and as a means of affording them relief in a less degrading manner than is done under the present Poor Law. Pauper and philanthropic labour, then, differ essentially from self-supporting labour in being 'non-profitable'

* Not included in this edition.

modes of employment; that is to say, they yield so bare an equivalent for the sum expended upon the labourers, that none, in the ordinary way of trade can be found to provide the means necessary for putting them into operation: while pauper labour differs from philanthropic labour, in the fact that the funds requisite for 'setting the poor on work' are provided by law as a matter of social policy, whereas, in the case of philanthropic labour, the funds, or a part of them, are supplied by voluntary contributions, out of a desire to improve the labourers' condition. There are, then, two distinguishing features, in all philanthropic labour – the one is, that it yields no profit (if it did it would become a matter of trade), and the other, that it is instituted and maintained from a wish to benefit the labourer. [. . .]

Viewed economically, philanthropic and pauper work may be said to be the regulators of the minimum rate of wages – establishing the lowest point to which competition can possibly drive down the remuneration for labour; for it is evident, that if the self-supporting labourer cannot obtain greater comforts by the independent exercise of his industry than the parish rates or private charity will afford him, he will at once give over working for the trading employer, and declare on the funds raised by assessment or voluntary subscription for his support. Hence, those who wish well to the labourer, and who believe that cheapness of commodities is desirable 'only', as Mr Stewart Mill says, 'when the cause of it is, that their production costs little labour, and not when occasioned by that labour's being ill-remunerated'; and who believe, moreover, that the labourer is to be benefited solely by the cultivation of a high standard of comfort among the people – to such, I say, it is evident, that a Poor Law which reduces the relief to able-bodied labourers to the smallest modicum of food consistent with the continuation of life must be about the greatest curse that can possibly come upon an over-populated country, admitting, as it does, of the reduction of wages to so low a point of mere brutal existence as to induce that recklessness and improvidence among the poor which is known to give so strong an impetus to the increase of the people. A minimised rate of parish relief is necessarily a minimised rate of wages, and admits of the labourers' pay being reduced, by pauper competition, to little short of starvation; and such, doubtlessly, would have been the case long ago in the scavaging trade by the employment of parish labour, had not the Philanthropic Association instituted the system of street-orderlies, and by the payment of a higher rate of wages than the more grinding parishes afforded – by giving the men 12s. instead of 9s. or even 7s. a week – prevented the remuneration of the regular hands being dragged down to an approximation to the parish level. Hence, rightly viewed, philanthropic labour – and, indeed, pauper labour too – comes under the head of a remedy for low wages, as pre-venting, if properly regulated, the undue depreciation of industry from excessive competition, and it is in this light that I shall now proceed to consider it.

The several plans that have been propounded from time to time, as remedies for an insufficient rate of remuneration for work, are as multifarious as the circumstances influencing the three requisites for production – labour, capital, and land. I will here run over as briefly as possible – abstaining from the ex-pression of all opinion on the subject – the various schemes which have been proposed with this object, so that the reader may come as prepared as possible to the consideration of the matter.

The remedies for low wages may be arranged into two distinct groups, viz., those which seek to increase the labourer's rate of pay *directly*, and those which seek to do so *indirectly*.

The *direct* remedies for low wages that have been propounded are:

A. *The establishment of a standard rate of remuneration for labour.* This has been proposed to be brought about by three different means, viz.:

1. By law or government authority; either (a) fixing the min-imum rate of wages, and leaving the variations above that point to be adjusted by competition (this, as we have seen, is the effect of the Poor Law); or, (b) settling the rate of wages generally by means of local boards of trade for *conseils de prud'hommes*, consisting of delegates from the workmen and employers, to determine, by the principles of natural equity, a *reasonable* scale of remuneration in the several trades, their decision being binding in law on both the employers and the employed.

2. By public opinion; this has been generally proposed by those who are what Mr Mill terms 'shy of admitting the interference of authority in contracts for labour', fearing that if the law intervened it would do so rashly and ignorantly, and desiring to compass by *moral* sanction what they consider useless or dangerous to attempt to bring about by *legal* means. 'Every employer,' says Mr Mill, 'they think, *ought* to give *sufficient wages*,' and if he does not give such wages willingly, he should be compelled to do so by public opinion.

3. By trade societies or combination among the workmen; that is to say, by the payment of a small sum per week out of the wages of the workmen, towards the formation of a fund for the support of such of their fellow operatives as may be out of employment, or refuse to work for those employers who seek to give less than the standard rate of wages established by the trade.

B. *The prohibition of stoppages or deductions of all kinds from the nominal wages of workmen.* This is principally the object of the Anti-Truck Society, which seeks to obtain an Act of Parliament, enjoining the payment in full of all wages. The stoppages or extortions from workmen's wages generally consist of:

1. Fines for real or pretended misconduct.
2. Rents for tools, frames, gas, and sometimes lodgings.
3. Sale of trade appliances (as trimmings, thread, &c.) at undue prices.
4. Sale of food, drink, &c., at an exorbitant rate of profit.
5. Payment in public-houses; as the means of inducing the men to spend a portion of their earnings in drink.
6. Deposit of money as security before taking out work; so that the capital of the employer is increased without payment of interest to the work people.

C. *The institution of certain aids or additions to wages*; as –

1. Perquisites or gratuities obtained from the public; as with waiters, box-keepers, coachmen, dustmen, vergers, and others.
2. Beer-money, and other 'allowances' to workmen.
3. Family work; or the co-operation of the wife and children as a means of increasing the workman's income.

4. Allotments of land, to be cultivated after the regular day's labour.
5. The parish 'allowance system', or relief in aid of wages, as practised under the old Poor Law.

D. *The increase of the money value of wages*; by –
  1. Cheap food.
  2. Cheap lodgings; through building improved dwellings for the poor, and doing away with the profit of sub-letting.
  3. Co-operative stores: or the 'club system' of obtaining provisions at wholesale prices.
  4. The abolition of the payment of wages on Sunday morning, or at so late an hour on the Saturday night as to prevent the labourer availing himself of the Saturday's market.
  5. Teetotalism; as causing the men to spend nothing in fermented drinks, and so leaving them more to spend on food.

Such are the *direct* modes of remedying low wages, viz., either by preventing the price of labour itself falling below a certain standard; prohibiting all stoppages from the pay of the labourer; instituting certain aids or additions to such pay; or increasing the money value of the ordinary wages by reducing the price of provisions.

The *indirect* modes of remedying low wages are of a far more complex character. They consist of, first, the remedies propounded by political economists, which are –

A. *The decrease of the number of labourers*; for gaining this end several plans have been proposed, as –
  1. Checks against the increase of the population, for which the following are the chief Malthusian proposals:
      a. Preventive checks for the hindrance of impregnation.
      b. Prohibition of early marriages among the poor.
      c. Increase of the standard of comfort, or requirements, among the people; as a means of inducing prudence and restraint of the passions.
      d. Infanticide; as among the Chinese.
  2. Emigration; as a means of draining off the surplus labourers.
  3. Limitation of apprentices in skilled trades; as a means of preventing the undue increase of particular occupations. This, however, is advocated not by economists, but generally by operatives.

4. Prevention of family work; or the discouragement of the labour of the wives and children of operatives. This, again, cannot be said to be an 'economist' remedy.

B. *Increase of the circulating capital, or sum set aside for the payment of the labourers.*

1. By government imposts. 'Governments,' says Mr Mill, 'can create additional industry by creating capital. They may lay on taxes, and employ the amount productively.' This was the object of the original Poor Law (43 Eliz.), which empowered the overseers of the poor to 'raise weekly, or otherwise, by taxation of every inhabitant, &c., such sums of money as they shall require for providing a sufficient stock of flax, hemp, wool, and other ware or stuff, to set the poor on work.'

2. By the issue of paper money. The proposition of Mr Jonathan Duncan is, that the government should issue notes equivalent to the taxation of the country, with the view of affording increased employment to the poor; the people being set to work as it were upon credit, in the same manner as the labourers were employed to build the market-house at Guernsey.

C. *The extension of the markets of the country*; by the abolition of all restrictions on commerce, and the encouragement of the free interchange of commodities, so that, by increasing the demand for our products, we may be able to afford employment to an extra number of producers.

The above constitute what, with a few exceptions, may be termed, more particularly, the 'economist' remedies for low wages.

D. *The regulation of the quantity of work done by each workman, or the prevention of the undue economising of labour.* For this end, several means have been put forward.

1. The shortening the hours of labour, and abolition of Sunday-work.

2. Alteration of the mode of work; as the substitution of day-work for piece-work, as a means of decreasing the stimulus to over-work.

3. Extension of the term of hiring; by the substitution of annual engagements for daily or weekly hirings, with a view to the prevention of 'casual labour'.

4. Limitation of the number of hands employed by one capitalist; so as to prevent the undue extension of 'the large system of production'.

5. Taxation of machinery; with the object, not only of making it contribute its quota to the revenue of the country, but of impeding its undue increase.

6. The discountenance of every form of work that tends to the making up of a greater quantity of materials with a less quantity of labour; and consequently to the expenditure of a greater proportion of the capital of the country on machinery or materials, and a correspondingly less proportion on the labourers.

E. *'Protective imposts', or high import duties on such foreign commodities as can be produced in this country*; with the view of preventing the labour of the comparatively untaxed and uncivilised foreigner being brought into competition with that of the taxed and civilised producer at home.

F. *'Financial reform', or reduction of the taxation of the country*; as enabling the home labourer the better to compete with the foreigner.

The two latter proposals, and that of the extension of the markets, may be said to seek to remedy low wages by expanding or circumscribing the foreign trade of the country.

G. *A different division of the proceeds of labour.* For this object several schemes have been propounded:
1. The 'tribute system' of wages; or payment of labour according to the additional value which it centres on the materials on which it operates.
2. The abolition of the middleman; whether 'sweater', 'piecemaster', 'lumper', or what not, coming between the employer and employed.
3. Co-operation: or joint-stock associations of labourers, with the view of abolishing the profit of the capitalist employer.

H. *A different mode of distributing the product of labour;* with the view of abolishing the profit of the dealer, between the producer and consumer – as co-operative stores, where the consumers club together for the purchase of their goods directly of the producers.

I. *A more general and equal division for the wealth of the country*: for attaining this end there are but two known means:

1. Communism; or the abolition of all rights to individual property.
2. Agapism; or the voluntary sharing of individual possessions with the less fortunate or successful members of the community.

These remedies may, with a few exceptions (such as the tribute system of wages, and the abolition of middlemen), be said to constitute the socialist and communist schemes for the prevention of distress.

J. *Creating additional employment for the poor*; and so removing the surplus labour from the market. Two modes of effecting this have been proposed:

1. Home colonisation, or the cultivation of waste lands by the poor.
2. Orderlyism, or the employment of the poor in the promotion of public cleanliness. and the increased sanitary condition of the country.

K. *The prevention of the enclosure of commons*; as the means of enabling the poor to obtain gratuitous pasturage for their cattle.

L. *The abolition of primogeniture*; with the view of dividing the land among a greater number of individuals.

M. *The holding of the land by the State*, and equal apportionment of it among the poor.

N. *Extension of the suffrage among the people*; and so allowing the workman, as well as the capitalist and the landlord, to take part in the formation of the laws of the country. For this purpose there are two plans:

1. 'The freehold-land movement', which seeks to enable the people to become proprietors of as much land as will, under the present law, give them 'a voice' in the country.
2. Chartism, or that which seeks to alter the law concerning the election of members of Parliament, and to confer the right of voting on every male of mature age, sound mind, and non-criminal character.

O. *Cultivation of a higher moral and Christian character among the people*. This form of remedy, which is advocated by many, is based on the argument, that, without some mitigation of the 'selfishness of the times', all other schemes for improving the condition of the people will be either evaded by the cunning or the rich, or defeated by the servility of the poor.

The above I believe to be a full and fair statement of the several plans that have been proposed, from time to time, for alleviating the distress of the people. This enumeration is as comprehensive as my knowledge will enable me to make it; and I have abstained from all comment on the several schemes, so that the reader may have an opportunity of impartially weighing the merits of each, and adopting that, which in his own mind, seems best calculated to effect what, after all, we every one desire – whether protectionist, economist, free-trader, philanthropist, socialist, communist, or Chartist – the good of the country in which we live, and the people by whom we are surrounded.

Now we have to deal here with that particular remedy for low wages or distress which consists in creating additional employment for the poor. The increase of employment for the poor was the main object of the 43 Eliz., for which purpose, as we have seen, the overseers of the several parishes were empowered to raise a fund by assessments upon the property of the rich, for providing 'a sufficient stock of flax, hemp, wool; and other ware or stuff, to set the poor on work'. But though economists, to this day, tell us that 'while, on the one hand, industry is limited by capital, so, on the other, every increase of capital gives, or is capable of giving, additional employment to industry, and this without assignable limit,'* nevertheless the great difficulty of carrying out the provisions of the original Poor Law has consisted in finding a market for the products of pauper labour, for the frequent gluts in our manufactures are

---

* This is Mr. Mills's second fundamental proposition respecting capital (see *Principles of Pol. Econ.* p. 82, vol. i.). 'What I intend to assert is,' says that gentleman, 'that the portion of capital which is destined to the maintenance of the labourers may – supposing no increase in anything else – be indefinitely increased, without creating an impossibility of finding them employment – in other words, if there are human beings capable of work, and food to feed them they may always be employed in producing something.'

sufficient to teach us that it is one thing to produce and another to dispose of the products; so that to create additional employment for the poor something besides capital is requisite: it is necessary either that they shall be engaged in producing that which they themselves immediately consume, or that for which the market admits of being extended.

The two plans proposed for the employment of the poor, it will be seen, consist (1) in the cultivation of waste lands; (2) in promoting public cleanliness, and so increasing the sanitary condition of the country. The first, it is evident, removes the objection of a market being needed for the products of the labour of the poor, since it proposes that their energies should be devoted to the production of the food which they themselves consume; while the second seeks to create additional employment in effecting that increased cleanliness which more enlightened physiological views have not only made more desirable, but taught us to be absolutely necessary to the health and enjoyment of the community.

The great impediment, however, to the profitable employment of the poor, has generally been the unproductive or unavailing character of pauper labour. This has been mainly owing to the fact that the able-bodied who are deprived of employment are necessarily the lowest grade of operatives; for, in the displacement of workmen, those are the first discarded whose labour is found to be the least efficient, either from a deficiency of skill, industry, or sobriety, so that pauper labour is necessarily of the least productive character.

Another great difficulty with the employment of the poor is, that the idle, or those to whom work is more than usually irksome, require a stronger inducement than ordinary to make them labour, and the remuneration for parish work being necessarily less than for any other, those who are pauperised through idleness (the most benevolent among us must allow there are such) are naturally less than ever disposed to labour when they become paupers. All pauper work, therefore, is generally unproductive or unavailing, because it is either inexpert or unwilling work. The labour of the in-door paupers, who receive only their food for their pains, is necessarily of the same compulsory character as slavery; while that of the out-door paupers, with the remuneration often cut down to the lowest subsisting point, is scarcely of a more willing or more availing kind.

Owing to this general unproductiveness (as well as the difficulty of finding a field for the profitable employment of the unemployed poor), the labour of paupers has been for a long time past directed mainly to the cleansing of the public thoroughfares. Still, from the degrading nature of the occupation, and the small remuneration for the toil, pauper labourers have been found to be such unwilling workers that many parishes have long since given over employing their poor even in this capacity, preferring to entrust the work to a contractor, with his paid self-supporting operatives, instead.

[. . .]

5

SIGHTS OF LONDON

Mayhew presents us with a marvellously rich and detailed picture of London at the time of the Great Exhibition. The Metropolis, as he depicts it, is not so much a series of fine public buildings and charted streets, as a gigantic system of production, consumption and waste disposal. Mayhew is interested in streets, in the sights and sounds and use of space. Markets, docks and certain localities were particularly noteworthy as was the subterranean world of the sewers. Degenerationalist themes figure prominently in Mayhew's London.

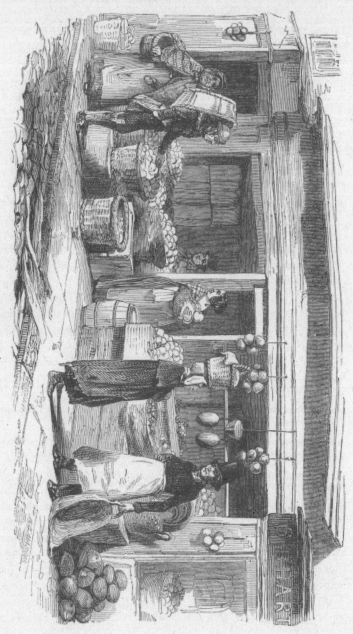

ORANGE-MART, DUKE'S PLACE

[from a daguerreotype by Beard]

Of the orange and nut market
[*volume i. pp.86,87*]
In Houndsditch there is a market supported principally by coster-mongers, who there purchase their oranges, lemons, and nuts. This market is entirely in the hands of the Jews; and although a few tradesmen may attend it to buy grapes, still it derives its chief custom from the street-dealers, who say they can make far better bargains with the Israelites (as they never refuse an offer) than they can with the Covent-garden salesmen, who generally cling to their prices. This market is known by the name of 'Duke's-place', although its proper title is St James's-place. The nearest road to it is through Duke's-street, and the two titles have been so confounded that at length the mistake has grown into a custom.

Duke's-place – as the costers call it – is a large square yard, with the iron gates of a synagogue in one corner, a dead wall forming one entire side of the court, and a gas-lamp on a circular pavement in the centre. The place looks as if it were devoted to money-making – for it is quiet and dirty. Not a gilt letter is to be seen over a doorway; there is no display of gaudy colour, or sheets of plate-glass, such as we see in a crowded thoroughfare when a customer is to be caught by show. As if the merchants knew their trade was certain, they are content to let the London smoke do their painter's work. On looking at the shops in this quarter, the idea forces itself upon one that they are in the last stage of dilapid-ation. Never did property in Chancery look more ruinous. Each dwelling seems as though a fire had raged in it, for not a shop in the market has a window to it; and, beyond the few sacks of nuts exposed for sale, they are empty, the walls within being blackened with dirt, and the paint without blistered in the sun, while the door-posts are worn round with the shoulders of the customers, and black as if charred. A few sickly hens wander about, turning over the heaps of dried leaves that the oranges have been sent over in, or roost the time away on the shafts and wheels of the nearest truck. Excepting on certain days, there is little or no business stirring, so that many of the shops have one or two shutters up, as if a death had taken place, and the yard is quiet as an inn of court. At a little distance the warehouses, with their low ceilings, open fronts, and black sides, seem like dark holes or coal-stores; and, but for the mahogany backs of chairs showing at the first floors, you would scarcely believe the houses to be inhabited, much more to be elegantly furnished as they are. One of the drawing-rooms that I entered here was warm and red with morocco leather, Spanish mahogany, and curtains and Turkey carpets; while the ormolu chandelier and the gilt frames of the looking-glass and pictures twinkled at every point in the fire-light.

The householders in Duke's-place are all of the Jewish persuasion, and among the costers a saying has sprung up about it. When a man has been out of work for some time, he is said to be 'Cursed, like a pig in Duke's-place'.

Almost every shop has a Scripture name over it, and even the public-houses are of the Hebrew faith, their signs appealing to the followers of those trades which most abound with Jews. There is the 'Jeweller's Arms', patronised greatly of a Sunday morning, when the Israelite jewellers attend to exchange their trinkets and barter amongst themselves. Very often the counter before 'the bar' here may be seen covered with golden ornaments, and sparkling with precious stones, amounting in value to thousands of pounds. The landlord of this house of call is licensed to *manufacture* tobacco and cigars. There is also the 'Fishmonger's Arms', the resort of the vendors of fried soles; here, in the evening, a concert takes place, the performers and audience being Jews. The landlord of this house too is licensed to manufacture tobacco and cigars. Entering one of these houses I found a bill announcing a 'Bible to be raffled for, the property of — '. And, lastly, there is 'Benjamin's Coffee-house', open to old clothesmen; and here, again, the proprietor is a licensed tobacco-manufacturer. These facts are mentioned to show the untiring energy of the Jew when anything is to be gained, and to give an instance of the curious manner in which this people support each other.

Some of the nut and orange shops in Duke's-place it would be impossible to describe. At one sat an old woman, with jet-black hair and a wrinkled face, nursing an infant, and watching over a few matted baskets of nuts ranged on a kind of carpenter's bench placed upon the pavement. The interior of the house was as empty as if it had been to let, excepting a few bits of harness hanging against the wall, and an old salt-box nailed near the gas-lamp, in which sat a hen, 'hatching', as I was told. At another was an excessively stout Israelite mother, with crisp negro's hair and long gold earrings, rolling her child on the table used for sorting the nuts. Here the black walls had been chalked over with scores, and every corner was filled up with sacks and orange-cases. Before one warehouse a family of six, from the father to the infant, were busy washing walnuts in a huge tub with a trap in the side, and around them were ranged measures of the wet fruit. The Jewish women are known to make the fondest parents; and in Duke's-place there certainly was no lack of fondlings. Inside almost every parlour a child was either being nursed or romped with, and some little things were being tossed nearly to the ceiling, and caught, screaming with enjoyment, in the jewelled hands of the delighted mother. At other shops might be seen a circle of three or four women – some old as if grandmothers, grouped admiringly round a hook-nosed infant, tickling it and poking their fingers at it in a frenzy of affection.

The counters of these shops are generally placed in the open streets like stalls, and the shop itself is used as a store to keep the stock in. On these counters are ranged the large matting baskets, some piled up with dark-brown polished chestnuts – shining like a racer's neck – others filled with wedge-shaped Brazil-nuts, and rough hairy cocoa-nuts. There are heaps, too, of newly-washed walnuts, a few showing their white crumpled kernels as a sample of their excellence. Before every doorway are long pot-bellied boxes of oranges, with the yellow fruit just peeping between the laths on top, and lemons – yet green – are ranged about in their paper jackets to ripen in the air.

In front of one store the paving-stones were soft with the sawdust emptied from the grape-cases, and the floor of the shop itself was whitened with the dry powder. Here stood a man in a long tasselled smoking-cap, puffing with his bellows at the blue bunches on a tray, and about him were the boxes with the paper lids thrown back, and the round sea-green berries just rising above the sawdust as if floating in it. Close by, was a group of dark-eyed women bending over an orange-case, picking out the rotten from the good fruit, while a sallow-complexioned girl was busy with her knife scooping out the damaged parts, until, what with sawdust and orange-peel, the air smelt like the pit of a circus.

Nothing could be seen in this strange place that did not, in some way or another, appertain to Jewish customs. A woman, with a heavy gold chain round her neck, went past, carrying an old green velvet bonnet covered with feathers, and a fur tippet, that she had either recently purchased or was about to sell. Another woman, whose features showed her to be a Gentile, was hurrying toward the slop-shop in the Minories with a richly quilted satin-lined coat done up in her shawl, and the market-basket by her side, as if the money due for the work were to be spent directly for house-keeping.

At the corner of Duke's-street was a stall kept by a Jew, who sold things that are eaten only by the Hebrews. Here in a yellow pie-dish were pieces of stewed apples floating in a thick puce-coloured sauce.

One man that I spoke to told me that he considered his Sunday morning's work a very bad one if he did not sell his five or six hundred bushels of nuts of different kinds. He had taken 150*l*. that day of the street-sellers, and usually sold his 100*l*. worth of goods in a morning. Many others did the same as himself. Here I met with every attention, and was furnished with some valuable statistical information concerning the street-trade.

Of London street-markets on a Saturday night
[*volume i. pp.9,10*]

The street-sellers are to be seen in the greatest numbers at the London street-markets on a Saturday night. Here, and in the shops immediately adjoining, the working-classes generally purchase their Sunday's dinner; and after pay-time on Saturday night, or early on Sunday morning, the crowd in the New-cut, and the Brill in particular, is almost impassable. Indeed, the scene in these parts has more of the character of a fair than a market. There are hundreds of stalls, and every stall has its one or two lights; either it is illuminated by the intense white light of the new self-generating gas-lamp, or else it is brightened up by the red smoky flame of the old-fashioned grease lamp. One man shows off his yellow haddock with a candle stuck in a bundle of firewood; his neighbour makes a candlestick of a huge turnip, and the tallow gutters over its sides; whilst the boy shouting 'Eight a penny, stunning pears!' has rolled his dip in a thick coat of brown paper, that flares away with the candle. Some stalls are crimson with the fire shining through the holes beneath the baked chestnut stove; others have handsome octohedral lamps, while a few have a candle shining through a sieve: these, with the sparkling ground-glass globes of the tea-dealers' shops, and the butchers' gaslights streaming and fluttering in the wind, like flags of flame, pour forth such a flood of light, that at a distance the atmosphere immediately above the spot is as lurid as if the street were on fire.

The pavement and the road are crowded with purchasers and street-sellers. The housewife in her thick shawl, with the market-basket on her arm, walks slowly on, stopping now to look at the stall of caps, and now to cheapen a bunch of greens. Little boys, holding three or four onions in their hand, creep between the people, wriggling their way through every interstice, and asking for custom in whining tones, as if seeking charity. Then the tumult of the thousand different cries of the eager dealers, all shouting at the top of their voices, at one and the same time, is almost bewildering. 'So-old again,' roars one. 'Chestnuts all 'ot, a penny a score,' bawls another. 'An 'aypenny a skin, blacking,' squeaks a boy. 'Buy, buy, buy, buy, buy – bu-u-uy!' cries the butcher. 'Half-quire of paper for a penny,' bellows the street stationer. 'An 'aypenny a lot ing-uns.' 'Twopence a pound grapes.' 'Three a penny Yarmouth bloaters.' 'Who'll buy a bonnet for fourpence?' 'Pick 'em out cheap here! Three pair for a halfpenny, bootlaces.' 'Now's your time! beautiful whelks, a penny a lot.' 'Here's ha'p'orths,' shouts the perambulating confectioner. 'Come and look at 'em! here's toasters!' bellows one with a Yarmouth bloater stuck on a toasting-fork. 'Penny a lot, fine russets,' calls the apple woman: and so the Babel goes on.

One man stands with his red-edged mats hanging over his back and chest, like a herald's coat; and the girl with her basket of walnuts lifts her brown-stained fingers to her mouth, as she screams, 'Fine warnuts! sixteen a penny, fine war-r-nuts.' A boot-maker, to 'ensure custom', has illuminated his shop-front with a line of gas, and in its full glare stands a blind beggar, his eyes turned up so as to show only 'the whites', and mumbling some begging rhymes, that are drowned in the shrill notes of the bamboo-flute-player next to him. The boy's sharp cry, the woman's cracked voice, the gruff, hoarse shout of the man, are all mingled together. Sometimes an Irishman is heard with his 'fine ating apples'; or else the jingling music of an unseen organ breaks out, as the trio of street singers rest between the verses.

Then the sights, as you elbow your way through the crowd, are equally multifarious. Here is a stall glittering with new tin sauce-pans; there another, bright with its blue and yellow crockery, and sparkling with white glass. Now you come to a row of old shoes arranged along the pavement; now to a stand of gaudy tea-trays; then to a shop with red handkerchiefs and blue checked shirts, fluttering backwards and forwards, and a counter built up outside on the kerb, behind which are boys beseeching custom. At the door of a tea-shop, with its hundred white globes of light, stands a man delivering bills, thanking the public for past favours, and 'defying competition'. Here, alongside the road, are some half-dozen headless tailors' dummies, dressed in Chesterfields and fustian jackets, each labelled, 'Look at the prices', or 'Observe the quality'. After this is a butcher's shop, crimson and white with meat piled up to the first-floor, in front of which the butcher himself, in his blue coat, walks up and down, sharpening his knife on the steel that hangs to his waist. A little further on stands the clean family, begging; the father with his head down as if in shame, and a box of lucifers held forth in his hand – the boys in newly-washed pinafores, and the tidily got-up mother with a child at her breast. This stall is green and white with bunches of turnips – that red with apples, the next yellow with onions, and another purple with pickling cabbages. One minute you pass a man with an umbrella turned inside up and full of prints; the next, you hear one with a peepshow of Mazeppa, and Paul Jones the pirate, describing the pictures to the boys looking in at the little round windows. Then is heard the sharp snap of the percussion-cap from the crowd of lads firing at the target for nuts; and the moment afterwards, you see either a black man half-clad in white, and shivering in the cold with tracts in his hand, or else you hear the sounds of music from 'Frazier's Circus', on the other side of the road, and the man outside the door of the penny concert, beseeching you to 'Be in time – be in time!' as Mr Somebody is just about to sing his favourite song of the 'Knife Grinder'. Such, indeed, is the riot, the struggle, and the scramble for a living, that the confusion and uproar of the New-cut on Saturday night have a bewildering and saddening effect upon the thoughtful mind.

Each salesman tries his utmost to sell his wares, tempting the passers-by with his bargains. The boy with his stock of herbs offers 'a double 'andful of fine parsley for a penny'; the man with the donkey-cart filled with turnips has three lads to shout for him to their utmost, with their 'Ho! ho! hi-i-i! What do you think of this here? A penny a bunch – hurrah for free trade! *Here's* your turnips!' Until it is seen and heard, we have no sense of the scramble that is going on throughout London for a living. The same scene takes place at the Brill – the same in Leather-lane – the same in Tottenham-court-road – the same in Whitecross-street; go to whatever corner of the metropolis you please, either on a Saturday night or a Sunday morning, and there is the same shouting and the same struggling to get the penny profit out of the poor man's Sunday's dinner.

Since the above description was written, the New-cut has lost much of its noisy and brilliant glory. In consequence of a new police regulation, 'stands' or 'pitches' have been forbidden, and each coster, on a market night, is now obliged, under pain of the lock-up house, to carry his tray, or keep moving with his barrow. The gay stalls have been replaced by deal boards, some sodden with wet fish, others stained purple with blackberries, or brown with walnut-peel; and the bright lamps are almost totally superseded by the dim, guttering candle. Even if the pole under the tray or 'shallow' is seen resting on the ground, the policeman on duty is obliged to interfere.

The mob of purchasers has diminished one- half; and instead of the road being filled with customers and trucks, the pavement and kerb-stones are scarcely crowded.

The Sunday morning markets
[*volume i. pp. 10, 11*]

Nearly every poor man's market does its Sunday trade. For a few hours on the Sabbath morning, the noise, bustle, and scramble of the Saturday night are repeated, and but for this opportunity many a poor family would pass a dinnerless Sunday. The system of paying the mechanic late on the Saturday night – and more particularly of paying a man his wages in a public-house – when he is tired with his day's work lures him to the tavern, and there the hours fly quickly enough beside the warm tap-room fire, so that by the time the wife comes for her husband's wages, she finds a large portion of them gone in drink, and the streets half cleared, so that the Sunday market is the only chance of getting the Sunday's dinner.

Of all these Sunday-morning markets, the Brill, perhaps, furnishes the busiest scene; so that it may be taken as a type of the whole.

The streets in the neighbourhood are quiet and empty. The shops are closed with their different-coloured shutters, and the people round about are dressed in the shiney cloth of the holiday suit. There are no 'cabs', and but few omnibuses to disturb the rest, and men walk in the road as safely as on the footpath.

As you enter the Brill the market sounds are scarcely heard. But at each step the low hum grows gradually into the noisy shouting, until at last the different cries become distinct, and the hubbub, din, and confusion of a thousand voices bellowing at once again fill the air. The road and footpath are crowded, as on the over-night; the men are standing in groups, smoking and talking; whilst the women run to and fro, some with the white round turnips showing out of their filled aprons, others with cabbages under their arms, and a piece of red meat dangling from their hands. Only a few of the shops are closed, but the butcher's and the coal-shed are filled with customers, and from the door of the shut-up baker's, the women come streaming forth with bags of flour in their hands, while men sally from the halfpenny barber's smoothing their clean-shaved chins. Walnuts, blacking, apples, onions, braces, combs, turnips, herrings, pens, and corn-plaster, are all bellowed out at the same time. Labourers and mechanics, still unshorn and undressed, hang about with their hands in their pockets, some with their pet terriers under their arms. The pavement is green with the refuse leaves of vegetables, and round a cabbage-barrow the women stand turning over the bunches, as the man shouts, 'Where you like, only a penny.' Boys are running home with the breakfast herring held in a piece of paper, and the side-pocket of the apple-man's stuff coat hangs down with the weight of the halfpence stored within it. Presently the tolling of the neighbouring church bells breaks forth. Then the bustle doubles itself, the cries grow louder, the confusion greater. Women run about and push their way through the throng, scolding the saunterers, for in half an hour the market will close. In a little time the butcher puts up his shutters, and leaves the door still open; the policemen in their clean gloves come round and drive the street-sellers before them, and as the clock strikes eleven the market finishes, and the Sunday's rest begins. [. . .]

Of Covent-garden market
[*volume i. pp.81–83*]
On a Saturday – the coster's business day – it is computed that as many as 2,000 donkey-barrows, and upwards of 3,000 women with shallows and head-baskets visit this market during the fore-noon. About six o'clock in the morning is the best time for viewing the wonderful restlessness of the place, for then not only is the 'Garden' itself all bustle and activity, but the buyers and sellers stream to and from it in all directions, filling every street in the vicinity. From Long Acre to the Strand on the one side, and from Bow-street to Bedford-street on the other, the ground has been seized upon by the market-goers. As you glance down any one of the neighbouring streets, the long rows of carts and donkey-barrows seem interminable in the distance. They are of all kinds, from the greengrocer's taxed cart to the coster's barrow – from the showy excursion-van to the rude square donkey-cart and brick-layer's truck. In every street they are ranged down the middle and by the kerb-stones. Along each approach to the market, too, nothing is to be seen, on all sides, but vegetables; the pavement is covered with heaps of them waiting to be carted; the flagstones are stained green with the leaves trodden under foot; sieves and sacks full of apples and potatoes, and bundles of broccoli and rhubarb, are left unwatched upon almost every doorstep; the steps of Covent-garden Theatre are covered with fruit and vegetables; the road is blocked up with mountains of cabbages and turnips; and

men and women push past with their arms bowed out by the cauliflowers under them, or the red tips of carrots pointing from their crammed aprons, or else their faces are red with the weight of the loaded head-basket.

The donkey-barrows, from their number and singularity, force you to stop and notice them. Every kind of ingenuity has been exercised to construct harness for the costers' steeds; where a buckle is wanting, tape or string make the fastening secure; traces are made of rope and old chain, and an old sack or cotton hand-kerchief is folded up as a saddle-pad. Some few of the barrows make a magnificent exception, and are gay with bright brass; while one of the donkeys may be seen dressed in a suit of old plated carriage-harness, decorated with coronets in all directions. At some one of the coster conveyances stands the proprietor, arranging his goods, the dozing animal starting up from its sleep each time a heavy basket is hoisted on the tray. Others, with their green and white and red load neatly arranged, are ready for starting, but the coster is finishing his breakfast at the coffee-stall. On one barrow there may occasionally be seen a solitary sieve of apples, with the horse of some neighbouring cart helping himself to the pippins while the owner is away. The men that take charge of the trucks, whilst the costers visit the market, walk about, with their arms full of whips and sticks. At one corner a donkey has slipped down, and lies on the stones covered with the cabbages and apples that have fallen from the cart.

The market itself presents a beautiful scene. In the clear morning air of an autumn day the whole of the vast square is distinctly seen from one end to the other. The sky is red and golden with the newly-risen sun, and the rays falling on the fresh and vivid colours of the fruit and vegetables, brighten up the picture as with a coat of varnish. There is no shouting, as at other markets, but a low murmuring hum is heard, like the sound of the sea at a distance, and through each entrance to the market the crowd sweeps by. Under the dark Piazza little bright dots of gas-lights are seen burning in the shops; and in the paved square the people pass and cross each other in all directions, hampers clash together, and ex-cepting the carters from the country, every one is on the move. Sometimes a huge column of baskets is seen in the air, and walks away in a marvellously steady manner, or a monster railway van, laden with sieves of fruit, and with the driver perched up on his high seat, jolts heavily over the stones. Cabbages are piled up into stacks as it were. Carts are heaped high with turnips, and bunches of carrots like huge red fingers are seen in all directions. Flower-girls, with large bundles of violets under their arms, run past, leaving a trail of perfume behind them. Wagons, with their shafts sticking up in the air, are ranged before the salesmen's shops, the high green load railed in with hurdles, and every here and there bunches of turnips are seen flying in the air over the heads of the people. Groups of apple-women, with straw pads on their crushed bonnets, and coarse shawls crossing their bosoms, sit on their porter's knots, chatting in Irish, and smoking short pipes; every passer-by is hailed with the cry of, 'Want a baskit, yer honor?' The porter, trembling under the piled-up hamper, trots along the street, with his teeth clenched and shirt wet with the weight, and staggering at every step he takes.

Inside, the market all is bustle and confusion. The people walk along with their eyes fixed on the goods, and frowning with thought. Men in all costumes, from the coster in his corduroy suit to the greengrocer in his blue apron, sweep past. A countryman, in an old straw hat and dusty boots, occasionally draws down the anger of a woman for walking about with his hands in the pockets of his smock-frock, and is asked, 'if that is the way to behave on a market-day?' Even the granite pillars cannot stop the crowd, for it separates and rushes past them, like the tide by a bridge pier. At every turn there is a fresh odour to sniff at; either the bitter aromatic perfume of the herbalists' shops breaks upon you, or the scent of oranges, then of apples, and then of onions is caught for an instant as you move along. The broccoli tied up in square packets, the white heads tinged slightly red, as it were, with the sunshine, – the sieves of crimson love-apples, polished like china, – the bundles of white glossy leeks, their roots dangling like fringe, – the celery, with its pinky stalks and bright green tops, – the dark purple pickling-cabbages, – the scarlet carrots, – the white knobs of turnips, – the bright yellow balls of oranges, and the rich brown coats of the chesnuts – attract the eye on every side. Then there are the apple-merchants, with their fruit of all colours, from the pale yellow green to the bright crimson, and the baskets ranged in rows on the pavement before the little shops. Round these the customers stand examining the stock, then whispering together over their bargain, and counting their money. 'Give you four shillings for this here lot, master,' says a coster, speaking for his three companions. 'Four and six is my price,' answers the salesman. 'Say four, and it's a bargain,' continues the man. 'I said my price,' returns the dealer; 'go and look round, and see if you can get 'em cheaper; if not, come back. I only wants what's fair.' The men, taking the salesman's advice, move on. The walnut merchant, with the group of women before his shop, peeling the fruit, their fingers stained deep brown, is busy with the Irish purchasers. The onion stores, too, are surrounded by Hibernians, feeling and pressing the gold-coloured roots, whose dry skins crackle as they are handled. Cases of lemons in their white paper jackets, and blue grapes, just seen above the sawdust, are ranged about, and in some places the ground is slippery as ice from the refuse leaves and walnut husks scattered over the pavement.

Against the railings of St Paul's Church are hung baskets and slippers for sale, and near the public-house is a party of countrymen preparing their bunches of pretty coloured grass – brown and glittering, as if it had been bronzed. Between the spikes of the railing are piled up square cakes of green turf for larks; and at the pump, boys, who probably have passed the previous night in the baskets about the market, are washing, and the water dripping from their hair that hangs in points over the face. The kerb-stone is blocked up by a crowd of admiring lads, gathered round the bird-catcher's green stand, and gazing at the larks beating their breasts against their cages. The owner, whose boots are red with the soil of the brick-field, shouts, as he looks carelessly around, 'A cock linnet for tuppence,' and then hits at the youths who are poking through the bars at the fluttering birds.

Under the Piazza the costers purchase their flowers (in pots) which they exchange in the streets for old clothes. Here is ranged a small garden of flower-pots, the musk and mignonette smelling sweetly, and the scarlet geraniums, with a perfect glow of coloured air about the flowers, standing out in rich contrast with the dark green leaves of the evergreens behind them. 'There's myrtles, and larels, and boxes,' says one of the men selling them, 'and there's a harbora witus, and lauristiners, and that bushy shrub with pink spots is health.' Men and women, selling different articles, walk about under the cover of the colonnade. One has seedcake, another small-tooth and other combs, others old caps, or pig's feet, and one hawker of knives, razors, and short hatchets, may occasionally be seen driving a bargain with a countryman, who stands passing his thumb over the blade to test its keenness. Between the pillars are the coffee-stalls, with their large tin cans and piles of bread and butter, and protected from the wind by paper screens and sheets thrown over clothes-horses; inside these little parlours, as it were, sit the coffee-drinkers on chairs and benches, some with a bunch of cabbages on their laps, blowing the steam from their saucers, others, with their mouths full, munching away at their slices, as if not a moment could be lost. One or two porters are there besides, seated on their baskets, breakfasting with their knots on their heads.

As you walk away from this busy scene, you meet in every street barrows and costers hurrying home. The pump in the market is now surrounded by a cluster of chattering wenches quarrelling over whose turn it is to water their drooping violets, and on the steps of Covent Garden Theatre are seated the shoeless girls, tying up the halfpenny and penny bundles.

Of the Old Clothes Exchange
[*volume ii. pp.26,27*]
The trade in second-hand apparel is one of the most ancient of callings, and is known in almost every country, but anything like the Old Clothes Exchange of the Jewish quarter of London, in the extent and order of its business, is unequalled in the world. There is indeed no other such place, and it is rather remarkable that a business occupying so many persons, and requiring such facilities for examination and arrangement, should not until the year 1843 have had its regulated proceedings. The Old Clothes Exchange is the latest of the central marts, established in the metropolis.

Smithfield, or the Cattle Exchange, is the oldest of all the markets; it is mentioned as a place for the sale of horses in the time of Henry II. Billingsgate, or the Fish Exchange, is of ancient, but uncertain era. Covent-garden – the largest Fruit, Vegetable, and Flower Exchange – first became established as the centre of such commerce in the reign of Charles II; the establishment of the Borough and Spitalfields markets, as other marts for the sale

of fruits, vegetables, and flowers, being nearly as ancient. The
Royal Exchange dates from the days of Queen Elizabeth, and
the Bank of England and the Stock Exchange from those of
William III, while the present premises for the Corn and Coal
Exchanges are modern.

Were it possible to obtain the statistics of the last quarter of a
century, it would, perhaps, be found that in none of the important
interests I have mentioned has there been a greater increase of
business than in the trade in old clothes. Whether this purports a
high degree of national prosperity or not, it is not my business at
present to inquire, and be it as it may, it is certain that, until the
last few years, the trade in old clothes used to be carried on
entirely in the open air, and this in the localities which I have
pointed out in my account of the trade in old metal as comprising
the Petticoat-lane district. The old clothes trade was also pursued
in Rosemary-lane, but then – and so indeed it is now – this was
but a branch of the more centralised commerce of Petticoat-lane.
The head-quarters of the traffic at that time were confined to a
space not more than ten square yards, adjoining Cutler-street.
The chief traffic elsewhere was originally in Cutler-street, White-
street, Carter-street, and in Harrow-alley – the districts of the
celebrated Rag-fair.

The confusion and clamour before the institution of the present
arrangements were extreme. Great as was the extent of the business transacted, people wondered how it could be accomplished,
for it always appeared to a stranger, that there could be no order
whatever in all the disorder. The wrangling was incessant, nor
were the trade-contests always confined to wrangling alone. The
passions of the Irish often drove them to resort to cuffs, kicks, and
blows, which the Jews, although with a better command over
their tempers, were not slack in returning. The East India Company, some of whose warehouses adjoined the market, frequently
complained to the city authorities of the nuisance. Complaints
from other quarters were also frequent, and sometimes as many as
200 constables were necessary to restore or enforce order. The
nuisance, however, like many a public nuisance, was left to
remedy itself, or rather it was left to be remedied by individual
enterprise. Mr L. Isaac, the present proprietor, purchased the
houses which then filled up the back of Phil's-buildings, and

formed the present Old Clothes Exchange. This was eight years ago; now there are no more policemen in the locality than in other equally populous parts.

Of Old Clothes Exchanges there are now two, both adjacent, the one first opened by Mr Isaac being the most important. This is 100 feet by 70, and is the mart to which the collectors of the cast-off apparel of the metropolis bring their goods for sale. The goods are sold wholesale and retail, for an old clothes merchant will buy either a single hat, or an entire wardrobe, or a sackful of shoes, – I need not say *pairs*, for odd shoes are not rejected. In one department of 'Isaac's Exchange', however, the goods are not sold to parties who buy for their own wearing, but to the old clothes merchant, who buys to sell again. In this portion of the mart are 90 stalls, averaging about six square feet each.

In another department, which communicates with the first, and is two-thirds of the size, are assembled such traders as buy the old garments to dispose of them, either after a process of cleaning, or when they have been repaired and renovated. These buyers are generally shopkeepers, residing in the old clothes districts of Marylebone-lane, Holywell-street, Monmouth-street, Union-street (Borough), Saffron-hill (Field-lane), Drury-lane, Shoreditch, the Waterloo-road, and other places of which I shall have to speak hereafter.

The difference between the first and second class of buyers above mentioned, is really that of the merchant and the retail shopkeeper. The one buys literally anything presented to him which is vendible, and in any quantity, for the supply of the wholesale dealers from distant parts, or for exportation, or for the general trade of London. The other purchases what suits his individual trade, and is likely to suit regular or promiscuous customers.

In another part of the same market is carried on the *retail* old clothes trade to any one – shopkeeper, artisan, clerk, coster-monger, or gentlemen. This indeed, is partially the case in the other parts. 'Yesh, inteet,' said a Hebrew trader, whom I con-versed with on the subject, 'I shall be clad to shell you one coat, sir. Dish von is shust your shize; it is verra sheep, and vosh made by one tip-top shnip.' Indeed, the keenness and anxiety to trade – whenever trade seems possible – causes many of the frequenters of these marts to infringe the arrangements as to the manner of the traffic, though the proprietors endeavour to cause the regulations to be strictly adhered to.

The second Exchange, which is a few yards apart from the other, is known as Simmons and Levy's Clothes Exchange, and is unemployed, for its more especial business purposes, except in the mornings. The commerce is then wholesale, for here are sold collections of unredeemed pledges in wearing apparel, consigned there by the pawn-brokers, or the buyers at the auctions of unredeemed goods; as well as draughts from the stocks of the wardrobe dealers; a quantity of military or naval stores, and such like articles. In the afternoon the stalls are occupied by retail dealers. The ground is about as large as the first-mentioned exchange, but is longer and narrower.

In neither of these places is there even an attempt at architectural elegance, or even neatness. The stalls and partitions are of unpainted wood, the walls are bare, the only care that seems to be manifested is that the places should be dry. In the first instance the plainness was no doubt a necessity from motives of prudence, as the establishments were merely speculations, and now everything but business seems to be disregarded. The Old Clothes Exchanges have assuredly one recommendation as they are now seen – their appropriateness. They have a threadbare, patched, and second-hand look. The dresses worn by the dealers, and the dresses they deal in, are all in accordance with the genius of the place. But the eagerness, crowding, and energy, are the grand features of the scene; and of all the many curious sights in London there is none so picturesque (from the various costumes of the buyers and sellers), none so novel, and none so animated as that of the Old Clothes Exchange.

Business is carried on in the wholesale department of the Old Clothes Exchanges every day during the week; and in the retail on each day except the Hebrew Sabbath (Saturday). The Jews in the old clothes trade observe strictly the command that on their Sabbath day they shall do no manner of work, for on a visit I paid to the Exchange last Saturday, not a single Jew could I see engaged in any business. But though the Hebrew Sabbath is observed by the Jews and disregarded by the Christians, the Christian Sabbath, on the other hand, is disregarded by Jew and Christian alike, some few of the Irish excepted, who may occasionally go to early mass, and attend at the Exchange afterwards. Sunday, therefore, in 'Rag-fair', is like the other days of the week (Saturday excepted); business closes on the Sunday, however, at 2 instead of 6.

On the Saturday the keen Jew-traders in the neighbourhood of the Exchanges may be seen standing at their doors – after the synagogue hours – or looking out of their windows, dressed in their best. The dress of the men is for the most part not disting-uishable from that of the English on the Sunday, except that there may be a greater glitter of rings and watch-guards. The dress of the women is of every kind; becoming, handsome, rich, tawdry, but seldom neat.

The London Dock
[*volume iii. pp.302,303*]

I shall now give a brief statement of the character, condition, and capacity of the London Dock. After which, the description of the kind of labour performed there; and then the class of labourers performing it will follow in due order.

The London Dock occupies an area of ninety acres, and is situated in the three parishes of St George, Shadwell, and Wapping. The population of those three parishes in 1841 was 55,500, and the number of inhabited houses 8,000, which covered a space equal to 338 acres. This is in the proportion of twenty-three inhabited houses to an acre and seven individuals to each house. The number of persons to each inhabited house is, despite of the crowded lodging-houses with which it abounds, not beyond the average for all London. I have already shown that Bethnal-green, which is said to possess the greatest number of low-rented houses, had only, upon an average, seventeen inhabited houses to each acre, while the average through London was but 5.5 houses per acre. So that it appears that in the three parishes of St George's-in-the-East, Shad-well, and Wapping, the houses are more than four times more crowded than in the other parts of London, and more numerous by half as many again than those even in the low-rented district of Bethnal-green. This affords us a good criterion as to the character of the neighbourhood, and, consequently, of the people living in the vicinity of the London Dock.

The courts and alleys round about the dock swarm with low lodging-houses; and are inhabited either by the dock-labourers, sackmakers, watermen, or that peculiar class of the London poor who pick up a living by the water-side. The open streets themselves have all more or less a maritime character. Every other shop is either stocked with gear for the ship or for the sailor. The windows of one house are filled with quadrants and bright brass sextants, chronometers, and huge mariners' compasses, with their cards trembling with the motion of the cabs and waggons passing in the street. Then comes the sailors' cheap shoe-mart, rejoicing in the attractive sign of 'Jack and his Mother'. Every public-house is a 'Jolly Tar', or something equally taking. Then come sailmakers, their windows stowed with ropes and lines smelling of tar. All the grocers are provision-agents, and exhibit in their windows the cases of meat and biscuits; and every article is warranted to keep in any climate. The corners of the streets, too, are mostly monopolised by slop-sellers; their windows particoloured with bright red-and-blue flannel shirts; the doors nearly blocked up with hammocks and 'well-oiled nor'-westers'; and the front of the house itself nearly covered with canvas trousers, rough pilot-coats, and shiny black dreadnoughts. The passengers alone would tell you that you were in the maritime districts of London. Now you meet a satin-waistcoated mate, or a black sailor with his large fur cap, or else a Custom-house officer in his brass-buttoned jacket.

The London Dock can accommodate 500 ships, and the warehouses will contain 232,000 tons of goods. The entire structure cost 4,000,000l. in money: the tobacco warehouses alone cover five acres of ground. The wall surrounding the dock cost 65,000l. One of the wine-vaults has an area of seven acres, and in the whole of them there is room for stowing 60,000 pipes of wine. The warehouses round the wharfs are imposing from their extent, but are much less lofty than those at St Katherine's; and being situated at some distance from the dock, goods cannot be craned out of the ship's hold and stowed away at one operation. According to the last half-yearly report, the number of ships which entered the dock during the six months ending the 31st of May last was 704, measuring upwards of 195,000 tons. The amount of earnings during that period was 230,000l. and odd, and the amount of expenditure nearly 121,000l. The stock of goods in the warehouses last May was upwards of 170,000 tons.

As you enter the dock the sight of the forest of masts in the distance, and the tall chimneys vomiting clouds of black smoke, and the many coloured flags flying in the air, has a most peculiar effect; while the sheds with the monster wheels arching through the roofs look like the paddle-boxes of huge steamers. Along the quay you see, now men with their faces blue with indigo, and now gaugers, with their long brass-tipped rule dripping with spirit from the cask they have been probing. Then will come a group of flaxen-haired sailors chattering German; and next a black sailor, with a cotton handkerchief twisted turban-like round his head. Presently a blue-smocked butcher, with fresh meat and a bunch of cabbages in the tray on his shoulder; and shortly afterwards a mate, with green paroquets in a wooden cage. Here you will see sitting on a bench a sorrowful-looking woman, with new bright cooking tins at her feet, telling you she is an emigrant preparing for her voyage. As you pass along this quay the air is pungent with tobacco; on that it overpowers you with the fumes of rum; then you are nearly sickened with the stench of hides, and huge bins of horns; and shortly afterwards the atmosphere is fragrant with coffee and spice. Nearly everywhere you meet stacks of cork, or else yellow bins of sulphur, or lead-coloured copper-ore. As you enter this warehouse, the flooring is sticky, as if it had been newly tarred, with the sugar that has leaked through the casks; and as you descend into the dark vaults, you see long lines of lights hanging from the black arches, and lamps flitting about midway. Here you sniff the fumes of the wine, and there the peculiar fungus-smell of dry rot; then the jumble of sounds as you pass along the dock blends in anything but sweet concord. The sailors are singing boisterous nigger songs from the Yankee ship just entering; the cooper is hammering at the casks on the quay; the chains of the cranes, loosed of their weight, rattle as they fly up up again; the ropes splash in the water; some captain shouts his orders through his hands; a goat bleats from some ship in the basin; and empty casks roll along the stones with a heavy drum-like sound. Here the heavily-laden ships are down far below the quay, and you descend to them by ladders; whilst in another basin they are high up out of the water, so that their green copper sheathing is almost level with the eye of the passenger; while above his head a long line of bowsprits stretches far over the quay; and from them hang spars and planks as a gangway to each ship. [. . .]

The West India Docks
[*volume iii. pp.310,311*]

The West India Docks are about a mile and a half from the London Docks. The entire ground that they cover is 295 acres, so that they are nearly three times larger than the London Docks, and more than twelve times more extensive than those of St Katherine's. Hence they are the most capacious of all the great warehousing establishments in the port of London. The export dock is about 870 yards, or very nearly half-a-mile in length by 135 yards in width; its area, therefore, is about 25 acres. The import dock is the same length as the export dock, and 166 yards wide. The south dock, which is appropriated both to import and export vessels, is 1,183 yards, or upwards of two-thirds of a mile long, with an entrance to the river at each end; both the locks, as well as that into the Blackwall basin, being forty feet wide, and large enough to admit ships of 1,200 tons burden. The warehouses for imported goods are on the four quays of the import dock. They are well contrived and of great extent, being calculated to contain 180,000 tons of merchandise; and there has been at one time on the quays, and in the sheds, vaults, and warehouses, colonial produce worth 20,000,000*l.* sterling. The East India Docks are likewise the property of the West India Dock Company, having been purchased by them of the East India Company at the time of the opening of the trade to India. The import dock here has an area of 18 acres, and the export dock about 9 acres. The depth of water in these docks is greater, and they can consequently accommodate ships of greater burden than any other establishment on the river. The capital of both establishments, or of the united company, amounts to upwards of 2,000,000 of money. The West India import dock can accommodate 300 ships, and the export dock 200 ships of 300 tons each; and the East India import dock 84 ships, and the export dock 40 ships, of 800 tons each. The number of ships that entered the West India Dock to load and unload last year was 3008, and the number that entered the East India Dock 298. [. . .]

The transition from the London to the West India Docks is of a very peculiar character. The labourers at the latter place seem to be more civilised. The scrambling and scuffling for the day's hire, which is the striking feature of the one establishment, is scarcely distinguishable at the other. It is true there is the same crowd of labourers in quest of a day's work, but the struggle to obtain it is neither so fierce nor so disorderly in its character. And yet, here the casual labourers are men from whom no character is demanded as well as there. The amount of wages for the summer months is the same as at the London Dock. Unlike the London Dock, however, no reduction is made at the East and West India Docks during the winter.

The labour is as precarious at one establishment as at the other. The greatest number of hands employed for any one day at the East and West India Docks in the course of last year was nearly 4,000, and the smallest number about 1,300. The lowest number of ships that entered the docks during any one week in the present year was 28, and the highest number 209, being a difference of 181 vessels, of an average burden of 300 tons each. The positive amount of variation, however, which occurred in the labour during the briskest and slackest weeks of last year was a difference of upwards of 2,500 in the number of extra workmen employed, and of about 2,000*l*. in the amount of wages paid for the six days' labour. I have been favoured with a return of the number of vessels that entered the East and West India Docks for each week in the present year, and I subjoin a statement of the number arriving in each of the first fourteen of those weeks. In the 1st week of all there were 86, the 2nd 47, the 3rd 43, the 4th 48, the 5th 28, the 6th 49, the 7th 46, the 8th 37, the 9th 42, the 10th 47, the 11th 42, the 12th 131, the 13th 209, and the 14th 85. Hence it appears, that in the second week the number of ships coming into dock decreased nearly one-half; in the fifth week they were again diminished in a like proportion, while in the sixth week they were increased in a similar ratio; in the twelfth week they were more than three times what they were in the eleventh, in the thirteenth the number was half as much again as it was in the twelfth, and in the fourteenth it was down below half the number of the thirteenth, so that it is clear that the subsistence derived from dock labour must be of the most fickle and doubtful kind.

The St Katherine's Dock
[*volume iii. pp.311,312*]

Nor are the returns from St Katherine's Dock of a more cheerful character. Here it should be observed that no labourer is employed without a previous recommendation; and, indeed, it is curious to notice the difference in the appearance of the men applying for work at this establishment. They not only have a more decent look, but seem to be better behaved than any other dock-labourers I have yet seen. The 'ticket' system is here adopted – that is to say, the plan of allowing only such persons to labour within the docks as have been satisfactorily recommended to the company, and furnished with a ticket by them in return – this ticket system, says the statement which has been kindly drawn up expressly for me by the superintendent of the docks, may be worth notice, at a time when such efforts are making to improve the condition of the labourers. It gives an identity and *locus standi* to the men which casual labourers cannot otherwise possess, it connects them with the various grades of officers under whose eyes they labour, prevents favouritism, and leads to their qualifications being noted and recorded. It also holds before them a reward for activity, intelligence, and good conduct; because the vacancies in the list of preferable labourers, which occur during the year, are invariably filled in the succeeding January by selecting, upon strict inquiry, the best of the extra-ticket labourers, the vacancies among the permanent men being supplied in like manner from the list of preferable labourers, while from the permanent men are appointed the subordinate officers, as markers, samplers, &c.

Let us, however, before entering into a description of the class and number of labourers employed at St Katherine's, give a brief description of the docks themselves. The lofty walls, which constitute it in the language of the Custom-house a place of special security, enclose an area of 23 acres, of which 11 are water, capable of accommodating 120 ships, besides barges and other craft; cargoes are raised into the warehouses out of the hold of a ship, without the goods being deposited on the quay. The cargoes can be raised out of the ship's hold into the warehouses of St Katherine's in one-fifth of the usual time. Before the existence of docks, a month or six weeks was taken up in discharging the cargo of an East-Indiaman of from 800 to 1200 tons burden, while 8 days were necessary in the summer and 14 in the winter to unload a ship of 350 tons. At St Katherine's, however, the average time now occupied in discharging a ship of 250 tons is twelve hours, and one of 500 tons two or three days, the goods being placed at the same time in the warehouse: there have been occasions when even greater despatch has been used, and a cargo of 1100 casks of tallow, averaging from 9 to 10 cwt. each, has been discharged in seven hours. This would have been considered little short of a miracle on the legal quays less than fifty years ago. In 1841, about 1,000 vessels and 10,000 lighters were accommodated at St Katherine's Dock. The capital expended by the dock company exceeds 2,000,000 of money.

The business of this establishment is carried on by 35 officers, 105 clerks and apprentices, 135 markers, samplers, and foremen, 250 permanent labourers, 150 preferable ticket-labourers, proportioned to the amount of work to be done. The average number of labourers employed, permanent, preferable, and extras, is 1096; the highest number employed on any one day last year was 1713, and the lowest number 515, so that the extreme fluctuation in the labour appears to be very nearly 1200 hands. The lowest sum of money that was paid in 1848 for the day's work of the entire body of labourers employed was 64l. 7s. 6d., and the highest sum 214l. 2s. 6d., being a difference of very nearly 150l. in one day, or 900l. in the course of the week. The average number of ships that enter the dock every week is 17, the highest number that entered in any one week last year was 36, and the lowest 5, being a difference of 31. Assuming these to have been of an average burden of 300 tons, and that every such vessel would require 100 labourers to discharge its cargo in three days, then 1,500 extra hands ought to have been engaged to discharge the cargoes of the entire number in a week. This, it will be observed, is very nearly equal to the highest number of the labourers employed by the company in the year 1848.

The remaining docks are the Commercial Docks and timber ponds, the Grand Surrey Canal Dock at Rotherhithe, and the East Country Dock. The Commercial Docks occupy an area of about 49 acres, of which four-fifths are water. There is accommodation for 350 ships, and in the warehouses for 50,000 tons of merchandise. They are appropriated to vessels engaged in the European timber and corn trades, and the surrounding warehouses are used chiefly as granaries – the timber remaining afloat in the dock until

it is conveyed to the yard of the wholesale dealer and builder.
The Surrey Dock is merely an entrance basin to a canal, and can
accommodate 300 vessels. The East Country Dock, which adjoins
the Commercial Docks on the south, is capable of receiving 28
timber-ships. It has an area of 6½ acres, and warehouse-room
for 3700 tons.

In addition to these there is the Regent's Canal Dock, between
Shadwell and Limehouse, and though it is a place for bonding
timber and deals only, it nevertheless affords great accommodation
to the trade of the port by withdrawing shipping from the river.

The number of labourers, casual and permanent, employed at
these various establishments is so limited, that, taken altogether,
the fluctuations occurring at their briskest and slackest periods
may be reckoned as equal to that of St Katherine's. Hence the
account of the variation in the total number of hands employed,
and the sum of money paid as wages to them, by the different dock
companies, when the business is brisk or slack, may be stated as
follows:

At the London Dock the difference between
   the greatest and smallest number is   2,000 hands
At the East and West India Docks   2,500 hands
At the St Katherine's Dock   1,200 hands
At the remaining docks say   <u>1,300</u> hands

Total number of dock labourers thrown out of   7,000
   employ by the prevalence of easterly winds

The difference between the highest and lowest
   amount of wages paid at the London Dock is   £1,500
At the East and West India Docks   £1,875
At the St Katherine's Dock   £900
At the remaining docks   <u>£975</u>
                 £5,250

From the above statement then it appears, that by the prevalence
of an easterly wind no less than 7,000 out of the aggregate number
of persons living by dock labour may be deprived of their regular
income, and the entire body may have as much as 5250*l.* a week
abstracted from the amount of their collective earnings, at a period
of active employment. But the number of individuals who depend
upon the quantity of shipping entering the port of London for their

daily subsistence is far beyond this amount. Indeed we are assured by a gentleman filling a high situation in St Katherine's Dock, and who, from his sympathy with the labouring poor, has evidently given no slight attention to the subject, that taking into consideration the number of wharf-labourers, dock-labourers, lightermen, riggers and lumpers, shipwrights, caulkers, ships' carpenters, anchor-smiths, corn-porters, fruit and coal-meters, and indeed all the multifarious arts and callings connected with shipping, there are no less than from 25,000 to 30,000 individuals who are thrown wholly out of employ by a long continuance of easterly winds. Estimating then the gains of this large body of individuals at 2s. 6d. per day, or 15s. per week, when fully employed, we shall find that the loss to those who depend upon the London shipping for their subsistence amounts to 20,000l. per week, and, considering that such winds are often known to prevail for a fortnight to three weeks at a time, it follows that the entire loss to this large class will amount to from 40,000l. to 60,000l. within a month, – an amount of privation to the labouring poor which it is positively awful to contemplate. Nor is this the only evil connected with an enduring easterly wind. Directly a change takes place a glut of vessels enters the metropolitan port, and labourers flock from all quarters; indeed they flock from every part where the workmen exist in a greater quantity than the work. From 500 to 800 vessels frequently arrive at one time in London after the duration of a contrary wind, and then such is the demand for workmen, and so great the press of business, owing to the rivalry among merchants, and the desire of each owner to have his cargo the first in the market, that a sufficient number of hands is scarcely to be found. Hundreds of extra labourers, who can find labour nowhere else, are thus led to seek work in the docks. But, to use the words of our informant, two or three weeks are sufficient to break the neck of an ordinary glut, and then the vast amount of extra hands that the excess of business has brought to the neighbourhood are thrown out of employment, and left to increase either the vagabondism of the neighbourhood or to swell the number of paupers and heighten the rates of the adjacent parishes.

6

CULTURE AND BELIEF

The phrase 'popular culture' was unknown in mid-Victorian England but Mayhew certainly conceived of a culture that was peculiar to the poor and of variations particular to specific groups and occupations. He chose to interview for the second edition of London Labour and the London Poor representatives of the professionals – clowns, tumblers, gymnasts, dancers, comedians, musicians, singers, fire-eaters, pavement artists, actors, Punch and Judy men and the like – who delivered 'entertainment' and 'amusement' that appealed. From them he received vivid descriptions of their practices – for example, an entire script of a Punch and Judy production and detailed accounts of Guy Fawkes celebrations past and present. Probably he felt that the inclusion of such extraordinary material would help boost the sales of his work, especially as the issue of noise nuisance was very topical. Mayhew asked questions of these people about their audiences and, when he interviewed men, women and children from other walks of life, he asked questions of the poor about their use of such leisure as they had. He was also alive to the part that religion, whether organised or unorganised, played or did not play in the lives of the people. The influence of religion, in terms of morality and ordered living, was of interest to him. In his interviews he frequently asked what the individuals knew of Scripture, whether they attended Church or Chapel and what, if anything, they believed. Mayhew's work provides historians with much of what they know about popular culture and belief in the London of the Great Exhibition.

PUNCH'S SHOWMEN
[from a photograph]

Punch
[*volume iii. pp.43–60*]

The performer of Punch that I saw was a short, dark, pleasant-looking man, dressed in a very greasy and very shiny green shooting-jacket. This was fastened together by one button in front, all the other button-holes having been burst through. Protruding from his bosom, a corner of the pandean pipes was just visible, and as he told me the story of his adventures, he kept playing with the band of his very limp and very rusty old beaver hat. He had formerly been a gentleman's servant, and was especially civil in his manners. He came to me with his hair tidily brushed for the occasion, but apologised for his appearance on entering the room. He was very communicative, and took great delight in talking like Punch, with his call in his mouth, while some young children were in the room, and who, hearing the well-known sound of Punch's voice, looked all about for the figure. Not seeing the show, they fancied the man had the figure in his pocket, and that the sounds came from it. The change from Punch's voice to the man's natural tone was managed without an effort, and instantaneously. It had a very peculiar effect.

'I am the proprietor of a Punch's show,' he said. 'I goes about with it myself, and performs inside the frame behind the green baize. I have a pardner what plays the music – the pipes and drum; him as you see'd with me. I have been five-and-twenty year now at the business. I wish I'd never seen it, though it's *been* a money-making business – indeed, the best of all the street hexhibitions I may say. I am fifty years old. I took to it for money gains – that was what I done it for. I formerly lived in service – was a footman in a gentleman's family. When I first took to it, I could make two and three pounds a day – I could so. You see, the way in which I took first to the business was this here – there was a party used to come and "cheer" for us at my master's house, and her son having a hexhibition of his own, and being in want of a pardner, axed me if so be I'd go out, which was a thing that I degraded at the time. He gave me information as to what the money-taking was, and it seemed to me that good, that it would pay me better nor service. I had twenty pounds a-year in my place, and my board and lodging, and two suits of clothes, but the young man told me as how I could make one pound a day at the Punch-and-Judy business, after a little practice. I took a deal of persuasion, though, before I'd join him – it was beneath my dignity to fall from a footman to a showman. But, you see, the French gennelman as I lived with (he were a merchant in the city, and had fourteen clerks working for him) went back to his own country to reside, and left me with a written kerrackter; but that was no use to me: though I'd fine recommendations at the back of it, no-one would look at it; so I was five months out of employment, knocking about – living first on my wages and then on my clothes, till all was gone but the few rags on my back. So I began to think that the Punch-and-Judy business was better than starving after all. Yes, I should think anything was better than that, though it's a business that, after you've once took to, you never can get out of – people fancies you know too much, and won't have nothing to say to you. If I got a situation at a tradesman's, why the boys would be sure to recognise me behind the counter, and begin a-shouting into the shop (they *must* shout, you know): "Oh, there's Punch and Judy – there's Punch a-sarving out the customers!" Ah, it's a great annoyance being a public kerrackter, I can assure you, sir; go where you will, it's "Punchy, Punchy!" As for the boys, they'll never leave me alone till I die, I know; and I suppose in my old age I shall have to take to the parish broom. All our forefathers died in the workhouse. I don't know a Punch's showman that hasn't. One of my pardners was buried by the workhouse; and even old Pike, the most noted showman as ever was, died in the workhouse – Pike and Porsini. Porsini was the first original street Punch, and Pike was his apprentice; their names is handed down to posterity among the noblemen and footmen of the land. They both died in the workhouse, and, in course, I shall do the same. Something else *might* turn up, to be sure. We can't say what this luck of the world is. I'm obliged to strive very hard – very hard indeed, sir, now, to get a living; and then not to get it after all – at times, compelled to go short, often.

'Punch, you know, sir, is a dramatic performance in two hacts. It's a play, you may say. I don't think it can be called a tragedy hexactly; a drama is what we names it. There is tragic parts, and comic and sentimental parts, too. Some families where I performs will have it most sentimental – in the original style; them families is generally sentimental theirselves. Others is all for the comic, and then I has to kick up all the games I can. To the sentimental folk I am obliged to perform werry steady and werry slow, and leave out all comic words and business. They won't have no ghost, no coffin, and no devil; and that's what I call spiling the performance entirely. It's the march of hintellect wot's a doing all this – it is, sir. But I was a going to tell you about my first jining the business. Well, you see, after a good deal of persuading, and being drew to it, I may say, I consented to go out with the young man as I were a-speaking about. He was to give me twelve shillings a week and my keep, for two years certain, till I could get my own show things together, and for that I was to carry the show, and go round and *collect*. Collecting, you know, sounds better than begging; the pronounciation's better like. Sometimes the people says, when they sees us a coming round, "Oh, here they comes a-begging" – but it can't be begging, you know, when you're a-hexerting your-selves. I couldn't play the drum and pipes, so the young man used to do that himself, to call the people together before he got into the show. I used to stand outside, and patter to the figures. The first time that ever I went out with Punch was in the beginning of August, 1825. I did all I could to avoid being seen. My dignity was hurt at being hobligated to take to the streets for a living. At fust I fought shy, and used to feel queer somehow, you don't know how like, whenever the people used to look at me. I remember werry well the first street as ever I performed in. It was off Gray's Inn, one of them quiet, genteel streets, and when the mob began to gather round I felt all-overish, and I turned my head to the frame instead of the people. We hadn't had no rehearsals afore-hand, and I did the patter quite permiscuous. There was not much talk, to be sure, required then; and what little there was, consisted merely in calling out the names of the figures as they came up, and these my master prompted me with from inside the frame. But little as there was for me to do, I know I never could have done it, if it hadn't been for the spirits – the false spirits, you see (a little drop of gin), as my master guv me in the morning. The first time as ever I made my appearance in public, I collected as much as eight shillings, and my master said, after the performance was over, "You'll do!" You see I was partly in livery, and looked a little bit decent like. After this was over, I kept on going out with my master for two years, as I had agreed, and at the end of that time I had saved enough to start a show of my own. I bought the show of old Porsini, the man as first brought Punch into the streets of England. [. . .]

'I gave him thirty-five shillings for the stand, figures and all. I bought it cheap, you see, for it was thrown on one side, and was of no use to any one but such as myself. There was twelve figures and the other happaratus, such as the gallows, ladder, horse, bell, and stuffed dog. The characters was Punch, Judy, Child, Beadle, Scaramouch, Nobody, Jack Ketch, the Grand Senoor, the Doctor, the Devil (there was no Ghost used then), Merry Andrew, and the Blind Man. These last two kerrackters are quite done with now. The heads of the kerrackters was all carved in wood, and dressed in the proper costume of the country. There was at that time, and is now, a real carver for the Punch business. He was dear, but werry good and hexcellent. His Punch's head was the best as I ever seed. The nose and chin used to meet quite close together. A set of new figures, dressed and all, would come to about fifteen pounds. Each head costs five shillings for the bare carving alone, and every figure that we has takes at least a yard of cloth to dress him, besides ornaments and things that comes werry expensive. A good show at the present time will cost three pounds odd for the stand alone – that's including baize, the frontispiece, the back scene, the cottage, and the letter cloth, or what is called the drop-scene at the theatres. In the old ancient style, the back scene used to pull up and change into a gaol scene, but that's all altered now.

'We've got more upon the comic business now, and tries to do more with Toby than with the prison scene. The prison is what we calls the sentimental style. Formerly Toby was only a stuffed figure. It was Pike who first hit upon hintroducing a live dog, and a great hit it were – it made a grand alteration in the hexhibition, for now the performance is called Punch and Toby as well. There is one Punch about the streets at present that tries it on with three dogs, but that ain't much of a go – too much of a good thing I calls it. Punch, as I said before, is a drama in two hacts. We don't drop the scene at the end of the first – the drum and pipes strikes up instead. The first act we consider to end with Punch being taken to prison for the murder of his wife and child. The great difficulty in performing Punch consists in the speaking, which is done by a call, or whistle in the mouth, such as this here.' [He then produced the call from his waistcoat pocket. It was a small flat instrument, made of two curved pieces of metal about the size of a knee-buckle, bound together with black thread. Between these was a plate of some substance (apparently silk), which he said was a secret. The call, he told me, was tuned to a musical instrument, and took a considerable time to learn. He afterwards took from his pocket two of the small metallic plates unbound. He said the composition they were made of was also one of the 'secrets of the purfession'. They were not tin, nor zinc, because 'both of them metals were poisons in the mouth, and hinjurious to the constit-ution.'] 'These calls,' he continued, 'we often sell to gennelmen for a sovereign a-piece, and for that we give 'em a receipt how to use them. They ain't whistles, but calls, or unknown tongues, as we sometimes names 'em, because with them in the mouth we can pronounce each word as plain as any parson. We have two or three kinds – one for out-of-doors, one for in-doors, one for speaking and for singing, and another for selling. I've sold many a one to gennelmen going along, so I generally keeps a hextra one with me. Porsini brought the calls into this country with him from Italy, and we who are now in the purfession have all learnt how to make and use them, either from him or those as he had taught 'em to. I larnt the use of mine from Porsini himself. My master whom I went out with at first would never teach me, and was werry partickler in keeping it all secret from me. Porsini taught me the call at the time I bought his show of him. I was six months in perfecting myself in the use of it. I kept practising away night and morning with it, until I got it quite perfect. It was no use trying at home, 'cause it sounds quite different in the hopen hair. Often when I've made 'em at home, I'm obliged to take the calls to pieces after trying 'em out in the streets, they've been made upon too weak a scale. When I was practising, I used to go into the parks, and fields, and out-of-the-way places, so as to get to know how to use it in the hopen hair. [. . .]

'The fust person who went out with me was my wife. She used to stand outside, and keep the boys from peeping through the baize, whilst I was performing behind it; and she used to collect the money afterwards as well. I carried the show and trumpet, and she the box. She's been dead these five years now. Take one week with another, all through the year, I should say I made then five pounds regular. I have taken as much as two pounds ten shillings in one day in the streets; and I used to think it a bad day's business at that time if I took only one pound. You can see Punch has been good work – a money-making business – and beat all mechanics right out. If I could take as much as I did when I first began, what must my forefathers have done, when the business was five times as good as ever it were in my time? Why, I leaves you to judge what old Porsini and Pike must have made. Twenty years ago I have often and often got seven shillings and eight shillings for one hexhibition in the streets: two shillings and three shillings I used to think low to get at one collection; and many times I'd perform eight or ten times in a day. We didn't care much about work then, for we could get money fast enough; but now I often show twenty times in the day, and get scarcely a bare living at it arter all. That shows the times, you know, sir – what things was and is now. Arter performing in the streets of a day we used to attend private parties in the hevening, and get sometimes as much as two pounds for the hexhibition. This used to be at the juvenile parties of the nobility; and the performance lasted about an hour and a half. For a short performance of half-an-hour at a gennelman's house we never had less than one pound. A performance outside the house was two shillings and sixpence; but we often got as much as ten shillings for it. I have performed afore almost all the nobility. Lord — was particular partial to us, and one of our greatest patronisers. At the time of the Police Bill I met him at Cheltenham on my travels, and he told me as he had saved Punch's neck once more; and it's through him principally that we are allowed to exhibit in the streets. Punch is exempt from the Police Act. If you read the hact throughout, you won't find Punch mentioned in it. But all I've been telling you is about the business as it was. What it *is*, is a werry different consarn. A good day for us now seldom gets beyond five shillings, and that's between myself and my pardner, who plays the drum and pipes. Often we are out all day, and get a mere nuffing. Many days we have been out and taken nuffing at all – that's werry common when we dwells upon horders. By dwelling on horders, I means looking out for gennelmen what want us to play in front of their houses. When we strike up in the hopen street we take upon a haverage only threepence a show. In course we *may* do more, but that's about the sum, take one street performance with another. Them kind of performances is what we calls "short showing". We gets the halfpence and hooks it. A "long pitch" is the name we gives to performances that lasts about half-an-hour or more. Them long pitches we confine solely to street corners in public thorough-fares; and then we take about a shilling upon a haverage, and more if it's to be got – we never turns away nuffing. [. . .]

'Hampstead, tho', ain't no good; they've got too poor there. I'd sooner not go out at all than to Hampstead. Belgrave-square, and all about that part, is uncommon good; but where there's many chapels Punch won't do at all. I did once, though, strike up hopposition to a street preacher wot was a holding forth in the New-road, and did uncommon well. All his flock, as he called 'em, left him, and come over to look at me. Punch and preaching is two different creeds – hopposition parties, I may say. We in generally walks from twelve to twenty mile every day, and carries the show, which weighs a good half-hundred, at the least. Arter great exertion, our woice werry often fails us; for speaking all day through the "call" is werry trying, 'specially when we are chirruping up so as to bring the children to the vinders. The boys is the greatest nuisances we has to contend with. Wherever we goes we are sure of plenty of boys for a hindrance; but they've got no money, bother 'em! and they'll follow us for miles, so that we're often compelled to go miles to awoid 'em. Many parts is swarming with boys, such as Vitechapel. Spitalfields, that's the worst place for boys I ever come a-near; they're like flies in summer there, only much more thicker. I never shows my face within miles of them parts. Chelsea, again, has an uncommon lot of boys; and wherever we know the children swarm, there's the spots we makes a point of awoiding. Why, the boys is such a hobstruction to our performance, that often we are obliged to drop the curtain for 'em. They'll throw one another's caps into the frame while I'm inside on it, and do what we will, we can't keep 'em from poking their fingers through the baize and making holes to peep through. Then they will keep tapping the drum; but the worst of all is, the most of 'em ain't got a farthing to bless themselves with, and they *will* shove into the best places. Soldiers, again, we don't like, they've got no money – no, not even so much as pockets, sir. Nusses ain't no good. Even if the mothers of the dear little children has given 'em a penny to spend, why the nusses takes it from 'em, and keeps it for ribbins. Sometimes we can coax a penny out of the children, but the nusses knows too much to be gammoned by us. Indeed, servants in generally don't do the thing what's right to us – some is good to us, but the most of 'em will have poundage out of what we gets. About sixpence out of every half-crown is what the footman takes from us. We in generally goes into the country in the summer time for two or three months. Watering-places is werry good in July and August. Punch mostly goes down to the sea-side with the quality. Brighton, though, ain't no account; the Pavilion's done up with, and therefore Punch has discontinued his visits. We don't put up at the trampers' houses on our travels, but in generally inns is where we stays; because we considers ourselves to be above the other showmen and mendicants. At one lodging-house as I stopped at once in Warwick, there was as many as fifty staying there what got their living by street performances – the greater part were Italian boys and girls. There are altogether as many as sixteen Punch-and-Judy frames in England. Eight of these is at work in London, and the other eight in the country; and to each of these frames there are two men. We are all acquainted with one another; are all sociable together, and know where each other is, and what they are a-doing on. When one comes home, another goes out; that's the way we proceed through life. It wouldn't do for two to go to the same place. If two of us happens to meet at one town, we jine, and shift pardners, and share the money. One goes one way, and one another, and we meet at night, and reckon up over a sociable pint or a glass. We shift pardners so as each may know how much the other has taken. It's the common practice for the man what performs Punch to share with the one wot plays the drum and pipes – each has half wot is collected; but if the pardner can't play the drum and pipes, and only carries the frame, and collects, then his share is but a third of what is taken till he learns how to perform himself. The street performers of London lives mostly in little rooms of their own; they has generally wives, and one or two children, who are brought up to the business. Some lives about the Westminster-road, and St George's East. A great many are in Lock's-fields – they are all the old school that way. Then some, or rather the principal part of the showmen, are to be found about Lisson-grove. In this neighbourhood there is a house of call, where they all assembles in the evening. There are a very few in Brick-lane, Spitalfields, now; that is mostly deserted by showmen. The West-end is the great resort of all; for it's there the money lays, and there the showmen abound. We all know one another, and can tell in what part of the country the others are. We have intelligence by letters from all parts. There's a Punch I knows on now is either in the Isle of Man, or on his way to it.'

Punch talk

' "Bona parlare" means language; name of patter. "Yeute munjare" – no food. "Yeute lente" – no bed. "Yeute bivare" – no drink. I've "yeute munjare", and "yeute bivare", and, what's worse, "yeute lente". This is better than the costers' talk, because that ain't no slang at all, and this is a broken Italian, and much higher than the costers' lingo. We know what o'clock it is, besides.'

Scene with two Punchmen

' "How are you getting on?" I might say to another Punchman. "Ultra cateva," he'd say. If I was doing a little, I'd say, "Bonar". Let us have a "shant a bivare"– pot o' beer. If we has a good pitch we never tell one another, for business is business. If they know we've a "bonar" pitch, they'll oppose, which makes it bad.

' "Co. and Co." is our term for partner, or "questa questa", as well. "Ultray cativa" – no bona. "Slumareys" – figures, frame, scenes, properties. "Slum"– call, or unknown tongue. "Ultray cativa slum" – not a good call. "Tambora" – drum; that's Italian. "Pipares" – pipes. "Questra homa a vardring the slum, scapar it, orderly" – there's someone a looking at the slum. Be off quickly. "Fielia" is a child; "Homa" is a man; "Dona", a female;

"Charfering-homa" – talking-man, policeman. Policemen can't interfere with us, we're sanctioned. Punch is exempt out of the Police Act. Some's very good men, and some on 'em are tyrants; but generally speaking they're all werry kind to us, and allows us every privilege. That's a flattery, you know, because you'd better not meddle with them. Civility always gains its esteem.'

The Punchman at the theatre

'I used often when a youth to be very fond of plays and romances, and frequently went to theatres to learn knowledge, of which I think there is a deal of knowledge to be learnt from those places (that gives the theatres a touch – helps them on a bit). I was very partial and fond of seeing Romeau and Juliet; Otheller; and the Knights of St John, and the Pretty Gal of Peerlesspool; Macbeth and the Three Dancing Witches. Don Goovarney pleased me best of all though. What took me uncommon were the funeral purcession of Juliet – it affects the heart, and brings us to our nat'ral feelings. I took my ghost from Romeau and Juliet; the ghost comes from the grave, and it's beautiful. I used to like Kean, the principal performer. Oh, admirable! most admirable he were, and especially in Otheller, for then he was like my Jim Crow here, and was always a great friend and supporter of his old friend Punch. Otheller murders his wife, ye know, like Punch does. Otheller kills her, 'cause the green-eyed monster has got into his 'art, and he being so extremely fond on her; but Punch kills his'n by accident, though he did not intend to do it, for the Act of Parliament against husbands beating wives was not known in his time. A most excellent law that there, for it causes husbands and wives to be kind and natural one with the other, all through the society of life. Judy irritates her husband, Punch, for to strike the fatal blow, vich at the same time, vith no intention to commit it, not knowing at the same time, being rather out of his mind, vot he vas about. I hope this here will be a good example both to men and wives, always to be kind and obleeging to each other, and that will help them through the mainder with peace and happiness, and will rest in peace with all mankind (that's moral). It must be well worded, ye know, that's my beauty.' [. . .]

The history of Punch

'There are hoperas and romarnces. A romarnce is far different to a hopera, you know; for one is interesting, and the other is dull and void of apprehension. The romarnce is the interesting one, and of the two I likes it the best; but let every one speak as they find – that's moral. *Jack Sheppard*, you know, is a romarnce, and a fine one; but Punch is a hopera – a huproar, we calls it, and the most pleasing and most interesting of all as was ever produced. Punch never was beat and never will, being the oldest performance for many hundred years, and now handed down to prosperity (there's a fine moral in it, too). [. . .]

'Punch commences with a song. He does roo-too-rooey, and sings the "Lass of Gowrie" down below, and then he comes up, saying, "Ooy-ey; Oh, yes, I'm a coming. How do you do, ladies and gents?" – ladies always first; and then he bows many times. "I'm so happy to see you," he says; "Your most obedient, most humble, and dutiful servant, Mr Punch." (Ye see I can talk as affluent as can be with the call in my mouth.) "Ooy-ey, I wishes you all well and happy." Then Punch says to the drum-and-pipes man, as he puts his hand out, "How do you do, master? – play up; play up a hornpipe: I'm a most hexcellent dancer;" and then Punch dances. Then ye see him a-dancing the hornpipe; and after that Punch says to the pipes, "Master, I shall call my wife up, and have a dance;" so he sings out, "Judy, Judy! my pratty creetur! come upstairs, my darling! I want to speak to you" – and he knocks on the play-board. – "Judy! Here she comes, bless her little heart!"

Enter JUDY.

PUNCH. What a sweet creature! what a handsome nose and chin!
   [*he pats her on the face very gently*]
JUDY. [*slapping him*] Keep quiet, do!
PUNCH. Don't be cross, my dear, but give me a kiss.
JUDY. Oh, to be sure, my love. [*they kiss*]
PUNCH. Bless your sweet lips! [*hugging her*] This is melting moments.
   I'm very fond of my wife; we must have a dance.
JUDY. Agreed. [*they both dance*]
PUNCH. Get out of the way! You don't dance well enough for me.
   [*he hits her on the nose*] Go and fetch the baby, and mind and take care of it, and not hurt it.
                                                    [JUDY *exaunts*

JUDY. [*returning back with baby*] Take care of the baby, while I go
and cook the dumplings.

PUNCH. [*striking Judy with his right hand*] Get out of the way! I'll
take care of the baby.

[JUDY *exaunts*

PUNCH [*sits down and sings to the baby*] –

  Hush-a-by, baby, upon the tree-top,
  When the wind blows the cradle will rock;
  When the bough breaks the cradle will fall,
  Down comes the baby and cradle and all.
  [*baby cries*]

PUNCH. [*shaking it*] What a cross boy! [*he lays it down on the play-
board, rolls it backwards and forwards to rock it to sleep, and sings again*]
  Oh, slumber, my darling, thy sire is a knight,
  Thy mother's a lady so lovely and bright;
  The hills and the dales, and the tow'rs which you see,
  They all shall belong, my dear creature, to thee.

[PUNCH *continues rocking the child. It still cries, and he takes it up in his
arms, saying,* What a cross child!]

[. . .]

Guy Fawkes
[*volume iii. pp.64–72*]

The practice of burning guys, and lighting bonfires, and letting off
fireworks, is now generally discontinued, and particularly as regards
the public exhibitions at Blackheath and Peckham Rye. The
greatest display of fireworks, we are inclined to believe, took place
in the public streets of the metropolis, for up to twelve o'clock at
night, one might occasionally hear reports of penny cannons, and
the jerky explosions of crackers.

Guy Fawkes (man)
[*volume iii. pp.68–70*]

'I'm in the crock'ry line, going about with a basket and changing
jugs, and glass, and things, for clothes and that; but for the last
eight years I have, every Fifth of November, gone out with a guy.

GUY FAWKES

It's a good job for the time, for what little we lay out on the guy we don't miss, and the money comes in all of a lump at the last. While it lasts there's money to be made by it. I used always to take the guy about for two days; but this last year I took him about for three.

'I was nineteen year old when I first went out with a guy. It was seeing others about with 'em, and being out of work at the time, and having nothing to sell, I and another chap we knocked up one between us, and we found it go on pretty well, so we kept on at it. The first one I took out was a very first-rater, for we'd got it up as well as we could to draw people's attention. I said, "It ain't no good doing as the others do, we must have a tip-topper." It represented Guy Fawkes in black velvet. It was about nine feet high, and he was standing upright, with matches in one hand and lantern in the other. I show'd this one round Clerkenwell and Islington. It was the first big 'un as was ever brought out. There had been paper ones as big, but ne'er a one dressed up in the style mine was. I had a donkey and cart, and we placed it against some cross-rails and some bits of wood to keep him steady. He stood firm because he had two poles up his legs, and being lashed round the body holding him firm to the posts – like a rock. We done better the first time we went out than we do lately. The guy must have cost a sovereign. He had a trunk-hose and white legs, which we made out of a pair of white drawers, for fleshings and yellow boots, which I bought in Petticoat-lane. We took over 3*l.* with him, which was pretty fair, and just put us on again, for November is a bad time for most street trades, and getting a few shillings all at once makes it all right till Christmas.

'A pal of mine, of the name of Smith, was the first as ever brought out a big one. His wasn't a regular dressed-up one, but only with a paper apron to hang down the front and bows, and such-like. He put it on a chair, and had four boys to carry it on their shoulders. He was the first, too, as introduced clowns to dance about. I see him do well, and that's why I took mine in hand.

'The year they was chalking "No Popery" all about the walls I had one, dressed up in a long black garment, with a red cross on his bosom. I'm sure I don't know what it meant, but they told me it would be popular. I had only one figure, with nine bows, and that tidiwated all about him. As we went along everybody shouted out

"No Popery!" Everybody did. He had a large brimmed hat with a low crown in, and a wax mask. I always had wax ones. I've got one at home now I've had for five year. It cost two-and-six-pence. It's a very good-looking face but rather sly, with a great horse-hair beard. Most of the boys make their'n devils, and as ugly as they can, but that wouldn't do for Christians like as I represent mine to be.

'One year I had Nicholas and his adviser. That was the Emperor of Russia in big top-boots and white breeches, and a green coat on. I gave him a good bit of mustachios – a little extra. He had a Russian helmet hat on, with a pair of eagles on the top. It was one I bought. I bought it cheap, for I only gave a shilling for it. I was offered five or six for it afterwards, but I found it answer my purpose to keep. I had it dressed up this year. The other figure was the devil. I made him of green tinsel paper cut out like scale armour, and pasted on to his legs to make it stick tight. He had a devil's mask on, and I made him a pair of horns out of his head. Over them was a banner. I was told what to do to make the banner, for I had the letters writ out first, and then I cut 'em out of tinsel paper and stuck them on to glazed calico. On this banner was these words:

> "What shall I do next?"
> "Why, blow your brains out!"

That took immensely, for the people said "That is wery well." It was the time the war was on. I dare say I took between 3*l*. and 4*l*. that time. There was three of us rowed in with it, so we got a few shillings a-piece.

'The best one I ever had was the trial of Guy Fawkes. There was four figures, and they was drawn about in a horse and cart. There was Guy Fawkes, and two soldiers had hold of him, and there was the king sitting in a chair in front. The king was in a scarlet velvet cloak, sitting in an old arm-chair, papered over to make it look decent. There was green and blue paper hanging over the arms to hide the ragged parts of it. The king's cloak cost sevenpence a-yard, and there was seven of these yards. He had a gilt paper crown and a long black wig made out of some rope. His trunks was black and crimson, and he had blue stockings and red boots. I made him up out of my own head, and not from pictures. It was just as I thought would be the best way to get it up, out of my own head.

I've seed the picture of Guy Fawkes, because I've got a book of it at home. I never was no scholar, not in the least. The soldiers had a breast-plate of white steel paper, and baggy knee-breeches, and top-boots. They had a big pipe each, with a top cut out of tin. Their helmets was the same as in the pictures, of steel paper, and a kind of a dish-cover shape, with a peak in front and behind. Guy was dressed the same kind as he was this year, with a black velvet dress and red cloak, and red boots turning over at top, with lace sewed on. I never made any of my figures frightful. I get 'em as near as I can to the life like.

'I reckon that show was the best as I ever had about. I done very well with it. They said it was a very good sight, and well got up. I dare say it cost me, with one thing and another, pretty nigh 4l. to get up. There was two of us to shove, me and my brother. I know I had a sovereign to myself when it was over, besides a little bit of merry-making.

'This year I had the apprehension of Guy Fawkes by Lord Suffolk and Monteagle. I've followed up the hist'ry as close as I can. Next year I shall have him being burnt, with a lot of faggits and things about him. This year the figures cost about 3l. getting up. Fawkes was dressed in his old costume of black velvet and red boots. I bought some black velvet breeches in Petticoat-lane, and I gave 1s. 9d. for the two pair. They was old theatrical breeches. Their lordships was dressed in gold scale-armour like, of cut-out paper pasted on, and their legs imitated steel. They had three-corner cock'd hats, with white feathers in. I always buy fierce-looking masks with frowns, but one of them this year was a-smiling — Lord Monteagle, I think. I took the figures as near as I can form from a picture I saw of Guy Fawkes being apprehended. I placed them figures in a horse and cart, and piled them up on apple-chests to the level of the cart, so they showed all, their feet and all. I bind the chests with a piece of table-cover cloth. The first day we went out we took 2l. 7s., and the second we took 1l. 17s., and the last day we took 2l. 1s. We did so well the third day because we went into the country, about Tottenham and Edmonton. They never witnessed such a thing down them parts. The drummer what I had with me was a blind man, and well known down there. They call him Friday, because he goes there every Friday, so what they usually gave him we had. Our horse was blind, so we was obliged to have one to lead him in front and another to lead the blind drummer behind. We paid the drummer 16s. for the three days. We paid for two days 10s., and the third one most of it came in, and we all went shares. It was a pony more than a horse. I think we got about a 1l. a-piece clear, when we was done on the Friday night. It took me six weeks getting up in my leisure time. There was the Russian bear in front. He wore a monkey dress, the same as in the pantomimes, and that did just as well for a bear. I painted his face as near as I could get it, to make it look frightful.

'When I'm building up a guy we first gits some bags and things, and cut 'em out to the shape of the legs and things, and then sew it up. We sew the body and arms and all round together in one. We puts two poles down for the legs and then a cross-piece at the belly and another cross-piece at the shoulder, and that holds 'em firm. We fill the legs with sawdust, and stuff it down with our hands to make it tight. It takes two sacks of sawdust for three figures, but I generally have it give to me, for I know a young feller as works at the wood-chopping. We stand 'em up in the room against the wall, whilst we are dressing them. We have lots of chaps come to see us working at the guys. Some will sit there for many hours looking at us. We stuff the body with shavings and paper and any sort of rubbish. I sew whatever is wanted myself, and in fact my fingers is sore now with the thimble, for I don't know how to use a thimble, and I feel awkward with it. I design everything and cut out all the clothes and the painting and all. They allow me 5s. for the building. This last group took me six weeks, – not constant, you know, but only lazy time of a night. I lost one or two days over it, that's all.

'I think there was more Guy Fawkeses out this year than ever was out before. There was one had Guy Fawkes and Punch and a Clown in a cart, and another was Miss Nightingale and two soldiers. It was meant to be complimentary to that lady, but for myself I think it insulting to bring out a lady like that as a guy, when she's done good to all.

'They always reckon me to be about the first hand in London at building a guy. I never see none like them, nor no-one else I don't think. It took us two quire of gold paper and one quire of silver paper to do the armour and the banner and other things. The gold paper is 6d. a-sheet, and the silver is 1d. a sheet. It wouldn't look so noble if we didn't use the gold paper.

'This year we had three clowns with us, and we paid them 3s. a day each. I was dressed up as a clown, too. We had to dance about, and joke, and say what we thought would be funny to the people. I had a child in my arms made of a doll stuffed with shavings, and made to represent a little boy. It was just to make a laugh. Every one I went up to I told the doll to ask their uncle or their aunt for a copper. I had another move, too, of calling for "Bill Bowers" in the crowd, and if I got into any row, or anything, I used to call to him to protect me. We had no time to say much, for we kept on moving, and it loses time to talk.

'We took the guy round Goswell-road and Pentonville the first day, and on the second we was round Bethnal-green way, among the weavers. We went that way for safety the second day, for the police won't interrupt you there. The private houses give the most. They very seldom give more than a penny. I don't suppose we got more than 3s. or 4s. in silver all the three days.

'Sometimes we have rough work with the Irish going about with guys. The "No Popery" year there was several rows. I was up at Islington-gate, there, in the Lower-road, and there's loads of Irish live up there, and a rough lot they are. They came out with sticks and bricks, and cut after us. We bolted with the guy. If our guy hadn't been very firm, it would have been jolted to bits. We always nailed straps round the feet, and support it on rails at the waist, and lashed to the sides. We bolted from this Irish mob over Islington-green, and down John-street into Clerkenwell. My mate got a nick with a stone just on the head. It just give him a slight hurt, and drawed the blood from him. We jumped up in the donkey-cart and drove off.

'There was one guy was pulled out of the cart this year, down by Old Gravel-lane, in the Ratcliff-highway. They pulled Miss Nightingale out of the cart and ran away with her, and regular destroyed the two soldiers that was on each side of her. Sometimes the cabmen lash at the guys with their whips. We never say anything to them, for fear we might get stopped by the police for making a row. You stand a chance of having a feather knocked off, or such-like, as is attached to them.

'There's a lot of boys goes about on the 5th with sticks, and make a regular business of knocking guys to pieces. They're called guy-smashers. They don't come to us, we're too strong for that, but they only manage the little ones, as they can take advantage of. They do this some of them to take the money the boys have collected. I have had regular prigs following my show, to pick the pockets of those looking on, but as sure as I see them I start them off by putting a policeman on to them.

'When we're showing, I don't take no trouble to invent new rhymes, but stick to the old poetry. There's some do new songs. I usually sing out –

> Gentlefolks, pray
> Remember this day;
> 'Tis with kind notice we bring
> The figure of sly
> And villanous Guy,
> Who wanted to murder the king,
> By powder and store,
> He bitterly swore,
> As he skulk'd in the walls to repair,
> The parliament, too,
> By him and his crew,
> Should all be blowed up in the air.
>
> But James, very wise,
> Did the Papists surprise,
> As they plotted the cruelty great;
> He know'd their intent,
> So Suffolk he sent
> To save both kingdom and state.
> Guy Fawkes he was found
> With a lantern underground,
> And soon was the traitor bound fast:
> And they swore he should die,
> So they hung him up high,
> And burnt him to ashes at last.
> So we, once a-year,
> Come round without fear,
> To keep up remembrance of this day;
> While assistance from you
> May bring a review
> Of Guy Fawkes a-blazing away.

So hollo, boys! hollo, boys!
   Shout and huzza;
So hollo, boys! hollo, boys!
   Keep up this day!
So hollo, boys! hollo, boys!
   And make the bells ring!
Down with the Pope, and God save the Queen!

'It used to be King, but we say Queen now, and though it don't rhyme, it's more correct.

'It's very seldom that the police say anything to us, so long as we don't stop too long in the gangway not to create any mob. They join in the fun and laugh like the rest. Wherever we go there is a great crowd from morning to night.

'We have dinner on Guy Fawkes' days between one and two. We go to any place where it's convenient for us to stop at, generally at some public-house. We go inside, and leave some of the lads to look after the guy outside. We always keep near the window, where we can look out into the street, and we keep ourselves ready to pop out in a minute if anybody should attack the guy. We generally go into some by-way, where there ain't much traffic. We never was interrupted much whilst we was at dinner, only by boys chucking stones and flinging things at it; and they run off as soon as we come out.

'There's one party that goes out with a guy that sells it afterwards. They stop in London for the first two days, and then they work their way into the country as far as Sheerness, and then they sells the guy to form part of the procession on Lord-mayor's day. It's the watermen and ferrymen mostly buy it, and they carry it about in a kind of merriment among themselves, and at night they burn it and let off fireworks. They don't make no charge for coming to see it burnt, but it's open to the air and free to the public.

'None of the good guys taken about on the 5th are burnt at night, unless some gentlemen buy them. I used to sell mine at one time to the Albert Saloon. Sometimes they'd give me 15s. for it, and sometimes less, according to what kind of a one I had. Three years, I think, I sold it to them. They used to burn it at first in the gardens at the back, but after they found the gardens fill very well without it, so they wouldn't have any more.

'I always take the sawdust and shavings out of my guys, and save the clothes for another year. The clothes are left in my possession to be taken care of. I make a kind of private bonfire in our yard with the sawdust and shavings, and the neighbours come there and have a kind of a spree, and shove one another into the fire, and kick it about the yard, and one thing and another.

'When I am building the guy, I begin about six weeks before 5th of November comes, and then we subscribe a shilling or two each and buy such things as we wants. Then, when we wants more, I goes to my pals, who live close by, and we subscribe another shilling or sixpence each, according to how we gets on in the day. Nearly all those that take out guys are mostly street traders.

'The heaviest expense for any guy I've built was 4l. for one of four figures.'

Silly Billy
[*volume iii. pp.134–138*]

The character of 'Silly Billy' is a kind of clown, or rather a clown's butt; but not after the style of Pantaloon, for the part is comparatively juvenile. Silly Billy is supposed to be a schoolboy, although not dressed in a charity-boy's attire. He is very popular with the audience at the fairs; indeed, they cannot do without him. 'The people like to see Silly Billy,' I was told, 'much more than they do Pantaloon, for he gets knocked about more though, but he gives it back again. A good Silly,' said my informant, 'has to imitate all the ways of a little boy. When I have been going to a fair, I have many a time stopped for hours watching boys at play, learning their various games, and getting their sayings. For instance, some will go about the streets singing:

> Eh, higgety, eh ho!
> Billy let the water go!

which is some song about a boy pulling a tap from a water-butt, and letting the water run. There's another:

> Nicky nickey nite,
> I'll strike a light!

I got these both from watching children whilst playing. Again, boys will swear "By the liver and lights of a cobbler's lapstone!"'and their most regular desperate oath is,

> Ain't this wet? Ain't it dry?
> Cut my throat if I tells a lie.

They'll say, too, "S'elp my greens!" and "Upon my word and say so!" All these sayings I used to work up into my Silly Billy, and they had their success.

'I do such things as these, too, which is regularly boyish, such as "Give me a bit of your bread and butter, and I'll give you a bit of my bread and treacle." Again, I was watching a lot of boys playing at pitch-button, and one says, "Ah, you're up to the rigs of this hole; come to my hole – you can't play there!" I've noticed them, too, playing at ring-taw, and one of their exclamations is "Knuckle down fair, and no funking." All these sayings are very useful to make the character of Silly Billy perfect. Bless you, sir, I was two years studying boys before I came out as Silly Billy. But then I persevere when I take a thing in hand; and I stick so close to nature, that I can't go far wrong in that line. Now this is a regular boy's answer: when somebody says, "Does your mother know you're out?" he replies, "Yes, she do; but I didn't know the organ-man had lost his monkey!" That always went immense.

'It's impossible to say when Silly Billy first come out at fairs, or who first supported the character. It's been popular ever since a fair can be remembered. The best I ever saw was Teddy Walters. He's been at all the fairs round the universe – England, Ireland, Scotland, Wales, and France. He belonged to a circus when he went abroad. He's done Silly Billy these forty year, and he's a great comic singer beside. I was reckoned very clever at it. I used to look it by making up so young for it. It tires you very much, for there's so much exertion attached to it by the dancing and capering about. I've done it at the fairs, and also with tumblers in the street; only, when you do it in the street, you don't do one-half the business.

'The make-up for a Silly Billy is this: Short white trousers and shoes, with a strap round the ankle, long white pinafore with a frill round the neck, and red sleeves, and a boy's cap. We dress the head with the hair behind the ears, and a dab of red on the nose and two patches of black over the eyebrows. When I went to the fair I always took three pairs of white trousers with me. The girls used to get up playing larks with me, and smearing my white trousers with gingerbread. It's a very favourite character with the women – they stick pins into you, as if you were a pin-cushion. I've had my thighs bleeding sometimes. One time, during Greenwich, a ugly old woman came on the parade and kissed me, and made me a present of a silver sixpence, which, I needn't say, was soon spent in porter. Why, I've brought home with me sometimes toys enough to last a child a fortnight, if it was to break one every day, such as carts and horses, cock and breeches, whistles, &c. You see, Silly Billy is supposed to be a thievish sort of a character, and I used to take the toys away from the girls as they were going into the theatre, and then I'd show it to the Clown and say, "Oh, look what that nice lady's give me! I shall take it home to my mother."

   'I've done Silly Billy for Richardson's, and near every booth of consequence. The general wages is from 5s. to 7s. 6d. the day, but my terms was always the three half-crowns. When there's any fairs on, I can always get a job. I always made it a rule never to go far away from London, only to Greenwich or Gravesend, but not farther, for I can make it better in town working the concert-rooms. There are some who do nothing but Silly Billy; and then, if you take the year round, it comes to three days' work a week. The regular salary doesn't come to more than a pound a week, but then you make something out of those who come up on the parade, for one will chuck you 6d., some 1s. and 2s. 6d. We call those parties "prosses". I have had such a thing as 5s. give to me. We are supposed to share this among the company, and we generally do. These are the "nobbings", and may send up your earnings to as much as 25s. a week, besides drink, which you can have more given to you than you want.

   'When we go about the streets with tumblers, we mostly only sing a song, and dance, and keep the ring whilst the performance is going on. We also "nob", or gather the money. I never heard of a Silly Billy going out busking in tap-rooms and that. The tumblers like the Silly Billy, because the dress is attractive; but they are getting out of date now, since the grotesque clown is so much in the street. I went about with a school termed "The Demons", and very clever they was, though they've all broke up now, and I don't know what's become of them. There were four of them. We did middling, but we could always manage to knock up such a thing as 20s. each a week. I was, on and off, about six months with them. After their tumbling, then my turn would begin. The drummer would say: "Turn and turn about's fair play. Billy, now it's your turn. A song from Billy; and if we meet with any encouragement, ladies and gentlemen, the young man here will tie his legs together and chuck several summersets." Then I'd sing such a song as "Clementina Clements", which begins like this:

> You talk of modest girls,
>   Now I've seen a few,
> But there's none licks the one
>   I'm sticking up to.
> But some of her faults
>   Would make some chaps ill;
> But, with all her faults,
>   Yes, I love her still.
> Such a delicate duck was Clementina Clements;
> Such a delicate duck I never did see.

'There's one verse where she won't walk over a potato-field because they've got eyes, and another when she faints at seeing a Dutch doll without clothes on. Then she doesn't like tables' legs, and all such as that, and that's why she is "such a delicate duck". That song always tells with the women. Then I used to sing another, called "Wha do men and women marry for?" which was a very great favourite. One verse that went very well was:

> If a good wife you've got,
>   (But there's very few of those,)
> Your money goes just like a shot:
>   They're everlasting wanting clothes.
> And when you've bought 'em all you can,
>   Of course you cannot buy them more;
> They cry, Do you call yourself a man?
>   Was this what we got married for?

'When I danced, it was merely a comic dance – what we call a "roley poley". Sometimes, when we had been walking far, and pitching a good many times, the stones would hurt my feet awful with dancing.

'Pitching with tumblers is nothing compared to fair-parading. There you are the principal of the comic men after Clown, for he's first. We have regular scenes, which take twenty minutes working through. When the parade is slack, then comes the Silly Billy business. There's a very celebrated sketch, or whatever you call it, which Clown and Silly Billy do together, taking off mesmerism.

'Clown comes on, dressed up in a tall white hat, and with a cloak on. He says that he has just arrived from the island of Mititti, and that he's the great Doctor Bokanki, the most celebrated mesmeriser in the world. He says, "Look at me. Here I am. Ain't I mesmerised elephants? Ain't I mesmerised monkeys? and ain't I going to mesmerise him?" He then tells Silly Billy to sit in the chair. Then he commences passing his hands across his eyes. He asks Billy, "What do you see, Billy?" He turns his face, with his shut eyes, towards the crowd, and says, "A man with a big nose, sir, and such a many pimples on his face." "And now what do you see, Billy?" "Oh, ain't that gal a-winking at me! You be quiet, or I'll tell my mother." "Now what do you see, Billy?" "Nothink." Then the doctor turns to the crowd, and says, "Now, ladies and gentlemen, I shall touch him on the fakement at the back of his head which is called a bump. Oh, my eyes! ain't Billy's head a-swelling! This bump, ladies and gentlemen, is called a organ – not a church nor yet a chapel organ, nor yet one of them they grind in the street. And here's another organ," he says, putting his hand on Billy's stomach. "This here is called his wittling department organ, or where he puts his grub. I shall now touch him on another fakement, and make him sing." Then he puts his finger on Billy's head, and Billy sings:

> As I one day was hawking my ware,
> I thought I'd invent something novel and rare;
> For as I'm not green, and I know what's o'clock,
> So I'll have a go in at the pine-apple rock.
> Tol de ro lay, tol de ro lay.

'Then Billy becomes quiet again, and the doctor says, "I'll now, ladies and gentlemen, touch him on another fakement, and cause Billy to cry. This here is his organ of the handling department." Then he takes Billy's finger and bites it, and Billy begins to roar like a town bull. Then the doctor says, "I'll now, ladies and gentlemen, touch him on another fakement, whereby the youth can tell me what I've got in my hand." He then puts his hand in his coat-tail pocket, and says, "Billy, what have I got in my hand?" and Billy says, "Ah, you nasty beast! why it's a – it's a – it's a – oh, I don't like to say!" They do this a lot of times, Billy always replying, "Oh, I don't like to say!" until at last he promises that, if he won't tell his mother, he will; and then he says, "It's a small tooth-comb." "Very right, Billy; and what's in it?" "Why, one of them 'ere things that crawls." "Very right, Billy; and what is it?" "Why, it's a – it's a black-beetle." "Very right, Billy; look again. Do you see anything else?" "There's some crumbs." Then he tells Billy, that as he is such a good boy he'll bring him to; and Billy says, "Oh, don't, please, sir; one's quite enough." Then he brings him to, and Billy says, "Oh, ain't it nice! Oh, it's so golly! Here, you young woman, I wish you'd let me touch your bumps." Then, if the people laugh, he adds, "You may laugh, but it gives you a all-over sort of a feeling, as if you had drunk three pints of pickling vinegar."

'That's a very favourite scene; but I haven't give it you all, for it would fill a volume. It always makes a hit; and Billy has a rare chance of working comic attitudes and so on when the doctor touches his bumps.

'There's another very celebrated scene for Silly Billy. It's what we call the preaching scene. [. . .]

'I was in Greenwich fair, doing Silly Billy, when the celebrated disturbance with the soldiers took place. I was at Smith and Webster's booth (Richardson's that was), and our clown was Paul Petro. He had been a bit of a fighting man. He was bending down for Silly Billy to take a jump over him, and some of the soldiers ran up and took the back. They knocked his back as they went over, and he got shirty. Then came a row. Four of them pitched into Paul, and he cries out for help. The mob began to pelt the soldiers, and they called out to their comrades to assist them. A regular confusion ensued. The soldiers tumbled us about, and took off their belts. They cut Paul's forehead right open. I was Silly Billy, and I got a broomstick, and when one of the soldiers gave me a lick over the face with his belt, I pitched him over on the mob with my broomstick. I was tumbled down the steps among the mob, and hang me if they didn't pitch into me too! I got the awfullest nose you ever see. There was I, in my long pinafore, a-wiping up the blood, and both my eyes going as black as plums. I cut up a side place, and then I sat down to try and put my nose to rights. Lord, how I did look about for plaster! When I came back there was all the fair a-fighting. The fighting-men came out of their booths and let into the soldiers, who was going about flourishing their belts and hitting everybody. At last the police came; two of them was knocked down, and sent back on stretchers: but at last, when a picket was sent for, all the soldiers – there was about forty of them – were walked off. They got from six to nine months' imprisonment; and those that let into the police, eighteen months. I never see such a sight. It was all up with poor Silly Billy for that fair, for I had to wrap my face up in plaster and flannel, and keep it so for a week.

'I shouldn't think there were more than a dozen Silly Billys going about at the present time; and out of them there ain't above three first-raters. I know nearly all of them. When fairs ain't on they go about the streets, either with schools of tumblers or serenaders; or else they turn to singing at the concerts. To be a good Silly Billy, it requires a man with heaps of funniment and plenty of talk. He must also have a young-looking face, and the taller the man the better for it. When I go out I always do my own gag, and I try to knock out something new. I can take a candle, or a straw, or a piece of gingerbread, or any mortal thing, and lecture on it. At fairs we make our talk rather broad, to suit the audience.

'Our best sport is where a girl comes up on the parade, and stands there before going inside – we have immense fun with her. I offer to marry her, and so does Clown, and we quarrel as to who proposed to the young woman first. I swear she's my gal, and he does the same. Then we appeal to her, and tell her what we'll give her as presents. It makes immense fun. The girls always take it in good part, and seem to enjoy it as much as the mob in front. If we see that she is in any ways shy we drop it, for it's done for merriment, and not to insult; and we always strive to amuse and not to abuse our friends.'

Of the experience of a street-bookseller
[*volume i. pp.294–296*]

I now give a statement, furnished to me by an experienced man, as to the nature of his trade, and the class of his customers. Most readers will remember having seen an account in the life of some poor scholar, having read – and occasionally, in spite of the remonstrances of the stall-keeper – some work which he was too needy to purchase, and even of his having read it through at intervals. That something of this kind is still to be met with will be found from the following account:

'My customers, sir, are of all sorts,' my informant said. 'They're gentlemen on their way from the City, that have to pass along here by the City-road. Bankers' clerks, very likely, or insurance-office clerks, or such like. They're fairish customers, but they often screw me. Why only last month a gentleman I know very well by sight, and I see him pass in his brougham in bad weather, took up an old Latin book – if I remember right it was an odd volume of a French edition of Horace – and though it was marked only 8*d*., it was long before he would consent to give more than 6*d*. And I should never have got my price if I hadn't heard him say quite hastily, when he took up the book, 'The very thing I've long been looking for!' Mechanics are capital customers for scientific or trade books, such as suit their business; and so they often are for geography and history, and some for poetry; but *they're* not so screwy. I know a many such who are rare ones for searching into knowledge. Women buy very little of me in comparison to men; sometimes an odd novel, in one volume, when it's cheap, such as *The Pilot*, or *The Spy*, or *The Farmer of Inglewood Forest*, or *The Monk*. No doubt some buy *The Monk*, not knowing exactly what sort of a book it is, but just because it's a romance; but some young men buy it, I know, because they have learned what sort it's like. Old three vol. novels won't sell at all, if they're ever so cheap. Boys very seldom buy of me, unless it's a work about pigeons, or something that way.

'I can't say that odd vols. of Annual Registers are anything but a bad sale, but odd vols. of old Mags. [magazines], a year or half-year bound together, are capital. Old London Mags., or Ladies', or Oxford and Cambridges, or Town and Countrys, or Universals, or Monthly Reviews, or Humourists, or Ramblers, or Europeans, or any of any sort, that's from 40 to 100 years old, no matter what they are, go off rapidly at from 1s. 6d. to 3s. 6d. each, according to size, and binding, and condition. Odd numbers of Mags. are good for little at a stall. The old Mags. in vols. are a sort of reading a great many àre very fond of. Lives of the Princess Charlotte are a ready penny enough. So are Queen Carolines, but not so good. Dictionaries of all kinds are nearly as selling as the old Mags., and so are good Latin books. French are only middling; not so well as you might think.'

My informant then gave me a similar account to what I had previously received concerning English classics, and proceeded: 'Old religious books, they're a fair trade enough, but they're not so plentiful on the stalls now, and if they're black-letter they don't find their way from the auctions or anywhere to any places but the shops or to private purchasers. Mrs Rowe's *Knowledge of the Heart* goes off, if old. Bibles, and Prayer-books, and Hymn-books, are very bad.' [This may be accounted for by the cheapness of these publications, when new, and by the facilities afforded to obtain them gratuitously.] 'Annuals are dull in going off; very much so, though one might expect different. I can hardly sell "Keepsakes" at all. Children's books, such as are out one year at 2s. 6d. apiece, very nicely got up, sell finely next year at the stalls for from 6d. to 10d. Genteel people buy them of us for presents at holiday times. They'll give an extra penny quite cheerfully if there's "Price 2s. 6d." or "Price 3s. 6d." lettered on the back or part of the title-page. School-books in good condition don't stay long on hand, especially Pinnock's. There's not a few people who stand and read and read for half an hour or an hour at a time. It's very trying to the temper when they take up room that way, and prevent others seeing the works, and never lay out a penny theirselves. But they seem quite lost in a book. Well, I'm sure I don't know what they are. Some seem very poor, judging by their dress, and some seem shabby genteels. I can't help telling them, when I see them going, that I'm much obliged, and I hope that perhaps next time they'll manage to say "thank ye", for they don't open their lips once in twenty times. I know a man in the trade that goes dancing mad when he has customers of this sort, who aren't customers. I dare say, one day with another, I earn 3s. the year through; wet days are greatly against us, for if we have a cover people won't stop to look at a stall. Perhaps the rest of my trade earn the same.' This man told me that he was not unfrequently asked, and by respectable people, for indecent works, but he recommended them to go to Holywell-street themselves. He believed that some of his fellow-traders *did* supply such works, but to no great extent.

Street-vocalists
[*volume iii. pp.190–204*]

The street-vocalists are almost as large a body as the street musicians. It will be seen that there are 50 Ethiopian serenaders, and above 250 who live by ballad-singing alone.

Street negro serenaders
[*volume iii. pp.190,191*]

At present I shall deal with the Ethiopian serenaders, and the better class of ballad-singers. Two young men who are of the former class gave the following account. Both were dressed like decent mechanics, with perfectly clean faces, excepting a little of the professional black at the root of the hair on the forehead:

'We are niggers,' said one man, 'as it's commonly called; that is, negro melodists. Nigger bands vary from four to seven, and have numbered as many as nine; our band is now six. We all share alike.' 'I,' said the same man, 'was the first who started the niggers in the streets, about four years ago. I took the hint from the performance of Pell and the others at the St James's. When I first started in the streets I had five performers, four and myself. There were the banjo-player, the bones, fiddle, and tambourine. We are regularly full-dressed, in fashionable black coats and trowsers, open white waistcoats, pumps (bluchers some had, just as they could spring them), and wigs to imitate the real negro head of hair. Large white wrists or cuffs came out after. It was rather a venturesome 'spec, the street-niggers, for I had to find all the clothes at first start, as I set the school a-going. Perhaps it cost me 6s. a head all round – all second-hand dress except the wigs, and each man made his own wig out of horse-hair dyed black, and sewn with black thread on to the skin of an old silk hat. Well, we first started at the top of the Liverpool-road, but it was no great success, as we weren't quite up in our parts and didn't play exactly into one another's hands. None of us were perfect, we'd had so few rehearsals. One of us had been a street-singer before, another a street-fiddler, another had sung nigger-songs in public-houses, the fourth was a mud-lark, and I had been a street-singer. I was brought up to no trade regularly. When my father died I was left on the world, and I worked in Marylebone stone-yard, and afterwards sung about the streets, or shifted as I could. I first sung in the streets just before the Queen's coronation – and a hard life it was. But, to tell the truth, I didn't like the thoughts of hard labour – bringing a man in so little, too – that's where it is; and as soon as I could make any sort of living in the streets with singing and such-like, I got to like it. The first "debew", as I may say, of the niggers, brought us in about 10s. among us, besides paying for our dinner and a pint of beer a-piece. We were forced to be steady you see, sir, as we didn't know how it would answer. We sang from eleven in the morning till half-past ten at night, summer time. We kept on day after day, not rehearsing, but practising in the streets, for rehearsing in private was of little use – voices are as different in private rooms and the public streets as is chalk from cheese. We got more confidence as we went along. To be sure we had all cheek enough to start with, but this was a fresh line of business. Times mended as we got better at our work. Last year was the best year I've known. We start generally about ten, and play till it's dark in fine weather. We averaged 1l. a week last year. The evenings are the best time. Regent-street, and Oxford-street, and the greater part of St James's, are our best places. The gentry are our best customers, but we get more from gentlemen than from ladies. The City is good, I fancy, but they won't let us work it; it's only the lower parts, Whitechapel and Smithfield ways, that we have a chance in. Business and nigger-songs don't go well together. The first four days of the week are pretty much alike for our business. Friday is bad, and so is Saturday, until night comes, and we then get money from the working people. The markets, such as Cleveland-street, Fitzroy-square (Tottenham-court-road's no good at any time), Carnaby-market, Newport-market, Great Marylebone-street, and the Edgware-road, are good Saturday nights. Oxford-street is middling. The New-cut is as bad a place as can be. When we started, the songs we knew was "Old Mr Coon", "Buffalo Gals", "Going ober de Mountain", "Dandy Jim of Carolina", "Rowly Boly O", and "Old Johnny Booker". We stuck to them a twelvemonth. The "Buffalo Gals" was best liked. The "bones" – we've real bones, rib-of-beef bones, but some have ebony bones, which sound better than rib-bones – they tell best in "Going ober de Mountain", for there's a symphony between every line. It's rather difficult to play the bones well; it requires hard practice, and it brings the skin off; and some men have tried it, but with so little success that they broke their bones and flung them away. The banjo is the hardest to learn of the lot. We have kept changing our songs all along; but some of the old ones are still sung. The other favourites are, or were, "Lucy Neale", "O, Susannah", "Uncle Ned", "Stop dat Knocking", "Ginger Blue", and "Black-eyed Susannah". Things are not so good as they were. We can average 1l. a-piece now in the week, but it's summer-time, and we can't make that in bad weather. Then there's so many of us. There's the Somer's-town "mob" now in London; the King-street, the four St Giles's mobs, the East-end (but they're white niggers), the two Westminster mobs, the Marylebone, and the Whitechapel. We interfere with one another's beats sometimes, for we have no arrangement with each other, only we don't pitch near the others when they're at work. The ten mobs now in London will have 50 men in them at least; and there's plenty of stragglers, who are not regular niggers: there's so many dodges now to pick up a living, sir. The Marylebone and Whitechapel lots play at nights in penny theatres. I have played in the Haymarket in the "New Planet", but there's no demand for us now at the theatres, except such as the Pavilion. There are all sorts of characters in the different schools, but I don't know any runaway gentleman, or any gentleman of any kind among us, not one; we're more of a poorer sort, if not to say a ragged sort, for some are without shoes or stockings. The "niggers" that I know have been errand-boys, street-singers, turf-cutters, coal-heavers, chandlers, paviours, mud-larks, tailors, shoe-makers, tin-men, bricklayers' labourers, and people who have had no line in particular but their wits. I know of no connection

with pickpockets, and don't believe there is any, though pickpockets go round the mobs; but the police fling it in our teeth
that we're connected with pickpockets. It's a great injury to us is
such a notion. A good many of the niggers – both of us here likes
a little drop – drink as hard as they can, and a good many of them
live with women of the town. A few are married. Some niggers
are Irish. There's Scotch niggers, too. I don't know a Welsh one,
but one of the street nigger-singers is a real black – an African.'

Statement of another Ethiopian serenader
[*volume iii. pp.191–194*]
'It must be eight years ago,' he commenced, 'since the Ethiopian
serenading come up – aye, it must be at least that time, because the
twopenny boats was then running to London-bridge, and it was
before the *Cricket* was blown up. I know that, because we used to
work the boats serenading. I used to wear a yellow waistcoat, in
imitation of them at the St James's Theatre.

'The first came out at St James's Theatre, and they made a deal
of money. There were five of them – Pell was bones, Harrington
was concertina, I think, White was violin, Stanwood the banjo,
and Germain the tambourine. I think that's how it was, but I can
easy ascertain. After them sprang up the "Lantum Serenaders" and
the "Ohio Serenaders", the "South Carolina Serenaders", the
"Kentucky Minstrels", and many other schools of them; but Pell's
gang was at the top of the tree. Juba was along with Pell. Juba was
a first class – a regular A1 – he was a regular black, and a splendid
dancer in boots.

'As soon as I could get in to vamp the tunes on the banjo a little,
I went at it, too. I wasn't long behind them, you may take your
oath. We judged it would be a hit, and it was fine. We got more
money at it then than we do at any game now. First of all we
formed a school of three – two banjos and a tambourine, and after
that we added a bones and a fiddle. We used to dress up just the
same then as now. We'd black our faces, and get hold of a white
hat, and put a black band round it, or have big straw hats and high
collars up to the ears. We did uncommonly well. The boys would
follow us for miles, and were as good as advertisements, for they'd
shout, "Here's the blacks!" as if they was trumpeting us. The first
songs we came out with were "Old Joe", "Dan Tucker", and

"Going ober de Mountain", and "O come along, you sandy boys". Our opening chorus was "The Wild Racoon Track", and we finished up with the "Railway Overture", and it was more like the railway than music, for it was all thumping and whistling, for nobody knowed how to play the banjo then.

'When I went out pitching first I could sing a good song; but it has ruined my voice now, for I used to sing at the top – tenor is the professional term.

'It wasn't everybody as could be a nigger then. We was thought angels then. It's got common now, but still I've no hesitation in saying that, keep steady and sober, and it works well to the present day. You can go and get a good average living now.

'We could then, after our "mungare" and "buvare" (that's what we call eat and drink, and I think it's broken Italian), carry home our 5s. or 6s. each, easy. We made long days, and did no night-work. Besides, we was always very indifferent at our business, indeed. I'd be blowed if I'd trust myself out singing as I did then: we should get murdered. It was a new thing, and people thought our blunders was intended. We used to use blacking then to do our faces – we got Messrs. Day and Martin to do our complexion then. Burnt cork and beer wasn't so popular then.

'I continued at the nigger business ever since. I and my mate have been out together, and we've gone out two, and three, or four, up to eleven in a school, and we've shared better when eleven than when we was two. The highest we've got in a day has been 1l. 6s. each, at the Portsmouth review, when Napier went out with the fleet, above two years ago. We walked down to Portsmouth a-purpose. We got 14s. 6d. each – and there was five of us – at the launch of the *Albert*.

'The general dress of the nigger is a old white hat and a long-tailed coat; or sometimes, when we first come out, in white waist-coats and coats; or even in striped shirts and wigs, and no hats at all. It's all according to fancy and fashion, and what takes.

'When we go to a cheap concert-room, such as the Albion, Ratcliffe-highway, or the Ship and Camel, Bermondsey, our usual business is to open with a chorus, such as "Happy are we", though, perhaps, we haven't had a bit of grub all day, and been as wretched as possible; and then we do a song or two, and then "crack a wid", as we say, that is, tell an anecdote, such as this:

'Three old niggers went to sea on a paving-stone. The first never had any legs, the next never had any arms, and the other was strip stark naked. So the one without any legs said, "I see de bird; so the one without any arms took up a gun and shot it, and the one without any legs run after it, and the one that was strip stark naked put it in his pocket. Now, you tell me what pocket that was?"

'Then another says, "In his wainscoat pocket." Then I return, "How can he if he was naked? Can you give the inflammation of that story? Do you give it up?" Then he says, "No, won't give it up." Then I say, "Would you give it up if you had it." Then he says, "Yes!" and I reply, "The inflammation of that is the biggest lie that ebber was told."

'Sometimes we do conundrums between the songs. I ask, "Can you tell me how to spell blind pig in two letters?" and then he, remembering the first story, answers, "Yes, the biggest lie that ebber was told." "No, that's not it." Then I continue, "p, g; and if you leave the i out it must be a blind pig, Jim."

'Then we go on with the concert, and sing perhaps, "Going ober de Mountain" and "Mary Blane", and then I ask such conundrums as these:

'"Why is mahogany like flannel?" "Because they are both used to manufacture into drawers;" and then we do this rhyme,

Because mahogany makes drawers to put your clothes in,
and flannel makes drawers to put your toes in.

'Perhaps we do another conundrum, such as this: "Supposing you nigger was dead, what would be the best time to bury you?" One says, "I shan't suppose." Another says, "I don't know." And then I say, "Why, the latter end of the summer;" and one asks, "Why, Jim?" "Because it's the best time for black-berrying." Then I cry out, "Now, you niggers, go on with the consort;" and one of them will add, "Now, Jim, we'll have that lemoncholy song of Dinah Clare, that poor girl that fell in the water-butt and got burnt to death."

'Another of our dialogues is this one: "Did I ebber tell you about that lemoncholy occurrence, Mary Blane, the young girl that died last night in the house that was burned down this morning, and she's gone to live in a garret?" "I shall call and see her." "You can't." "Cos why?" "Cos she moved from where

she lives now; she's gone to live where she used to come from."
"Did you ever see her broder Bill?" "No; he's dead." "What!
broder Bill dead, too?" "Yes; I seed him this morning, and axed
him how he was." "Well, and what did he told you?" "He told
me he was wery well, thankye, and he was going to lib along with
Dinah; and he'd only been married three weeks. So I asked him
how many children he'd got. He said he'd only got one. So I said,
"Dere something very dark about that, and I don't think all
goes right, if you was to have a son in three weeks." So he said,
"Look you here, sir; if the world was made in six days, it's
debblish hard if we can't make a son in three weeks." "Go on
with the consort."

'Another of our dialogues is this: "Did I ever tell you, Jim, about
my going out a-riding?" "Neber." "Well, then, I'll told you, I had
two dollars in my pocket." "Had you?" "And I thought I'd do it
gentleman-tell-like." "Yes." "So I went to the libery dealer."
"Who?" The libery dealer – the man that keeps the horses'
stable." "Oh! golly! you mean the stable-man." "Yas. Well, I axed
him if he could lend me a horse to ride on;" so he said, he'd only
got one horse." "Wall?" "And that was a grey mare. I thought that
would do just as well. "Of course." "And I axed him what that
would cost me? and he said he should charge me two dollars for
that – so I paid the two dollars." "Wall?" "And he put me the spurs
on my boots, and he put de bridle on the horse's back." "The
bridle on the horse's back! – what did he do with the bit?" "He
neber had a bit at all; he put the stirrups in the mouth." "Now
stop – you mean, he put the saddle on the back, and the bridle in
the mouth." "I know it was something. Den they put me on the
saddle, and my feet on the bridle." "You mean he put your foot
in the stirrups." "So I went out very well." "So the mare begun
for to gallop, so I caught hold of the tummel of the saddle." "The
tummel!" "Yes, Jim, the tummel." "No, no; you means the
pummel." "Wall, hab it the pummel – you knows – but, but,
I know, I'm right. So I caught hold of the mane, and I got on
berry well till I come to a hill, when the mare began to gollop
hard down the hill, because she was shy." "What was she shy at?"
"She saw a new-found-out-land dog crossing the wood." "A
new-found-out-land dog crossing the road!" "Yes; so I thought
I'd try and stop her: so I stuck my knees into her side, and my spur

into her, and by golly, she went too fast." "And did she now?" "Till she falled down and broke her knees." "Poor thing!" "Aye, and pitched poor nigger on his head; so I got up and tought I'd take the debil of a mare back to the stable. So when I got back I told the libbery man about it." "Yas, the stable-man." "And he said I must pay 2l. 10s." "What for?" "For repairing the mare; so I said I wouldn't; so he said he would take me before the court, and I said he might take me down the alley, if he liked; so I thought I had better go and insult a man ob de law about it. So I went to the man ob the law's house and pulled at the servant, and out comed the bell." "No; you means pulled the bell, and out comed the servant. Wall?" "I said, Can you conform me is de man ob de law at home?" so she told me he was out, but the man ob de law's wife was at home, so down she come. So I said I wanted to insult the man ob de law, and she said, "Insult me; I do just as well." So she says, "Plane yourself." So I said, Well, den, supposing you was a grey mare, and I hired you for two dollars to ride you, and you was rader rusty, and went too fast for me, and I wanted to stop you, and I stuck my knees in your side, and my spur into you, and you falled down and broke your knees, how could I help it?" So she flung the door in my face and went in. So now go on with the consort."

'Sometimes, when we are engaged for it, we go to concert-rooms and do the nigger-statues, which is the same as the *tableaux vivants*. We illustrate the adventures of Pompey, or the life of a negro slave. The first position is when he is in the sugar-brake, cutting the sugar cane. Then he is supposed to take it to be weighed, and not being weight, he is ordered to be flogged. My mate is then doing the orator and explaining the story. It's as nice a bit of business as ever was done, and goes out-and-out. You see, it's a new thing from the white ones. The next position is when he is being flogged, and then when he swears revenge upon the overseer, and afterwards when he murders the overseer. Then there's the flight of Pompey, and so on, and I conclude with a variety of sculptures from the statues, such as the Archilles in Hyde-park, and so on. This is really good, and the finest bit of business out, and nobody does it but me; indeed it says in the bill – if you saw it – "for which he stands unrivalled".

'We sometimes have a greenhorn wants to go out pitching with us – a "mug", we calls them; and there's a chap of the

name of "Sparrow-back", as we called him, because he always
wore a bob-tailed coat, and was a rare swell; and he wished to
go out with us, and we told him he must have his head shaved
first, and Tom held him down while I shaved him, and I took
every bit of hair off him. Then he underwent the operation of
mugging him up with oil-colour paint, black, and not forgetting
the lips, red. Ah, he carried the black marks on him for two
months afterwards, and made a real washable nigger. We took
him with us to Camberwell fair, and on the way he kept turning
round and saying how strong he smelt of turps, and his face was
stiff. Ah, he was a serenader! How we did scrub it into him
with a stiff brush! When we washed at a horse-trough, coming
home, he couldn't get a bit of the colour off. It all dried round
his nose and eyes.

'When we are out pitching, the finest place for us is where there
is anybody sick. If we can see some straw on the ground, or any
tan, then we stays. We are sure to play up where the blinds are
down. When we have struck up, we rattle away at the banjos, and
down will come the servant, saying, "You're to move on; we
don't want you." Then I'll pretend not to understand what she
says, and I'll say, "Mary Blane did you ask for? O yes, certainly,
Miss;" and off we'll go into full chorus. We don't move for less
than a bob, for sixpence ain't enough for a man that's ill. We
generally get our two shillings.

'Sometimes gents will come and engage us to go and serenade
people, such as at weddings or anything of that sort. Occasionally
young gents or students will get us to go to a house late in the
morning, to rouse up somebody for a lark, and we have to beat
away and chop at the strings till all the windows are thrown up.
We had a sovereign given us for doing that.

'The Christmas time is very good for us, for we go out as waits,
only we don't black, but only sing; and that I believe – the singing,
I mean – is, I believe, the original waits. With what we get for to
play and to go away, and what we collect on boxing Monday,
amounts to a tidy sum.

'There's very few schools of niggers going about London now. I
don't think there are three schools pitching in the streets. There's
the Westminster school – they have kettle-drums and music-
stands, and never sings; and there's the New Kent-road gang, or

Houghton's mob, and that's the best singing and playing school out; then a St Giles's lot, but they are dicky – not worth much. The Spitalfields school is broke up. Of course there are other niggers going about, but to the best of my calculation there ain't more than 40 men scattered about.

'Houghton's gang make the tour of the watering-places every year. I've been to Brighton with them, and we did pretty well there in the fine season, making sure of 30s. a week a man; and it's work that continues all the year round, for when it's fine weather we do pitching, and when it's wet we divide a school into parties of two, and go busking at the public-houses.' [. . .]

A standing patterer
[*volume i. pp.233,234*]

Some standing patterers are brought up to the business from childhood. Some take to it through loss of character, or through their inability to obtain a situation from intemperate habits, and some because 'a free life suits me best'. In a former inquiry into a portion of this subject, I sought a standing patterer, whom I found in a threepenny lodging-house in Mint-street, Southwark. On my inquiring what induced him to adopt, or pursue, that line of life, he said:

'It was distress that first drove me to it. I had learnt to make willow bonnets, but that branch of trade went entirely out. So, having a wife and children, I was drove to write out a paper that I called "The People's Address to the King on the Present State of the Nation". I got it printed, and took it into the streets and sold it. I did very well with it, and made 5s. a day while it lasted. I never was brought up to any mechanical trade. My father was a clergyman [here he cried bitterly]. It breaks my heart when I think of it. I have as good a wife as ever lived, and I would give the world to get out of my present life. It would be heaven to get away from the place where I am. I am obliged to cheer up my spirits. If I was to give way to it, I shouldn't live long. It's like a little hell to be in the place where we live [crying], associated with the ruffians that we are. My distress of mind is awful, but it won't do to show it at my lodgings – they'd only laugh to see me down-hearted; so I keep my trouble all to myself. Oh, I am heartily sick of this street work – the insults I have to put up with – the drunken men swearing at me. Yes, indeed, I am heartily sick of it.'

This poor man had some assistance forwarded to him by bene- volent persons, after his case had appeared in my letter in the *Morning Chronicle*. This was the means of his leaving the streets, and starting in the 'cloth-cap trade'. He seemed a deserving man.

The wooden-legged sweeper
[*volume ii. pp.486–488*]

This man lives up a little court running out of a wide, second-rate street. It is a small court, consisting of some half-dozen houses, all of them what are called by courtesy 'private'.

I inquired at No. 3 for John – 'The first-floor back, if you please, sir'; and to the first-floor back I went.

Here I was answered by a good-looking and intelligent young woman, with a baby, who said her husband had not yet come home, but would I walk in and wait? I did so; and found myself in a very small, close room, with a little furniture, which the man called 'his few sticks', and presently discovered another child – a little girl. The girl was very shy in her manner, being only two years and two months old, and as her mother said, very ailing from the difficulty of cutting her teeth, though the true cause seemed to be want of proper nourishment and fresh air. The baby was a boy – a fine, cheerful, good-tempered little fellow, but rather pale, and with an unnaturally large forehead. The mantelpiece of the room was filled with little ornaments of various sorts, such as bead-baskets, and over them hung a series of black profiles – not portraits of either the crossing-sweeper or any of his family, but an odd lot of heads, which had lost their owners many a year, and served, in company with a little red, green, and yellow scripture- piece, to keep the wall from looking bare. Over the door (inside the room) was nailed a horse-shoe, which, the wife told me, had been put there by her husband, for luck.

A bed, two deal tables, a couple of boxes, and three chairs, formed the entire furniture of the room, and nearly filled it. On the window-frame was hung a small shaving-glass; and on the two boxes stood a wicker-work apology for a perambulator, in which I learnt the poor crippled man took out his only daughter at half-past four in the morning.

'If some people was to see that, sir,' said the sweeper, when he entered and saw me looking at it, 'they would, and in fact they *do* say, "Why, you can't be in want." Ah! little they know how we starved and pinched ourselves before we could get it.'

There was a fire in the room, notwithstanding the day was very hot; but the window was wide open, and the place tolerably ventilated, though oppressive. I have been in many poor people's 'places', but never remember one so poor in its appointments and yet so free from effluvia.

The crossing-sweeper himself was a very civil sort of man, and in answer to my inquiries said:

'I know that I do as I ought to, and so I don't feel hurt at standing at my crossing. I have been there four years. I found the place vacant. My wife, though she looks very well, will never be able to do any hard work; so we sold our mangle, and I took to the crossing: but we're not in debt, and nobody can't say nothing to us. I like to go along the streets free of such remarks as is made by people to whom you owes money. I had a mangle in — Yard, but through my wife's weakness I was forced to part with it. I was on the crossing a short time before that, for I knew that if I parted with my mangle and things before I knew whether I could get a living at the crossing I couldn't get my mangle back again.

'We sold the mangle only for a sovereign, and we gave two-pound-ten for it; we sold it to the same man that we bought it of. About six months ago I managed for to screw and save enough to buy that little wicker chaise, for I can't carry the children because of my one leg, and of course the mother can't carry them both out together. There was a man had the crossing I've got; he died three or four years before I took it; but he didn't depend on the crossing – he did things for the tradespeople about, such as carpet-beating, messages, and so on.

'When I first took the crossing I did very well. It happened to be a very nasty, dirty season, and I took a good deal of money. Sweepers are not always civil, sir.

'I wish I had gone to one of the squares, though. But I think after — street is paved with stone I shall do better. I am certain I never taste a bit of meat from one week's end to the other. The best day I ever made was five-and-sixpence or six shillings; it was the winter before last. If you remember, the snow laid very thick on the ground, and the sudden thaw made walking so uncomfortable, that I did very well. I have taken as little as sixpence, fourpence, and even twopence. Last Thursday I took two ha'pence all day. Take one week with the other, seven or eight shillings is the very outside.

'I don't know how it is, but some people who used to give me a penny, don't now. The boys who come in wet weather earn a great deal more than I do. I once lost a good chance, sir, at the corner of the street leading to Cavendish-square. There's a bank, and they pay a man seven shillings a week to sweep the crossing: a butcher in Oxford Market spoke for me; but when I went up, it unfortunately turned out that I was not fit, from the loss of my leg. The last man they had there they were obliged to turn away – he was so given to drink.

'I think there are some rich crossing-sweepers in the city, about the Exchange; but you won't find them now during this dry weather, except in by-places. In wet weather, there are two or three boys who sweep near my crossing, and take all my earnings away. There's a great able-bodied man besides – a fellow strong enough to follow the plough. I said to the policeman, "Now, ain't this a shame?" and the policeman said, "Well, *he* must get his living as well as you." I'm always civil to the police, and they're always civil to me – in fact, I think sometimes I'm too civil – I'm not rough enough with people.

'You soon tell whether to have any hopes of people coming across. I can tell a gentleman directly I see him.

'Where I stand, sir, I could get people in trouble everlasting; there's all sorts of thieving going on. I saw the other day two or three respectable persons take a purse out of an old lady's pocket before the baker's shop at the corner; but I can't say a word, or they would come and throw me into the road. If a gentleman gives me sixpence, he don't give me any more for three weeks or a month; but I don't think I've more than three or four gentlemen as gives me that. Well, you can scarcely tell the gentleman from the clerk, the clerks are such great swells now.

'Lawyers themselves dress very plain; those great men who don't come every day, because they've clerks to do their business for them, they give most. People hardly ever stop to speak unless it is to ask you where places are – you might be occupied at that all day. I manage to pay my rent out of what I take on Sunday, but not lately – this weather religious people go pleasuring.

'No, I don't go now – the fact is, I'd like to go to church, if I could, but when I come home I am tired; but I've got books here, and they do as well, sir. I read a little and write a little.

'I lost my leg through a swelling – there was no chloroform then. I was in the hospital three years and a half, and was about fifteen or sixteen when I had it off. I always feel the sensation of the foot, and more so at change of weather. I feel my toes moving about, and everything; sometimes, it's just as if the calf of my leg was itching. I *feel* the rain coming; when I see a cloud coming my leg shoots, and I know we shall have rain.

'My mother was a laundress – my father has been dead nineteen years my last birthday. My mother was subject to fits, so I was forced to stop at home to take care of the business.

'I don't want to get on better, but I always think, if sickness or anything comes on –

'I am at my crossing at half-past eight; at half-past eleven I come home to dinner. I go back at one or two till seven.

'Sometimes I mind horses and carts, but the boys get all that business. One of these little customers got sixpence the other day for only opening the door of a cab. I don't know how it is they let these little boys be about; if I was the police, I wouldn't allow it.

'I think it's a blessing, having children [referring to his little girl] – that child wants the gravy of meat, or an egg beaten up, but she can't get it. I take her out every morning round Euston-square and those open places. I get out about half-past four. It is early, but if it benefits her, that's no odds.'

Street-seller of saws
[*volume i. pp.362–363*]

From one of the street-traders in saws I had the following account
of his struggles, as well as the benefit he received from teetotalism,
of which he spoke very warmly. His room was on the fourth floor
of a house in a court near Holborn, and was clean and com-
fortable-looking. There were good-sized pictures, in frames, of
the Queen, the Last Supper, and a Rural Scene, besides minor
pictures: some of these had been received in exchange for saws
with street-picture-sellers. A shelf was covered with china ornaments, such as are sold in the streets; the table had its oil-skin
cover, and altogether I have seldom seen a more decent room. The
rent, unfurnished, was 2*s.* a week.

'I've been eight years in this trade, sir,' the saw-seller said, 'but I
was brought up to a very different one. When a lad I worked in a
coal-pit along with my father, but his behaviour to me was so cruel,
he beat me so, that I ran away, and walked every step from the
north of England to London. I can't say I ever repented running
away – much as I've gone through. My money was soon gone
when I got to London, and my way of speaking was laughed at.
[He had now very little of a provincial accent.] That's fourteen year
back. Why, indeed, sir, it puzzles me to tell you how I lived then
when I did live. I jobbed about the markets, and slept, when I
could pay for a lodging, at the cheap lodging-houses; so I got into
the way of selling a few things in the streets, as I saw others do. I
sold laces and children's handkerchiefs. Sometimes I was miserable
enough when I hadn't a farthing, and if I managed to make a
sixpence I got tipsy on it. For six weeks I slept every night in the
Peckham Union. For another five or six weeks I slept every night
in the dark arches by the Strand. I've sometimes had twenty or
thirty companions there. I used to lie down on the bare stones, and
was asleep in a minute, and slept like a top all night, but waking was
very bad. I felt stiff, and sore, and cold, and miserable. How I lived
at all is a wonder to me. About eleven years ago I was persuaded
to go to a Temperance Meeting in Harp-alley [Farringdon-street],
and there I signed the pledge; that is, I made my mark, for I can't
read or write, which has been a great hinder to me. If I'd been a
scholar a teetotal gent. would have got me into the police three

years ago, about the time I got married. I did better, of course, when I was a teetotaller – no more dark arches. I sold a few little shawls in the streets then, but it was hardly bread and butter and coffee at times. Eight year ago I thought I would try saw-selling: a shopkeeper advised me, and I began on six salt saws, which I sold to oil-men. They're for cutting salt only, and are made of zinc, as steel would rust and dirty the salt. The trade was far better at first than it is now. In good weeks I earned 16s. to 18s. In bad weeks 10s. or 12s. Now I may earn 10s., not more, a week, pretty regular: yesterday I made only 6d. Oilmen are better customers than chance street-buyers, for I'm known to them. There's only one man besides myself selling nothing but saws. I walk, I believe, 100 miles every week, and that I couldn't do, I know, if I wasn't teetotal. I never long for a taste of liquor if I'm ever so cold or tired. It's all poisonous.'

The saws sold are 8-inch, which cost at the swag-shops 8s. and 8s. 6d. a dozen; 10-inch, 9s. and 9s. 6d.; and so on, the price advancing according to the increased size, to 18-inch, 13s. 6d. the dozen. Larger sizes are seldom sold in the streets. The second man's earnings, my informant believed, were the same as his own.

The wife of my informant, when she got work as an embroideress, could earn 11s. and 12s. At present she was at work braiding dresses for a dressmaker, at 2½d. each. By hard work, and if she had not her baby to attend to, she could earn no more than 7½d. a day. As it was she did not earn 6d.

7

THE POOR AT HOME
Poverty and the domestic economy

Throughout his work for the Morning Chronicle *Mayhew exhibited great interest in the domestic economy in its many manifestations. This interest showed itself in the content of his interviews, of course: examples can be found in other sections of this volume. He also showed himself adept at using materials collected by others in order to delve deeper into the experiences of being poor and experimented with other ways of accumulating data. Included here are the text of a questionnaire administered to street orderlies at the point of recruitment by the Parish of St Mary Paddington, Mayhew's statistical summary of the results and some of his conclusions, and his own attempt to survey the population of a cheap lodging-house using a collective interview technique. Interview material from a cats'-meat carrier, a street-seller of dogs' collars and a street-seller of cutlery reminds us that Mayhew used the interviews as a vehicle for commentary on the problems facing poor families.*

THE STREET-SELLER OF CROCKERY-WARE

BARTERING FOR OLD CLOTHES

[from a daguerrotype by Beard]

THE POOR AT HOME

Questionnaire of street-orderlies
[*volume ii. pp.264–268*]

Before any man is employed as a street-orderly, he is called upon to answer certain questions, and the replies from 67 men to these questions supply a fund of curious and important information – important to all but those who account the lot of the poor of no importance. In presenting these details, I beg to express my obligations to Mr Colin Mackenzie, the enlightened and kindly secretary of the Association.

I shall first show what is the order of the questioning, then what were the answers, and I shall afterwards recapitulate, with a few comments, the salient characteristics of the whole.

The questions are after this fashion; the one I adduce having been asked of a scavager to whom a preference was given:

THE PARISH OF ST MARY, PADDINGTON
Questions asked of Parish Scavagers, applying for employment as Street-Orderlies, with the answers appended.

Name?	W— C—
Age?	35 years
How long a scavenger?	Three months
What occupation previously?	Gentleman's footman
Married or single?	Married
Reading, writing, or other education?	Yes
Any children?	One
Their ages?	Three years
Wages?	Nine shillings per week
Any parish relief?	No

What and how much food the applicants have usually purchased in a week

Meat?	2s. 6d.
Bacon?	None
Fish?	None
Bread?	2s.
Potatoes?	4d.
Butter?	6d.
Tea and sugar?	1s.
Cocoa?	None
What rent they pay?	2s.
Furnished or unfurnished lodgings?	Unfurnished
Any change of dress?	No
Sunday clothing?	No
How many shirts?	Two shirts
Boots and shoes?	One pair
How much do they lay out for clothes in a year?	I have nothing but what I stand upright in
Do they go to church or chapel?	Sometimes
If not, why not?	It is from want of clothes
Do they ever bathe?	No
Does the wife go out to, or take in work?	Yes
What are her earnings?	Uncertain
Do they have anything from charitable institutions or families?	No
When ill; where do they resort to?	Hospitals, dispensaries, and the parish doctor
Do their children go to any school; and what?	Paddington
Do they ever save any money; how much, and where?	
How much do they spend per week in drink?	
Do not passers by, as charitable ladies, &c., give them money; and how much per week?	No

Such are the questions asked, and I now give the answers of 67 individuals.

Their ages were:

10 were from 20 to 30	15 from 50 to 60
13 were from 30 to 40	4 from 60 to 70
24 were from 40 to 50	1 over 70

The greatest number of any age was 7 persons of 45 years.

Their previous occupations had been:

22 labourers	1 haybinder
3 at the business 'all their lives'	1 gaslighter
3 dustmen	1 dairyman
3 ostlers	1 ploughman
2 stablemen	1 gardener
2 carmen	1 errand boy
2 porters	1 fur dresser
2 gentlemen's servants	1 fur dyer
2 greengrocers	1 skinner
1 following dust-cart	1 leather dresser
1 excavator	1 letter-press printer
1 gravel digging	1 paper stainer
1 stone-breaking in the yards	1 glass blower
1 at work in the brick-fields	1 farrier
1 at work in the lime-works	1 plasterer
1 vendor of goods	1 licensed victualler
1 coal porter	1 clerk
1 sweep	

Therefore, of 67 scavagers,
12 had been artisans
55 had been unskilled workmen

Hence about five-sixths belong to the unskilled class of operatives.

Time of having been at scavagering

3 'all their lives' at the business	4 from 5 to 10 years
1 about 27 years	34 from 1 to 5 years
6 from 15 to 20 years	13 twelve months and less
6 from 10 to 15 years	

Hence it would appear, that few have been at the business a long time. The greater number have not been acting as scavagers more than five years.

State of education – Could they read and write?

45 answered yes	5 could read only
4 replied that they could read and write	12 could do neither
	1 was deaf and dumb

Hence it would appear, that rather more than two-thirds of the scavagers have received some little education.

Did they go to church or chapel?

22 answered yes	1 not often
9 went to church	17 never went at all
4 went to chapel	1 was ashamed to go
4 went to the Catholic chapel	1 went out of town to enjoy himself
1 went to both church and chapel	
5 went sometimes	2 made no return (1 being deaf and dumb)

Thus it would seem, that not quite two-thirds regularly attend some place of worship; that about one-eleventh go occasionally; and that about one-fourth never go at all.

Why did they not go to church?

12 had no clothes
55 returned no answer (1 being deaf and dumb)

Hence of those who never go (19 out of 67), very nearly two-thirds (say 12 in 19) have no clothes to appear in.

Did they bathe?

59 answered no	2 returned 'sometimes'
3 replied yes	1 was deaf and dumb
2 said they did in the Thames	

Hence it appeared, that about seven-eighths never bathe, although following the filthiest occupation.

Were they married or single?

56 were married, 6 were single, 5 were widowers.

Thus it would seem, that about ten-elevenths are or have been married men.

How many children had they?

1 had 15	6 had 1 each
1 had 6	16 had none (6 of these
2 had 5 each	being single men)
11 had 4 each	2 returned their family
19 had 3 each	as grown up without
9 had 2 each	stating the number

Consequently 51 out of 61, or five-sixths, are married, and have families numbering altogether 165 children; the majority had only 3 children, and this was about the average family.

What were the ages of their children?

11 were grown up	80 between 1 and 10
2 between 30 and 40	8 were 1 year and under
9 between 20 and 30	5 were returned at home
49 between 10 and 20	1 returned as dead

One-half of the scavagers' children, therefore, are between 1 and 10 years of age; the majority would appear to be 8 years old.
Some were said to be grown up, but no number was given.

Did their children go to school?

13 answered yes	2 returned no
13 to the National School	1 replied that his children were
5 to the Ragged School	'not with him'
2 to Catholic	22 (of whom 16 had no
2 to Parish	children, and 1 was deaf
6 to local schools	and dumb) made no reply
1 replied that he went sometimes	

From this it would seem, that a large majority – 41 out of 51, or four-fifths – of the parents who have children send them to school.

Did their wives work?

15 returned no	12 answered yes
6 said their wives were 'unable'	1 sold cresses
1 had lost the use of her limbs	15 made no return
2 did, but 'not often'	(11 having no wives and
4 did 'when they could'	1 being deaf and dumb)
10 worked 'sometimes'	

Hence two-fifths of the wives (22 out of 56) do no work, 16 do so occasionally, and 13, or one-fourth, are in the habit of working.

What were wives' earnings?

10 returned them as 'uncertain'	1 at 2s. to 4s. per week
1 'didn't know'	1 at 3s. or 4s. per week
1 estimated them at 1s. 6d. per week	1 at 3d. or 4d. per day
1 at 1s. to 2s. per week	43 gave no returns (having either no wives, or their wives not working)
2 at 2s. per week	
3 at 2s. or 3s. per week	1 was deaf and dumb
2 at about 3s. per week	

So that, out of 29 wives who were said to work, 16 occasionally and 13 regularly, there were returns for 23. Nearly half of their earnings were given as uncertain from their seldom doing work, while the remainder were stated to gain from 1s. to 4s. per week; about 2s. 6d. perhaps would be a fair average.

What wages were they themselves in the habit of receiving?

3 had 16s. 6d. per week	15 had 9s. per week
2 had 16s. per week	4 had 8s. per week
28 had 15s. per week	5 had 7s. per week
3 had 14s. 6d. per week	4 had 1s. 1½d. a day and 2 loaves
1 had 14s. per week	
2 had 12s. per week	

Hence it is evident, that one-half receive 15s. or more a week, and about a fourth 9s.

It was not the parishes, however, but the contractors with the parishes, who paid the higher rates of wages: Mr Dodd, for St Luke's; Mr Westley, for St Botolph's, Bishopsgate; Mr Parsons, for Whitechapel; Mr Newman, for Bethnal-green, &c.

These wages the scavagers laid out in the following manner:

For rent, per week

1 paid 4s.	33 paid 2s.	1 lived rent free.
1 paid 3s. 6d.	4 paid 1s. 6d.	1 paid for board and lodging
8 paid 3s.	1 paid 1s. 3d.	
14 paid 2s. 6d.	2 paid 1s.	1 lived with mother

Hence it would appear, that near upon half the number paid 2s. rent. The usual rent paid seems to be between 2s. and 3s., five-sixths of the entire number paying one or other of those amounts. Only three lived in furnished lodgings, and the rents of these were, respectively, two at 2s. 6d. and the other at 2s.

For bread, per week

1 expended 5s. 3d.	13 expended 2s.
1 expended 5s.	4 expended 1s. 6d.
1 expended 4s. 7d.	1 expended 1s. 9d.
1 expended 4s. 6d.	4 two loaves a day from parish
1 expended 4s. 3d.	3 gave a certain sum per week
7 expended 4s.	to their wives or mothers
13 expended 3s. 6d.	to lay out for them, and
8 expended 3s.	1 boarded and lodged
3 expended 2s. 6d.	1 was deaf and dumb
4 expended 2s. 3d.	

Thus it would seem, that the general sum expended weekly on bread varies between 2s. and 4s. The average saving from free-trade, therefore, would be between 4d. and 8d., or say 6d., per week.

For meat, per week

4 expended 4s.	1 expended 8d.
5 expended 3s. 6d.	2 expended 6d.
11 expended 3s.	1 once a week
12 expended 2s. 6d.	4 had none
1 expended 2s. 4d.	5 no returns (3 of this number
5 expended 2s.	gave a weekly allowance to
4 expended 1s. 6d.	wives or mothers, 1 was
1 expended 1s. 2d.	deaf and dumb, and 1 paid
9 expended 1s.	for board and lodging)
2 expended 10d.	

By the above we see, that the sum usually expended on meat is between 2s. 6d. and 3s. per week, about one-third of the entire number expending that sum. All those who expended 1s. and less per week had 9s. and less for their week's labour. The average saving from the cheapening of provisions would here appear to be between 5d. and 6d. per week at the outside.

For tea and sugar, per week

2 paid 2s. 6d.	5 paid 1s. 3d.
1 paid 2s. 4d.	5 paid 1s. 2d.
1 paid 2s. 3d.	13 paid 1s.
19 paid 2s.	2 paid 8d.
2 paid 1s. 9d.	5 no returns
4 paid 1s. 8d.	1 deaf and dumb
12 paid 1s. 6d.	1 board and lodging
5 paid 1s. 4d.	3 making allowances

The sum usually expended on tea and sugar seems to be between 1s. 6d. and 2s. per week.

For fish, per week

3 expended 1s.	4 allowed so much per
5 expended 8d.	week to wives, or
23 expended 6d.	mother, or landlady
8 expended 4d.	1 deaf and dumb
23 expended nothing	

Hence one-third spent 6d. weekly in fish, and one-third nothing.

For bacon, per week

1 expended 1s.	1 expended 4d.
2 expended 10d.	43 expended nothing
1 expended 9d.	4 allowances to wives, &c.
5 expended 8d.	1 deaf and dumb
9 expended 6d.	

The majority (two-thirds), therefore, do not have bacon. Of those that do eat bacon, the usual sum spent weekly is 6d. or 8d.

For butter, per week

1 expended 1s. 8d.	1 expended 3d.
24 expended 1s.	2 expended nothing
11 expended 10d.	4 made allowances
12 expended 8d.	1 deaf and dumb
11 expended 6d.	

Thus one-third expended 1s., and about one-sixth spent 10d.; another sixth, 8d.; and another sixth, 6d. a week, for butter.

For potatoes, per week

1 spent 1s.	6 spent 4d.
2 spent 10d.	28 spent nothing
6 spent 8d.	4 made allowances
1 spent 7d.	1 deaf and dumb
18 spent 6d.	

About one-fourth spent 6d.; the greater proportion however (nearly one-half), expended nothing upon potatoes weekly.

For clothes, yearly

2 expended 2l.	1 had 2 pairs of boots a
2 expended 1l. 10s.	year, but no clothes
2 expended 1l. 5s.	2 expended 'not much'
3 expended 1l.	2 got them as they could
1 expended 18s.	1 expended a few shillings
1 expended 17s.	1 said it 'all depends'
1 expended 15s.	2 returned 'nothing'
4 expended 12s.	1 was deaf and dumb
1 expended 10s.	6 made no return
34 couldn't say	

Hence 43 out of 67, or nearly two-thirds, spent little or nothing upon their clothes.

Had they a change of dress?

28 had a change of dress	1 was deaf and dumb
38 had not	

Above one-half, therefore, had no other clothes but those they worked in.

Had they any Sunday clothing?

20 had some	21 made no return
45 had none	1 deaf and dumb

More than two-thirds, then, had no Sunday clothes.

How many shirts had they?

10 had 3 shirts	2 had 1 shirt
54 had 2 shirts	1 was deaf and dumb

The greater number, therefore, had two shirts.

How many shoes had they?

27 had 2 pairs

39 had 1 pairs

1 was deaf and dumb

Thus the majority had only one pair of shoes.

How much did they spend in drink?

1 expended 2*s*. a week

1 expended 1*s*. or 2*s*. a week

2 expended 1*s*. 6*d*. a week

4 expended 1*s*. a week

1 expended 6*d*. a week

1 expended 3*d*. or 5*d*. a week

7 said they 'couldn't say'

2 expended nothing

1 said he 'wouldn't say'

1 said 'that all depends'

2 said they 'had none to spend'

2 expended nothing

44 gave no return (1 deaf and dumb)

Hence answers were given by one-third, of whom the greatest number 'couldn't say' (?) Of the ten who acknowledged spending anything upon drink, the greater number, or 4, said they spent 1*s*. a week only.

But?

Did they save any money?

36 answered no

31 gave no reply (1 being deaf and dumb)

What did they in case of illness coming upon themselves or families?

28 went to the dispensary

8 went to the hospital

6 went to the parish doctor

3 wives went to the lying-in hospital

1 went to the workhouse

2 said 'nothing'

1 'never troubled any'

8 made no reply (1 being deaf and dumb)

The greater number, then, go, when ill, to the dispensary.

Were they in receipt of alms?

56 answered no

2 answered sometimes

3 answered yes

6 made no returns (1 being deaf and dumb)

Did the passers-by give them anything?

49 answered no	1 answered very seldom
2 answered sometimes beer	12 no returns (1 being deaf
1 answered never	and dumb)
2 answered seldom	

Did they receive any relief from their parishes?

56 replied no	1 had a 4-lbs. loaf
4 had 2 loaves and 1s. a day	1 had 15 lbs. of bread
as wages	2 answered 'not at present'
1 had 4 loaves a week	2 made no returns

Thus the greater proportion (five-sixths), it will be seen, had no relief; two of those who had relief received 9s. wages a week, and two others only 7s., while four received part of their wages from the parish in bread.

These analyses are not merely the characteristics of the applicant or existent street-orderlies; they are really the annals of the poor in all that relates to their domestic management in regard to meat and clothes, the care of their children, their church-going, education, previous callings, and parish relief. The inquiry is not discouraging as to the character of the poor, and I must call attention to the circumstance of how rarely it is that so large a collection of facts is placed at the command of a public writer. In many of the public offices the simplest information is as jealously withheld as if statistical knowledge were the first and last steps to high treason. I trust that Mr Cochrane's example in the skilful arrangement of the returns connected with the Association over which he presides, and his courteous readiness to supply the information, gained at no small care and cost, will be more freely followed, as such a course unquestionably tends to the public benefit.

It will be seen from these statements, how hard the struggle often is to obtain work in unskilled labour, and, when obtained, how bare the living. Every farthing earned by such workpeople is necessarily expended in the support of a family; and in the foregoing details we have another proof as to the diminution of the purchasing fund of the country, being in direct proportion to the diminution of the wages. If 100 men receive but 7s. a week each for their work, their yearly outlay, to 'keep the bare life in them,' is 1820*l.* If they are paid 16*s.* a week, their outlay is 4160*l.*; an expenditure of 2340*l.* more in the productions of our manufactures, in all textile, metal, or wooden fabrics; in bread, meat, fruit, or vegetables; and in the now necessaries, the grand staple of our foreign and colonial trade – tea, coffee, cocoa, sugar, rice, and tobacco. *Increase your wages, therefore, and you increase your markets*. For manufacturers to underpay their workmen is to cripple the demand for manufactures. To talk of the over-production of our cotton, linen, and woollen goods is idle, when thousands of men engaged in such productions are in rags. It is not that there are too many makers, but too few who, owing to the decrease of wages, are able to be buyers. Let it be remembered that, out of 67 labouring men, three-fourths could not afford to buy proper clothing, expending thereupon 'little' or 'nothing', and, I may add, *because* earning little or nothing, and so having scarcely anything to expend. [. . .]

Mayhew's survey of the inmates of a lodging-house

Cheap lodging-houses
[*volume iii. pp.312–318*]

I now come to the class of cheap lodging-houses usually frequented by the casual labourers at the docks. It will be remembered, perhaps, that I described one of these places, as well as the kind of characters to be found there. Since then I have directed my attention particularly to this subject; not because it came first in order according to the course of investigation I had marked out for myself, but because it presented so many peculiar features that I thought it better, even at the risk of being unmethodical, to avail myself of the channels of information opened to me rather than defer the matter to its proper place, and so lose the freshness of the impression it had made upon my mind.

On my first visit, the want and misery that I saw were such, that, in consulting with the gentleman who led me to the spot, it was arranged that a dinner should be given on the following Sunday to all those who were present on the evening of my first interview; and, accordingly, enough beef, potatoes, and materials for a suet-pudding, were sent in from the neighbouring market to feed them every one. I parted with my guide, arranging to be with him the next Sunday at half-past one. We met at the time appointed, and set out on our way to the cheap lodging-house. The streets were alive with sailors, and bonnetless and capless women. The Jews' shops and public-houses were all open, and parties of 'jolly tars' reeled past us, singing and bawling on their way. Had it not been that here and there a stray shop was closed, it would have been impossible to have guessed it was Sunday. We dived down a narrow court, at the entrance of which lolled Irish labourers smoking short pipes. Across the court hung lines, from which dangled dirty-white clothes to dry; and as we walked on, ragged, unwashed, shoeless children scampered past us, chasing one another. At length we reached a large open yard. In the centre of it stood several empty costermongers' trucks and turned-up carts, with their shafts high in the air. At the bottom of these lay two young girls huddled together, asleep. Their bare heads told their mode of life, while it was evident, from their muddy Adelaide boots, that they had walked the streets all night. My companion tried to see if he knew them, but they slept too soundly to be roused by gentle means. We passed on, and a few paces further on there sat grouped on a door-step four women, of the same character as the last two. One had her head covered up in an old brown shawl, and was sleeping in the lap of the one next to her. The other two were eating walnuts; and a coarse-featured man in knee-breeches and 'ankle-jacks' was stretched on the ground close beside them.

At length we reached the lodging-house. It was night when I had first visited the place, and all now was new to me. The entrance was through a pair of large green gates, which gave it somewhat the appearance of a stable-yard. Over the kitchen door there hung a clothes-line, on which were a wet shirt and a pair of ragged canvas trousers, brown with tar. Entering the kitchen, we found it so full of smoke that the sun's rays, which shot slanting down through a broken tile in the roof, looked like a shaft of light cut through the fog. The flue of the chimney stood out from the bare brick wall like a buttress, and was black all the way up with the smoke; the beams, which hung down from the roof, and ran from wall to wall, were of the same colour; and in the centre, to light the room, was a rude iron gas-pipe, such as are used at night when the streets are turned up. The floor was unboarded, and a wooden seat projected from the wall all round the room. In front of this was ranged a series of tables, on which lolled dozing men. A number of the inmates were grouped around the fire; some kneeling toasting herrings, of which the place smelt strongly; others, without shirts, seated on the ground close beside it for warmth; and others drying the ends of cigars they had picked up in the streets. As we entered the men rose, and never was so motley and so ragged an assemblage seen. Their hair was matted like flocks of wool, and their chins were grimy with their unshorn beards. Some were in dirty smock-frocks; others in old red plush waistcoats, with long sleeves. One was dressed in an old shooting-jacket, with large wooden buttons; a second in a blue flannel sailor's shirt; and a third, a mere boy, wore a long camlet coat reaching to his heels, and with the ends of the sleeves hanging over his hands. The features of the lodgers wore every kind of expression: one lad was positively handsome, and there was a frankness in his face and a straightforward look in his eye that strongly impressed me with a sense of his honesty, even although I was assured he was a confirmed pickpocket. The young thief who had brought back the 11½ d. change out of the shilling that had been entrusted to him on the preceding evening, was far from prepossessing, now that I could see him better. His cheek-bones were high, while his hair, cut close on the top, with a valance of locks, as it were, left hanging in front, made me look upon him with no slight suspicion. On the form at the end of the kitchen was one whose squalor and wretchedness produced a feeling approaching to awe. His eyes were sunk deep in his head, his cheeks were drawn in, and his nostrils pinched with evident want, while his dark stubbly beard gave a grimness to his appearance that was almost demoniac; and yet there was a patience in his look that was almost pitiable. His clothes were black and shiny at every fold with grease, and his coarse shirt was so brown with long wearing, that it was only with close inspection you could see that it had once been a checked one: on his feet he had a pair of lady's side-laced boots, the toes of which had been cut off so that he might get them on. I never beheld so gaunt a picture of famine. To this day the figure of the man haunts me.

The dinner had been provided for thirty, but the news of the treat had spread, and there was a muster of fifty. We hardly knew how to act. It was, however, left to those whose names had been taken down as being present on the previous evening to say what should be done; and the answer from one and all was that the new-comers were to share the feast with them. The dinner was then half-portioned out in an adjoining outhouse into twenty-five platefuls – the entire stock of crockery belonging to the estab-lishment numbering no more – and afterwards handed into the kitchen through a small window to each party, as his name was called out. As he hurried to the seat behind the bare table, he commenced tearing the meat asunder with his fingers, for knives and forks were unknown there. Some, it is true, used bits of wood like skewers, but this seemed almost like affectation in such a place: others sat on the ground with the plate of meat and pudding on their laps; while the beggar-boy, immediately on receiving his portion, danced along the room, whirling the plate round on his thumb as he went, and then, dipping his nose in the plate, seized a potato in his mouth. I must confess the sight of the hungry crowd gnawing their food was far from pleasant to contemplate; so, while the dinner was being discussed, I sought to learn from those who remained to be helped, how they had fallen to so degraded a state. A sailor lad assured me he had been robbed of his mariner's ticket; that he could not procure another under 13s.; and not having as many pence, he was unable to obtain another ship. What could he do? he said. He knew no trade: he could only get employ-ment occasionally as a labourer at the docks; and this was so seldom, that if it had not been for the few things he had, he must have starved outright. The good-looking youth I have before spoken of wanted but 3l. 10s. to get back to America. He had worked his passage over here; had fallen into bad company; been imprisoned three times for picking pockets; and was heartily wearied of his present course. He could get no work. In America he would be happy, and among his friends again. I spoke to the gentleman who had brought me to the spot, and who knew them all well. His answers, however, gave me little hope. The boy, whose face seemed beaming with innate frankness and honesty, had been apprenticed by him to a shoe-stitcher. But, no! he preferred vagrancy to work. I could have sworn he was a trust-worthy lad, and shall never believe in 'looks' again.

The dinner finished, I told the men assembled there that I should come some evening in the course of the week, and endeavour to ascertain from them some definite information concerning the persons usually frequenting such houses as theirs. On our way home, my friend recognised, among the females we had before seen huddled on the step outside the lodging-house, a young woman whom he had striven to get back to her parents. Her father had been written to, and would gladly receive her. Again the girl was exhorted to leave her present companions and return home. The tears streamed from her eyes at mention of her mother's name; but she would not stir. Her excuse was, that she had no clothes proper to go in. Her father and mother were very respect-able, she said, and she could not go back to them as she was. It was evident, by her language, she had at least been well educated. She would not listen, however, to my friend's exhortations; so, seeing that his entreaties were wasted upon her, we left her, and wended our way home.

Knowing that this lodging-house might be taken as a fair sample of the class now abounding in London, and, moreover, having been informed by those who had made the subject their peculiar study, that the characters generally congregated there constituted a fair average of the callings and habits of those who resort to the low lodging-houses of London, I was determined to avail myself of the acquaintances I made in this quarter, in order to arrive at some more definite information upon those places than had yet been made public. The only positive knowledge the public have hitherto had of the people assembling in the cheap lodging-houses of London is derived chiefly from the Report of the Constabulary Commissioners, and partly from the Report upon Vagrancy. But this information, having been procured through others, was so faulty, that having now obtained the privilege of personal inspec-tion and communication, I was desirous of turning it to good account. Consequently I gave notice that I wished all that had dined there on last Sunday to attend me yesterday evening, so that I might obtain from them generally an account of their past and present career. I found them all ready to meet me, and I was assured that, by adopting certain precautions, I should be in a fair way to procure information upon the subject of the cheap lodging-houses of London that few have the means of getting. However, so as to be able to check the one account with another, I put myself in communication with a person who had lived for upwards of four months in the house. Strange to say, he was a man of good education and superior attainments – further than this I am not at liberty to state. I deal with the class of houses, and not with any particular house, be it understood.

The lodging-house to which I more particularly allude makes up as many as 84 'bunks', or beds, for which 2*d*. per night is charged. For this sum the parties lodging there for the night are entitled to the use of the kitchen for the following day. In this a fire is kept all day long, at which they are allowed to cook their food. The kitchen opens at 5 in the morning, and closes at about 11 at night, after which hour no fresh lodger is taken in, and all those who slept in the house the night before, but who have not sufficient money to pay for their bed at that time, are turned out. Strangers who arrive in the course of the day must procure a tin ticket, by paying 2*d*. at the wicket in the office, previously to being allowed to enter the kitchen. The kitchen is about 40 feet long by about 40 wide. The 'bunks' are each about 7 feet long, and 1 foot 10 inches wide, and the grating on which the straw mattress is placed is about 12 inches from the ground. The wooden partitions between the 'bunks' are about 4 feet high. The coverings are a leather or a rug, but leathers are generally preferred. Of these 'bunks' there are five rows, of about 24 deep; two rows being placed head to head, with a gangway between each of such two rows, and the other row against the wall. The average number of persons sleeping in this house of a night is 60. Of these there are generally about 30 pickpockets, 10 street-beggars, a few infirm old people who subsist occasionally upon parish relief and occasionally upon charity, 10 or 15 dock-labourers, about the same number of low and precarious callings, such as the neighbourhood affords, and a few persons who have been in good circumstances, but who have been reduced from a variety of causes. At one time there were as many as 9 persons lodging in this house who subsisted by picking up dogs' dung out of the streets, getting about 5*s*. for every basketful. The earnings of one of these men were known to average 9s. per week. There are generally lodging in the house a few bone-grubbers, who pick up bones, rags, iron, &c., out of the streets. Their average earnings are about 1s. per day. There are several mud-larks, or youths who go down to the water-side when the tide is out, to see whether any article of value has been left upon the bank of the river. The person supplying this information to me, who was for some time resident in the house, has seen brought home by these persons a drum of figs at one time, and a Dutch cheese at another. These were sold in small lots or slices to the other lodgers.

The pickpockets generally lodging in the house consist of hand-kerchief-stealers, shoplifters – including those who rob the till as well as steal articles from the doors of shops. Legs and breasts of mutton are frequently brought in by this class of persons. There are seldom any housebreakers lodging in such places, because they require a room of their own, and mostly live with prostitutes. Besides pickpockets, there are also lodging in the house speculators in stolen goods. These may be dock-labourers or Billingsgate porters, having a few shillings in their pockets. With these they purchase the booty of the juvenile thieves. 'I have known,' says my informant, 'these speculators wait in the kitchen, walking about with their hands in their pockets, till a little fellow would come in with such a thing as a cap, a piece of bacon, or a piece of mutton. They would purchase it, and then either retail it amongst the other lodgers in the kitchen or take it to some 'fence', where they would receive a profit upon it. The general feeling of the kitchen – excepting with four or five individuals – is to encourage theft. The encouragement to the 'gonaff' [a Hebrew word signi-fying a young thief, probably learnt from the Jew 'fences' in the neighbourhood] consists in laughing at and applauding his dexter-ity in thieving; and whenever anything is brought in, the 'gonaff' is greeted for his good luck, and a general rush is made towards him to see the produce of his thievery. The 'gonaffs' are generally young boys; about 20 out of 30 of these lads are under 21 years of age. They almost all of them love idleness, and will only work for one or two days together, but then they will work very hard. It is a singular fact that, as a body, the pickpockets are generally very sparing of drink. They are mostly libidinous, indeed universally so, and spend whatever money they can spare upon the low prostitutes

round about the neighbourhood. Burglars and smashers generally
rank above this class of thieves. A burglar would not condescend
to sit among pickpockets. My informant has known a house-
breaker to say with a sneer, when requested to sit down with the
'gonaffs', 'No, no! I may be a thief, sir; but, thank God, at least I'm
a respectable one.' The beggars who frequent these houses go
about different markets and streets asking charity of the people that
pass by. They generally go out in couples; the business of one of
the two being to look out and give warning when the policeman is
approaching, and of the other to stand 'shallow'; that is to say, to
stand with very little clothing on, shivering and shaking, sometimes with bandages round his legs, and sometimes with his arm
in a sling. Others beg 'scran' [broken victuals] of the servants at
respectable houses, and bring it home to the lodging-house, where
they sell it. You may see, I am told, the men who lodge in the
place, and obtain an honest living, watch for these beggars coming
in, as if they were the best victuals in the City. My informant knew
an instance of a lad who seemed to be a very fine little fellow, and
promised to have been possessed of excellent mental capabilities if
properly directed, who came to the lodging-house when out of a
situation as an errand-boy. He stayed there a month or six weeks,
during which time he was tampered with by the others, and
ultimately became a confirmed 'gonaff'. The conversation among
the lodgers relates chiefly to thieving and the best manner of
stealing. By way of practice, a boy will often pick the pocket of
one of the lodgers walking about the room, and if detected declare
he did not mean it.

The sanitary state of these houses is very bad. Not only do the
lodgers generally swarm with vermin, but there is little or no
ventilation to the sleeping-rooms, in which 60 persons, of the
foulest habits, usually sleep every night. There are no proper
washing utensils, neither towels nor basins, nor wooden bowls.
There are one or two buckets, but these are not meant for the use
of the lodgers, but for cleaning the rooms. The lodgers never
think of washing themselves. The cleanliest among them will do
so in the bucket, and then wipe themselves with their pocket-
handkerchiefs, or the tails of their shirts.

A large sum to be made by two beggars in one week is 20s.;
or 10s. apiece, one for looking out, and the other for 'standing

shallow'. The average earnings of such persons are certainly below 8s. per week. If the Report of the Constabulary Force Commissioners states that 20s. per week is the average sum earned, I am told the statement must have been furnished by parties who had either some object in overrating the amount, or else who had no means of obtaining correct information on the subject. From all my informant has seen as to the earnings of those who make a trade of picking pockets and begging, he is convinced that the amount is far below what is generally believed to be the case. Indeed, nothing but the idle, roving life that is connected with the business, could compensate the thieves or beggars for the privations they frequently undergo.

After obtaining this information, I attended the lodging-house in pursuance of the notice I had given, in order to ascertain from the lodgers themselves what were the callings and earnings of the different parties there assembled. I found that from 50 to 60 had mustered purposely to meet me, although it was early in the evening, and they all expressed themselves ready to furnish me with any information I might require. The gentleman who accompanied me assured me that the answers they would give to my questionings would be likely to be correct, from the fact of the number assembled, as each would check the other. Having read to them the account (in the *Morning Chronicle*) of my previous interview with them, they were much delighted at finding themselves in print, and immediately arranged themselves on a seat all round the room. My first question was as to the age of those present. Out of 55 assembled, I found that there were; 1 from 60 to 70 years old, 4 from 50 to 60, 1 from 40 to 50, 15 from 30 to 40, 16 from 20 to 30, and 18 from 10 to 20. Hence it will be seen that the younger members constituted by far the greater portion of the assembly. The 18 between 10 and 20 were made up as follows: There were 3 of 20 years, 8 of 19 years, 3 of 18 years, 4 of 17 years, 1 of 16 years, and 2 of 15 years. Hence there were more of the age of 19 than of any other age present.

My next inquiry was as to the place of birth. I found that there were 16 belonging to London, 9 to Ireland, 3 to Bristol, 3 to Liverpool, 2 were from Norfolk, 2 from Yorkshire, 2 from Essex, 2 from Germany, and 2 from North America. The remaining 14 were born respectively in Macclesfield, Bolton, Aylesbury, Seacomb, Deal,

Epping, Hull, Nottinghamshire, Plumstead, Huntingdonshire, Plymouth, Shropshire, Northamptonshire, and Windsor. After this I sought to obtain information as to the occupations of their parents, with a view of discovering whether their delinquencies arose from the depraved character of their early associations. I found among the number, 13 whose fathers had been labouring men, 5 had been carpenters, 4 millers and farmers, 2 dyers, 2 cabinet-makers, a tallow-chandler, a wood-turner, a calico-glazer, a silversmith, a compositor, a cotton-spinner, a hatter, a grocer, a whip-maker, a sweep, a glover, a watchmaker, a madhouse-keeper, a bricklayer, a ship-builder, a cow-keeper, a fishmonger, a mill-wright, a coast-guard, a ropemaker, a gunsmith, a collier, an undertaker, a leather-cutter, a clerk, an engineer, a schoolmaster, a captain in the army, and a physician.

I now sought to learn from them the trades that they themselves were brought up to. There were 17 labourers, 7 mariners, 3 weavers, 2 bricklayers, and 2 shoemakers. The rest were respectively silversmiths, dyers, black-smiths, wood-turners, tailors, farriers, caulkers, French polishers, shopmen, brickmakers, sweeps, ivory-turners, cowboys, stereotype-founders, fishmongers, tallow-chandlers, ropemakers, miners, bone-grubbers, engineers, coal-porters, errand-boys, beggars, and one called himself 'a prig'.

I next found that 40 out of the 55 could read and write, 4 could read, and only 11 could do neither.

My next point was to ascertain how long they had been out of regular employment, or to use their own phrase, 'had been knocking about'. One had been 10 years idle; one, 9; three, 8; two, 7; four, 6; five, 5; six, 4; nine, 3; ten, 2; five, 1; three, 6 months, and one, 2 months out of employment. A bricklayer told me he had been eight summers in, and eight winters out of work; and a dock-labourer assured me that he had been 11 years working at the dock, and that for full three-fourths of his time he could obtain no employment there.

After this, I questioned them concerning their earnings for the past week. One had gained nothing, another had gained 1s, eleven had earned 2s.; eight, 3s.; nine, 4s.; five, 5s.; four, 6s.; four, 7s.; six, 8s.; one, 10s.; one, 11s.; and one, 18s. From three I received no answers. The average earnings of the 52 above enumerated are 4s. 11d. per week.

Respecting their clothing, 14 had no shirts to their backs, 5 had no shoes, and 42 had shoes that scarcely held together.

I now desired to be informed how many out of the number had been confined in prison; and learnt that no less than 34 among the 55 present had been in gaol once, or oftener. Eleven had been in once; five had been in twice; five, in 3 times; three, 4 times; four, 6 times; one, 7 times; one, 8 times; one, 9 times; one, 10 times; one, 14 times; and one confessed to having been there at least 20 times. So that the 34 individuals had been imprisoned altogether 140 times; thus averaging four imprisonments to each person. I was anxious to distinguish between imprisonment for vagrancy and imprisonment for theft. Upon inquiry I discovered that seven had each been imprisoned once for vagrancy; one, twice; one, 3 times; two, 4 times; one, 5 times; two, 6 times; two, 8 times; and one, 10 times; making in all 63 imprisonments under the Vagrant Act. Of those who had been confined in gaol for theft, there were eleven who had been in once; seven, who had been in twice; two, 3 times; three, 6 times; one, 8 times, and two, 10 times; making a total of 77 imprisonments for thieving. Hence, out of 140 incarcerations, 63 of those had been for vagrancy, and 77 for theft; and this was among 34 individuals in an assemblage of 55.

The question that I put to them after this was, how long they had been engaged in thieving? and the following were the answers: one had been 15 years at it; one, 14 years; two, 12 years; three, 10 years; one, 9 years; one, 8 years; two, 7 years; one, 6 years; two, 5 years; three, 4 years; and one, 3 years; one, 18 months; one, 7 months; two, 6 months; and one, 2 months. Consequently, there were, of the half-hundred and odd individuals there assembled, thieves of the oldest standing and the most recent beginning.

Their greatest gains by theft, in a single day, were thus classified. The most that one had gained was 3d., the greatest sum another had gained was 7d.; another, 1s. 6d.; another, 2s. 6d.; another, 6s.; five had made from 10s. to 15s.; three from 1l. to 2l.; one from 2l. to 3l.; six from 3l. to 4l.; one from 4l. to 5l.; two from 20l. to 30l.; and two from 30l. to 40l. Of the latter two sums, one was stolen from the father of the thief, and the other from the till of a counter when the shop was left unoccupied, the boy vaulting over the counter and abstracting from the till no less than seven 5*l*. notes, all of which were immediately disposed of to a Jew in the immediate neighbourhood for 3*l*. 10*s*. each.

The greatest earnings by begging had been 7*s*. 6*d*., 10*s*. 6*d*., and 1*l*.; but the average amount of earnings was apparently of so precarious a nature, that it was difficult to get the men to state a definite sum. From their condition, however, as well as their mode of living whilst I remained among them, I can safely say begging did not seem to be a very lucrative or attractive calling, and the lodgers were certainly under no restraint in my presence.

I wanted to learn from them what had been their motive for stealing in the first instance, and I found upon questioning them, that ten did so on running away from home; five confessed to have done so from keeping flash company, and wanting money to defray their expenses; six had first stolen to go to theatres; nine, because they had been imprisoned for vagrants, and found that the thief was better treated than they; one because he had got no tools to work with; one because he was 'hard up;' one because he could not get work; and one more because he was put in prison for begging.

The following is the list of articles that they first stole: six rabbits, silk shawl from home, a pair of shoes, a Dutch cheese, a few shillings from home, a coat and trousers, a bullock's heart, four 'tiles' of copper, fifteen and sixpence from master, two handker-chiefs, half a quartern loaf, a set of tools worth 3*l*., clothes from a warehouse, worth 22*l*., a Cheshire cheese, a pair of carriage lamps, some handkerchiefs, five shillings, some turnips, watch-chain and seals, a sheep, three and sixpence, and an invalid's chair. This latter article, the boy assured me he had taken about the country with him, and amused himself by riding down hill.

Their places of amusement consisted, they told me, of the following: The Britannia Saloon, the City Theatre, the Albert Saloon, the Standard Saloon, the Surrey and Victoria Theatres when they could afford it, the Penny Negroes, and the Earl of Effingham concerts.

Four frequenters of that room had been transported, and yet the house had been open only as many years, and of the associates and companions of those present, no less than 40 had left the country in the same manner. The names of some of these were curious. I subjoin a few of them: The Banger, The Slasher, The Spider, Flash Jim, White-coat Mushe, Lankey Thompson, Tom Sales [he was hung], and Jack Sheppard.

Of the fifty-five congregrated, two had signed the temperance pledge, and kept it. The rest confessed to getting drunk occasion-ally, but not making a practice of it. Indeed, it is generally allowed that, as a class, the young pickpockets are rather temperate than otherwise; so that here, at least, we cannot assert that drink is the cause of the crime. Nor can their various propensities be ascribed to ignorance, for we have seen that out of 55 individuals 40 could read and write, while 4 could read. It should be remembered, at the same time, that out of the 55 men only 34 were thieves. Neither can the depravity of their early associations be named as the cause of their delinquencies, for we have seen that, as a class, their fathers are men rather well to do in the world. Indeed their errors seem to have rather a physical than either an intellectual or a moral cause. They seem to be naturally of an erratic and self-willed temperament, objecting to the restraints of home, and incapable of continuous application to any one occupation what-soever. They are essentially the idle and the vagabond; and they seem generally to attribute the commencement of their career to harsh government at home.

According to the Report of the Constabulary Force Commiss-ioners, there were in the metropolis 1839, 221 of such houses as the one at present described, and each of these houses harboured daily, upon an average, no less than eleven of such characters as the foregoing, making in all a total of 2431 vagrants and pickpockets sheltered by the proprietors of the low lodging-houses of London. The above twopenny lodging-house has, on an average, from fifty to sixty persons sleeping in it nightly, yielding an income of nearly 3l. per week. The threepenny lodging-houses in the same neigh-bourhood average from fifteen to twenty persons per night and produce a weekly total of from 20s. to 25s. profit, the rent of the houses at the same time being only from 5s. to 6s. per week. [. . .]

Of the life of a street-seller of dog-collars
[*volume i. pp.359,360*]

From [a] well-known vendor of these articles [. . .] I had the following sketch of his history:

'I was born in Brewer-street, St James,' he said, in answer to
my questions; 'I am 73 years of age. My father and mother were
poor people; I never went to school; my father died while I was
young; my mother used to go out charing; she couldn't afford
to pay for schooling, and told me, I must look out and yearn
my own living while I was a mere chick. At ten years of age I
went to sea in the merchant sarvice. While I was in the merchant
sarvice, I could get good wages, for I soon knowed my duty. I
was always of an industrious turn, and never liked to be idle;
don't you see what I mean. In '97 I was pressed on board the
Inconstant frigate; I was paid off six months arterwards, but hadn't
much to take, and that, like all other young men who hadn't
larned the dodges of life, I spent very soon; but I never got
drunk – thank God!' said the old man, 'I never got drunk, or I
shouldn't ha' been what I am now at 73 years of age. I was drafted
into the *Woolwich* 44-gun ship; from her to the *Overisal*.' I inquired how the name of the ship was spelt; 'Oh I am not scholard
enough for that there,' he replied, 'tho' I did larn to read and
write when abord a man of war. I larned myself. But you must
look into a Dutch dictionary, for it's a Dutch name. I then
entered on board the *Amphine* frigate, and arter I had sarved some
months in her, I entered the merchant sarvice again, and arter
that I went to Greenland to the whale-fishery – they calls me here
in the college [he is now an inmate of Greenwich Hospital]
"Whaler Ben", but I arnt affronted – most on 'em here have
nicknames. I went three voyages besides to the West Ingees. I
never got drunk even there, though I was obliged to drink rum; it
wouldn't ha' done to h'a drunk the water *neat*, there was so many
insects in it. When my sailor's life was over I comes to Liverpool
and marries a wife – aye and as good a wife as any poor man ever
had in England. I had saved a goodish bit o' money, nearly 300*l.*,
for I was not so foolish as some of the poor sailors, who yearns
their money like horses and spends it like asses, I say. Well we sets
up a shop – a chandler shop – in Liverpool: me and my old

'ooman does; and I also entered into the pig-dealing line. I used to get some of my pigs from Ireland, and some I used to breed myself, but I was very misfortunate. You recollect the year when the disease was among the cattle, in course you recollects that; well, sir, I lost 24 pigs and a horse in one year, and that was a good loss for a poor man, wer'n't it? I thought it werry hard, for I'd worked hard for my money at sea, and I was always werry careful, arter I knowed what life was. My poor wife too used to trust a good deal in the shop, and by-and-by, behold you, me and my old 'ooman was on our beam ends. My wife was took ill too — and, for the purpose of getting the best adwice, I brings her to London, but her cable had run out, and she died, and I've been a poor forlorned creatur' ever since. You wouldn't think it, but arter that I never slept on a bed for seven years. I had blankets and my clothes — but what I means is that I never had a bed to lie on. I sold most of my bits o' things to bury my wife. I didn't relish applying to the parish. I kept a few sticks tho', for I don't like them ere lodging-houses. I can't be a werry bad kerackter, for I was seven years under one landlord, and I warrant me if I wanted a room agin he would let me have one. Arter my wife died, knowing some'at about ropes I gets work at Maberley's, the great contractors — in course you knows him. I made rope traces for the artillery; there's a good deal of leather-work about the traces, and stitching them, you see, puts me up to the making of dogs'-collars. I was always handy with my fingers, and can make shoes or anythink. I can work now as well as ever I could in my life, only my eyes isn't so good. Ain't it curious now, sir, that wot a man larns in his fingers he never forgets? Well being out o' work, I was knocking about for some time, and then I was adwised to apply for a board to carry at one of them cheap tailors, but I didn't get none; so I takes to hawking link buttons and key rings, and buys some brass dog-collars; it was them brass collars as made me bethought myself as I could make some leather ones. Altho' I had been better off I didn't think it any disgrace to get a honest living. The leather collars is harder to make than the brass ones, only the brass ones wants more implements. There are about a dozen selling in the streets as makes brass-collars — there's not much profit on the brass ones. People says there's nothing like leather, and I thinks they are right. Well, sir, as I was a-telling you, I commences the leather-collar making, – in course I didn't make 'em as well at first as I do now. It was werry hard lines at the best of times. I used to get up at 4 o'clock in the morning in the summer time, and make my collars; then I'd turn out about 9, and keep out until 7 or 8 at night. I seldom took more than 2s. per day. What profit did I get out of 2s.? Why, lor bless you, sir! if I hadn't made them myself, I shouldn't have got no profit at all. But as it was, if I took 2s., the profits was from 1s. to 1s. 6d.; howsomever, sometimes I didn't take 6d. Wet days too used to run me aground altogether; my rheumatics used to bore me always when the rain come down, and then I couldn't get out to sell. If I'd any leather at them times I used to make it up; but if I hadn't none, why I was obligated to make the best on it. Oh, sir! you little knows what I've suffered; many a banyan day I've had in my little room – upon a wet day – aye, and other days too. Why, I think I'd a starved if it hadn't a been for the 'bus-men about Hungerford-market. They are good lads them there 'bus lads to such as me; they used to buy my collars when they didn't want them. Ask any on 'em if they know anything about old Tom, the collar-maker, and see if they don't flare up and respect me. They used sometimes to raffle my collars and give 'em back to me. Mr Longstaff too, the landlord of the Hungerford Arms – I believe it's called the Hungerford Hotel – has given me some-thing to eat very often when I was hungry, and had nothing myself. There's what you call a hor'nary there every day. You knows what I mean – gentlemen has their grub there at so much a head, or so much a belly it should be, I says. I used to come in for the scraps, and werry thankful I was for them I can assure you. Yes, Mr Longstaff is what you may call a good man. He's what you calls a odd man, and a odd man's always a good man. All I got to say is, 'God bless him!' he's fed me many time when I've been hungry. I used to light upon other friends too, – landlords of public-houses, where I used to hawk my collars; they seemed to take to me somehow; it wer'n't for what I spent in their houses I'm sure, seeing as how I'd nothing to spend. I had no pension for my sarvice, and so I was adwised to apply for admission to "the house here" [Greenwich Hospital]. I goes to Somerset-House; another poor fellow was making a application at the same time; but I didn't nothing till one very cold day, when

I was standing quite miserable like with my collars. I'd been out several hours and hadn't taken a penny, when up comes the man as wanted to get into the house, running with all his might to me. I thought he was going to tell me he had got into the house, and I was glad on it, for, poor fellow, he was werry bad off; howsomever he says to me, 'Tom,' says he, 'they wants you at the Admirality.' 'Does they?' says I, and 'cordingly away I goes; and arter telling the admiral my sarvice, and answering a good many questions as he put to me, the admiral says, says he, 'The order will be made out; you shall go into the house.' I think the admiral knowed me or somethink about me, you see. I don't know his name, and it wouldn't ha' done to have axed. God bless him, whoever he is, I says, and shall say to my dying day; it seemed like Providence. I hadn't taken a ha'penny all that day; I was cold and hungry, and suffering great pain from my rheumatics. Thank God,' exclaimed the old man in conclusion, 'I am quite comfortable now. I've everythink I want except a little more tea and shuggar, but I'm quite content, and thank God for all his mercies.'

The old man informed me moreover that he did not think there were more than half-a-dozen street-sellers besides himself who made leather collars; it was a poor trade, he said, and though the other makers were younger than he was, he 'could lick them all at stitching'. He did not believe, he told me, that any of the collar-sellers sold more than he did – if as many – for he had friends that perhaps other men had not. He makes collars now sometimes, and wishes he could get some shopkeeper to sell them for him, and then maybe, he says, he could obtain a little more tea and shuggar, and assist a sister-in-law of his whom he tells me is in great distress, and whom he has been in the habit of assisting for many years, notwithstanding his poverty. The old man, during the recital of his troubles, was affected to tears several times – especially when he spoke of his wife, and the distress he had undergone – and with much sincerity blessed God for the comforts that he now enjoys.

The home comforts of a cats'-meat carrier
[*volume i. p.183*]

The generality of the dealers wear a shiny hat, black plush waist-coat and sleeves, a blue apron, corduroy trousers, and a blue and white spotted handkerchief round their necks. Some, indeed, will wear two and three handkerchiefs round their necks, this being fashionable among them. A great many meet every Friday after-noon in the donkey-market, Smithfield, and retire to a public-house adjoining, to spend the evening.

A 'cats' meat carrier' who supplied me with information was more comfortably situated than any of the poorer classes that I have yet seen. He lived in the front room of a second floor, in an open and respectable quarter of the town, and his lodgings were the perfection of comfort and cleanliness in an humble sphere. It was late in the evening when I reached the house. I found the 'carrier' and his family preparing for supper. In a large morocco leather easy chair sat the cats' meat carrier himself; his 'blue apron and black shiny hat' had disappeared, and he wore a 'dress' coat and a black satin waistcoat instead. His wife, who was a remarkably pretty woman, and of very attractive manners, wore a 'Dolly Varden' cap, placed jauntily at the back of her head, and a drab merino dress. The room was cosily carpeted, and in one corner stood a mahogany 'crib' with cane-work sides, in which one of the children was asleep. On the table was a clean white table-cloth, and the room was savoury with the steaks, and mashed potatoes that were cooking on the fire. Indeed, I have never yet seen greater comfort in the abodes of the poor. The cleanliness and wholesomeness of the apartment were the more striking from the unpleasant associations connected with the calling.

It is believed by one who has been engaged at the business for 25 years, that there are from 900 to 1,000 horses, averaging 2 cwt. of meat each – little and big – boiled down every week; so that the quantity of cats' and dogs' meat used throughout London is about 200,000 lbs. per week, and this, sold at the rate of 2½ *d.* per lb., gives 2,000*l.* a week for the money spent in cats' and dogs' meat, or upwards of 100,000*l.* a year, which is at the rate of 100*l.*-worth sold annually by each carrier. The profits of the carriers may be estimated at about 50*l.* each per annum.

The capital required to start in this business varies from 1*l.* to 2*l.* The stock-money needed is between 5*s.* and 10*s.* The barrow and basket, weights and scales, knife and steel, or blackstone, cost about 2*l.* when new, and from 15*s.* to 4*s.* second-hand.

Street-seller of cutlery
[*volume i. pp.339,340*]

'We has to walk farther to sell our goods, and people beat us down so terrible hard, that we can't get a penny out of them when we do sell. Sometimes they offers me 9*d.*, yes, and often 6*d.* for an 8½*d.* knife; and often enough 4*d.* for one that stands you in 3¾*d.* – a ¼*d.* profit, think of that, sir. Then they say, "Well, my man, will you take my money?" and so as to make you do so, they'll flash it before your eyes, as if they knew you was a-starving, and would be sure to be took in by the sight of it. Yes, sir, it is a very hard life, and we has to put up with a good deal – a good deal – starvation and hard-dealing, and insults and knockings about, and all. And then you see the swag-shops is almost as hard on us as the buyers. The swag-men will say, if you merely makes a remark, that a knife they've sold you is cracked in the handle, "Oh, is it; let me see whereabouts;" and when you hands it to 'em to show it 'em, they'll put it back where they took it from, and tell you, "You're too particular by half, my man. You'd better go and get your goods somewhere else; here take your money, and go on about your business, for we won't sarve you at all." They'll do just the same with the scissors too, if you complains about their being a bit rusty. "Go somewhere else," they'll say, "We won't sarve you." Ah, sir, that's what it is to be a poor man; to have your poverty flung in your teeth every minute. People says, "to be poor and seem poor is the devil;" but to be poor, and be treated like a dog merely because you are poor, surely is ten thousand times worse. A street-seller now-a-days is looked upon as a "cadger", and treated as one. To try to get a living for one's self is to do something shameful in these times.'

The man then gave me the following history of himself. He was a kindly-looking and hearty old man. He had on a ragged fustian jacket, over which he wore a black greasy-looking and tattered oilskin coat – the collar of this was torn away, and the green baize lining alone visible. His waistcoat was patched in every direction, while his trousers appeared to be of corduroy; but the grease and mud was so thick upon them, that it was difficult to tell of what material they were made. His shoes – or rather what remained of them – were tied on his feet with pieces of string. His appearance altogether denoted great poverty.

'My father was a farmer, sir. He had two farms, about 800 acres in all. I was one of eleven (ten sons and one daughter). Seven years before my father's death he left his farm, and went to live on his money. He had made a good bit at farming; but when he died it was all gone, and we was left to shift as we could. I had little or no education. My brothers could read and write, but I didn't take to it; I went a bird's-nesting, boy-like, instead, so that what little I did larn I have forgot. I am very sorry for that now. I used to drive the plough, and go a-harrowing for father. I was brought up to nothing else. When father died, I thought as I should like to see London. I was a mere lad – about 20 – and so I strolled up to town. I had 10s. with me, and that, with a bundle, was all that I possessed in the world. When I got to London I went to lodge at a public-house – the Red Lion – in Great Wild-street; and while I was there I sought about for work, but could not get any; when all was gone, I was turned out into the streets, and walked about for two days and two nights, without a bed, or a bit to eat, unless what I picked out of the gutter, and eat like a dog – orange-peel and old cabbage-stumps, indeed anything I could find. When I was very hard put to it, I was coming down Drury-lane, and I looked in, quite casual like, to ask for a job of work at the shop of Mr Bolton, the needle-maker from Redditch. I told him as how I was nigh starving, and would do anything to get a crust; I didn't mind what I put my hand to. He said he would try me, and gave me two packets of needles to sell – they was the golden-eyed ones of that time of day – and he said when I had got rid of them I was to come back to him, and I should have two packets more. He told me the price to ask – sixpence a paper – and away I went like a sand-boy, and got rid of the two in an hour and a half. Then I went back, and when I told him what I'd done, he shook hands with me, and said, as he burst out laughing, "Now, you see I've made a man of you."

Oh, he was an uncommon nice gentleman! Then he told me to keep the shilling I had taken, and said he would trust me with two more packets. I sold them, and two others besides, that day. Then, he says, 'I shall give you something else, and he let me have two packets of tailors' needles and half a dozen of tailors' thimbles. He told me how to sell them, and where to go, and on them I did better. I went round to the tailors' shops and sold a good lot, but at last they stopped me, because I was taking the bread out of the mouths of the poor blind needle-sellers what supplies the journey-men tailors at the West-end. Then Mr Bolton sent me down to one of his relations, a Mr Crooks, in Fetter Lane, who was a Sheffield man, and sold cutlery to the hawkers; and Mr Crooks and Mr Bolton set me up between them, and so I've followed the line ever since. I dare say I shall continue in it to my dying day. After I got fairly set agoing, I used to make – take good and bad, wet and dry days together – 18s. a week; three shillings a day was what I calculated on at the least, and to do that I was obligated to take between 2l. and 3l. a week, or about eight or nine shillings each day. I went on doing this for upwards of thirty year. I have been nearly forty years, altogether, in the streets, selling cutlery. I did very tidy till about four years back – I generally made from 18s. to 1l. a week up to that time. I used to go round the country – to Margate, Brighton, Portsmouth – I mostly travelled by the coast, calling at all the sea-port towns, for I always did best among the sailors. I went away every Spring time, and came to London again at the fall of the year. Sixteen year ago, I married the widow of a printer – a pressman – she had no money, but you see I had no home, and I thought I should be more comfortable, and so I have been – a great deal more comfortable – and so I should be now, if things hadn't got so bad. Four year ago, as I was a telling you, it was just after the railways had knocked off work, things began to get uncommon bad – before then, I had as good as 30s. or 40s. stock, and when things got slack, it went away, little by little. I couldn't make profit enough to support me and my old woman – she has got the rheumatics and can't earn me a halfpenny or a farden in the world; she hasn't done so for years. When I didn't make enough to live upon, of course I was obligated to break into my stock; so there it kept going shilling by shilling, and sixpence by sixpence, until I had got nothing left to work upon – not a halfpenny. You see, four or five months ago, I was took very bad with the rheumatic fever and gout. I got wet through in the streets, and my clothes dried on me, and the next day I was taken bad with pains in my limbs, and then everything that would fetch me a penny went to the pawn-shop; all my own and my old woman's clothes went to get us food – blankets, sheets and all. I never would go nigh the parish; I couldn't bring myself to have the talk about it. When I got well and out into the streets again, I borrowed 2s. or 3s. of my landlady – I have lived with her these three years – to get my stock again, but you see that got me so few things, that I couldn't fetch myself up. I lost the greater portion of my time in going backards and forrards to the shop to get fresh goods as fast as I sold them, and so what I took wasn't enough to earn the commonest living for me and my missus. Since December we have been nearly starving, and that's as true as you have got the pen in your very hand. Sunday after Sunday we have been with-out a bit of dinner, and I have laid a-bed all day because we have had no coal, and then been obligated to go out on Monday morning without a bit of victuals between my lips. I've been so faint I couldn't hardly walk. I've picked the crusts off the tables of the tap-rooms where I have been to hawk my goods, and put them in my pocket to eat them on the sly. Wet and dry I'm obligated to be out; let it come down ever so hard I must be in it, with scarcely a bit of shoe, and turned 60 years old, as I am. Look here, sir,' he said, holding up his foot, 'look at these shoes, the soles is all loose, you see, and let water. On wet days I hawk my goods to respectable shops; tap-rooms is no good, decent people merely get insulted there. But in most of the shops as I goes to people tells me, "My good man it is as much as we can do to keep ourselves and our family in these cutting times." Now, just to show you what I done last week. Sunday, I laid a-bed all day and had no dinner. Monday, I went out in the morning without a morsel between my lips, and with only 8½ d. for stock-money; with that I bought a knife and sold it for a shilling, and then I got another and another after that, and that was my day's work – three times 3½ d. or 10½ d. in all, to keep the two of us. Tuesday, I sold a pair of small scissors and two little pearl-handled knives, at 6d. each article, and cleared 10½ d. on the whole, and that is all I did. Wednesday, I sold a razor-strop for 6d., a four-bladed knife for a shilling, and a small

hone for 6*d*.; by these I cleared 10*d*. altogether. Thursday, I sold a
pair of razors for a shilling, clearing by the whole 11½*d*. Friday, I
got rid of a pair of razors for 1*s*. 9*d*., and got 9*d*. clear.' I added up
the week's profits and found they amounted to 4*s*. 3½*d*. 'That's
about right,' said the man, 'out of that I shall have to pay 1*s*. for my
week's rent; we've got a kitchen, so that I leave you to judge how
we two can live out of what's remaining.' I told him it wouldn't
average quite 6*d*. a day. 'That's about it,' he replied, 'we have half a
loaf of bread a day, and that thank God is only five farthings now.
This lasts us the day, with two-penny-worth of bits of meat that my
old woman buys at a ham-shop, where they pare the hams and puts
the parings by on plates to sell to poor people; and when she can't
get that, she buys half a sheep's head, one that's three or four days
old, for then they sells 'em to the poor for 1½*d*. the half; and these
with ¾*d*. worth of tea, and ½*d*. worth of sugar, ¼*d*. for a candle, 1*d*.
of coal – that's seven pounds – and ¾*d*. worth of coke – that's half
a peck – makes up all we gets.' [These items amount to 6½*d*. in all.]
'That's how we do when we can't get it, and when we can't, why
we lays in bed and goes without altogether.'

8

PAUPERS AND CRIMINALS

For all the innovatory quality of his work as a social investigator, Mayhew was very much a man of his times. He was deeply influenced by middle-class radicalism and committed to its civilising mission. Work was central to his thinking. Like his contemporaries, he believed that an aptitude for labour was a direct measure of the restraint and discipline upon which social order rested and that the non-formation of habits of industry was closely bound up with the growth of pauperisation and the consequent descent of the labouring classes into the dangerous classes.

A DINNER AT A CHEAP LODGING-HOUSE

London vagrants

[volume iii. pp.368–396]

The evils consequent upon the uncertainty of labour I have already been at considerable pains to point out. There is still one other mischief attendant upon it that remains to be exposed, and which, if possible, is greater than any other yet adduced. Many classes of labour are necessarily uncertain or fitful in their character. Some work can be pursued only at certain seasons; some depends upon the winds, as, for instance, dock labour; some on fashion; and nearly all on the general prosperity of the country. Now, the labourer who is deprived of his usual employment by any of the above causes, must, unless he has laid by a portion of his earnings while engaged, become a burden to his parish, or the state, or else he must seek work, either of another kind or in another place. The mere fact of a man's seeking work in different parts of the country, may be taken as evidence that he is indisposed to live on the charity or labour of others; and this feeling should be encouraged in every rational manner. Hence the greatest facility should be afforded to all labourers who may be unable to obtain work in one locality, to pass to another part of the country where there may be a demand for their labour. In fine, it is expedient that every means should be given for extending the labour-market for the working classes; that is to say, for allowing them as wide a field for the exercise of their calling as possible. To do this involves the establishment of what are called the 'casual wards' of the different unions throughout the country. These are, strictly speaking, the free hostelries of the unemployed workpeople, where they may be lodged and fed, on their way to find work in some more active district. But the establishment of these gratuitous hotels has called into existence a large class of wayfarers, for whom they were never contemplated. They have been the means of affording great encouragement to those vagabond or erratic spirits who find continuity of application to any task specially irksome to them, and who are physically unable or mentally unwilling to remain for any length of time in the same place, or at the same work – creatures who are vagrants in disposition and principle; the wandering tribe of this country; the nomads of the present day.

'The right which every person apparently destitute possesses, to demand food and shelter, affords,' says Mr Pigott, in the *Report on Vagrancy*, 'great facilities and encouragement to idle and dissolute persons to avoid labour, and pass their lives in idleness and pillage. There can be no doubt that of the wayfarers who, in summer especially, demand admission into workhouses, the number of those whom the law contemplates under the titles of "idle and disorderly", and "rogues and vagabonds", greatly exceeds that of those who are honestly and *bona fide* travelling in search of employment, and that it is the former class whose numbers have recently so increased as to require a remedy.'

It becomes almost a necessary result of any system which seeks to give shelter and food to the industrious operative in his way to look for work, that it should be the means of harbouring and fostering the idle and the vagabond.

To refuse an asylum to the vagrant is to shut out the traveller; so hard is it to tell the one from the other.

The prime cause of vagabondism is essentially the non-inculcation of a habit of industry; that is to say, the faculty of continuous application at a particular form of work, has not been engendered in the individual's mind, and he has naturally an aversion to any regular occupation, and becomes erratic, wandering from this thing to that, without any settled or determined object. Hence we find, that the vagrant disposition begins to exhibit itself precisely at that age when the first attempts are made to inculcate the habit of continuous labour among youths. This will be seen by the table in the opposite page (taken from the Returns of the Houseless Poor), which shows the greatest number of inmates to be between the ages of fifteen and twenty-five.

The cause of the greater amount of vagrancy being found among individuals between the ages of fifteen and twenty-five (and it is not by the table alone that this fact is borne out), appears to be the

THE AGES OF APPLICANTS FOR SHELTER AT THE CENTRAL ASYLUM, PLAYHOUSE-YARD, WHITECROSS-STREET, IN THE YEAR 1849

Children under a year old

Age in months	Number of applicants
< 1	17
1	4
2	42
3	21
4	14
5	14
6	26
7	30
8	7
9	14
10	7
11	5

Aged over a year

Age in years	Number of applicants
1	28
2	22
3	28
4	30
5	36
6	39
7	56
8	38
9	92
10	108
11	104
12	107
13	177
14	102
15	268
16	259
17	380
18	336
19	385
20	296

Age in years	Number of applicants
21	335
22	386
23	295
24	399
25	122
26	238
27	219
28	238
29	84
30	294
31	56
32	91
33	105
34	98
35	186
36	98
37	63
38	56
39	42
40	117
41	63
42	91
43	49
44	42
45	91
46	28
47	35
48	56
49	84
50	108
51	28
52	46
53	44
54	21
55	49
56	35
57	27
58	35
59	27
60	35

Age in years	Number of applicants
61	7
62	14
63	7
64	14
65	12
66	6
67	10
68	7
69	4
70	7
71	4
72	6
73	7
74	6
75	7
76	6
77	2
78	4
79	0
80	2

irksomeness of any kind of sustained labour when first performed. This is especially the case with youth; and hence a certain kind of compulsion is necessary, in order that the habit of doing the particular work may be engendered. Unfortunately, however, at this age the self-will of the individual begins also to be developed, and any compulsion or restraint becomes doubly irksome. Hence, without judicious treatment, the restraint may be entirely thrown off by the youth, and the labour be discarded by him, before any steadiness of application has been produced by constancy of practice. The cause of vagrancy then resolves itself, to a great extent, into the harshness of either parents or employers; and this it will be found is generally the account given by the vagrants themselves. They have been treated with severity, and being generally remarkable for their self-will, have run away from their home or master to live while yet mere lads in some of the low lodging-houses. Here they find companions of the same age and character as themselves, with whom they ultimately set out on a vagabond excursion through the country, begging or plundering on their way.

Another class of vagrants consists of those who, having been thrown out of employment, have travelled through the country, seeking work without avail, and who, consequently, have lived on charity so long, that the habits of wandering and mendicancy have eradicated their former habits of industry, and the industrious workman has become changed into the habitual beggar.

'Having investigated the general causes of depredation, of vagrancy, and mendicancy,' say the Constabulary Commissioners, in the Government Reports of 1839 (p. 181), 'as developed by examinations of the previous lives of criminals or vagrants in the gaols, we find that scarcely in any cases is it ascribable to the pressure of unavoidable want or destitution, and that in the great mass of cases it arises from the temptation of obtaining property with a less degree of labour than by regular industry.' Again, in p. 63 of the same Report, we are told that 'the inquiries made by the most experienced officers into the causes of vagrancy manifest, that in all but three or four per cent the prevalent cause was the impatience of steady labour.' My investigations into this most important subject lead me, I may add, to the same conclusions. In order to understand the question of vagrancy thoroughly, however, we must not stop here; we must find out what, in its turn, is the cause of this impatience of steady labour; or, in other words, we must ascertain whence comes the desire to obtain property with a less degree of labour than by regular industry. Now, all 'steady labour' – that is to say, the continuance of any labour for any length of time – is naturally irksome to us. We are all innately erratic – prone to wander both in thought and action; and it is only by a vigorous effort, which is more or less painful to us at first, that we can keep ourselves to the steady prosecution of the same object, to the repeated performance of the same acts, or even to continuous attention to the same subject. Labour and effort are more or less irksome to us all. There are, however, two means by which this irksomeness may be not only removed, but transformed into a positive pleasure. One is, by the excitement of some impulse or purpose in the mind of the workman; and the other, by the inculcation of a habit of working. Purpose and habit are the only two modes by which labour can be rendered easy to us; and it is precisely because the vagrant is deficient in both that he has an aversion to work for his living, and wanders through the country without an object, or, indeed, a destination. A love of industry is not a gift, but a habit; it is an accomplishment rather than an endowment; and our purposes and principles do not arise spontaneously from the promptings of our own instincts and affections, but are the mature result of education, example, and deliberation. A vagrant, therefore, is an individual applying himself continuously to no one thing, nor pursuing any one aim for any length of time, but wandering from this subject to that, as well as from one place to another, because in him no industrial habits have been formed, nor any principle or purpose impressed upon his nature.

Pursuing the subject still further, we shall find that the cause of the vagrant's wandering through the country – and indeed through life – purposeless, objectless, and *unprincipled*, in the literal and strict meaning of the term, lies mainly in the defective state of our educational institutions; for the vagrants, as a class, it should be remembered, are not 'educated'. We teach a lad reading, writing, and arithmetic, and believe that in so doing we are developing the moral functions of his nature; whereas it is often this ability to *read merely* – that is to say, to read without the least moral perception – which becomes the instrument of the youth's moral depravity. The *Jack Sheppard* of Mr Harrison Ainsworth is borrowed from the circulating library, and read aloud in the low lodging-houses in the evening by those who have a little education, to their companions who have none; and because the thief is there furbished up into the hero – because the author has tricked him out with a sort of brute insensibility to danger, made 'noble blood flow in his veins', and tinselled him over with all kinds of showy sentimentality – the poor boys who listen, unable to see through the trumpery deception, are led to look up to the paltry thief as an object of admiration, and to make his conduct the *beau idéal* of their lives. Of all books, perhaps none has ever had so baneful an effect upon the young mind, taste, and principles as this. None has ever done more to degrade literature to the level of the lowest licentiousness, or to stamp the author and the teacher as guilty of pandering to the most depraved propensities. Had Mr Ainsworth been with me, and seen how he had vitiated the thoughts and pursuits of hundreds of mere boys – had he heard the names of the creatures of his morbid fancy given to youths at an age when they needed the best and truest counsellors – had he seen these poor little wretches, as I have seen them, grin with delight at receiving the degrading titles of 'Blue skin', 'Dick Turpin', and 'Jack Sheppard', he would, I am sure, ever rue the day which led him to paint the most degraded and abandoned of our race as the most noble of human beings. What wonder, then, that – taught either in no school at all, or else in that meretricious one which makes crime a glory, and dresses up vice as virtue – these poor lads should be unprincipled in every act they do – that they should be either literally actuated by no principles at all, or else fired with the basest motives and purposes, gathered from books which distort highway robbery into an act of noble enterprise, and dignify murder as justifiable homicide?

Nor are the habits of the young vagrant less cultivated than his motives. The formation of that particular habit which we term industry, and by which the youth is fitted to obtain his living as a man, is perhaps the most difficult part of all education. It commences at an age when the will of the individual is beginning to develop itself, and when the docile boy is changed into the impatient young man. Too great lenity, or too strict severity of government, therefore, becomes at this period of life dangerous. If

the rule be too lax, the restless youth, disgusted with the mono-
tony of pursuing the same task, or performing the same acts, day
by day, neglects his work – till habits of indolence, rather than
industry, are formed, and he is ultimately thrust upon the world,
without either the means or the disposition of labouring for his
living. If, on the other hand, the authority of the parent or master
be too rigidly exercised, and the lad's power of endurance be taxed
too severely, then the self-will of the youth is called into action;
and growing restless and rebellious under the tyranny of his
teachers, he throws off their restraint, and leaves them – with a
hatred, instead of a love of labour engendered within him. That
these are two of the primary causes of vagrancy, all my inquiries
have tended to show. The proximate cause certainly lies in the
impatience of steady labour; but the cause of this impatience is
referable to the non-formation of any habit of industry in the
vagrant, and the absence of this habit of industry is usually due to
the neglect or the tyranny of the lad's parent or master. This is
no theory, be it remembered. Whether it be the master of the
workhouse – where the vagrants congregate every night – whether
it be the young vagrant himself, or the more experienced tramp,
that speaks upon the subject, all agree in ascribing the vagabondism
of youth to the same cause. There is, however, another phase of
vagrancy still to be explained; viz. the transition of the working
man into the regular tramp and beggar. This is the result of a habit
of dependence, produced in the operative by repeated visits to
the casual wards of the unions. A labouring man, or mechanic,
deprived of employment in a particular town, sets out on a journey
to seek work in some other part of the country. The mere fact of
his so journeying to seek work shows that he has a natural
aversion to become a burden to the parish. He is no sooner,
however, become an inmate of the casual wards, and breakfasts
and sups off the bounty of the workhouse, than he learns a most
dangerous lesson – he learns how to live by the labour of others.
His sense of independence may be shocked at first, but repeated
visits to the same places soon deaden his feelings on this score; and
he gradually, from continual disuse, loses his habit of labouring,
and ultimately, by long custom, acquires a habit of 'tramping'
through the country, and putting up at the casual wards of the
unions by the way. Thus, what was originally designed as a means

of enabling the labouring man to obtain work, becomes the instrument of depriving him of employment, by rendering it no longer a necessity for him to seek it; and the independent workman is transformed after a time into the habitual tramper, and finally into the professional beggar and petty thief. Such characters, however, form but a small proportion of the great body of vagabonds continually traversing the country.

The vagrants are essentially the non-working, as distinguished from the hard-working, men of England. They are the very opposite to the industrious classes, with whom they are too often confounded. Of the really destitute working-men, among the vagrants seeking relief at the casual wards, the proportion is very small; the respectable mechanics being deterred by disgust from herding with the filth, infamy, disease, and vermin congregated in the tramp-wards of the unions, and preferring the endurance of the greatest privations before subjecting themselves to it. [. . .]

Characteristics of the various classes of vagrants

I now come to the characteristics of vagrant life, as seen in the casual wards of the metropolitan unions. The subject is one of the most important with which I have yet had to deal, and the facts I have collected are sufficiently startling to give the public an idea of the great social bearings of the question; for the young vagrant is the budding criminal.

Previously to entering upon my inquiry into this subject, I consulted with a gentleman who had long paid considerable attention to the question, and who was, moreover, in a position peculiarly fitted for gaining the greatest experience, and arriving at the correctest notions upon the matter. I consulted, I say, with the gentleman referred to, as to the Poor Law officers, from whom I should be likely to obtain the best information; and I was referred by him to Mr Knapp, the master of the Wandsworth and Clapham Union, as one of the most intelligent and best-informed upon the subject of vagrancy. [. . .]

He told me that he considered a casual ward necessary in every union, because there is always a migratory population, consisting of labourers seeking employment in other localities, and destitute women travelling to their husbands or friends. He thinks a casual ward is necessary for the shelter and relief of such parties, since the law will not permit them to beg. These, however, are by far the smaller proportion of those who demand admittance into the casual ward. Formerly, they were not five per cent of the total number of casuals. The remainder consisted of youths, prostitutes, Irish families, and a few professional beggars. The youths formed more than one-half of the entire number, and their ages were from twelve to twenty. The largest number were seventeen years old – indeed, he adds, just that age when youth becomes disengaged from parental control. These lads had generally run away, either from their parents or masters, and many had been reared to a life of vagrancy. They were mostly shrewd and acute youths; some had been very well educated. Ignorance, to use the gentleman's own words, is certainly not the prevailing characteristic of the class; indeed, with a few exceptions, he would say it is the reverse. These lads are mostly distinguished by their aversion to continuous labour of any kind. He never knew them to work – they are, indeed, essentially the idle and the vagabond. Their great inclination is to be on the move, and wandering from place to place; and they appear, he says, to receive a great deal of pleasure from the assembly and conversation of the casual ward. They are physically stout, healthy lads, and certainly not emaciated or sickly. They belong especially to the able-bodied class, being, as he says, full of health and mischief. When in London, they live in the day-time by holding horses, and carrying parcels from the steam-piers and railway termini. Some loiter about the markets in the hope of a job, and others may be seen in the streets picking up bones and rags, or along the water-side searching for pieces of old metal, or anything that may be sold at the marine-store shops. They have nearly all been in prison more than once, and several a greater number of times than they are years old. They are the most dishonest of all thieves, having not the least respect for the property of even the members of their own class. He tells me he has frequently known them to rob one another. They are very stubborn and self-willed. They have often broken every window in the oakum-room, rather than do the required work. They are a most difficult class to govern, and are especially restive under the least restraint; they can ill brook control, and they find great delight in thwarting the authorities of the workhouse. They are particularly fond of amusements of all kinds. My informant has often heard them discuss the merits of the different actors at the minor theatres and saloons. Sometimes they will elect a chairman, and get up a regular debate, and make speeches from one end of the ward to the other. Many of them will make very clever comic orations; others delight in singing comic songs, especially those upon the workhouse and gaols. He never knew them love reading. They mostly pass under fictitious names. Some will give the name of 'John Russell', or 'Robert Peel', or 'Richard Cobden'. They often come down to the casual wards in large bodies of twenty or thirty, with sticks hidden down the legs of their trousers, and with these they rob and beat those who do not belong to their own gang. The gang will often consist of a hundred lads, all under twenty, one-fourth of whom regularly come together in a body; and in the casual ward they generally arrange where to meet again on the following night. In the winter of 1846, the guardians of Wandsworth and Clapham, sympathising with their ragged and wretched appearance, and desirous of affording them the means of obtaining an honest livelihood, gave my informant instructions to offer an asylum to any who might choose to remain in the workhouse. Under this arrangement, about fifty were admitted. The majority were under seventeen years of age. Some of them remained a few days – others a few weeks – none stopped longer than three months; and the generality of them decamped over the wall, taking with them the clothes of the union. The confinement, restraint, and order of the workhouse were especially irksome to them. This is the character of the true vagrant, for whom my informant considers no provision whatsoever should be made at the unions, believing as he does that most of them have settlements in or around London. [. . .]

He tells me he is convinced that it is the low lodging-houses and the casual wards of the unions that offer a ready means for youths absconding from their homes, immediately on the least disagreement or restraint. [. . .] A boy after running away from home, generally seeks shelter in one of the cheap lodging-houses, and there he makes acquaintance with the most depraved of both sexes. The boys at the house become his regular companions, and he is soon a confirmed vagrant and thief like the rest. The youths of the vagrant class are particularly distinguished for their libidinous propensities. They frequently come to the gate with a young prostitute, and with her they go off in the morning. With this girl, they will tramp through the whole of the country. They are not remarkable for a love of drink, – indeed, my informant never saw a regular vagrant in a state of intoxication, nor has he known them to exhibit any craving for liquor. He has had many drunkards under his charge, but the vagrant is totally distinct, having propensities not less vicious, but of a very different kind. He considers the young tramps to be generally a class of lads possessing the keenest intellect, and of a highly enterprising character. They seem to have no sense of danger, and to be especially delighted with such acts as involve any peril. They are likewise characterised by their exceeding love of mischief. The property destroyed in the union of which my informant is the master has been of considerable value, consisting of windows broken, sash-frames demolished, beds and bedding torn to pieces, and rags burnt. They will frequently come down in large gangs, on purpose to destroy the property in the union. They generally are of a most restless and volatile disposition. [. . .]

They are perfectly organised, so that any regulation affecting their comforts or interests becomes known among the whole body in a remarkably short space of time. [. . .]

The juvenile vagrants constitute one of the main sources from which the criminals of the country are continually recruited and augmented. Being repeatedly committed to prison for disorderly conduct and misdemeanour, the gaol soon loses all terrors for them; and, indeed, they will frequently destroy their own clothes, or the property of the union, in order to be sent there. Hence they soon become practised and dexterous thieves, and my informant has detected several burglaries by the property found upon them. The number of this class is stated, in the Poor Law Report on Vagrancy, to have been, in 1848, no less than 16,086, and they form one of the most restless, discontented, vicious, and dangerous elements of society. At the period of any social commotion, they are sure to be drawn towards the scene of excitement in a vast concourse. During the Chartist agitation, in the June quarter of the year 1848, the number of male casuals admitted into the Wandsworth and Clapham Union rose from 2501 to 3968, while the females (their companions) increased from 579 to 1388.

Of the other classes of persons admitted into the casual wards, the Irish generally form a large proportion. At the time when juvenile vagrancy prevailed to an alarming extent, the Irish hardly dared to show themselves in the casual wards, for the lads would beat them and plunder them of whatever they might have – either the produce of their begging, or the ragged kit they carried with them. Often my informant has had to quell violent disturbances in the night among these characters. The Irish tramp generally makes his appearance with a large family, and frequently with three or four generations together – grandfather, grandmother, father, and mother, and children – all coming at the same time. In the year ending June, 1848, the Irish vagrants increased to so great an extent that, of the entire number of casuals relieved, more than one-third in the first three quarters, and more than two-thirds in the last quarter, were from the sister island. [. . .]

These constitute the two large and principal classes of vagrants. The remainder generally consist of persons temporarily destitute, whereas the others are habitually so. The temporarily destitute are chiefly railway and agricultural labourers, and a few mechanics travelling in search of employment. These are easily distinguishable from the regular vagrant; indeed, a glance is sufficient to the practised eye. They are the better class of casuals, and those for whom the wards are expressly designed, but they only form a very small proportion of the vagrants applying for shelter. In the height of vagrancy, they formed not one per cent of the entire number admitted. Indeed, such was the state of the casual wards, that the destitute mechanics and labourers preferred walking through the night to availing themselves of the accommodation. Lately, the artisans and labourers have increased greatly in proportion, owing to the system adopted for the exclusion of the habitual vagrant, and the consequent decline of their number. The working man travelling in search of employment is now generally admitted into what are called the receiving wards of the workhouse, instead of the tramp-room, and he is usually exceedingly grateful for the accommodation. [. . .]

Of the original occupations or trades of the vagrants applying for relief at the different unions throughout the country, there are no returns. As, however, a considerable portion of these were attracted to London on the opening of the Metropolitan Asylums for the Houseless Poor, we may, by consulting the Society's yearly Reports, where an account of the callings of those receiving shelter in such establishments is always given, be enabled to arrive at some rough estimate as to the state of destitution and vagrancy existing among the several classes of labourers and artisans for several years.

The following table, being an average drawn from the returns for seventeen years of the occupation of the persons admitted into the Asylums for the Houseless Poor, which I have been at considerable trouble in forming, exhibits the only available information upon this subject, synoptically arranged:

Factory employment	1 in every	3
Hawkers	1 in every	4
Labourers (agricultural)	1 in every	12
Seamen	1 in every	12
Char-women and washer-women	1 in every	13
Labourers (general)	1 in every	17
Wadding-makers	1 in every	35
Smiths and iron-founders	1 in every	36
Weavers	1 in every	38
Brick-makers	1 in every	39
Rope-makers	1 in every	41
Braziers	1 in every	55
Paper-makers and stainers	1 in every	58
Skin-dressers	1 in every	58
Basket-makers	1 in every	62
Bricklayers, plasterers, and slaters	1 in every	62
Gardeners	1 in every	67
File-cutters	1 in every	70
Sawyers	1 in every	73
Turners	1 in every	74
Wire-workers	1 in every	75
Cutlers	1 in every	77
Harness-makers and saddlers	1 in every	80
Stonemasons	1 in every	88
Dyers	1 in every	94
Chimney-sweeps	1 in every	97
Errand boys	1 in every	99
Porters	1 in every	99
Painters, plumbers, and glaziers	1 in every	119
Cabinet-makers and upholsterers	1 in every	128
Shoemakers	1 in every	130

Compositors and printers	1 in every	142
Brush-makers	1 in every	145
Carpenters, joiners, and wheelwrights	1 in every	150
Bakers	1 in every	167
Brass-founders	1 in every	177
Tailors	1 in every	177
Comb-makers	1 in every	178
Coopers	1 in every	178
Surveyors	1 in every	198
Fell-mongers	1 in every	203
Average for all London	1 in every	219
Glass-cutters	1 in every	229
Bedstead-makers	1 in every	235
Butchers	1 in every	248
Bookbinders	1 in every	255
Mendicants	1 in every	256
Engineers	1 in every	265
Miners	1 in every	267
Lace-makers	1 in every	273
Poulterers	1 in every	273
Furriers	1 in every	274
Straw-bonnet-makers	1 in every	277
Trimming and button-makers	1 in every	277
Ostlers and grooms	1 in every	286
Drovers	1 in every	297
Hairdressers	1 in every	320
Pipe-makers	1 in every	340
Clerks and shopmen	1 in every	346
Hatters	1 in every	350
Tin-men	1 in every	354
Tallow-chandlers	1 in every	364
Servants	1 in every	377
Cork-cutters	1 in every	380
Jewellers and watchmakers	1 in every	411
Umbrella-makers	1 in every	415
Sailmakers	1 in every	455
Carvers and gilders	1 in every	500
Gunsmiths	1 in every	554
Trunk-makers	1 in every	569

Chair-makers	1 in every	586
Fishmongers	1 in every	643
Tanners	1 in every	643
Musicians	1 in every	730
Leather-dressers and curriers	1 in every	802
Coach-makers	1 in every	989
Engravers	1 in every	1,133
Shipwrights	1 in every	1,358
Artists	1 in every	1,374
Drapers	1 in every	2,047
Milliners and dressmakers	1 in every	10,390

Of the disease and fever which mark the course of the vagrants wheresoever they go, I have before spoken. The 'tramp-fever', as the most dangerous infection of the casual wards is significantly termed, is of a typhoid character, and seems to be communicated particularly to those who wash the clothes of the parties suffering from it. This was likewise one of the characteristics of cholera. That the habitual vagrants should be the means of spreading a pestilence over the country in their wanderings will not be wondered at, when we find it stated in the Poor Law Report on Vagrancy, that 'in very few workhouses do means exist of drying the clothes of these paupers when they come in wet, and it often happens that a considerable number are, of necessity, placed together wet, filthy, infested with vermin, and diseased, in a small, unventilated space.' 'The majority of tramps, again,' we are told, 'have a great aversion to being washed and cleaned. A regular tramper cannot bear it; but a distressed man would be thankful for it.' [. . .]

The causes and encouragements of vagrancy are twofold, – *direct* and *indirect*. The roving disposition to which, as I have shown, vagrancy is *directly* ascribable, proceeds (as I have said) partly from a certain physical conformation or temperament, but mainly from a non-inculcation of industrial habits and moral purposes in youth. The causes from which the vagabondism of the young *indirectly* proceeds are:

1. The neglect or tyranny of parents or masters. (This appears to be a most prolific source.)
2. Bad companions.

3. Bad books, which act like the bad companions in depraving the taste, and teaching the youth to consider that approvable which to all rightly constituted minds is morally loathsome.

4. Bad amusements – as penny-theatres, where the scenes and characters described in the bad books are represented in a still more attractive form. Mr Ainsworth's *Rookwood*, with Dick Turpin 'in his habit as he lived in', is now in the course of being performed nightly at one of the East-end saloons.

5. Bad institutions – as, for instance, the different refuges scattered throughout the country, and which, enabling persons to live without labour, are the means of attracting large numbers of the most idle and dissolute classes to the several cities where the charities are dispensed. [. . .]

A really fine-looking lad of eighteen gave me the following statement. He wore a sort of frock-coat, very thin, buttoned about him, old cloth trousers, and bad shoes. His shirt was tolerably good and clean, and altogether he had a tidy look and an air of quickness, but not of cunning:

'My father,' he said, 'was a bricklayer in Shoreditch parish, and my mother took in washing. They did pretty well; but they're dead and buried two years and a half ago. I used to work in brick-fields at Ball's-pond, living with my parents, and taking home every farthing I earned. I earned 18*s.* a week, working from five in the morning until sunset. They had only me. I can read and write middling; when my parents died, I had to look out for myself. I was off work, attending to my father and mother when they were sick. They died within about three weeks of each other, and I lost my work, and I had to part with my clothes; before that I tried to work in brick-fields, and couldn't get it, and work grew slack. When my parents died I was thirteen; and I sometimes got to sleep in the unions; but that was stopped, and then I took to the lodging-houses, and there I met with lads who were enjoying themselves at push-halfpenny and cards; and they were thieves, and they tempted me to join them, and I did for once – but only once. I then went begging about the streets and thieving, as I knew the others do. I used to pick pockets. I worked for myself, because I thought that would be best. I had no fence at all – no pals at first, nor anything. I worked by myself for a time. I sold the handkerchiefs I got to Jews in the streets, chiefly in

Field-lane, for 1s. 6d., but I have got as much as 3s. 6d. for your real fancy ones. One of these buyers wanted to cheat me out of 6d., so I would have no more dealings with him. The others paid me. The "Kingsmen" they call the best handkerchiefs – those that have the pretty-looking flowers on them. Some are only worth 4d. or 5d., some's not worth taking. Those I gave away to strangers, boys like myself, or wore them myself, round my neck. I only threw one away, but it was all rags, though he looked quite like a gentleman that had it. Lord Mayor's day and such times is the best for us. Last Lord Mayor's day I got four handkerchiefs, and I made 11s. There was a 6d. tied up in the corner of one handkerchief; another was pinned to the pocket, but I got it out, and after that another chap had him, and cut his pocket clean away, but there was nothing in it. I generally picked my men – regular swells, or good-humoured looking men. I've often followed them a mile. I once got a purse with 3s. 6d. in it from a lady when the Coal Exchange was opened. I made 8s. 6d. that day – the purse and handkerchiefs. That's the only lady I ever robbed. I was in the crowd when Manning and his wife were hanged. I wanted to see if they died game, as I heard them talk so much about them at our house. I was there all night. I did four good handkerchiefs and a rotten one not worth picking up. I saw them hung. I was right under the drop. I was a bit startled when they brought him up and put the rope round his neck and the cap on, and then they brought her out. All said he was hung innocently; it was she that should have been hung by herself. They both dropped together, and I felt faintified, but I soon felt all right again. The police drove us away as soon as it was over, so that I couldn't do any more business; besides, I was knocked down in the crowd and jumped upon, and I won't go to see another hung in a hurry. He didn't deserve it, but she did, every inch of her. I can't say I thought, while I was seeing the execution, that the life I was leading would ever bring me to the gallows. After I'd worked by myself a bit, I got to live in a house where lads like me, big and little, were accommodated. We paid 3d. a-night. It was always full; there was twenty or twenty-one of us. We enjoyed ourselves middling. I was happy enough: we drank sometimes, chiefly beer, and some-times a drop of gin. One would say, "I've done so much", and another, "I've done so much;" and stand a drop. The best I ever heard done was 2l. for two coats from a tailor's, near Bow-church,

Cheapside. That was by one of my pals. We used to share our money with those who did nothing for a day, and they shared with us when we rested. There never was any blabbing. We wouldn't do one another out of a farthing. Of a night some one would now and then read hymns, out of books they sold about the streets – I'm sure they were hymns; or else we'd read stories about Jack Sheppard and Dick Turpin, and all through that set. They were large thick books, borrowed from the library. They told how they used to break open the houses, and get out of Newgate, and how Dick got away to York. We used to think Jack and them very fine fellows. I wished I could be like Jack (I did then), about the blankets in his escape, and that old house in West-street – it is a ruin still. We played cards and dominoes sometimes at our house, and at pushing a halfpenny over the table along five lines. We struck the halfpenny from the edge of the table, and according to what line it settled on was the game – like as they play at the Glass-house – that's the "model lodging-house" they calls it. Cribbage was always played at cards. I can only play cribbage. We have played for a shilling a game, but oftener a penny. It was always fair play. That was the way we passed the time when we were not out. We used to keep quiet, or the police would have been down upon us. They knew of the place. They took one boy there. I wondered what they wanted. They catched him at the very door. We lived pretty well; anything we liked to get, when we'd money: we cooked it ourselves. The master of the house was always on the look-out to keep out those who had no business there. No girls were admitted. The master of the house had nothing to do with what we got. I don't know of any other such house in London; I don't think there are any. The master would sometimes drink with us – a-larking like. He used us pretty kindly at times. I have been three times in prison, three months each time; the Compter, Brixton, and Maidstone. I went down to Maidstone fair, and was caught by a London policeman down there. He was dressed as a bricklayer. Prison always made me worse, and as I had nothing given me when I came out, I had to look out again. I generally got hold of something before I had been an hour out of prison. I'm now heartily sick of this life. I wish I'd been transported with some others from Maidstone, where I was tried.'

[. . .]

Statement of a returned convict
[*volume iii. pp.386–388*]
I shall now give the statement of a man who was selected at random from amongst a number such as himself, congregated in one of the most respectable lodging-houses. He proved, on examination, to be a returned convict, and one who had gone through the severest bodily and mental agony. He had lived in the bush, and been tried for his life. He was an elderly-looking man, whose hair was just turning grey, and in whose appearance there was nothing remarkable, except that his cheek-bones were unusually high, and that his face presented that collected and composed expression which is common to men exposed to habitual watchfulness from constant danger. He gave me the following statement. His dress was bad, but differed in nothing from that of a long-distressed mechanic. He said:

'I am now 43 [he looked much older], and had respectable parents, and a respectable education. I am a native of London. When I was young I was fond of a roving life, but cared nothing about drink. I liked to see "life", as it was called, and was fond of the company of women. Money was no object in those days; it was like picking up dirt in the streets. I ran away from home. My parents were very kind to me; indeed, I think I was used too well, I was petted so, when I was between 12 and 13. I got acquainted with some boys at Bartlemy-fair a little before that, and saw them spending lots of money and throwing at cock-shies, and such-like; and one of them said, "Why don't you come out like us?" So afterwards I ran away and joined them. I was not kept shorter of money than other boys like me, but I couldn't settle. I couldn't fix my mind to any regular business but a waterman's, and my friends wouldn't hear of that. There was nine boys of us among the lot that I joined, but we didn't all work together. All of 'em came to be sent to Van Dieman's Land as transports except one, and he was sent to Sydney. While we were in London it was a merry life, with change of scene, for we travelled about. We were successful in nearly all our plans for several months. I worked in Fleet Street, and could make 3*l.* a week at handkerchiefs alone, sometimes falling across a pocket-book. The best handkerchiefs then brought 4*s.* in Field-lane. Our chief enjoyments were at the "Free and Easy", where all the thieves and young women went, and sang and danced. I had a young woman for a partner then; she went out to Van Diemen's Land. She went on the lift in London [shopping and stealing from the counter]. She was clever at it. I carried on in this way for about 15 months, when I was grabbed for an attempt on a gentleman's pocket by St Paul's Cathedral, on a grand charity procession day. I had two months in the Old Horse [Bridewell]. I never thought of my parents at this time – I wouldn't. I was two years and a half at this same trade. One week was very like another, – successes and escapes, and free-and-easies, and games of all sorts, made up the life. At the end of the two years and a half I got into the way of forged Bank-of-England notes. A man I knew in the course of business, said, "I would cut that game of 'smatter-hauling' [stealing handkerchiefs], and do a little 'soft' [pass bad notes]. So I did, and was very successful at first. I had a mate. He afterwards went out to Sydney, too, for 14 years. I went stylishly dressed as a gentleman, with a watch in my pocket, to pass my notes. I passed a good many in drapers' shops, also at tailors' shops. I never tried jewellers, they're reckoned too good judges. The notes were all finnies [5l. notes], and a good imitation. I made more money at this game, but lived as before, and had my partner still. I was fond of her; she was a nice girl, and I never found that she wronged me in any way. I thought at four months' end of retiring into the country with gambling-tables, as the risk was becoming considerable. They hung them for it in them days, but that never daunted me the least in life. I saw Cashman hung for that gunsmith's shop on Snow-hill, and I saw Fauntleroy hung, and a good many others, but it gave me no uneasiness and no fear. The gallows had no terror for people in my way of life. I started into the country with another man and his wife – his lawful wife – for I had a few words with my own young woman, or I shouldn't have left her behind me, or, indeed, have started at all. We carried gambling on in different parts of the country for six months. We made most at the E. O. tables, – not those played with a ball, they weren't in vogue then, but throwing dice for prizes marked on a table. The highest prize was ten guineas, but the dice were so made that no prize could be thrown; the numbers were not regular as in good dice, and they were loaded as well. If anybody asked to see them, we had good dice ready to show. All sorts played with us. London men and all were taken in. We made most at the races. My mate and his wife told me that at the last Newmarket meeting we attended, 65l. was made, but they rowed in the same boat. I know they got a deal more. The 65l. was shared in three equal portions, but I had to maintain the horse and cart out of my own share. We used to go out into the roads [highway robbery] between races, and if we met an "old bloke" [man] we "propped him" [knocked him down], and robbed him. We did good stakes that way, and were never found out. We lived as well as any gentleman in the land. Our E. O. table was in a tilted cart. I stayed with this man and his wife two months. She was good-looking, so as to attract people. I thought they didn't use me altogether right, so at Braintree I gave another man in the same way of business 25l. for his kit – horse, harness, tilted-cart, and table. I gave him two good 5l. notes and three bad ones, for I worked that way still, not throwing much of a chance away. I came to London for a hawker's stock, braces and such-like, to sell on the road, just to take the down off [remove suspicion]. In the meantime, the man that I bought the horse, &c., of, had been nailed passing a bad note, and he stated who he got it from, and I was traced. He was in a terrible rage to find himself done, particularly as he used to do the same to other people himself. He got acquitted for that there note after he had me "pinched" [arrested]. I got "fullied" [fully committed]. I was tried at the "Start" [Old Bailey], and pleaded guilty to the minor offence [that of utterance, not knowing the note to be forged], or I should have been hanged for it then. It was a favourable sessions when I was tried. Thirty-six were cast for death, and only one was "topped" [hanged], the very one that expected to be "turned up" [acquitted] for highway robbery. I was sentenced to 14 years' transportation. I was ten weeks in the *Bellerophon* hulk at Sheerness, and was then taken to Hobart Town, Van Dieman's Land, in the *Sir Godfrey Webster*. At Hobart Town sixty of us were picked out to go to Launceston. There [at Launceston] we lay for four days in an old church, guarded by constables; and then the settlers came there from all parts, and picked their men out. I got a very bad master. He put me to harvest work that I had never even seen done before, and I had the care of pigs as wild as wild boars. After that I was sent to Launceston with two letters from my master to the superintendent, and the other servants thought I had luck to get away from Red Barks to Launceston, which was 16 miles off. I then worked in a Government potato-field; in the Government charcoal-works for about 11 months; and then was in the Marine department, going by water from Launceston to George Town, taking Government officers down in gigs, provisions in boats, and such-like. There was a crew of six [convicts] in the gigs, and four in the watering-boats. All the time I consider I was very hardly treated. I hadn't clothes half the time, being allowed only two slop-suits in a year, and no bed to lie on when we had to stay out all night with the boats by the river Tamar. With 12 years' service at this my time was up, but I had incurred several punishments before it was up. The first was 25 lashes, because a bag of flour had been burst, and I picked up a capful. The flogging is dreadfully severe, a soldier's is nothing to it. I once had 50 lashes, for taking a hat in a joke when I was tipsy; and a soldier had 300 the same morning. I was flogged as a convict, and he as a soldier; and when we were both at the same hospital after the flogging, and saw each other's backs, the other convicts said to me, "D— it, you've got it this time;" and the soldier said, when he saw my back, "You've got it twice as bad I have." "No", said the doctor, "ten times as bad – he's been flogged; but you, in comparison, have only had a child's whipping." The cats the convicts were then flogged with were each six feet long, made out of the log-line of a ship of 500 tons burden; nine over-end knots were in each tail, and nine tails whipped at each end with wax-end. With this we had half-minute lashes; a quick lashing would have been certain death. One convict who had 75 lashes was taken from the triangles to the watch-house in Launceston, and was asked if he would have some tea, – he was found to be dead. The military surgeon kept on saying in this case, "Go on, do your duty." I was mustered there, as was every hand belonging to the Government, and saw it, and heard the doctor. When I was first flogged, there was inquiry among my fellow-convicts, as to "How did D— (meaning me) stand it – did he sing?" The answer was, "He was a pebble;" that is, I never once said, "Oh!" or gave out any expression of the pain I suffered. I took my flogging like a stone. If I had sung, some of the convicts would have given me some lush with a locust in it [laudanum hocussing], and when I was asleep would have given me a crack on the head that would have laid me straight. That first flogging made me ripe. I said to myself, "I can take it like a bullock." I could have taken the flogger's life at the time, I felt such revenge. Flogging always gives that feeling; I know it does, from what I've heard others say who had been flogged like myself. In all I had 875 lashes at my different punishments. I used to boast of it at last. I would say, "I don't care, I can take it till they see my backbone." After a flogging, I've rubbed my back against a wall, just to show my bravery like, and squeezed the congealed blood out of it. Once I would not let them dress my back after a flogging, and I had 25 additional for that. At last I bolted to Hobart Town, 120 miles off. There I was taken before Mr H—, the magistrate, himself a convict formerly, I believe from the Irish Rebellion; but he was a good man to a prisoner. He ordered me 50, and sent me back to Launceston. At Launceston I was "fullied" by a bench of magistrates, and had 100. Seven years before my time was up I took to the bush. I could stand it no longer, of course not. In the bush I met men with whom, if I had been seen associating, I should have been hanged on any slight charge, such as Brittan was and his pals.'

I am not at liberty to continue this man's statement at present: it would be a breach of the trust reposed in me. Suffice it, he was in after days tried for his life. Altogether it was a most extraordinary statement; and, from confirmations I received, was altogether truthful. He declared that he was so sick of the life he was now leading, that he would, as a probation, work on any kind of land anywhere for nothing, just to get out of it. He pronounced the lodging-houses the grand encouragements and concealments of crime, though he might be speaking against himself, he said, as he had always hidden safely there during the hottest search. A policeman once walked through the ward in search of him, and he was in bed. He knew the policeman well, and was as well known to the officer, but he was not recognised. He attributed his escape to the thick, bad atmosphere of the place giving his features a different look, and to his having shaved off his whiskers, and pulled his nightcap over his head. The officer, too, seemed half-sick, he said.

It ought also to be added, that this man stated that the severity of the Government in this penal colony was so extreme, that men thought little of giving others a knock on the head with an axe, to get hanged out of the way. Under the discipline of Captain Macconochie, however, who introduced better order with a kindlier system, there wasn't a man but what would have laid down his life for him.

Lives of the boy inmates of the casual
wards of the London workhouses

[*volume iii. pp.388–396*]

[. . .]

'I'm a native of Wisbeach, in Cambridgeshire, and am sixteen. My father was a shoemaker, and my mother died when I was five years old, and my father married again. I was sent to school, and can read and write well. My father and step-mother were kind enough to me. I was apprenticed to a tailor three years ago, but I wasn't long with him; I runned away. I think it was three months I was with him when I first runned away. It was in August – I got as far as Boston in Lincolnshire, and was away a fortnight. I had 4s. 6d. of my own money when I started, and that lasted two or three days. I stopped in lodging-houses until my money was gone, and then I slept anywhere – under the hedges, or anywhere. I didn't see so much of life then, but I've seen plenty of it since. I had to beg my way back from Boston, but was very awkward at first. I lived on turnips mainly. My reason for running off was because my master ill-used me so; he beat me, and kept me from my meals, and made me sit up working late at nights for a punishment: but it was more to his good than to punish me. I hated to be confined to a tailor's shopboard, but I would rather do that sort of work now than hunger about like this. But you see, sir, God punishes you when you don't think of it. When I went back my father was glad to see me, and he wouldn't have me go back again to my master, and my indentures were cancelled. I stayed at home seven months, doing odd jobs, in driving sheep, or any country work, but I always wanted to be off to sea. I liked the thoughts of going to sea far better than tailoring. I determined to go to sea if I could. When a dog's determined to have a bone, it's not easy to hinder him. I didn't read stories about the sea then, not even *Robinson Crusoe*, – indeed I haven't read that still, but I know very well there is such a book. My father had no books but religious books; they were all of a religious turn, and what people might think dull, but they never made me dull. I read Wesley's and Watts's hymns, and religious magazines of different connections. I had a natural inclination for the sea, and would like to get to it now. I've read a good deal about it since – Clark's *Lives of Pirates*, *Tales of Shipwrecks*, and other things in penny numbers (Clark's I got out of a library though). I was what people called a deep boy for a book; and am still. Whenever I had a penny, after I got a bellyful of victuals, it went for a book, but I haven't bought many lately. I did buy one yesterday – the *Family Herald* – one I often read when I can get it. There's good reading in it; it elevates your mind – anybody that has a mind for studying. It has good tales in it. I never read *Jack Sheppard*, – that is, I haven't read the big book that's written about him; but I've often heard the boys and men talk about it at the lodging-houses and other places. When they haven't their bellies and money to think about they sometimes talk about books; but for such books as them – that's as *Jack* – I haven't a partiality. I've read *Windsor Castle*, and *The Tower* – they're by the same man. I liked *Windsor Castle*, and all about Henry VIII, and Herne the hunter. It's a book that's connected with history, and that's a good thing in it. I like adventurous tales. I know very little about theatres, as I was never in one.

'Well, after that seven months – I was kindly treated all the time – I runned away again to get to sea; and hearing so much talk about this big London, I comed to it.'

[. . .]

'I was a week in London before I knew where I was. I didn't know where to go. I slept on door-steps, or anywhere. I used often to stand on London-bridge, but I didn't know where to go to get to sea, or anything of that kind. I was sadly hungered, regularly starved; and I saw so many policemen, I durstn't beg – and I dare not now, in London. I got crusts, but I can hardly tell how I lived. One night I was sleeping under a railway-arch, somewhere about Bishopsgate-street, and a policeman came and asked me what I was up to? I told him I had no place to go to, so he said I must go along with him. In the morning he took me and four or five others to a house in a big street. I don't know where; and a man – a magistrate, I suppose he was – heard what the policeman had to say, and he said there was always a lot of lads there about the arches, young thieves, that gave him a great deal of trouble, and I was one associated with them. I declare I didn't know any of the other boys, nor any boys in

London – not a soul; and I was under the arch by myself, and only that night. I never saw the policeman himself before that, as I know of. I got fourteen days of it, and they took me in an omnibus, but I don't know to what prison. I was committed for being a rogue and something else. I didn't very well hear what other things I was, but "rogue" I know was one. They were very strict in prison, and I wasn't allowed to speak. I was put to oakum some days, and others on a wheel. That's the only time I was ever in prison, and I hope it will always be the only time. Something may turn up – there's nobody knows. When I was turned out I hadn't a farthing given to me. And so I was again in the streets, without knowing a creature, and without a farthing in my pocket, and nothing to get one with but my tongue. I set off that day for the country. I didn't try to get a ship, because I didn't know where to go to ask, and I had got ragged, and they wouldn't hear me out if I asked any people about the bridges. I took the first road that offered, and got to Greenwich. I couldn't still think of going back home. I would if I had had clothes, but they were rags, and I had no shoes but a pair of old slippers. I was sometimes sorry I left home, but then I began to get used to travelling, and to beg a bit in the villages. I had no regular mate to travel with, and no sweetheart. I slept in the unions whenever I could get in – that's in the country. I didn't never sleep in the London workhouses till afterwards. In some country places there were as many as forty in the casual wards, men, women, and children; in some, only two or three. There used to be part boys, like myself, but far more bigger than I was; they were generally from eighteen to twenty-three: London chaps, chiefly, I believe. They were a regularly jolly set. They used to sing and dance a part of the nights and mornings in the wards, and I got to sing and dance with them. We were all in a mess; there was no better or no worse among us. We used to sing comic and sentimental songs, both. I used to sing 'Tom Elliott', that's a sea song, for I hankered about the sea, and 'I'm Afloat'. I hardly know any but sea-songs. Many used to sing indecent songs; they're impudent blackguards. They used to sell these songs among the others, but I never sold any of them, and I never had any, though I know some, from hearing them often. We told stories sometimes; romantic tales, some; others blackguard kind of tales, about bad women; and others about thieving and roguery; not so much about what they'd done themselves, as about some big thief that was very clever at stealing, and could trick anybody. Not stories such as Dick Turpin or Jack Sheppard, or things that's in history, but inventions. [. . .]

'Sometimes there was fighting in the casual wards. Sometimes I was in it, I was like the rest. We jawed each other often, calling names and coming to fight at last. At Romsey a lot of young fellows broke all the windows they could get at, because they were too late to be admitted. They broke them from the outside. We couldn't get at them from inside. I've carried on begging, and going from union to union to sleep, until now. Once I got work in Northampton with a drover. I kept working when he'd a job, from August last to the week before Christmas. I always tried to get a ship in a sea-port, but couldn't. I've been to Portsmouth, Plymouth, Bristol, Southampton, Ipswich, Liverpool, Brighton, Dover, Shoreham, Hastings, and all through Lincolnshire, Nottinghamshire, Cambridgeshire, and Suffolk – not in Norfolk – they won't let you go there. I don't know why. All this time I used to meet boys like myself, but mostly bigger and older; plenty of them could read and write, some were gentlemen's sons, they said. Some had their young women with them that they'd taken up with, but I never was much with them. I often wished I was at home again, and do now, but I can't think of going back in these rags; and I don't know if my father's dead or alive [his voice trembled], but I'd like to be there and have it over. I can't face meeting them in these rags, and I've seldom had better, I make so little money. I'm unhappy at times, but I get over it better than I used, as I get accustomed to this life. I never heard anything about home since I left. I have applied at the Marine Society here, but it's no use. If I could only get to sea, I'd be happy; and I'd be happy if I could get home, and would, but for the reasons I've told you.' [. . .]

Of the character of the vagrants frequenting the unions in the centre of the metropolis, and the system pursued there, one description will serve as a type of the whole.

At the Holborn workhouse (St Andrew's) there are two casual wards, established just after the passing of the Poor Law Amendment Act in 1834. The men's ward will contain 40, and the women's 20. The wards are underground, but dry, clean, and comfortable. When there was a 'severe pressure from without', as a porter described it to me, as many as 106 men and women have been received on one night, but some were disposed in other parts of the workhouse away from the casual wards.

'Two years and a half ago, "a glut of Irish" [I give the words of my informant] came over and besieged the doors incesantly; and when above a hundred were admitted, as many were remaining outside, and when locked out they lay in the streets stretched along by the almshouse close to the workhouse in Gray's-inn-lane.' I again give the statement (which afterwards was verified) *verbatim*: 'They lay in camps,' he said, 'in their old cloaks, some having brought blankets and rugs with them for the purpose of sleeping out; pots, and kettles, and vessels for cooking when they camp; for in many parts of Ireland they do nothing – I've heard from people that have been there – but wander about; and these visitors to the workhouse behaved just like gipsies, combing their hair and dressing themselves. The girls' heads, some of them, looked as if they were full of caraway seeds – vermin, sir – shocking! I had to sit up all night; and the young women from Ireland – fine-looking young women; some of them finer-looking women than the English, well made and well formed, but uncultivated – seemed happy enough in the casual wards, singing songs all night long, but not too loud. Some would sit up all night washing their clothes, coming to me for water. They had a cup of tea, if they were poorly. They made themselves at home, the children did, as soon as they got inside; they ran about like kittens used to a place. The young women were often full of joke; but I never heard an indecent word from any of them, nor an oath, and I have no doubt, not in the least, that they were chaste and modest. Fine young women, too, sir. I have said, "Pity young women like you should be carrying on this way," (for I felt for them) and they would say, "What can we do? It's better than starving in Ireland, this workhouse is." I used to ask them how they got over, and they often told me their passages were paid, chiefly to Bristol, Liverpool, and Newport, in Monmouthshire. They told me that was done to get rid of them. They told me that they didn't know by whom; but some said, they believed the landlord paid the captain. Some declared they knew it, and that it was done just to get rid of them. Others told me the captain would bring them over for any trifle they had; for he would say, "I shall have to take you back again, and I can charge my price then." The men were uncultivated fellows compared to the younger women. We have had old men with children who could speak English, and the old man and his wife could not speak a word of it. When asked the age of their children (the children were the interpreters), they would open the young creatures' mouths and count their teeth, just as horse-dealers do, and then they would tell the children in Irish what to answer, and the children would answer in English. The old people could never tell their own age. The man would give his name, but his wife would give her maiden name. I would say to an elderly man, "Give me your name." "Dennis Murphy, your honour." Then to his wife, "And your name?" "The widdy Mooney, your honour." "But you're married?" "Sure, then, yes, by Father — ." This is the case with them still. Last night we took in a family, and I asked the mother — there was only a woman and three children — her name. "The widdy Callaghan, indeed, then, sir." "But your Christian name?" "The widdy [widow]," was the only answer. It's shocking, sir, what ignorance is, and what their sufferings is. My heart used to ache for the poor creatures, and yet they seemed happy. Habit's a great thing — second nature, even when people's shook. The Irishmen behaved well among themselves; but the English cadgers were jealous of the Irish, and chaffed them, as spoiling their trade — that's what the cadging fellows did. The Irish were quiet, poor things, but they were provoked to quarrel, and many a time I've had to turn the English rips out. The Irish were always very thankful for what they had, if it was only a morsel; the English cadger is never satisfied. I don't mean the decent beat-out man, but the regular cadger, that won't work, and isn't a good beggar, and won't starve, so they steal. Once, now and then, there was some suspicion about the Irish admitted, that they had money, but that was never but in those that had families. It was taken from them, and given back in the morning. They wouldn't have been admitted again if they had any amount. It was a kindness to take their money, or the English rascals would have robbed them. I'm an Englishman, but I speak the truth of my own countrymen, as I do of the Irish. The English we had in the casual wards were generally a bad cadging set, as saucy as could be, particularly men that I knew, from their accent, came from Nottinghamshire. I'd tell one directly. I've heard them, of a night, brag of their dodges – how they'd done through the day – and the best places to get money. They would talk of gentlemen in London. I've often heard them say —, in Piccadilly, was good; but they seldom mentioned names, only described the houses, especially club-houses in St James's-street. They would tell just where it was in the street, and how many windows there was in it, and the best time to go, and "you're sure of grub", they'd say. Then they'd tell of gentlemen's seats in the country – sure cards. They seldom give names, and, I believe, don't know them, but described the houses and the gentlemen. Some were good for bread and money, some for bread and ale. As to the decent people, we had but few, and I used to be sorry for them when they had to mix with the cadgers; but when the cadgers saw a stranger, they used their slang. I was up to it. I've heard it many a night when I sat up, and they thought I was asleep. I wasn't to be had like the likes o' them. The poor mechanic would sit like a lost man – scared, sir. There might be one deserving character to thirty cadgers. We have had gipsies in the casual wards; but they're not admitted a second time, they steal so. We haven't one Scotch person in a month, or a Welshman, or perhaps two Welshmen, in a month, among the casuals. They come from all counties in England. I've been told by inmates of "the casual", that they had got 2s. 6d. from the relieving officers, particularly in Essex and Suffolk – different unions – to start them to London when the "straw-yards" [the asylums for the houseless] were opened; but there's a many very decent people. How they suffer before they come to that! you can't fancy how much; and so there should be straw-yards in a Christian land – we'll call it a Christian land, sir. There's far more good people in the straw-yards than the casuals; the dodgers is less frequent there, considering the numbers. It's shocking to think a decent mechanic's houseless. When he's beat out, he's like a bird out of a cage; he doesn't know where to go, or how to get a bit – but don't the cadgers!' The expense of relieving the people in the casual ward was twopence per head, and the numbers admitted for the last twelve months averaged only twelve nightly. [. . .]

9

CLASSIFICATION OF THE WORKERS
AND NON-WORKERS

In no respect did Mayhew's self-image as a natural scientist find greater expression than in his passion for classification and the making of categories and sub-categories. Mayhew was convinced that the ways in which information was ordered into meaningful units held the key to generalisation, social analysis and the discovery of natural systems. In these extracts we see him at work searching for a uniform basis for the organising and arrangement of the labouring and non-labouring population into coherent divisions. He was also fascinated by the idea of mapping characteristics of the poor on the basis of statistical information. Much later Charles Booth was to adopt this technique.

GANG OF COAL-WHIPPERS AT WORK BELOW BRIDGE

[*from a sketch*]

CLASSIFICATION OF THE WORKERS
AND NON-WORKERS

Of the workers and non-workers
[*volume iv. pp.3–12*]

[. . .] all society would appear to arrange itself into four different classes:

1. THOSE THAT WILL WORK
2. THOSE THAT CANNOT WORK
3. THOSE THAT WILL NOT WORK
4. THOSE THAT NEED NOT WORK

Under one or other section of this quadruple division, every member, not only of our community, but of every other civilised State, must necessarily be included; the rich, the poor, the industrious, the idle, the honest, the dishonest, the virtuous, and the vicious – each and all must be comprised therein.

Let me now proceed specially to treat of each of these classes – to distribute under one or other of these four categories the diverse modes of living peculiar to the members of our own community, and so to enunciate, for the first time, the natural history, as it were, of the industry and idleness of Great Britain in the nineteenth century.

It is no easy matter, however, to classify the different kinds of labour scientifically. To arrange the several varieties of work into 'orders', and to group the manifold species of arts under a few comprehensive genera – so that the mind may grasp the whole at one effort – is a task of a most perplexing character. [. . .] It is impossible, however, to proceed with the present inquiry without making some attempt at systematic arrangement; for of all scientific processes, the classification of the various phenomena, in connection with a given subject, is perhaps the most important;

indeed, if we consider that the function of cognition is essentially *discriminative*, it is evident, that without distinguishing between one object and another, there can be no knowledge, nor, indeed, any perception. Even as the seizing of a particular difference causes the mind to *apprehend* the special character of an object, so does the discovery of the agreements and differences among the several phenomena of a subject enable the understanding to *comprehend* it. What the generalisation of events is to the ascertainment of natural laws, the generalisation of things is to the discovery of natural systems. But classification is no less dangerous than it is important to science; for in precisely the same proportion as a correct grouping of objects into genera and species, orders and varieties, expands and assists our understanding, so does any erroneous arrangement cripple and retard all true knowledge. The reduction of all external substances into four elements by the ancients — earth, air, fire, and water — perhaps did more to obstruct the progress of chemical science than even a prohibition of the study could have effected.

But the branches of industry are so multifarious, the divisions of labour so minute and manifold, that it seems at first almost impossible to reduce them to any system. Moreover, the crude generalisations expressed in the names of the several arts, render the subject still more perplexing.

Some kinds of workmen, for example, are called after the *articles they make* — as saddlers, hatters, boot-makers, dress-makers, breeches-makers, stay-makers, lace-makers, button-makers, glovers, cabinet-makers, artificial-flower-makers, ship-builders, organ-builders, boat-builders, nailers, pin-makers, basket-makers, pump-makers, clock and watch makers, wheel-wrights, ship-wrights, and so forth.

Some operatives, on the other hand, take their names not from what they make, but from the *kind of work they perform*. Hence we have carvers, joiners, bricklayers, weavers, knitters, engravers, embroiderers, tanners, curriers, bleachers, thatchers, lime-burners, glass-blowers, seamstresses, assayers, refiners, embossers, chasers, painters, paper-hangers, printers, book-binders, cab-drivers, fish-ermen, graziers, and so on.

Other artisans, again, are styled after the *materials upon which they work*, such as tin-men, jewellers, lapidaries, goldsmiths, braziers, plumbers, pewterers, glaziers, &c. &c.

And lastly, a few operatives are named after the *tools they use*; thus we have ploughmen, sawyers, and needlewomen.

But these divisions, it is evident, are as unscientific as they are arbitrary; nor would it be possible, by adopting such a classification, to arrive at any practical result. [. . .]

If, with the view of obtaining some more precise information concerning the several branches of industry, we turn our attention to the Government analysis of the different modes of employment among the people, we shall find that for all purposes of a scientific or definite character the Occupation Abstract of the Census of this country is comparatively useless. Previous to 1841, the sole attempt made at generalisation was the division of the entire industrial community into three orders, viz.:

I. *Those employed in Agriculture*.
   1. Agricultural Occupiers.
     a. Employing Labourers.
     b. Not employing Labourers.
   2. Agricultural Labourers.
II. *Those employed in Manufactures*.
   1. Employed in Manufactures.
   2. Employed in making Manufacturing Machinery.
III. *All other Classes*.
   1. Employed in Retail Trade or in Handicraft, as Masters or Workmen.
   2. Capitalists, Bankers, Professional, and other educated men.
   3. Labourers employed in labour not Agricultural – as Miners, Quarriers, Fishermen, Porters, &c.
   4. Male Servants.
   5. Other Males, 20 years of age.

The defects of this arrangement must be self-evident to all who have paid the least attention to economical science. It offends against both the laws of logical division, the parts being neither distinct nor equal to the whole. In the first place, what is a manufacturer ? and how is such an one to be distinguished from one employed in handicraft ? How do the workers in metal, as the 'tin manufacturers', 'lead manufacturers', 'iron manufacturers' – who are one and all classed under the head of manufacturers – differ, in an economical point of view, from the workers in wood, as the carpenters and joiners, the cabinet-makers, ship-builders, &c., who are all classed under the head of handicraftsmen ? [. . .]

The Occupation Abstract of the Census of 1841, though far more comprehensive than the one preceding it, is equally unsatisfactory and unphilosophical. In this document the several members of Society are thus classified:

1. *Persons engaged in Commerce, Trade, and Manufacture.*
2. *Agriculture.*
3. *Labour, not Agricultural.*
4. *Army and Navy Merchant Seamen, Fishermen, and Watermen.*
5. *Professions and other pursuits requiring education.*
6. *Government, Civil Service, and Municipal and Parochial Officers.*
7. *Domestic Servants.*
8. *Persons of Independent Means.*
9. *Almspeople, Pensioners, Paupers, Lunatics, and Prisoners.*
10. *Remainder of Population. including Women and Children.*

Here it will be seen that the defects arising from drawing distinctions where no real differences exist, are avoided, those engaged in handicrafts being included under the same head as those engaged in manufacture; but the equally grave error of confounding or grouping together occupations which are essentially diverse, is allowed to continue. Accordingly, the first division is made to include those who are engaged in trade and commerce as well as manufacture, though surely – the one belongs strictly to the distributing, and the other to the producing class – occupations which are not only essentially distinct, but of which it is absolutely necessary for a right understanding of the state of the country that we know the proportion that the one bears to the other. Again, the employers in both cases are confounded with the employed, so that, though the capitalists who supply the materials, and pay the wages for the several kinds of work are a distinct body of people from those who do the work, and a body, moreover, that it is of the highest possible importance, in an economical point of view, that we should be able to estimate numerically, – no attempt is made to discriminate the one from the other. Now these three classes, distributors, employers, and operatives, which in the Government returns of the people are jumbled together in one heterogeneous crowd, as if the distinctions between Capital, Labour, and Distribution had never been propounded, are precisely those concerning which the social inquirer desires the most minute information. [. . .]

He, therefore, who would seek to elaborate the natural history of the industry of the people of England, must direct his attention to some social philosopher, who has given the subject more consideration than either princes or Government officials can possibly be expected to devote to it. Among the whole body of economists, Mr Stuart Mill appears to be the only man who has taken a comprehensive and enlightened view of the several functions of society. [. . .]

Now, from the above it will appear, that there are four distinct classes of workers:

1. ENRICHERS, or those who are employed in producing utilities fixed and embodied in material things, that is to say, in producing exchangeable commodities or riches.
2. AUXILIARIES, or those who are employed in aiding the production of exchangeable commodities.
3. BENEFACTORS, or those who are employed in producing utilities fixed and embodied in human beings, that is to say, in conferring upon them some permanent good.
4. SERVITORS, or those who are employed in rendering some service, that is to say, in conferring some temporary good upon another.

Class 1 is engaged in investing *material* objects with qualities which render them serviceable to others.
Class 2 is engaged in aiding the operations of Class 1.
Class 3 is engaged in conferring on *human beings* qualities which render them serviceable to themselves or others.
Class 4 is engaged in giving a pleasure, averting a pain (during a longer or shorter period), or preventing an inconvenience, by performing some office for others that they would find irksome to do for themselves.

Hence it appears that the operations of the first and third of the above classes, or the Enrichers and Benefactors of Society, tend to leave some *permanent acquisition* in the improved qualities of either persons or things, – whereas the operations of the second and fourth classes, or the Auxiliaries and Servitors, are limited merely to promoting either the labours or the pleasures of the other members of the community. [. . .]

For the more perfect comprehension, however, of the several classes of society, let me subjoin a table in round numbers, calculated from the census of 1841, and including among the first items both the employers as well as employed:

Engaged in Trade and Manufacture	3,000,000
Engaged in Agriculture	1,500,000
Engaged in Mining, Quarrying, and Transit	750,000
Total Employers and Employed	5,250,000
Domestic Servants	1,000,000
Independent persons	500,000
Educated pursuits (including Professions and Fine Arts)	200,000
Government Officers (including Army, Navy, Civil Service, and Parish Officers)	200,000
Alms-people (including Paupers, Prisoners, and Lunatics)	200,000
	7,350,000
Residue of Population (including 3,500,000 wives and 7,500,000 children)	11,000,000
	18,350,000

Now, of the 5,250,000 individuals engaged in Agriculture, Mining, Transit, Manufacture and Trade, it would appear that about one million and a quarter may be considered as employers; and, consequently, that the remaining four millions may be said to represent the numerical strength of the operatives of England and Scotland. Of these about one million, or a quarter of the whole, may be said to be engaged in producing the materials of wealth; and about a quarter of a million, or one-sixteenth of the entire number, in extracting from the soil the substances upon which many of the manufacturers have to operate.

The artisans, or those who are engaged in the several handicrafts or manufactures operating upon the various materials of wealth thus obtained, are distinct from the workmen above-mentioned, belonging to what are called skilled labourers, whereas those who are employed in the collection, extraction, or growing of wealth, belong to the unskilled class.

An artisan is an *educated* handicraftsman, following a calling that requires an apprenticeship of greater or less duration in order to arrive at perfection in it; whereas a labourer's occupation needs no education whatever. Many years must be spent in practising before a man can acquire sufficient manual dexterity to make a pair of boots or a coat; dock labour or porter's work, however, needs neither teaching nor learning, for any man can carry a load or turn a wheel. The artisan, therefore, is literally a handicrafts-man – one who by practice has acquired manual dexterity enough to perform a particular class of work, which is consequently called 'skilled'. The natural classification of artisans, or skilled labourers, appears to be according to the materials upon which they work, for this circumstance seems to constitute the peculiar quality of the art more than the tool used – indeed, it appears to be the principal cause of the modification of the implements in different handicrafts. [. . .]

The most natural mode of grouping the artisans into classes would appear to be according as they pursue some *mechanical* or *chemical* occupation. The former are literally mechanics or handi-craftsmen – the latter chemical manufacturers. The handicraftsmen consist of: (1) The workers in silk, wool, cotton, flax, and hemp – as weavers, spinners, knitters, carpet-makers, lace-makers, rope-makers, canvas-weavers, &c. (2) The workers in skin, gut, and feathers – as tanners, curriers, furriers, feather dressers, &c. (3) The makers up of silken, woollen, cotton, linen, hempen, and leathern materials – as tailors, milliners, shirt-makers, sail-makers, hatters, glove-makers, saddlers, and the like. (4) The workers in wood, as the carpenters, the cabinet-makers, &c. (5) The workers in cane, osier, reed, rush, and straw – as basket-makers, straw-plait manufacturers, thatchers, and the like. (6) The workers in brick and stones – as bricklayers, masons, &c. (7) The workers in glass and earthenware – as potters, glass-blowers, glass-cutters, bottle-makers, glaziers, &c. (8) The workers in metals – as braziers, tinmen, plumbers, gold-smiths, pewterers, copper-smiths, iron-founders, blacksmiths, white-smiths, anchor-smiths, locksmiths, &c. (9) The workers in paper – as the paper-makers, cardboard-makers. (10) The chemical manu-facturers – as powder-makers, white-lead-makers, alkali and acid manufacturers, lucifer match-makers, blacking-makers, ink-makers, soap-boilers, tallow-chandlers, &c. (11) The workers at the superlative or extrinsic arts – that is to say, those which have no manufactures of their own, but which are engaged in adding to the utility or beauty of others – as printing, bookbinding, painting, and decorating, gilding, burnishing, &c.

The circumstances which govern the classification of *trades* are totally different from those regulating the division of work. In trade the convenience of the purchaser is mainly studied, the sale of such articles being associated as are usually required together. Hence the master coachmaker is frequently a harness manufacturer as well, for the purchaser of the one commodity generally stands in need of the other. The painter and house-decorator not only follows the trade of the glazier, but of the plumber, too; because these arts are one and all connected with the 'doing up' of houses. For the same reason the builder combines the business of the plasterer with that of the bricklayer, and not unfrequently that of the carpenter and joiner in addition. In all of these businesses, however, a distinct set of workmen are required, according as the materials operated upon are different.

We are now in a position to proceed with the arrangement of the several members of society into different classes, according to the principles of classification which have been here laid down. [. . .]

CLASSIFICATION OF THE
WORKERS AND NON-WORKERS
OF GREAT BRITAIN

THOSE WHO *WILL* WORK

1. *Enrichers*, as the Collectors, Extractors, or Producers of Exchangeable Commodities.
2. *Auxiliaries*, as the Promoters of Production, or the Distributors of the Produce.
3. *Benefactors*, or those who confer some permanent benefit, as Educators and Curators engaged in promoting the physical, intellectual, or spiritual wellbeing of the people.
4. *Servitors*, or those who render some temporary service, or pleasure, as Amusers, Protectors, and Servants.

THOSE WHO *CANNOT* WORK

5. *Those who are provided for by some public institution*, as the inmates of workhouses, prisons, hospitals, asylums, almshouses, dormitories, and refuges.

6. *Those who are unprovided for*, and incapacitated for labour, either from want of power, from want of means, or from want of employment.

THOSE WHO *WILL NOT* WORK

7. *Vagrants*
8. *Professional beggars*
9. *Cheats*
10. *Thieves*
11. *Prostitutes*

THOSE WHO *NEED NOT* WORK

12. *Those who derive their income from rent*
13. *Those who derive their income from dividends*
14. *Those who derive their income from yearly stipends*
15. *Those who derive their income from obsolete or nominal offices*
16. *Those who derive their income from trades in which they do not appear*
17. *Those who derive their income by favour from others*
18. *Those who derive their support from the head of the family*

Map showing the number of persons to every 100 acres, or

THE DENSITY OF THE POPULATION

in each of the counties of England and Wales, in 1851

Counties printed black are those in which the population is above the average density.
Counties left white are those in which the population is below the average density.
The average has been calculated from the last returns of the Registrar-General.

Map showing the number who signed the marriage register with marks in every 100 persons married

or THE INTENSITY OF IGNORANCE

in each county of England and Wales

The counties printed black are those in which the number who signed the marriage register with marks is above the average.

The counties left white are those in which the number who signed the marriage register with marks is below the average.

The average has been calculated for the ten years from 1839 to 1848.

Map showing the number of the criminal offenders to every 10,000 acres of the population, or

THE INTENSITY OF THE CRIMINALITY

in each county of England and Wales

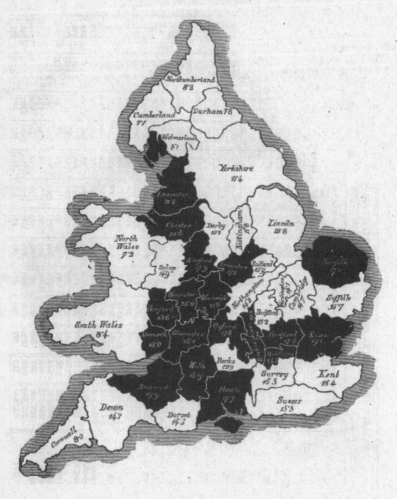

Counties printed black are those in which the number of criminals is above the average.
Counties left white are those in which the number of criminals is below the average.
The average has been calculated from the returns for the last ten years.

Map showing

THE CRIMINALITY OF FEMALES

every 100,000 of the female population, in each county of England and Wales

Counties printed black are those in which the number of criminal females is above the average.
Counties left white are those in which the number of criminal females is below the average.
The average is taken for the last 10 years.

The average for all England and Wales is 62 in every 100,000 of the female population.
The average for all Middlesex (the highest) is 110 in every 100,000 of the female population.
The average for all Derby (the lowest) is 23 in every 100,000 of the female population.

10

ANSWERS TO CORRESPONDENTS

London Labour and the London Poor *began life as a serial publication that was issued in twopenny weekly parts between 1851 and 1852. Each part was enclosed in a wrapper on which Mayhew printed information and inquiries sent in by his readers together with his replies. Items, whether praiseworthy, critical, engaging or slight, reveal the unique and fascinating relationship which Mayhew enjoyed with his readers. These exchanges also provided Mayhew with a platform upon which to air newly-developing ideas and methods. In the extracts printed here, for instance, he solicits statistical information; declares his attitude to 'promiscuous charity'; makes clear his conviction that employment alone will solve the problem of poverty among the able-bodied poor; describes his foundation of a 'Loan Office for the Poor'; allows a journeyman tailor and a draper their say; engages in debates about free trade, capitalism and the working classes, and the causes of prostitution; publishes a letter describing the contents of the library of a model lodging-house and prints a description of the* Coal-Whippers' Journal. *'Answers to Correspondents' were included in the single-volume binding in which the weekly parts were issued at the time the project collapsed. They do not appear in the 1861 edition. In the first edition individual items were neither numbered nor, in general, dated.*

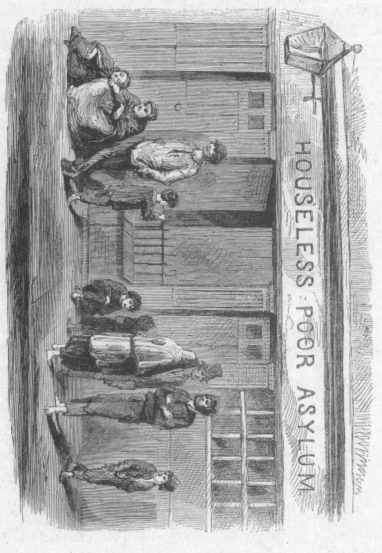

ASYLUM FOR THE HOUSELESS POOR, CRIPPLEGATE

[from a sketch]

ANSWERS TO CORRESPONDENTS

[*printed and bound with the single-volume edition of* London Labour
and the London Poor *of 1851–2. They are unpaginated.*]

An account has been given among the notices to correspondents of
the several occupations which will be treated of in this work, on
the completion of the volume concerning the street-folk. In the
meantime, the several operatives, trade societies, and employers,
will do the Author, and it is hoped themselves and the public, a
considerable service by forwarding such facts connected with their
trade, as may have come under their own *personal* experience.

MR MAYHEW would feel obliged by the name and address of
the writers being added to all communications – not with a view
to publication, but as a guarantee of respectability and good faith.
MR MAYHEW (for obvious reasons) never prints the names of
those from whom he receives his information, but leaves the
public to look to him alone as the person responsible for the truth
of the statements here published; it is therefore necessary for his
own credit sake, that he should be furnished with the means of
ascertaining the credibility of his informants, before pledging
himself to the authenticity of any facts with which they may
supply him. All anonymous communications will henceforth be
unattended to.

The statistical information that MR MAYHEW desires is of three
kinds – First, concerning the earnings of individuals – Secondly,
the income and expenditure, objects and government of trade
societies – and Thirdly, the *kind* of cheap labour by which the
'cutting' masters in the several trades are enabled to undersell the
more liberal employers.

1st. The earnings of individual operatives should be proved by
the account-books of the employers or employed, both of which
will be highly valuable, especially if extending over a series of
years. Each of the account-books of the operatives, however,

should be accompanied by a statement as to whether it represents the earnings of a person who is *fully*, *partially*, or only *casually*, employed; also, whether the workman is a *quick*, *average*, or *slow* hand. Of course all such books (or statistical documents of any kind indeed) as may be entrusted to MR MAYHEW for the purposes of this work, will be carefully preserved, and when done with faithfully returned.

2nd. The Trade Society statistics that MR MAYHEW would be thankful for, are statements of the number of members in and out of society for a series of years – the wages of society men during the same time, specifying the cause of any rise or fall – the subscriptions paid by members, and how much of these is devoted to trade purposes, and how much to 'philanthropic' (if any) – the income and expenditure of the society for each year as far back as possible – the sums paid annually to the unemployed, as well as the yearly number of unemployed members – the amount given every year to the sick, (specifying if possible the prevailing diseases of the trade) – the sums disbursed to the superannuated, as well as the gross amount paid at death of the members, setting forth the number of individuals in each case – the sums paid for insurance of tools, if any – the amount disbursed to tramps – the number of employers who pay society prices, and if possible the number of those who do not (the last items especially, should be given for as long a period as possible, so that an estimate may be formed as to the prospects of the trade). MR MAYHEW would also be glad to know what are the trade regulations concerning apprentices – the term of apprenticeship – the number usually taken – the premium paid – and the remuneration of the apprentice. The hours of labour recognised by the society, and the duration of the brisk and slack seasons, would likewise be useful, as well as whether the men are paid day-work or piece-work. It would further be desirable to know the cost and causes of any strikes that may have taken place, and the opinion of the more intelligent members, of the trade thereupon. MR MAYHEW wishes moreover to be furnished with facts as to whether the late reduction in the price of food has been followed by a commensurate reduction in the rate of wages, and whether at the time of the imposition of the income or any other tax, the wages of the operatives were reduced to an equal extent. MR MAYHEW is aware that such has been the case in many trades, but he is desirous of ascertaining whether the reduction has been general, and if not, of learning the nature of the exceptions.

3rd. As to the nature of the cheap labour by which the cutting masters in the different trades are enabled to undersell the more liberal employers, MR MAYHEW wishes to know: first, whether the cheap labourers employed belong to the less skilful portion of the trade – as boys, 'improvers', old men, &c.; or to the less respectable – as the drunken, the idle, and the dishonest; or the less expensive – that is to say, those who will put up with a coarser diet, as foreigners, Irishmen, &c., and those who have their subsistence found them, either by the State, as paupers and criminals, or by their connections and relations, as wives and children. Also whether there are any 'aids to wages' among the cheaper labourers in the several trades, as 'allotments', 'relief', &c. &c. Moreover, it would be advisable to make known whether the cheap workers are obliged to find security, and if so, to what extent – whether they are bound to provide any and what articles that it is usual for the more liberal employers in the trade to find for their workpeople – whether they are bound to buy their materials, tools, or food, of their employers, and if so, the prices charged by them compared with others. If they are boarded or lodged by their employers, the quality and quantity of provisions, and style of accommodation found them. If there are fines, the nature of the offences for which they are imposed, and the amount exacted. If middlemen are customary, then should be stated the sum paid *to* such middlemen by the employer, and the sum paid *by* them to the employed; if, on the other hand, there be a large number of small working masters in the trade, it would be desirable to know the lowest sum required by an operative to commence manufacturing on his own account – the usual hours of labour among the small masters – the rate of working, that is to say, the quantity of work done by them in a given time – the number who work on the Sunday – the time lost in finding a market for the goods when finished – the advantages taken of their necessities by the tradesmen to whom they sell – the kind of assistants the small masters employ, and the wages they pay.

Statistical information on the above points, in connection with any of the trades, or indeed in connection with any other trade, will be of the utmost value. Such information need not concern London alone, but the provinces as well, for it is MR MAYHEW's intention not to confine the work to the artisans and labourers of the Metropolis solely.

MR MAYHEW would further be thankful for accounts as to the individual expenditure of operatives. These would be of the greatest service, as the means of arriving at the number of ounces of solid food consumed by working men in particular trades, so that the quantity may be contrasted with other trades, as well as with the dietaries of paupers and prisoners. A statement of the sum spent in intoxicating liquors would do good in tending to check a most pernicious custom.

In conclusion, MR MAYHEW begs to state, that he would likewise be glad to be furnished with a brief account of the experience, privations, and struggles of those working men whose lives have been unusually chequered, and the publication of which is likely to prove interesting or useful to their fellow-workmen, or the public generally.

Money donated for the London Poor

L. C. F. presents her compliments to MR MAYHEW, and begs to enclose half a sovereign, to be disposed of as he may think proper, to any of the distressed persons mentioned in his account of the *London Poor*. She heartily wishes that she could make it more, but her circumstances do not admit of it at present, though she trusts ere long to be able to send another donation; and will also, when possible, subscribe to the *Friendly Association of Costermongers*, as described in MR MAYHEW's work. Should the two Young Flower Girls, or the little Cress Girl, mentioned by MR MAYHEW, be still in distress, her own sympathies go first with the young in sorrow. So much sin as well as misery may be prevented, by timely aid in supplying them with stock to pursue their honest trading, that one might hope whilst assisting them in their means of support, to be also aiding (however humbly), in 'saving souls alive'. But MR MAYHEW will be, of course, the best judge where so sadly small a sum can be made of the most avail.

[MR MAYHEW has handed over the half-sovereign, kindly forwarded by L. C. F., to his Publisher, Mr John Howden. MR MAYHEW has, in his dealings with the poorer classes, seen too many instances of the evils of promiscuous charity, to consent to become the dispenser of alms. The most dangerous lesson that can possibly be taught to any body of people whatsoever is, that there are other means of obtaining money than by working for it. Benevolence, however kind in its intentions, does oftentimes more harm than even the opposite principle. To bestow alms upon a struggling, striving man, is to destroy his independence, and to make a beggar of one who *would* work for his living. It is to teach such an one to trust to others for his subsistence, rather than to convince him that he himself contains within his own frame the means of providing for his own sustenance – indeed, it is to change the self-supporting animal into the mere vegetable; for the main distinction between animal and vegetable life is, that the one seeks its own food and the other has it brought to it. MR MAYHEW, while he wishes to arouse the public to the social necessity of enabling every person throughout the kingdom to live in comfort by his labour, has no wish to teach the humbler classes that they can possibly obtain a livelihood by any other means. All that the better part of the working-classes desire is, to live by their industry; and those who desire to live by the industry of others, form no portion of the honest independent race of workmen in this country whom MR MAYHEW wishes to befriend. The deserving poor are really those who *cannot* live by their labour, whether from under-payment, want of employment, or physical or mental incapacity; and these MR MAYHEW wishes, and will most cheerfully do all he can, at any time and in any way, to assist. If the poverty arise from unfair payment, we should demand from the employers a fair living price for the work. If, on the other hand, it arise from want of employment, then we should seek to obtain work for those who cannot themselves procure it; and if from disability, we should use our influence to get them admission to some asylum specially devoted to the alleviation of their particular sufferings; or, if there be no such asylum, then we should endeavour to found some one of the kind wanted.

MR MAYHEW been thus explicit as to the principles which guide him, because he wishes it to be known that, for several reasons, he has no desire to fill the post of dispenser of alms. In the first place, it is necessary that, for the honour of the office he has taken upon himself, he should be placed beyond even the remotest suspicion. He has therefore determined to accept no place of pecuniary trust whatsoever; and in accordance with this resolve, he has handed over such money as has been forwarded to him for distribution among the poor, to Mr John Howden, with the view of making it the nucleus of an institution that he is most anxious to see established, viz., a 'Loan-Office for the Poor', where small advances may be obtained on approved security, at a moderate rate of interest. This appears to Mr Mayhew not only to overcome all the objections to alms-giving, but to afford the same pecuniary assistance to those who stand in need of it, without degrading them into beggars. Such an institution would also go far to put a stop to the exorbitant rates of interest now charged by those who trade upon the necessities and destitution of the indigent, – such as the dolly-shops, pawnbrokers, stock-money lenders, tally-shops, and many like iniquities. Those gentlemen and ladies who would not object to serve upon the committee of such an institution, are requested to forward their names to the Office, 69, Fleet-street, and those who think sufficiently well of its objects to contribute towards its capital, will oblige by making their post-office orders payable to Mr John Howden, who has kindly consented to act as Honorary Secretary for the time being. It is proposed to pay three, or, if possible, four per cent. interest for all contributions made to the institution, the sums contributed by the subscribers being lent out at five per cent., and the difference devoted to the expenses of the institution.] [. . .]

[Mr Mayhew, however, wishes it to be distinctly understood, that he in no way pledges himself to the principles here asserted from time to time. It should be remembered he is collecting facts, and merely avails himself of the *waste* pages of this periodical as a means of recording the opinions which are forced upon him in the course of his investigations (such opinions being at all times carefully excluded from the work itself). He reserves to himself therefore (as a person unconnected with party), the right of changing or modifying his sentiments as often as a more enlarged series

of facts may present new views to his mind. It is in this light that he
wishes his speculations to be received – for speculations they are,
though, perhaps based upon a greater number of phenomena than
any economist has as yet personally obtained. For the present he
can only declare his determination to follow the facts, whithersoever they may lead (for he has no object but the truth), and if he
be open to the charge of generalising, before he has made himself
acquainted with all the particulars, he at least has a greater right to
do so than any economist of the present day – seeing that he is
perhaps the first who has sought to evolve the truths of the Labour
Question by personal investigation. As yet political economy has
been a purely arm-chair science – gentlemen who troubled their
heads about the matter have done *no more than* trouble their heads:
they have sat beside a snug sea-coal fire and tried to excogitate, or
think out the several matters affecting the working-classes – even
as Adam Smith, the great founder of the science, retired for twelve
years to an obscure village in Scotland to dream upon the laws
concerning production and the producers. And yet it is upon the
cobweb philosophy thus spun out that the whole of the legislation
of the present day is made to depend!

MR MAYHEW will at all times be glad to listen patiently to any
new ideas, though he must object to a disgorging of the old ones, in
opposition to the sentiments he here propounds; he will also be
pleased to receive any additional facts from working men, whose
greater experience may cause them to detect omissions and errors
in the enumeration of circumstances given here or hereafter. A
desire for the public good precludes party bigotry.] [. . .]

A journeyman on coconuts

[. . .]

C. B., of Portland Town, says: 'Being a subscriber to your useful
work, *London Labour*, I take it to the shop to read, for I am a
journeyman tailor. There is a passage at page 89, that some of my
shopmates find great fault with, and don't believe you are stating
correct, when you say that cocoa nuts are generally spelt 'coker'.
They wish to know in what work of M'Culloch's they are spelt as
such, and how long they have been entered as such at the Custom
House; for they cannot find them spelt so in any work they have

seen. You will please to answer this on the wrapper of *London Labour*, and you will much oblige me, as I defend you as well as I am able.' [The orthography is 'coker' in M'Culloch's *Commercial Dictionary*; and they are certainly so written at the Customs, and by all fruit brokers. MR KEELING (of the firm of Keeling and Hunt) was the first gentleman who made MR MAYHEW acquainted with the commercial distinction.] [. . .]

The library of a model dwelling-house
[. . .]

Model Lodging House
2, Charles Street, Drury Lane

SIR,
We, the undersigned inmates of the above Model Lodging House, collectively beg to be allowed to disburden ourselves of the undue odium heaped upon us so mercilessly in the invidious aspersions of your correspondent last week. If the mis-statement of your informant is not refuted, the public will naturally infer that the common habits of the Lodgers present a scene of savage life, and that the interior displays the constant aspect of a perfect Babel; being, as erroneously asserted, 'the scene of dirt and disorder, with noise, confusion, and intemperance abounding from morning till night'.

Though there is no separate Reading Room, yet we have a small library, composed of books (presented by members of the Society, by whom the house was established) which, though not engaging the taste of all, is at times resorted to.

The books most in request being *Chambers's Information* and Tracts. Besides this, however, we have a list of Periodicals sub-scribed for by the Lodgers – these are eagerly and attentively read as they appear. The character of these works will, we think, sufficiently speak in our defence, for whilst occupied in their perusal, which happens at all spare intervals of leisure, the time so spent must prove the untruth of the alleged disorder, &c.

The following is a list of Weekly Publications taken in, viz:
London Labour – from the first
Household Words
Tomlins's Help to Self-Educators

The Builder
Mechanics' Magazine
Knight's Cyclopaedia of the Industry of All Nations
Expositor
Chambers's Journal
The People's and Howitt's Journal
Family Herald
London Journal
Weekly Dispatch

With these few remarks we leave this statement in your hands for candid inquiry, which if resorted to will assuredly reverse the unfavourable impression your strictures are calculated to produce on the public mind.

We remain,

Your constant Readers,

J. JOHNSON, THOS. PASSMORE, W. R. ROBINSON,
J. E. AUBREY (*lodgers resident between three and four years*)

A. KATES, WM. SMITH, JOHN SMITH, H. POWELL,
FREDK. HARCOURT, JAS. TAYLOR
(*lodgers resident between two and three years*)

JOSEPH YATES, E. WOLSTENHOLME, GEORGE HUNT,
W. HIND (*lodgers resident between one and two years*)

F. SMITH, THOMAS TROTMAN, J. GREEN, J. LUSH
(*lodgers resident between six and twelve months*)

The above list of names might have been considerably extended had it been requisite.

[Since the above was forwarded, a letter bearing the signatures of the first two persons named in the above list, has been received, stating that there is 'not a single scintilla of truth' in the information furnished by me respecting the Model Lodging House in Charles Street, Drury Lane, and adding that the doors of that particular Model 'are never even nominally closed till midnight, and never rigorously at that hour'.]

[. . .]

Free-trade and the working man

1st October, 1851

The gentleman is in error. On revision, he will perceive, that the contrasted accounts went to show that the man had lost almost as much by free-trade as he had gained. If food had been cheapened since 1846, employment had become scarcer; so that he could afford to have five loaves per week before free-trade, and only four loaves per week since. Hence though the man had gained by the repeal of the corn laws one penny in every seven pence he laid out in bread, he had, nevertheless, been able to earn one loaf less per week since 1846 than he could before then, that is to say, he had gained 4*d*., and lost 7*d*. by the measure. In meat, however, he had gained 6*d*. a week; but then in rent he had lost 4*d*.; in potatoes, 1*d*.; in tea, 1*d*.; and in beer 2*d*. per week; that is to say, he had since 1845 been able to afford less of the three last-mentioned articles. Thus, the gains would appear to be – bread, 4*d*., and meat, 6*d*. per week, or 10*d*. altogether; whereas the losses are – rent, 4*d*.; potatoes, 1*d*.; tea, 1*d*.; beer 2*d*.; and bread, 7*d*.; or 15*d*. altogether; so that there would seem to be a net loss of 5*d*. per week to this man since free-trade. This should have been more fully explained in the article, though the whole bearing of it inclines to the same result. Mr. Mayhew was inquiring of a man who made soldiers' trousers what he had gained by free-trade. He was one of the very poor who were to be so much benefited by the measure. Meat he *never* tasted, and his weekly consumption of bread was two loaves per week, the saving in which was 2*d*. His wages had not been decreased, nor was his work less, so that he was a clear gainer of 2*d*. in about 7*s*. a week, or 1*d*. in every 3*s*. 6*d*. of his earnings!! It would appear that those who earn about 15*s*. a week, and whose wages have not yet been reduced, save perhaps 1*s*. by the change (see the article on Street-Orderlies); and those whose wages have been reduced are, of course, considerable losers by the alteration. To the tradesman and capitalist, however, whose profits depend not, like wages, upon the price of food, the change of course is a clear gain; each pound being worth at least a guinea, since free-trade. [. . .]

A draper on surveying his trade

SIR,

Having read your very excellent work, the *London Labour and Poor*, ever since its first publication, I remember having seen in some of the back numbers an intimation to one of your correspondents that it was your intention in course of time to treat of that class of the London labour, the *Drapers*. I am myself a Draper's Assistant, and having some little practical knowledge of the business, I should feel a great pleasure in giving you any information on the subject, as far as my knowledge of the peculiarities of the trade goes, if you have not already completed your inquiries; and if what little assistance I can render you in your arduous undertaking is worthy of your acceptance, I should feel the greatest pleasure in contributing my mite to the immense funds of information that you have collected. A letter addressed to me, or an answer in the next number of your *London Labour and Poor*, stating the nature of the information you require on the subject, shall meet with my earnest attention.

P.S. I have enclosed one of my employer's cards, to whose house, should you write, you will please address for me.'

[The information required upon this and, indeed, every other trade is, (1) the division of labour in the trade, citing the nature of the work performed by the different classes of workmen; (2) the hours of labour; (3) the labour market, or the mode of obtaining employment; (4) the tools employed and who finds them; (5) the rate and mode of pay to each different class of workmen, dividing the wages or salaries into two classes, the 'fair' and the 'unfair'; (6) the deductions from the pay in the form of fines, 'rents', or stoppages of any kind; (7) the additions to wages in the shape of perquisites, premiums, allowances, &c.; (8) a history of the wages of the trade, with the dates of increase or decrease in the pay, and the causes thereof; (9) the brisk and slack season of the trade, with statement of the causes on which they depend, as well as the number of extra hands required in the brisk season as compared with the slack; (10) the rate of pay to those who are 'taken on' only during the brisk season; (11) the amount of surplus labour in the trade and the cause of it, whether from (a) overwork, (b) undue increase of the people in the trade, (c) change from yearly to weekly hirings, (d) excessive economy of labour, as 'large system' of business, (e) introduction of women; (12) the badly-paid trade – (a) the history and causes of it, (b) what is the cheap labour employed, or how do the cheap workers differ from those who are better paid: are they less skilful, less trustworthy, or can they *afford* to take less, deriving their subsistence from other sources? (c) is the badly-paid trade maintained chiefly by the labour of apprentices, women, &c., &c.? (d) is it upheld by middlemen, 'sweaters', or the like? (e) are the men injured by *driving* (that is, by being made to do more work for the same money) or by *grinding* (that is, by being made to do the same or more work for less money), or are they injured from a combination of both systems? (f) who are the employers paying the worse wages? – are they 'cutting men', that is to say, men who are reducing the mens' wages as a means of selling cheap; or are they 'grasping men', who do it merely to increase their profits; or small capitalists, who do it in order to live? Proofs should be given of all stated. Accounts of earnings and expenditure are of the greatest importance; also descriptions of modes of life and habits, politics, religion, literature, and amusements of the trade; estimates of the number in trade with the proportion belonging to the better aud the worse paid class, and the quantity of surplus hands. If any trade and benefit society, an account of it would be desirable; if not, what do men, in case of sickness?] [. . .]

The causes of prostitution

[. . .]

J. B., it will be seen, falls into the same fallacy as the Glasgow correspondent, assuming that girls are seduced through frequenting Casinos; surely the true rendering is, that they frequent such places either *because* they have been already seduced and have become shameless, or because they are of a *seducible* disposition. Is it compatible with the character of a modest girl, to visit a place which she knows is resorted to by women of loose character, and whither she is aware gentlemen go only to become acquainted with such people? and, even supposing her innocence led her to such a place (of which strong proof would be required), would she not, if really modest, and if she had not been previously depraved, object to dance with men whose acquaintance she had formed thus promiscuously? It would seem that we might as well believe that a girl who accompanied a man to a brothel was *seduced* by him. That there are many cases of heartless deception, no one can have the least doubt; but that modest-minded women visit Casinos, and that it requires much persuasion to induce a young lady who is in the habit of frequenting them to abandon herself to vicious practices, surely no man of common sense can believe. As was before said, girls who go to such places are seducible, and *therefore* seduced. Nor can MR MAYHEW believe that it is *directly* a love of dress and gaiety that leads to prostitution. Prostitution is really and truly woman's crime; and the same propensity as induces men to live by thieving, cheating, or begging, rather than labouring, disposes the generality of loose women to adopt prostitution as a mode of livelihood. The Constabulary Commissioners, who are the only gentlemen that have scientifically investigated the causes of crime, have laid it down, from the testimony and experience of the most observing persons, that crime in the majority of instances arises from 'a disposition to acquire property with a less degree of labour than by ordinary industry'. Twist and turn the matter over as we please, we must end at this point, simply because it assumes nothing, and expresses the bare fact. Crime of all kinds, women's as well as men's, is, generally speaking, but still of course with exceptional cases, the consequence of an indisposition to labour for a living; that is to say, if a certain person possessing no property will not work for the food and comforts he or she requires in order to live, such a person in such a case can only obtain them dishonestly, or, in other words, criminally. Do not let it be understood that it is here intended to imply that such is the case universally. Heaven forbid! The meaning is, simply, that this cause of crime is the *more general* one. The love of dress is not the direct cause of prostitution, which arises rather from the disposition to obtain fine clothes other than by working for them. This is usually the *primum mobile* to vicious courses – the love of ease, and getting their wants and desires satisfied with as little difficulty and in as pleasant a manner as possible.

Nevertheless there are many other causes leading directly to the same result, and the love of admiration is necessarily one of these. What proportion of the prostitutes are led to adopt their line of life from an indisposition to earn what they require, and what proportion from a love of personal admiration, it is difficult at present to say; but, perhaps, we may even here draw this line – the prostitutes who proceed from the *poorer* classes of society become depraved because they perceive that greater creature-comforts can be obtained in our community by immoral practices than by regular industry; whereas those prostitutes who proceed from the *middle* classes are led to adopt a vicious life principally from the craving for admiration, of which the love of dress, society, and display are the consequences rather than the causes. The prostitutes of the 'superior classes', on the other hand (and we must all admit there are such prostitutes), become debased purely from the love of admiration, because *they* can have no mercenary motive for pursuing such a course of conduct. The above appear to be the two prime causes of prostitution. The poorer girls take to it mainly from the irksomeness and deficient remuneration of labour among us; while those belonging to the wealthier class adopt the same course chiefly from an undue love of admiration. But this refers only to the class who *take* to prostitution, and, as was said in a previous number, there are two other distinct classes of loose women whom J. B. confounds. Those who are *driven* to prostitution, either through want or seduction, are of course the most pitiable, and at the same time the most hopeful of all the three classes; but these consist of by far the smallest number. Those who, on the other hand, take to prostitution either through an indisposition to work for their living, or from a love of admiration, as well as the third class, or, those who are *bred* to a vicious course of life, being early depraved or allowed by their parents to associate with whomsoever and go whithersoever they please, are the most difficult of all to deal with. To this latter class, it will be seen, appertain the remarks made by J. B. concerning parents' neglect of their daughters. That this is a fruitful source of prostitution – perhaps, indeed, the most fruitful of all those above mentioned – such people as have eyes in their heads and brains at the back of them must have been long convinced. How else can we explain the fact that the greater number of prostitutes belong to the humbler classes of society? In middle-class life the girl is, of course, seldom or never permitted out of her parents' sight; indeed so strict a supervision is maintained over the daughter's conduct, that no opportunity of erring is afforded; but, among the humbler classes, it should be remembered that we have reached that state of society (the admiration of economists) which compels the wife to labour for her living; and, consequently, to absent herself from home, and to transfer her care from her children to some factory, or other place of labour. Hence, the daughters of our people are, perforce, brought up in our gutters and channels, and depraved often by vicious intercourse long ere any passion or love could have led to such a result. Gentlemen ask from their easy chairs how are we to cure this. The answer is, it never can be cured until we find a remedy for the social evils of which such things are the necessary results. In the degradation of our women we suffer for the infamy and callous selfishness of our men. Those causes of prostitution which consist in defective moral and religious training are purposely omitted here, because they have a *negative* rather than a *positive* influence on the result – such training serving simply to *check* the operation of the natural principles leading to that end, and the want of it consequently permitting them to act uncontrolled. MR MAYHEW is much obliged to J. B. for his thoughts on the subject, and would be happy to hear from him again. [. . .]

The *Coal-Whippers' Journal*

[. . .]

[The London coal-whippers have forwarded a Prospectus of a new journal which is about to be published by some members of their own body. These labouring men have long been celebrated for the many classical scholars included among their ranks; but curious as classical scholarship may be when found among such a class, still intelligence in a periodical will prove of much greater value. It is hoped therefore that the coal-whippers will not be so anxious to display their learning as their sense. If they will but avoid a perhaps pardonable demonstration of their scholastic acquirements, and determine to deal with the labour question judicially rather than emotionally, eschewing all that may savour of the platform – if they will but adhere to plain matters of fact, collecting and making known the statistics of labour, and so contributing their mite of truth to the general knowledge fund on this difficult question, they may be the means of doing incalculable good, not only to their own people, but to the great body of labouring men throughout the country. Let them rest assured that the labourer is to be benefited solely by truth. No revolution in any country what-soever can ever make two and two anything but four. If the working men are wronged, then let them demonstrate how the treatment they receive violates the laws of right, and depend upon it there are enough people wishing right to prevail, ultim-ately to put an end to wrong. The process may seem a slow one, but there is no hastening it *by force* – conviction alone can work the change. MR MAYHEW himself believes that the working men of England are grossly wronged by capitalists. All production is according to the very first principles of political economy – a partnership between the man of money and the man of muscles, in which the monied man agrees to advance to the working man his share of the produce in the form of wages. Look at the labour question in whatever light we may, these are the very elements of it. It may offer some violence to the pride of the capitalist to be told that his labourers are partners in his business, but common sense and justice admit of no other view being taken of the transaction. That this fundamental contract is violated, and that the labourer *does not get his fair share of the produce at the present day, none can doubt* – the padlock, to quote a solitary instance, which is made for a halfpenny, is sold for a shilling. In place of the original compact a new law has been instituted, by which the *necessities* of the working man – instead of equity – are made to determine the value of his labour. This is what is called the law of supply and demand, which taking no heed of the result (this is to say, whether the value of the materials on which the workman has exercised his skill has been doubled or increased even a hundred-fold by the operation), says, that the proportion of the wealth which is to come to the labourer is to be regulated by no other principle than what the capitalist can induce or force of him (by starvation or chicanery) to accept. Now this to MR MAYHEW appears to be the very reverse of justice, and contrary to the fundamental principles of the very science of which it is said to be a part. Unfortunately, however, the law of supply and demand has got to be recognised by the rulers of the land, and to be considered almost as a part of the commercial creed of the country – the last 'new commandment', as it were – against which it is political blasphemy to raise one's voice. Until the injustice of this principle is exposed and made generally known, there is no hope for the labouring man; for a necessary corollary (and certainly a most convenient one to all employers) of the law of supply and demand is the dogma of free labour, which asserts that in any way to restrict the liberty of the capitalist to buy his labour in the cheapest market and sell it (of course) in the dearest, is to interfere with the 'rights of commerce'. This, however, would seem to perpetrate an even greater iniquity than the present wage-law – and that solely for the benefit of the capitalist – *at the expense, moreover, of both producer and consumer*, giving rise at once to underpaid workmen and overcharged purchasers – to cheap labour and dear commodities *for the mere aggrandisement of the middleman*. To buy labour at the cheapest possible rate, without any regard to the value of the produce, is to defraud the producer, and to sell it at the dearest possible rate (without any regard to the prime cost of the commodity), is to swindle the purchaser. Surely this was the principle of trade which guided the dealings of Ikey Solomons, the Jew fence, and yet he was tried at the Old Bailey and transported for putting it in practice. In the case of the receiver of stolen goods, the main iniquity consists in not paying a fair price for the labour of the article purchased; and indeed it is often this buying of the articles far below their equitable value that constitutes the chief evidence as to the guilty knowledge of the receiver. If no restriction whatever is to be placed upon the dealings of capitalists, and they are to have full liberty to buy in the cheapest market – despite the principles of justice – then why in the name of common sense prosecute the receiver or the thief, when their whole crime consists in not paying a proper price for the labour of the commodities they obtain? Under these circumstances it behoves the great body of working men to protest loudly – but calmly and resolutely – against the iniquity of the law of supply and demand, and against the doctrine of free labour which seeks to make the remuneration of workmen depend on the greed of commercial men rather than the principles of justice. There are no men who can make this apparent better than the coal-whippers – no men who have had greater experience of the atrocities that can be perpetrated under the *free labour* principle, and none who if they will but tell all they know, and all they have seen, and tell it dispassionately – appealing to the consciences rather than the passions of their fellow-creatures – can do more to bring about that state of right and truth which all good men desire. This is the sole object MR MAYHEW has in view – all he wishes is to make the public aware of the infamies that can be practised upon the labourer when the trader is allowed to use him as his own brutalising love of gain may dictate; he hopes by showing these things to induce some change in our social state (though at present he hardly knows *what* change) by which the workman may ensure *his fair share of the produce*. There are many means proposed to obtain this end. Protection Chartism, Co-operative Societies, Socialism, Communism, and many other social and political panacea; but with these, MR MAYHEW has in his present vocation nothing to do, and he wishes it to be distinctly known and understood – without reservation or cavil – that he is in no way connected with any social or political party or sect whatever. MR MAYHEW is neither Chartist, Protectionist, Socialist, Communist, nor Co-operationist; but a mere collector of facts, endeavouring to discover the several phenomena of labour with a view of arriving ultimately at the laws and circumstances affecting, and controlling the operation and rewards of the labourer, as well as of showing the importance of the poor and the working-classes as members of the State. [. . .]

A letter from a bricklayer's labourer

[J. W., of James-street, Gray's-inn-road, a bricklayer's labourer, sends a long and valuable communication touching the condition and earnings of the workmen in his trade. Among other things, he states that a great many of the constant hands have been reduced from 3s. and 3s. 6d. per day to 2s. 8d. *since the repeal of the Corn Laws*. MR MAYHEW will be happy to hear again from J. W., should he have any fresh facts to communicate.] [. . .]

A debate about labour and capital between
F.B.B. and Henry Mayhew

[F.B.B., of Alfred-street, Bedford-square, sends a letter in answer
to certain observations printed among the Notices to Correspondents in Number 10. It is impossible to give the entire document,
but the following extracts are sufficient to show the spirit and
arguments of the writer. MR MAYHEW's comments are given
between brackets.]

Sir, – Allow me to say, that I think your observations on labour
and capital, in No. 10 of *London Labour*, very erroneous and mis-
chievous, and calculated to mislead the working-classes. I may
observe, by the way, that I am no capitalist or employer of labour.
You assert that 'the working men of England are grossly wronged
by capitalists'; and 'that the labourer does not get his fair share of
the produce at the present day', you add, 'none can doubt.' Now
I beg to say that I, in common with many thousand others, very
much 'doubt', nay, distinctly 'deny', the truth of your assertion.
Political economists consider that the wages of the labourer are his
share of the produce [the halfpenny out of the shilling padlock];
and they believe this share is necessarily regulated by the law of
supply and demand. [A share is a portion regulated by equity, and
not by a scramble.] If wages are to be thus regulated, I desire to
know by what other standard can they be regulated? To talk of
'conscience' and 'justice', is to use vague terms of no definite
meaning. [!] The dictates of 'conscience' depend upon organisation and education; what one man's conscience teaches, another
man's denies. [Does truth depend on the same circumstances?
To what organisations and in what schools does 2 + 2 = 5? So
of moral truth.] There is no definite and invariable standard of
right. [So that Rush and Greenacre were condemned to death for
not conforming to the fashion of the time.] The same is true of
'justice'. The law of supply and demand is evidently a law of
nature [though justice and right are not], and to interfere with it
would introduce endless confusion and mischief. Would you
compel a capitalist to give a certain amount of wages, irrespective
of all risks and losses, and the profits which he calculates necessary
to repay him for capital, knowledge, and superintendence? Surely
this would be gross injustice, if it were practicable!' [The returns of

the capitalist then are to be regulated by the principle of justice, while the remuneration of the working man is to be left to a scramble, or the law of supply and demand. What MR MAYHEW desires is, that the amount coming to both parties should be regulated by the eternal principles of equity (if F. B. B. can understand such things) – the same as all partnerships are. If the labourer and capitalist are not partners, then, of course, the equitable principle does not hold; but as this partnership is the fundamental axiom of political economy, why surely the principle which is used to determine the 'rights' (the word is quoted, in obedience to the prejudices of F. B. B.) of partners should be applied to settle what is due to the labourer as well as the capitalist.] You and others, who declaim on this subject, never consider the population question – the overcrowding of the labour market. This, I am convinced, is the chief source of our social evils. The fault of low wages is not in the capitalists, but in the labourers, who overcrowd the labour market, and compete with each other. If the working-classes have no prudence, no self-denial, they ought surely to bear the consequences of their deficiency in this respect – not the capitalist. If they will recklessly increase the population of their own class, they must take the natural consequences in the lowering of wages. Other classes practise self-denial in this respect [the highest personage in the realm, for instance; but capitalists never are family men, of course]. It might be hoped, that if the working-classes were duly informed on the subject, and were better educated, and this may be expected from national education, they would at length learn wisdom and prudence; which will never be the case, so long as they are put upon a false scent, and are taught, by unreflecting sentimentalists, that they are entirely blameless, and that all the fault and wrong is with the capitalist and the Government. It is very easy and very cheap benevolence to indulge in vague generalities and high-sounding declamation about 'conscience' and 'justice' – 'injustice', 'wrong', and 'oppression', but not so easy to prove where the 'wrong' and 'injustice' lie. [Because, according to F.B.B., wrong and injustice are mere conventional phantasms – things of organisation and education.] From the style of your writing, you appear to belong to the class of impulsive sentimentalists (see *Edinburgh Review*, on 'English Socialism'), who are too

apt to suffer their feelings to overbear their reason and judgment — a more dangerous class to take up any 'cause' I cannot
conceive, or one more likely to do injury to those whose interests
they advocate.

[Excepting *those*, be it observed, who allow their reason and judgment to overpower their feelings, a class of which, it may be added,
the Devil himself is the apt and sublime archetype. MR MAYHEW
has printed the above letter — abuse and all — because he thinks it
may be taken as a fair sample of the present fashionable economical
creed — a creed which does not hesitate to tell us that 'justice',
'right', and 'conscience' are matters of 'organisation' and 'education', mere whimsies of the stomach, or bugbears of the nerves, or
dogmata of the schools; for the propounders of such doctrines,
being unable to perceive that conscience is the exercise of judgment on moral propositions, and justice the perception of moral
equality or equity, are likewise unable to perceive that to deny the
existence of the conscience is to deny that there is any such faculty
as judgment in man, while to make equity and other moral truths
mere conventions is to reduce the most fundamental truths of all,
viz. those which depend on a perception of equality, to matters
of pure fashion. The population question, in which F.B.B. goes
'the whole hog', like Stuart Mill — declaring that there is no hope
for the workmen of this country until they imitate the Catholic
priests and register vows in heaven of perpetual celibacy — is one of
which MR MAYHEW purposes exposing the fallacy in its due place.
Suffice it, for the present, that he believes the superabundance of
labourers in this kingdom to be due to the creation of 600,000,000
of steam men (which is the estimated power of the aggregate
machinery of England) within the last hundred years — a fact of
which economists and populationists never condescend to take
the least notice — though where the difference can be between a
steam-engine performing all the functions of the labourer, and
oftentimes of the artisan, and a human machine doing simply what
the thing of brass and iron does — it is beyond common-sense to
discover. The entire number of human operatives in England and
Wales are not more than 4,000,000 — the steam operatives are at
the least 150 times as many, or 600,000,000 — and when it is
remembered that these competing steam labourers are things that

can work night and day without any sense of fatigue – without cravings or desires – without children to feed and educate, or wives to support and clothe – it surely must be evident to all at what fearful odds the mere creature of flesh and blood – of stomach, brain and (though F.B.B. and his school object, still it must be added) *heart* – must enter the field against them. And yet, knowing the enormous rate at which the steam population has been increasing in this country during the last century – at the rate of no less than 6,000,000 of steam labourers per annum – Mr Stuart Mill and others, when writing about remedies for low wages, do not hesitate to tell us that there is no hope for the working man until he is taught to restrain his passions – stigmatising all who object to their 'preventives' and 'checks' as sentimentalists, who suffer impulse and feeling to overbear reason and judgment. Verily, as Coleridge declared, the heart often reasons much sounder and clearer than the head. Moreover, the extraordinary anomaly with these writers is, that while crying out loudly for the non-increase of human labourers, they say not one word against the propagation of the steam ones; for, with a lop-sidedness peculiar to such logicians, they attribute almost every evil in the land to the fact of there being 4,000,000 workmen to supply nearly 20,000,000 of individuals with food, clothing, shelter, warmth, light and, indeed, every necessary and luxury that human nature can either demand or desire – declaring that one-fifth of the population are far too many to create the wealth required for the sustenance and enjoyment of the whole, and a good part of the world besides; and that, consequently, the labour market of the country is over-stocked to such a degree that distress and want must be the necessary portion of a considerable number; but (mark the absurdity) never even so much as hinting the while that the 600,000,000 of steam rival operatives which have been created within the last century have in any way tended to induce the overstocking of the said labour market, not venturing to propose that *capitalists* should be taught to restrain *their* passions (for wealth) and made to refrain from annually bringing so many steam labourers into existence. That there are too many steam-engines and mechanical labourers is proved by the repeated gluts in the Manchester and other markets – such gluts being admitted on all hands to be the necessary consequences of over-production. Manchester manufacturers, however, while they admit the over-production, attribute the glut rather to under-consumption, saying that it is impossible there can be too much calico till every man and woman in the kingdom has a super-abundance of under-clothing. But how is it possible for working men and women to avail themselves of the superabundance of materials for shirts, shifts, and petticoats, when the only thing they have to give in exchange for such articles is their labour? and of this, by the invention of machinery, the division of labour, and the large system of production, we are daily depriving them – or in others seeking how to produce more wealth with fewer labourers. When the economy of labour is the ruling principle of the science of manufacture, how can we wonder that the superabundance of labourers is due solely to the unrestrained sensuality of the working-classes? With 600,000,000 of steam men to help to do the work of the nation, no wonder that a considerable portion of the 4,000,000 of human creatures can get little or no work to do! But we are told steam-engines create work for the human machines. There must be, it is said, some man or child to tend them; whereas human machines are pure social incumbrances, causing no addition what-soever to the aggregate demand for labour. Every fresh pair of feet that come into the world do not create a demand for an extra pair of shoes - nor each new back want clothing – nor another head require additional shelter – nor another stomach additional food to be produced. Certainly not. The steam-man is the greatest of national blessings – our fellow-man the greatest of national curses.

But in order that the natural additions to the aggregate demand for labour, created by each new workman who is brought into existence, should have free play, it is necessary that there be a corresponding demand for the workman's own labour. If he be not employed, of course he cannot employ others to make his shoes – his coats, grow his bread, or build his house: for if deprived of work by his steam competitor, then he must go barefoot, bare-backed, empty-bellied, and houseless, - the fate of thousands in this country, as witness the handloom-weavers, the sawyers, &c. Even to reduce the workman's wages, is to decrease the aggregate amount of work to be done in the kingdom. The national income, which is estimated at £300,000,000 sterling per annum, may be said to consist of three equal parts: £100,000,000 going to replace capital; £100,000,000 being the gross amount of profits accruing to the capitalists; and £100,000,00 the gross amount of wages received by the labourers. The latter, or wage fund, constitutes the great purchasing fund of the country, for the whole of this is (with the most trifling exceptions) consumed; whereas the profit fund is mainly (perhaps more than half) saved with a view of increasing the capital of the capitalists. Hence, to decrease the wage fund is consequently to decrease the purchasing fund of the community. F.B.B. should not venture to write on subjects to which he has evidently paid but little attention, and to which he can contribute no new ideas. This magpie mania for mere chattering is one of the worst signs of the times. MR MAYHEW must decline replying to all similar communications for the future.]

[. . .]

APPENDIX I: MAYHEW'S TABLES OF CONTENTS
AND LISTS OF ILLUSTRATIONS
FROM THE 1862 EDITION

A. Tables of Contents

Volume 1: *Contents*
THE STREET–FOLK
Wandering tribes in general   1
Wandering tribes in the country   2
The London street-folk   3
Costermongers   4
Street-sellers of fish   61
Street-sellers of fruit and vegetables   79
Stationary Street-sellers of fish, fruit, and vegetables   97
The street Irish   104
Street-sellers of game, poultry, rabbits, butter, cheese, and eggs   120
Street-sellers of trees, shrubs, flowers, roots, seeds, and branches   131
Street-sellers of green stuff   145
Street-sellers of eatables and drinkables   158
Street-sellers of stationery, literature, and the fine arts   213
Street-sellers of manufactured articles   323
The women Street-sellers   457
The children Street-sellers   466

Volume 2: *Contents*
THE STREET–FOLK
Introduction   1
Street-sellers of second-hand articles   5
Street-sellers of live animals   47
Street-sellers of mineral productions and natural curiosities   81
The street-buyers   103
The street-Jews   115
Street-finders or collectors   136
The streets of London   181
Chimney-sweepers   338
Crossing-sweepers   465

Volume 3: *Contents*

THE STREET–FOLK
The destroyers of vermin   I
Street-exhibitors   43
Street-musicians   158
Street–vocalists   190
Street–artists   204
Exhibitors of trained animals   214
Skilled and unskilled labour   221
Garret-masters   221
The coal-heavers   233
Ballast-men   265
Lumpers   288
The dock-labourers   300
Cheap lodging-houses   312
The transit of Great Britain and the Metropolis   318
London watermen, lightermen, and steamboat-men   327
London omnibus-drivers and conductors   336
London cab-drivers   351
London carmen and porters   357
London vagrants   368
Meeting of ticket-of-leave men   430

Volume 4: *Contents*

THE AGENCIES AT PRESENT IN OPERATION WITHIN THE METROPOLIS, FOR
THE SUPPRESSION OF VICE AND CRIME, *by the Rev. William Tuckniss, B. A.*
Universal desire for investigation   xi
Mere palliatives insufficient to check the growth of crime   xi
Decrease of crime doubtful   xii
General desire to alleviate misery   xiii
Guthrie on great cities   xiv
Social position of London   xv
Agencies at work in London   xvii
    Their number and income   xvii
Curative agencies   xviii
    British and Foreign Bible Society   xix
    Society for Promoting Christian Knowledge   xix
    Institution for Reading the Word of God in the Open Air xix
    Theatre Services   xix
    London City Mission   xx
    Church of England Scripture Readers' Society   xxii
    Religious Tract Society   xxiii
    Pure Literature Society   xxiii
Preventive agencies   xxiv
    National Temperance Society   xxiv
    United Kingdom Alliance   xxiv
    Free Drinking Fountain Association   xxv
    Ragged School Union   xxv

Preventive agencies (continued)
    Society for Improving the Condition of the Labouring Classes   xxv
    Female Servants' Home Society   xxvi
    Female Aid Society   xxvii
    Training Institutions for Servants   xxvii
    Field Lane Night Refuges   xxvii
    Dudley Stuart Night Refuge   xxvii
    Houseless Poor Asylum   xxviii
    House of Charity   xxviii
    Foundling Hospital   xxviii
    Society for the Suppression of Mendicity   xxviii
    Association for Promoting the Relief of Destitution   xxviii
    Association for the Aid and Benefit of Dressmakers and Milliners   xxix
    Young Women's Christian Association and West-end Home   xxix
    Society for Promoting the Employment of Women   xxx
    Metropolitan Early Closing Association, &c.   xxx
Repressive and punitive agencies   xxx
    Society for the Suppression of Vice   xxxi
    The Associate Institution   xxxi
    Society for Promoting the Observance of the Lord's Day   xxxiv
    Society for the Prevention of Cruelty to Animals   xxxiv
Reformative agencies   xxxiv
    Reformatory and Refuge Union   xxxiv
    Reformative agencies for fallen women   xxxv
    Magdalen Hospital   xxxvi
    London by Moonlight Mission   xxxvii
    Society for the Rescue of Young Women and Children   xxxvii
    London Female Preventive and Reformatory Institution   xxxvii
Concluding remarks   xxxviii

INTRODUCTION AND CLASSIFICATION, *by Henry Mayhew*   I
Workers and non-workers   2
    Classification of ditto   11
Those who will work   12
    Enrichers   13
    Auxiliaries   16
    Benefactors   19
    Servitors   20
Those who cannot work   22
    Those who are provided for   22
    Those who are unprovided for   22
Those who will not work   23
    Vagrants or tramps   23
    Professional beggars   23
    Cheats and their dependants   24
    Thieves and their dependants   25
    Prostitutes and their dependants   27
Those that need not work   27
    Those who derive their income from rent   27
    Those who derive their income from dividends   27
    Those who derive their income from yearly stipends   27
    Those who derive their income from obsolete or nominal offices   27

Those that need not work (continued)
  Those who derive their income from trades in which they do
    not appear   27
  Those who derive their income by favour from others   27
  Those who derive their support from the head of the family   27

THE NON-WORKERS, *by Henry Mayhew*   28

PROSTITUTES.

THE PROSTITUTE CLASS GENERALLY, *by Henry Mayhew and*
Bracebridge Hemyng   35
Prostitution in ancient states   37
  The Jews, &c.   39
  Ancient Egypt   43
  Ancient Greece   45
  Ancient Rome   49
  The Anglo-Saxons   34
Prostitution among the barbarous nations   58
  African nations   58
  Australia   67
  New Zealand   71
  Islands of the Pacific   76
  North American Indians   84
  South American Indians   90
  Cities of South America   93
  West Indies   94
  Java   96
  Sumatra   99
  Borneo   103
Prostitution among the semi-civilised nations   104
  Celebes   107
  Persia   108
  The Affghans   111
  Kashmir   115
  India   117
  Ceylon   125
  China   129
  Japan   136
  The ultra-Gangetic nations   139
  Egypt   141
  Northern Africa   149
  Arabia, Syria, and Asia Minor   151
  Turkey   155
  Circassia   158
  The Tartar races   160
Prostitution among the mixed northern nations   163
  Russia   165
  Siberia   167
  Iceland and Greenland   172
  Lapland and Sweden   174
  Norway   177
  Denmark   179

Prostitution in civilised states   181
    Spain   191
    Amsterdam   195
    Belgium   195
    Hamburg   196
    Prussia – Germany   198
    Berlin   198
    Austria   200
    Modern Rome   201
    Turin   203
    Berne   204
    Paris   205

PROSTITUTION IN LONDON, *by Bracebridge Hemyng*   210
General remarks   210
Seclusives, or those that live in private houses and apartments   215
    The Haymarket   217
Degree of education among prostitutes   218
Board lodgers   220
    Autobiographies   220
Those who live in low lodging-houses   223
    Swindling Sail   223
    Lushing Loo   224
Sailors' women   226
    Visit to Ratcliff-highway   228
    Visit to Bluegate Fields, &c.   231
Soldiers' women   233
    Visit to Knightsbridge   235
Thieves' women   236
    Visit to Drury-lane, &c   236
Park women   242
    Examples   242
The dependants of prostitutes   246
    Bawds   246
    Followers of dress lodgers   247
    Keepers of accommodation houses   249
    Procuresses, pimps, and panders   250
    Fancy men   252
    Bullies   253
Clandestine prostitutes   255
    Female operatives   255
    Maidservants   257
    Ladies of intrigue and houses of assignation   258
Cohabitant prostitutes   259
    Narrative of a gay woman   260
Criminal returns   263
Traffic in foreign women   269

THIEVES AND SWINDLERS, *by John Binny*
Introduction   273
Sneaks, or common thieves   277
    Juvenile thieves   277
    Stealing from street-stalls   277

Sneaks, or common thieves (continued
    Stealing from the till   278
    Stealing from the doors and windows of shops   279
    Stealing from children   281
    Child stripping   281
    Stealing from drunken persons   282
    Stealing linen, &c.   283
    Robberies from carts   284
    Stealing lead from house-tops, copper from kitchens, &c.   285
    Robberies by false keys   286
    Robberies by lodgers   288
    Robberies by servants   289
    Area and lobby sneaks   290
    Stealing by lifting windows, &c.   292
    Attic or garret thieves   293
    A visit to the rookery of St Giles   294
    Narrative of a London sneak   301
Pickpockets and shoplifters   303
    Common pickpockets   306
    Omnibus pickpockets   309
    Railway pickpockets   310
    A visit to the thieves' dens in Spitalfields   311
    Narrative of a pickpocket   316
Horse- and dog-stealers   325
    Horse-stealing   325
    Dog-stealing   325
Highway robbers   326
    A ramble among the thieves' dens in the borough   330
Housebreakers and burglars   334
    Narrative of a burglar   345
    Narrative of another burglar   349
Prostitute thieves   355
    Prostitutes of the Haymarket   356
    Common street-walkers   360
    Hired prostitutes   361
    Park women   362
    Soldiers' women   363
    Sailors' women   365
Felonies on the River Thames   366
    Mudlarks   366
    Sweeping-boys   367
    Sellers of small wares   367
    Labourers on board ship   367
    Dredgermen or fishermen   368
    Smuggling   368
    Felonies by lightermen   368
    The river pirates   369
    Narrative of a mudlark   370
Receivers of stolen property   373
    Dolly-shops   373
    Pawnbrokers, &c.   374
    Narrative of a returned convict   376

Coining   377
  Coiners   378
  Forgers   380
Cheats   383
  Embezzlers   383
  Magsmen or sharpers   385
  Swindlers   388

BEGGARS, *by Andrew Halliday*
Introduction   393
Origin and history of the Poor Laws   394
  Statistics of the Poor Laws   397
  Report of the Poor Law Board   397
Street-beggars in 1816   398
Mendicant pensioners   399
Mendicity society   399
  Examples of applications   401
Begging-letter writers   403
  Decayed gentlemen   404
  Broken-down tradesmen   405
  Distressed scholar   405
  The Kaggs' family   406
Advertising begging-letter writers   410
Ashamed beggars   412
The swell beggar   413
Clean family beggars   413
Naval and military beggars   415
  Turnpike sailor   415
  Street-campaigners   417
Foreign beggars   419
  The French beggar   419
  Destitute Poles   420
  Hindoo beggars   423
  Negro beggars   425
Disaster beggars   427
  A shipwrecked mariner   428
  Blown-up miners   429
  Burnt-out tradesmen   429
  Lucifer-droppers   431
  Bodily afflicted beggars   431
  Seventy years a beggar   432
  Having swollen legs   433
  Cripples   433
  A blind beggar   433
  Beggars subject to fits   434
  Being in a decline   435
  Shallow coves   435
  Famished beggars   436

Disaster beggars (continued)
   The choking dodge   437
   The offal-eater   437
Petty trading beggars   438
   An author's wife   440
Dependants of beggars   441
   Referees   445
Distressed operative beggars   446
   Starved-out manufacturers   446
   Unemployed agriculturists   446
   Frozen-out gardeners   446
   Hand-loom weavers, &c.   447

B. Lists of Illustrations

Volume 1: *List of illustrations*

Portrait of Mr Mayhew   frontispiece
The London costermonger   on page 13
The coster-girl   on page 37
The oyster-stall   on page 49
The Orange-mart (Duke's Place)   on page 73
The Irish street-seller   on page 97
The wallflower-girl   on page 127
The groundsel-man   on page 147
The baked-potato man   on page 167
The coffee-stall   facing page 184
The coster-boy and -girl 'tossing the pieman'   facing page 196
Doctor Bokanky, the street herbalist   facing page 197
Illustrations of street-art, no. 1   facing page 224
Illustrations of street-art, no. 2   facing page 238
Hindoo tract-seller   facing page 239
'The Kitchen', Fox Court   facing page 250
The long-song seller   facing page 272
Illustrations of street-art, no. 3   facing page 278
Illustrations of street-art, no. 4   facing page 279
The book-auctioneer   facing page 296
The street-seller of nutmeg-graters   facing page 330
The street-seller of dog's collars   facing page 360
The street-seller of crockery-ware   facing page 361
The blind boot-lace seller   facing page 406
The street-seller of grease-removing composition   facing page 428
The Lucifer match-girl   facing page 429
The street-seller of walking-sticks   facing page 438
The street-seller of rhubarb and spice   facing page 452
The street-seller of combs   facing page 458

Volume 2: *List of illustrations*

London nightmen	frontispiece
A view in Petticoat-lane	facing page 36
A view in Rosemary-lane	facing page 37
The street dog-seller	facing page 54
The crippled street bird-seller	facing page 55
Street-seller of birds'-nests	facing page 72
The Jew old-clothes man	facing page 73
The bone-grubber	facing page 138
The mud-lark	facing page 139
The London dustman	facing page 172
View of a dust-yard	facing page 173
The London scavenger	facing page 226
Street orderlies	facing page 227
The able-bodied pauper street-sweeper	facing page 262
The rubbish-carter	facing page 263
The London sweep	facing page 346
One of the few remaining climbing-sweeps	facing page 347
The milkmaid's garland	facing page 370
The sweep's home	facing page 371
The sewer-hunter	facing page 388
Mode of cleansing cesspools	facing page 389
Flushing the sewers	facing page 424
The rat-catchers of the sewers	facing page 425
The bearded crossing-sweeper at the exchange	facing page 470
The crossing-sweeper that has been a maidservant	facing page 471
The Irish crossing-sweeper	facing page 480
The one-legged crossing-sweeper at Chancery-lane	facing page 481
The boy crossing-sweepers	on page 507

Volume 3: *List of illustrations*

Guy Fawkes	frontispiece
Rat-killing at sporting public-houses	facing page 8
Jack Black, rat-killer to Her Majesty	facing page 9
Punch's showman, with assistant	facing page 46
Street-telescope exhibitor	facing page 82
Street-acrobats performing	facing page 83
Street-conjuror	facing page 118
Circus-clown at fair	facing page 119
Street-performers on stilts	facing page 150
Old Sarah	facing page 151
Ethiopian serenaders	facing page 190
Interior of photographer's travelling caravan	facing page 191
A garret-master, or cheap cabinet-maker	facing page 226
Gang of coal-whippers at work below bridge	facing page 227
Coal-porters filling waggons at coal-wharf	facing page 262

Ballast-heavers at work in the pool   facing page 263
Lumpers discharging timber-ship in commercial dock   facing page 298
A dinner at a cheap lodging-house   facing page 299
Thames lightermen tugging away at the oar   facing page 334
Cab-driver   facing page 335
Street ticket-porter with knot   facing page 364
Vagrants in the casual ward of workhouse   facing page 365
Vagrant from the refuge in Playhouse-yard, Cripplegate   facing page 406
Vagrants from Asylum for the Houseless Poor   facing page 407
Ticket-of-leave men   facing page 430
Meeting of ticket-of-leave men   facing page 431

Volume 4: *Maps and tables illustrating the criminal statistics
of each of the counties of England and Wales in 1851*

Map showing the density of the population   page 451
    Table of ditto   page 452
Map showing the intensity of criminality   page 455
    Table of ditto   page 456
Map showing the intensity of ignorance   page 459
    Table of ditto   page 460
    Table of ignorance among criminals   page 462
    Table of degrees of criminality   page 464
    Comparative educational tables   page 465
Map showing the number of illegitimate children   page 467
    Table of ditto   page 468
Map showing the number of early marriages   page 471
    Table of ditto   page 472
Map showing the number of females   page 475
    Table of ditto   page 476
Map showing committals for rape   page 477
    Table of ditto   page 479
Map showing committals for assault with intent to ravish
    and carnally abuse   page 481
    Table of ditto   page 482
Map showing committals for disorderly houses   page 485
    Table of ditto   page 485
Map showing concealment of births   page 489
    Table of ditto   page 490
Map showing attempts at miscarriage   page 493
    Table of ditto   page 494
Map showing assaults with intent   page 497
    Table of ditto   page 498
Map showing committals for bigamy   page 499
    Table of ditto   page 500
Map showing committals for abduction   page 501
    Table of ditto   page 502
Map showing the criminality of females   page 503
    Table of ditto   page 504

Volume 4: *List of illustrations*

A midnight meeting – Rev. Baptist Noel speaking   frontispiece
Greek dancing-girl – *hetaira* – age of Socrates   page 45
Roman brothel – imperial era   page 47
Women of the Bosjes race   page 59
Girls of Nubia – making pottery   page 65
Women of the Sacs, or 'Sau-kies', tribe of American Indians   page 85
Dyak women – Borneo   page 103
Chinese woman – prostitute   page 129
Scene in the gardens of *Closerie des Lilas* – Paris   page 213
A night-house – Katie Hamilton's   page 217
The New-cut – evening   page 223
The Haymarket – midnight   page 261
Boys exercising at Tothill Fields' prison   page 301
Cell, with prisoner at crank labour, in the Surrey House of
     Correction   page 345
Friends visiting prisoners   page 377
Liberation of prisoners from Coldbath Fields' House of
     Correction   page 387

APPENDIX 2: A MAYHEW BIBLIOGRAPHY

Mayhew's own writings
[including plays, novels, books for young people, archival remains, and contemporary reviews of his work but excluding editorial roles in, for example, *Figaro in London* (1835–1839), *Punch* (1841–1842), *Comic Almanac* (1850) and *Morning News* (Jan 1859)]

Henry Mayhew (1834), *The Wandering Minstrel* [drama].

Henry Mayhew (1842), *What to Teach and How to Teach it; so that the child may become a good and wise man.*

Henry Mayhew (1844), *The Prince of Wales's Library* (Part I)

Henry and Augustus Mayhew (1847), *The Greatest Plague of Life: or the Adventures of a Lady in Search of a Good Servant.*

Henry and Augustus Mayhew (1847), *The Good Genius Who Turned Everything into Gold: or, The Queen Bee and the Magic Dress.*

Henry Mayhew (1847) 'What is the Cause of Surprise? And What Connection has it with Suggestion?' in *Douglas Jerrold's Shilling Magazine, 6.*

Henry and Augustus Mayhew (1848), *The Image of His Father: or a Tale of a Young Monkey.*

Henry and Augustus Mayhew (1849), *The Magic of Kindness.*

Henry Mayhew (1849–1850), 'Labour and the Poor' being Letters I-LXXXII in the *Morning Chronicle*, 19 Oct. 1849 to 12 Dec. 1850.

Henry and Augustus Mayhew (1850), *Fear of the World.*

Henry and Augustus Mayhew (1850), *Acting Charades.*

Henry Mayhew (1850), 'Labour and the Poor': speech at a public meeting, 28 October 1850, published in Committee of the Tailors of London (1850), *Labour and the Poor: Report of the Speech of Henry Mayhew Esquire, and the evidence adduced at a Public Meeting held at St Martin's Hall, Long Acre . . . for the purpose of exposing the falsehoods contained in the Morning Chronicle of Friday October 4 1850 on the Sweating or Domestic System . . .*

Henry Mayhew, letter to the *Economist*, 16 Nov. 1850 and 21 Dec. 1850.

Henry Mayhew (1851), *Low Wages: Their Causes, Consequences and Remedies* (Parts 1-4, Nov. and Dec. 1851)

Henry Mayhew (1851), 'Home is Home' in Viscount Ingestre (ed.), *Meliora: or Better Times to Come.*

Henry Mayhew and George Cruikshank (1851), *1851: or the Adventures of Mr and Mrs Sandboys.*

Henry Mayhew (1851), 'The Great Exhibition', *Edinburgh News and Literary Chronicle*, May–July 1851.

Henry Mayhew (1851–2) *London Labour and the London Poor*, 3 volumes published serially [first number probably appeared 14 Dec. 1850; last number appeared on 21 Feb 1852]; the British Library owns a volume in which these were bound together with *Answers to Correspondents* from the original wrappers. *Huntington Library, San Marino, Ca: FU 607* Henry Mayhew to Frederick James Furnivall, 4 May 1852.

Henry Mayhew (1854), *The Story of the Peasant-Boy Philosopher*.

Henry Mayhew (1855), *The Wonders of Science, or Young Humphrey Davy*.

Evidence of Henry Mayhew, Second Report of Select Committee of the House of Commons on Transportation 1856 (296), XVII. qq.3504, 3516, 3742.

Henry Mayhew (1856), 'On Capital Punishments' in Society for Promoting the Amendment of the Law (1856), *Three Papers on Capital Punishment*.

Henry Mayhew (1856), *The Rhine and the Picturesque Scenery*.

Henry Mayhew (1856), *How We Live in the World of London* [drama].

Henry Mayhew (1856), *The Great World of London* [part work], Parts 1-9 March-November.

Henry Mayhew (1856–7?) 'Punch on the Platform' [tour of personal performances].

Huntington Library, San Marino, Ca. HM 10774 18 April 1857 Henry Mayhew to A.L.

Henry and Augustus Mayhew (1857), *Paved with Gold* [part-work project which Henry Mayhew left after number 5].

Henry Mayhew (1858), *The Upper Rhine: The Scenery of its Banks and the Manners of its People*.

Henry Mayhew (1861–2), *London Labour and the London Poor*, 4 vols, Griffin, Bohn and Co.

Henry Mayhew (1861), *Young Benjamin Franklin*.

Henry Mayhew and John Binny (1862), *The Criminal Prisons of London and Scenes of Prison Life*.

Henry Mayhew (1863), *The Boyhood of Martin Luther*.

Henry Mayhew (1864), *German Life and Manners as Seen in Saxony at the Present Day*, 2 vols.

Henry Mayhew (1865), *The Shops and Companies of London and the Trades and Manufactures of Great Britain* [part-work to which he contributed].

Henry Mayhew (1865), *London Labour and the London Poor*, 4 vols, second printing of the 1862 edition.

Henry Mayhew (1871), *Report Concerning the Trade and Hours of Closing Usual Amongst the Licensed Victualling Establishments Now Open for the Unrestricted Sale of Beer, Wine and Spirits, at Certain So-called 'Working Men's Clubs', Distributed Throughout the Metropolis*.

Henry and Athol Mayhew [his son] (1874), *Mont Blanc* [drama].

Henry Mayhew and others (1874), *London Characters. Illustrations of the Humour, Pathos and Peculiarities of London Life*.

Contemporary reviews

Illustrated London News (29 November 1845), 'St James's Theatre – The Amateurs' [an account of Charles Dickens's production of *Every Man in his Humour* which includes an illustration of Mayhew in costume].

Spectator (27 October 1849), 'The Morning Chronicle on the State of the Poor'.

Frasers's Magazine (Number 41, January 1850), 'Labour and the Poor' [by J. M. Ludlow].

British Quarterly Review (Volume 11, May 1850) 'Review of the "Morning Chronicle" Correspondent on the State of the Poor in the Metropolis'.

Economist (18 November 1850), 'Distressed Populations', being unfavourable review of *Morning Chronicle* series 'Labour and the Poor'.

Eclectic Review (94, October 1851), Review of 'Labour and the Poor'.

The Athenaeum (15 November 1851), unsigned review of *London Labour and the London Poor*, pp.1199–201.

The Athenaeum (15 December 1855), p.1464, review of Henry Mayhew, *The Wonders of Science or Young Humphrey Davy*.

The Athenaeum (30 May 1863), p.714, review of Henry Mayhew, *The Boyhood of Martin Luther*.

Spectator (8 March 1856), 'New Serial: The Great World of London'.

Obituaries

Obituary, 'Henry Mayhew', in *The Times*, 27 July 1887.

'The Late Mr Henry Mayhew', in *London Illustrated News*, 91, 6 August 1887.

Obituary of Henry Mayhew, in *Punch*, 6 August 1887.

Some modern editions and selections

Dover Facsimile Edition (1968), Henry Mayhew, *London Labour and the London Poor*, 1862, 4 vols.

Caliban Edition (1980), *Morning Chronicle Survey of Labour and the Poor: The Metropolitan Districts*, with an introduction by Peter Razzell, 6 volumes.

J. L. Bradley (ed.) (1965) Henry Mayhew: *Selections from London Labour and the London Poor*, Oxford.

Anne Humpherys (ed.) (1971), *Voices of the Poor* [selections from Mayhew's *Morning Chronicle* Letters).

E. P. Thompson and E. Yeo (1971) (eds), *The Unknown Mayhew* (paperback edition) 1973.

Jules Ginswick (ed.) (1983), *Labour and the Poor in England and Wales 1849–1851*, 3 vols.

Victor Neuburg (ed.) (1985), *Henry Mayhew, London Labour and the London Poor, Selections*.

Modern authorities

James Bennett (1981), *Oral History and Delinquency: the Rhetoric of Criminology*, Chicago.

Raymond Chapman (1994), *Forms of Speech in Victorian Fiction*, Harlow.

David Englander (1991, published 1993), 'Criminality upon and beneath the Surface in Victorian London', *Criminal Justice History*, 12, Westport, Ct.

David Englander and Rosemary O'Day (eds) (1995), *Retrieved Riches: Social Investigation in Britain 1840–1914*, Aldershot.

David Englander (1995), 'Comparisons and Contrasts: Henry Mayhew and Charles Booth as Social Investigators', in David Englander and Rosemary O'Day (eds) (1995), *Retrieved Riches: Social Investigation in Britain 1840–1914*.

David Englander (1998), *Poverty and Poor Law Reform in 19th Century Britain, 1834-1914: From Chadwick to Booth*, Harlow.

David Englander (2000), 'From the Abyss: Pauper Petitions and Correspondence in Victorian London' in *London Journal*, 15.

M. M. Goldsmith (1985), *Private Vices, Public Benefits*, Cambridge.

Christopher Herbert (1991), *Culture and Anomie: Ethnographic Imagination in the Nineteenth Century*, Chicago and London.

Gertrude Himmelfarb (1984), *The Idea of Poverty, England in the Early Industrial Age* (1985 paperback edition), London and Boston.

Angela M. Hookham (1962), 'The Literary Career of Henry Mayhew', Unpublished M. A. thesis, University of Birmingham.

Anne Humpherys (1977), *Travels into the Poor Man's Country*, Athens, Georgia.

Gareth Stedman Jones (1983), *Languages of Class: Studies in English Working Class History, 1832–1982*, Cambridge.

Gareth Stedman Jones (1984), 'The Labours of Henry Mayhew, "Metropolitan Correspondent"', *London Journal*, 10 (1).

P. J. Keating (1971), *The Working Classes in Victorian Fiction*, London.

Raymond J. Kent (1981), *A History of British Empirical Sociology*.

Anne J. Kershen (1993), 'Henry Mayhew and Charles Booth: Men of their Times?' in Alderman, G. and Holmes, C. (eds), *Outsiders and Outcasts: Essays in Honour of William J. Fishman*, London.

Harland S. Nelson (1965), 'Dickens's "Our Mutual Friend" and Henry Mayhew's "London Labour and the London Poor"' in *Nineteenth Century Fiction*, 20.

Rosemary O'Day (1995), 'Interviews and investigations: Charles Booth and the Making of the Religious Influences Survey', in David Englander and Rosemary O'Day (eds) (1995), *Retrieved Riches: Social Investigation in Britain 1840–1914*.

P. E. Razzell and R. W. Wainwright (eds) (1973), *The Victorian Working Class*.

Raphael Samuel (1973), 'Mayhew and Labour Historians', *Bulletin of the Society for the Study of Labour History*, No. 26.

F. B. Smith (1979), 'Mayhew's Convict' in *Victorian Studies*, 22.

Sheila M. Smith (1980), *The Other Nation: The Poor in the English Novels of the 1840s and 1850s*, Oxford.

Harvey Peter Sucksmith (December 1969), 'Dickens and Mayhew: a further note', in *Nineteenth Century Fiction*, 24.

Edward Thompson (1967), 'The Political Education of Henry Mayhew', *Victorian Studies*, 11.

Edward Thompson (1971), 'Mayhew and the Morning Chronicle', in E. P. Thompson and E. Yeo (1971) (eds), *The Unknown Mayhew* (paperback edition 1973).

Karel Williams (1981), *From Pauperism to Poverty*, London.

Eileen Yeo, 'Mayhew as Social Investigator' in E. P. Thompson and E. Yeo (1971) (eds), *The Unknown Mayhew* (paperback edition 1973).

Eileen Yeo (1991), 'The Social Survey in Social Perspective, 1830–1930' in Martin Bulmer et al., *The Social Survey in Historical Perspective*, 1880–1940, Cambridge.

APPENDIX 3: MAYHEW'S AUTHORITIES

Authorities cited in the three-volumes-in-one edition of
London Labour and the London Poor, 1851

The listing of authorities pertains to those referred to in the 1851 single-bound three-volume edition of *London Labour and the London Poor*. This edition was selected because in it Mayhew relied less on his assistants for separate contributions than he did in the 1861-2 edition. (The list does not include citations in the *Morning Chronicle, Criminal Prisons of London* or in the 1861-2 edition of *London Labour and the London Poor*.) These citations range from what might be regarded as mere name-dropping, through poetry, songs and ditties to statistics and statutes.[1] In places it is difficult (even impossible) to differentiate Mayhew's sources one from another and so this list must be regarded with caution. Nevertheless it provides an entrée into a study of Mayhew's use of sources and engagement with contemporary works.[2]

Some scholars have disparaged him for merely importing statistics that were readily available at the time.[3] This was certainly true of some but not of other statistical data in *London Labour and the London Poor*. His topographical mapping and presentation of data was often distinctive.

If, however, we regard Mayhew primarily as a brilliant journalistic communicator, the range of his sources is more impressive and his work in making them available to a wider public more admirable. For instance, his concern for the application of anthropology, so often ignored by modern commentators, both reflected and fed the Victorian middle-class's obsession with exploration.

Mayhew's authorities
[John] Lydgate, 'London Lykpeny', i:8
William Shakespeare, i:8;.294; (*Cymbeline*) ii:339; (*Hamlet*), iii:6
[Ben] Jonson, i:8
[John] Ford, *Son's Darling*, i:8
[Francis] Beaumont and [John] Fletcher, i:8

1 Where Mayhew's source is imprecise, I have tried to supply a title by checking with the British Library Catalogue. Where no title can be supplied for more obscure authorities, I have attempted to include in square parentheses at least first names and/or the context in which Mayhew used the work. Entries are generally given volume by volume; only when the same authority is clearly intended in different volumes have I created composite entries – e.g. William Shakespeare.
2 Titles have been checked and corrected against the British Library catalogue.
3 E. Thompson & Eileen Yeo (eds), *The Unknown Mayhew: Selections from the Morning Chronicle,* Penguin Books, 1973, 7

[Samuel] Johnson, i:8

Charles Knight, London, i:8

John Stuart Mill. i:9; ii:305–7; iii:8–9, 28

Records of the Royal Society, i:57

Records of the Court of Common Council of London, Reigns of Elizabeth I, James I, James II, i:59

Vagrancy Laws passed by Parliament in the reign of Elizabeth I, i:59

Records of sales of varieties of fish in Billingsgate Market, i:63

Adam Smith, i:67; ii:305, 306

City missionaries, i:70

A Roman Catholic priest, i:115

Dr [Jonathan] Pereira (on nutritional value of fish), i:118, 119, 203 (treatise on diet)

Captain Perry (ditto) of his Polar Expedition, 1827, i:118

Experiments in nutrition at the Zoological Gardens of London, i:118

Sir John Ross (nutrition), i:119

Captain [John Dundas] Cochrane, [*Narrative of a Pedestrian*] *Journey through Russia and Siberian Tartary*,[4] i:255 (nutrition), 119

Sir John Franklin (nutrition), i:119

Dr [Alfred] Carpenter (nutrition), i:119

Mr Jacob Bentley (nutrition), i:119

Report of the Government Commissioners of Inquiry (?into the diet of the poor), i:120

Sir James Graham (dietaries of prisoners) Letter to the Chairman of Quarter Sessions, Jan 27 1843, i:120

[William] Cobbett, i:132

The Garden of Heaven (described as a Roman Catholic book), i:135

Dr [William] Withering (eminent botanist), i:142

Mr [Joseph] Strutt, *Sports and Pastimes of the People of England*, 1800, i:205, 216, 226, 273, 274

Dr Connolly (the ungovernability of the educated insane), i:213

[? William Thomas] Moncrieff, *Rochester* (popular farce), i:216

Fauchet, *Origine de la langue et poésie Française*, 1581, i:226

[George] Putenham, *Arte of English poesie*, 1589, i:226

The character of a street-seller of stationery, provided by a clergymen to Mr Knight, i:271

[Thomas] Sternhold and [John] Hopkins (psalmists and hymnists), i:283

Alexander Pope, i:294

Robert Burns, i:294

Lord Byron, i:294

[John] Milton, i:294

[Matthew] Prior, i:294

Walter Scott, i:294

[Edmund] Burke, i:294

[Samuel] Richardson's *Pamela*, i:294

4 Where possible the full title has been given by inserting missing words in Mayhew's original reference. Date of publication has also been supplied where possible.

Tom Paine, i:294

Testimony of a clergyman concerning provision for the poor, i:318–319

The Lacemakers' Appeal, i:364

Prospectus of the Street Mechanics, Labourers, Hawkers etc. Protection Association, Holborn, i:365

1841 Census returns of hawkers, hucksters and pedlars, i:377

Extract from Mayhew's material in the Morning Chronicle about lodging-houses, i:408

1839 Report of the Constabulary Commission concerning mendicants' lodging houses, i:408

Ratting advert, i:452

Advert for a ferret match, ii:56

Advert for warehouse of rag, bottle and kitchen stuff buyer, ii:108

45 letters destined for waste, ii:114

Dr [Neil] Arnott (on the composition and impact of street dust), ii:188

Erasmus Wilson (on the skin and lungs), ii:188

Board of Health reports (on dust in the metropolis), ii:189; (? on water-cleansing), ii:275–6

Mr John Bullar's report to Parliament (in his capacity as Hon. Secretary to the Association for the Promotion of Baths and Wash-houses), ii:189

Mr Hawes (consumption of soap in the metropolis), ii:190

Professor Clarke (ditto), ii:191

Board of Health, first report on the supply of water to the metropolis, ii:195–6

Mr Charles Cochrane (scientific calculations of dung deposits etc.), ii:196; (on payment of parish street-sweepers), ii:250; (street-orderlyism), ii:257–259, 270, 275

Sanitary Progress, ii:197

Oath of the London scavengers, ii:206

Extract from parish minute book (St Pancras), Nov 7 1839, ii:210

Regulations for the cleansing of city streets, ii:210–211.

[George] Crabbe (poet), ii:251

Reports of the National Philanthropic Association, ii:259–62

W. Haywood, Surveyor to the City Commission of Sewers, report 'upon street cleansing and in reference to the street-orderly system', ii:.271–275; report of the City Sewer Transactions and Works, Feb 12 1850, ii:405–6, 425, 430

Mr Lee of Sheffield (water-cleansing), ii:275, 276

Post Office Directory, ii:288

Monsieur [Jean Baptiste] Say (division of labour), ii:305; iii:8

Dr Andrew Ure, Philosophy of Manufactures, ii:306; (smoke) ii:341

Mr [?Henry]Thornton (on overpopulation), ii:307, 317, 322

Bishop [Hugh] Latimer from his Sermons, i:100 (on enclosures), ii:309

Roger Ascham (on enclosures) from Eden's History of the Poor, i:118, ii:309

[William] Harrison (on enclosures), ii:309

William Stafford, 1581 (on enclosures) from Pictorial History of England, 2, 960, ii:309

Francis Bacon, *History of King Henry VII*: Works, 5, 61, ii:309

Reports of the Commissioner of the Times newspaper, June 1845, ii::310

Report of the Poor Law Commissioners (1844), ii:320

Mr Pearse (army clothier), evidence given to the Select Committee on Army and Navy Appointments, ii:331

Mr Shaw, army clothier, his letter to the Chairman of the Committee on Army, Navy and Ordnance Estimates, ii:331

Records of the Smoke Prevention Committee, ii:339

Dr [David Boswell] Reid, chemist (smoke), ii:340–341

Professor [William Thomas] Brande (smoke), ii:341

Mr Beckett (smoke), ii:341

E[dward] Solly, Lecturer in Chemistry at the Royal Institution (smoke), ii:341

Mr Booth (smoke), ii:341–2

Professor [Michael] Faraday (smoke), ii:343

[John] Rickman's Table of Population of England and Wales between 1570 and 1750, ii:317

Report of Irish House of Lords into population of Ireland, 1731, ii:318

Hearth Money returns (Ireland), 1754–1788, ii:318

Newenham's inquiry into the population of Ireland, 1805, ii:318

Incomplete Irish census, 1813, ii:318

Censuses from 1821–1851, ii:317–18

Mr Baines, *History of the Handloom Weavers*, ii:334

Limerick and Clare Observer, ii:334

6th Annual Report of the Poor Law Commissioners, 1840, 31, ii:335

[William] Harrison's *Discourse* (preface to Holinshed's *Chronicles*), 1577, ii:338

Report of parliamentary inquiry into child chimney-sweeps (1817), ii:347–354

Mr Cook, ii:349

[Charles] Lamb (on sweeps) *Essays of Elia*, 1823, ii:366–7

Mr Luke Howard's observations of average temperatures, 1805–1830, ii:374

Board of Health report on fires, ii:380

Mr Payne, coroner of the City of London (on fires), ii:381

Mr Braidwood, director of the fire brigade, in evidence to parliament, ii:381

William Baddeley, engineer, ii:381

Mr Emmott, engineer of the Oldham water works, ii:382

Mr W. Lindley, engineer supervisor of Hamburg rebuilding, ii:382

Dr Paley in Report to the Metropolitan Commission of Sewers, ii:385

[John] Stow (antiquary), ii:389

Dr [George William] Lemon, *English Etymology* [1783], ii:389

Monsieur Dupin (classification), iii:5

Meeting at Buckingham Palace to discuss Great Exhbition, June 30 1849 (classification), iii:5

Mr McCulloch (produce of the potteries), ii:284

Mr Dodd (textile manufactures), ii:321

Mr Porter (causes of poverty), ii:325; his *Progress of the Nation*, 1847, ii:326

Henry Mayhew – quote from *Morning Chronicle* re timber-porters at the docks – ii:329

[Frederic William] Maitland, *History of London*, ii:403

[Publius or Caius Cornelius] Tacitus, *Life of Agricola*, ii:404

Sir George Staunton, ii:408

Committee of the House of Commons inquiry into sewers, 1848, ii:408–9

Board of Health Report: . . . application of sewer water and town manure to agricultural production, ii:411 [cites individual testimonies]

D.F. Fortescue, Board of Health, ii:411

Mr Forster (report on sewers), ii:411–414

Commissions of sewers, ii:414–423

Report on King's Scholars' Fund Sewer, 1849, ii:425

Report of surveyors to Commissioners of Sewers, Aug 31 1848, ii:427

Occupation Abstract of Census of 1841, iii:7

Irish Census, iii:7

Charles Babbage (manufacture), iii:7

Monsieur Guerry (statist), iii:30

Report of Poor Law Commissioners, 1848, iii:34

Biblical sources for prostitution etc, iii:39–43

G. Wilkinson, *Ancient Egypt*, iii:44

Mackinnon, *History of Civilization*, iii:46

[John] Potter, *Antiquities of Greece*, iii:46

Hase, *On the Ancient Greeks*, iii:46

[Philipp August] Boeck[h], *Public Economy of Athens*, iii:46

Sharon Turner (Anglo-Saxon marriage etc.), iii:55 [probably *The History of the Anglo-Saxons*, 1840][5]

Wilkins (ed.), *Leges Anglo-Saxonicae*, iii:55.

Napier, *Excursions in Southern Africa*, iii:56

Harriet Ward, *Five Years in Kaffir Land*, iii:57 [*The Cape and the Kaffirs: a Diary of Five Years' Residence in Kaffirland,* 1851][6]

Barrow, *Travels*, iii:57

Methuen, *Life in the Wilderness*, iii:59

[Thomas Edward] Bowdich's *Essay* [*on the Geography of North-Western Africa*, 1821], iii:61

Thompson and Allen, *Expedition to the Niger*, iii:61, 63

[Macgregor] Laird's *Voyage*, iii:61

J. E. Forbes, *Dahomey and the Dahomans*, iii:63

[Archibald] Dalziel's *History of Dahomey*, [1793] iii:63

Mr Leed's *Account*, iii:63

John Duncan, *Travels* [*in Western Africa*, 2 vols, 1847], iii:63

Adams, *Remarks on the West Coast*, iii:63

[John] Adams, *Sketches* [*taken during ten voyages to Africa*, 1823], iii:63

[Henry] Meredith, [*An*] *Account of the Gold Coast* [*of Africa*, 1812], iii:63

Isaac, *Travels on the East Coast* [*of Africa*], iii:64

5 Where Mayhew's reference is unclear, the most probable authority is supplied in square brackets.
6 The full title of the volume is supplied where it has not been possible to modify Mayhew's reference by inserting missing words.

620   LONDON LABOUR AND THE LONDON POOR

[James] Richardson, *Travels in the [Great Desert of] Sahara [in the years of 1845 and 1846*, 2 vols, 1848], iii:65

Jameson, Wilson and Hugh Murray, *Account of Africa,* iii:65

[Count] St Marie, *Visit to Algeria*, iii:65;151 [Count Sainte-Marie, *Algeria in 1845: A Visit to . . .* , 1846]

[James] Bruce [*Travels to Discover the Source of the Nile*, 5 vols, 1790] (on Abyssinian society), iii:66

Gogat (ditto), iii:66

Mr [Henry] Salt (ditto), [*A Voyage to Abyssinia*, 1814] iii:66

Sir [William] Cornwallis Harris (ditto), [*Highlands of Ethiopia*, 1844] iii:66

Ignatius Palme, *Travels in Kordosan*, iii:66

Werne, *Expedition up the White Nile*, iii:67

[Charles] Sturt, *Two Expeditions [into the Interior of New South Wales*, 2 vols, 1833] iii:71

[Charles] Sturt, *Expedition to Central Australia*, iii:71; *Voyage to the South Seas*, iii:84

[William] Westgarth, *Australia Felix*, iii:71

Leichardt, *Expeditions*, iii:71

[Christopher Pemberton] Hodgson, *Australian Settlements*, iii:71

[George Henry] Haydon, [*Five Years' Experience in] Australia Felix* [1846], iii:71

Stoke, *Discoveries*, iii:71

[George French Angas] Angus, *Savage Life and Scenes [in Australia and New Zealand*, 2 vols, 1847], iii:71, 76

Sir George Grey, *Journals [of Two Expeditions of Discovery in North-Western and Western Australia*, 2 vols, 1841], iii:71

[Edward John] Eyre's *Expedition [to Australia]*, iii:71

Pridden, *History [of Australia]*, iii:71

[lists other explorers who have described aboriginal life in iii:71]

Tyrone Power, *Pen and Pencil Sketches* (on New Zealand), iii:74

[Edward] Jerningham Wakefield [*Adventure in New Zealand*, 1845] (on New Zealand), iii:75, 76

Handbook of New Zealand by a Magistrate of the Colony, iii:76

Dieffenbach, *Travels*, iii:76

Brown (on the aborigines), iii:76

[George Samuel Windsor] Earl, *Travels*, iii:71,76

[George Samuel Windsor] Earl, *Eastern Seas* [1837], iii:99

[M. Lucet], *Rovings in the Pacific by a Merchant Long Resident in Tahiti*, 1851, iii:80, 94

Walpole, *Four Years in the Pacific*, iii:84, 94

[William] Ellis, *Tour Through Hawaii* [1822–5], iii:84; *Polynesian Researches* [1833], iii:84

Herman Melville, *Omoo* and *Typee*, iii:84

Progress of the Gospel in Polynesia, iii:84

Montgomery, *Narrative of Bennett and Tyerman's Voyage*, iii:84

[? brothers Henry or William] Williams, *Missionary Enterprise*, iii:84

[William Charles] Mariner, [*An Account of the Natures of the] Tonga Islands* [1817], iii:84

[Charles] Wilkes, [*Atlas to the Narrative of the*] *United States Exploring Expedition* [1844], iii:84, 90, 94

Ruschenberger, *Three Years in the Pacific*, iii:84, 94

Sir George Simpson, *Voyage round the World*, iii:84, 87, 88, 90 [*Narrarive of a Journey Round the World*, 1847]

[John] Coulter, *Travels in South America*, iii:84 [*Adventures on the Western Coast of South America*, 1847]; *Voyage in the Pacific*, iii:84 [*Adventures in the Pacific*, 1845]

Heckewelder (on North American Indians), iii:87

Hunter (ditto Narrative of Captivity), iii:88, 90

McLean (recent author on Hudson River tribes), iii:88, *Twenty-five Years Service in Hudson Bay*, iii:90

[George] Catlin, [*Catlin's Notes of*] *Eight Years Travels* [*and Residence in Europe . . . , 1848*], iii:90

[Jonathan] Carver, *Travels in North America*, iii:90

[? Sir Alexander] Mackenzie, *Memoirs, Official and Personal*, iii:90

[John] West, *Residence in the Red River Colony*, iii:90 [*The Substance of a Journal During a Residence at the Red River Colony, British North America*, 1827]; [*A Journal of a*] *Mission to the Indians of New Brunswick* [1827], iii:90

Drake, *Book of the Indians*, iii:90

Halkett, *Historical Notes*, iii:90

Buchanan, *Sketches of History*, iii:90

[Francis Hamilton] Buchanan, *Journey in the Mysore* [probably *A Journey from Madras through the Countries of Mysore . . .* , 3 vols, 1807], iii:125

[James] Robertson, *History of Missions to the Indians*, iii:90 [*History of the Mission . . . to Nova Scotia*, 1847]

[William] Robertson, *History of America* [1777 and several editions down to 1840], iii:90

[John Parish] Robertson, *Letters on South America* [1843], iii:93, 94

[John Parish] Robertson, *Letters on Paraguay* [1838], iii:93

Sir James Alexander, *Acadie*, iii:90 [*L'Acadie: Explorations in British America*, 1849]

Cleveland, *Voyages and Enterprises*, iii:90

Dunlop, *Travels in Central America*, iii:93

Captain Basil Hall, *Journal* [probably *Fragments of Voyages and Travels*, 9 vols, 1831–3], iii:93

Stephenson, *Incident of Travel in Central America*, iii:93

Stephenson, *Historical and Descriptive Narrative*, iii:93

Norman, *Rambles in Yucatan*, iii:93

[Charles] Waterton, *Wanderings in South America* [1825], iii:93

Southey, *History of Brazil*, iii:93

Southey, *History of the West Indies*, iii:94

[Thomas] Young, [*Narrative of a*] *Residence on the Mosquito Shore* [*during the years 1839, 1840 and 1841, 1842*], iii:93

Gardiner, *Travels in Brazil*, iii:93

[? Sir John] Hawkshaw, *Reminiscences*, iii:93

[Alexander von] Humboldt, *Personal Narrative*, iii:93

Prince [Henry William] Adalbert [of Prussia], *Travels [in the South of Europe and in Brazil,* 1849], iii:93

[John] Macgregor, *Progress of America,* [1847] iii:93

[Daniel Parish] Kidder, *[Sketches of] Residence [and Travel] in Brazil* [1845], iii:94

[Brantz] Mayer, *Mexico as it [was and as it] is,* [1844] iii:94

Matheson, *Travels in Brazil,* iii:94

[Alexander] Caldcleugh, *Travels in South America [during the years 1819, 1820 and 1821,* 1825] iii:94

[Henry] Capadose, *Sixteen Years in the West Indies; Antigua and the Antiguans,* [1845] iii:96

Breen, *Historical Account of St Lucia,* iii:94

Bidwell, *West Indies as they are,* iii:94 [probably a mistake for Richard Bickell, *West Indies as they are,* 1825]

[John] Stewart, *[A View of the Past and Present] State of [the Island of] Jamaica,* [1823] iii:94

[William] Lloyd, *Letters from the West Indies,* [1839] iii:94

[Frederick William Naylor] Bayley, *Four Years' Residence [in the West Indies,* 1830], iii:94

Washington Irving, *Life and Voyages of Columbus,* [1854, 1859] iii:94

[Robert] Baird, *Impressions [and Experiences] of the West Indies [and North America in 1849],* iii:94

[Thomas Stanford] Raffles, *History of Java,* [2 vols 1817], iii:94, iii:99

Crawford, *Indian Archepelago,* iii:99, 102, 108

(? Crawford), *Journal of the Indian Archepelago,* iii:102

Crawford, *Researches in India,* iii:125

[John] Crauford [sic], *Embassy to Siam [Journal of an Embassy from the Governor-General of India to the Courts of Siam . . . ,* 1828] iii:140

[John] Crauford [sic], *Embassy to Avar,* iii:140 [possibly an error for Michael Symes, *An Account of an Embassy to the Kingdom of Avar, sent by the Governor-General of India [in 1795],* 1800]

[John Splinter] Stavorinus, *Voyages* [1796–1799], iii:99

[William] Marsden, *[History of] Sumatra* [1811], iii:102

[John] Anderson, *Mission to the East Coast [of Sumatra in 1823]* [1826], iii:102

Brooke (on prostitution in Malaya), iii:104; *Journals,* iii:108

Keppel (on prostitution in Malaya), iii:104; *Voyage of the Dido,* iii:108

Mundy (on prostitution in Malaya), iii:104, 108

Belcher (on prostitution in Malaya), iii:104

Law (on prostitution in Malaya), iii:104

[John] Malcolm, *History of* Persia [1815], iii:111

Malcolm, *Memoir on Central India,* iii:125

Javier, *Three Years in Persia,* iii:111

[Moritz von] Kotzebue, *Embassy to Persia* [1819], iii:111 [*Narrative of a Journey into Persia, in the suite of the imperial Russian Embassy, in the year 1817*]

Brydges, *Narrative of the Embassy,* iii:111

[James Justinian] Morier, *Second Journey to Persia,* iii:111 [*A Journey Through Persia, Armenia and Asia Minor to Constantinople [in 1808 and 1809],* published 1812; *Second Journey* published 1818]

[Robert] Ker Porter, [*The Caucasus . . . during his*] *Travels* [1817–20], iii:111

Stocqueler, *Pilgrimage*, iii:111

[Mountstuart] Elphinstone, *Kabul*, iii:114 [*An Account of the Kingdom of Caubal . . .* , published 1815, 1839]

[Godfrey Thomas] Vigne, [*A Personal Narrative of a*] *Visit to Ghuzui*, [*Kabul, and Afghanistan*, 1840], iii:114

[Godfrey Thomas] Vigne, *Travels in Kashmir* [1844], iii:116

[Alexander] Burnes, *Kabul*, iii:114 [*Cabool, 1836, 1837 and 1838*], published 1842]

[Karl Alexander] Hugel, *Travels in Kashmir* [*and the Panjab*, 1845], iii:116

Moorcroft, *Travels in the Himalayan Provinces* [*of Hindustan and the Panjab, in Ladakh and Kashmir . . .* , 1841], iii:116

[George] Forster, *Travels from Bengal to England*, iii:116 [*A Journey from Bengal to England, through the northern part of India, Kashmire, Afghanistan and Persia . . .* , 1, 1790]

[Walter] Hamilton, [*The*] *East India Gazetteer 1815, containing particular descriptions of . . . Hindostan*, 1828], iii:116, 125

[François] Bernier, *Travels in the Empire of the Mogul*, iii:116 [*Travels in the Mogul Empire, 1656–1668*, transl. 1826 by Irving Brook]

Bishop [Reginald] Heber, *Journal*, iii:125 [probably refers to: *The Life of Reginald Heber by his wife*, 1830, with selections from his correspondence and private papers]

Asiatic Researces [sic], iii:125 [probably refers to *Asiatic Researches or Transactions of the Society* (Asiatic Society of Bengal); the index of the first 18 volumes was published in 1835]

Hugh Murray, [*An Historical and Descriptive*] *Account of* [*British*] *India* [1832; 4th edition published 1843], iii:125

Hugh Murray, *Description of China*, iii:136 [*An Historical and Descriptive Account of China*, 1836]

[Lt-Col James Tod, *Travels in Western India* [1839], iii:125

[Lt-Col James] Tod, *Annals of Rajasthan,* iii:125

Lancelot Wilkinson, *Second Marriage of Widows in India*, iii:125 [*Introduction to an Essay on the Second Marriages of Widows, by a Learned Brahman of Nagpore*, 1841]

Essays presented to Parliament in 1803, iii:125

[Charles] Grant, *Observations on Society and Morals among our Asiatic Subjects*, iii:125 [*Observations on the State of Society among the Asiatic Subjects of Great Britain, particularly in respect to morals . . .* , published 1797, 1813 etc.]

[Charles James C.] Davidson, [*Diary of*] *Travels* [*and Adventures*] *in Upper India* [1843], iii:125

Mayne, *Continental India*, iii:125

Campbell, *British India*, iii:125

[James] Campbell, *Excursions in Ceylon* [1843], iii:129

[James] Hough, [*A Reply to the Letters of the Abbé Dubois, on the State of*] *Christianity in India*, iii:125

Abbé [J. A.] Dubois, *Letters on the Hindus,* iii:125 [*Letters on the State of Christianity in India*, 1823]

[Henry] Bevan, *Thirty Years in India* [1839], iii:125

[Werner] Hoffmeister, *Travels in [Ceylon and Continental] India* [1848], iii:125

[James] Mill, *History of British India* [published in 1817, 1820, 1840, 1851 etc.], iii:125

Wilson, *Notes*, iii:125

Ferishta, *Mohammedan History*, iii:125

Penhoen, *Empire Anglais*, iii:125

Xavier (on prostitution in India), iii:125

Raymond (on prostitution in India), iii:125

Jaseigny (on prostitution in India), iii:125

L'Indie (on prostitution in India), iii:125

Conformité des coutumes des Indes Orienteaux avec celles des Juifs (on prostitution in India), iii:125

[Henry Charles] Sirr, *Ceylon and the Singhalese* [1850], iii:129 [*Ceylon and the Cingalese . . .*]

[Charles] Pridham, *History of Ceylon* [1849], iii:129 [*An Historical, Political and Statistical Account of Ceylon and its Dependencies*, 1849]

[Jonathan] Forbes, *Eleven Years in Ceylon* [1842], iii:129

[John] Davy, [*An Account of the*] *Interior of Ceylon* [1821], iii:129

[Robert] Knox, *Captivity in Ceylon* [1681], iii:129 [*A Historical Relation of the Island of Ceylon . . . together with an account of the captivity*, 1681]

[James Emerson] Tennent, *Christianity in Ceylon* [1850], iii:129

[George Leonard] Staunton (on China) [*An Authentic Account of an Embassy from the King of Great Britain to the Emperor of China*, 1797], iii:136

Tee Taing Leu (on China), iii:136

[? Thomas] Lee, *Code of Criminal Law*, iii:136 [possibly Thomas Lee, *A Dictionary of Practice in Civil Actions . . .* , 2 vols, 1825]

[John Francis] Davis, *The Chinese* [1836, 1846], iii:136

[Charles Friedrich August] Guttzlaff, *China Opened* [revised by A. Reed, 1838], iii:136

[Robert] Fortune, [*Three Years*] *Wandering in the North[ern Provinces] of China* [1847], iii:136

[George] Smith, [*A Narrative of an Exploratory*] *Visit to* [. . .] *the Consular Cities of China* [1847], iii:136

[Robert] Montgomery Martin, *China* [1847], iii:136

[Frederick Edwyn] Forbes, *Five Years in China* [*from 1842–1847*, 1848], iii:136

[Samuel Wells] Williams, *Survey of the Chinese Empire*, iii:136 [*The Middle Kingdom: A Survey*, 1848]

[G.] Tradescant Lay, [*The*] *Chinese as they are* [*:Their moral, social and political character*, 1841, 1843], iii:136

[Robert] Morrison, [*A*] *View of China* [*for Philological Purposes*, 1817], iii:136

[Thomas Taylor] Meadow[s], *Desultory Notes* [*on the Government and People of*] *China* [1847], iii:136

The Chinese Repository [1832–1851], iii:136

[Thomas] Thornton, *History of China* [1844], iii:136

[David] Abeel, [*Journal of a*] *Residence in China* [. . . *1830 to 1833*, 1835], iii:136

[Arthur Augustus Thurlow] Cunyngham[e], [*An Aide-de-Camp's*] *Recollections of Service* [*in China*, 1847], iii:136

[Walter Henry] Medhurst, *State of China*, iii:136 [*China: Its State and Prospects*, 1838]

Auguste Harpman, *Revue des deux mondes*, iii:136

[? William B.]Langdon, *China*, iii:136 [probably refers to William B. Langdon and Nathan Dunn, *10,000 Things Relating to China and the Chinese*, 1842]

De Guignes, *Voyage à Peking*, iii:136

Tomkin, *Journals and Letters*, iii:140

[George] Finlayson, [*The*] *Mission* [*to Siam . . . 1821–1822*, 1826], iii:140

White, *Journey*, iii:140

[Robert Gordon] Latham, [*The*] *Natural History of the Varieties of Man* [1850], iii:140

[Edward William] Lane, [*An Account of the Manners and Customs of the*] *Modern Egyptians* [1836, 1837], iii:149

[Sophia] Poole, [*The*] *Englishwoman in Egypt* [*Letters from Cairo . . . 1842, 1843 and 1844*, 1844], iii:149

[William Holt] Yates [translator], [*The Modern History and Condition of*] *Egypt* [1843], iii:149

J. A. St John, *Manners and Customs of Ancient Greece*, iii:146 [correct name and title: James Augustus Saint John, *The History of the Manners and Customs of Ancient Greece*, 1842]

[James Augustus] St John, *Egypt and Mohammed Ali* [1834], iii:149

[James Augustus] St John, *Egypt and Nubia* [1845], iii:149

[James Augustus] St John, *Oriental Album* [1848, 1851 etc], iii:149

Cadalvene & Breuvery, *L'Egypte*, iii:149

Mugin, *Histoire de l'Egypte*, iii:149

[Johann Ludwig] Burckhardt, *Arabic Proverbs* [1830], iii:149; *Travels in Arabia* [1829], iii:155; *Notes on the Bedouins* [1830], iii:155 [name sometimes rendered as John Lewis Burkhardt]

Expédition Française à l'Egypte, iii:149

[Carsten] Niebuhr, *Travels in Egypt*, iii:149 [*Voyage en Egypte (1761–1763)* 1841]; *Description de l'Arabie* [1779], iii:155

[William Makepeace] Thackeray, [*Notes of a Journey*] *from Cornhill to Cairo* [2nd edition 1846], iii:149

[Eliot] Warburton, [*The*] *Crescent and the Cross* [3rd edition, 1845], iii:149

Bayle St John, [*Two Years Residence in a*] *Levantine Family* [1850, 1856], iii:149

[Frederick] Henniker, *Travels*, iii:149 [probably refers to Frederick Henniker, *Notes During a Visit to Egypt . . .* , 1824]

[Thomas] Boaz, *Modern Egypt*, iii:149 [*Egypt: A Familiar Description of the Land, People and Produce*, 2nd edition 1850]

Clot Bey, *Aperçu Général sur l'Egypte*, iii:149

[Hermann Ludwig Heinrich von] Pueckler Muskau, *Egypt and Mehemet Ali*, iii:149 [*Egypt Under Mehemet Ali*, translated by H. R. Lloyd, 1850]

[J. Clark] Kennedy, *Algeria and Tunis* [*in 1845*, 1846], iii:151

[Michael] Russel, [*History and Present Condition of the*] *Barbary States* [1835, 1844], iii:151

[James Grey] Jackson, [An] Account [of the Empire of Marocco, 1809, 1811, 1814 editions], iii:151

[Filippo] Pananti, Narrative [of a Residence in Algiers . . . , 1818], iii:151

[Frederick William] Beechey [North Africa] iii:151 [Proceedings of the Expedition to Explore the Northern Coast of Africa . . . , 1828]

[Edward] Blaquière [North Africa] iii:151 [Letters from the Mediterranean . . . Tunis, 1813.]

Rev. Robert Walpole [on Turkish Empire], iii:152, 155, 158 [Memoirs Relating to European and Asiatic Turkey, 1817 etc.]

[Francis Rawdon] Chesney, Euphrates Expedition, iii:155 [The Expedition for the Survey of the Rivers Euphrates and Tigris . . . , 1850]

[John William Perry] Farren, Letters to Lord Lindsay, iii:155 ['Letter on the Present State and Prospects of Syria' in A. W. C. Lindsay, Letters on Egypt, Edom and the Holy Land, 1838]

Perrier, Syrie sous Mehemet Ali, iii:155

[John G.] Kinnear, Cairo, Petra, and Damascus [1841], iii:155

[Walter Keating] Kelly, Syria and the Holy Land [1844], iii:155

Poujolat, Voyage en Orient, iii:155

[William Francis] Ainsworth, Travels [and Researches] in Asia Minor [1842, 1852 etc.], iii:155

Blondel, Deux Ans en Syrie, iii:155

[Thomas] Skinner, Overland Journey, iii:155 [Adventures During a Journey Overland to India, 2 vols, 1836, 1837]

Sketches of Turkey by an American, iii:158

Castellan, Moeurs des Ottomanes, iii:158

[Charles] Macfarlane, Constantinople [in 1828] [1830] iii:158

Porter, Philosophical Transactions, iii:158

Lady M[ary] W[ortley] Montague, Letters, iii:158

[? James Augustus] St John, Notes, iii:158

[Thomas] Thornton (Asia Minor) iii:158 [probably refers to Thomas Thornton, The Present State of Turkey, 1807, 1809 etc.]

[? R.] Walsh (Asia Minor) iii:158 [probably refers to R. Walsh, A Resident of Constantinople, 1836]

Marshall (Asia Minor) iii:158

[? James] Slade's Travels (Asia Minor) iii:158

Arvieux, Voyages (Asia Minor) iii:158

[Anne Marie Hortense, Viesse de] Marmont, Turkey, iii:158 [The Present State of the Turkish Empire, translated by Sir F. Smith, 1839]

[Alexander] Russel[l], [The Natural History of] Aleppo [1794], (Asia Minor) iii:158

[Edmund] Spencer, [Travels in the] Western Caucasus [1838], iii:160

[Edmund] Spencer, Travels in Circassia [1837], iii:160, 163

Klapreth, Voyages dans le Caucase, iii:160, 163

Wilbraham, Travels (Caucasus), iii:160

Marigny, Three Voyages (Caucasus), iii:160

Levchine, Les Kirghia Kazaks, iii:163

Kohl, *Russia and the Russians*, iii:167

[? Johann Heinrich Schnitzler] La *Russie en 1844 – par un Homme d'Etat*, iii:167 [possibly Johann Heinrich Schnitzler, *Secret History of the Government and Court of Russia under the Emperors Alexander and Nicholas*, 2 vols, 1847]

Russia under Nicholas I, iii:167 [possibly a reference to Ivan Golovine's *Russia Under the Autocrat Nicholas the First*, 1846]

[Robert] Lyall, *Character of the Russians*, [1823], iii:167

Voyages de deux Francais, iii:167

[August Bozzi] Granville, *Travels* (Russia), iii:167 [*St Petersburg: A Journal of Travels to and from that Capital*, 2 vols, 1828, 1829]

[Ivan] Golovine, *Russia Under the Autocrat* [*Nicholas the First*, 1846], iii:167

[Richard Lister] Venables, *Domestic Manners of the Russians*, iii:167

Bourke, *St Petersburg and Moscow*, iii:167

[Edward Pett] Thompson, *Life in Russia* [*or the Discipline of Despotism*, 1848], iii:167

Jesse, *Notes by a Half Pay* (Russia) iii:167

[George Adolph] Erman, *Travels* [*in Siberia*, 1848] iii:167, 171

[? Moritz] Wrangell, *Nord de la Sibérie*, iii:171

[Charles Herbert] Cottrell, *Recollections of Siberia* [*in the years 1840 and 1841*, 1842], iii:171

[Peter] Dobell, *Travels* [*in Kamtchatka and Siberia*, 1830] iii:171

Parry, *Three Voyages* (Siberia) iii:171 [probably *Northern Regions, or Uncle Richard's Relation of Captain Parry's Voyages*, 1827]

[George Back] Bache, *Narrative of the Arctic Land Expedition . . . 1833 to 1835*, [1836] iii:171

[Richard] King, [*Narrative of a*] *Journey to the* [*Shores of the*] *Arctic Ocean* [1836], iii:171

[Alexander] Fisher, [*A Journal of a*] *Voyage of Discovery* [*to the Arctic Regions*, 1821], iii:172

[Sir John] Barrow, [*A Chronological History of Voyages*] *into the Arctic Regions*, 1818], iii:172

[John J. Shillinglaw] Shillinglan, *Arctic Discoveries*, iii:172 [*A Narrative of Arctic Discovery*, 1850]

Snow, *Arctic Regions*, iii:172

[William] Scoresby, *Arctic Countries*, iii:172 [*An Account of the Arctic Regions*, 1820]

[Ebenezer] Henderson, *Residence in Iceland*, iii:174 [*Iceland . . . or the Journal of a Residence in that Island . . .* , 1819]

[Uno von] Trail, *Letters on Iceland* [1780], iii:174

[Henry Home, Lord Kames] Kames, *Sketches of Man* (Iceland), iii:174 [correct title: *Sketches of the History of Man*, 1774 5 vols]

Gaimard, *Voyages en Islande* [*Iceland*], iii:174

[William Jackson] Hooker, *Tours in Iceland*, iii:174 [*Journal of a Tour in Iceland . . . 1809*, 1811]

[David] Crantz, *History of Greenland* [1820], iii:174

Account of Greenland, Iceland, &c, iii:174

Dillon, *Winter in Greenland*, iii:174

Barrow, *Visit to Iceland*, iii:174

Egede, *Description of Greenland*, iii:174

Graah, *Voyage to Greenland*, iii:174

Angelot, *Législation des Etats du Nord*, (Scandinavia) iii:177, 181

[Arthur de] Capel[l] Brooke, [*A*] *Winter in Lapland* [*and Sweden*, 1827], iii:177

Reichard, *Guide des Voyageurs*, iii:177

[John] Bramsen, *Letters of a Prussian Traveller* [1818], iii:177

[Samuel] Laing, *Tour in Sweden* [*in 1838*, 1839], iii:177; [*Journal of a*] *Residence in Norway* [1836], iii:179

Tryzell, *History of Sweden*, iii:177

Frankland, *Visits to Courts of Russia and Sweden*, iii:177

[Wilhelm] Wittich, [*A Visit to the*] *Western Coast of Norway* [1848], iii:179

[W. Bilton], *Two Summers in Norway* [1840 2 vols], iii:179

[Robert Gordon] Latham, *Norway and the Norwegians* [1840], iii:179

[Charles Boileau] Elliot, *Letters from the North of Europe* [1832], iii:179

[George] Mat[t]hew Jones, *Travels* [*in Norway, Sweden . . .* , 1827], iii:179

Clarke, *Travels*, iii:179

Count Bjornstyere, *Moral State of Norway*, iii:179

Buch, *Travels in Norway*, iii:179

[Edward] Price, *Wild Scenes in Norway*, iii:179 [*Views of Wild Scenery*, and *Journal*, 2nd edition 1853]

[William A.] Ross, [*A*] *Yacht Voyage to Norway*, [*Denmark and Sweden*, 1840], iii:179

Kraft, *Topographisk, Statistisk . . . Norge, Christiana*, 1820, 5 vols, 8vo, iii:179

[Robert] Bremner, *Excursions in Denmark*, [*Norway and Sweden*, 1840], iii:181

[Andreas Anderson] Feldborg, *Denmark Delineated* [1824], iii:181

Reports of 'official' returns

Returns of sales of varieties of wet fish, i:64–72

Aggregate sales of dried fish, i:77

Gross value of the several kinds of fish annually sold in the streets of London, i:77–8

Returns of wholesale fruit and vegetables handled annually in London markets, i:79–81

Proportion of green fruit sold by costermongers, i:86

Board of Trade Import records for oranges and lemons i:88–9

Returns of the quantities of dried fruit sold by costermongers, i:91

Returns of the quantities of oranges, lemons and nuts sold by costermongers, i:90

Returns of the quantities of fresh vegetables sold by costermongers, i:93

Returns of the numbers of persons admitted into The Asylum for the Houseless Poor, Play-house Yard, Cripplegate, over a period of 14 years, i:112

Record of Irish immigration into Liverpool (? supplied by a Liverpool magistrate), i:112

Returns of sales of poultry and game from the two great London markets, i:122

Returns of wholesales of trees, shrubs, flowers etc in London markets and proportion sold in streets, i:131

Market returns of the wholesale trade and street-sales of watercress, i:153

Returns of sales of trotters, i:173

Accounts kept by a street-seller of metalware, i:325-6

Relief of the Jews, ii:130

Return showing the extent, population, and police force in the Metropolitan Police district and the City of London, September 1850, ii:159

1841 Census return of sweeps, dustmen and nightmen in the metropolis, ii:162-3

Table showing numbers of inhabited houses and population in various parts of London, 1841-1851, ii:164

Table showing increase in population and population density etc 1841-1851, ii:165

Table showing the several divisions of the metropolis cleansed by the scavengers and parish men, etc., ii:186-7

Table showing comparative cost of town and country clothing, ii:194

Table of food consumed by and excreta of a horse per day, ii:194-5

Meteorological reports, table of surface water in the metropolis, by month, ii:202

Comparison of figures for rainfall provided by Royal Society, etc, ii:202

Professor Way's analysis of surface water in London, May 1850, ii:204-205

Table showing numbers of men engaged in dust-collection, scavenger and rubbish-carting, ii: 213-214.

Court of Common Council of London, cost of new thoroughfares in London, 1851, ii:279-280

1841 Census – showing those employed and those unemployed, ii

Constructed statistics

Estimates of the monetary value annually of sales of green fruit, dried fruit and vegetables by costermongers, i:95-96

Counting of street-stalls of fruit and vegetables, i:96

Estimates of sales of poultry and game on the London streets, i:125, 129, 130

Sales of trees and shrubs sold on London streets based on market returns and on purchases from nursery gardeners, i:134

Returns of nurserymen and market salesmen used to construct sales of cut flowers in the streets, i:137

Returns of nurserymen and market salesmen used to construct sales of flowers in pots and roots of flowers in the streets, i:139

Value of seeds sold annually on the streets, i:141

The quantity of branches forming the street horticultural trade, i:143-4

Monetary value of street-sales of green stuff (watercress, groundsel, chickweed and plantain, turf), i:158

Quantities of bread sold by vendors in the summer months, i:179; and extrapolated to the whole year, i:180

Estimates of sales of coffee and tea by vendors, i:186

Estimates of ginger-beer sales, i:189

Estimates of pepper-mint water sales, i:191

Estimates of street-sales of milk, i:192

Estimates of street-sales of curds and whey, i:193

Estimates of street-sales of rice-milk, i:194

Estimates of street-sales of water, i:195

Estimates of street-sales of pies, i:197

Estimates of street-sales of boiled puddings, i:197

Estimates of street-sales of plum duff, i:198

Estimates of street-sales of cakes, tarts etc, i:199

Estimates of street-sales of gingernuts etc, i:201

Estimates of street-sales of hot cross buns and Chelsea buns, i:201, 202

Estimates of street-sales of muffins and crumpets, i:202, 203

Estimates of street-sales of confectionary, i:205

Estimate of street-sales of cough drops, i:206

Summary of the capital and income of the street-sellers of eatables and drinkables, i:208–12

Summary of the capital and income of the street-sellers of stationery, literature and the fine arts, i:306–309

Listing of accommodation for patterers outside London, i:310–311

Summary of the capital and income of the street-sellers of manufactured articles, i:485–490

Summary of the capital and income of all classes of street-seller, ii:2ff.

Summary of the capital and income of the street-sellers of second-hand articles, live animals, mineral productions etc., ii:96–103

Listing of accommodation for patterers outside London, p310–311

Gross weight of animal dung deposited in streets of London annually, ii:195

Yearly totals of gross quantity of street-refuse, with proportionate quantity of 'Mac' collected from metropolitan thoroughfares, ii:198

Ratio of rainwater to mechanically-supplied water, ii:203

Table of division of labour, mode and rates of payment etc of London scavengers

Table of surface water in the metropolis, by month, ii:202

Table showing division of labour, mode and rates of payment etc. of operative scavagers, ii:219

Weekly food and rent budgets, ii:229–232, 295–296, 367

Tables comparing street-sweeping by machines and by hand etc. ii:239–240

Table showing men employed in scavaging by the metropolitan parishes and highway boards, their wages etc., ii:246–247

Table showing employment of street-orderlies, ii:260

Analysis of questionnaire completed by 67 applicants for employment as street-orderlies, ii:264–268

Report by the St Pancras parish into the introduction of a street-orderly system, ii:269–270

Table showing indebtedness of street-orderly system to Charles Cochrane, ii:270

Tables showing vehicular traffic on London thoroughfares in 1850, ii:282–283

Table regarding numbers of rubbish-carters, their wages and their work, ii:290–291

Table showing increase in population of England and Wales, 1570–1851, ii:317

Table showing increase in population of Scotland, 1755–1851, ii:317

Table showing increase in population of Ireland, 1731–1851, ii:318

Table showing increase in United Kingdom population, 1821–1851, ii:318

Tables showing increase in productions and commerce of the United Kingdom, 1801–1850, ii:319

Table showing number of paupers in England and Wales, annually 1840–1848 ii:320

Table showing the increase in the number of criminals in Eangland and Wales, 1805–1850

Calculation of soot produced by London houses, ii:343

Table showing houses at different rentals, ii:344

Table showing wages of operative chimney-sweeps, ii:359

Table showing master chimney-sweeps etc (collected by personal visits in each district), ii:362–363

Table showing number of bathers at London's public baths, with gender breakdown, ii:265

Table of causes of fire in the metropolis, 1833–1849 (compiled by W. Baddeley), ii:379

Table of damages done by fires in the metropolis, 1833–1849 (compiled by W. Baddeley), ii:380

Table of causes of fires analysed, ii:380

Table showing wet sewage discharge from two streets, ii:387

Table I showing density of population in counties of England and Wales, 1851, iii:6a and 6b[7]

Table of classification of workers and non-worker of Great Britain, iii:12–27

Table II of illiteracy by county (based on marriage-register evidence), 1839–1848, iii:18a & b

Table III showing illiteracy among criminals by county, iii:18c–18d

Graph showing relative degrees of criminality and illiteracy in the counties of England and Wales over a ten-year period, iii:18e

Table [in text] of offenders (by type) brought to notice of Metropolitan police, 1837, iii:33

Table [in text] of offenders brought to notice of Metropolitan police, 1837, collated with those in Liverpool, Bristol, Bath and Newcastle-upon-Tyne, iii:34

Table V Tabulated analysis of educational standards of all prisoners, 1839–1848, iii:34a

Map I of ignorance of England and Wales, iii:34b

Map II, iii:34c

Map III, iii:34d

7 Tables I-VII are not numbered in the 1851 edition.

Table VI of illegitimate births in England and Wales, 1845–1848, by county, iii:48a & b

Map IV of illegitimacy in England and Wales, iii:48c

Map V of early marriages among males in England and Wales, iii:48d

Table VII showing early marriages among males and females by county in England and Wales, 1841–1848, iii:48e–48f

Table VIII showing gender composition of population of England and Wales by county in 1851, iii:62a

Map VI showing number of females to every 100 males in the counties of England and Wales, iii:62b

Table IX showing criminality (rape statistics) by county in England and Wales, 1841–1850, iii:76a–b

Map VII showing number of persons committed for rape by counties in England Wales, iii:76c

Map VIII showing number of persons committed for carnally abusing girls by counties in England Wales, iii:76d

Table X showing number of persons committed for carnally abusing girls by counties in England Wales, 1841–1850, iii:76e–f

Map IX showing distribution of those committed for keeping disorderly houses in England and Wales, iii:87a

Table XII showing criminality with regard to concealing births by county in England and Wales, 1841–1848, iii:102a–b

Map X showing distribution of concealment of births per 10,000 illegitimate births in England and Wales, iii:102c

Map XI showing distribution of incidence of attempted abortion per 10,000 illegitimate births in England and Wales, iii:102d

Table XIII showing distribution of incidence of attempted abortion per 10,000 illegitimate births by county n England and Wales, 1841–1850, iii:102e

Table XIV showing distribution of incidence of attempted ravishing or carnal abuse by county n England and Wales, 1841–1850, iii:116a

Map XII showing distribution by county of incidence of committals for attempted ravishing or carnal abuse per 100,000 in England and Wales, iii:116b

Table XV showing distribution of incidence of committals for bigamy by county n England and Wales, 1841–1850, iii:132a

Map XIII showing distribution by county of incidence of committals for bigamy per every 100,000 marriages in England and Wales, iii:132b

Map XIV showing distribution by county of incidence of committals for abduction per every 10,000,000 of the male population in England and Wales, iii:132c

Table XVI showing distribution of incidence of abduction committals by county in England and Wales, 1841–1850, iii:132d

Table XVII showing relative amount of female and male criminality by county in England and Wales, 1841–1850, iii:148a

Map XV showing distribution by county of incidence of criminality of females per every 100,000 of the female population in England and Wales, iii:148b

Periodicals and newspapers cited

Lloyd's Numbers 25, his pennies, i:291
Reynolds' periodicals, especially his *Mysteries of the Court* 25, his pennies, i:290
Monthly Review (notice of Walter Scott's *Lord of the Isles*, 1815), i:231
London Journal, i:291
Family Herald, i:291
Penny Punch, i:291
Cork Examiner, ii:325
Facts and Figures, 1841, ii:327
British Friend of India Magazine, iii:125

Poems and ditties cited

Duck-legged Dick, i:15
A penn'worth of gin, i:172
One-a-penny, two-a-penny, hot-cross buns, i:201
One-a-penny, poker; two-a-penny, tongs!, i:201
Jane Willibred we did starve and beat her very hard, i:220, 228
Cardinal Wiseman's Lament, i:224
The Pope and Cardinal Wiseman [Now Lord John Russell did so bright . . .], i:227
Voice from the gaol or . . . the life of William Calcraft, the present hangman, i:225
If I'd as much money as i could tell, i:243
The very kittens on the hearth, i:244
To save a journey up the town, i:254
Edwin and Emma (Goldsmith), i:280
Celestial blessings hover round his head, i:281
Stranger, pause a moment, stay, i:281
Copy of verses of Mary May, i:281-2
Never to blend our pleasure or our pride (Wordsworth), ii:64
Cyllenius so, as fables tell, and Jove (Hughes of Tom Britton), ii:82
No Jews, no wooden shoes, ii:117
To see the Pope's blacke knight, a cloaked Frere (Bishop Hall), ii:205
'Martial Maid' (Beaumont and Fletcher), ii:205
But e'en in infancy decree, ii:333
Fear no more the heat o' the sun (Shakespeare, *Cymbeline*), ii:339
I've seen the adumbra tree in flower, white plumage on the crow, iii:125

Songs cited

The Pope he leads a happy life, 221
Buffalo gals, come out tonight, 221
The gay cavalier, 221
Jim along Josey, 221
There's a good time a-coming, 221
Drink to me only, 221
Kate Kearney, 221

Chuckaroo-choo, 221
Chockala-roony, 221
Pagadaway, 221
Hottypie, 221
I dreamed that I dwelt in marble halls, 221
The standard-bearer, 221
Just like love, 221
Whistle o'er the lave o't, 221
Widow Mackree, 221
I've been roaming, 221
Oh! that kiss, 221
The English gentleman, 221
The Pope he is coming; oh crikey, oh dear! [of the Smithfield martyrs, to the
    tune of 'The Campbells are coming'], 227
The Queen, the Pope and the Parliament, 227
Since Corder died on buystree, 228
Haynan, 228
Sir Topas, 275
The Earl of Dorset's song, 1665, 275
A cobbler there was and he lived in a stall, 275
Parnell's song, 275
The Cock-lane ghost, 275
Children in the wood, 275
Chevy chase, 275
Barbara Allen, 275
Gilderoy was a bonnie boy, 275
Prince Albert, 276
Jenny Lind, 276
Now Farnecombe's out and Musgrove's in, 276
Queer doings in Leather-lane, 276
Middlesex and victory! Or Grosvenor and Osborne forever, 277
Death of Queen Adelaide, 277
Elegy on the death of Sir Robert Peel, 277
On the awful fire at B. Caunt's, in St Martin's Lane, 277
Come all good Christians and give attention, 277
On the ninth day of September, eighteen hundred and forty-five, 277
Twas a dark foggy night, 278
The way to live happy together, 278
Ye banks and braes of Bonnie Doun, 279
The Merry Fiddler, 279
There's a good time coming, boys, 279
Nix, my Dolly, 279
The Girls of —shire, 279
Widow Mahoney, 279
Remember the glories of Brian the Brave, 279
Clementina Clemmina, 279
Lucy Long, 279

Erin go Bragh, 279
Christmas in 1850, 279
The death of Nelson, 279
The life and adventures of Jemmy Sweet, 279
The young May moon, 279
Hail to the Tyrol, 279
He was such a lushy cove, 279
The heart that can feel for another, 279
The amorous waterman of St John's Wood, 279
Robin the Beau, 279
The poachers, 279
The miller's ditty, 279
When I was first breeched, 279
The husband's dream, 280
Demon of the Sea (to the tune of The Brave Old Oak), 280
Pirate of the isles, 280
All people that on earth do dwell (adaptation of the hymn), 283
You feeling Christians look with pity, 399

Street dialogues cited
The old English John Bull v. the Pope's Bull of Rome, i:236
The lesson of the dog, i:237
Conversation between Achilles and the Wellington statue, i:237

Cocks (street forgeries) cited
Dying speeches, executioners' songs, death-verses:i:268–9
Sorrowful lamentation and last farewell of J.B.Rush, i:281
Life, trial and execution of Mary May, i:282
Come all good Christians, praise the Lord, i:283
Confession . . . of John Tawell the Quaker, i:283–4

Broadsheets cited
Trial of Mr and Mrs Manning for the murder of Mr Patrick O'Connor, i:284
  (includes other e.g.s)

Books cited
Annual Register, i:294
The Whitby tragedy, i:284 (also other e.gs. of murder pamphlets)
Listings of books for sale at station bookstalls for 1d or 2d, i:292
Philander and Sylvia, i:293
The English classics (*e.g. Vicar of Wakefield, Tom Jones,* i:293–4, *Pamela,* i:294)
(books too numerous to mention are listed in i:294–301)

Conundrums listed
The Nutcrackers . . . , i:285
I've got no wings, yet in the air, i:285
I am a word of letters seven, i:285

Statutes cited

Edicts of Edward II and Edward IV regarding minstrelsy, i:273

43 Elizabeth (Poor Law), ii:256

23 Henry VIII (statute of sewers), ii:389

25 Henry VIII c.13 (restriction on number of sheep and on enclosure), ii:309

5 & 6 Edward VI c.5 (maintenance of land in tillage), ii:305

50, George III c.41 (laws concerning hawkers and pedlars) i:58, vol ii:3

25 George III (law concerning licensed killing of game), i:120

28 George III c.48 (restricted number of child chimney sweeps etc), ii:346

6 George IV c.80 [ditto] i:58

1 & 2 William IV c.32 (law concerning licensed killing of game), i:120

Michael Angelo Taylor's Act, i:59

Police Act, 2 & 3 Victoria, i:59

'Recent act of parliament' banning use of muffin-seller's bell, i:202